ED VULLIAMY

Amexica

War Along the Borderline

REVISED AND UPDATED WITH
NEW MATERIAL

VINTAGE

1 3 5 7 9 10 8 6 4 2

Vintage
20 Vauxhall Bridge Road
London SW1V 2SA

Vintage is part of the Penguin Random House group of companies
whose addresses can be found at global.penguinrandomhouse.com

First published in the UK by The Bodley Head in 2010
First published in Vintage in 2011
This revised edition published in Vintage in 2020

penguin.co.uk/vintage

A CIP catalogue record for this book is available from the British Library

ISBN 9781529113662

Typeset in 10.8/12.55pt Walbaum MT Std by Jouve (UK), Milton Keynes
Printed and bound in Great Britain by Clays Ltd, Elcograf S.p.A.

Penguin Random House is committed to a sustainable future
for our business, our readers and our planet. This book is made
from Forest Stewardship Council® certified paper.

This is for my Father, J.S.P.V.

1919–2007

This updated edition is dedicated to the courage of Lydia Cacho and to the memory of our murdered journalist colleagues in Mexico

Contents

Author's Note

If you drink the water in Ciudad Juárez, there you stay, goes the saying – *Si bebes agua de Juárez, allí te queda*. It's not a reference to the quality of the drinking water, about which polemic abounds, but addiction to a dusty and dangerous but strong and charismatic city. In fact, it's a dictum that describes the mesmeric lure of the whole 2,000-mile borderland, of which Juárez and its sister-city on the US side, El Paso, form the fulcrum. I did drink the water, and although I didn't stay, I return over and over again.

The body of this book was published a decade ago, mostly written after a summer of reporting in 2008, then a gruelling but thrilling full-immersion five-month journey in 2009, along, across and around the frontier. Although I knew Ciudad Juárez beforehand, I was for the most part an explorer across strange land, an insatiably curious visitor, a traveller-with-notebook through a full-blown 'narco war', whatever that means now, raging across terrain of breathtaking beauty, and among the kindest, funniest, friendliest people in the world. I was bedazzled, bewitched, beguiled and appalled, and the book's strengths and weaknesses lie in the fact that so much of this was new to me.

I wanted to write one of the first books on this enthralling territory since the latest, present incarnation of the 'narco war' began, in December 2006. I knew from my work on the Italian Mafia that narco traffic was the best lens through which to measure much about the world we live in, and since those days of the late 1980s and early 1990s, the critical mass of international drug dealing had shifted to Mexico, and with it the violence narco traffic entails. Accomplished writers like Charles Bowden and Luís Alberto Urrea had by then written about drug war on and migration across this land, but not since President Felipe Calderón sent the Mexican army into Nuevo Laredo in 2006, detonating the present war. When I wrote *Amexica* four years later, one had to explain who Joaquín 'El Chapo' Guzmán, leader of the Sinaloa cartel, was; since which we've had a TV series about El Chapo, several seasons of *Narcos* on Netflix, plus a number of feature films, such as the awful *Sicarios* 1 & 2. There's been some wonderful writing and film-making too, and the trial-as-theatre of the man himself in New York. There's even an El Chapo leisurewear line in Mexico now, and licensed El Chapo craft beer.

Journalists are supposed to be ahead of the curve – that's our métier – but it's a bad place to be; the curve overtakes you in the outside lane. Those lonely desert byways a decade ago are now traffic jams of reporters and TV crews, quite rightly, as the border becomes a place of humanitarian disaster and – at the time of writing – mainmast of President Donald Trump's hateful lexicon, policy and re-election campaign. Hence this new edition and material, to bring *Amexica* up to date.

The frontier is still at once porous and harsh, a dichotomy that was the book's driving theme. Communities live across its cities and towns, like pairs of lungs, and a million people traverse it every day, legally, as do hundreds of billions of dollars' worth of goods annually ($614.5 billion in 2019). But tens of thousands are trapped at the frontier, trying to cross; thousands more die or disappear trying to do so. The border is also a front on which President Trump has fixated, presenting the borderline as a rampart against 'invasion', pledging his new wall to run its length.

For all the trans-border porosity, one crosses the line southbound, and, as Jack Kerouac wrote in *On the Road*: 'Just across the street, Mexico began. We looked with wonder. To our amazement, it looked exactly like Mexico.' Similarly, crossing the bridges northbound, one can leave places of palpable danger for the relative calm of Chula Vista in California, or El Paso, McAllen and Brownsville in Texas. And yet, in August 2019, El Paso lost its status as one of the safest cities of its size in America, not to any incursion by drug traffickers or migrants from Ciudad Juárez across the border, but to bullets fired by an anti-Hispanic racist from Dallas, who massacred twenty-two people out shopping at Walmart on a busy weekend before school term began.

The official militarisation of the frontier described in *Amexica* ten years ago has accelerated and entrenched, drawing an ever-harder line in the desert sand or along the Rio Grande. Ten years ago, the administration of Barack Obama continued the build-up of law enforcement and 'border protection' begun by his predecessors, Bill Clinton and George W. Bush, and clamped down on criminal immigrants, accelerating deportations to record levels. Now, Trump shocks his own country, collides with federal courts, and outrages the world with policies separating children from parents, appalling conditions of incarceration, wholesale round-ups of immigrants without papers − or criminal records. Some 59,000 asylum seekers (at the time of writing) have been sent back under so-called Migrant Protection Protocols and must 'Remain in Mexico', as the new policy is also known, to await their 'credible fear' interviews. Less than 1 per cent are successful.

The world has changed over the last ten years − Syria, climate change, disease − and on this border, yes and no; the more it changes, the more it stays the same. Since this book was first published, the primary, propelling narrative has shifted from narco traffic to migration. Ten years ago, the driving story was drug smuggling (and emergent domestic consumption), to which the theme of migration played an accompanying role, as cartels moved in on human trafficking.

But now hundreds of children are separated from their parents; the world is on the move, and much of it has converged on 'Amexica'. While ten years ago, most migrants were Mexicans in flight to the border from violence and poverty, now tens of thousands flee gangland violence in Guatemala, El Salvador and Honduras. In Ciudad Juárez, a 'little Havana' of Cuban migrants is established; Venezuelans crowd the bridges at Nuevo Laredo. People converge from Asia and Eastern Europe; Haitians arrive in Tijuana, fail to cross and settle; an encampment is established in Ciudad Acuña from the Great Lakes, Horn and Western countries of Africa, hoping to cross to Del Rio, Texas.

But violence, the cartels and their conviviality with government remain perennial, and ubiquitous. Not much along the frontier has really changed thematically – only the faces and names. Ten years ago, the task was to report on how Guzmán's Sinaloa cartel supplanted rivals along the border west of Juárez, for export mainly of cocaine, then, less successfully, confronted the Zetas and Gulf cartel further east. Now, with Guzmán jailed and his cartel fragmented, the 'plaza' is unquiet again, as the Cartel Jalisco Nueva Generación, CJNG, stakes its claim, based mainly on synthetic drugs and fentanyl, to fill a vacuum left by the claw-back on prescribed opioids in the US. Violence increased when the plates shifted ten years ago, and does so again.

The book was published as murder rates hit the highest since the Mexican Revolution of 1910; Juárez became the most dangerous city in the world in 2010, with Tijuana second. The homicide rate waned as Guzmán's cartel secured the border's western smuggling 'plazas', and Los Zetas those to the east, only to spike again since 2016. The year 2019 was the bloodiest yet in Mexico's recent history, counting 34,582 officially registered murders – a significant increase on the figure of 29,100 for 2018.[1] Ten years ago, Ciudad Juárez was murder capital of the world; now it's Tijuana. Five of the world's six most murderous cities in 2018 were in Mexico.[2] This is due substantially, but by no means only, to drug smuggling or dealing at some level, however great or small, its impact on society, and to impunity from justice for those who kill. The ravages of Covid-19, felt worldwide, impacted Mexico in singular ways during spring and early summer 2020, exposing a brutalised society. While crime rates plummeted around the world, in Mexico they soared, as cartels took advantage of distracted authorities to fight one another.[3] The month of March saw an average of ninety-eight murders every day, and April ninety-nine; nineteen people were killed in a single gun battle in Chihuahua on 3 April. As well as kill, the cartels tightened their grip on civil society by stepping into a vacuum of provision by the state. Images emerged of masked men from the Gulf cartel and CJNG distributing boxes of food and essential supplies to needy citizens, labelled as gifts from the cartel, as would be aid from an NGO or charity; other cartons of aid were stamped with the image of 'El Chapo' Guzmán.[4] Domestic violence and femicide, which increased worldwide during coronavirus, worsened so badly in Mexico as to count the murders of 964 women during the first three months of 2020. Opposition congresswoman Martha Tagle said that 'the deadliest pandemic for women in our country, more than the coronavirus, is femicidal violence'.[5] The oppressive culture that pertains in American-owned assembly plants along the border, so-called *maquiladoras* described in the ensuing chapter 'Eat off the Floor', reached a grotesque low during coronavirus, when – with most production across the US and Mexico ceased for safety reasons – employees in these factories were ordered to continue working, in close proximity to one another, and with no protective gear. In Tijuana and Ciudad Juárez, some workers went on unofficial strike, demanding social distancing and apposite protection, and risked losing their jobs.[6]

Ten years ago, the worst of the *femicidio* – mass murder of women – in Juárez had focused on young factory workers, abducted, violated and killed because they were what they were, women. Now, a horribly mutated *femicidio* appears also to target young, politicised and educated women because of what they *do*.

So why can't I stay away? Mainly for personal reasons that make the borderland and its people irresistible – friendships forged through and since *Amexica*.

But there are other, journalistic, reasons. The border was and remains a prism through which to examine our world, wherein the illicit economy bleeds into the supposedly legal one as high street banks launder profits of drug traffic with impunity. As the great anti-Mafia writer Roberto Saviano wrote, the Colombian narco lord Pablo Escobar was 'the Copernicus' of the narco traffic because he was 'the first to understand that it's not the world of cocaine that must orbit around the markets, but the markets that must rotate around cocaine'.[7]

Amexica ended with the story of how the Wachovia bank moved at least $373.63 billion of wired money from Mexico, plus $47 billion in cheques and $4.73 billion in cash, much of it proven to come from the Sinaloa cartel, without adequate checks. Europe and Britain's biggest bank, HSBC, was mentioned in the book, in the very early stages of a scandal that ended up with it too being caught moving El Chapo's money, without anyone from Wachovia or HSBC arrested, let alone jailed.[8] Following Guzmán's conviction in 2019, the US government's attempts to retrieve forfeiture of his alleged $14 billion value ignores the billions of his blood money sent swilling around the 'legal' economy by Wachovia and HSBC. These connections were made in *Amexica*, and they are starker than ever now – I call it the lie of legality.

Mainly, though, the border calls me back because of something newly disquieting and disturbingly hard to define that is happening in this place. As I wrote in *Amexica*, the violence, although extreme, has no 'cause' as such, beyond money and kudos. It is nihilistic and post-political, stitched into – and thereby brutalising – normal existence. I described Amexica ten years ago as 'a battlefield wrapped in everyday life', and that is all the more stark now. The jury at the 2018 Bayeux Awards – the 'Oscars' of war reporting – debated coverage of Mexico, with some experienced journalists, including the veteran of twenty conflicts Patrick Chauvel, insisting that 'this is not war'. But if not, what is it?

We have here the phenomenon of a new kind of twenty-first-century war in – apparently and supposedly – 'peacetime'. I cut my teeth as a war reporter in Bosnia and Iraq: 'real' wars with front lines and shells and bombs falling on besieged cities and towns; 'ethnic cleansing' and villages incinerated into the dust of their own stone. Yet the death toll in Mexico since 2006 – some 300,000, excluding the disappeared – is treble that of the war in Bosnia (though their respective populations are incomparable). The outrageous number of disappeared, officially 61,637 by the end of 2019, is 50 per cent higher than in all the Balkan wars between 1991 and 1999 – a theme inadequately treated in the original book, rectified here after remarkable changes in the way the disappeared are sought and identified.

Yet pulsating Juárez is not besieged Sarajevo. Part of the book's aim was to describe unspeakable violence in places where life goes on and quotidian encounters are generally a delight. I wrote then that the darker the shadows fall, the more lambent the colours, and this is all the more true now: the violence becomes unrelenting and unspeakable, yet in no place I know are the ready smile, the unnecessary chat, the twinkle-in-the-eye so pervasive. This carnage unfolds in places where the people go to school, to Mass and to market; the soccer league functions well, universities are generally good, shopping centres are open; street burritos and bakery pastries are delicious, restaurants are full again – and the vast majority of people are the most heart-warming you could hope to meet. We need a word for this, and perhaps, rather than exclude this kind of violence – like that in Northern Ireland for thirty-five years, Colombia for sixty-two – from a definition of 'war', we need to rethink what warfare is.

Since 2010, I've spent more time in Mexico as a friend to the people I met on the slipstream of *Amexica* than I have working, and this is both a joy and liberation, not least from the book and its story. It feels surreal, sometimes, but what fun to go with friends to watch 'El Tri', the national football team, or the Bravos play in Juárez, in their stadium a stone's throw from the border, all fun and food, passion and beer, or FC Tijuana Xoloitzcuintles de Caliente – try singing that when you've had a few – the 'Xolos'. There is no awe like confrontation with Mexico's past and the beauty of Mexico's landscape; and no better way to savour life than on Mexican time in the Mexican present with the right people, listening to Mexican music with Mexican tequila in a Mexican mood. I allow myself to feel as though I know the country a little better now than I did then.

But when it comes to the war, it is a vanity to say one 'knows' Mexico. As Bowden said, in his 2010 book about Juárez, *Murder City*, Mexico's war has no control room in which people know or direct what is happening. We will never really know what is going on, because no one does. I use the term 'black box' – there is none, no space or place wherein the answers lie. Mexico's war has no bottom, apparently no foreseeable end – and no ultimate explanation, which is why this book feels at once ten years old, but of yesterday and today.

I was chatting into the early hours during October 2019, at the home in Ciudad Juárez of reporter and author Sandra Rodríguez Nieto, who has covered the bloodletting at very close range and written a book about impunity. Also round the table was anthropologist Cecilia Ballí, who wrote the definitive academic thesis on *femicidio* in the city during the 1990s and 2000s; both writers feature importantly in what follows. With the tequila low in its bottle, Cecilia asked whether we'd ever been really happy. Sandra replied: 'Yes, my city makes me happy. I love Juárez; it kills people, but it also gives me a sense of life, unconnected to the killings, to do with its complexity, and its people.' I understand her entirely – ugly, strong, scary, marvellous Juárez. That's the point: Amexica looks normal, but it's not.

Los Angeles / Ciudad Juárez / London,
May 2020

Acknowledgements

The original book would not have happened without ten crucial people, their inspiration and help: David Rieff, whose idea of a holiday back in the late nineties was for the two of us to head for Ciudad Juárez in search of cowboy boots and stories. Tracy Bohan at the Wylie Agency, who urged me to turn a mess of ideas into a book. Then Will Sulkin at Bodley Head, and Eric Chinski at Farrar Straus and Giroux, who did just that. Leon Krauze and Tracy Wilkinson waved me off down the road from Mexico City, where Jorge Fregoso, Julián Cardona, Dudley Althaus and Cecilia Ballí were, thank God, along it.

To them, I now add Nicholas Skidmore at Vintage, whose faith in the original and encouragement now, resuscitates *Amexica* back to life. Ten years ago, Kay Peddle at Bodley Head and Eugenie Cha at Farrar Straus and Giroux guided the manuscript, to whom I now add Katherine Fry for her excellent edit. Since the original, deep thanks also to Jaqueline Ka and Austin Mueller at Wylie in New York, and Frances Coady at Picador, New York. Also the Fainting Robin Foundation in North Carolina, which part-funded research for this edition.

I thanked from the heart my colleagues and editors on the *Guardian* and *Observer*: John Mulholland, Paul Webster, Jo Tuckman, Holly Bentley, Arnel Hecimović, Finbar Sheehey and Allan Jenkins – and my professional mentors John Ware and Duncan Campbell. I need now to add, from both papers: Jane Ferguson, Ursula Kenny, Tracy McVeigh, Jessica Reed, Eric Hilaire, Richard Nelsson, Jason Rodrigues and Luc Torres. Perennial thanks are due to John Hooper, who replaced me for the *Guardian* in Rome, now with the *Economist*.

There is deep gratitude due to colleagues on other publications and TV stations. From the original edition: Tracy Wilkinson as above, of the *Los Angeles Times*; Sandra Rodríguez Nieto of *El Diario* in Ciudad Juárez; Jorge Fregoso as above, now of *Univision*; Alejandro Páez and Ignacio Álvarez Alvarado of *El Universal*, both in Mexico City; Juan Carlos Zuñiga and Marco Mendoza of *El Imparcial*, Hermosillo; Antonio Martínez Santoyo of *El Mañana* in Nuevo Laredo; Brenda Norrell of *Censored News* and *Narcosphere*; Marc Lacey, then of the *New York Times*; Alfredo Corchado of the *Dallas Morning News*; Dane Schiller, then of the *Houston Chronicle*; Dudley Althaus as above, now writing for the *San Antonio Express News*; Sacha Feinman, now in politics for the US Democratic Party; Jesse Bogan, then of *Forbes*; William Booth of the *Washington Post*; and Elena Cosentino of the BBC. Thanks always to Andrea di Robilant and Ferruccio Sansa, both formerly of *La Stampa*.

More doors opened on the slipstream of *Amexica* than I dared hope or imagine. Accordingly, my gratitude deepens to all those I met along that further road of the book's aftermath. Foremost among them are Jon Lee Anderson of the *New Yorker*; and Roberto Saviano, to whom I owe special thanks, Federica Campana and Gala Sicart Olavide. Lydia Cacho and Anabel Hernández, as per the text. In Mexico City: Enrique and Andrea Krauze, Marcela Turati and J. Jesús Esquivel of *Proceso*, Bertha Navarro Solares, David Brooks of *La Jornada*, Carmen Aristegui, Juan Villoro and the memory of Sergio González Rodríguez; and in Monterrey, Diego Enrique Osorno. Also: María Jimena Duzán of *La Semana* in Bogotá; Hector Abad in Medellín; Gustavo Gorriti in Lima; Patricio Fernández of *The Clinic* in Santiago de Chile; Carlo Italo Verdelli and Filippo Ceccarelli at *La Repubblica* in Rome; Ian Buruma and Michael Shea at the *New York Review of Books*, and Kate Linthicum of the *Los Angeles Times*. Also: Gala Sicart as above, Bill Swainson and Christopher MacLehose at the MacLehose Press; Susana Seijas of the Committee to Protect Journalists; Alan Rusbridger and Nick Davies, lately of the *Guardian*; and Angus McQueen of Ronachan Films.

Personal thanks in the original were to: in Los Angeles, John Cale and Nita Scott. In Tucson: Debra May, Phreddie and Olivia Bartolomaei, Elaine Mariole, Trudy Duffy, Bob and Peggy Feinman. To Mike Flores in Sells, AZ, and to what is now the memory of Charles

Bowden, then in Patagonia, AZ. To Molly Molloy in Las Cruces, NM; Diana Washington Valdez, Tom and Nadine Russell in El Paso; Don Henry and Leah Ford in Belmont; Lisa Hilton in Houston, Michael Seifert in Brownsville – all in Texas. To Raymundo Ramos in Nuevo Laredo, Mario Treviño in Reynosa and Julia Quiñones in Piedras Negras. Though they were acknowledged by inclusion in the text, I need to single out, in Ciudad Juárez: the memory, now, of Esther Chávez; also Paula Flores, Norma Andrade, Rosario Acosta, Marisela Ortíz and all those who lost family to, and campaigned over, the *femicidio* in that city – and now, the memory of Isabel Cabanillas de la Torre.

Personal gratitude was due then – and still is – to: Victoria Edgar, the memory of my father John Sebastian Vulliamy, to my mother Shirley Hughes, my daughters Elsa and Claudia, brother Tom, sister Clara and Mark Owen; Paul Gilroy and Vron Ware, Marcus and Cora Gilroy Ware; Marco 'El Sexto Sol' Roth, Mark Dowie and Wendy Schwarz, Kerry Dowson, Tom Rhodes. And Josh Lord at East Side Ink tattoos, New York, for his syncretic Virgin of Guadalupe, on my right shoulder, who kept me safe. Also to the Trattoria da Maria on Notting Hill Gate, and to the Frontline Club, Vaughan and Pranvera Smith, May Prior and all the staff.

There are important thanks to impart, since the original edition. Those mentioned in the dedication and cited in the Afterwords can presume themselves thanked personally, as well as professionally, especially, for emphasis: Ruben García, Pastor José Antonio Galván, Pastor Diego Robles, Pastor Lorenzo Ortíz and Glady Cañas Aguilar.

In Mexico: Homero, Betty and Chloe Aridjis, Laura Hernández, Laura Demeneghi. Also Roma Records, Mexico City; and in Ciudad Juárez, Centenario burritos, Bar Eugenie and the Rezizte bakery.

In New York: David Rieff again, Judith Thurman, Mimi (as in the text) and Antonia Doretti, Graciela Mochkofsky, Gabriel and Ismael Pasquini, Peter Godwin and Arabella Greene. In the US West and along the border: Ron and Jane Olson, and all at Munger Tolles & Olson in Los Angeles. To Larry and Eva Roth, Luis and Esther at the Ocean Beach Hotel, Erik Ortega and all at Ortega's, Ocean Beach. To Carlee's bar, Borrego Springs, and all who keep the Anza-Borrego State Park. In Canada: René Weisner and Brian Fitzpatrick.

In Italy: Olivella Foresta, Andrea, Matilde and Ludovico Ciolli. In

France: François Geffard, Rémy Ourdan, Florence Hartmann and Simone Hisler. In Poland: Monika Sneiderman, Bożena Dudko, Wojciech Tymowski, Olga Stanisławka, Alicja Kapuśckińska and Urszula Glensk. In Ireland: Maurice Earls, Peter Murtagh, Risteard Ó Domhnaill and Fiachna Ó Braonáin.

In the UK: Edna O'Brien, Paul Greengrass, Max Porter, Stephen Garrett, Tom Rhodes, Noel Bradshaw, Nicola Dahrendorf, Jon Swain, María de Vecchi, Isabella Mulholland, John Blake and Karen Brown, Melanie Jessop, Ilona Leighton-Gooddall, Jacqui Rae and the memory of Michael Jacobs. To Lorenzo and Marina Berni at Ristorante San Lorenzo; to Peter Florence and Cristina Fuentes La Roche from the Hay Festival; and from the Borris Festival, Vivienne Guinness. To James Youngman, Minel and Sacha, St John and St Elizabeth Hospital and the Royal Free Hospital.

Thanks to the following bookshops: University Bookstore, UACJ, and Librería Átenas in Ciudad Juárez; Librería Ático in Mexico City, and the branches of Cafebrería at Roma, Condesa and Polanco. In Los Angeles, the Last Bookstore; Battery Books and Vroman's Bookstore in Pasadena; Green Apple Books and the Black Bird Bookstore in San Francisco; Antigone Books, Tucson; the branches of Barnes & Noble in El Paso and at Union Square, New York; also in New York: Three Lives & Co., Strand Books and Compendium Books. In Dublin, Books Upstairs; and Daunt Books, Holland Park, London.

The final acknowledgement in the original *Amexica* was to an alley cat in Tuscon, called Echolls. Here it is to the memory of Lydia Cacho's dogs, Ulma and Luna – murdered by *sicarios* – and Petra, who survived the attempt to poison her.

Credits

Lyrics

When Sinatra Played Juárez
Words and Music by Tom Russell © 2001 Frontera Music (ASCAP)/Administered by Bug Music. All Rights Reserved Used by Permission.

Where The Dream Begins
Words and Music by Tom Russell © 2001 Frontera Music (ASCAP)/Administered by Bug Music. All Rights Reserved Used by Permission.

The Road It Gives, The Road It Takes Away
Words and Music by Tom Russell and Andrew Hardin © 2001 Frontera Music (ASCAP) and Alligator Farm Music (BMI)/Administered by Bug Music. All Rights Reserved Used by Permission.

Ilustrations

1. Amexica: the corpse of an executed man hangs, decapitated and handcuffed, from the Puente Rotario in Cuidad Juárez © Alex Tellez / *Periodico PM*
2. Joaquín Guzmán Loera: picture sourced from a Mexican police handout
3. Osiel Cárdenas Guillén © Getty images
4. The devil's highway © David Rochkind
5. Urban Frankenstein: children foraging in the aftermath of a massacre © 2010 by Julián Cardona. Reprinted by permission of Anderson Literary Management, LLC. All rights reserved
6. Here begins the homeland © Shaul Schwarz/Getty images
7. Urban Frankenstein: a body chained to a fence © Alejandro Bringas/Reuters
8. The human junkyard © 2010 by Julián Cardona. Reprinted by permission of Anderson Literary Management, LLC. All rights reserved
9. Wind of knives © Guillermo Arias/AP
10. The road it gives, and the road it takes away © Robert Yager
11. Eat off the floor ©Antonio Olmos Zazueta
12. Gateway to the Americas: migrants prepare to jump and ride a train © Photo by Gary Coronado/Palm Beach Post/ZUMA Press
13. Amexica © Robert King/Polaris/eyevine
14. Gateway to the Americas: the daily line to cross the border on foot © *New York Times*/Redux/eyevine
15. Iron river © Getty images
16. Santísima Muerte © Redux/eyevine
17. The Virgin of Guadalupe: tattoo © Josh Lord, East Side Ink, New York; photo © Arnel Hecimovic

Map

Amexica: The US–Mexican borderland © Finbarr Sheehy

Amexica: the US-Mexican borderland
Principal locations and cartel influence

Cartel influence: contested
Sinaloa cartel
Arellano Felix Organisation

Cartel influence: contested
Sinaloa cartel
Beltrán-Leyva cartel
Juárez cartel

RIO GRANDE

- Los Angeles

CALIFORNIA

ARIZONA

NEW ME

- Phoenix

Tohono O'Odham Indian Nation

Calexico

San Diego
Tijuana   Mexicali   San Luis

Yuma

Lukeville

- Tucson

Columbus

Sonoyta
El Sasabe

Nogales Douglas

Palomas

Nogales Agua Prieta

Caborca ●Altar

Ciudad Juárez

BAJA CALIFORNIA NORTH

SONORA

CHIHUA

- Hermosillo

Chihuah

Cartel influence: contested
Sinaloa cartel
Beltrán-Leyva cartel

M I

- Ciudad Obregón

PACIFIC OCEAN

BAJA CALIFORNIA SOUTH

Los Mochis ●

Culiacán ●

- La Paz

SINALO

Border key
≡ Existing fence
▬ Proposed fence
■ No fence

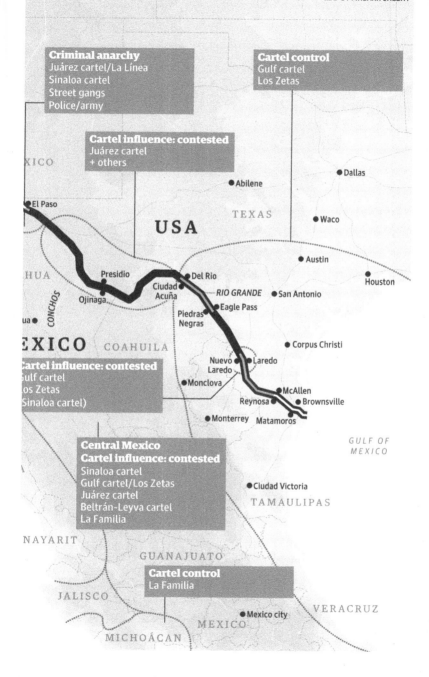

PROLOGUE

Amexica

As dawn breaks over the vast desert, the body is hanging from a concrete overpass known as 'Switchback Bridge'. It has been there for two hours – decapitated and dangling by a rope tied around the armpits. The sun begins to throw its rays across the busy intersection, with its rush-hour traffic and former American school buses carrying workers to sweatshops. It is still there an hour later, this grotesque, headless thing – swaying, hands cuffed behind its back – in the cold early-morning wind that kicks up dust and cuts through the Mexican border town of Ciudad Juárez, the most dangerous city in the world.

Next to their prey this morning – left hanging just as the factory shifts were about to change – the executioners, or *sicarios* as they are called, have hung a sheet, on which they have painted a message: '*Yo Lázaro Flores, apoyo a mi patron, el monte perros*' – 'I, Lázaro Flores, served my boss, the dog-fucker'. '*Atte. (Atencion), La Línea*' – 'Look out, The Line' – it concluded. A crowd assembles to watch in unsurprised silence. The straps underneath the corpse's armpits creak, and its feet flap in the wind, but the crowd remains gawping at this hideous, buckled thing, perhaps fearing, if they leave, they might take with them the curse of that which was done. So that before they could go, it must be dealt with, erased from view and from the morning. Finally, after three hours, firemen arrive and erect ladders in order to take the carcass down, wrap it in canvas, put it in a red van, and drive it away to the morgue, to be examined and 'read' for any message contained in the mutilations. And so Juárez could get on with a day that would see another four narco murders before it was out. Which was an unusually low count: with the year 2009 but a month old, 227 people have already been killed in this city on Mexico's border with the United States.

La Línea is a recent mutation of what was once the Juárez narco-trafficking cartel run by Amado Carrillo Fuentes, known by the *nom de narco* 'Lord of the Skies', so called because of the fleet of Boeing planes that was at his disposal for smuggling cocaine from Colombia. But *La Línea* is now just one of the miasma of factions and interests – cartels, street gangs, corrupt police units, military detachments – fighting with ever more inventive twists of violence for the 'Plaza', the river of drugs running north through Juárez into El Paso and from there across the US. Fighting, too, for the resultant plazas of Juárez and northern Mexico themselves: for where the river runs through, people will drink, and as a direct consequence of the Mexican cartels' near-monopoly of the supply of narcotics to the United States, northern Mexico is ravaged by crack and methamphetamine addiction, and by the bloody battles for terrain on which to sell them. The sheet, known as a *narcomanta*, and its message, known as a *narcomensaje*, are common features of the executions, designed to charge the slaying with menace or even opacity: Lázaro Flores was not the dead man's name, but that of a prominent local businessman – something for the city, and indeed Mr Flores, to ponder.

This macabre, barbaric execution, in November 2008, took the number of murders in the anarchic city of two million people to about 1,300 that year. The toll would cap 1,700 before the end of December. The national figure of those killed across Mexico reached over 5,400 in 2008. In 2009, despite successive waves of military reenforcements and a promise by Mayor José Reyes Ferriz on 1 January that Juárez 'cannot have another year like that' the toll was even higher: 2,657 people murdered, making Ciudad Juárez the world's most murderous city, with 192 homicides per 100,000 citizens. The total of those murdered across Mexico in 2009 reached 7,724.[1] This means that by the end of that year, more than 16,000 people had been killed since Mexican president Felipe Calderón launched a military offensive against the cartels in December 2006, with many of the victims mutilated, like this man, horribly and carefully, then exhibited to convey some message or threat. By summer 2010, the total killed since December 2006 had exceeded 24,000. The killing is everywhere across Mexico, but concentrated along the border with the USA – 2,100 miles long, the busiest border in the world and a place that belongs to both countries, and yet to neither.

Ciudad Juárez lives cheek by jowl with the United States and its 'twin city' El Paso, on the other side of the frontier. Sometimes the proximity is surreal: from the campus of the University of Texas in El Paso, one sees, in the foreground, the diligent enjoyment of life – students strolling to and fro. Across mid-distance, less than half a mile away, runs the border in two forms: an articulately harsh wall decorated with barbed wire and the trickle of the Rio Grande. And beyond the boundary, one of the poorest barrios – or *colonias* as they are called here – in Mexico: a bleached, ramshackle shanty town called Anapra, thrown up out of wood and corrugated iron on the edge of a burgeoning city. The desert dirt and dust on which Anapra is built are criss-crossed by outlaw electricity supply cables to the barrio huts. El Paso and Juárez form the heart of, and midway point along, this singular strip of land conjoining two countries. The borderland is a place of paradox: of opportunity and poverty, promise and despair, love and violence, beauty and fear, sex and church, sweat and family. Even the frontier itself is a dichotomy, simultaneously porous and harsh. The US border patrol recognises the contradiction in its recruiting billboard on Interstate 19 north of Nogales, Arizona, advertising 'A Career in Borders, But No Boundaries'.

The frontier itself can be brutal. In 1994, the United States initiated 'Operation Gatekeeper' in San Diego, 'Operation Hold the Line' in El Paso and another similar operation in the Rio Grande Valley. Since then, under five administrations (Bill Clinton's twice, George W. Bush's twice and now Barack Obama), the border has become a military front line, along which runs more than 600 miles of fence enhanced by guard posts, search-lights and heavily armed patrols. In places where there is no fence, there are infrared cameras, sensors, national guard soldiers and SWAT teams from other, specialist law-enforcement columns, like the Drug Enforcement Adminstration and Bureau of Alcohol, Tobacco, Firearms and Explosives, plus the newly empowered border patrols and their own special forces, called BORTAC and BORSTAR. From the other side, apart from the tidal wave of drugs and migrants smuggled across the border, there are the killings: of Border Patrol agent Robert Rosas in Southern

California in August 2009, shot when he tried to interdict an armed incursion; and of the respected rancher Rob Krentz near Douglas, Arizona, when he chanced upon what were believed to be smugglers moving across his land.

There is a striking contrast between the asphalt of the United States and the instantaneous jumble and tumble of Mexico. When you fly over the border, you see streets arranged in a grid on the US side give way suddenly to those, if arranged at all, like a crazy-quilt. And the discrepancy is even greater between poverty on the US side and poverty on the Mexican side. One is struck by a stark, brazen inequality of wealth and power as one crosses the line, be it through the busy, click-clunk-click-clunk of turnstiles between sprawling Mexicali and tiny Calexico, or along the remote desert road between Lukeville, Arizona, and Sonoyta, Sonara; or over the trickle of the Rio Grande from El Paso into the cauldron of Juárez; the lustier flow between Eagle Pass and Piedras Negras or the last remaining cross-border ferry, between Los Ebanos, Texas, and Díaz Ordaz, Tamaulipas.

But the border is, as I say, porous. The more the United States builds its fence, enhances its technological stockade and empowers its patrols and customs officers, the more people cross the border *legally* – currently about a million of them every day. Families live astride the frontier; workers, shoppers, relatives and schoolchildren commute across the line; it takes twenty minutes to walk from downtown El Paso to main-street Juárez, from what is supposed to be the First World into what looks like the Third, yet is not. More commercial traffic crosses the US–Mexico border than any other in the world, currently worth some \$367.4 billion a year.[2] Five million trucks cross the border annually, and thousands of freight train wagons each day, carrying goods from across the Americas into the USA, and from China via the Mexican port of Lázaro Cárdenas – as well as southwards, bringing exports from the United States. A necklace of thousands of sweatshop assembly plants, called *maquiladoras*, has been established all along the border to provide the US with cheap labour just across its own frontier. American and Mexican fire services answer each other's calls and, during 2008, more than fifty victims of the drug violence in Ciudad Juárez were treated for multiple gunshot wounds at Thomason Hospital in El Paso. The border country has its own music, '*norteño*', and its own Spanglish slang spoken on both sides of the frontier, a lexicon that sometimes just jumbles the two languages together, as on the door of a bar in El Paso: '*Minores and Personas Armadas Strictly No Entrada*'. Friends may address each other as 'Mano!' mixing 'hey, man' with the Spanish '*hermano*' – brother. Across Mexico, a bicycle is a '*bicicleta*', but on the border it can be a '*baica*'. Someone's wife can be his '*waifa*' rather than '*esposa*'. In the US, a Chicano gangbanger is a '*vato*', but on the border he's a '*cholo*'.[3] Then there's the word for diarrhoea: '*turista*' – tourist, for obvious reasons. Perhaps the most useful border term of all is *rasquache* or *rasquachismo*, defined by the writer Tomás Ybarra-Frausto as being 'to posit a bawdy, spunky consciousness, to seek to subvert and turn ruling paradigms upside down. It is a witty, irreverent and impertinent posture', and if it doesn't define the borderline, there is certainly no shortage of it.[4]

The borderland is a territory in its own right, astride the line, estranged from both Washington and Mexico City, the centres of power whence decrees about its daily life are issued often without much understanding of how the borderland works or fails to work. There is as much seamlessness across the border as there is contrast. There is as much that bonds the two sides of the frontier as there is that divides them, though these adhesives and points of commonality are being tested and strained by the narco war. Gloria Anzaldúa, who revolutionised the Chicana writing of her generation, called the border '*una herida abierta* – an open wound – where the Third World grates against the First and bleeds. And before a scab forms, it haemorrhages again, the lifeblood of two countries merging to form a third country – a border culture.'[5] The borderland has an identity and flavour of daily life that spans the frontier, and I call this land – 2,100 miles long and about 50 miles wide, from the Pacific to the Gulf – *Amexica*. Now, because of the flood tide of narcotics running through and along it, Amexica is a battlefield, but a battlefield wrapped in everyday life. And for all its inquietude, the border is every bit as charismatic, complex and irresistible as it is fearful and terrifying.

'Amexica' is not just a play on words. The original and proper term for the Náhuatl-speaking Aztec people who migrated south to build their great city at Tenochtitlán – later Mexico City – and found their empire is 'Mexica' (pronounced 'Meshica'), and they came from just north of the border, around the so-called 'Four Corners' where New Mexico, Colorado, Arizona and Utah meet. The Chicano consciousness movement of US Latinos during the 1960s resurrected the notion of a cradle land of the Mexica people – in the northern (or south-western, to the Americans) deserts – called 'Aztatlán', or just 'Aztlán'. This land was important to Mexica creation mythology, based, like the border today, upon a concept of duality and complementary opposition. The creator God Ometeotl incorporates both male and female, and his/her children, Quetzalcoatl and Tezcatlipoca, are both allies and adversaries, representing harmony and conflict, balance and change.[6] According to some accounts, it was from Aztatlán that the primary God, Huitzilopochtli, led the Mexica south to what would become their imperial capital.[7] It was in what Mexicans now think of as the northern desert borderland that Huitzilopochtli was born to his mother, Coatlicue, primal mother and principal goddess of fertility and destruction, womb and tomb, who wore a skirt of serpents and a necklace of human hands and hearts.

The Spanish word for a border is *La Frontera*, with all the intended connotations of the word 'frontier' – as in the American 'Last Frontier'. While the south-western USA is 'the frontier' in American parlance and nineteenth century folklore, so *El Norte* – the same terrain, through Mexican eyes – struck a similar chord of mystique in the lore of both Spanish conquistadores and Mexicans after them. Before it actually became a border, what is now the borderland was a territory charged with the myth of exploration, risk, opportunity, outlaw glamour and danger. '*El Norte*' was symbolically charged in ancient Mexica legend: according to the Aztecs' coloured system of the flat world's four directions, north was white: its stone was white flint, and the white Ceiba tree, the tree of abundance, was said to grow there. But north was also associated with death and winter, and was the way to the underworld. More recently, while the Americans had Billy the Kid, Mexicans had El Zorro; to Americans, the cowboy is in the south-west; to Mexicans, *el vaquero* is in the north – they are the same personage in the same place, on *La Frontera*. Miguel Olmos Aguilera, a quietly spoken musicologist who directs the Cultural Studies Department at the *Colegio De La Frontera del Norte* in Tijuana, posits, in conversation, that 'the *"Frontera"* has always had an imaginative and emotional meaning, as well as a geographical one. Since pre-Hispanic days, it has been a place in the imagination of death and fame, suffering and heroism, as well as a reality which kills people.[8]

To citizens of the United States the word 'America' usually refers only to that country. To the rest of the continent, though, it refers to the entire continent – as well as to Mexico City's most famous football team, Club América. Mexico's powerful and ubiquitous symbol and icon, the Virgin of Guadalupe, is the Mother of God and Queen of Mexico – but she is also Empress of the Americas, all of them. There is, furthermore, academic debate about how and whence the masculine word 'Mexico' emerged – 'Mexica', like 'America', having been initially feminine.[9]

The border was created by the Treaty of Guadalupe Hidalgo in 1848, which ended the US–Mexican wars, after which the Gadsden Purchase of 1853, known in Mexico as the Sale of La Mesilla, pushed what is now Arizona and New Mexico south of the Gila river to the present frontier.[10] Ever since, people have kept arriving on the border, not just to cross it, but to remain by it. The more the populations grow, the more each pair of twin cities is bound together, the closer the two countries have become – an adhesion now challenged by the narco war. The demographics of migration across the border are, meanwhile, astounding: one in five Mexicans either visits or works in the United States at one time or another in their lives.[11] But *Amexica* is not about (to use that dreaded shorthand expression) 'the Hispanicisation of the USA', or that moment in 1996 when salsa overtook ketchup as the United States' favourite condiment. True, the Hispanic population of the United States now takes Amexica to and beyond the Canadian border, and especially to such places as Los Angeles of course, and thence Chicago, New York and the Carolinas. But this book is not about the estimated twelve million Mexicans and 28 million Mexican Americans living legally in the United States nor (probably) another 28 million illegal Mexican residents. It is about the quintessence of 'Amexica', the borderland itself.

Amexica found me as much as I found it. For years, I have worked along the borderline: narratives about international trucking and sweatshop factories, abducted women and the breathtaking desert, all set against a backdrop of adventure and hard grind, love and lust, achievement and tribulation, scintillescent light and occult shadows.

This is a place of impenitent heat by day and bitter winds cutting through the darkness of night. I have been a war reporter on many battlegrounds, yet nowhere has violence been so strange and commanded such revulsion and compulsion as it does along the borderline. War deepens the dichotomies, intensifying Amexica's magnetic field. It darkens the already opaque shade, making the colours even more lambent. The edge gets edgier but the ready smile more winning; the danger deepens but the welcome becomes warmer. The perversion of values makes the everyday more valuable; the feral physical cruelty of the slaughter accentuates the borderland's spirituality and its sensuality. The narco war has a suffocating claustrophobia about it, in counterpoint to the unique beauty and infinite *scale* of the landscape – the eternity of desert and sky that form its backdrop. The distances are all the more liberating but they are deceptive, and savage also: something is always about to happen in Amexica, hence the dread and expectation, apprehension and tenterhooks of every moment.

This is not a story with a beginning, middle and end, it is a slice of very recent, unfinished history. Or to take from Brian DeLay's introduction to his greatest of all books written about the border, *War of a Thousand Deserts*: 'This is a shared story. This is American history, Mexican history and Indian history.' This book is not so much about a war as it is a view of a singular place in time of war. It is about the ways in which war impacts Amexica, but it also shows how the war is a consequence of other – mainly economic – degradations and exploitations, quite apart from drugs, from which the border's people have suffered. A suffering due not least to the fact that narco cartels are corporations like any other, applying the commercial logic and following the same globalised 'business models' as the multiplicity of legal enterprises that have wreaked a different kind of havoc along the borderline. Indeed, the drug violence is in many ways a direct result of the deprivation and misery caused by the legal globalised economy. The cartels are not pastiches of multinational capital – they are pioneers of it, integral to it, and apply its rules and logic (or, rather, lack of rules and logic) to their marketplace just as would any other commercial enterprise.

The book is also a journey from west to east, Pacific to Gulf. It begins in Tijuana, opposite San Diego, where two cartels are locked in battle. Thence into the deserts of Sonora and Arizona, and the deadly trails followed by half of all illegal migrants into the US across the border – a business being commandeered by the narco cartels. The kernel of the voyage is Ciudad Juárez, where the idea of a war between cartels implodes into criminal anarchy and terrible suffering from violence, addiction and deprivation. The road then winds through breathtaking country, on the US side in Texas and on the Rio Grande's right bank into cities like Ciudad Acuña and Piedras Negras, utterly transformed by the arrival not so much of drug cartels as *maquiladora* factories. Next is the border's main trade corridor and temple of its commercial porosity, from Nuevo Laredo into Laredo, Texas. This is the truck route between Mexico and the USA: it is also where the latest drug war began, for the trade is contaminated by a river of smuggled drugs. The journey ends in the border's richest and most complex territory in terms of history and identity: Tamaulipas on the Mexican side and the Rio Grande Valley in Texas, between which the cartels' drugs flow north – and the guns run south across the borderline to the terrifying 'Zetas', a paramilitary cartel.

The voyage will not only be a geographical one. It will afford a glimpse behind the insistently glamorous associations which the drug business enjoys. When the narco trafficker looks in the mirror, he sees not a criminal, but a romantic bandit. As Roberto Saviano, author of the remarkable book *Gomorrah*, about the Neapolitan Camorra syndicates, put it in conversation: 'They love to think of themselves as Scarface; it's their favourite movie.'[12] But because of the singular product in which the narco *traficante* deals, the media and society also see in the narco more than a little bit of Scarface, thanks to the packaging of drug culture by our media and mass culture. We have become vogueishly obsessed with 'fair trade' consumerism to the point that supermarket chains compete with each other's rhetoric about where and how the mange-tout peas are grown by happy African villagers. Multinational coffee-shop chains strive to make consumers feel good about the 'sustainable' Andean or Indonesian plantations their particular brand of latte comes from. But this pop-moral advertising lexicon does not apply to the origins of drugs: public fascination with celebrity drug-addiction has exempted drugs from the touchy-feely vocabulary of 'ethical' consumerism. For all the concern, however laudable, with the lives ruined to make cheap clothes or an unethical cappuccino, few ever stop to ask how many lives just went up a supermodel's nose – the opposite, indeed: the same media that pontificates about ethical consumerism treats celebrity drug-taking as fodder for tittle-tattle gossip, laced with a giggly – only slightly disapproving – waggle of the forefinger. Or even excessive sympathy for the stars in rehabilitation, or admiration for gutsy appearances on reality TV. *Amexica* offers a backstage pass, access all areas, behind the celebrity gossip and those glittering cocaine nights in Los Angeles, New York, London and Madrid.

There is another way in which the narco war fits into our contemporary modus vivendi that makes it very much a war of its time. It is the first real twenty-first-century war, because it is about, in the end, nothing. Mexico's war is a conflict of the post-political era. It is being fought in an age of belligerent hyper-materialism as an ideology in itself, the leading exponents of which run their corporations or banks with personal greed as their sole credo, and their brands as icons of this post-modern religion. Until this hyper-materialist era, the human race has populated a world where, unfortunately, Muslims and Jews fight each other, communists and fascists, Serbs and Croats, Tutsis and Hutus, American or British soldiers and Islamic insurgents, and so on. We may all have different readings of why they do this, but they do so – at least nominally – for a cause, faith or tribal identity, however crazy. But Mexico's war (some do not like calling it a war) has not even the pretence of a propelling cause. Mexicans are mutilating, decapitating, torturing and killing each other ostensibly over money and the drug-smuggling routes that provide it. Some would argue that all wars are fought indirectly over money and resources, be they wars of empire fought in the nineteenth century until 1918, or wars of ideology or religion in the twentieth century. But most of the savage violence in Mexico is for the smaller profits of the domestic market and local street corner, meted out for its own sake. There is no financial stake in killing a street addict. There are regional and clan identities, to the states of Tamaulipas, or Sinaloa, but they are fluid and subject to too many whimsical alliances and betrayals for the war to be defined as tribal as it is in, say, Rwanda. Mexico's war has no ideological pretentions or window dressing – its only cover is that it was originally fought, like other, lesser, Mafia wars, over the now diversified product lines that get America (and

Europe) high. But the *casus belli* is now even more vacuous than that. The narco war is fought for the accoutrements of a new post-modern social kudos, social performance, the ability to show off the right labels, brands and products in accordance with advertising; to wear the right clothes, to be accompanied by the appropriately desirable girl, chatter on the latest mobile phone with the latest 'applications', own the right gadget and drive the right SUV. For these definitions of status, thousands die. The narco war is fought on YouTube and mobile phones as well as in the streets and back-room torture chambers: cartels use YouTube to threaten rivals and public officials, boast of their killing and set up rogue 'hot spot' digital sites to broadcast their savagery and invite comments. One such site hosted from El Paso received more than 320,000 hits and posted more than 1,000 comments.[13] Murders, mutilations and executions are posted on the Internet, themselves a blend of cyber-sado-pornography. Unlike the cyber-strutting of al-Qaeda, from whom it is sometimes argued they got the idea, the narcos use digital communication not as a weapon of insane Holy War, but with something approaching a sense of humour with which to goad and boast across cyberspace — gift-wrapping their real-life bloodlust in the electronic ether of titillation and non-meaning.

The post-moral vulgarity of 'mainstream' capitalist culture from which these digitally-savvy narcos get their ideas in turn rises to meet them in its own product lines, demonstrating, reciprocally, just how 'mainstream' the narcos themselves are; how much they belong to, and are symptomatic of, the contemporary cultural-economic landscape, rather than estranged from it. In summer 2010, the MAC cosmetics line, owned by Estée Lauder, was set to launch a new couture and make-up range inspired by young girls working in the *maquiladoras* of Juárez, with an 'outre' edge provided by the fact that — as everyone knows — hundreds of these girls have been abducted, violated and murdered — a kind of 'Feminicidio Chic'. The lines, designed by Laura and Kate Mulleavy, sisters behind avant-garde fashion label Rodarte, was to feature off-white chiffon and lace garments, lipstick and nail polish in shades such as Sleepwalker, Juárez and Ghost Town, inspired by the 'lines of women workers making their way to factory jobs in the middle of the night,' according to a company press release. MAC's proposal met, thankfully, with uproar from activist groups such as Women on the Border, whose Executive Director Elvia Arriola called the proposed launch 'exploitative of women's pain'. In July 2010, MAC mumbled that it would change the product names and donate $100,000 to a charity in Juárez, while the wretched Mulleavy sisters chirped that 'We never intended to make light of this serious issue and we are truly sorry.'

At the time of writing, though, the Ubisoft company, which develops computer games, has no plans to cancel its launch of a rip-roaring new entertainment called 'Call of Juárez: The Cartel'. Players are invited on the company's website to thrill themselves by living out the city's misery and carnage on their computer screens and 'take the law into [their] own hands' on a 'bloody road trip from Los Angeles to Juárez'. Previewed graphics show gunmen dressed in Stetsons and flak vests roaming grim city streets toting shotguns and a Kalashnikov.*

One striking feature of the post-political war is that neither the political left nor right has managed to muster the slightest resistance. There is no significant trade union, nor any revolutionary or overtly workers' movement against the narco cartels (though civil society organisations doing their level best tend to be of the left). Similarly, there is no sign of a rightist, fascistic or vigilante movement for law and order (at least not on the Mexican side of the border); the army's role is a mercurial one, and no Mussolini figure to the right of President Calderón has come to the fore. Instead, a war that is quintessentially materialist and largely male meets resistance from two quarters that do not belong to conventional politics. The post-political, materialist war meets resistance from the 'pre-political' clergy and church groups more than any other constituency of society – both Catholic (though not entirely from the organised Church) and reformed. And the male war meets resistance from strong women, as individuals, organisations – and in the home. That these social quarters provide the only measureable, let alone cogent, counterweight to narco violence at street level is something with which a secular mass media, forever seeking policy

* 'Cartel video game riles US–Mexico border residents' by Julián Cardona and Alejandro Martinez-Cabrera, Reuters, Thursday February 17, 2011.

options and conventional political or military 'solutions', is deeply and visibly uncomfortable, not least because they all, serially, fail.

This was the kind of war being fought by the cartels during the two weeks over Christmas in 2008:

- A man masquerading as a fisherman, calling himself Enrique Portocarrero, is arrested in Colombia for designing and building twenty fibre-glass submarines to bring cocaine ashore in Mexico. He was known as 'Captain Nemo'[14]
- A sudden escalation of declamatory *narcomantas* in public places, usually naming and warning local police officials, reached a zenith in every sense, hung from Monterrey cathedral and ominously denouncing President Calderón himself for favouring the Sinaloa cartel over its principal rival, the Gulf cartel[15]
- A member of President Calderón's personal and permanent bodyguard was arrested and charged for being in the employ of – and feeding secrets about the president's policies and movements to – the Beltrán Leyva brothers cartel
- After five men were arrested and charged in El Paso alone for procuring firearms in Texas and smuggling them into Mexico, US Secretary of State Condoleezza Rice insisted that the lifting of a ban on semi-automatic weapons had nothing to do with the vast quantities of such weapons seized in Mexico[16]
- The decapitated bodies of twelve federal army soldiers are found in the southern state of Guerrero, the most audacious single execution of serving military personnel since the Mexican revolution of 1910. They are gagged by the arms and feet when executed, with a message reading: 'For Every One of Mine You Kill, We Kill Ten'[17]
- The US National Drug Assessment Threat report for 2009 declares that 'The Mexican drug-trafficking organisations represent the greatest organised crime threat to the United States'

During the first two weeks of the New Year, 2009:

- Twenty-one people are killed within forty-eight hours in and around Ciudad Juárez
- Twenty-seven people are killed within one week in Baja California

- A television station in Monterrey is attacked with grenades after reporting on narco murders[18]
- General Mauro Enrique Tello Quiñones, who left the army to work as a security consultant for the mayor of Cancún in his efforts against the narcos, is abducted, tortured and executed along with two adjutants. Among those arrested in connection with the murder are Cancún's police chief and several of his senior officers[19]
- In Tijuana, Santiago Meza López is arrested, charged with disintegrating 300 bodies in acid
- Four decapitated seventeen-year-olds are among twenty-one people killed in Tijuana during the first week of the year[20]
- Twenty-one senior law-enforcement officers in Tijuana are arrested for protecting the Arellano Félix cartel. There is speculation as to whether this is a genuine offensive by authorities trying to clean up corruption, or said authorities working for the rival Sinaloa cartel

The transition from Christmas 2009 into the New Year, 2010, went thus:

- During the first four days of December, twenty-five are killed in Ciudad Juárez, as the city is blanketed by a rare snowfall, bringing the annual total of dead to 2,390 for a single city[21]
- It emerges that only 2 per cent of the much-vaunted $1.4 billion 'Mérida Initiative' of aid from the United States to Mexico to help fight the cartels has arrived in the recipient country due to bureaucratic problems, contracting rules and difficulties getting helicopters to Mexico[22]
- Thirteen Zeta gangsters are killed as Mexican marines burst through the gates of a narco compound outside Monterrey. Several passers-by, including a twelve-year-old girl, are injured by intense fire. The Zetas call for help, which arrives in the form of a dozen armed vehicles that then engage an army patrol it meets on the way[23]
- An American teacher and school district councillor from Southern California, Bobby Salcedo, is abducted and killed in Durango while visiting his wife's home town of Gómez Palacio during a twinning celebration between his town and hers. Four others were also kidnapped and killed

- A special forces naval ensign, Melquisedet Angulo Córdova, was killed during the shoot-out that eliminated Beltrán Leyva. Two days after his official funeral, gunmen burst into the home of Angulo Córdova's family, killing four of his immediate family, including his mother[27]
- The body of thirty-six-year-old Hugo Hernández, abducted in Sonora on 2 January, turns up in Los Mochis, Sinaloa, though not in one piece. His torso is in one location, his severed arms and legs boxed in another place, and his skull found in another. But his face had been flayed, left near the city hall of Los Mochis, sewn to a soccer ball[28]
- The death toll in Ciudad Juárez for only the first week of the New Year, 2010, reaches the abominable figure of fifty-nine[29]

On New Year's Eve, a week before Mr Hernández's face was discovered tied to a football in Los Mochis, the bound, beaten and tortured bodies of two men had also been found nearby, with their hands tied behind their backs. A message beside them read: 'This Territory Already Has An Owner'. But the twist was this: these last deaths of 2009 were bodies hanging from an overpass, just like the headless man from 'Switchback Bridge' in Juárez.[30]

CHAPTER ONE

La Plaza

My friend Jorge Fregoso and I were drinking a beer at a bar in a labyrinth of quiet alleyways away from central Tijuana one Saturday afternoon in September 2008 when the shooting started. It targeted an art-deco mansion in the sedate Misión del Pedregal suburb. Federal army trucks arrived to its left, state police shock troops to the right. Few shots were fired from inside the building, it seemed, but a deafening fusillade of fire was aimed at the villa. Only next day was it revealed to have procured, for the authorities, Eduardo Arellano Félix – 'The Doctor' – chief of the clan trying to defend the plaza of drug traffic between Tijuana and California for his Arellano brothers syndicate from the raiding Sinaloa cartel. Misión del Pedregal is clearly marked as being, says the sign adjacent to Arellano's house, a *'Vecinos Vigilando'*, Neighbourhood Watch, zone – yet, says a woman cleaning her porch opposite Arellano's next day, 'I didn't think there was anyone living in that house.' What followed the announcement were seventy-two hours of carnage even by Tijuana standards, which took the death toll for the city to 462 in the year 2008, and caused even the local *El Sol de Tijuana* newspaper, accustomed to such things, to run the headline *'Baño de Sangre'*, bloodbath.

Fregoso, a reporter for the local Síntesis TV news channel, and I receive our first alert shortly after 3 p.m. on the Monday when we are called to a *colonia* called Libertad, where a corpse lies slumped in the dirt beneath a rung of steps made of tyres. A crowd of young people arrives to observe the busy forensic aftermath in a disconcertingly knowing silence, punctuated by the odd giggly joke or mobile phone call, while some 30 metres away the iron wall that marks the border with the USA also looks on, the old fence made of metal landing sheets used by the US air force from Vietnam to Iraq in 1991.

Three young women from the forensic team (wearing identical grey shirts, black jeans and pony tails) take careful photographs and notes, then, like the accompanying trucks full of balaclava-covered federal police, speed off to a different location, Mariano Matamoros, and a major artery on the city's outskirts where another corpse lies, visible by the green light of a Pemex gas station. The windscreen of the victim's Ford Explorer (with California plates) is pitted with three bullet holes, and he seems to have made a run into the street, followed by twenty-five further shots, each shell casing marked by a blue number on a yellow card. Before the forensic women have even finished here, we are immediately summoned across dirt tracks — tearing, zigzagging, between cement buildings — to a crossing of back streets in the Casablanca district, and a lifeless body beside the doorway of a corner shop painted with yellow flowers. When the ninja-clad cops pull back the sheet, we see a teenager shot at point-blank range in the face, blood oozing onto the flagstones, and a watching girl turns away to weep into her mobile phone. But now the night really begins.

Fregoso, with his access to police communications, receives the news so fast that we hurtle our orange Volkswagen between the fourth and fifth jeeps of a machine-gun-toting police convoy (to the hooting fury of jeep number five) heading for the next slaughter. The cordon of plastic tape reading '*Precuación*' is not even in place yet outside the 9/4 minimart in Villa Foresta, in theory selling '*Vinos y licores*', where a blanket covers the remains of the security guard, with two more dead inside. There is wild wailing from the womenfolk as this body outside was revealed: his flesh has been grated into something like raw kebab meat by fire at point-blank range from a Kalashnikov, or *cuerno de chivo* — goat's horn — as an AK-47 is known around here. Further screams follow the sight of those killed inside the store, brought out on stretchers and loaded into the white 'DIF' Forensic Department truck now carrying five former people. The shop, says the *susurro* — the rustling whisper through the crowd — was a stash for drugs being loaded for export aboard two cars, presumably intended to join the 65,000 that cross from Tijuana into San Diego every day, but which the police now tow away. Meanwhile, heavy-set men in sharp suits arrive to look from a slight distance, embracing each other in a way that suggested burdensome comradeship and solace, but little sadness. Any attempt to speak to them is rebuffed with menacing silence and a glare. One of them goes over to console a young woman clutching a baby, in paroxysms of grief, beneath a mural advertising Viper auto alarms.

Yonkes – repair yards for fixing up cars with second-hand parts – are a hallmark of Tijuana's byways, and next morning another group of *sicarios* – or maybe the same squad – return to Villa Foresta in brazen, broad noonday light, past the mural of a girl in a bikini sprawled over an SUV and into gate number one of *Yonke Cristal*, killing one man whose body, wearing a red shirt, is visible through the bars of a red gate. Two other corpses are hidden behind a white van, the skeletal metal frames of the vehicles all around, detached wheel hubs like prying eyes, and the words *'Jesucristo Excelsior'* carved into the hillside above. This is now Tuesday, and on Wednesday morning Tijuana awakes to the news that while the city slept, three more bodies were found in an abandoned van and another in a car. The van has been dumped in a quarter called Los Álamos, at a meeting point between ramshackle hillside *colonias*, a smart gated community and an electronics factory, and the dead men have been tortured, mutilated and strangled – one of them handcuffed. People killed and dumped in vehicles are known in this war as *'encajuelados'*, literally 'entrunked'. The body in the car is that of a police officer called Mauricio Antonio Hernando Flores. It is his personal car, and the officer had parked beneath a great statue of an open-armed figure of Christ, presiding over Tijuana in imitation of Rio de Janeiro, with its engine running, just past 1 a.m. apparently awaiting someone. Whoever shot him, leaving his body to be discovered slumped in the blood-soaked driver's seat, knew him, and was expected at the scene.

There are two kinds of cop-killings in the narco war. One was illustrated in January 2008 when the narcos crossed some line in the etiquette of drug warfare. The *sicarios'* car pulled off a main road onto the dirt track into the wretched *colonia* of Loma Bonita. They would have parked next to the Swap Meet jumble-sale hangar and walked to what is now a vacant lot for sale, marked by a white wooden cross, where officer Margarito Zaldano lived. They entered the house and executed not only Zaldano but also his wife Sandra and twelve-year-old daughter Valeria. Zaldano's crime? Being a cop and doing his job trying to arrest criminals who were protected by his own police force. The other kind of slaying of police officers – or *la chota*, as they are known on the border, the fuzz – involves those who become embroiled with the narcos, work for them or add to the income of their day job by moonlighting for the cartels, often with the same uniforms and weapons. These officers get caught out if they renege on a deal, charge too much for their services, oversights or information, or if their work for one cartel becomes irksome to another. Mexicans joke that a police officer is offered a simple career choice: *plata o plomo* – silver or lead – and many, while they can get it, inevitably opt for the former. After the killing of Officer Flores, the authorities, in contrast to their outpouring of tribute to Zaldano back in January, refused to fuss much over this latest execution of one of their colleagues by a single *tiro de gracia* – a 'mercy' shot to the head. In Tijuana, as elsewhere, the municipal police can be working for one cartel, the state police with another, and the *Federales* with yet another. None of this happens in a vacuum.

Like every war, this carnage has a history, and we need to understand the background to the narco cartels' business, lest the war appear to be the senseless bloodletting it is not. Or, at least, was not at first. Indeed, one needs to know one's Mafia history as much as that of any major player in the global economy and polity, because the syndicates are more powerful, more astute, and handle higher turnovers than most multinational corporations, as well as fuel our society with their products. The drug cartels were prototypes and pioneers of globalisation; the Neapolitan 'Camorra' was the first multinational into post-communist Eastern Europe, harvesting Kalashnikovs produced under Soviet licence. The Camorra was also among the first capitalist enterprises to penetrate communist China, dealing in textiles and drugs coming into the port of Naples. Now that the 'legal' global economy is in crisis, narco cartels respond to their own crisis within that economy in their own – but by no means separate – way.

Unlike their Italian counterparts, the Mexican cartels cannot trace their origins to the eighteenth century, but they were drug-dealing before the Italians. The smuggling syndicate based in Ciudad Juárez was not only the first narco syndicate run by a woman, 'La Nacha', Ignacia Jasso, but among the first to trade in heroin to the USA, after the market for supplying America with alcohol, during Prohibition, came to an end in 1933. The Mexican heroin-growing and opium market in Sinaloa gained impetus during the Second World War, when the United States signed an agreement to buy opium to meet its wartime medical needs.[1] The Mexican narco smugglers did start dealing in drugs on a major scale at the same time as the Italians, towards the end of the 1960s, when it became clear that demand from the United States and Europe was insatiable. 'The narco economy,' wrote Guillermo Ibarra, an economist at Sinaloa State University, 'and family remittances from the United States actually keep our state on its feet.'[2]

At first, Mexico's role was that of producer, of 'Mexican Mud' heroin, poppies for which were ideally suited to the climate of the Pacific coast state of Sinaloa, home of the 'classic' narco cartels – then and now. Two initiatives by the US government during the 1970s and '80s changed things, and in part laid the foundations for the modern cartels. First, during the 1970s, the United States steered the Mexican government through 'Operation Condor', which succeeded in all but destroying indigenous Mexican heroin production, incinerating and defoliating the Sinaloan poppy crops, in dichotomous partnership with the same Mexican political apparatus that had ruled in close co-existence with – protected by and protecting – the *gomeros*, or heroin barons, so called because of the gummy texture of their merchandise.

Second, Washington embarked on its covert backing of right-wing Contra rebels against the Sandinista government in Nicaragua.[3] The Contras would be armed with weapons secretly transported from the US, with the criminal underworld acting as supplier and mediator. But the arms had to be paid for in 'currency' that would not call attention to itself, and they were: in cocaine from Colombia. Luckily for all involved, narcotic science and narcotic fashion both coincided with Washington's interests, as well as those of the cartels in Colombia and Mexico. Just as the US needed Colombia's natural currency to procure and pay for arms to the Contras, cocaine was becoming the drug of choice: in powdered form for American entertainment and other smart circles, and in its chemical derivative form, crack, on the street and in the ghetto. The Mexicans became the courier service for arms in one direction and cocaine in the other – a service that became known as the 'Mexican Trampoline'. Mexico's cartels combined three things to act as a conduit in flooding America with crack and cocaine: their knowledge of smuggling routes as old as the border itself, the unofficial acquiescence of the Reagan administration, and their conviviality with Mexico's Institutional Revolutionary Party, which had ruled since 1917. In so doing, they realised, as novelist Don Winslow put it: 'that their real product isn't drugs, it's the two-thousand-mile border they share with the United States. Land can be burned, crops can be poisoned, people can be displaced, but that border isn't going anywhere.'[4]

As masters of the border, Mexican narcos were in a position to assume control of the hemisphere. Cocaine supply routes through the Caribbean and Miami were strangled by US authorities still earnest about fighting a 'war on drugs', which only increased the flow through Mexico, which it was impossible to throttle. The Mexican traffickers demanded that their Colombian suppliers pay not in cash for the necessary transportation, but in kind; and the percentage of cocaine payable as commission for the delivery service increased, and increased. So that now, according to the US Drug Enforcement Administration, 90 per cent of all drugs entering the United States do so as part of Mexican cartel business. The major imports are still cocaine and marijuana, though recent Mexican mass-production of methamphetamine accounts for most US consumption of the drug, as it does across Latin America. The bust of a methamphetamine factory in Argentina in September 2008 involved predominantly Mexican nationals. Drug-enforcement agencies also blame Mexican cartels for the sudden spike in heroin availability, and the precipitous fall in street prices, from $5,000 per ounce in 2004 to $1,000 per ounce in 2008.

But when we talk about 'The Mexicans' we talk not about a homogenous organisation; quite the reverse. We talk about cartels operating, during this period, under licence from the authorities. Franchised by municipal, state and federal government officials and police forces, the system was based, through an organised network of corruption on what is called the *'Plaza'* – a word used in Spanish to mean a place of gathering, be it a square in the centre of a town, or the *Plaza de Toros* – a bullring – or the jurisdiction of a police or military force. Apart, crucially, from its eastern stretch towards the Gulf, the border was strategically carved into drug-smuggling 'Plazas', each considered the territory of a sub-division of the original Sinaloan mafia, which would pay the authorities for protection and cooperation – with percentages shaved off at every level, to the top – on its turf. In return, the mafia would finger freelance or rival operators so that the authorities could give the impression of an authentic enforcement operation.[5]

Even if it sometimes feels a bit like train-spotting, we need to be familiar with the names and heritage of the major trafficking organisations that operate the trade worth an estimated $323 billion a year[6] – pushing drugs into the veins of the wretched, up the noses of the rich, and frying the brains of the young. People refer to 'the Mafia' as though it were some amorphous alien force or – worse – a romantic brotherhood operating to some code of honour laid down by 'Godfather' Corleone, a Marlon Brando don. 'Mafia' is a useful generic term, but applies properly only to Cosa Nostra of Sicily, the syndicate with which the world is most familiar because of its history and mythic presence in mass culture. But in Mexico, as in Italy, the dramatis personae of narco traffic is more complicated than 'the Mafia', and we need to know the cast.

The pioneer of Mexico's narco trafficking mafia was Pedro Avilés Pérez, from Sinaloa, who escalated the smuggling of marijuana and heroin into the United States during the late 1960s. But the original Mexican Godfather was Miguel Ángel Félix Gallardo, a protégé of Avilés' who took over his operation after Avilés was killed in a shootout with the police in 1978. Félix Gallardo founded the Guadalajara cartel and became perhaps the biggest narco trafficker in the world during his zenith. In 1985, however, a calamity changed the cartel, the Mexican government's conviviality with it, and US complicity with that relationship. An undercover agent for the US Drugs Enforcement Administration, Enrique 'Kiki' Camarena, was fingered, kidnapped and tortured to death in Guadalajara (there is evidence that the CIA knew and may even have trained the people who did it, to a point that relations between the two agencies have never since fully recovered).

The truth behind Camarena's death has eluded all attempts at excavation, but whatever that truth, Washington demanded that Mexico do something – and that something was to arrest Félix Gallardo. In 1989, Gallardo was convicted for ordering Camarena's abduction and murder, but from jail he sought to keep his organisation together, allocating its various component Plazas in which to operate. There was even a council, held in an expensive Acapulco hotel, to which the jailed Gallardo sent messengers to clarify the Plazas, exhort the cartels to cooperate against their common enemy, US law enforcement, and offer advice on how to negotiate with the Mexican authorities and impose discipline.[7]

Gallardo's vision was one which in Italy is called a *Pax Mafiosa* – the Mafia's peace – whereby criminal syndicates know their place with reference to each other, law enforcement knows its place in the same scheme of things, the product keeps flowing, and politicians understand that this kind of quiet comes at a price – protection. A *Pax Mafiosa* can guarantee the politician votes, and a power base, in return for nothing more than the tranquillity of a blind eye at least, or cover for, even adherence to, a particular cartel at best. But this is not how the criminal mind works. If the cartels are greedy, why should they not become even greedier? If their modus operandi is to break laws, why would their modus vivendi be keep to them? When things become bloody in the world of narco trafficking, and the peace is blown apart, this means power is shifting, disintegrating or resisting disintegration and being claimed across the ordained Plazas. When Cosa Nostra famously blew up the anti-Mafia judges Giovanni Falcone and Paolo Borsellino in 1992, it was taken wrongly to be a sign of the Mafia's strength. Cosa Nostra was reeling from what the judges had achieved against them, and – crucially – the tables were turning across the Plazas of Italy. Cosa Nostra was being overtaken by new – leaner and meaner – operators: the Camorra of Naples and 'Ndrangheta of Calabria. The old guard was in trouble, the Plaza unquiet. Nor, in Mexico, could such a momentous event as Gallardo's arrest occur without leaving a vacuum, any more than any of his lieutenants could resist trying to fill it. The Guadalajara cartel split, different branches claiming its mantle: one, led by Gallardo's nephews and nieces, established the Tijuana cartel: another, led by Joaquín Guzmán – *El Chapo* or Shorty – founded the Sinaloa cartel and a third formed the Juárez cartel. But the shattering of *Pax Mafiosa* did not result in a reduction in the flow of drugs, it means only that control of the flow, of the Plazas, is up for grabs. It has also come to mean, in Mexico, that unfettered greed and a terrible surplus has created a new Plaza on home turf, contaminating Mexico itself. And so a draft map of the present war came to be drawn.

The most famous Plaza, that between Tijuana and California, was featured in Steven Soderbergh's film *Traffic*. It was run by the Tijuana cartel, or Arellano Félix Organisation, the AFO, but is now contested. The Tijuana cartel is the only one to claim a direct (but disputed) family connection to Gallardo: Gallardo had five nephews, the Arellano Félix brothers – Eduardo, arrested that Saturday in Misión Pedregal, was the last to remain at large. Joaquín '*El Chapo*' Guzmán's first round of offensives on the border followed the borderline itself, west to east, starting in the early 1990s in Tijuana, soon after Gallardo's arrest, when Guzmán claimed the *Padrino*'s mantle. In those days, the AFO kept Guzmán at bay: the early 1990s were the days of the 'Narco Juniors' in Tijuana, who flaunted a style that the recent violence has only just forced out of date. The brothers and their entourage would cruise the city and its nightlife, dressing outrageously, on their motorcycles or in SUV *trocas*. In many ways, they invented a narco style of yuppie razzmatazz. The AFO most infamously perpetrated the highest hit against the Catholic Church by any crime syndicate, when its hit men killed Cardinal Juan Jesús Posadas Ocampo, on 24 May 1993 at Guadalajara airport.

The AFO can be said to be prime movers in changing the rules of engagement to include women and children as well as clerics – something the 'old guard' narcos prided themselves in avoiding. In August 2008, Jesús Rubén Moncada – aka '*El Güero Loco*' the Crazy Blond – was arrested in Los Angeles for a famous massacre in 1998 of nineteen people, including a baby clutched in its mother's arms, on a villa veranda near Ensenada, down the coast south of Tijuana. He had been living illegally in LA for ten years.[8] In 2002, the cartel's leader, Ramón Arellano Félix, was shot and killed by federal police. And in the latest round of violence since 2006, the AFO has been subjected to a battering by Guzmán's cartel, which abated only recently when his man in Tijuana, Eduardo García Simental, known as '*El Teo*', was arrested in January 2010. The arrest of Eduardo Arellano Félix that Saturday afternoon in 2008 leaves his sister Enelda as commander of the Tijuana clan (a first for a woman since Ignacia Jasso in Juárez during Prohibition), while Eduardo's nephew, Fernando Sánchez Arellano, 'The Engineer', runs the street operation. Enelda is an important figure, because narco trafficking had become a male domain – until now, when more and more women have become engaged in the business. Drug trafficking is seen as a more dignified profession than prostitution, as women elect to serve as smugglers, with a better chance of passing border controls and checkpoints than men. There have been some major arrests of women, and the body of María José González, singer and winner of the Sun Festival beauty pageant, was found by a road in Culiacán in spring 2009 near that of her drug-trafficking husband and a sign reading 'Don't Throw Trash'. The authorities believe she had become involved with the Sinaloa cartel, one of many beauty queens to become cartel mascots, then victims of their rivals.[9]

A stretch of land between Tijuana and Ciudad Juárez is variously controlled by an organisation that switches allegiance to bigger cartels in order to operate. It was once run by two brothers called Arturo and Alfredo Beltrán Leyva, who come from the same range of mountains as *Chapo* Guzmán, near the town of Guamúchil, in Sinaloa. For years, the Beltrán Leyva brothers operated their stretch of frontier on behalf of the Sinaloa cartel, to which they were allied. They acted also as a security wing for Guzmán, overseeing squads of *sicarios* and protecting *El Chapo*'s lieutenants and their families. But two things happened in rapid succession: in December 2007, while Guzmán's cartel was fighting the Gulf cartel and its military wing, the Zetas, leaders from the Beltrán Leyva cartel held a treacherous meeting with the Zetas in Veracruz, purportedly to discuss opening a space for the brothers in Central Mexico, independently of Guzmán. The meeting fitted into a series the Zetas were said to be holding, offering their services as hit men for a 'super-cartel' comprising anyone prepared to challenge Guzmán.[10] In January 2008, a month after the meeting, Alfredo Beltrán Leyva was arrested, and in this moment lay a turning point in the war. Guzmán is said to have commented that Beltrán Leyva's meeting with the Zetas necessitated his having to 'cut off that arm of the organisation'. The Beltrán Leyva clan deserted Guzmán, convinced that he had delivered Alfredo to the authorities in order to court, or even secure, their favour. The younger brother, Arturo Beltrán Leyva, '*El Alfa*', exacted revenge on senior public officials, including the Federal Police Commissioner, and on Guzmán's son, Edgar Guzmán López, whom his *sicarios* gunned down in a shopping mall in May 2008. As head of security for Guzmán, Arturo had the home addresses of the families of his senior affiliates, and the violence unleashed by Beltrán Leyva against his former protector's entourage accounts for some of the worst recent killing in Sinaloa.

Over Christmas and New Year 2009–10, a government offensive against the Beltrán Leyva cartel reached high drama. On 16 December, a unit of naval special forces, backed by helicopter cover, stormed Arturo's dwelling complex in Cuernevaca, shot and killed him – the highest narco drug lord to be assassinated by the military since President Calderón's offensive, and the first since Ramón Arellano Félix in 2002. Beltrán Leyva's bloodied corpse was subject by his military assassins to an official rite associated with the narcos themselves. Photographs showed his jeans pulled down to his knees and his torso adorned with rows of bloodied $100 bills, and in another shot with spiritual accoutrements. Such a display angered commentators such as Jorge Chabat in *El Universal*, who called the rite 'the typical modus operandi of narco traffickers',[11] but that newspaper, like others, eagerly published the images.[12]

During the raid of 16 December, an ensign from the commando unit, Melquisedet Angulo Córdova, aged thirty, had been killed as Beltrán Leyva's bodyguards exchanged fire. He was buried with full military honours, and the response of Beltrán Leyva's supporters was immediate. The day after the commando's hometown funeral in the state of Tabasco, gunmen burst into his grieving family's home, killing his mother, sister, brother and an aunt.[13] By targeting the immediate family of military personnel serving in the war against them, the narcos had escalated the stakes in Mexico's war by yet another notch, but the authorities' response was equally swift. With both senior Beltrán Leyva brothers removed, leadership of the cartel fell to the younger Héctor Beltrán Leyva. He remains at large, but on 2 January 2010, another brother, Carlos, was taken by a bloodless swoop in the Sinaloan capital of Culiacán. The government could not have made itself clearer: the war was being cranked up still further. But who stood to gain? The President, of course; but also, said the whisper on the street – which on the border is called a *susurro*, a rustle of leaves – the Sinaloa cartel, who had everything to win from the government's war against its rivals, as the government well knows.

Ciudad Juárez was always the core of Amexica, formerly '*El Paso Del Norte*' – portal to the North – a trading route long before the border and a smuggling route as old as the line itself. *La Nacha Jasso* was the unchallenged heroin and then marijuana queen of Juárez from the legalisation of alcohol until the 1970s. But the modern Juárez cartel was forged by Amado Carrillo Fuentes, who emerged as a force after he attached himself to the most powerful drug lord of the central border area, Pablo Acosta Villarreal, during the 1980s. Acosta operated out of the isolated town of Ojinaga, opposite Presidio in Texas, and in an unparalleled series of interviews with the writer Terrence Poppa, detailed how his syndicate enjoyed the protection of the state and federal police, politicians and army.[14] But, spotting his chance, Carrillo arranged for his mentor to be killed by federal officers during a raid on his home village of Santa Elena in 1987, which involved cooperation with forces from the US side. In his excellent account of Carrillo's building of the Juárez cartel, *Down by the River*, Charles Bowden relates how Carrillo paid a federal commander a million dollars to mount the raid and ensure Acosta's death.[15] Carrillo Fuentes then shifted the cartel's power base to Juárez itself and strengthened it: in the mid-1990s, according to the DEA, the Juárez cartel was the biggest drug trafficker in the world, shifting more than 50 per cent of all narcotics consumed in the USA. In 1996, Carrillo died during facial surgery – if he did die: mystery still surrounds his passing, with all four surgeons engaged for the operation subsequently murdered. Violence in Juárez followed his death, as Carrillo Fuentes' heir and brother, Vicente, tried to secure the terrain, but even that bloodbath was moderate compared to the present savagery in the city, which is supposed to have begun when Joaquín Guzmán's Sinaloa cartel laid siege in 2007. Whether the Juárez cartel remains a force in the labyrinth of competing interests that are killing across the city today has yet to be ascertained; but one can only presume that its present incarnation, *La Línea*, retains potency in the maelstrom, alongside some 500 street gangs, the Sinaloa cartel, different strata of corrupt police forces and the armed forces. How fitting, and gruesome, that '*La Línea*' is also a common term in everyday parlance for the border itself.

As a man who perceives himself as heir to the Avilés/Gallardo empire, Joaquín *El Chapo* Guzmán saw the Plaza of his Sinaloa cartel as a national one, almost of birthright. The moment Gallardo was arrested, Guzmán, who had built solid alliances with cocaine exporters in Colombia, declared war first on those whom he disdained as pretenders in Tijuana and, with time, every other criminal organisation in Mexico. Guzmán was captured, however, early into his leadership of the cartel, in 1993. It was from jail, in luxury confinement at El Puente Grande maximum-security prison near Guadalajara, that – US intelligence sources believe – Guzmán adapted his tactics to build alliances in public office and high politics. Perhaps because of those contacts, Guzmán escaped spectacularly in 2001, just before he was due to be extradited to the United States, thus becoming poster boy for the latest wave of cult narco folk heroism. 'Breakout Of The Millennium' was the title of one *narcocorrido* ballad commemorating the escape. Another, by Los Buitres (The Vultures) and broadcast across radio airwaves, juke boxes, the Internet and YouTube goes: 'He sleeps at times in houses / At times in tents / Radio and rifle at the foot of the bed / And sometimes his roof is a cave / Guzmán is everywhere.' Guzmán is semi-literate, but issues communiqués boasting that he pays out five million dollars a month to corrupt officials, and makes sudden, brazen appearances like that in May 2005 at a restaurant in Nuevo Laredo (on Gulf cartel terrain he was contesting at the time), when some forty diners found the doors suddenly locked by his gunmen. The clientele was asked not to use cell phones while Guzmán and his entourage enjoyed their own meal and drinks, after which *El Chapo* himself pulled out thousands of dollars in cash and paid for everyone in the house.[16]

From jail, Guzmán had directed successive assaults on the border Plazas, which chronologically followed the frontier from west to east. After Tijuana came Juárez, following Carrillo's death. But it was after Guzmán had escaped that he launched the offensive which detonated this latest phase of the war by unleashing his forces, unsuccessfully, against the Gulf cartel in 2005, and in pursuit of the prize: Nuevo Laredo, the busiest commercial border crossing in the world. The offensive in Nuevo Laredo was both an end and a beginning: it was the last of Guzmán's first round of attacks but also the onset of the current war, taking the violence to another level altogether. Some expert observers believe that Guzmán has become something of a figurehead, a symbolic narco monarch who wields less power than notoriety, and that the cartel is now run by others with lower profiles but greater ruthlessness, Ismael '*El Mayo*' Zambada – who in 2010 gave a unique interview to *El Universal*, boasting about the cartel's prowess – and Ignacio Coronel until he was killed by Mexican troops in July 2010. It is often speculated, on the *susurro*, that if it was part of the Mexican government's strategy to restore a *Pax Mafiosa* by backing one cartel in its bid for a monopoly, then that cartel would be the Sinaloa. But it is now too late to pursue such a goal, because of the ferocious power wielded by Guzmán's main rival, the Gulf cartel.

Until 2005, the drama was mainly among and between Sinaloans moving up to the border, which initially excluded the only syndicate to whom Gallardo had conceded its own indigenous terrain, the Gulf cartel, based in the north-eastern state of Tamaulipas, opposite deep south Texas. At the time of writing, it is too early to discern any specific outcome to the offensive launched by President Calderón in December 2006, but one partial result is clear: the Gulf cartel and what was formed as its military wing, Los Zetas, have held their terrain against both their rivals and the army. While *Chapo* Guzmán remains Mexico's most powerful drug lord, and his cartel appears to remain that closest to political power, the Zetas' insurgency and resilience makes them the Mexican government's gravest problem, along with the very different nightmare of the anarchy in Ciudad Juárez. For this reason, the Gulf cartel and Zetas warrant special attention.

Unlike the other syndicates with leaderships from Sinaloa, the Gulf cartel grew out of – and is fiercely proud of – its territory and home state, which runs along the border from Nuevo Laredo to the mouth of the Rio Grande. The cartel was founded by a whiskey bootlegger from the 1930s, Juan Nepomuceno Guerra, when he moved into the marijuana and heroin business during the 1970s. He is said to have had the only rival on his terrain, Casimiro Espinoza, killed.

That murder, in 1984, was reportedly organised by Guerra's nephew, Juan García Ábrego, and marks the birth of the modern Gulf cartel. By moving the cartel into cocaine, García Ábrego became the first drug trafficker to make the FBI's Ten Most Wanted list, and was duly arrested and extradited to the USA in 1996, leaving the leadership contested but easily won by Osiel Cárdenas Guillén. Cárdenas, who hailed from a poor ranch on the outskirts of Matamoros, consolidated his power within the cartel by killing his rival, Chava Gómez — earning himself the nickname '*El Mata Amigos*', the friend-killer — and led it from his home city until being arrested during a gun battle in 2003. He was subsequently extradited to the US in 2007, and sentenced in Houston to twenty-five years in jail in February 2010, after a trial held in secret. Cárdenas, in his way, defines the present narco war: from a very humble background in the police force, he sought not to manipulate high politics, but secured his position within the cartel and against its competitors by recruiting an enforcement wing trained by former members of special service military units, which Cárdenas named *Los Zetas*, after their leader Arturo Guzmán's call sign in the police, Z1.

The Zetas emerged to take over the cartel as a syndicate in their own right (a position facing a challenge from within the cartel at the time of writing). They are now one of the most terrifying and formidable drug-trafficking organisations in the world with a paramilitary army estimated by the DEA to number 4,000 highly trained soldiers. Arturo Guzmán and his deputies Rogelio González, 'Z2', and Heriberto Lazcano, known as 'Z3', enticed former members of Mexico's special airborne anti-drug military unit, the GAFE, to defect and train up others. Some of the Zetas' troops were reportedly trained by the US at Fort Benning in Georgia, but this has not conclusively been proved. After 'Z1' Guzmán was killed in 2002 and 'Z2' Rogelio captured in 2004, Lazcano, a former commando in the Mexican GAFE special forces, took on the leadership. The recruiting continues: the Zetas, calling themselves a '*Grupo Operativo*', hung a 'narcomanta' banner from a bridge in Nuevo Laredo in 2008 calling for men with 'Military Experience' to call a displayed number. 'We offer a good salary, food and medical care for your families,' it taunted. The Gulf/Zetas claim as part of their territory the most lucrative smuggling point on the border and a prize coveted by any cartel: the freight road and rail bridges that cross the Rio Grande between Nuevo Laredo and Laredo, Texas – the busiest commercial border-crossing point in the world. In 2005, the Sinaloa cartel attacked, in pursuit of a share of the contaminated traffic that crosses the frontier every day. The assault was the beginning of the current war, the latest and most vicious phase not just in the long history of narco violence, but in Mexico's history since the revolution of 1910.

Meanwhile, the Zetas have all but secured their goal of a route down the Gulf Coast and into Central America, affording direct access to the traditional cocaine-producing country of Colombia, and new export markets of the drug in Peru and Venezuela. The advantages of coastal supremacy were illustrated by a novel haul on 16 June 2009: dozens of mysteriously dead sharks in two containers brought ashore by the marine authorities at the Gulf port of Progreso turned out to have had their bellies stuffed with bags containing a total of 1,965 lbs of cocaine.[17] In order to secure a clear route to the cocaine producing countries, the Zetas are combating the Sinaloa cartel in guerrilla warfare in Guatemala. The Zetas are the cartel with the best international connections to markets in Britain and Europe, aligned with their opposite numbers: the 'Ndrangheta of Calabria. When in September 2008 some 175 operatives for the Gulf cartel were arrested by US authorities – to whose intelligence services the cartel is known as 'The Company' – ten were in Calabria.[18] The alliance is important in the light of remarks made by the then Mexican attorney general, Eduardo Medina Mora, in March 2009, saying that the crack-down against cross-border traffic was forcing Mexican cartels to shift their attentions and potentially their operations, and 'focus more closely on Europe'.[19] The alliance is equally cogent in the wake of recent briefings by the Mexican diplomatic service indicating that a slight decline in cocaine consumption in the USA entails a surplus needing to be shipped somewhere – which may partly explain why Britain, Spain and other European countries serviced by the 'Ndrangheta have now overtaken the US in the consumption per capita of cocaine and its 'cooked' derivatives.

An alliance between the Zetas and 'Ndrangheta is also logical in terms of narco social style. Although the parallels are not exact, some similar progression can be traced in the decline of the 'classical' Sicilian Cosa Nostra as matching that of the Félix Gallardo federation during the 1980s, as both were overtaken by more ferocious syndicates emerging from poorer backgrounds and without pretensions to become 'Godfather' figures – epitomised by the Zetas from Tamaulipas (challenging Sinaloa) and 'Ndrangheta from Calabria (challenging Sicily). In Mexico as in Italy, there is a ubiquitous nostalgia, however misplaced, for 'old time' gangsters with almost aristocratic pretensions for their codes of 'honour', debonair style and political connections. But they have been superseded, both generationally and in terms of savagery: in the Italian instance by the Camorra and 'Ndrangheta, and in Mexico by the leaner and meaner Zetas, who came from a background of rural slums, urban street gangs and the police or military academies. In both cases, the old Fedora or Western Stetson has been replaced by a shaven buzz-cut and tattoos; the appointment with a politician by that with a personal martial arts trainer. Osiel Cárdenas was an auto-mechanic before joining the police, and as a modest dresser is seen as the style guru of this transition to what one could call 'Generation Z' in the genealogy, without end, of drug dealing. In February 2010, however, there was a sudden and violent rupture between the Gulf cartel and Zetas, and infighting which cut a swathe of murder across Tamaulipas. The Gulf/Zeta syndicate had become a victim of is own success: its grip on that section of the border so strong it had led to a calm in which the Zetas' enforcement role left them with little to do beyond becoming a cartel in their own right. The might they then claimed to wield was too much for the Gulf cartel old guard, which had resisted Cárdenas, and which the Zetas in theory served. By early 2011, some of this Gulf cartel leadership guard had even done the unthinkable: sided with the erstwhile enemy, the Sinaloa cartel and others in a new, if flimsy, alliance: 'Carteles Unidos', United Cartels, against the terrifying Zetas. After the shooting by the Zetas in February 2011 of two US agents that resulted in the death of ICE customs agent Jaime Zapata – a watershed moment – the 'united' cartels were even more anxious to distance themselves from the paramilitaries, in fear of reprisals from north of the border. During spring 2011, the discovery of mass graves across Tamaulipas brought not only the internecine struggle but also the entire war to a gruesome nadir.

The Zetas are, moreover, leaving an ever-heavier footprint within the United States. Apart from their deep penetration of the most important border hub city of Houston, they have been linked to appalling violence in the deep south. In August 2008, five men were found with their throats slit in Columbiana, Alabama; they had been tortured with electric shocks. The FBI claims the victims owed a debt of $400,000 to the Gulf cartel. During the big raid against the Gulf cartel in September 2008, twelve of its operatives were arrested in Atlanta, where authorities reported an increasing level of cartel-related violence. In 2001, a haul of $4.1 million in Gulf cartel cash was uncovered in Atlanta, and another $2.3 million in Houston. In the United States, the battle for distribution is now essentially between Guzmán and the Gulf. After the swoop against the Gulf cartel in September 2008, 750 affiliates to the Sinaloa cartel were arrested by another famous round-up across the USA, Operation Xcellerator, in February 2009. Some $46o million in cash was seized, along with 24,000 lbs of cocaine and 1,200 lbs of methamphetamine.

In its essence, then, Mexico's cartel war is becoming a three-way battle between the army, Guzmán and the Zetas – but there is a final and more recent addition to the list: *La Familia*. *La Familia* emerged during the 1990s as a syndicate entirely indigenous to the state of Sinaloa's coastal southern neighbour, Michoacán. It was devoted to claiming drug-trafficking from and across the state for its own against a subsidiary of Guzmán's, the Milenio cartel, run by a family called Valencia. According to some reports, the rift was due to rivalry over a woman between a member of the Valencias and the man who founded *La Familia*, Nazario Moreno González, known as '*El Más Loco*' – The Craziest One – killed by the Mexican army in 2010. *La Familia* 'came out' with a famous incident on 6 September 2006, when twenty masked men burst into a low-rent discotheque, the *Sol y Sombra* in Morelia, the state capital, and bowled five decapitated heads across the floor, accompanied by a message that was bizarre even by the wayward standards of narco communication: '*La Familia* does not kill for money. It does not kill women. It does not kill the innocent. Only those who deserve to die. Know that this is divine justice.' *El Más Loco* prosletysed from a book mixing quotations from the Scriptures with his own excruciating mantras, such as: 'Don't View Your Obstacles As Problems But Accept Them and Discover In Them The Opportunity To Improve Yourself'.

To fight off its Sinaloan neighbours, the emergent *Familia* had elected to be trained by the Zetas. In 2007, however, *La Familia* decided to carve an identity for itself, throwing off the Zetas, who were coming to dominate the *Familia*, as had been their intention all along. The response to the rebuff from Tamaulipas was a brazen act of terrorism against civilians: a bomb was thrown at crowds of families celebrating the Mexican tradition of '*El Grito*' – the Cry of Independence – on the night of 15 September, the eve of Mexico's Independence Day. It killed eight people and injured more than 100 in the president's home city of Morelia. *La Familia* sent a flurry of messages to local media disavowing the attack, and hung *narcomensajes* accusing the Zetas of responsibility. After the swoops against first the Gulf cartel and then Guzmán, the US authorities next targeted operatives working for *La Familia*, with 305 arrested during mid-October 2009 by a sting known as Project Coronado. The concentration of arrests was around Dallas, where seventy-seven were arrested for operating a distribution network feeding Illinois, Minnesota and Mississippi.

As the year 2006 drew to a close, some 2,000 people had been killed in violence between the cartels, mostly in Nuevo Laredo and Michoacán. Against this mayhem, on 11 December 2006, only ten days after he had been sworn in, the newly elected President of Mexico, Felipe de Jesús Calderón Hinjosa, mobilised 40,000 troops. Calderón, a Harvard-trained lawyer and devout conservative Catholic from Morelia, was the second president to be elected as a leader of the National Action Party (PAN), of which he had been a co-founder, succeeding PAN's first president, Vicente Fox, a former executive for the Coca Cola company in Mexico. For the previous seventy-two years, Mexico had been ruled without interruption by the Institutional Revolutionary Party, which had become more institutional than revolutionary by building and managing a byzantine system of government by corrupt patronage, thereby exercising political party power or influence in every pore of the social fabric to a degree unknown elsewhere in the West. Fox's victory in 2000 was seen at the time to have broken with a stifling epoch, liberating Mexico into the Elysian fields of free-market capitalist meritocracy. His victory was an overwhelmingly urban one and especially resounding along the border. Fox won every border state and sixteen of the nineteen electoral districts adjacent to the United States.[20] It is seen by commentators in the USA and Mexico as unfortunate that the narco violence coincides with the transition to a genuinely capitalist free market in Mexico; but it is essential to the argument of this book that the violence is not, however, a counterforce against what the title of one learned account of this mutation in the country's history calls 'opening Mexico'.[21] The violence occurs not despite but, in large part, *because* of these changes; it is at best an inevitable side-effect of 'opening Mexico', and at worst an integral feature of it.

It would have been almost impossible for the narco cartels to operate without the help of the PRI; they mirrored and were part of the party's pyramidal, monopolistic system of patronage. But a newly competitive economic environment and the defeat of the PRI obliged the cartels to look again at their own operations, tighten international alliances and diversify their merchandise beyond the cocaine line that had been the main product of its boom years, the 1970s and '80s, during cohabitation with the PRI. Now, a new generation of cartel leaders, typified by Osiel Cárdenas, expanded their catalogue range and strengthened their production and supply of synthetic drugs like methamphetamine or crystal meth. And with cocaine consumption declining in the United States, they also returned to the best-seller of yore, heroin, researching new permutations suitable to the latest taste – such as the craze for 'cheese heroin' in Texas, mixing heroin with over-the-counter drugs to make it cheaper, more impactful and longer-lasting. These are products of 'open' Mexico's Fox–Calderón era.

President Calderón's foursquare young spokeswoman, Alejandra Sota Mirafuentes, meets me at the Brasserie Lipp (the one in Mexico City, not Paris, and part of an international luxury hotel complex) to insist, over mineral water: 'We cannot turn a blind eye to criminality. The power of the cartels has become a very real threat to the security of the Mexican state – the ability to buy off local and state authority, even federal government. For years,' she says of the PRI epoch, 'the authorities just gave in.' But, 'this is very important: Mexico has changed, politically. If in the past, the government was greedy and wanted to take advantage of the cartels, that is no longer the case.' The initial intervention in Michoacán, she says, 'opened the body, and once the body was opened, we could see that it had contracted severe cancer: Juárez, Sinaloa, Tamaulipas, whole regions were controlled by the cartels'. It seems odd that this bright young woman – let alone Calderón's government – had not known that all along. President Calderón has, after all, needed to purge his own apparatus of corruption in an initiative he called 'Clean House'. His former acting police chief, Gerardo Garay, was arrested for protecting the Beltrán Leyva brothers, and his 'drug czar', Noé Ramírez, for taking a $450,000 bribe from the Sinaloa cartel. Both are awaiting trial, both have denied wrong-doing. Operation Clean House had failed, however, to net another of Mexico's apparently trustworthy drug czars, José Luis Santiago Vasconcelos, who was warmly embraced by Washington, and the man who extradited Osiel Cárdenas. Vasconcelos was killed in a mysterious plane crash over Mexico City in November 2008 and six months later, in May 2009, a DEA report named him as being on the payroll of the Beltrán Leyva cartel.[22]

The thrust of the offensive, says Sota, is to challenge the cartels militarily while 'aggressively' reforming the legal system and institutions, starting with the federal structure. The task, she says, 'begins with the military, but by the end of the presidential term, we aim to have established an honest and well-structured federal police. We start with the military because we cannot count on the municipal and state police. In a number of places, the traffickers control the police'. So that is official, at least. As is this: 'The military is going to stay in there for as long as it takes.' As long as what takes? 'So long as it takes for the state to fulfil its basic obligations: public security and the collection of taxes, which are currently threatened by and even subverted and imitated by levies imposed by the cartels.' Strangely, and with estimable honesty, Sota adds: 'The president is clear: the fight is not against drugs, it is against the violence and the ability of criminal organisations to subvert the state. The president knows that drugs will not disappear.'

That is the map at the outset, the template of the cartel war, to bear in mind as one explores the border, though there is no predicting how the lines on the map will blur or demarcate the narcotopology. However, a journey along the map as it stands entails, loosely, three stages: first, the road from Tijuana to Ciudad Juárez, across terrain of warfare between the Sinaloa, Tijuana and Beltrán Leyva cartels. Then a meltdown in Juárez, as the cartel pyramids collapse into a murderous anarchy. Finally, from Ciudad Acuña and Nuevo Laredo eastwards, the road leads into a land where there was, between 2005 and 2010, relatively less fighting, but which is the most terrifying stretch along the border. Until early 2010, this was terrain subject to an iron reign consolidated by the Zetas and Gulf cartel; it is only now that they are no longer synonymous with one another, the 'classical' and military wings at internecine war with each other.

With the election of Barack Obama, the map has also changed at the level of US government. After decades of the United States seeing the narco-trafficking problem as essentially an all-Mexican one, there is now a sense of officially acknowledged 'co-responsibility' over crucial areas of policy. During visits to Mexico City by Secretary of State Hillary Clinton and the president himself, the matter of arms trafficking from the USA to Mexico, previously taboo, has been addressed. There has been acknowledgement of the fundamental fact that the root cause of the crisis is addiction to drugs in American society. In March 2009, President Obama announced a Janus-faced package with two themes: man the border defences, while also attacking the root causes of addiction. He increased the allocations of all federal agencies along the border, with $700 million that year towards personnel and technology, and more to come. President Obama said he would upgrade intelligence-gathering, and improve cross-border interdiction, but also that he would 'redouble' efforts to diminish demand for drugs in the US and staunch the flow of weapons from the US to Mexico. 'It's really a two-way situation here,' said the president, speaking a language never before heard from the White House. 'The drugs are coming north, we're sending funds and guns south.'[23]

The reality on the ground is mercurial and in places much worse than the map suggests, because if the map shows a war caused by fighting between cartels for smuggling routes and a consequent government crackdown, it does not show another, monstrous reason for the war: that the Mexican side of the borderline has become a place accursed by addiction to hard drugs. This seems of little consequence to the United States, and is virtually taboo in Mexico, but is the cause of most of the killing and most wretched of circumstances in the drug war. All warfare creates resultant 'sideshow' horrors. The consequential sideshow of America's addiction to hard drugs supplied from Mexico, and both countries' war against the traffic, are two-fold: first, the ravages of hard drugs along the border, and subsequently, the feral war for control of this domestic 'Plaza', which is just as savage as that for narcotic exports, if not more so. Fundamental to Mexican government strategy and to the thinking of the DEA is that to fragment the cartels is to weaken them, thereby damaging drug traffic and reducing violence. 'We want it to be disorganised,' says Eileen Zeidler, spokeswoman for the DEA in San Diego, of the cartels' fragmentation since President Calderón's offensive. 'If they're not organised, they don't function. We want it to fall apart.'[24] Ms Zeidler's boss, the DEA's chief of intelligence, Anthony Placido, went so far as to call the violence a 'sign of success', and to speak of 'wounded, vulnerable' cartels.[25] But fragmentation does not mean a weakening of narco traffic, it simply nuances the market: the domestic Plaza is fought over by the plethora of gangs that serve the big cartels when drugs cross the frontier, but fight one another when dealing on home turf, bringing death and misery to the *colonias*. Like any other corporation, the cartels nowadays 'outsource' – as corporate jargon has it – much of their business to sub-contractors such as street gangs or corrupt police forces who tender for a slice of the profits. Narco outsourcing even has a name: *el derecho de piso* – the right of tender, of passage and it is a murdering business as street gangs and other interests vie and kill for the contracts.

Our journey begins where the desert sun sets into the Pacific at Amexica's western edge, the frontier between Tijuana and San Diego. The latter is not really a border town – it is too big, too Californian. But one can already feel the frontier at the 12th Street and Imperial transit centre, which during the early morning stages a two-way rush hour through the mumbling homeless pushing their belongings in supermarket carts: of people arriving for work from Tijuana, and people leaving for work in Tijuana.

The blue line trundles towards the railway yards and dockland base of the US Pacific Fleet, frigates and masts thick with radar, and painted murals illustrate the 'History of Our Community' at Barrio Logan (a Hispanic settlement named after an Irish pioneer), featuring a Mesoamerican Indian blowing into a conch shell, fishermen hauling their catch and porpoises. Through factories and the lights and smoke of dawn, Rosebud Law Enforcement services and Tactical Assault Gear is right next door to Rosa's Mexican Diner, just as it would be anywhere else in America. But anywhere else is not the suburb of Chula Vista, two miles north of Tijuana, nor San Ysidro, end of the line – and of the United States. Thirty minutes south of downtown San Diego, on the platform teeming by 7.30 in the morning, the two-way rush hour is in full swing, as is a McDonald's, which is a border hub of its own: customs agents, girls laden with huge packs of diapers, Mexican businessmen who have fled to Chula Vista but return each day to work in Tijuana and Mexican ladies on their way to clean American toilets are all eating breakfast . . . and there it is: the concrete barrier, the footbridge, and beyond it, Mexico. *Aquí Empieza la Patria* – Here Begins the Homeland – is Tijuana's municipal motto, and a Mexican flag, defiantly and desperately giant, with its eagle clutching a snake on a cactus, which legend has it predicted the birth of the nation, flies in America's face, at the border.

CHAPTER TWO

Aquí Empieza la Patria –
Here Begins the Homeland

Tijuana's image north of the border was always that of a festive party town. And for the Americans who poured into 'TJ' by the thousands every day, and by the tens of thousands every weekend, it was. 'You are in the Most Visited City in the World' claims the sign above Ave-nida Revolución, and whether statistically true or not, people thronged here to savour Mexican exotica, buy souvenirs, drink Margaritas by the jug (at an age younger than the USA permits), get teeth fixed cheaply, invest in a spare pair of spectacles and, latterly, buy Viagra or Prozac and other medications for a fraction of the price back home. Tijuana grew during the nineteenth century, after the loss of 'Alta California' to the USA in 1848. The downtown area acquired its reputation for selling an ersatz 'Mexico' to North Americans in 1915, when Tijuana decided to echo that year's great Panama–California Exposition in San Diego with a fair of its own called the *Feria Típica Mexicana*, to lure visitors across the border. Since which the city has specialised in sombreros, reproduction Aztec bric-a-brac, ponchos and other trinkets that actually have nothing to do with the coun-try's sixth largest city of 1.5 million people. Every Mexican border city and town divides itself between indigenous northern '*Norteños*', '*Sureños*' from the south and '*Chilangos*' from the capital. There is even a constituency which calls itself '*Fronterizos*', from the border itself – and these are crucial points of identity.[1] Over half of the population of Tijuana does come from 'traditional' southern Mexico, not to live according to some folklore kitsch, but to work in sweat-shop *maquiladora* factories or eke out some other living in desperately poor *colonias* on the city's outskirts. For the southerners, or those from El Salvador, Honduras and Guatemala, Tijuana can be harsh, unwelcoming, dangerous and violent. Attacks on Mixtecs, Mayas or Zapotecs are routine. Until recently, when vast estates of uniform housing were built around the city, whole communities from South and Central America lived on the *dompes*, or landfills, of domestic and industrial rubbish.[2]

Tijuana's reputation for naughtiness grew during Prohibition, soon after the *Feria*, when the city became a magnet for those seeking not only off-the-peg Mexico but also alcohol, gambling and the go-go good-time vices that accompanied them. The existence of the biggest naval base on the Pacific edge at San Diego guaranteed steady off-duty customers in addition to civilian tourists. But the narco war has changed all this, so that now, says Enrico Rodríguez in his empty shop full of unbrowsed jewellery, trinkets and Western wear, 'I cross myself every time I make a sale, and have not crossed myself for two days.' No one wants a polaroid picture taken of themselves wearing a sombrero next to an old donkey painted black and white like a zebra, and the strippers pole-dance pretty much to one another. Apart, perhaps, from the odd scurvy vagabond from California, too stoned to care about any potential danger, and, of course, the local backsliders, equipped with a limited supply of greenbacks. The famous district around the cross streets of Avenida Revolución and Constitución is now more about sleaze than aphrodisia. On its uppers, Mermaid's Club and Hotel, with Western saloon-style swing doors, is forced to offer 'Two Massages for the Price of One'. The Adelita Bar (est. 1962), with the Hotel Coahuila situated conveniently next door, has seen better days, now hoping to attract guests with neon signs of girls wearing *bandolero* bullet belts and brandishing Kalashnikov machine guns. A passing *gringo*, I am ushered inside with desperate insistence and quickly introduced by a heavily tattooed doorman to comely Gabriela in a glittering, fluorescent turquoise bikini and train of plastic feathers like a peacock's. She asks if I would like to buy her a drink while the doorman, whose height reaches as far as Gabriela's articulate bust, runs down a list of offers — including stiff alcohol, sex and a card game — very easily refused. The cavernous depths are not quite empty: a group of Mexican men share a bottle of tequila while their female company sip sodas and a lone, pallid American with a goatee and skin that has not seen daylight for a good while watches the writhing pole-dancer. But that's about it for the night, concedes the doorman. The Narco Juniors, as they became known, once cocks-of-the-walk, have disappeared too. Since war broke out, the modern *narcotraficante*, out of prudence and self-preservation keeps a low profile, partying at the villa and entertaining ladies through home delivery rather than brazenly in public — as they did not long ago.

How well she remembers those days. How could she ever forget — when the Narco Juniors were in their prime: flashing their wealth around Tijuana, dripping gold with a scantily dressed beauty hanging from each arm? Cruising in their SUVs, taking over nightclubs in which they would only drink champagne. Cristina Palacios Hodoyán, lighting ultra-thin cigarettes with a gold lighter held in her ultra-thin fingers, remembers them with a sorrow in her eyes that even her polished demeanour cannot hide. How could she forget the Juniors, when two of her three sons were among them? The eldest, Alejandro, was kidnapped twice — once in 1996, and again the following year, since when he has never been seen again. The youngest, Alfredo, became known as '*El Lobo*', the Wolf, and is serving 176 years in a Mexican jail, convicted of multiple murder and criminal association. 'I had wanted them to become lawyers, or go into their father's business as civil engineers,' their mother reflects. After finishing her cigarette, she picks at a smoked salmon sandwich, at a table in the Merlot Restaurant, near Tijuana Country Club, where the better class of people go. Mrs Palacios turns sixty-nine the day after we have dinner, and says she plans a quiet meal with close friends, nothing extravagant.

Her boys had had the city at their feet. As heirs to the Palacios Hodoyán family, they enjoyed automatic membership of and access to the 'Club Campestre' and so-called '*Instituo Set*', alumnae of the elite Tijuana Institute. There was an auspicious future in their father Ramírez's legitimate businesses if they wanted it. Alfredo was confirmed into the Church by the then Bishop of Tijuana, a family friend who would become Cardinal Posadas Ocampo, assassinated by the very cartel Alejandro and Alfredo later joined. 'Ocampo was very dear to us,' recalls Cristina, 'known and loved by Tijuana'. Born in the USA, the boys could cross the border any time, and set up in business there if they preferred, with their father's rolodex of clients at their disposal. And the Hodoyán brothers were heading that way, until Ramón Arellano Félix arrived in town from Sinaloa.

'I remember Ramón,' says Cristina with a shudder. 'He always wore a mink coat, even on a hot day, and shorts – with a big golden cross against his bare chest. There was a place by a tree where children had always played with tricycles and bicycles, and later they might meet up there in the evening, chatting up the girls or boys. Alex was in college studying law, aged about twenty-five, Alfredo was eighteen or nineteen. And Ramón Arellano Félix and the boys from Sinaloa used to come up to the tree, presenting themselves as interesting and exciting, flashing their money, and the girls wanted to be seen with them.'[3]

'So that the people who would start bringing drugs into my house – only I didn't know that at the time – were children I had known since kindergarten,' says Cristina Palacios. 'Ramón would take them to the clubs. He would walk in and commandeer a table, even if it was taken, just send the people away. He would buy champagne for his company all night; but if you talked to anyone else, you were considered a traitor. Any time, they could take someone out and kill them, and they did. Once you were in, you were in, and there was no way out. My sons had become part of it all, they were among people who would laugh while cutting someone's fingers off, or chop someone into pieces for fun. All this I learned later, when Alex had been captured and Alfredo was in prison.'

On 11 September 1996, 'Alejandro disappeared in Guadalajara. And from September to February he was in custody, held by General Jesús Gutiérrez Rebollo of the Mexican army.' During this time, in December 1996, General Gutiérrez Rebollo was appointed to the top post as Mexico's 'drug czar', leading the government's effort against the cartels, not least because of his success in procuring Alejandro Hodoyán. Alejandro was 'singing', telling the general all he knew about his AFO cartel.

It emerged when Alejandro talked to his family, says Cristina, that the confessions were ill-gotten, and that the general had played a vile game with his quarry. 'The soldiers,' recalls Mrs Palacios, 'used electric shocks on his eyes and feet, and burned him with cigarettes and lighters to get him to talk. Gutiérrez Rebollo,' she goes on, 'had arrived later, after others had tortured him, so that Alex felt beholden to him and would tell him everything.' In late November, once he had softened his prisoner, Rebollo called in prosecutors from Mexico City, who recorded a videotaped confession in which Alejandro, between gulps of water, recalls how his partners in the cartel would 'laugh after a murder, and go off and have a lobster dinner.' Killing, he told his captors, 'is a party for them, it's a kick'. Alejandro told the prosecutors that he had started running errands for the cartel, progressed to running drugs across the border and then joined a unit of *sicarios*. After they had the information they needed, the Mexican Public Defence Department handed Alejandro over to the Americans, who were preparing an indictment against the AFO. 'We also now know,' Mrs Palacios adds with a shiver, 'that the Americans were aware this was how he was forced to talk.'[4]

'On February 10 1997,' she continues, 'Alejandro was flown to San Diego, he told me, and put in custody by the FBI and DEA. At that point, both my sons were in San Diego, in different prisons, because Alfredo had been arrested too. But Alejandro was not arrested, it was worse than that: he was to become a protected witness. "I know a lot of things," he told me, "and I need protection."' But he had no protection: what they did not tell Alex was that everything he had said in Mexico City had been leaked by the Ministry of Public Security to the Tijuana cartel, and that General Gutiérrez Rebollo was working all along for the Juárez cartel. Only two months after taking office in his new job at the apex of Mexico's supposed anti-cartel offensive, Gen. Gutiérrez Rebollo was convicted of collaboration with Amado Carrillo Fuentes – the general even lived in a villa owned by the 'Lord of the Skies'.

After ten days in DEA custody in San Diego, 'Alejandro was asked to testify against his brother,' says Cristina. Alfredo Hodoyán, her younger son, had been charged with murder and was about to be extradited for trial in Mexico. He was in an impossible position between the rock of family loyalty and the hard place of his own survival. Mrs Palacios says: 'Alejandro ran back to Tijuana. By then, he was a condemned man: by the AFO for having squealed to Gutiérrez Rebollo, and by the Juárez cartel for belonging to a rival.' Alejandro hid at home. Two weeks later, Cristina was driving her son in the family's SUV: 'We were in a parking lot, when a truck blocked our way. Men surrounded us, with guns, and told us to get out of the car.

I said no. They didn't have masks or anything. Then they pulled Alex out and drove away. I never saw him again.' She lights another ultra-thin cigarette, draws in the smoke with a deep breath and says, 'It all made sense. They're all working for one cartel or another. When I went through a police album of intelligence officers, I found the face of the man I saw in the van, who kidnapped my Alejandro. But I still have Alfredo. He is in jail in Matamoros, and we are trying to get the sentence reduced.' Alfredo Hodoyán had been extradited to Mexico shortly after his brother's disappearance, held in Mexico City and convicted on several counts of murder.

All this is in the past, she insists. Cristina has updated her expectations of herself, working with parents or families of people kidnapped and probably killed by narco traffickers – trying to pressurise the authorities into tracking their lost loved ones, and doing something that only very rarely happens: go after the kidnappers and killers. 'The problem is, though,' Cristina continues in a matter-of-fact way, 'most of these people, once kidnapped, were dissolved in acid.' We are joined by Fernando Ocegueda Flores, whose son, also called Fernando, was taken from the family home, he says, on 10 February 2007. 'The police were so uncooperative, even obstructive, that at first I thought they themselves had taken my son,' he says. 'Then the whisper from neighbours told me that it had been the Arellano Félix Organisation. From the authorities, all this time, I have had nothing, zero, no investigation, not even a reply. I went crazy, and decided to conduct my own investigation. For two years, I searched – I went to everyone I knew in the cartel and asked them point blank to tell me. I went to their houses, I knocked on their doors in rage'. 'We were worried,' says Cristina, 'that he would not survive this line of investigation.' 'Someone did this, and I had to find out who,' retorts Fernando. Finally, he says, 'I went to a very dangerous place, and they put me in a car and I talked to this man. My request had gone high up the chain, and they told me my son had been killed and the body dissolved in acid.'

On 24 January 2009, Federal police raided a *narcotraficantes'* party at a ritzy seaside resort on the coastal highway from Tijuana to Ensenada, and arrested one Santiago Meza López, universally known and wanted in Tijuana as *'El Pozolero'*, the stew-maker. *Pozole* is a popular ragout made of pork, vegetables and seasonings, but this is not what Meza was brewing. He confessed to having disposed of some 300 corpses by dissolving them in vats of lye or hydrochloric acid, initially at the service of the AFO but defecting to the Sinaloa cartel, for which he was paid $600 a week.[5] Meza's confession was a straightforward one: he would fill a vat with water and two bags of lye, don a pair of protective gloves and goggles, boil the pinkish brew and dispose of the bodies delivered at his lair by truck, one by one.

Accordingly, Fernando Ocegueda came to know that the answer to his and hundreds of other distraught families' questions lay along the road south-eastwards from Tijuana to the satellite *colonia* of Colina de Florido, a place of shrivelled orchards, ramshackle houses, home to the Silza propane gas terminal. Up a dirt track into the desert lies the hamlet of Ojo de Agua, the Eye of Water, above which are two small graveyards nestled into the hillside. The *Pozolero*'s lair is surrounded by a blue tarpaulin and guarded by an encampment of bored *federales*. It is a square of ground, about 30 by 30 yards, enclosed by walls of grey breeze-blocks, open to the sky, with a little hut in the corner. For a tip of 400 pesos ($32), the *federales* open the padlock and slide the heavy white gate, for a guided tour. Across the compound, earth is piled in mounds, and blue plastic barrels are scattered across the dirt. Two steel containers stand beside a cistern at the top of the slight incline on which the lair is built. 'This is where he put them into the acid,' says the federal police captain, in a plain-speaking, unadorned way, but with something between a grimace and a smile.

The unofficial tour is economically informative: 'They would have been brought by truck, and unloaded over here,' says the captain, striding around, 'then taken here, probably on wheelbarrows, put into the vats, and there you go, no more bodies!' But a potent smell rises through the afternoon heat: the inimitable, sickly sweet, putrid smell of death and decomposition, of human remains. 'It's always stronger when it gets hot, around this time of day,' observes the captain, as though by way of apology. So the *Pozolero* was not as thorough in executing his task as the public were led to believe – nor, clearly, were the police investigators whose duty it is, in theory, to collect any remaining DNA on the site, seal it, endeavour to identify the dead and seek out their relatives. In fact, here we are, stomping around a crime scene that is abandoned but littered with evidence. 'We haven't noticed any sign of the detectives for three months – no one, nothing, we're just told to stay here and . . . well, watch for anyone who arrives,' complains the bored captain. This was August 2009, seven months after the arrest and confession. The captain points into the cistern, from which an especially pungent stench ascends into the afternoon. 'There's still plenty down there,' he informs, kindly but unnecessarily. And not only 'down there' – we take a look inside one of the blue plastic barrels, and there is the gum of a lower jaw, with teeth still attached, which somehow escaped dissolution. At the bottom of one of the steel tanks, there is raw flesh, and jelly-like human tissue.

There are also quite a few remnants from the recreational life led by the stew-maker and whatever apprentices he needed to practise his craft: a barbecue, several dozen empty Tecate beer cans strewn here and there, bits of seafood in the dust and a thriving marijuana plant. The arrest was made in January and in the little hut in the corner of the settlement, the *Pozolero*'s Christmas tree remains, complete with decorations made of festive red velvet ribbon and sparkly tinsel.

During the recent war, the killing has become qualitatively, as well as quantitatively, more grotesque – savage mutilations, decapitations, tortures to a point of perverse cruelty. The carnage has come to require a deviant sense of innovation, a twisted creativity: 'bone-tickling' involves scraping the bone with an ice-pick sunk through the flesh. Doctors are employed to ensure that those being questioned or tortured do not lose consciousness or die too soon. Methods of execution are almost inventive in their calculated atrocity: one of the Arellano brothers' victims was left tied to a chair and his hands chopped off, so that he bled slowly to death, alone. The killing has been extended to include families and children among the victims. This is not entirely new: at one point during the 1980s, Félix Gallardo needed to deal with an encroachment into his Guadalajara business by an interloper called Héctor Palma. Gallardo tasked one of his operatives to seduce Palma's wife and run off with the lady and her children – which he did. One day, the cuckolded Palma received a package by courier. It contained his wife's severed head. He learned later that Gallardo's man, Clavel Moreno, had proceeded to push his children to their deaths off a bridge. Palma built a special little chapel in their memory.

The children of some lesser narcos attend Valentína Gómez Farias primary school in Tijuana. The school is kept beautifully clean and the children, wearing red uniforms, chirp around the playground before settling in for lessons with orderly discipline. One morning in March 2008, however, the children arrived to find a message for them to bear in mind as they prepared their futures in the community: twelve festering corpses piled across the road from the school gates, naked, tortured and with tongues cut – people who talked too much. It was a lesson to the pupils not to do the same, says the principal, Miguel Ángel González Tovar, simultaneously courteous and exhausted as he understates what he tries to do in running a school where 'the children of narcos, children of police officers and children of ordinary workers attend. The situation is very delicate. There are evil people in our area, but they still send their children to school.

'It was terrifying,' he says of that morning in March. 'The children were terrified, the staff were terrified and I had to pretend not to be terrified, but everyone knew what was happening. It was a warning, and it means what it means. We try to teach here, to teach against that message, like an island of education and peace and security for the children, but we are fighting a form of barbarism here, and cannot be isolated from what is going on outside. That is not easy, however. They gave me a CCTV video camera, but it doesn't work. They gave me an alarm button, but that's broken. It's terribly sad, a situation we despise, are scared of but fight against.'

Dr Antonio Irán Muñoz, a forensic pathologist assigned to the Baja California state prosecutor's department in Tijuana, talks about how 'each different mutilation leaves a clear message. They have become a kind of folk tradition. If the tongue is cut out, it means they talked too much – a snitch, or *chupro*. A man who squealed on the clan has his finger cut off and maybe put in his mouth.' This is logical, a traitor is known as a *'dedo'* – a finger. Sometimes fingers are stuck up the rectum. 'If you are castrated,' continues Dr Muñoz, 'you may have slept with or looked at the woman of another man in the business. Severed arms could mean that you stole from your consignment, severed legs that you tried to walk away from the cartel.

Decapitation is another thing altogether: it is simply a statement of power, a warning to all, like public executions of old. The difference is that in normal times, the dead were "disappeared" or dumped in the desert. Now, they are executed and displayed for all to see, so that it becomes a war against the people.'

At another school, in the deserted resort of Rosarito Beach down the coast from Tijuana, an official visit is being put together on the tarmac basketball pitch. Víctor Hugo, a fifteen-year-old pupil at the Abraham Lincoln Secondary School No. 32, was gunned down in a narco shoot-out earlier this year, for reasons that are still unclear. And today, the recently appointed state prosecutor of Baja California, Rommel Moreno Manjarrez, has chosen the school to make a speech reassuring teenagers that there is a force out there trying to hold the *traficantes* to account. 'The police are now with us, and there is new hope against violence,' says the prosecutor. And the pupils applaud; '*Viva México!*' shouts one.

Prosecutor Moreno stepped into a difficult job when he became state attorney general in 2007. His predecessor, Antonio Martínez Luna, stepped down after a video released in May that year by a known drug dealer accused Martínez of protecting the Sinaloa cartel; he even had a nickname: '*El Blindado*' – the bullet-proof. The trafficker in the video was found dead soon after it was released so the veracity cannot be tested. Mr Martínez, now reported to be living in the United States, has denied all connections with the Sinaloa cartel, but he stepped down and Moreno was appointed nonetheless to clean up the image of a pivotal office during a drug war.

It had seemed worth giving Moreno the benefit of the doubt. When we first met in 2008, he seemed immediately engaging, not least because he had studied law at Sapienza University in Rome, and taken many trips to Sicily to learn from his mentor, the great anti-Mafia judge Giovanni Falcone. He has an affable if somewhat vague manner, and we enjoyed sharing recollections of the inimitable Falcone, and speaking Italian in Tijuana. He remembered, too, the campaign by another mutual acquaintance, brave Leoluca Orlando, who mobilised a mass popular movement against Cosa Nostra called '*La Rete*', the network. 'This is what I want to see here in Mexico,' said Moreno. 'A culture in the magistrature similar to that in Italy, committed to going after the Mafia, supported by movements in the civil society like that organised by Orlando.' It all sounded good, and I was hoping to talk on, towards an elusive point in the discourse, the bit about efficacy, arrests and convictions. But Moreno did not make himself available for a follow-up conversation for weeks afterwards.

Most mornings, I hovered about like a courtier at various official engagements that featured Moreno and a rolling dramatis personae, like an acting troupe in repertoire, also featuring City Mayor Jorge Ramos and José Osuna Millán, Governor of Baja California. The format was always the same: the panel sat in the shade of a large open-sided marquee and applauded one another's speeches about combating the cartels, after which its members were served cool drinks by waitresses in high heels and mini-skirts. On one occasion, launching a fleet of high-tech vehicles for use by the state police, that morning's edition of the Tijuana newspaper *El Mexicano* carried a front-page story about the murder of Adriana Alejandra Ruíz Muñiz, a model and cheerleader for the local soccer team, *Xoloitzcuintles de Caliente.*[6] The horrific scene of her death had been found filmed on the mobile phone of one José Carlos Meza, known also as '*El Charlie*' in narco circles, who had been detained and put under investigation by Moreno's department. Meza protested his innocence, claiming that Adriana Alejandra was an informant for the police, furnishing the authorities with information on Guzmán's man in Tijuana, Eduardo García Simental, *El Teo.* Meza implied that Adriana Alejandra had been *El Teo*'s lover, and provided what he claimed to be the name of the man who duly kidnapped and killed her. Adriana Alejandra had her fingernails pulled out and the bones in her fingers broken during the interrogation, after which she was decapitated.

While the paper told the story and Rommel Moreno made speeches, Dr Muñoz, in the forensic autopsy department of Moreno's prosecution service, is inspecting Adriana Alejandra's corpse on his slab. He is anxious to oblige my request to join him while he conducts his analysis of the corpse, in order to develop and illustrate his de-coding of mutilations with a visual aid. But Prosecutor Moreno's assistant says this is impossible, beyond the prosecutor's authority, a matter for the courts. Dr Muñoz is annoyed, for he is considering this case carefully, weighing up the various hypotheses: 'that it could be the big narcos, as they say, or that this is a crime specifically against a woman, a so-called "crime of passion" by a common criminal. And this is, actually, my inclination in this case. I've looked very carefully at how the fingers have been broken, and it has not been done very well – you could almost call it careless, or reckless, and when the narcos are torturing an informant, the tracks they leave are never careless. They would have sliced the fingers off at the joints, not merely crushed them, maybe so as to send them to someone. But my job is not to pass judgement of this kind, I'm not a police officer and the police do not ask me who I think did it, or why. My job is to make a report, and the rest is up to the prosecutors and investigators, and – how can I say this? – that's where the farce begins. The authorities don't look at any of this socially or forensically.' Dr Muñoz produces a bullet from a plastic bag and brandishes it between his thumb and forefinger. 'If I find bullets from the same weapon in different bodies that are brought to me, and put this in my report, but no one takes any notice. The narcos give us signs, they leave unique marks, like fingerprints, only the authorities do not heed them. They have the files, they have the register of weapons, but they will not make an inventory, bullet by bullet.'

Dr Muñoz gets out a pen and draws four boxes, labelled: 'Me', 'Prosecutor's Office', 'Judge' and 'Jail'. 'For every hundred bodies sent to me, twenty go to the prosecutor's office, ten go before the judge and one ends up in jail – no, fewer; in less than one per cent of cases do they ever get the real killer. And that one per cent is probably not a criminal boss, it'll be the little guy. Meanwhile, they convict people for things they couldn't possibly have done.' There are not many people in Mexico, or anywhere, brave enough to speak so freely and boldly from inside the system about their own employer, but there is no stopping Dr Muñoz. 'There is a woman called Jacinta, from the south, a Mixtec lady who is supposed to have kidnapped six armed federal agents all by herself. The strategy of the authorities is show business. They need to make a spectacle out of these cases – you can see, whenever they do catch a narco, they parade them, with all the drugs and guns. It is pure theatre, to impress the president like I as a child tried to impress my father. To the press, they feed this phrase '*presunto responsable*' – presumed responsible – what on earth does that mean? Is that conviction by a court? It's a lot of rubbish. And all the while, I have these victims of torture and mutilation brought before me, knowing that they will never catch the people who did this. But I love my profession, I love my job. It combines medicine and law in practice: the corpse is my patient, and my job is to interrogate the corpse, to ask it questions. Because the dead cannot speak, I have to find ways of getting them to tell me what happened.'

Tijuana is a strong city, and, after all, the local Mexicans are still here even if the tourists are not. A 'Fab Four' Beatles tribute is sold out. Taking your lady for a skinny-vanilla-frappuccino at a branch of the D'Volada chain – a Mexican Starbucks – is a cool date, especially if it has wi-fi so that no one need actually talk. 'Sanborns' is a landmark institution which characterises any Mexican city, combining a restaurant and rendezvous with a small department store, and Tijuana's is no exception, brimful every Sunday lunchtime, its waitresses in their hallmark 'traditional' costumes with wings on their shoulders. The *Cinépolis* is packed for the latest movie glorifying violence – fantasy violence – made up the coast in Hollywood.

After reading all that Hemingway and D. H. Lawrence, I decided I really must sample a *corrida* at the bullring near the border fence by the sea, only to be reminded how little I admired either writer, and despise this supposed 'entertainment' as yet another knackered bull is slashed according to plan and his carcass hauled off with ropes. But couples cheer, the band plays and ladies wave handkerchiefs at the matinée idol matador clad in the regalia of Old Spain.

Far more authentic is the *Sótano Suizo* pub, which was heaving on the Sunday that Eduardo Félix Arellano was being flown to the capital, but not because of him. There was another, different arrival in Mexico City that day: by the Chivas soccer team from Guadalajara, for the match Mexicans call *El Clásico*, against Club América. On screen in Tijuana, both teams unleash attack after attack in a tremendous game-to-the-death, Chivas winning 2–1. A joyful Guadalajara fan in the bar, Adán, likens snatching victory in the capital and seat of power to 'robbing your boss's house, and fucking his wife on the way out'. But the temperature of *El Clásico* was nothing compared to that eight months later for Mexico's make-or-break World Cup qualifying match against none other than its neighbour, the USA: the transborder Amexica derby. Quite apart from its complex piquancy

on the border, there is history to this fixture. Mexicans find it hard
to admit that Americans play very good football nowadays, and it is
a deeply-held belief that while the *gringo* subjugates Mexico, there is
one thing that the boys in green do better than their northern neighbours: play soccer. Or so they thought, until a terrible night during
the 2002 World Cup in Japan, when the USA dismissed Mexico 2–0
in a knock-out round. The wound cut deep, and right to the top.
Before the game, then President Vicente Fox proposed to George
W. Bush that the two might watch the game together at a venue on
the border, as a gesture of friendship between the two nations. But
the dismissive answer came back from an aide: since the game was
being played in Asia, the president would be asleep at that time of
night. America slept through its historic victory while Mexico was
wide-eyed with anguish.

Now, with Mexico trailing the US in the 2010 World Cup qualifying table, defeat today in Mexico City would entail a serious risk of
shameful elimination from the finals in South Africa while the
gringo sailed through. The Americans score first: Mexico 0, USA 1,
in Mexico City. Adán from last time cracks the inevitable sullen joke
about the boss robbing YOUR house this time, and fucking YOUR
wife. But then Israel Castro equalises with a glorious shot from 27
yards and with minutes to go, Miguel Sabah controls a perfect cross
to score the winner for Mexico. Then one of those things happens, as
they do, by word of mouth from bar to bar, *colonia* to *colonia*: head
for the border. Which they do, by the thousands, on foot and in hooting, flag-waving motorcades. They paint their faces, stick fingers
through the fencing, and sing their songs. Finally, the whooping
crowd blocks the frontier traffic crossing and six are arrested. 'Look,'
says my friend Delgado, trying to explain, 'we clean their toilets, we
pick their fruit and water their lawns. But we can beat them in
football.'

The Sunday crowds fill Tijuana Cathedral, outside which market
stalls sell unmistakably Mexican devotional accoutrements: it may
trouble the Vatican, but it is of deep meaning to many devout Mexicans that the Virgin of Guadalupe, national symbol and 'Empress of
the Americas', can also represent Coatlicue, mother of the Aztec primary god. Such dichotomy – ubiquitous in the 'folk Catholicism'

practised in Mexico – is incomprehensible to dogmatic Christians, just as the ambivalence of the Mexica gods themselves was incomprehensible to the conquistadores, whose religion the Mexica incorporated into their own. During the Credo, a text message arrives on the Archbishop's phone to say that Eduardo Félix Arellano was arrested during that shoot-out at the villa. 'It is a time of challenge for us, as Christians and as citizens whose quality of life and lives themselves are in real and immediate danger,' says Archbishop Rafael Romo. 'The violence is now strategic, against all society, and this is the difference. Not to mention the problems that the drugs cause in our diocese. What we can do is offer resistance, and an affirmation of hope.' Most of the narco aristocracy, and more than a few of the *sicarios*, though, are devout Catholics, or at least they go through the motions of devotion – baptism, church marriage, cash donations and confession. There is even an unofficial narco 'saint', Santo Jesús Malverde, a bandit with a Robin Hood legacy to whose shrine in Sinaloa devout traffickers pay homage with devotional pledges – *mandas* – in return for the Holy outlaw's blessing. During the 1980s, the narcos actively aligned themselves with the Church's conservative wing against priests advocating Liberation Theology.

Archbishop Romo is direct for a man of his austere authority. 'They expect to come to us and talk about what they do. Our word to them is clear: we will talk about these things, these dangers. If they think they are religious, we will debate them, urge them to leave behind this evil and these activities against God. They are like those "Ultra" football fans that come to the stadium – they support your team but the club doesn't want them there to behave like that, but it is still your team and you are not supposed to turn them away. Moreover, it is not easy in the barrios for priests dealing with them face to face.'

This was October 2008. Perhaps the bishop would have replied more severely had we spoken some months later – after a terrible narco execution in July of 2009. Father Habacuc Hernández and two seminarians training for the priesthood were ordered out of their pick-up truck on the road into Ciudad Altamirano, 180 miles south of Mexico City and repeatedly shot. Hernández had travelled by horseback and truck for hundreds of miles across mountainous terrain to serve his scattered community. He was one of ten children from a poor family who had worked for a while, illegally, in Texas. Villagers believed he must have fallen foul of instructions by the narcos not to meddle in their affairs.[7]

On the Day of the Dead, 1 November 2008, the daily *El Sol de Tijuana* carried a front page which looked like a heavy-metal album cover, with a hooded skeleton brandishing a scythe and a headline quoting a carefully timed pronouncement by the bishop: ROMO: LA SANTA MUERTE NO EXISTE — Holy Death does not exist. The archbishop was taking a public swipe in a popular paper at the cult in which the borderline is steeped, on both sides. *La Santísima Muerte* — Most Holy Death — adorns car windshields, T-shirts, mobile phone holders and hangs as a silver pendant on chests all along the borderline. To the uninitiated, they look like trinkets from a Goth shop at Camden Market in London or the Lower East Side of New York, but they are not. Most cogently, wayside shrines to *La Santísima Muerte*, also called *La Señora de las Sombras* — Lady of the Shadows — have been erected on the outskirts of most cities skirting the border on the Mexican side. In these shrines, built as little temples, she stands, the hooded skeleton holding the orb of the world in one hand and her scythe in the other. She usually wears a crown or mitre, and her cloak is often white, but sometimes painted in the colours of the rainbow. In some shrines, the skeleton is a real one, draped in fabrics. And around her, offerings are made: cigarettes, fruit, photographs of the deceased. Candles are lit to her, which bear her image on glass around the wax. Messages and petitions are written, asking for protection. Sometimes she is adorned with flowers.

This cult has its origins in the syncretism between Catholicism and pre-Columbian faiths and the cult of death, and has been dated to the eighteenth century. In the 1960s, the first public sanctuary to *Santísima Muerte* was built in the poor Tepito neighbourhood of Mexico City. In 2005, the cult was removed from the Mexican government's list of religious rites licensed to practise, and only since then has it captured the imagination of the criminal young, winning a rapidly expanding number of devotees among narco traffickers and the street gangs affiliated with them. *Santísima Muerte* has become an icon to which drug dealers and killers plead for protection against their own death, a talisman and mass cult accompanying the war. Though *Santísima Muerte* is regarded outside the country as yet another exotic piece of Mexican mumbo-jumbo, the cult can make one's flesh crawl as one watches others pull over their cars and whisper their devotions to her at these shrines. *La Santísima Muerte* has a calculated didactic iconography. In mystical Catholicism, the figure of the Antichrist — the notion of Satan in the guise of the returned Messiah — is more terrifying than the devil himself, because of the deceit. Perhaps that is why the Antichrist is so rarely portrayed in Christian art (among the few portrayals is Luca Signorelli's very unsettling depiction in the Orvieto cathedral of Satan preaching to the prayerful masses, wearing a mask of Jesus). The point is this: all the accoutrements of *La Santísima Muerte* echo exactly the iconography of devotion to Mary Mother of Christ in general, and the Virgin of Guadalupe in particular — the shrines, offerings, prayers, flowers and candles decorated with her image. *La Santísima Muerte* is not, like Satanism, an inversion of the faith. Rather, she wears the garb of faith — like the Antichrist, she is not an inversion but a masquerader.

In conversation, most priests are afraid to fathom the cult and its potency, while authorities are afraid enough to attack it both legally and physically. In Tijuana, almost all the roadside chapels which stood in 2008 had by the summer of 2009 been demolished — by the army, said Mayor Jorge Ramos, though the military will not accept official responsibility. Demolished, but not gone. One especially prominent one had been erected above the concrete sweep of the Abelardo Rodríguez Dam. High above the reservoir, I remember the shrine: painted white, with low front walls through which one could enter into a space for offerings and pleadings for intercession; the 'saint' looking out from behind a real human skull, adorned with a headshawl of rainbow colours and wearing a mitre over which necklaces of beads were strewn. The hideous figure usually clutched a bunch of fresh flowers, regularly laid. The shrine is now demolished: jagged masonry and broken bricks, but there remains a defiant shrine within the rubble, crammed with candles bearing the image of *La Santa Muerte*, a few of them still burning. The butts of cigarettes given in offering are lined up in neat rows, wedged in the broken masonry. Cigars have been left, and personal trinkets. To the side is a mound of hundreds of empty glass candle-holders, most of them decorated with the familiar figure — hundreds of people have been this way since the destruction, and there is more: messages painted on the shrine's toppled walls, now scattered across the terrain. 'Though they destroy you, I still believe in you,' reads one. The next one says: 'They have taken my child, my parent, my penance, my condolence.' Watching us all this while, guarding the rubble of the shrine, is a black Ford F-150 truck with darkened windows and a CD hanging from the rear view mirror. Next day, I return to find a different vehicle, a Toyota truck this time. I wander over, cheerily, dumb *gringo* complimenting the shrine. The truck's passenger window is open, and there are two men sitting in it; the younger looks straight ahead, out of the window, at the shrine. The older man turns towards me, stares, nods twice and stares again. *'Vete a la chingada'* – go fuck yourself – he says nonchalantly, and without further word flicks the electronic switch to close his window.

The Day of the Dead in Mexico is syncretism in action, a profoundly charged entwinement of ancient faiths with imported Christianity, of Aztec communion with the underworld with the Catholic days of All Saints (1 November) and All Souls (2 November). Elaborate meals are cooked, and special breads baked to share with the departed. Musicians are hired to sing them ballads and laments, toys brought for dead children, special prayers whispered and rites observed. Most feasts across the country are held in cemeteries, but in Tijuana this can be the occasion for a family reunion astride the border itself – by the beach where California and Mexico meet. This may sound more idyllic than it is. The turquoise ocean looks distantly seductive, but this is a scrappy piece of land divided by a mesh fence, which is the border – across and through which families sit down for picnic lunch, one half on the American side, the other in Mexico. This is the last stretch of fence along the whole border as flimsy as this, and during earlier visits to Tijuana, it was an evening pastime to come down to the *playa* and watch people climb over and run for it. Sometimes boys used to pose atop the fence, balancing, while family members or tourists took pictures, before darting into the United States of America, knowing that the border patrol, the *migra*, would catch some, but could not catch all. Another favourite crossing point was a dry cement canal running between Tijuana and the USA, along which so-called 'roadrunners' would hurtle at dusk, timing their sprint across the *territorio de nadie* – no man's land – between passes by the *migra* patrols and helicopters above.[8] These days, fence-hopping as a spectator sport at sundown is over; it ended after the Clinton administration mounted 'Operation Gatekeeper' in 1994, overseen and enforced by the then United States Attorney in San Diego, Alan Bersin, now 'border czar' for President Barack Obama. But the crossings continue and so do the picnics as a matter of weekend ritual, especially on the first day of November.

The Giovanni family assembles: Salvador Giovanni on the Mexican side with his daughter, Jessica, holding her baby, Jorge, so that the child's father, her husband Ricardo, can play with his son – a game of finger-tickling through the mesh, the international border – and catch up on his wife's weekly news from the southern side of the border. Salvador's other daughter Chantelle, a student of criminal justice at San Diego University, has also come to the US side 'for the first time, when I heard that my brother could meet his wife and baby at the fence', along with her boyfriend Luis – so it becomes quite a Sunday reunion, only with an international frontier running through it. 'It sure is a picnic with a difference,' says Salvador in perfect English, cutting his son a slice of water melon to a size that will fit through the fence. Dollar bills as well as tamales get passed to and fro through the wire. 'Some of us can't get across at all, and others who did cannot go back again if they return to this side – like my son-in-law. He made it over, got a job, earns money and sends most of it back – what father of a girl and grandfather of a little baby in this town is going to have a problem with that?' Salvador 'spent a while over there myself, working in Los Angeles. But they were different times. We used to come and go as we pleased. For ten years, I worked in an auto shop and came home every two weeks.' Not any longer: Jessica and her husband kiss through the wire, she lingers a moment, sadness flickers in her eyes, Dad tickles his baby, and it's time to go. 'I gotta work,' says Ricardo, and slouches back across the parking lot. However, says Salvador Giovanni, the US will soon end these traditional Sunday picnics and replace the mesh fence with the reinforced version that already runs for over 700 of the 2,100 miles of border. It is concentrated at and around urban centres, so that these family assemblies become a vulnerable point in America's defences. 'But the thing is,' says Salvador, 'there's always a chance', and he gestures towards a no man's land at the fence's edge, near the ocean.

'Every six or seven days, a big group just makes a run for it and the Americans know as well as the Mexicans that they can't catch everyone – there's always a few who'll dodge the cameras and infra-red lights, and God bless 'em.'

Some make it, others are caught and deported – after hours, days, sometimes years in the United States. An afternoon at the border dump for deportees shows most of the deported to be like Natalia González, aged thirty-eight, who lived twenty-two years making batteries in Los Angeles before a check on documentation by the immigration authorities. 'There's work here in the *maquilas*,' she says, 'but my son's in LA, so I don't know what to do next.' But there is another small constituency among the deportees, says Víctor Clark Alfaro, for years a campaigner for human rights in Tijuana, a minor-ity extremely useful to the cartels: 'they speak English, they have contacts across the USA, many have been in gangs like the Latin Kings and Mexican Mafia, one third have been in prisons, they know about drugs and how to use weapons. They cover up their gang tattoos when they cross, are dumped without work, but quickly find it.' A man with teardrop tattoos arrives in the pound, the kind of tat-toos you get as a gang member, or in prison. Julio César is a confident and friendly, if intimidating, alumnus of Huntsville jail in Texas, America's capital of capital punishment, where he served time for dealing in amphetamine. 'You're looking at my tattoos, ain'tcha?' He speaks the obvious with a blend of menace and amusement. 'Yeah, I got 'em, and you know what for, don't you?' Though César is not going to elaborate, I recall having it explained to me in a scary quar-ter of east Los Angeles by gang members with teardrop tattoos that for each person you killed a teardrop was filled in. They were a form of initiation into and protection by the Mexican Mafia or some other gang inside and outside jail. César sheds many tears of ink, two of them filled in. He says that in the three jails in which he served time in America, 'I got looked after by the *Raza* ['the race', as Mexicans call themselves by way of assertion in the USA], 'by the brother-hood.' By which brotherhood? Mexican Mafia? Latin Eagles? Latin Kings? I ask. 'Now that'd be telling,' César says, but concedes: 'One of those.' It is a conversation I probably could not have had were César not in the compound and overseen by the police – and that he cannot continue for the same reason. César was due to be deported in 1993, but the jail lost his records, he says, so he remained inside until 2001, got deported, slipped back into California for five years and was caught yet again: 'just because I like to smoke'. Now back, 'I'm going to get whatever work I can find here in TJ that'll get me the money to get back there', he says. 'I have some contacts. TJ's cool, only there's no way for an honest man to make a living, if you understand what I'm sayin'.'

Others who cross the border are never seen again: they are never greeted by the relatives to whom they were headed, nor are they received back home, unless it is aboard a plane, in a coffin paid for by the Mexican government. For some in Tijuana, *Día de los Muertos* 2008 has a special purpose, which is to pay homage to those who died in the deserts of America on their way to what they had intended to be a better life – the theme which dominates and defines the next stage of this book's journey along the border. The procession of homage in Tijuana is by those who survived the journey but were deported, and now assembled at the Salabrini hostel, which receives deposited, homeless deportees from the United States. Each marcher carries a white cross bearing the name of a compatriot who died attempting to make it to the USA – of exposure in the desert, heat or cold, thirst or hunger, attack by bandits or venomous snakes. The deportee marchers walk as far as the Mexican side of the fence, onto which, after saying prayers beside a little shrine of flowers and candles, they affix the crosses. 'Lord, hear our prayer,' chants Revd Luis Kendzerski, 'for the migrants and the poor, the abandoned and the dead, of the border.' Of every ten who die, he says, two are women or children.

East of Tijuana, through Tecate, along Mexican Highway 2, there is the first of many heart-stopping moments along this journey: the heat of early afternoon rises from the land below the road and across the desert, stretching into Southern California and on, it seems, for eternity. Hues of red, pink and burnt sienna wrap the distance, ascending into the smoky-blue haze of sky as it meets the horizon. There is complete stillness in the apparently boundless landscape. On the Mexican side, the road leaves Tecate onto a high mountain ridge and a parallel border road on the Californian side through leafy glades to a lonely but hospitable little town called Jacumba, with a spa motel, and into the cauldron of Imperial Valley. Here, the crossing into Mexico connects two towns with names that place both of them didactially in 'Amexica'. They are called Calexico and Mexicali, California and Mexico spliced and shared. Much of the Imperial and Mexicali Valleys lies below sea level, and both cities cohabit in a geological bowl in which air is trapped, so that neither the pungent stench of livestock, feed-lots and fertilizer on the US side nor the waft of chemicals drifting on the breeze from Mexicali can escape. Though this is a desert, Imperial Valley boasts some of the most productively fertile farmland in the western United States, thanks to the All-American canal, running from the Colorado river and benefitting farmers on both sides of the border, due not only to intended irrigation but also to an unforeseen life-source in the Mexicali valley: seepage. Water seeping from the canal created wetlands in the desert and has been pumped from the ensuing aquifer by farmers on the Mexican side, and used to grow crops. Until, that is, April 2009, when the rebuilding of the canal along 23 miles of watertight concrete was completed, saving an estimated 3.1 million acre-feet of water per year.[9] The canal lining was seen in California as a popular environmental and economical recovery of lost water for use by farmers in the Imperial Valley Irrigation District and domestic taps in the Metropolitan Water District of San Diego. Except on the border, in Calexico, which sided with the outraged Mexican farmers. A former mayor, Alex Perrone, argued that 'economically, if Mexicali loses, we will watch Calexico die. We're near totally dependent on the development and spending power of more than a million people on the other side. If the water goes, the farms suffer and the industries suffer. And if they suffer, Calexico suffers.' And so, concludes Perrone, who was born in Mexicali, 'We opposed the lining of the canal. Water is scarce, and our joint community has been developed around what has been available. Now the farmers are losing land over there, because the water is limited. This'll stop creating jobs, which means you contract the economy. It impacts on the agro-businesses, the people who sell the seed and fertilizer, or supply and maintain the machinery, and then it will impact us.'

But in this sweltering valley, and across the land to the east, water – *agua* – has a significance way beyond matters of irrigation and farmland. Along Highway 98, the road from Interstate 8 down into Calexico, the temperature rises with every mile – well over 100 degrees – and blue plastic tanks have been placed along it at regular intervals. Above them fly blue flags, and each is marked with the word *AGUA*, stencilled in white paint. There is a connection between these water posts and a plot in the cemetery at nearby Holtville, where those who died in the desert without a name are buried. This road takes us out of California now, into the state of Arizona and on to the narrative that lies behind both the water stations and the cemetery – that of the desert as graveyard. For something else is happening here, which has nothing to do with the canal, and whereby even a few drops of *agua* can make the difference between life and death.

CHAPTER THREE

El Camino del Diablo –
The Devil's Highway

There was a northern road, cut wood-blackened and
flower-sided; wing feather bowstring, down feather bowstring-sided /
On that side, North, bad were my thoughts. And I uprooted it,
broke it, threw it down, stamped on it/ Thus you may wish and
plan, various kinsmen.
*Opening speech in preparation for war, Tohono O'odham tribal
ceremony.*[1]

The hinges of hell would cool this land; it is a pyrexia, and breath-
lessly still. Not a zephyr to disturb the simmering air. Beneath the
mesquite trees, creosote bush and agave cacti with blades like drawn
swords, are thousands of holes in the dust, some burrowed by kanga-
roo rats to escape the sun. These animals have kidneys that can
reabsorb water and concentrate urine so as not to lose fluid; their
nasal passages are designed in order to recycle any moisture from
breath they exhale. Also invisible until the impenitent heat has
abated are kit foxes, whose dens are so ubiquitous that it seems there
must be hundreds of them in just two square miles. Not so: this animal changes dens frequently, and changes vixens with every season,
but never leaves its terrain and always rests underground during the
day.[2] The spindly branches of the ocotillo appear like a fan of
parched, dead sticks – only they are alive, hibernating, feigning dry
death. They would spring to verdant life with the slightest fall of
rain or during a desert storm, for weeks if not months, storing the
water, then return into their disguise of mummified kindling. And
when its leaves do grow, and flowers that look like flames blossom
from its stems, there is a spike behind each tiny leaf, to punish and
warn off any thirsty animal tempted by sapless thirst to steal its
moisture with a refreshing bite. The 'Teddy Bear' cholla cactus, back
lit, looks as cuddly as a furry toy, but its spines are barbed and stick

to anyone who brushes against them. Its big cousin, *cylindropuntia fulgida*, aka the Jumping Cholla, has treacherously weak joints that can dislodge themselves and, it appears, fly into the skin, implanting their spikes. Then there is the Arizona barrel, with fish-hooked spines that can bury themselves into your flesh, and cannot be removed. At dawn and dusk, rattlesnakes appear along the pathways, flicking their forked tongues, and the wilderness echoes with the haunting range of howls, yaps, cries and growls of the coyotes – songs of the trickster in Native American lore, one of the most resilient, cunning and adaptable of all animals on earth, even in this barren land. In the legend of the Navajo, north of here, the First Coyote flipped a blanketful of stars into the heavens, creating the Milky Way.[3]

In this xerosis of the land, any organism that has been shed to desiccate in the dust cracks underfoot like old parchment. Discarded snakeskin lies by the wayside, dry as burned paper. The stillness itself is immense: only broken by the occasional dart of a lizard across the rock, or the flight of a black-and-white backed woodpecker through the cavity it has excavated into the wall of a mighty saguaro within which it nests and whose fluids it extracts. The only persistent movement is on high, circling eagles on the fly, ready to dive at any chipmunk or jackrabbit with the audacity to move across country at this time of the afternoon. Or else vultures, seeking out those who could not make it. In the distance lies a boundless world and a constant drama of colour and light; of predator, prey and survival. The immensity stretches into the Cabeza Prieta, or 'Dark Head', mountain range of western Arizona – black volcanic peaks laid bare by millennia of erosion, and coloured a smoky indigo as evening considers its options. There are other dark colours, from granite and mica, which beneath the unrelenting sun create a haze of navy blue across the wild: the Diablo Mountains, Growler Valley, Scarface Mountain, Black Mountain, Gunsight Hills, Alamo Wash, John the Baptist Mountains . . . As the writer Luis Alberto Urrea said: 'the poems on the map read like a dirge'.[4]

The esteemed Mexican naturalist Ezequiel Ezcurra wrote that his 'work in the Gran Desierto changed my stereotype image of a competitive nature, where killing and conquering was the rule for the survival of selfish genes, into a different and somewhat opposing view: Life is driven not by contest, but by symbiosis and a drive for reproduction. It is not so much about supremacy as it is about co-operation of organisms and passion of the senses.'[5] And that is all very well, but for an animal or plant to evolve and endure this terrain takes millennia of natural selectivity and mutation. To be a frail human in this land is quite another matter, for over all this presides the sun. There are some scattered signs of Homo sapiens. Off a hiking trail running through the Buenos Aires Wildlife Refuge in southern Arizona, abandoned: empty plastic five-litre water canisters, grimy shoes, soiled fake Nike track-suit ziptops, school backpacks with pictures of Hannah Montana, a shaving set, exercise books, used batteries – all collecting sand and fading in the heat. Most poignantly of all, a pocket photograph album, the images bleached, just discernible, show a group of people smiling at what appears to be a celebratory meal of mostly seafood. There are three men with moustaches, three big ladies in best dresses; another man plays a guitar. These things are discarded slices from a journey being undertaken out there, in the baked distance.

This trail of dust – which winds south from Wellton, Arizona, over the Mohawk Canal and out across the US Air Force Barry Goldwater bombing range and Cabeza Prieta National Wildlife Refuge – was named by Spanish explorers who used it as an exploratory route north from their mission at Caborca, now in Sonora, in the mid sixteenth century. The name, marked in square Y 23 on the map of Yuma County you buy at the gas station, is *El Camino del Diablo*, the Devil's Highway.

The *Camino del Diablo* was an ancient trail first laid by Pima tribes native to the Sonoran Desert, but the route was pioneered for the historical record by order of Francisco Vásquez de Coronado, governor of Nueva Galicia, initially in pursuit of a mythical cluster of seven cities of gold called Cíbola. A missionary and explorer, Melchor Díaz, is said to have set out from Coronado's encampment near Caborca, to seek Cíbola and establish a route to the Sea of Cortez, into which the Colorado flows. The hardships encountered by Díaz's expedition earned the road its name. It was mapped more than a century later by the man whose memory remains ubiquitous across northern Mexico and southern Arizona, Father Eusebio Francisco Kino. Father Kino – a seventeenth-century missionary, philosopher and astronomer – converted, but also defended the rights of, the

Pima and was the first to chart not only the Devil's Highway, but also the water springs along it, called *tinajas*. Knowledge of the *tinajas* had been a means of survival and of wisdom among the Pima, and the instinct for locating them separates real desert people from transient inhabitants and boarders even today. In 1775, a band of 200 colonists under Juan Bautista de Anza endured the highway's hardships on their way from what is now Tubac, Arizona, to found the city of San Francisco.

The Devil's Highway won back its name in May 2001, when fourteen migrants recruited by criminal *'coyotes'* in the Mexican state of Veracruz, were found dead from dehydration and exposure. Their smugglers, heading from a border crossing west of the Mexican town of Sonoyta for the Arizona town of Ajo, became hopelessly lost on a doomed meander across some of the most unforgiving terrain.[6] The last stragglers were rescued in an operation no agent at Wellton's little border patrol station will ever forget, just south of a lovely palm-lined oasis and aquifer of water from the Colorado, and a service station on the freeway called 'Dateland', which sells date milkshakes. They were just fourteen among the many who die; but in Mexico, they were, absurdly, turned into folk martyrs by the country that exports people – through desperate poverty – across the border into America.

There are names for the players in this business of people-smuggling: the migrants are known as *pollos*, chickens, and those that recruit them therefore *polleros*, chicken-runners, working for *coyotes*, who control the networks. Bottom of the criminal ladder are the *guías*, the guides, who actually do the walk. To the border patrol, the migrants are 'wetbacks', even if all they have crossed is sand, otherwise 'bodies', 'wets' or 'tonkies'. Mexicans use the word *mojados* themselves: literally, wetted. The border patrol, of immigration police, is, of course, *la migra*.

The causes of migration from Mexico into the United States – about which much has been written – are deep and many, but are all variations on the theme of extreme poverty in criminally unequal Mexico, the lure of the economic superpower along its northern border and that country's demand for cheap labour. The first Mexicans came in flight from the revolution of 1910, and to fill jobs created by the First World War – leading to the establishment of the border patrol in 1924. During the Great Depression, as now, opportunities for work shrank and migrants were made less welcome, only to return dramatically with the Second World War. Such was the demand for cheap labour after 1941 that the US government devised the Bracero Program to regulate it (the name comes from the Spanish word *brazo*, an arm), whereby employers could register immigrant workers and pay them specified wages for specific work over specific periods. The demographics and economics of the modern border began as many employers preferred to use the programme as cover to pay lower wages to illegal immigrants, while the migrants themselves would settle on the Mexican side of the border when their time was up, rather than return to the interior, in order to sign up again for further work in the United States. With the war over, migrants continued to flow north, so that the US felt obliged to mount 'Operation Wetback' in 1954, a round-up of illegal 'aliens'. The abolition of the Bracero Program in 1964 led directly to a second and even more momentous step in forging the border's population and economy: an agreement between Washington and Mexico City the following year to allow the building of the *maquiladora* assembly plants on the Mexican side of the line, 'bonded' for duty-free export across the frontier. The scheme, a precursor to the North American Free Trade Agreement, was devised primarily so that American corporations could pay Third World wages just across the southern border, and in Mexican terms to find employment for *braceros* returning home en masse, but remaining on the frontier.[7]

The direct cause of the deaths along the Devil's Highway in 2001 was a sudden exodus of migrants from the time-honoured border crossings into San Diego, El Paso, and cities along the Rio Grande Valley, into the deadly wilderness, in response to the boldest offensive against illegal immigration the US government had hitherto mounted. In 1994, Bill Clinton's administration escalated Washington's perennial battle with three 'Operations': 'Gatekeeper' in San Diego, 'Hold the Line' in El Paso and 'Operation Rio Grande' in the valley – three fronts which constituted a genesis of the process intensified by President George W. Bush after the al-Qaeda attacks of 11 September 2001. President Clinton's Operations proceeded chronologically from west to east, with 'Gatekeeper' overseen by the then US Attorney for San Diego and Imperial Counties, Alan Bersin, defying his own favourite description of the trans-border community as 'San Tijuana'. 'Gatekeeper' brought the first stretches of the present-day border fence, night-vision cameras, infrared spy cameras, a reinforced border patrol and high-tech sensors that could detect movement. And it worked: by the end of the decade, figures for arrested migrants had plummeted – in the cities. But from the point of view of those smuggling migrants, let alone those being smuggled, 'Gatekeeper' entailed not a suspension of operations but a by-passing of the concentrations of fencing, technology and border patrol – and a redirection along the *Camino del Diablo*. The fourteen *pollos* who died near Wellton were only fourteen of what Enrique Morones – founder of a humanitarian organisation called Border Angels, which placed those blue water stations along the road to Calexico – believes to be 10,000 people who have died in the desert since the inception of Operation Gatekeeper. But numbers are of as little use on the border as they are in the desert. There is simply no way of knowing how many have crossed and died, or how many have crossed and survived; how many corpses will never be found for each one that is. Or how many Mexicans or Central Americans are still illegally but busily working away in America for each one who is dead or deported. All we can know is what a friar called Francisco Salazar already knew in 1650 when he wrote that the *Camino del Diablo* was 'a vast graveyard of the unknown dead . . . the scattered bones of human beings slowly turning to dust'.[8] There is no sign of the exodus along this widened *Camino del Diablo* abating – only of it becoming better organised, and exposed to different dangers and cruelties, now that narco cartels are taking over the business end of things.

The Reverend Robin Hoover of the First Christian Church on Speedway in Tucson leans back in his chair, feet on the desk, soles in my face, and describes his many good works. He dismisses descriptions of the work of others, like Morones and his Border Angels, as 'exaggerated'. He points out that I 'must be the thousandth journalist' to interview him. 'CNN were here only last week.' But there is a reason for his attitude. He has saved lives and gathered valuable information that no one else in America has compiled about deaths in the desert.

During the 1980s, the decade of President Ronald Reagan's support for military regimes and fascist militias in South and Central America, an ecumenical cadre of clerics together with some 500 congregations based on the border and in a network across America organised the Sanctuary Movement to protect political refugees from death squads in El Salvador and Guatemala, and the murderous US-backed regimes in Chile, Argentina and elsewhere. From his time with the Sanctuary Movement, Revd Hoover went on to establish and run another organisation, Humane Borders, which agitates on behalf of migrants and organises the placement of lines of water stations throughout Southern Arizona, and especially along what Revd Hoover's data shows to be the new corridors of death. One is across the land of the Tohono O'odham – 'Desert People' – Native American tribe, their 'reservation', across which the border now cuts like a gash, cutting off its people on the US side from Mexico and vice versa. The other is a corridor running either side of Interstate 19 between Nogales on the border and Tucson, 70 miles north. These two corridors account for 42 per cent of recorded deaths in Arizona, says Revd Hoover, which in turn account for half the total deaths along the entire border. The clusters of corpses on Revd Hoover's screen show, he says, 'that although we had an overall reduction year over year until 2007, the numbers of migrants dying is now on the rise again. If the border patrol and new security measures were effective, the numbers dying would be dropping. But they are not: in the mid 2000s, we were seeing one hundred deaths a year. Over the last three years [to 2009], that figure has increased to two hundred, and the reason is that, as we can see from this diagram [and he flicks to another chart] the more the roads are patrolled, the more the migrants cross more remote and dangerous terrain. The deaths occur further from the roads, where you may be less likely to get caught, but less likely to make it.' The collation and analysis is estimably thorough: maps from 2005 show the majority of deaths between 5,000 and 6,000 metres from paved roads. The latest figures show them at least 9,000 metres away. 'The distance from the roads where people are perishing has nearly doubled,' says Revd Hoover. 'We are the authority for mapping this shit out – the government doesn't do it.' In August 2010, details of work by the Pima County Chief Medical Examiner's office was published, showing the migration crisis to have totally transformed its work, with 20 per cent of its examinations performed on border-crossers. The office had 'admitted' 1,700 corpses over the preceding decade, and 81 for the months of June and July 2010 alone.

Revd Hoover calculates that 'up to twenty-five per cent cross using contacts they know – relatives or cousins – people concerned with the well-being of everyone in the group, should anything go wrong. That leaves a huge majority, about seventy per cent, in the hands of the *coyotes* whose only interest in getting you there will be a bit of extra pay, but who will not wait if something goes wrong, walking across country where a twisted ankle is a death sentence.'

The fourteen dead on the Devil's Highway in May 2001 had used as their point of departure in Mexico the border town of Sonoyta. At that time, Sonoyta was abuzz with human traffic: the main square bustling with movement. Coaches from the interior disgorged load after load of people from the south, ready for the journey. The town was full of flophouses where itinerants would stay cheaply, and be picked up by prowling *polleros* and *coyotes*. Now, Sonoyta is quiet – uncannily quiet. The town seems to have shut. '*Chapo*' Guzmán chose Sonoyta as the location to deliver an order, according to US intelligence, that operatives for his cartel 'use their weapons to defend their loads at all costs' while crossing into Arizona.⁹ So, informs a dentist in Sonoyta: 'the *polleros* have gone. This is now a place for another kind of crossing. You will see them only at night, and it is a good thing not to see them. From here, the bad guys now transport drugs, not other people.' The *Ajo Copper News* on the US side gives a weekly update on shootings in Sonoyta, while the sheriff's log is a litany of drug seizures. For the *pollos*, says the dentist, 'you need to go to Altar'.

Altar, some 30 miles south-east of Sonoyta and 60 miles back from the frontier, is by no means the most dangerous town in the border-land, but it is one of the eeriest. There is no way of arriving in Altar without being thoroughly checked out, heart-in-mouth, for there is no reason why a *gringo* like me would be in this place, other than to pry into its main trade. Altar is the new hub, in the western half of the borderland, for the arrival of migrants in transit from southern Mexico and Central America. In the heat of late morning, stalls along the sides of the square, and up the back streets, are selling the equipment needed for the crossing and ordeal ahead: black backpacks, black T-shirts, camouflaged combat pants, flashlights – and, of course, the necessary spiritual protections: key rings, prayer cards and purses for change bearing the image of the Virgin of Guadalupe and San Judas Tadeo, cousin of Jesus Christ and the patron saint of lost causes, to whom one turns in time of difficulty.

Throughout the town are flophouses of the kind a while back found in Sonoyta – shelters where migrants pay between $3 and $5 for a bunk-bed made of wood, used blankets and the possibility of a mattress stained with dried semen and sweat. There are dormitories like those on Panteón Street, into which we are not admitted by an administrator apparently nervous about the other men lounging around the reception area – *polleros* plying their trade, preparing to bake chicken in the desert. There is one shelter, however, which is free, and where there is a welcome, the *Centro Comunitario de Atención al Migrante y Necesitado* (CCAMYN – the Community Centre for Assistance to the Migrant and Needy), supported by the diocese of Hermosillo, the state capital. The centre, clean and wholesome, is run by Marcos Burruel, who was once a quality control supervisor at the brewery in Tecate, using his sense of smell to pick out a substandard brew, but who now uses similar instincts to prevent anyone who has been drinking alcohol to sleep here, or a *pollero* disguised as a migrant but looking for custom from conniving his way into the dormitory. At CCAMYN, there are clean mattresses and linen for the deserving. Outside is a carved plaque and dedication: '*A Los Caídos En Los Desiertos de la Muerte*' – To the fallen in the deserts of death. '*En memoria de aquellos que por buscar una mejor vida / Lo único que encontraron fue la muerte*' – In memory of those who searched for a better life / But the only thing they met was death.

We sit and talk while the shelter is closed during the day. 'How different it was when I was a boy here,' recalls Burruel. 'There were no fences, and people would cross and come back, cross and come back. Which they still do – there's much more coming and going than one hears about. Most get taken straight off the bus, the *coyote* is waiting there. They're cunning – the migrant may say, "I'm looking for Roberto, or *El Tigre*", and the *coyote* will say, "I'm *El Tigre*'s friend" and make a fake phone call: 'Hey, *Tigre*, your people from Chiapas have arrived.' And if they don't want to go, they're sometimes taken with violence and held until they pay. The authorities don't give a shit, and do nothing – besides, there's always a deal between the police and the *coyotes*: the police can get one hundred pesos for each migrant, which is more than they earn working for the police.'

Burruel estimates that 'about eighty per cent of the people who cross know of the dangers, but many don't have a clue. From here to Tucson or Phoenix can take them four to five days, but the *coyotes* tell them it'll take three to four hours. It's become a dirty business. Not just the heat, but kidnapping. Every day there's kidnapping, here in Altar and the desert. They kidnap the wetbacks and ask for ransom [Burruel uses the term *mojado*, 'wetback' migrant, although he is Mexican and though there is no river here]. They hold them for days, weeks, I have no way of knowing how many just disappear. They kidnapped and held a crowd of them in that house just across the street there', and he gestures behind him, through the window.

Burruel, a slight man wearing a beige shirt, talks about his work and his charge with a certain detachment, for all his commitment, as though such an attitude may protect him from the many people in Altar who disapprove of him, and of whom he is clearly afraid. 'The migrants are here because they're eager to cross, but know nothing apart from what they heard back in the villages, where they see the *coyote* as someone important. In some ways, I'm here to help them in this madness: I feed people, give a bed to a few – but I must also make them aware of what's about to happen. I warn them about kidnapping, show them videos about the dangers. And some do change their mind. They see the films and decide to go back. One time a man kept asking to change the video, and that's how I knew he was a *coyote* infiltrating the shelter. That's how my trouble begins.

'What I do here,' Burruel continues, 'angers the *coyotes*. If I talk about the dangers, this upsets them.' But, as he has implied, it is more serious than that. 'Here in Altar, other people have come who are part of organised rackets, to kidnap people; criminals who are not *coyotes* but related to the drug-trafficking cartels. The drug smugglers use Altar too, to stash and transport drugs and to tax the *polleros*. And this is very dangerous for me. They insult me, threaten me, tell me they're going to kill me.' Burruel is suddenly haunted, loses his detachment, and confides: 'Since I got my job here, I've been terrified of the night.'

Most of the narcos and *coyotes* working Altar are from Sinaloa, says Burruel, 'as are the *bajadores* – bandits – who come with guns and rob people before they cross'. What his conversation drives towards is a recent development: that the traffic in migrants between here and the border crossing town of El Sasabe is being taken over by the cartels. 'The narcos control the frontier. From here to Sasabe, the *coyotes* have to pay a tax to the mafia, which they collect from the poor *pollos*, between 700 and 1,200 pesos [$50-$80] for each. If they don't pay, the narcos stop the truck and beat hell out of the driver, maybe beat the migrants and burn the bus.

'So why do I do this job? I must be crazy, I know. It's not because I think it matters, because it doesn't. Actually, what I try to do is point-less, against their business. It's because I believe in God, and because the priest is a friend of mine. But I'm only human, and of course I'm afraid. I'm also, by the way, a postman, and must do my rounds now.' These duties delivering mail, he says, afford a break, a breath of air beyond the stifling claustrophobia of this deceptively sleepy town, apparently calm but saturated with the movement and violence of which Burruel speaks.

But there is more to learn. In the thicket of back streets behind the square is a shop selling clothing, aimed like every other at the migrants' needs, but a little less like a military surplus store than the stalls: there are children's clothes and sunhats that are neither black nor camouflage. The shop is run by Amanda Ortíz Reina, wife of a man I had met briefly when he was mayor of Altar a decade ago, Francisco García Aten, a schoolmaster who had warned then that drug dealers would move in on the smuggling of migrants. In 2009, Ms Ortíz herself campaigned to win the office her husband occupied until 2003, on a ticket challenging the power of organised crime in town, but was beaten by her rival, Rafael Rivera Vidrio, who refuses to see us.

Ms Ortíz, by contrast, admits two unannounced strangers rolling up on her doorstep – after a brief but visible sizing up – and makes sweet tea, to drink with cakes served on a tray with a paper doily. She came to Altar aged twenty, to marry, in a city 'where everyone knew each other and supported one another'. Most of the population 'worked in the fields, like my father, and no one got rich from the collective farms, but they fed us. It was companionable, and we lived in symbiosis with the desert.' But now, 'incomers from Sinaloa have taken over the town and subjugated the local authorities and police. This has escalated even over the past two or three years; things have changed even since the government began the offensive.' So far as the cartels are concerned, Ms Ortíz posits tentatively, the terrain is contested between Guzmán and those loyal to the Beltrán Leyva clan, now allied to the Gulf cartel. 'While they fight each other for the Plaza, they both extort from the migrants, up to one hundred dollars per head smuggled, I understand.' But there is a twist to the cartels' involvement. As they swing their organisational muscle behind migration, so 'it becomes more efficient. And safer, in some ways though not in others. Our indications are that there is less rape by the *coyotes*, less robbery by bandits, less harassment on the way to the drop houses, less of anything that will attract the authorities' attention to the drugs, or get in the way of the money. But there is a terrible price to pay for this. Once they reach safety, the migrants are at their mercy.'

Then Ms Ortíz reverts from this distant menace to what is before her. 'My greatest worry for our town,' she concludes, 'is that children along the border are growing up with this as their world. My sons used to play in the streets; now that is simply too dangerous. We're terrified of the kids from Sinaloa, but the criminals become role models for the young people. When I ran for mayor, the old people wanted me, but the young people voted against me – when we used to go into town campaigning, there would be kids of twelve or thirteen years old, with walkie-talkies, reporting on our movements – to whoever. The truth no one wants to admit is that the young don't want to take a stand against what is happening. They're happy with this new culture, these new opportunities; they're growing up with it. Many parents have left, leaving us who remain scared, alone and frustrated. We're afraid to talk to our neighbours, because we're unsure who we are talking to.' As we look around her shop, minibuses heave by, up the little street and out across the land where the Buckhorn cactus changes colour in response to stress, turning a purple colour in times of severe drought or cold, then blooms in the many colours of fire during spring – the desert's mixed messages to those about to cross it.

They sit in what shade they can find around the main square, and wait, plan, figure out the next move. They are people in flight from what they have left behind, and in fear of what lies ahead. Some are on their way, others on their way back. The latter have less to lose now and are readier to talk. 'We knew the risks, and we took them,' reflects Ramón from Tabasco, who has now crossed twice, and been deported twice, 'and that's enough'. Ramón has paid *coyotes* $1,200 since he left home near Villahermosa four months ago, 'and there's nothing left. I have nothing for it but to go home, where there is nothing'. There are a lot of 'nothings' in that sentence, *mucha nada*. Ramón has a tooth missing, wears a pale blue shirt and a smile incongruous to his lot. He worked the land back home, 'where it's very beautiful, but I couldn't feed my family, I could hardly feed myself'. The second crossing was the worst, says Ramón's friend Víctor from Chiapas, with whom he teamed up on the bus from Villahermosa. 'The first time we crossed and were picked up by the *migra* as soon as we found the main road. We were back in El Sasabe within three days. But the second time, it was hotter, we walked longer. The first guides knew their way, it was just bad luck the *migra* spotted us. But the second pair were useless, a couple of *pendejos* [idiots]. They thought they were the real thing, but in the end they were *cobardes* [cowards, weaklings] who argued between themselves. After two days, we were still on the Indian reservation, they said, when we should have been near the freeway services where the bus would take us to Phoenix. We were spotted by helicopter, and this time all the *migra* were Mexican, real *sabelotodos* – smartasses – kids like I would walk past in the street back home, but they called us all kinds of shit.'

There are much edgier people in Altar embarking on their first journey across, on which they have staked their life. Some do not want to talk at all, and groups of boys with tattoos and cropped hair switch their conversation to an indigenous language as soon as we approach. But one man, Rodolfo, manages a joke. He is travelling with two cousins to join his eldest son in Minnesota, where, he says, 'I've heard about the cold in winter and how it'll kill me, but now I'm more worried about the heat.' The bridge home to Jalisco is burned: 'All I own I have put into this journey,' he says. 'I sold my house and my animals to pay the *coyote* and to buy clothes and things we need for the trip. Yes, I know the risks, but we have to take them; I cannot sell even the little I grow any more, the prices for produce are so low I'm paying to grow it, so we'll pray all day, and leave before dark.'

The road from Altar to El Sasabe, across a spectacular landscape called the *sierrita*, is a route to take during daylight. A sporadic flow of rickety white minibuses crammed with migrants, or open-backed cattle trucks with wooden slats to contain the human load, account for the only traffic to speak of. Minibuses kick up dust and the Arizona plates get us waved down and pulled over by men in bomber jackets and jeans. There is no demand for money, no sign of weapons, but there are plenty of questions, nods of disapproval and partial belief at the answer that we are researching migration patterns – one does not mention the words 'drug' or 'trafficking' around here. And there are stories told, whether true or false, with menace: about a hamlet called Los Molinos where a carload full of people was 'shot off the road, with everybody killed'. Ten miles on, however, approaching El Sasabe, the incinerated skeleton of a minibus adorns the roadside. During 2010, swathes of the land across the horizon of buttes visible from this road became 'no-go' areas, into and out of which people could not travel, with access routes barred by roadblocks manned by gunmen from either the Sinaloa or Beltrán Leyva cartel – and villagers completely cut off.

The town of El Sasabe itself is set slightly back from the border, giving the migrants a diagonal line to walk before they cross, hoping to avoid the concentrations of agents around the town of the same name in Arizona. It is low-slung, a main drag of buildings made of bricks on hastily applied cement, including the Super Coyote Café selling fresh water. The migrants line up at a makeshift hut to register with a branch of the Mexican public safety ministry called Grupo Beta. These men and women wearing orange T-shirts and driving orange jeeps, have a peculiar role: a kind of migrant services branch of the government's social welfare administration, the *'Desarrollo Integral de la Familia'*. Grupo Beta agents take the names of those crossing, lest they be needed or never heard of again. They fill the migrants' water cannisters and even provide maps of the US side, where there is disquiet among the authorities as to whether Grupo Beta is helping to save lives or facilitating, if not encouraging, illegal immigration. One agent, called Alemán, remarks that 'we are doing the best we can. We're not encouraging them, we just try to stop them from dying.' He says that 'the flow of migration has slowed down, because it's getting much harder. We all know now that just over there, not only are the border patrol waiting for them, but even the National Guard.' And waiting in numbers recently increased by Homeland Security Secretary Janet Napolitano who was, until summoned by President Obama, governor of Arizona, the promised but parched land, receding from view up the Devil's Highway. A group of migrants camp down in the dust, wearing black hoodies and carrying their backpacks, and joke that it is in the interest of Grupo Beta to help them, because if they make it, the government benefits from the money they send home. But if they die, the government has to pay for the coffin and the plane to carry it. 'That would be the first time the government did anything for me,' cracks Jorge, a young man from Chilpancingo. 'If only they had given me that kind of money when I was back home!'

Only one trafficker is prepared to mumble a few words. Introducing himself reluctantly as Mario, he is a lean youth with spiky hair and a T-shirt reading 'Metal Rock On'. He says between cigarettes that he has been doing this for two years, after losing his job in Ciudad Obregón in the south of the state. 'I'm good,' he assures us, but adds nervously, 'You can write that all these people will make it to Phoenix' – as if he could know. One's mind runs back to the famous guide, Antonio López Ramos, who accompanied those who died on the Devil's Highway in 2001. He was identified by all the survivors as having a fleck of dyed red hair, for which he was nicknamed 'Red Rooster', and was apparently as cocky as this young man in El Sasabe now, who even echoes López's reported dress sense. Eleven miles of wall are under construction here: steel poles that mark the frontier as it disappears through scrub and creosote, being filled with concrete and standing four inches apart, a service dust-road along the American side – nothing but desert grass to the south. Suddenly, about four miles west of the hamlet, it stops, and the border continues as a line of squat metal bollards, around and over which the migrants will go, into the furnace.

The journey had been easier than Vicente Sánchez Morín feared.[10] A bus arrived as promised to take him and a cousin from Cintalpa in the west of Chiapas to the airport at Tuxtla Gutiérrez, from where a charter plane flew them to Hermosillo. 'I had never flown,' says Vicente, 'that was the only time I was scared, before we crossed the border.' From Hermosillo, another bus drove them to Altar, though there had been a breakdown and short delay at a place called San Agustín – Vicente remembered the name because it is the same as his brother's, whom he was to join in Denver. Agustín had a good job, or jobs, in Colorado: working fields and orchards during summer, fixing cars and casual shifts packing meat in winter. The crossing at El Sasabe had been 'easy', said Vicente, 'we went at night, the guide knew where he was going'. By now, they were in a party of ten, including a man from Apizaco, in Tlaxcala, who said nothing and who Vicente did not trust. 'He wore a black T-shirt and camouflage pants, he was always watching people, he never talked or seemed worried.' A minibus duly appeared, Vicente could not remember where, but we worked out it would have waited for them at Arivaca, 20 miles from Sasabe, with a connection to Interstate 19. Vicente saw the lights of Tucson at dusk, 'and I thought it was Phoenix already. They told us in Altar that's where we were headed and I'd told Agustín to pick me up there.' The van arrived in Phoenix during the heat of afternoon in May 2009 – Vicente does not know where, although: 'I know where it is now,' he says, safely in the care of a church group. 'I've been back to look at it a couple of times.'

When the van arrived the group of men were corralled into the back of a building in the outskirts of town. 'There was a group of four people waiting for us, and they were scary to us. By now, I had been separated from my cousin, at the place where the bus picked us up in the dark. The mood had changed. It wasn't like they were trying to get us to our relatives, it was like we were going to jail.' Weirdly, 'the man from Apizaco, who we had thought was one of us, knew them, like he suddenly switched sides'. The windows of the house were blackened, the door locked, the men left alone. 'Everything had gone wrong. I had no idea what was happening. Some hours later, more men came, with guns. These were completely different people. They were wearing masks, while the other people we had dealt with until now showed their faces, though they never told us their names. They'd had nicknames, the one who took us through the desert was called *La Flecha*, the arrow. Now I was really scared. Then they took all our papers, our money. Two days passed, maybe one night and a day. I tried to keep count with a man from Campeche. It was only when I finally found Agustín by telephone that I realised what was happening. It was almost more terrifying for him.' Agustín had been contacted by telephone and asked for $3,000 to buy his brother's freedom. 'He panicked completely. He hadn't expected anything like it. He'd sent me $1,000 for my trip, and hadn't anything like that kind of money. He was running around, asking anyone he knew. They told him that if he didn't find it within a week, they'd kill me. I knew nothing about all this.'

Vicente is a rugged man who looks older than his age of thirty-two, though he is physically fit. He tells his story in the office of a church as though it were happening to someone else. He wears a clean shirt, pressed slacks, smart shoes with buckles on them. Vicente is one of more than 1,000 people from Mexico and Central America whom Phoenix police have freed from captivity – in the city becoming known as the 'kidnap capital of America'.[11] Out of 368 kidnapping cases handled by the Phoenix Police Department in 2008, says spokesman Tommy Thompson, seventy-eight were calls to migrant drop houses. During the first six months of 2009, another sixty-eight had been identified or raided after emergency calls. In a raid on another drop house in a suburb called El Mirage, conditions had been even more frightening, some thirty men kept half-naked and pistol-whipped, their relatives shaken down for $5,000 before the property was raided in June 2009.[12] This is the delivery end of the narcos' taking over of the migrant business, using their contacts in the drug distribution network, based on street gangs and family associations, to recruit those prepared to hold migrants to ransom. Phoenix, now America's fifth city, has long been a destination for Mexican migrants, and especially from Sinaloa. According to the police department, Sinaloan gang members cruise the bars in Phoenix frequented by people from their towns back home, Culiacán and Los Mochis, recruiting for migrant kidnap operations, offering to pay cash advances with the balance payable upon receipt of the relatives' ransom money. As the mortgage market crashes, so the work is made easier by the number of properties to rent, which has increased by 75 per cent since 2000.

'We waited, and after a day they brought us some food,' says Vicente. 'They provided water, but no food until now. A woman came to help the men give it out – she told us she was "cooking for them", but I think I know what that means. This time a man showed his face. They needed more money, he said, and they asked us for the names of the relatives waiting for us. A man said he wouldn't give it, and they hit him, and told him: "If you want to live, give us the name and number." I gave them Agustín's number in Denver, which I had learned by heart.'

After four days, police stormed the property, without major incident. 'It happened quickly and suddenly. They took our names, and arranged for our relatives to be contacted. I didn't know how the police found us; I know now, but I'm unable to say.' Vicente, which I do not think is his real name, avoided deportation by agreeing to testify against the man from Tlaxcala. For the moment, Vicente is safe in Salt Lake City, protected by his church and US law enforcement. Vicente will probably get deported in the end, says the pastor looking after him at the evangelical sect to which Vicente belonged back in Mexico. And if so? 'I'll try again,' says Vicente. In October 2010, the cost of the cartels' takeover of migration could be counted by the single worst massacre of the entire war to days: the summary execution of 72 migrants, mostly from Honduras, held at San Fernando in Tamaulipas, at the other end of the border. Believed to have been kidnapped by the Zetas, the group apparently refused to pay the extra levies demanded and paid with their lives, apart from a sole survivor who lived to bear witness to the atrocity.

The agricultural centre of Caborca, 60 kilometres west of Altar, is regarded as the Spaniards' point of departure along the *Camino del Diablo*. At least, the histories have it that the expedition set out from an Indian village near Caborca, leaving the possibility that this may have been Pitiquito, where the loveliest church in the area nestles between the back streets of town and fields beyond. The cool and the damp, musky scent of plaster and stone inside the chapel of the San Diego del Pitiquo Mission, give relief on a baking hot afternoon, especially when the walls speak as they do. Built in 1687, the aisles were decorated in 1719 with monochrome frescos depicting Death and Glory, a magnificent eagle's head representing St John the Evangelist, a bull's head for St Luke, a majestic Virgin of the Apocalypse and skeletal figure of all-conquering death, pointing the way towards the Resurrection by prophesying the exact month and year of Christ's crucifixion, as in the Book of Daniel.[13] 'All the bikers want their photo taken underneath it,' laughs the priest, Father Claudio Murrieta. He is in his mid-forties, handsome, energetic, forever at work around the fields or at his computer writing a history of this corner of Sonora. Pitiquito was an Indian village, where a Mission farm was established, run by the church, while Altar was a military garrison — different foundations which led to very different histories. Altar became a city of commerce, legal and illegal, while Pitiquito remained agricultural, a place of orchards and crops: cotton, wheat — and eventually asparagus. But this last was emblematic of what has happened here since the government of President Carlos Salinas de Gortari ended the system of village landholding, privatising communally owned lots of farmland known as *ejidos* during the 1980s and allowing agribusinesses to take over the peasants' plots. 'Asparagus was new here: it was the big business crop which takes the nutrients and leaves the land barren,' says Father Murrieta, 'it is typical of the system now, exploiting the land and the people, bad production for quick profit, and low wages.'

We set off in the priest's truck to survey the scourge of poverty that followed President Salinas' privatisation of the *ejidos* — and the ensuing arrival of narco ranches on the land. The initial buyers were big landowners who turned the self-sufficient peasants (who were also small traders in their produce) into serfs, or else the rural unemployed. It is about this process, and its devastation of Mexican agriculture, along with the NAFTA free trade agreement, that Father Murrieta is writing his book. 'This is a route I do every day,' he says, 'to keep an eye on what's happening.' Which is, he says, 'that the average Mexican salary in the fields is fifteen pesos [about 8 pence or 12 cents] a day' — in a country where prices are not far below those in the United States. We pull up at a hamlet called La Estación, beside a disused railway line in the shadow of the spectrally beautiful Cerros mountains. Another of President Salinas' rackety ideas was to privatise Mexico's railways, selling thousands of miles of track to American freight rail companies and ultimately closing the entire passenger network. Behind us is the old station — once a bustle of meeting and greeting, arrivals to and departures from this now still and subjugated community, the building in ruins.

Father Murrieta greets a woman putting her washing through a mangle, chickens clucking around her ankles on the scrap of land surrounding the shack that is her home. 'She once farmed this land herself, when it was communal,' says Father Murrieta. 'But the privatisation was a pre-condition imposed by the Americans for entry into the free trade zone. The peso collapsed around the same time, and none of the peasants could afford even a slice of land. So first came the big ranchers with political connections,' he continues, 'then American agribusiness, buying up vineyards like that one, owned by a winery in California' – and he points to rows of vines, climbing the hillsides. Dogs lie in the shade of the mesquite trees; in a yard, a girl gets ready for a date, washing and applying make-up beside a tub of water with a cracked mirror balanced against a rusty pump. Along the dirt road adjacent to the railway line, posters have been erected by the rival political parties, PRI and PAN, for an upcoming election. The candidates' faces beam out at the hamlet. 'They're just messing with the people,' scoffs Father Murrieta, 'there's no difference between them, so they agree to fight it out with each other for the right to steal from the village' – and we agree that this is hardly a phenomenon unique to Mexico. In the yard of a bigger house with acacia trees in front of it, is parked an incongruously brand-new SUV with tinted windows. 'It's not hard to spot the ones who are working for the narcos,' Father Murrieta says with a shrug, 'but these are just the footsoldiers. After the landowners and the Americans, the narcos came, needing to clean money and stash drugs. They may keep horses, but obviously they don't farm.'

In late October 2009, an agricultural union leader called Margarito Montes Parra, who had tried to defend the rights of peasants, was ambushed by gunmen and killed while visiting Sonora. The Worker, Peasant and Popular General Union of which he was president is based in Oaxaca, but Montes Parra was trying to organise fishermen off the Sonoran coast, and arbitrate disputes involving the Yaqui Indian tribe. He had repeatedly criticised the authorities for protecting narco traffickers, and his son Adrián had also been shot here in Sonora in 2007, a murder the authorities said was linked to narcos buying land. On 30 October, Mr Montes was leaving a ranch with a party of families when a convoy of three trucks sped by, firing

AK-47s at the small crowd. In all, fourteen people were killed, including four children.[14]

This war has butchery for its badge, or cachet, and it was also not far from here that a massacre of unimaginable brutality took place. A white SUV was found abandoned, and inside it a stew of mutilated bodies – hacked, chopped, castrated, decapitated; literally, cutlets of severed head, arm, leg and torso crammed into the vehicle with no relation one to the other until they were matched by the forensic police. Unpublishably gruesome pictures of the discovery and its aftermath were taken by the authorities, showing the deeply disturbing sight of human pieces laid out on a tarpaulin across the floor of a hangar. It is a scene from Hell from which even Hieronymus Bosch in his most vividly imaginative moments of pious terror would have flinched.

We drive through this terrain with Father Murrieta, the Cerros mountains cloud-capped in mid-distance, and pass a compound by the old railway, fenced off by chainlink topped with barbed wire, with a gas cylinder and trucks and trailers parked up on the gravel within. 'That's them,' Father Murrieta says, 'transferring, and loading up drugs; they don't even bother to hide it.' He accelerates, for this is not a place to be caught snooping. Soon, there's a fine-looking ranch with a wide gateway, and horses visible behind a fence along the driveway lined with cypress trees. 'That's another,' Father Murrieta says almost nonchalantly. 'You're now driving past quite a big operation. They have some fine stables there, but that is not their line of business.' He confirms Amanda Ortíz's diagnosis: the warring factions here are the Sinaloa and Beltrán Leyva cartels, the latter representing the Zetas' western front. We tell the priest that we slept a second night in Caborca, wary of Altar, to which Father Murrieta retorts, with laughter: 'You fell for the appearance of things, did you? For sure, you're more likely to get kidnapped in Altar, or your car hijacked. But there's a much greater chance of getting killed in Caborca, even if it looks quiet. It's far more dangerous, because that's where the infrastructure the narcos need is located: distribution centres, support industries – packaging, transport, that kind of thing.' He points past a burned-out former cotton mill, American-owned now, but deserted: 'There's an important archaeological site over there, which no one can visit after a narco bought the land.'

Father Murrieta is now livid and needs some refreshment. The advantage of being a parish priest in Mexico is that the old ladies of the village are delighted to cook lunch for he who nourishes them with communion each Sunday. Father Murrieta registers no objection, as we are welcomed into María Bonilla's little house for a hearty meal of pasta and beans, with a bottle of Tecate for the priest, over which he tells a funny story. The Father had always wanted, he relates, to go for a beer-drinking holiday during the Munich Oktoberfest, and recently he made it. There had been a convention in the Veneto, after which most of the faithful wanted to go to Rome, 'apart from the priests!' he jokes. So Father Murrieta and a friend headed for Bavaria, 'and we lived on beer and potatoes for a few days. They had glasses THIS BIG!' and he raises a hand above the lace tablecloth to illustrate the height of a stein. 'But oh dear, the hotels were so expensive. We used to go up to the airport and sleep there, on the seats, then back to the *bierkeller* in the morning. Which was fine, but if I go again, I'll save up for a bed.'

Of the two 'corridors' along which Revd Hoover's charts showed people dying in the largest numbers, the more deadly was the land of the Tohono O'odham Native American tribe, for whom smuggling, and the US government's war against smuggling, constitute just the latest chapter in a history of striving against – and living with – subjugation and persecution ever since the white man, first Spanish, then American, stepped on its ancient land. The O'odham were a people from what the Spanish called the 'Pimería Alta' region, unified by traditions and the O'odham language, but for centuries the tribe lived and were bound in groups without tribal government or centralised secular leadership. The O'odham had no formal laws; individuals and families were expected to maintain 'order and proper decorum, and people who went against customs were asked to leave', writes the historian of the tribe, Winston P. Erickson.[15] They farmed with no idea of private land ownership, but were constantly raided for goods, food and women by people they described with the O'odham word for 'enemy' – *Apache*. Their land was crossed by the Coronado expeditions, missions established by the Spanish, and colonisation accelerated after the discovery of mines in Sonora. The O'odham were quick to show an interest in the growth of wheat as a crop, and European tools with which to grow it, which led the Spanish to think they might be potential converts to Catholicism. In the last years of the seventeenth century, the tribe was caught between the Spanish military's abuse and the favour of Father Kino, whose shrine at Magdalena in Mexico remains a pilgrimage route for many O'odham Catholics. When the Spanish moved permanently on to their land in the early 1700s, in search of gold and silver, the O'odham came to distrust them, hiding their sources of precious metals – and the Spanish responded ruthlessly and violently towards the O'odham and their neighbours, the Yaqui. In 1821 both tribes exchanged Spanish for brief Mexican rule, and in 1848 the border between the US and Mexico was drawn across O'odham land. 'The splitting of O'odham land between two countries inconvenienced the O'odham somewhat, but it would be many years before strong enforcement of border policies would occur,' writes Erickson, with understatement.[16] Under US law, he continues, 'the O'odham had few or no rights as intruding Anglos took what they wanted and ignored the rights of the native peoples'. By the turn of the century, the killing and destruction of the O'odham and their ways had begun in earnest: the reservation was designated across 4,800 square miles, as cut off as it was expansive, and the cash economy ravaged the O'odham and Yaqui ways of living, as many native people migrated to Tucson in search of employment as construction workers, railroad labourers or domestic servants, or to the copper mines of Ajo. During the 1930s, the first border fence was erected, although the O'odham remained – and remains – the only tribe in the United States which enrols Mexican citizens and allows them to vote in tribal elections. The tribe is one of the poorest in the south-western USA, with an average annual income of $8,000 per family and about one third of its citizens unemployed.

When the world's press descended on southern Arizona after the deaths of the 'Yuma 14' in 2001, the Tohono O'odham tribal authorities greeted visitors with pride and courtesy. The chairman, officials and employees of the tribe would discuss education and the dilemma between retaining the native Uto-Aztecan language and culture while giving young O'odham a chance in modern America. Now, attempts to contact the tribe officially disappear down a black hole – messages to its gatekeeper Pete Delgado hit a brick wall. Even one of

America's most respected and tenacious reporter on Native American affairs, the indefatigable Brenda Norrell, is forever, through an estimable website called 'Censored News' and others, hammering at the door in search of answers to questions about abuse of land, heritage and people by construction of the border fence. In the eyes of some tribal members, their authorities, having vowed to oppose yet another invasion by the white man in his attempt to reinforce the border with fences and hundreds of agents, have instead cooperated with the militarisation of their own land. The tribe is again exploited, caught again between a rock and a hard place: between smugglers of drugs and migrants exploiting the poverty of its people, and US authorities trying to stop them.

People cannot be silenced, however, and where there is grievance the courageous talk, whether out of rage, pride, despair or all three. Mike Flores is one such person. 'Who are you?' he asks by way of introduction, in the inimitable way in which Native Americans ask the question, with an implied enquiry after one's ancestry. Flores is a Native 'Amexican' in the deepest sense. He lives in a caravan on a patch of land behind the roadside café on the main highway through Sells, but his father comes from Quitovac, across the border carved through his ancient land, and migrated north to Ajo in the United States – just west of the reservation – to work in a copper mine. Flores's mother was born beside a natural spring, a *tinaja*, in what has since become the Organ Pipe Cactus National Monument park, adjacent to the border on the US side.

Flores is a true son of this land we are calling borderland, but with an identity that precedes any borders and transcends Spanish colonisation, Mexico, the arrival of the white man and the United States. Spiritually, he feels close to the Mexica, calling himself a 'traditional', according to the ancient beliefs of his ancestors, rather than what are called 'progressives' who converted to and still accept the Catholic faith. 'My grandfather told me: This is our way, the four directions, the four winds and what we call *him'dag*, the way, the journey. When I went [to Teotihuacán] to see the pyramids, I felt part of *that*,' he insists; 'those people were looking at things the way I do, they saw it the way we see it, and that's not surprising, they came from here.' I foolishly mention the journey of the Mexica to Tenochtitlan from around here, but Flores scoffs: 'Oh yeah, people have all these anthropologies and sociologies and all kinds of "ologies", but I'm an O'odham, not an 'ologist – all I know is what I was told by my father and grandfather, which was what they had been told by their fathers and grandfathers: that I can rub the dirt on my face anywhere between Alaska and Mexico City, and call it me, because that's where I come from.' The uniquely complex and beautiful emblem of the Tohono O'odham tribe portrays the human journey within the scheme of *him'dag*: a small figure, representing birth, stands atop a circular maze which winds, via a penultimate point in the far corner of the pattern, to a 'dark centre' of eternal life, in which one is cleansed and reflects back on knowledge gained during the journey. Just now, reports the O'odham paper *The Runner*, *him'dag* is a subject taught in school on the reservation, and a popular one. Pupils are reported to look forward to the special day of the week when traditional food replaces the usual junk served at lunchtime.

Flores would have learned how the Creator God I'itoi led his ancestors from the underworld, up into this land; he would call months *masads* or moons, the first being the *eda wa'ugad masad*, backbone month, beginning with the winter solstice to commence an annual cycle divided into halves, with its mid-point as the summer cactus-wine feast on the longest day.[17] During the 1970s, Flores became involved in the militant American Indian Movement, and 'I still feel the war, like it never ended'. Flores wears an AIM hat when we meet for breakfast in Sells. 'Right behind my caravan is where the US army set up its first base on our land. And sometimes at night, it's like I can hear our warriors preparing for battle. The past is very close by around here, you know – it's with us all the time. And the ancestors are watching to see how we deal with this latest situation. The land has fallen sick from being raped over and over. First, the white man, then the border, now this: ninja guys prowling around, helicopters flyin' over making the people and the horses scared.' Flores spits words of fire but with an expression of deep calm that is disarming and compelling, his vocabulary ablaze, but his eyes wide, voice soft.

The border patrol has Flores's unmitigated contempt: 'They come from Texas, South Carolina, upstate New York, and they don't know jack shit about this land. They act the tough guy, but if you put any of 'em out on the land under the sun without their toys, they'd be dead in two days. I can walk for weeks across this land, light and dark, 'cause I know it, I know where the springs are and what to eat. We've been close to the land for all time, we understand these things – how the birds hatch, how the water flows, how lizards stay cool in 110 degrees, so we can imitate them. But these guys: they think they're big boys but they ain't nothing on this land.' Which makes it even more offensive to Flores that 'they're interfering with *him'dag*, the way itself. We can't get the elders to perform the sacred rites from the Mexican side because they don't have the papers. Last year, we held our traditional ceremony, and it's the custom for our warriors to hunt a Pronghorn deer; it has to be caught, cooked and eaten in the correct way. But last year, the border patrol drove up on the warriors, handcuffed and detained them for eight hours, for having a weapon on their homeland.' Such audacity is 'overstepping the line', fumes Flores. 'It's part of the same shit that gets these kids in gangs who are twenty-one, twenty-two years old, using drugs and alcohol, and I get on my soap box and tell 'em that's not the way, that's the way the white man sent us. He taught us that to get anyone's attention you gotta show 'em a thousand dollars and that's what it's come to on the rez. Whoever offers the money gets their way.' This affects the tribal authorities too, says Flores. 'There's a switch in tactics,' he continues. 'At first, the tribal leadership opposed the border fence. But they feel more confident now, against us of the old way, 'cause they've seen a little money in it. Now they're happier about co-operating with anyone who wants to trample on this land, whatever they're messing in.'

We drive south, off the main highway running parallel to the border and down the road towards the frontier, marked with an arrowhead as 'Indian 19', leaving behind the shacks and trailers, the land rising so that we are surrounded by agave, chollas, mesquite and creosote. To the east, a conic mountaintop rises above the other desert peaks along the ridge and pierces the horizon like the tip of an arrow. Flores says: 'That's Baroquivari, which our ancestors considered the centre of the universe'; and one feels a strong sensation from the passive but passionate way in which he says this, and from the mountain itself. 'It's the land which keeps us going,' he says again. 'We and the land are the same.' We pass a compound of buildings and a holding pen for people, signed 'Law Enforcement Area', out of which a bus bearing the name and insignia of the Wackenhut security company tears towards and past us. This is one of the vehicles that commutes between the law-enforcement area and the border, taking illegal immigrants apprehended in – or rescued from, depending on how you look at it – the expanse, corralled and now shipped to the border and dumped on the other side to make their way back to Altar whence they came. 'One time,' says Flores, 'the tribal police stopped one of those buses and found the guards had stolen a tortoise from the desert. You know, to keep as a pet – a beautiful desert tortoise. That's how they see our land.' After 19 miles of Indian Highway 19, the paved road veers left towards an outpost community of trailers called San Miguel, clinging to the border, while we take a dirt track to the right, at the end of which is a clearing in the desert scrub, a border patrol van, electronic surveillance tower, fence made of steel poles of alternating height, and a heavy electronic gate. This is a pedestrian thoroughfare, which is not an official 'Port of Entry' but a passageway for members of the tribe only, upon production of ID. Behind it is an old fence made of sticks linked by two strands of rusty wire, intended – with little success, usually – to stop cattle wandering between the United States and Mexico. This latter was the border until recently. And beyond both these frontiers, across earth identical to that on which we stand, lies a place with two names: Flores calls it the continuation of ancient Tohono O'odham tribal land. The world beyond the tribe calls it Mexico. 'On the weekend,' says Flores, 'there used to be a market here. People would bring stalls and line them up along the border and sell tacos and clothes and stuff over the fence. That doesn't happen any more.' The markets, recalling those Day of the Dead picnics at Tijuana beach – themselves soon to be a thing of the past – are hard to imagine in the empty silence under the gaze of the border patrol and, no doubt, its quarry of smugglers on the other side.

On the edge of Sells is Poltergeist Lane. No one seems to know its real name: it was baptised by the gangs that patrol it, and tag the empty houses: 'Poltergeist Northside,' reads one graffito. This is the newer housing on the reservation, considered better than the trailers or shacks in which many O'odham live. One of the local gangs, explains a boy putting up a flier for a tribal rock poetry event in the café, is called the 'Dream Walkers', because 'they can kill you in your sleep, by spiking your dreams with curses and stuff'.

'There's a lot going on out there at night,' says Angelita Ramón, who lives at number 18 Poltergeist Lane, pointing past the creosote bushes. 'A lot of people coming through the wash right there, a lot of drugs coming through. I hear them, and it keeps me awake.' But Mrs Ramón's sleeplessness and struggle arise from the impact of all this movement on her own family. In the living room of her house, two daughters busy themselves with housework, cooking and television; but her three sons are present only as portraits on the wall. One 'committed suicide after the police took him into the desert one time and gave him a hard time. He was so mad at them, he killed himself; he was sixteen,' says Angelita. A second, Joseph: 'he's in jail, in New Mexico . . . they say he shot . . . you know . . . oh, I don't know . . . He's very protective of me now – always calling to see if I'm okay.' And there's the third: Bennett, who died a death so strange and unexplained 'it's driving me over the edge'.

At four thirty in the morning of Friday 9 April 2002, Bennett Palacio, aged eighteen and known as 'BJ', was walking home to Sells from a party following a baseball game. He turned from a dirt track onto the main road near a village called Cowlic, where he was struck by a border patrol vehicle and killed. Ever since, his mother and stepfather Ervin Ramón have avowed that Bennett had stumbled upon a drug transfer involving members of the border patrol on the dirt track, and was killed after making a getaway run onto the asphalt. It would not be so far-fetched: the FBI's Operation Lively Green in Arizona and the associated Operation Tarnished Star in Oklahoma resulted in ninety cases being brought against serving soldiers and government agents for drug smuggling in this region; among them were 13 guilty pleas entered during a single trial in Tucson in 2005, including a National Guard Sergeant Robert Baker, jailed for smuggling cocaine and getting other soldiers to do so.[18] Between 2001 and 2004, sixty-nine members of the military, border patrol, prison guards, law enforcement and other public employees had been convicted of accepting bribes to help smuggle cocaine.[19]

After years of tribulations through the courts – the Ramón family constantly spurned by tribal and federal authorities alike – and the emergence of court papers naming two drivers behind the collision who were never called as witnesses, the Ninth Circuit Court of Appeals in February 2006 and May 2007 rejected the family's action for unlawful death. The driver concerned was ruled not criminally responsible for killing Bennett Palacio. Applications to talk to the border patrol about the case for this book, as well as the wider issues of migration and rescue, were informally accepted during approaches made locally, but declined in Washington.

'Year after year, the pressures have eroded who we are as an original people,' says Ofelia Rivas, organiser of O'odham Voice Against the Wall, a campaign against the means of fortification of the border. 'Now, it's not just a border,' she says, 'it's a wall across our land. It stops people crossing, including our elders, and has already disturbed our burial sites. Some of our ceremonies are in Mexico, and I can't go. We've had tribal members on the American side arrested and deported while visiting relatives on their own tribal land, because they came from Mexico and didn't have the right papers. It's even disrupted the pathways of mountain lions which have to find new areas of habitation because they can't migrate. This is our ancestry, not a Kokopelli on someone's coffee mug! I'm fifty-three years old, and fifty-three is just fifty-three – but even I can remember when we got water out of water holes, and had to understand the land in order to eat and organise the year. I saw it all change during the 80s and 90s – the young people became lost, television took over our lives, then the militarisation. Twenty years from now', Ms Rivas predicts, 'our children will look back and say: "That is when it happened, the second destruction of our people." And it's all happening at such speed, after so many thousands of years. For all time, we just went to what's now Mexico and visited families, and people would come here. The authorities don't seem to realise that we have the spirits walking before us when we have to do these things. You must understand that we feel the eyes of our ancestors upon us, and have to explain to them that our history's being eradicated at this pace.' On the road off the reservation, into Tucson, a sign with a picture of smiling young O'odham reads: 'We lived and survived the desert for more than 500 years. Will we survive the next 500?'

Some 28,000 O'odham live on the US side of the border, and only an estimated 2,000 on the Mexican side, most of whom prefer to be called by the name the Spanish gave them, *Papagos*. Towards their villages, through the Sonora Desert, is some of the most majestic land in the Americas, over which tower the Saguaro cacti, monarchs of the desert, and the organ pipes, with rounded ribs and fruit from which the O'odham make jelly, wine and seed meal. As do the people of Quitovac, which lies up a track from the main road between Altar and Sonoyta. Quitovac is a village of fifty people, the largest single *Papago* settlement on the Mexican side, with a kindergarten that prepares children for 'Mexican school' in Sonoyta. A lady called Leticia keeps the little village *bodega* selling tortillas and household basics. She says that 'teachers come from Sells to run special programmes in O'odham traditions and culture, but the children tend to lose it when they grow older – and hardly ever go over to the American side because they get arrested if they don't have papers. They'll grow up as Mexicans, and only go to Sells if they need to see a doctor at the hospital . . . Most of our families are on the American side, but it's hard to visit them, and almost all traditional activities happen on the American side, apart from religious pilgrimages,' says Leticia. 'Most of us here are Catholic, and make pilgrimages to Magdalena more than the traditional rites; most of us still like to be called *Papagos*, like our parents called us, not O'odham.' This is more significant than it seems: for while Flores and Rivas feel quintessentially of the borderland in its most ancient sense, and an identity endangered by the white man, and now by the materialism of the cartels and the fight against them, the O'odham on the Mexican side seem less discontented, even though their culture has been thoroughly more eroded by Hispanic culture and religion. It is relevant that indigenous Mexicans became full citizens of the nation upon independence in 1810; Native Americans in the USA not until 1924.

Sitting on a chair outside his home is Eugenio Ortega Velasco, aged seventy-eight and the last man to speak the O'odham language in Mexico. 'At least I think so,' he says. 'When I was young, I moved around the whole territory, both sides of the border. There was work on the US side, and we used to go all the time, to and fro, and to visit family. Then, one by one, all my brothers and sisters went to work in the US, and never came back. Nothing much has changed since then, apart from the fact that it's very hard for most people to cross the border. I could if I wanted to' – he produces a pass with his photograph on it, valid for a year – 'but I don't feel the inclination. It's so much trouble – all those guards.' He folds his dog-eared letter from the Department of Homeland Security with a dismissive air, puts it back in his pocket and adjusts the brim of his hat downward, as the sun sinks low over the earth. Then he shifts his chair for no reason, and continues staring out in silence across the desert, from the porch of the house in which he was born.

The Tohono O'odham's cash-cow casino, on an annex of the reservation called San Javier, south of Tucson, is packed this summer Saturday night. The song belting out beneath a full moon after a thunderstorm is called '*Contrabando y Traición*' – 'Contraband And Treason' – and it is the one the audience has been waiting for. The young people on the lawn behind the amphitheatre whoop and sing along; the elderly folk and families in the more expensive seats 'rattle their jewellery'. The number, with its swaying accordion and rollicking bass line, is about a couple, Emilio and 'Camelia the Texan', smuggling drugs from Tijuana into San Ysidro, 'their car tyres replete with bad weed'. They cruise through a questionnaire at customs, make it to Los Angeles and collect the cash, which they split, Emilio telling his partner that he is now proceeding north to meet the love of his life. Upon receipt of this news, 'Seven shots sound; Camelia kills Emilio', but when the police arrive, they find only a *pistola tirade*, a dropped pistol – 'of Camelia and the money, nothing ever more was known'. The song was an early hit for the band on stage, Los Tigres del Norte, recorded in 1972, when the now middle-aged men were teenagers. Though not the first *narcocorrido*, it was the first to become a hit on every jukebox and across every dance floor in Mexico.[20] It was so popular that the band recorded two sequels: the first in which Camelia is tracked and gunned down by rival *traficantes* in Guadalajara, and a second, 'The Son Of Camelia', about her offspring killing five members of the Tijuana cartel and hunting down others to avenge his mother's murder. Los Tigres – three brothers and a cousin – are the kings of the genre they created, the undergrowth of which now provides a soundtrack to the narco war. They are the originals who have gone glitzy and international while the seeds, or some would say weeds, they planted grow thick and healthy, for the glorification of criminals.

Tonight, Los Tigres are dressed in flagrant red silk emblazoned with shameless gold; their pants skin-tight to show their bulging efforts to best advantage, their heels are high and their posturing lusty, for these are the pin-up boys of *narcocorrido*, from the state of Sinaloa, via San José, California; where they moved in their teens. Tucson – a name derived from the O'odham phrase '*Chuk Shon*', at the foot of a black hill – is 70 miles from Mexico and not strictly a border town, so much as a border hub. The south side of the city lies on what is regarded as the wrong side of the railway tracks: a burgeoning and mettlesome Mexican-American community, umbilically connected across the border. And tonight it's all bandanas with the Mexican flag. For all the Tigres' bravura as the godfathers of *narcocorrido*, this is a family outing. The entire Mexican-American spectrum is here: elderly couples with their children and grandchildren, boys in baggy shorts and tattoos on their shins and gaggles of girls pressed up against the fence at the front of the standing area. Jorge Hernández, the bandleader, raises his stetson with a debonair bow to the crowds and presents the musicians: '*mi hermano Raúl, mi hermano Hernán, mi primo Oscar*', my brother, my brother, my cousin.

Next up is a blustering number called '*El Avión de la Muerte*' – 'The Airplane Of Death'. It is a true story, supposedly, compiled from news reports, featuring the narco Manuel Atilano, captured and tortured by the Mexican army into flying them to his cartel's hideaway landing strip in Sinaloa. Atilano, however, seizes control of the plane and broadcasts details of his treatment over the radio: '*Con pinzas machacaron Partes nobles de su cuerpo*' – with pincers they crushed the noble parts of his body. The song ends with an act of heroism, as Atilano changes his plan to crash the aircraft into a police compound when he sees a schoolyard full of children next door, and instead plunges himself and his captors to their deaths against a hillside, bidding fond farewell to his friends in the landing strip's control tower – '*adiós a sus amigos camaradas de aviación*.'

Los Tigres have no connection to any cartel, but one is left uncertain whether the brazen inclusion (on a tape, of course) of rasping, rapid automatic machine-gun fire which carries along Los Tigres' next song called *Pacto de Sangre*, 'Pact Of Blood' is being faithful to their roots or offensively tasteless. There is no uncertainty, however, about how much the audience relishes all this gaudery: the gunfire, which sweeps in stereo from stage left to stage right, gets 'em dancing with even more splash and splurge.

Jorge Hernández puts it this way: 'Poor people idolise the narcos: they admire their bravery, and they want to be like them. When you sing the songs, the audience feel that they're living through the characters, as if they were watching a film. That's why people love the *corrido*. It lets them dream.'[22] Within weeks of tonight's concert, Los Tigres would become involved in their share of controversy. The band pulled out of an appearance at the prestigious Las Lunas music awards show because its organisers refused to allow them to play their latest song: *'La Granja'*, 'The Farm', a critique of President Calderón's offensive against the narco cartels, accompanied by a video showing pigs representing politicians getting rich on the back of the poor.[23] This peacockery is the razzmatazz side of this genre. However, more recently emerged *narcocorrido* bands are sometimes recruited to sing the glories of one particular cartel over another, a hero against a villain or, more usually, against the army. This, of course, makes them fair game for a rival cartel.

In a separate but chilling incident, the most famous murder of a musician occured in Matamoros, the easternmost city on the Mexican side of the border, on 1 December 2007: that of twenty-eight-year-old Zayda Peña, the raven-haired singer for Los Culpables – the Guilty Ones – a best-selling band. Peña, who sung a famous hit entitled *'Tiro de Gracia'* – a single 'mercy-shot' to the head – was staying at a motel in Matamoros after a concert the previous evening when gunmen came to the door and opened fire, killing a male companion and the hotel manager. Peña was taken to hospital and given emergency surgery, but as she emerged from the operating theatre a squad of *sicarios* was waiting in the corridor to deliver a *'Tiro de Gracia'* through the recovering star patient's head. 'Nothing, nothing, nothing,' was the response of the Tamaulipas state prosecutor's office when asked for possible trails in search of Peña's killers.[24] Ms Peña's mother has been working for the prosecutor's office since 2007, the year of her daughter's murder.

The Spanish word for 'walnuts' is *'nogales'*, and there are two towns of that name, facing each other across the border south of Tucson, so called because of the walnut trees that grew wild and in orchards across the verdant slopes that rise into Mexico from the thirsting desert of Arizona. On the southern edges of Nogales, Sonora, is a new building, opened to great fanfare, called *'Camino a Casa'* – the road home – another border project of the government's *Desarrollo Integral de la Familia*, or DIF. The brief is simple: to gather children who have been smuggled north across the border, caught and deported, and to get them home. But the process is complicated: in the clinically clean reception area, a couple, Cesar and Yvet, waits. He wears a white T-shirt and tattoos, she wears lines of exhaustion and her cheeks are tear-stained. They are in their thirties, from Acapulco where, says César, 'there is nothing for a family', and had crossed just east of Nogales, into the desert. They were caught near the town of Patagonia, having paid one *coyote* $1,000 in Acapulco and a further $400 in supplements in Altar and along the way. They had been deported separately, their daughter Francesca brought to *Camino a Casa*. Cesar signs a last piece of paper, and the security guard retreats through a magnetically locked door. Some time later it opens, emitting a chorus of high-pitched, young farewells – '¡Adiós, Francesca!' – and the couple's daughter, aged twelve, runs into her weeping mother's arms. 'There's nothing more to say really, thank you,' says Cesar, sweeping his womenfolk towards the door. 'We're going to find the bus home.' Across the road, other children chirrup and run around an urban schoolyard; Francesca shoots them a glance of envy, takes her mother's hand, and disappears back to Acapulco.

At first, the imposing María Mayela Alessi Cuevas appears as a set of long, painted fingernails with a woman and shoulder-padded jacket attached. She is the impeccably dressed director of this branch of *Camino a Casa* and runs the place with a mixture of no-nonsense authority and a degree of compassion, no doubt. She took the job when her husband moved his business to Nogales. Ms Alessi explains the situation with straightforward clarity. 'We get about five hundred a month,' she says, 'of whom twenty per cent are fetched by their families and eighty per cent are sent home.' When they cross into the United States, most have both parents living there, and are forwarded by relatives who put them in the care of *coyotes*. 'Some cross the desert, some through the official Ports of Entry (PoEs) with false visas or fake documents, with other families. They get asked what their name is, questions about things on the papers, get confused and get caught. A child's instinct is to tell the truth, and if the customs ask "is that your mom?" they give the game away. Often they're drugged to sleep when they cross but the customs wake them up, and when they're drowsy they make even more mistakes; we sometimes get girls who have had their hair cut to look like boys in the fake papers.' They, however, are the lucky ones. 'For the ones who cross the desert, things are harder,' says Ms Alessi. 'We get girls who have been raped, as young as twelve, and some are pregnant after having been raped on the way north. Others sustain physical injuries: we had a group deported after they had been in a car crash, a chase by the border patrol – one boy was in a wheelchair, his bones broken from his feet to his hip. Often we'll get one left behind by their brothers or sisters – two who made it and one who didn't, with everyone traumatised, and parents trying to get in touch from the USA. They sometimes think when they come here they're being arrested and going to jail. When the child is introduced to their parents or, more often, grandparents, they usually burst into tears. A few have so little to go back to that one or two older ones want to stay and work here; but most, by the time they get here, all they want to do is go home. So much that they often try to escape, break the windows at night to try and run for it.'

Most of the children, Ms Alessi explains, come from the south; then the bombshell: 'most of the kids from Sonora, from around here, are being used by the cartels as *burros* – donkeys – to carry drugs, some as young as thirteen. They cross over, know the territory and deliver the drugs, then try to hitchhike their way home and get caught. The Americans don't arrest them because they're minors, and the cartels know that. And some of them are doing and selling the drugs they run – it's a way of paying them.' Ms Alessi leaves us, with permission to talk without supervision to the children.

Two large recreation rooms off the courtyard house boys and girls respectively. In each, about a hundred faces traverse the spectrum of youthful emotion. Some are puckish, full of mischief; some are melancholy, even lachrymose. Some of the boys wear their courage – or their fear – behind an appearance of steadfastness, even aggression. Some of the girls wear theirs behind a mask of exuberance, while others wear their distrust out loud. The boys speak first, with César

Magaña cursing the *pocho* – Mexican-American – *migra* agent who 'kicked me in the back' when he was apprehended after two days walking. His father in North Carolina had paid the *coyote* who had taken him from Tabasco and 'things had been going well, until we were chased by the *migra*, first in a truck and then, when we dived into the trees on the mountainside, they were on foot. They caught us, kicked and punched us and said "that's for making us run, *mojados*!" They were all *pochos*, apart from one, and the *gringo* wasn't kicking!' Next to César is Marcos – aged sixteen from Campeche, with a heavier air, speaking more softly. 'After three days, we were desperate,' he says, his gaze far off. 'By then, we were looking for the *migra* to get caught, looking for them to save us. My father had paid the *coyote*, and I had to pay no more; I was told to follow everything the man called Zepeda said; I had to meet him off the bus in Altar. But Zepeda was a liar; he didn't know the way and got lost. They got us on a night it rained so hard you couldn't see in front of you. One day, nothing to drink; another day, wet through. When the border patrol caught us, they were kind – they knew we were pleased to see them. The older men ran, but we walked towards the border patrol, because all we wanted was to go home.'

Two girls sit silently, more shy than taciturn it turns out, not because of us but of the others. Xóchitl, sixteen, and Itzel, a year younger, are not the usual Mexican mixed *Mestizo*: they are pure Aztec, from Veracruz. Everything is '*más o menos*', they say, more or less. Do they want to go home? More or less. Was it frightening in the desert? More or less. Then Xóchitl adds: 'It was okay, until our friend was gone. Then the guide was gone. There were eight of us left, and we didn't know where we were, in the dark, in the night. After they found us, they brought three of us here, but I have no idea what happened to the others.' 'I don't care about Texas any more,' says another boy, Adan, aged fourteen, from San Luis Potosí. 'I don't want a rich blonde *gringa* from Dallas. I thought I did – it's what I imagined, that and my mama and papi, but I was wrong. I don't care about anything else now – I don't even want to see my parents in Texas – I just want to go home.'

A show of hands is hardly a scientific way to gauge opinion, but sometimes it suffices, and when asked whether they wanted to go home or try again, only one hand out of about eighty is raised in favour of the latter. This is Gabriel, aged seventeen, from Cacahoatán in Guatemala, with no return ticket. It is strange he is here; the DIF in theory only administers to Mexican citizens, those from further south being regarded with greater contempt than Mexicans in the USA. 'I came on the train,' he says. 'All the way, with my uncle. In the south of Mexico, they robbed us, and again in Nogales; the first time was Mexicans, the second time was Salvadoreans. This town was our last chance, my uncle said. And after a day, the helicopter came over us – we scattered. I lost my uncle, and ended up here. The lady who processed me said not to tell anyone where I am from, and that I could leave with some others, and try again. I have to try again.' He is seventeen, but seems either twelve or thirty-five he is so strong-willed, but so poignantly and utterly alone and a child.

'This place is the middle of nowhere,' says Arturo from Hidalgo. 'I hate it. They give you two tortillas a day and some water. That's it. They don't let us play football in case we try to escape; and we wait – wait for them to find our relatives and for our relatives to raise the money to get us home.' I had naively assumed that because the poetically named *Camino a Casa* was a government agency, the government might pay a bus fare to see these children home. 'Of course the government doesn't pay,' scolds a girl called Magdalena from Chiapas, and with a wisdom and humour she really should not possess at fifteen: 'The government only pays if you're in a coffin.' And at last, everyone laughs, a hollow but badly needed laugh, and we talk about football and the inevitable rivalry of *El Clásico* – felt as keenly by the girls as the boys – between Chivas and Club América.

'América' is a beautiful word, especially when it is the name of a child. And the group marooned in the purgatorial care of *Camino a Casa* in Nogales is sustained by its collective fascination with, and care for, the shelter's most heart-searing resident: América, aged four. In any other life she would be headed for the stage; as it is, heaven knows what awaits her. The little girl's parents are living in Florida, and she was sent across the border by relatives in her native Acapulco, ostensibly to join them. However, Ms Alessi had explained, 'the *coyotes* took her to the border with two others, aged five and six, in the middle of the night, sent them through the fence and pointed to a house, saying: "If you follow the lights and go into that house, your parents will come and pick you up." They did, the children walked up to the door, and the Americans called the border patrol. They were dumped at 4 a.m. in the deportation pound on the Mexican side, alone, with no explanation or adult present. They're not supposed to deport minors after 6 p.m., but in practice they don't care. So we went to get them, and América is still here while we try to locate her family.' This has taken two weeks so far, without success.

There is a teenaged boy called Francisco and a girl called Lizabeth who are very proud of their special role in minding América. 'Things can happen to a little girl that she cannot understand,' says Francisco, horribly perceptive. 'And we cannot let you talk to her without our presence,' affirms Lizabeth, thirteen, with authority. 'I want to go back to Acapulco,' cheeps little América, 'because there is a fairground there, and my mother [that would be her grandmother] has my lovely pair of boots there, in the *Calle de Chile*.' The child starts blowing kisses down the corridor. 'Then I got trapped,' she says suddenly. 'I went through the gate to play, and the men came. But now I'm going and after the fair my mother and me will sit and watch Amy on television.'

There is a sudden frisson along the corridor, the sun glinting through the frosted glass ceiling and firing a ricocheted shaft of light across the tiled floor. Amy is a character in a TV soap the children know from home, and they want América to sing, as she does. One of her favourite songs is by Danna Paola, who plays the title role of Amy in the hit Telenovela *Amy La Niña de la Mochila Azul*. América walks towards the shaft of sunlight and stands for a moment, gathering the words in her head, eyes closed. Then she opens them, takes a deep breath and sings: *Fiesta, Fiesta/La vida es fiesta/Escucha tu Corazón/Fiesta, fiesta/Que poco cuesta/Dar un poquito de amor.*

How little is that, to give a little love. Then América stops; everyone claps; she smiles a big, sunny grin, claps herself too, and bursts into tears.

The Business End of a .12-Gauge –
Barrett and Morgan's War

The Gadsden Hotel in Douglas, Arizona, is grander than it probably needs to be nowadays. But that doesn't stop one catching one's breath walking into the lobby, to behold those marble columns, that imperious winding stairway, and walls echoing with the sounds of Wild West war along the borderline. Built in 1907, the hotel bears the name of Lieutenant James Gadsden, president of the South Carolina Canal and Rail Road Company, rabid Southern nationalist, advocate of States' Rights and slavery. Later, he became US ambassador to Mexico, and secured the purchase in 1853 of all land, including southern Arizona, south of the Gila River, for the United States from Mexico. The purchase was a territorial postscript to the Treaty of Guadalupe Hidalgo of 1848 which ended the Mexican-American war, though some around here would say that the war was still being fought, for the borderline here is fraught with tension. In late March 2010, a respected rancher called Rob Krentz was shot dead by Mexicans coming through his land, fuelling rage as well as grief, and strengthening the hand of a growing anti-smuggling, counter-migration vigilante movement. A month later, the Arizona state governor Jan Brewer signed into law a measure enabling police to stop and demand that immigrants produce documents proving their status as legal residents, on pain of arrest and deportation if there were none. The measure was eyed by other border states with a view to similar legislation, and polarised Arizona. Thousands of protesters took to the streets of Phoenix and Tucson and sheriffs for two counties, Pima and Yuma, said they would not enforce the new law.

But the border road has now led us east of Tucson and Pima Counties, into hard-line Cochise County, via the gun stores and bike repair shops of Sierra Vista, a vigilante stronghold, in the wild south-east corner of Arizona, where rancher Krentz was shot dead. Here lie two neighbouring towns, both of them former copper-mining centres: Bisbee, a hip, liberal outpost and arts centre, and gritty Douglas with its Gadsden Hotel, built before Arizona became a state on St Valentine's Day 1912, and while Geronimo was still leading troops of the Apache against both Americans and Mexicans. For all the quick-draw legends and pomp of the hotel's surroundings, Butch Barrett dresses casually in the searing heat, for our appointment in the lobby. Barrett was for decades a customs special agent in this corner of Arizona, riding horseback and fighting regular hand-to-hand shoot-outs with narco traffickers from Agua Prieta over the border. During his time patrolling this land, the territory between Nogales and Arizona's eastern border with New Mexico had become known as 'Cocaine Alley'. But to Barrett and a partner of his called Lee Morgan, this country was both home and castle.

Not many stories like those of Barrett and Morgan's war get to be told first-hand any more, in the days of high-tech border policing, with sensors and virtual fencing. But Lee Morgan set it out in a memoir called *The Reaper's Line*, which tells it like this: 'The outlaw took aim with his Blazer and went for Miller's plump, round silhouette. The agent dropped the spikes and took aim at the driver with a .12-gauge pump shotgun. Looking down the business end of the .12-gauge convinced the smuggler he was about to commit a grave mistake.'[1]

Morgan's book is the best action movie never made about the border: a latter-day high-noon Western set largely at midnight, because Morgan was in the thick of the nascent years of the narco war, which he saw coming a decade away. After graduating from Border Patrol Academy in 1975, Morgan was initially stationed in Douglas, but worked across America and the Caribbean in the immigration service's anti-drug task force before returning as a customs special agent in 1987. After which he and Barrett fight perpetual, total war on two fronts: against their quarry, the smugglers, and against what they call 'REMFs' – rear echelon mother fuckers – who get paid by the taxpayer to push pens in Washington and throughout the bureaucracy. 'What did I learn from my first gunfight as a federal agent?' Morgan writes rhetorically. 'Well, I learned that as usual the REMFs are wrong and the grunts know what they need in the field to get the job done.'

For this book, access to the current border patrol was, sadly, declined by Washington – so what better than to hear it like it was? As a special agent out of uniform, Morgan teamed up with Barrett and another agent called Allan Sperling on horse patrol. Both Morgan and Barrett were Vietnam veterans, though, says Morgan, while 'I've seen my share of hell when the shit hit the fan in the jungle, Butch saw some really BAD shit. Try to imagine floating in a body of water so thick with bloated bodies that you actually had to lance the corpses with a bayonet so they would sink.' Back from fighting the Vietcong, Morgan's and Barrett's enemies were the Agua Prieta cartel, allied to Ciudad Juárez, and Morgan's favourite horse was called Cougar. Through the turn of the decade, Morgan and Barrett ride against the bareback narcos, fight shoot-outs against them and apprehend them in unarmed combat; it is late twentieth-century Wild West desert war, as thrilling as it is ominous of what is to come in the twenty-first: 'I yelled to the asshole that I would blow his face off if he brought the barrel of his rifle up. I hate to cap a guy if I don't absolutely have to. God-fearingly correct in his decision, the outlaw dropped his assault weapon to the floorboard and raised his hands above his head.' During an incursion by Mexican soldiers protecting the cartel: 'let me be perfectly clear about this: these armed black uniforms were not patrolling Mexico. They had invaded our country and were conducting military combat manoeuvres on US soil.' As for the narcos themselves: Morgan respects the mules carrying *la merca* – the dope. 'You know how those mountain-climbing pro dudes use the picks and pitons to ascend a rocky mountain bluff that goes straight up? Mickey Mouse crap! We've seen mules go up the same incline using only their bare fingers and tennis-shoe-covered toes.' On the narcos themselves, however: 'Being the chickenshits these behind-the-border backshooters are, any show of superior force causes them to run like scared jack rabbits being chased by coyotes.' And: 'But the Mexican outlaw wasn't quite done yet. The son of a bitch fought Butch tooth and nail while he kept hitting the accelerator with the tip of his cowboy boot. The truck kept surging and spinning in a tight circle like a wounded duck with one wing shot off.'

Not only did Butch Barrett's son get married on the magnificent staircase at the Gadsden Hotel, he also joined the Border Patrol recently, 'and I'm mighty proud of that', says his father, for all

Barrett's misgivings about the service these days. His were 'days when you had to provide your own horses and saddles', he recalls, 'until the REMFs were persuaded by a couple of successes we had that we deserved us a team of four. But it worked – tracking 'em down on horseback proved very successful. We knew the terrain, we knew how to get 'em and we got 'em. It was another world back then: pre 9/11, pre-technology, pre Generation X and Generation Me before it – but more heroes, I'm tellin' ya. Yes, they'll laugh at you now, but we did it for God and country. Some did it for the highs and the adrenalin, but they likely pulled out from the sheer terror of having someone carrying a load and trying to kill you to get it through.' We sit in armchairs at an old, low wooden table. There is no tea, coffee or beer, just talk and a big empty lobby around us. 'The kids now, they do it mostly for the money, and because it's a job. I don't blame them, but it's just an existence nowadays – in our time, you had to prove yourself, produce bodies, getcha hands dirty and take 'em on. The dope smugglers project this image of being the macho man, but they cry like babies when you got 'em in handcuffs.'

But, says Barrett, 'I still talk to some of the young agents. They're no fools, and they get into situations when they need a little old-school advice, particularly when it comes to dealing with the people with their feet under desks. That was the only mistake I made, to get promoted behind a desk! The problem is what it always was: the REMFs in Washington DC. They'd come down in my day, look around for fifteen minutes with the press secretary, and we'd offer them a tour out with us, good to go. But they never even sat in a car with us.'

Butch is proud of Douglas, but unsure about what that frontier has done to Douglas of late. 'If you go to City Hall and look at the portraits of the mayors, you'll find that the white guys suddenly stop and after a certain time, around 1980 when Phelps Dodge [the copper mining company] up and went, they're all Mexican. Well, I don't say I have a problem with that, except if the town is Mexican, then there's going to be a lot of them in the smuggling trade, you know, part of the picture. There's going to be a situation where you have a guy in law enforcement and his cousins are across the border. And he's going to get a call saying "hey, we'd like you to join the customs service and do as you're told", let this car through or turn a blind eye there. And that's gonna be said by your cousin on the other side, and it's going to be an offer you can't refuse. And that has happened, because I know it has.' There was a customs officer, says another agent, who was passed by the same pretty girl every day: '*¡Hola!*' she would say, smiling and waving, until, to script, he asked for her number. After a little rendezvous and one or two drinks, a car load of men arrived at the supposedly discreet bar with a briefcase containing $250,000 in cash, put it on the table and made a suggestion: take the money, or we call your wife – now. All he had to do is what he'd always done: wave back, and wave her through, only now he was in – and once in, there's no way out.[3]

Long before the Obama administration finally found a buzzword to admit the United States' 'co-responsibility' for Mexico's drug war, Lee Morgan wrote: 'Maybe we, as the decadent, arrogant *Norte-americanos*, should start questioning our own insatiable appetite for drugs.' He was also on top of the smuggling of guns to the south, when the matter was taboo: after one terrifying 'surreptitious excursion' to Agua Prieta, a man whom Morgan was trailing was arrested with 'enough ammo to start a small war', which indicated, along with Morgan's progressive seizures of weaponry from China, that the business ends of .12-gauge shotguns would soon be superseded by those of AK-47, AR-15 and TEC-9 machine guns. No one saw the narco war coming, writes Morgan, because: 'We have an entertainment and media industry that thrives on keeping our vegetating minds stuffed with compost . . . so there's no real need to think for yourself in America.' And his conclusion: 'The border is a line of barbwire and spiked pillars that seems only to serve as a symbol of one man's futile lifetime endeavours, his attempts to define Mother Nature's boundaries, as well as man's national claims to a piece of what no human can ever call his own possession. Men will always be willing to fight and die in follies of nationalism, but they will never be able to continually control their own borders.'

Morgan and I meet further along the road, in San Antonio on the river walk opposite the Alamo which, we note with amusement, has become Texas' leading tourist attraction and icon of the Texan revolution against Mexico, despite having fallen to the Mexican army during the famous battle of 1836, with all but two of its defenders killed. In smart casuals, he looks younger, and certainly trimmer than the rugged desert rat on the inside cover of his book, clutching binoculars.

'We were wild,' says Morgan. 'We were outta control, socially unacceptable. But we were effective. Now, it's all just policy, policy, policy and orders from the top. The good people are getting thrown out, pushed aside – "do it our way or get out of our way" – and it's been like that ever since we told 'em this was coming, that the drug lords were getting serious, like these people in Washington don't want to be told the truth. They don't understand the drug lords, they don't get it that you can't deal with them. Look at the things they do to people! You can't offer 'em a better job because they don't want to be in any other business unless it's another form of crime.'

And there is a surprise by the Alamo. Morgan and Barrett had a mentor in the customs service, a man called James Rayburn – the team leader, a slightly older man who knew every grain of sand in the desert and taught Morgan a few of the tricks in the book. Rayburn has joined us, for a chat by the river. They are two of the best special agents their service ever had, but have trouble figuring out the silly computerised machine that distributes timed tickets in the parking lot, for display on the dashboard of the truck they have driven into town from hill country. These men don't like to be controlled, and good for them. Both men smoke, and enjoy their cigarettes. Morgan and I order Mexican Dos Equis beer; Rayburn wants a Bud Lite. Rayburn's expertise, among many things, was to run informants in Mexico – people regarded, says Morgan, by defence attorneys as 'Judases' and by prosecutors as 'a painful but necessary black plague'.

On 2 July 1998, the Clinton administration signed an accord with the Mexican presidency of Ernesto Zedillo that became known as the 'Brownsville Agreement'. The agreement obliged US law-enforcement agencies – principally customs, the DEA and FBI – to notify, through the embassy in Mexico City, the Mexican attorney general's office of their undercover investigations and informants. Intelligence agencies, markedly the CIA, were exempt. 'For us border narcs, it was like being the only blind son of a bitch at a poker table,' objects Morgan. 'Everyone is reading your cards but you!' In practice, the accord meant that a Mexican government deeply infiltrated by narco cartels was being informed who the snitches were, to disastrous effect in Douglas alone, and on informers run by Morgan, one of them was infiltrating a syndicate manufacturing and smuggling methamphetamine. But after being informed by their government who the informer was, the smugglers avoided a sting Morgan had prepared for them at the local Motel 6 in Douglas. Instead, the informer became one of three out of the four undercover spies working for Morgan across the border in Agua Prieta to be gunned down soon after the Brownsville Agreement.

The events recalled the cornerstone murder of DEA agent Kiki Camarena in 1985, to which James Rayburn, sipping on his Bud, has a connection. Rayburn had controlled an informer, Benito Suárez, who was commandeered by US customs to look for Camarena, kidnapped on instructions of the Godfather himself, Miguel Félix Gallardo. But when Suárez arrived in Sinaloa, the Gallardo clan appeared suspicious of his timely return from Arizona. He and a fellow Mexican informer based in Phoenix were taken to a private house in Jalisco where Suárez was tortured and beaten, and believed he heard Camarena's voice in an adjoining room. Afterwards, the two men were driven to a cliff edge, and Suárez put in the driver's seat while his friend's face was crushed by the butt of an AK-47, and Suárez was whiplashed at the base of his skull. But as the car was pushed over the cliff to the bottom of the canyon, Suárez was miraculously thrown from it, and survived. Rayburn did all he could to have his man rescued out of Mexico and carried across the Bridge of the Americas from Ciudad Juárez into El Paso. 'The last time I saw him when he went hunting for Camarena,' says Morgan, who took turns with Rayburn driving Suárez to physiotherapy, he had been a 'healthy young man with fire in his eyes and a zest in his heart for life. But what met me at his apartment door on my first visit was the pitiful remains of a man I didn't recognise.' Suárez died of AIDS in 1998, a secret he preferred to keep rather than be treated, after being repeatedly sodomised during torture.

'It was the beginning of the end,' reflects Rayburn. 'After the Brownsville Agreement, it became almost impossible to do an effective undercover operation; it became harder to deal with Washington than to fight the criminals. When you go undercover, the REMFs hate it while you're doing it, then go on TV and claim all the credit when you pull the outlaws in. Nothing substitutes human intelligence and infiltration, and that's something we're losing, just as the drug lords are gaining it. While it gets harder for us to infiltrate them, they'll use relatives and friends to infiltrate us, they'll call a cousin on the US side and tell 'em: "Hey, we need you to work in border law enforcement — for us", and there ain't no saying no to them. We've seen it happen; we arrested one of our own customs people smuggling cocaine for a drug boss called Yolanda Molina. They told us to our faces, years ago: "if we can't beat you with weapons, we'll infiltrate you" — I had that told to my face by a man I arrested. We reported this, but no one listened. And sure enough, next we knew, the assistant special agent in charge of Nogales had been working for them all along.' They were referring to Richard Padilla Cramer, another decorated Vietnam veteran who served three decades in law enforcement, locking up corrupt officials, busting drugs and promoted to become attaché for immigration and customs enforcement at the US embassy in Mexico City. By which time, according to the prosecution case at the time of writing, as Cramer waits to stand trial, Cramer was selling his knowledge to the cartels, a treachery dating back to his days as head of ICE in Nogales, Arizona. 'This,' said Rene Andreu, former assistant head of the ICE customs division in Tucson, 'is impossible to grasp.'[4] 'We didn't believe it,' hoots Morgan, 'must've talked with him a thousand times — all that time, he was one of them.' Cramer has yet to stand trial and has denied all wrongdoing.

'When they called us cowboys,' Morgan ponders, 'it was intended as an insult. I was told I had a John Wayne attitude — well, what in hell's wrong with that? Dammit, the smugglers sure have a John Wayne attitude: they live like smugglers and expect to die like smugglers, and we were the same. You gotta know your enemy, you gotta know his terrain better 'n he does. The way we did the job was to get inside the smuggling organisation and hit it head-on. We were working with the inside view of how they work, who they are, what they do — get to know the basics, and the pressures they're under. That's what I try to tell the young guys now: get to know 'em, don't look down on them — but we could never do it now; I just wouldn't be allowed to work the way we did. We were in the right place at the right time.'

Since it is a beautiful afternoon by the river, another round of beers seems in order, and we turn the conversation to a favourite subject: reading tracks, or 'cutting for sign', as it is known in the trade, a skill that precedes even mankind's presence in the desert, where covering and detecting tracks are everything. The Red Fox walks the desert in such a way that its hind paws fall near or directly onto its fore prints – known in zoology as a 'direct register' – obliterating the forepaw tracks; it changes coat with the seasons for both insulation and camouflage, taking on what is called a 'dark morph' when necessary.[5] The art of covering and 'cutting' sign was perfected by Native Americans for hunting animals, and latterly by law enforcement for hunting humans. There is a special unit of the border patrol on the Tohono O'odham reservation called the 'Tracking Wolves', cutting for sign. And of course, sign-cutting was perfected by men like Morgan, Rayburn and Barrett. You need to know, says Morgan, the difference between a chevron and a starburst imprint, when a mat of some kind had been attached to the shoes, when footprints have been swept away by the last person in a convoy, walking backwards and brushing the terrain, as tribal raiders have done ever since this arid land was inhabited. And to read the sign that tells you exactly when these movements occurred, for your quarry may be near, or too far; the kind of thing you learn from whether the track of a bug runs over or beneath a footprint.

Back in the lobby of the Gadsden Hotel, Butch Barrett had recalled the romance of sign-cutting. 'It was something handed down to us country boys,' he says. 'My father used to take me hunting animals when I was twelve years old, and the first thing I learned was how to read their tracks. So I took that knowledge, and applied it to hunting people. The real hunt starts when you get off the roads: working out when a footprint isn't a real footprint, when they've made a mistake trying to lay a false trail – that's something the best of the young 'uns who are interested in getting results love to ask us about. "Back in your day," they say, "when you used to cut for sign. . ." and they ask us how it was done.'

By the river, Morgan confesses: 'I'm still always looking for tracks. Habitually, every time I go for a walk. Fact is: it worked. All these sensors and gadgets, they break, they malfunction. [He imitates a dumb voice on the end of the phone:] "I'm sorry, the system's down." And they can lie. But the ground can't lie. A piece of fibre caught by a cactus can't lie. The smallest shift in the sand on terrain you know can't lie. Just like a border fence can hold you up for twenty minutes, but it can't arrest you – it don't have no John Wayne attitude. Unlike the drug lords, watching all this and laughing.' They might also be laughing at a report by the General Accounting Office filed in August 2009 finding the Secure Border Initiative launched by President George Bush in 2005 to be running seven years behind the schedule it set for putting the latest gizmos in place, and running millions of dollars over budget because of maintenance bills. The 'virtual fence' system designed by Boeing had 'fallen prey to weather and mechanical problems', said the report by the GAO's Richard M. Stana. The total bill will come to $6.5 billion over twenty years, he estimated. During the same week as the report's publication, the government extended Boeing's contract for another year.[6] In 2010, President Obama conceded that the 'virtual fence' was an absurdity, and cancelled it.

The cartels will also, says Morgan, 'be wondering how all this'll enhance their ability to infiltrate us deeper, corrupt the system and keep the money flowing around'. He pauses. 'Kinda strange, ain't it, how Washington got all this technology, but never goes after the money – billions of dollars of it? Billions of dollars moving around the US banks, and going back into Mexico. They never go after it. That ever strike you as strange?'

The heresy has been spoken: Morgan, who saw the war coming, now wonders about the money-go-round that circles between Mexico and the United States, just as the late sun aims its last, deep rays against the Alamo. There are hundreds of billions of dollars in drug profits swilling around the US banking system out there, and US Customs veteran Lee Morgan II would like to know a hell of a lot more about who is moving it. Further along the border road from Morgan, Barrett and Rayburn's terrain of eastern Arizona, an anthropologist at the University of Texas, El Paso, Howard Campbell, suggests that we should try re-labelling the narco cartels, because of the money-go-round, calling them the Sinaloa-Phoenix-Denver cartel, the Juárez-El Paso-Chicago cartel or the Gulf-Houston-Atlanta cartel, so as to more accurately reflect their sphere of influence. It is out across the desert towards Campbell's seat of El Paso and its twin city of Ciudad Juárez that the road now beckons. But first, one last round with the horsemen of the John Wayne attitude, a toast to the reaper and his line in the sand.

CHAPTER FOUR

Urban Frankenstein

'If Juárez is a city of God, that is because the Devil is scared to come here' – *street* dicho, *or saying.*

'Ciudad Juárez: right now I'd say it's the safest city in Mexico' – *Lt. Col. Jorge Alberto Berecochea, upon taking over the 6th police district, March 2009*[1]

Of all the enthralling landscapes in America, none is more complicated in its awful beguilement than that southward from the balcony outside room 262 on the upper floor of the La Quinta Motel on Geronimo Avenue in El Paso, Texas – with a sixpack, a lime, hot salsa and bag of tortilla chips for company. In mid-distance runs the border. And beyond the boundary lies the factory smoke, the sea of lights, the lure and menace of the most charismatic and daunting of cities: Ciudad Juárez. While El Paso is the United States' second safest city of its size, with only sixteen homicides in 2008, Juárez is currently the most dangerous city in the Americas and, by some counts, the world. The scene is especially striking at dusk, when fleets of cast-off American school buses have done their rounds taking home the day shift in the *maquiladora* sweatshop factories, so that a layer of grey dust stirs around and settles on the lanes and the labyrinth of outlaw electrical wires supplying the *colonia* shacks.

To get here, the road from eastern Arizona has crossed the border state of New Mexico on the US side, and western Chihuahua, on what many Americans living on the frontier still call 'Old Mexico' when wishing to convey a rugged affection. The small town of Columbus, New Mexico, faces Palomas, Chihuahua, across an expanse of otherwise wild and empty land populated by ghosts from the Mexican revolution – the Pancho Villa park is nearby. Alima McMillan lives in remote Columbus but enjoyed her work across the border at a medical centre in Palomas, where mayor Estanislao García was kidnapped and shot dead the week after Ms McMillan and I met in September 2009. Ms McMillan had already decided that the eruption of violence in the town a short walk from where we had lunch in a café should prevent her from carrying on her regular surgeries there. Quite often, victims of the violence would appear at the border crossing in need of help, like a teenaged boy the previous week, who had been beaten, shot, doused with diesel fuel and set on fire. Palomas had been a place to which visitors from New Mexico went regularly to get teeth fixed and buy cheap medicines until new arrivals in town, says McMillan, 'put the fear of God into everyone and started clearing the territory'. Palomas was turned quite suddenly into a three-way battlefield between the army, the Juárez and Sinaloa cartels, now a place in which one family remains dominant, among the silence, the emptied houses, new narco villas, and the army Blackhawk helicopters overhead, 'flying their noses right up to the line', says Ms McMillan, 'to blow a bit of Mexican dust into Columbus'. From Columbus, the road clings to the border through a village called Malpais – bad country – a suburb of El Paso called Sunland Park, which is nonetheless still in New Mexico, then across the Texas state line, but cheek by jowl with the rusting iron fence, the barbed wire and the *colonia* of Anapra, which tumbles down into Ciudad Juárez, just yards away from the highway into downtown El Paso.

The scene from El Paso across the border is all the more surreal on the night of the *Grito* – the cry – commemorating Mexico's independence from Spain in 1810. This is the United States, but on a stage at the northern end of San Jacinto Square, a full mariachi band launches a night of festivity to precede the day commemorating that on which the Mexican nation was born 199 years before. '*¡Viva La independencia!*' shouts the singer, in a long, very tight cocktail dress from which she bursts. '*¡Viva!*' answers back the crowd of several thousand families, cuddling teenagers, and old ladies with Indian faces from Mexico's deep south, wrinkled with hard work, smiling beneath the round brims of their hats. '*¡Viva México!*' shouts the singer, the *Grito* – the cry – itself. '*¡Viva!*' replies the crowd as the band strikes up the national anthem, whereupon the crowd stands still, hands across the chest, clutching the heart, here in Old El Paso. Long lines wait for food served from stalls – sweet fried churros, tacos and shredded beef, though the longest queue approaches the sign promising 'Turkey Breast, Bratwurst, Hamburgers'. Other stalls have games: pop the balloon and win a 3-foot-high plaster cherub for the garden, or a big cuddly gorilla.

Down a side street, a lone van with flashing lights advertises 'Sodas, Aguas, Gatorades', and plays a tune more disturbing than jolly. As well he might, given what is happening over the border in Ciudad Juárez. The crowd of some 10,000 in El Paso can hear its counterpart across the river four times the size, the whooping and music that happens only rarely in a city that lives under effective, self-imposed, curfew. At 11.00, fireworks fill the skies both sides of the border, bursting with a sound like gunfire – thereby concealing the fusillades of murderous, real gunfire across Juárez at exactly that moment. In fact, some of the witnesses to the killing of ten people in a drug rehabilitation centre thought the rasp of A K-47s was a part of the celebrations.

The killers burst in through the gateway of the *Anexo de Vida* – annexe of life – rehabilitation centre in the heart of Barrio Azul, a poor *colonia* of little streets, and threw a grenade into the first room on their right, occupied by a sixteen-year-old guard. Inside the room next morning, a mattress is splattered with blood, the floor next to it saturated, but the teenager seems to have made it through the door before falling to the ground where his workout weights still lie. The killers have soaked his blood into the soles of their heavy boots and stamped it around in horribly clear footprints – that anyone who cared to solve the crime might examine, only no one ever seems to solve the crimes.

The cement and whitewashed walls of Barrio Azul are staked out with the blue graffiti tag of the local *pandilla*, or gang, the BAZUL, to claim the *colonia* and remember: '*In Memoriam, Zaiko y Nordiano*', presumably two street-fighting 'brothers' who died 'defending' it. A dog rests in the stinking trash strewn along Via Juan Escutia. A burned-out building is likewise tagged by the BAZUL, next door to which a neat pink house with flower pots on the window sills flies the flag for Independence Day. Turning into Via Jaime Nuño, there is the entrance to the *Anexo de Vida*. The words '*Para enfermos de drogadicción y alcoholismo*' are written in careful letters on the white paint – for the sick from drug addiction and alcoholism. Only there is no '*vida*' in this place now, chains on its padlocked gates, and a black tarpaulin hiding the aftermath of the horror unleashed just as the mayor of Juárez, José Reyes Ferriz, rang the bell and shouted the *Grito* last night. The previous week, seventy-five people had been killed in Juárez, including one man beheaded and another hung to die by handcuffs from a chain-link fence. And this was only a few days since 3 September, when seventeen people were killed at another rehab clinic, the *Aliviane*, a few blocks from city hall and the downtown bridge to El Paso. Black-clad gunmen had burst into the *Aliviane* and lined up the young male inmates against a wall before summarily executing them. The father of one of the dead said that his son had completed his rehabilitation, but went back to *El Aliviane* for prayer meetings.

We clamber onto the roof and down into the courtyard of the *Anexo de Vida*, still a mess thirteen hours after the killing, the hiding and flight. Sneakers are discarded in piles, crates are upturned and furniture scattered across the ground – following the painted signs to the *'Ruta de Evacuacíon'*. Off the courtyard are the rooms that were death chambers overnight, and still stink of the sickly-sweet stench of sticky blood which congeals in pools around us – wrapped in the other scents of what was until last night a rehabilitation centre run by poor people for people below poverty: stale sweat, rotting broccoli piled up in boxes, and the ashes of a fire on which dinner was being cooked. It does not take a policeman to work out what happened, only there is little sign of any police work, and no question of guarding the crime scene, or preventing us from contaminating it, nor the young boys who follow us inside, scavenging for souvenirs and things left behind to sell: medical drugs, tools, pairs of shoes, packets of cookies.

After the killing of the teenaged guard, the carnage then divides into two directions, along each side of the courtyard. To their left, the death squad headed towards the room of the centre's director, who seems to have made it outside, where a pond of his blood putrefies on the cement. Next were the quarters of the vice-director, a woman whose room is a pitiless sight: blood splattered across her floral bed spread, and rushing to the floor beside it where she seems to have been raked with bullets, then horrible smears where she appears to have collapsed onto her sofa beneath the window. Now, two boys play and cast their eyes over the ransacked drawers, taking two baseball caps. The dead woman's handbag lies on an armchair – it contains Christian magazines and a paperback guide to sacred sites in the Holy Land. Her CD collection is scattered on the floor – *Metal En Rosas*, a compilation of Guns 'n' Roses, and Radiohead. Curiously, only a single bullet casing lies on the floor; perhaps the children have taken the rest. Or maybe even the police.

The assassins moved past the main dormitory, in which mattresses still lie, and posters line the wall warning that *'La Adicción Es Una Enfermedad'*. And in this room a man now appears, wearing a Dallas Cowboys cap, returning to pick up the set of tools and shoes he left behind in the flight last night. 'I used to sleep over there, at the end. It happened about eleven o'clock,' he testifies. 'We were watching the boxing on TV. We heard the explosion, then the shooting, and hid under the mattresses at the end there. The whole thing took about two minutes.' How were they dressed? He doesn't remember. Why did they do this? 'I have no idea. The people who ran this centre did it just by themselves, and we came by ourselves, after they had taken us off the streets. We never received any threats, and we never threatened anyone. We hid nothing from the *narcotraficantes*, and we had nothing to hide from the *narcotraficantes*.' He breaks open a packet of biscuits, and eats. No, he will not give his name – *'Anónimo'*, he insists – and no, no photograph. The death squad proceeded to the room at the far left-hand corner, where two beds are now empty, in between which is a pool of blood so thick that it is still sticky underfoot, thirteen hours later, its darker coating over the still congealing red glistening in the shaft of sunlight that penetrates the door.

Meanwhile, another squad of executioners continued on from the entrance up the courtyard's right flank, past a storage area, the *'Área de Fumar'* and cooking yard, where blackened pots hang in which soup would have been cooked, and a metal tub for washing clothes. The grate of the fire that warmed, well, the last supper, is still full of ash. The scene in the next small room suggests that the killers were looking for something – a mattress overturned and shot to shreds, but no sign of murder. In the far right corner, however, there is a brutal scene, in and outside the *Enfermería* – the medical centre. In the courtyard is another pool of blood, and the wall is pitted with bullet holes. Whoever came to investigate the scene has scrawled *'CUERPO I'* – Corpse I – on a piece of paper placed on the ground. Inside the infirmary is a fearsome sight: a cupboard of medicines has been ransacked, with much of its contents left, and a closed door shot through with a bullet. There is a pool of blood by the door, but someone seems to have forced a desperate way out, like a trapped beast, for his blood is splattered all over the bullet-riddled wall outside and the metal door — ajar — is gnarled at the base, as he staggered and fell outside to become '*CUERPO* F'.

This room must have been a sanctuary of sorts: there are sports trophies and a bookcase with several editions of the same paperback Bible. This collection belonged to a man called José Ángel Torres, who obviously read, maybe even taught, English, for he had several copies of a volume called *Famous Christians*. He had potted cactus plants, a CD/cassette player and had just sipped at a plastic bottle of Diet Coke when his murderers arrived: it is about 7/8 full. To the rear of this hospital reception area is a bunk-bed, more copious blood, and a label reading '*CUERPO* H', next to a cabinet behind which is the doctor's stethoscope, on the floor. As we rummage around trying to recreate the crime, an SUV with blackened windows pulls up in the otherwise empty street outside the gate. Having climbed in, there is no quick way out — we're trapped. While it remains there, motionless, the flesh creeps with goose pimples for all the 35-degree heat, and one's vision blurs with fear. Then it purrs away.

Oddly, there are *CUERPO* F, H and I, but no *CUERPO* A, B, C, D, E or G. Either too much trouble or the kids had taken the labels as souvenirs. It doesn't matter — no one is going to look for the men wearing the boots that left further bloodied marks here in this corner. Although that is not what they are saying at the press conference in the Chihuahua state offices. 'We continue in our unrelenting work against the criminals,' affirms Patricia González, state prosecutor, with as little menace as hapless Rommel Moreno in Tijuana. 'We have shown the world that the struggle against organised crime is resolved and determined.' The new police chief is 'confident in our continuing investigations' into this latest carnage in yet another rehabilitation centre. Being the police chief of Juárez is work on a high wire. In February 2009, the narco traffickers decided that Chief Roberto Orduña, a retired army major who had been in office since May 2008, should go. After the purging of 300 police officers accused of working for the cartels, the narcos vowed to kill a police officer every forty-eight hours until Orduña resigned, starting with his operations director Sacramento Pérez Serrano and three of his staff. On 20 February, Orduña – who had lived in the police station for several months – quit his post and fled the city. He had replaced another chief who had also fled to live in El Paso. The mayor of Juárez, José Reyes Ferriz, has also received death threats, one in spring 2010 written on a severed pig's head, and keeps houses on both sides of the border. Interviewed in El Paso, he vows: 'I am not going to give in.' After inviting me to attend a summer cultural festival in Juárez, the mayor lists the things he needs, including an encrypted radio network so that he and the police do not have to constantly listen to the knocking sound followed by a *narcocorrido* with which the cartels hack in to announce that another officer has been or will be shot. Reyes Ferriz has been menaced by communiqués threatening to kill and decapitate him, even in El Paso, if he 'continues to help you know who', as one message put it.[2] The mayor and authorities decline to speculate on what the message – implying favour towards one cartel over another – could have meant. The governor of Chihuahua, José Reyes Baeza, was also the target of an assassination attempt: a car in his convoy was hit by machine-gun fire in February 2009. This time, one of the five gunmen, an ex-soldier, was arrested. These people preside over a city that was in January 2010 confirmed as having the world's highest homicide rate, by a group based in Mexico City called the Citizens Council for Public Security and Social Justice. The organisation calculated Juárez as killing 191 citizens per 100,000, way ahead of second-placed San Pedro Sula in Honduras with 119, New Orleans with 69, Medellín in Colombia with 62 and Cape Town with 60.[3] What characterises the killing in Juárez – or what fails to characterise it – is that no one knows who the killers are, or what they seek to gain from the killing. There is no reason why a 'drug lord', as newspapers call the cartel leaders, would want to liquidate ten wretched addicts in a rehab centre.

A week after the mayor shouted the *Grito* of independence, the black plastic sheet covering the gate of the *Anexo de Vida* in Barrio Azul has been removed. Inside, the blood has been whitewashed away with limestone; all that is left are bullet holes, mattresses, a Toronto Blue Jays cap and a newspaper from the day of the massacre (which would itself become the next day's front page). Its cover carries vividly illustrated coverage of the previous day's atrocity, but the paper is open at the pin-up spread showing a girl wearing a studded leather bikini, gagged at the mouth and bound in chains.

I had first crossed the Rio Grande into Juárez in 1981 for the same two reasons as anyone: the opening line of Bob Dylan's 'Just Like Tom Thumb's Blues' ('When you're lost in the rain in Juárez, and it's Eastertime too'), and to gawp at the salacity and audacity with which anything and everything was for sale. And although the fleshpot, the dope-den and the Kentucky Bar in which Marilyn Monroe celebrated her divorce from Arthur Miller are certainly not the 'real' Juárez, they are not entirely deceptions either. Not because Juárez was superficially a playground of danger and vice for visitors but because it was and remains, above all, a marketplace of the purest, unfettered kind. Juárez is a pioneer of, and monument to, economic deregulation. When I returned two decades later in 1999, Ciudad Juárez was ready to implode, and has now imploded. The implosion was not sudden, and its roots are deep. Juárez is at once a very singular city and one that encapsulates many things common to most other cities, though in extremis.

Juárez lies, so they say, *entre algo y la nada* – between something and nothing. It is a city of transit: a military, then road, then railway junction. A pivot of Spanish colonisation, it is the oldest settlement along what is now the border, established as *Misión de Nuestra Señora de Guadalupe de los Mansos del Paso del Norte* in 1659, as Spanish explorers and then traders and missionaries prepared to cross what they called the *Río del Norte* – what Mexicans now call the Río Bravo and Americans the Rio Grande. ('*Mansos*' was a loaded and thoroughly unpleasant Spanish colonial word applied to those indigenous to the area, equivalent to 'the tamed', or 'meek' – the subjugated.)[4] Paso del Norte was a commercial junction and entrepôt for trade between New Spain and its province of New Mexico, then between independent Mexico and its northern reaches.

Until the international border was drawn across Juárez's face in 1848, along a line following the river as it takes a sharp eastward turn, there was little on its northern left bank; only after the frontier was etched, was the city of El Paso established on the US side. The metropolis on the Mexican right bank expanded as a market centre for the surrounding cotton fields, but towards the end of the nineteenth century had become urbanised by the arrival of the Mexican Central northbound railway from Mexico City, which connected Paso del Norte to the railroad network that had woven an industrial infrastructure across the United States. The railway brought hundreds of thousands of Mexicans to the doorstep of the USA and the siding yards of the new American sister city and transport hub, so that a flow of goods and human traffic now connected the border city to the industrialising USA. Letters sent from El Paso by a German immigrant, Ernst Kohlberg, describe the border city on the US side as 'nearly the end of the world, and the last of creation', while in El Paso del Norte on the Mexican side, after a reinforcement of cavalrymen, he had 'never seen so many cutthroats together at one time'. The businessmen of the city, he noted, were each extorted for $160 for the military's stay. 'The money will not be lost if no other party gets control,' he wrote, but, 'if another crowd gets the upper hand, they will declare the levying of the tax as illegal and make us pay again.'[5] Whether Kohlberg's remark was a more apposite prediction of the arrival of the PRI and PAN or of the drug cartels is a matter of subjective judgement in hindsight.

In 1888, El Paso del Norte changed its name to Ciudad Juárez, in honour of Benito Juárez, president of Mexico during the 1860s, who had used the city as his headquarters. For a short while, the city even acted as Mexico's provisional national capital, while Juárez's republican forces fought French intervention in Mexico. Juárez became a capital city of a different kind during the Mexican revolution of 1910, of which it was the cradle. In the reconstruction that followed, Juárez grew into a manufacturing base in its own right, making copper wire. But the city's economic recovery from the revolutionary violence was also due to a thriving trade in smuggling during the prohibition of alcohol in the USA between 1919 and 1933. Juárez meanwhile opened its doors to anyone wishing to come and consume banned firewater rather than have it illegally delivered. And so the city's reputation for opportunism in illicit markets was born, enhanced by the shift, orchestrated by Ignacia '*La Nacha*' Jasso González, from alcohol to heroin once the former was legalised over the river. *La Nacha* was dope queen of Juárez until the 1970s, by which time another wave of commerce was about to engulf the city with far greater impact: the *maquiladoras*. Hundreds of thousands of Mexicans would arrive in Juárez from the interior and desperately poor south, not to cross the border, but to work on it, in the proliferation of assembly plants that suddenly spread throughout the borderland like an invasion of bland low-rise Lego bricks. Initially, and for complex reasons of exploitation and demographics, the majority of those employed in these soul-destroying factories were young women. Juárez attracted more *maquiladoras* than any other city along the border, and therefore more workers, but did not create an infrastructure to house or shelter them, let alone keep them warm, light their shacks, or school their children. Let alone protect them from the nightmarish kind of metropolis that resulted from this smash 'n' grab of cheap labour. For the big landowners, markedly the Bermúdez family, after whom Juárez's biggest *maquiladora* park is named, and by whom it is owned, the industrial explosion was a boon beyond their wildest dreams. As the photographer who has captured this city's descent, Julián Cardona, puts it: 'The rich of the city had paid the politicians to raise taxes from the poor, in order to turn the place where they lived into an urban Frankenstein.'

I met Cardona long after first seeing his work: he had curated shocking, striking pictures for a book called *Juárez, The Laboratory of Our Future*, with a text by Charles Bowden, which I had bought in 1998. The volume proved even more pessimistically prescient than it dared presume when published. Juárez has indeed become, since then, the laboratory of our futures: a prototype for the post-political global economy and now also the arena for post-political war that that economy has produced in the city. A decade after *The Laboratory of Our Future*, Bowden would reflect, in another book about the city: 'Juárez is not behind the times. It is the sharp edge slashing into a time called the future . . . This is not some breakdown of the social order. This is the new order'.[6]

Off a road leading south-east from the city – past road bridges built by the big landowners to connect their properties to the industrial parks – a dirt track turns into the scrub, towards the main cemetery. The concrete gateway and breeze-block walls are tagged by gangs when they come to bury their casualties: 'RIP Hulk' and 'RIP Oxxy'. 'RIP Onza' refers to someone named after the Spanish word for an ounce. In one corner is a section marked with white paint on a yellow wall: the *Fosa Común*, the common grave, stretching into the desert – mound after mound of earth beneath which lie those unidentified who died in Juárez without a name, though some have blank wooden name-boards, and others even have crosses and name plates, only those are bare too. Some, oddly, have flowers placed in memory – perhaps by a fellow patient at a rehab clinic, a fellow addict, or a family member who dare not give their murdered loved one a name. Traffic from over the horizon sends a distant hum of life from the road running through the army checkpoint and out into the desert, and a northerly wind scatters stray garbage and rustles the petals left in memory of the anonymous dead.

Hugo de León, proprietor of *Marmolería Hugo*, one of the headstone salesmen at the entrance of the cemetery, watches the funeral cortèges come and go, and reckons that 'about eighty per cent are to do with fighting over drugs – and too many of the dead are young. But some of the funerals still bring the mariachis and have a party.' Some are without names, he suggests, 'because the family couldn't afford to get the body from the morgue', and some 'because no one dared come forward to claim the body in case they got killed as well'. Of course, many of those buried in other parts of the cemetery do have names: 'We've had eighty bodies in the last five days, most from the violence, and most of them went over there, to the regular cemetery,' says de León. The walls to the 'regular cemetery' are tagged like the entrance: 'RIP Flozo 2008', and 'Sad Dog'. There are photographs on some of the headstones, like that of Miguel Ángel Juan Pavilla, who turns his firm, almost belligerent gaze out across the cemetery, having been killed the night of the *Grito* in 2009 – possibly one of the victims in the Barrio Azul rehab centre – just before his nineteenth birthday. He had a strong jaw, close-cropped hair and a blue zip jacket with 'Rocket' emblazoned across it. Someone has put a pink teddy bear on the grave of Luis Ramos Vega, killed on 20 June 2009, aged twenty, and picked out the letters TQM in pebbles – *Te Quiero Mucho*, I want you so much. They have also left a bottle of Coca-Cola in which yellow and white flowers are placed, struggling to drink the soda into their stalks. Beyond the latest headstones, the gravediggers have done their hefty workload well: deep, fresh holes dug already, mounds of earth beside them, ready to welcome tomorrow's harvest.

* * *

If Juárez is a city of God, that is because the Devil is scared to come here, goes the old *dicho*, or saying. But Julián Cardona, braver than the Devil, remains in Juárez and is building himself a new home here, to which his German Shepherd guard dog El Santo is only just acclimatising. In November 2008, Cardona and I had embarked on a forensic tour of the scene around the decapitated body suspended from 'Switchback Bridge' on the day of the killing. The *narcomensaje* was itself a puzzle. 'I, Lázaro Flores, served my boss, the dog-fucker' – but that was not the dead man's name. Lázaro Flores is a prominent businessman – with no connection to this killing – who owns an event palace and narrowly escaped kidnapping allegedly by police officers working for *La Línea*. There was also written a menace to a named senior police officer, whose son was rumoured to have defected from *La Línea* to another trafficking cadre. Around the time of the execution, *La Línea* took to publishing lists of police officers it was about to execute on public *narcomensajes*. A list of twenty-six officers was posted at a dog-racing track just before Christmas 2008, above the bodies of four civilians, one of them wearing a Santa Claus hat.

'Switchback Bridge' overpass is officially called *Puente Rotario*, after the Rotary Club whose cogwheel emblem it bears, right next to where the body was hung. It is one of the city's busiest junctions, so there would have been no shortage of witnesses, especially at 4.30 a.m., with the morning tide of shift workers just then heading for the *maquiladoras*. Hundreds of people must have seen it done. How quickly and surreptitiously can a vehicle or possibly a small convoy of vehicles pull up on an overpass, unload a bloody victim, suspend him between the hoardings advertising Frutti Sauce and Comida Express fast food, tie and fasten the ropes, and hang the sheet bearing the message? The killers would have driven their getaway vehicle passing a late sports bar called Hooligans, the GMC car concession and a *maquiladora* belonging to Honeywell, which would have changed shifts while the headless body was being hung there.

The severed head of the victim, from Sinaloa, was found days later in the *Plaza de los Periodistas* – Journalists' Square – at the foot of a statue of a boy hawking newspapers, a celebration of old Juárez's pride in itself as the cradle of a free press during the Mexican revolution. The message to journalists could not have been more articulate.

A few days later, on 14 November 2008, one of the leading reporters on crime in Juárez, Armando Rodríguez of the local paper *El Diario* – who had reported on both the execution at 'Switchback Bridge' and the discovery of the head beneath the statue – was shot dead while warming up his car. His eight-year-old daughter, whom he was taking to school, was in the passenger seat.[7]

'There's a lot of world-class business here,' says Cardona, as we pass the *maquiladoras* along the executioners' getaway route. 'And these worlds entwine, they're inseparable,' he explains. 'Young families come north, the girl gets a job in the *maquila* and the man is sexually potent but economically impotent. But he can earn money working for the narcos, part of a waiting labour force, and if he has a habit himself, which he probably has, he turns to crime and drug dealing to maintain it. So his addiction becomes an economic activity in the marketplace. If you keep things separate,' counsels Cardona, 'you will not understand what is happening in this city. Narco – *Maquiladoras* – Migration, that's the triangle, they're all related. And of course, there's narco money in the construction you see everywhere.' We pass the iron girder skeleton of a building that never seems to get finished; it was under construction when I was here seven years previously, and it still is. 'Narco installation art,' says Cardona. And later, a car with its windscreen shot out: 'the new Juárez window design'. In the waggish parlance of Juárez, recent architecture is categorised as being of the 'Early Narco', 'Mid Narco' or 'High Narco' periods. A series of arches proclaim the entrance to the upscale *Rincón San Marcos*, or St Mark's Corner, a gated community of villas inevitably re-christened *Rincón San Narcos* on the street. Around a pleasant green is arranged a quiet retreat of mansions, each more garish than the next, and advertisements for facial and cosmetic surgery. Here is a metaphor for the economy of power in Juárez. Outside some villas are vehicles marked with *maquila* corporate logos, and in the forecourt of others belonging to well-known drug barons, are powerful four-wheel drives with blackened windows – which are now illegal in Juárez, but what the hell.

In Juárez, the map of the cartel war frays. Any preconceptions about combat between narco-trafficking structures dissipate into a delta of violence. The chains of narco command have, apparently, collapsed.

Something else is happening, something differently terrifying and more murderous. Before proceeding, there is a cautionary word from one of the more renowned Mexican journalists to call Juárez his home, Alejandro Páez Varela, Editor of *El Universal*. Páez is back home from Mexico City to greet a group of friends at a cultural centre called *Cafebrería* – coffeebookshop – and launch his novel, *Corazón de Kalashnikov*, about two women who become involved with narcos. The *Cafebrería* is an agreeable space, an oasis in Juárez, frequented by a slice of life in the city whose existence is scarcely acknowledged outside it: a beleaguered intelligensia with tortoise-shell spectacles and pony tails gathers together to talk on white sofas beneath an ironwork staircase. But even this is considered worthy of the cartels' attention. The *Cafebrería* is run by José Pérez Espino and his wife Claudia. José is a former reporter with *El Universal* and runs the Juárez alternative news website Almargen. In January 2010, he posted this message on his Facebook page: 'I am afraid for my life. I've been a journalist for 20 years and I've overcome many threats. A person has threatened me with death. I know that he could be an extortionist as there are very many of them. I just wanted to post this information here.'

Red wine is served after Páez's reading from his book. Then Páez tells me: 'Juárez has been ruled by the Juárez cartel, it is true. But forget what you have read and heard about who controls what. Whoever the controllers are, they leave those who remain in the city to fight a battle to the finish, which involves the extermination of rivals and others. This has become crazy warfare, not even necessarily between the Sinaloa and the Juárez cartels, it is anarchy. Yes, they are all there, Juárez, Sinaloa and Zetas trying to get in. But the pyramids have collapsed, and not one of the big bosses in the battle for Juárez has been touched, not one – they are far away. This is a fight between the groups and gangs on the ground that used to work for them, and it has become a massacre.'

Julián Cardona cautions that 'it simply doesn't make sense, as the media and government think, to draw lines between cartels in Juárez. Along the smuggling corridors into the US, maybe, but not on the streets. The cartels cannot even see those lines themselves here any more. Of course the drug cartels exist, they are players, but they are no longer the main reason for the violence here. Look at this as a factory. You have a product and a production line. There are bosses, managers, middle management, line workers, accountants, bankers, shippers – they are all part of the process, but they never meet each other and most of them are not directly employed by the corporation. We'll have counted 1,700 dead in this city by the end of the year [he said, rightly, in September 2008] and in most cases, the executioners don't even know which cartel, if any, they're working for. If they change sides, from someone far from here who is part of the Juárez cartel to someone far from here in the Sinaloa cartel, they won't know it. All they have is their assigned task, their piece of turf, and maybe an order to do this, do that, or kill someone. Not why, or who for. They have no idea about the big money, or who their bosses are.'

This comes as a partial surprise (if anything surprises in Juárez), subverting the official 'map' of the cartel war. But it is utterly convincing. The notion that the cartel war has imploded and no longer explains the bloodshed in Juárez is a heresy against the versions of what is happening as expounded by the US and Mexican governments and many of the media in both countries. It fundamentally challenges the notion of carefully staged cartel war on a narco Monopoly board, as well as that of a government 'offensive' against drug dealing in the city. The heresy was formulated by two reporters, Cardona and his friend Ignacio Alvarado Álvarez, who ran the investigative Almargen media service now run by Pérez Espino from *Cafebrería*, but who has since been persuaded by his co-citizen Páez to work at *El Universal* in the capital. 'I have a family,' Alvarado says, explaining his decision to leave Juárez.

But we had first met when Ignacio was still living in Juárez, with Cardona, later in the morning after the decapitated corpse was hung from the overpass, in the inimitable and inevitable Sanborn's coffee house, for what was for me an unforgettable briefing. The cartels, explained Ignacio, have 'substituted the old pyramidal chain of command for the same concession or franchising system as any other corporation marketing any product or service in the globalised economy'. It takes a moment to realise how sarcastically funny Alvarado is being about the legal economy around us. 'You know how a corporation will not do its own detailed work any more – no! – that's not cost effective, that's monopolistic. So like a good capitalist, the cartel outsources, puts contracts out to tender, gives other people a chance to compete in order to reduce its own costs. Why should drug traffickers be any different? They're a business like any other. The cartels have got much more democratic in the capitalist sense: out-sourced, meritocratic and opportunistic,' he says, half-laughing, his eyes widening in mischief, disgust and fear. 'There really are far more opportunities for the small investor nowadays, with of course a higher risk, and more people getting killed. But think of the freedom to operate! The small guy pays a commission for the cartel's control over corrupt officials and the border, and occasionally they'll tell you who to kill, though not necessarily. The cartels don't need to control the streets, because they cannot, so they franchise them, they get other people to kill and die. The problem is: what happens if they have outsourced so much that they lose control completely? Do you see outsourcing making modern capitalism any more efficient? Of course not, it's a complete mess! So the cartels find that it's not so much that they need not control the streets, but they *cannot*.' 'What wealthy drug lord,' adds Cardona, 'would want to try and control *this*?

'I used to call my town a city of two economies,' Cardona continues, ordering *huevos rancheros*, 'one legal, the other illegal. But now that both are globalised, the dividing line has gone. Both the *maquilas* and the drug Plaza are based on the notion that the market will find its proper balance, and the market alone will dictate how Juárez will do business. And that is exactly what has happened. The "legal" economy brought hundreds of thousands of people to Juárez, me included, to work in *maquilas*, as I did, and offers to pay them three dollars a shift. The illegal market needs people, and offers better opportunities, to double that money for street dealing, multiply it by ten for a carrier, and by a hundred for killing. The *maquila* jobs market can't support what it created, so it sends you to get sucked into the other market, the parallel drug market, where you get paid in kind, you become an addict, you cut the drugs to sell, so that your addiction becomes an activity in the market, and you become an economic agent. When the recession comes, the *maquilas* find cheaper labour in Asia, so more people lose their jobs and turn in even greater numbers to buying, taking and selling drugs. And killing.'

Long before Juárez became the economic model for an inflation of killing, it was often in its history a place of tussling between smugglers of goods into the USA. But now, this late-capitalist, post-modern battlefield is for a Plaza that did not show up on the 'map' in Chapter One. A Plaza which is more fiendish in its violence than any war over trafficking into the USA: the battle for the internal drug market of Juárez — indeed of Mexico itself. In the aftermath of the cartel war and the throes of this new conflict, Juárez is blighted by drug addiction, markedly to crack and methamphetamine. Indeed, one reason Ignacio Alvarado gave for the erosion of cartel structures and boundaries, especially in Juárez, is 'that Mexico has become a country with a vast internal consumer market for drugs that is deliberately underestimated by government lies, and too anarchic for the cartels to control, even if they wanted to'. 'If we divide the drug market into eras,' says Cardona, 'we can see the smuggling era as that of the cartels — the monopoly capitalist era, if you like — and the explosion of domestic drug-taking as that of the free market, of criminal anarchy. Before, in the monopoly era, everyone knew their place: drug lords, the politicians, state police, local police, mid-narcos and gangs. Now, Juárez has become a formless, horizontal hierarchy, responding to the free market — some become very rich, most go into the trash.' Juárez is a city of 500 *colonias* with no municipal facilities to keep up with what were (until the recent recession) its 8,000 weekly arrivals. In each *colonia*, wasteland is drug-dealing territory for one of the 500 *colonia* gangs, apart from big spaces in the outlaying barrios like Anapra. There, says Cardona, 'the waste spaces are controlled by a gang called the police'.

Each *colonia* also has what in Tijuana were called *tienditas* — little shops — outlets for cocaine, marijuana, synthetic drugs and heroin. In Juárez they are called *picaderos*, sometimes marked by a shoe tied to a nearby telegraph wire. As the cartel pyramids collapse, so they lose control of the burgeoning domestic market for drugs, each *picadero* claiming and operating its own Plaza, protected by the local gang. The more the domestic Plaza expands, the looser the grip of the cartels, and the need for them to operate not so much a chain of command, but an affiliation system of 'outsourced' gangs. As a result, Juárez is now being fought over by a Pandora's Box of warring interests. Some of them are street gangs collated into a federation called *Los Aztecas*, which in turn serves *La Línea*, a street-level resurgence of the old Juárez cartel thought wrongly to have been shattered by

Guzmán. Another federation of gangs is the *Artistas Asesinos*, affiliated to the Sinaloa cartel's siege of Juárez, as are *Los Mexicles*, also
at the pleasure of Guzmán, who will kill anyone they can find who
had any business with *La Línea*. An especially vicious animosity
exists between *La Línea*'s *Aztecas* and *Los Mexicles*, since the latter
defected from the *Aztecas* to join Guzmán. This betrayal led to a riot
in Juárez prison in March 2009 in which twenty-one *Mexicles* were
killed by *Aztecas*, reportedly with official sanction. Then there are
the various police forces. In January 2009, the police chief tasked
with gang-busting, Francisco Ledesma, turned out to have himself
been a coordinator for *La Línea*, and was murdered. Partly as a
result, the rogue element in Chihuahua state police, formerly a wing
of the Juárez cartel, is now believed to be an independent force of its
own. The municipal police has meanwhile been liberated by the
domestic market from its attachment to politicians and cartels, and
can operate as it wishes. The army and federal police, supposedly in
town to quell this murderous farrago, we shall consider later.

There is some idea abroad that the killings are contained within
one sector of society, or in the shanty barrios, but not in town or the
exclusive quarters. Not at all: we drive to a smart villa currently
'under administration', where nine bodies were found recently, just
opposite a fancy hall called *La Cité*, let out for weddings and functions. Then along the Avenida Rivera Lara, past Desperado's disco
and rodeo, into the Calle Sierra del Pedregal, to arrive at a white,
gated property where up to thirty-six bodies (depending on which
account one heeds) were found buried beneath the patio in March
2007. At another house at 3363 Parsioneros, known as the House of
Death, twelve bodies were found buried. These were killings over
which controversy raged, with reports that an informant for the US
government was part of the cell that carried them out, and that those
who 'ran' him in the customs service were warned in advance of most
murders and knew that the massacre – in which state police officers
on the Juárez cartel payroll took part – was ongoing.[8] In the yard
behind the House of Death, the picture of a mysterious and beautiful
woman has been attached to the wall and 'shot' in the mouth, as
though she were used for target practice. 'The general pattern was,'
says Cardona, 'that if you exhibit the bodies, you are not killing for
the police. If you hide them, either you are killing for the police or

you are the police.' On the roadside round the corner from the House of Death, a police recruitment poster features a ninja-cop in a balaclava, and the words: '*Juárez te necesita!*' – Juárez needs you.

Only guesswork could explain why the satellite town of Riveras del Bravo is where it is: about an hour's drive from Ciudad Juárez, clinging to the borderline on the city's eastern edge. According to the *susurro*, these communities of relentlessly identical little houses – built to install *maquila* workers previously living in cardboard shacks – were erected where they were to suit landowners acquainted with politicians making the decisions, with both set to gain financially from an agreed deal over some far-flung location. Or maybe it is just that the city authorities somehow thought it a good idea to hurriedly throw up this maze of streets on a swamp by the river, on what were previously paddy fields and cotton plantations, cut off from the city, with no attempt at transport connections apart from a single bus route downtown. There has apparently been some idea for a park in which children could play: the remains of a rusting roundabout are still there, half-submerged in the swamp water seeping from the Rio Bravo. And anyway, to build all these houses during the *maquiladora* boom appears now to have been optimistic: since the emergence of cheaper labour in Asia and the onset of recession, row upon row of them have been abandoned and ransacked after their owners were laid off and returned home to the south. The PFK gang – whoever they are – seems to have made crack dens in most of them, tagging the walls or else incinerating them. On one street, four houses in a row are burned out, whether as a result of gang warfare or just pyromaniac recreation. Another posse in town is, apparently, the MK 18, which has taken over a row of empty houses leading down to an open sewer, so that the stink of excretia wafts on the breeze through its territory. At the end of Rivera de Zempoala, two lookout guards stand watch with a walkie-talkie. Ten years ago, this was a city of cardboard boxes growing out of the mire; now it is a showcase for the urban Frankenstein. As so often, the only respite or sign of resistance emanates from the church, surrounded by a high fence with a locked gate ever since the priest's computers were stolen. Here, children abandoned all day while both parents work at the *maquilas* can find a meal and company, lining up in shifts – girls, then boys – chatting over polystyrene plates divided into three sections of beans, pasta and a tortilla, before adjourning to the common room to watch Michael Jackson videos. When the priest, Father Ruberto Ramos, is out doing his rounds, the centre is run by Alfredo Aguilar, once a gang fighter on these streets, now a recent father and guardian of the next generation. 'Here, they are left alone,' he says, by way of opening our conversation. Left alone by whom? 'By their parents, older youths, their families. We deal with trauma from sexual harassment by fathers and elders; the most common form is violation of girls by their stepfathers, and in some cases a man will kill the children of the woman he takes on, if she has them from a previous marriage.' Next to his desk, Aguilar's computer has a screensaver showing a paradisal tropical scene – waterfalls, birds and lush vegetation.

'The little ones are abandoned when their parents go to work,' says Aguilar, 'and fall prey to everything imaginable. We try to give them shelter, some glimpse of other values. It's not easy – we have ten-year-old boys trying to hit on girls who are even younger, because it's what they see at home. There's so much violence in their lives, so many drugs and that too starts in the home: five to ten people living in a tiny house, on top of one another, with abuse, violence against the children, no privacy and no one able to sleep. So most of the gangbangers are fifteen to sixteen years old, some as young as thirteen. I was one of them, not serious, but I grew up among these people, girls raped, boys joining gangs and getting killed; I lived with them.' Aguilar, twenty-eight years old, wants to make a point rather than deliver a confessional. 'The main point,' he argues, 'is that these are people spat out by the *maquiladora* factory system, and out of that come the gangs and the drugs. These people arrived from Veracruz, Tabasco, Oaxaca to work in the *maquilas* and when the *maquila* spits you out, drug dealing becomes a way of staying, a way of living. You stay and survive the best you can, or you leave and your house becomes a crack den. But not only the *maquilas*: the city has spat these people out, too. No wonder truancy is a problem if you have six small primary schools for seven thousand families and no secondary school.' To get to secondary school in Ciudad Juárez can be a two- to three-hour cross-town journey each way because the bus routes are arranged like a fan from outlying places like this. Every retired American school bus converges from the *colonias* on the city centre as its destination; there is no transport between one satellite and another, so pupils must travel via what is considered by most to be a no-go downtown zone before daylight in the morning and after dark at night.

Father Ramos returns a few days later, and tells me: 'When I first came here, I was doing many children's funerals, children who had died after accidents at home – well, I say accidents, I mean they were killed by their stepfathers – raping them and killing them. I found that in order to have a lover, a woman had to agree to this choice: kill the child or lose the man. I had six of those funerals in my first two years.' Then Father 'Beto' as he is universally known, relates a few statistics. 'There are twenty thousand houses in this *colonia*, of which eight thousand are now abandoned,' leaving more than 60,000 people living in 12,000 tiny houses. The proportion of empty houses is high, even for Juárez, though the figures for the city itself make terrifying reading. A report by the *Colegio de la Frontera del Norte*, published in January 2010, found that there are 116,000 vacant houses across the city, out of a total housing stock of 416,000 units. The empty dwellings, says the report, 'result from the economic downturn that began in 2001, and the depopulation has increased greatly in the past two years because of the recession, violence and insecurity. Many migrants who came from southern Mexico to work in the *maquiladora* industry have decided to return to their places of origin. Others have migrated to the United States. Various neighborhoods contain mostly deserted and vandalized houses. In addition, statistics from the tax administration offices show that since 2008, more than 10,670 businesses have closed, the majority according to the business leaders, due to the economic crisis and the insecurity. There are many factory buildings vacant and these cannot be sold for any price to manufacturers due to the current conditions. The vacancy rate in industrial real estate is now at 14 per cent. Many of these businesses have abandoned Juárez.' The author of the report, COLEF researcher César Fuentes, told the *Diario* newspaper. 'The economic, public security and social crises in the city have important repercussions in terms of economic and social viability. It is difficult for someone to invest in the city if they know that they will become victims of extortion, robbery and kidnapping.'

*   *   *

'The border is all about trash,' says Cardona. 'Think of Juárez as per-petual motion by different kinds of trash: someone else's trashed fridge or car recycled; turning human beings into trash in the *maquilas*, dead human trash in the rehab centres – though you can't re-fit the dead people in a *'yonke'* and put them up for sale like you can the trashed cars.' We hold this conversation on a ridge of precar-ious housing above the sprawling *colonia* of Poniente, to which Cardona originally came himself, from the state of Zacatecas, to work in a *maquila*. Brought up by his grandparents in the country, he has stayed ever since, apart from a spell back home, during which he tried to organise resistance to the break-up of communally held and farmed land, after privatisation. But neither the campaign against big landowners grabbing the little holdings nor a love affair worked out. So he headed back north, settling into the miasma of little dwellings spread beneath us. Cardona surveys the panorama, with its views of downtown El Paso in one direction, and to the south, burgeoning breeze-block and cement housing crawling down into the valley and up the other side, dogs and children scattered across the maze of streets and radio masts piercing the sky. 'More than half a million people,' says Cardona, 'and only a single high school. Anyone who can't make it, throw them on the trash heap.'

In the eye of this storm, and at the far corner of Sanborn's café in the business district of Juárez, Sandra Rodríguez Nieto sips a cup of green tea. Even more striking for her courage than for her beauty, Ms Rodríguez is one of the senior reporters on the principal local paper, *El Diario*. She is direct about the peril in which she lives and works.

To do her job, Rodríguez must drive by night through zones of the city few dare penetrate, to listen to people who may know the answers to questions that seem unanswerable. She recalls an even-ing on which she had to abruptly end a conversation with a man who calmly announced he was informing on the cartels to the authori-ties. Although the job is becoming increasingly dangerous, Ms Rodríguez remains tied to the city and to her work here. But, she acknowledges, 'I am very, very concerned for some of the reporters who have young families. There was a colleague of mine, a young woman with a child, who was going to do a story, and I said, "Let me do it – I don't have children." But this woman said, "I have to, like a duty, because it is my job." She wasn't looking for fame, because we don't have bylines anymore. She just knew we all have to carry on with this task to expose what is going on.'

But what is going on in Ciudad Juárez, Sandra? 'Above all, we are talking about a culture of total impunity,' Rodríguez says. That word — "Impunidad" — is the title of a book on which she is working. 'Impunity starts at the top, with the people like those who arranged for the building of Riberas del Bravo where it is, on a marsh, who created the monster of a city purely for reasons of personal gain. The entire urbanisation of the city is a criminal enterprise'. And it goes all the way from those in power to the very bottom, and everyone in between: right down to the kids growing up in this criminal city, who never go to school, who instead go over to the narcos. All the way down to the 16-year-old boy I wrote a story about who killed his mother and father and little sister. When I asked him why, he said, 'Because I could.'

The message to reporters in this city implicit in the murder of Armando Rodríguez, after the head of the victim hanging from 'Switchback Bridge' was found in 'Journalists' Square', could not have been more articulate. But in Juárez — while newspapers elsewhere in the country have been silenced by the cartels, and some 58 reporters killed — *El Diario* continued to publish detailed, daily accounts of the bloodbath despite and since the murder of Armando Rodríguez (no relation to Sandra, though of course they knew each other as colleagues). The response of the cartels — or whoever the killers are — came on 16 September 2010, when a *Diario* photojournalist, Luis Carlos Santiago, and a young intern working with him were attacked by gunmen as they left the paper's office for lunch. Santiago was killed and the intern wounded. A week later, *El Diario* published a dramatic front-page open letter addressed 'To the Leaders of the Different Organisations That Are Fighting for Control of Juárez' and titled 'What Do You Want From Us?' The editorial, significantly, addressed the criminals as 'the de facto authorities in this city,' avoiding the word 'cartel' so as to encompass all possibilities regarding who the killers might be — including politicians, police, gangs and the army. 'We ask you to explain what you want from us, what we should try to publish or not publish,' wrote the editors, adding, with a chill, 'so we know what to expect.'

The open letter was wrongly reported in the United States as a sign that *El Diario* was going the way of newspapers like *El Manana*, further downriver in Nuevo Laredo, which has agreed, very reasonably, not to report the slaughter in order to protect the lives of its own reporters after an editor was murdered and its offices attacked. But *El Diario*'s intentions in publishing its editorial were quite the reverse: 'We cannot stop reporting what is happening here,' Sandra Rodríguez says. 'It is our duty, and we all of us feel it strongly — that we have a truth to tell, and we are committed to this first of all, because this is our community and because we know it better than anybody'.

As importantly, but unreported in the US, *El Diario*'s open letter went on to lambast the Chihuahua state secretary for education and culture, Guadalupe Chacón Monarrez, who had accused the media of becoming 'partners' in the violence by reporting it because, she said, 'psychological terrorism is achieved through communication.' 'What is it she wants us to say with respect to that?' countered the paper. 'That we will stop publishing?' Chacón Monarrez, the paper asserted, 'has created a smokescreen, to hide the incapacity of the authorities who have not done their job.' Unlike its journalists, who have done theirs beyond every call of duty.

Indeed, it is hard to imagine journalism as brave and dangerous as the kind Rodríguez and her colleagues practise in this murderous demimonde. The writer Charles Bowden urges that if the Pulitzer Prize is worth what it claims to be, it should be awarded with honours to the staff of *El Diario*, whose concerns are very much those of the United States as well as Mexico, and whose offices are, after all, only a short walk from Texas. 'If the Pulitzer stands for publishing the truth against the might of governments and at risk of your life,' Bowden says, 'then this year [in 2011], the nabobs of American journalism have it easy: give all the newspaper prizes to the people of *El Diario*.'

A spaghetti junction of slip roads connects US Interstate 10, as it skirts within yards of the border fence and roars through El Paso, with the Patriot Freeway that runs north from the frontier. Today, the cars are arrayed in all their glistening glory. No, not those above on the freeway, but in Lincoln Park below, where they are attended to with loving care by people from the tough barrios on the edge of town. A 1968 Impala Caprice convertible from the fourth generation of Chevrolet's iconic line is flanked by two Mexican flags and has the slogan *'Viva La Raza'* emblazoned across the bonnet in palace script. Its interior consists of puffy cream-coloured cushioning. A 1961 Impala, in burgundy, has the famous 'bubbleback' roofline and bears the motto 'Low Riding Girl'. Indeed, in front of the car is a child's doll dressed in a micro-skirt in the colours of the Mexican flag – next to which is a real live girl to match, subject of quite a few photos as she poses against the vehicle on the highest of heels, showing off the hair she combs, her legs, tattoos and, supposedly, the 1961 Impala. The car seats are upholstered in – what else? – green, white and red with 'Chicano Power' embroidered into them. The occasion is a heart-warming one: the Chicano Arts festival – part car show, part family cook-out, part gang convention, part arts fair, part afternoon disco, part Mesoamerican costume parade for children. On the concrete stilts supporting the freeway are graffiti paintings of the pyramids at Teotihuacán and the assertion: 'Lincoln Park: *El Corazón de El Paso'*, the heart of El Paso. The pillars cast shadows in long straight lines along which rows of people, mostly extended families, align their deckchairs in order to eat barbecued picnics, their lines rotating like the shadow cast by a sundial, in order to stay in the shade. But the real matter in hand is the battle of the car clubs, which loosely reflect neighbourhoods and even gangs – or clans – and in which mutual respect and rivalry co-exist in roughly equal measure: the Oldies Car Club of New Mexico pitched against the Imperials of El Paso, the Latin Pride Car Club against the Natural High Car Club, the Our Story Car Club against the Ekztazy Car Club. 'It's about cars, it's about Chicano pride and it's about your own pride in your own club, which is your brother's,' says Alejandro Dávila from eastern El Paso – an imposing man with the Aztec calendar tattooed on his shoulder and a two-headed serpent on his shin below the cargo pants. 'It all started here, man – hot rods, Zoot Suits, that's our heritage here in El Paso and we're conscious of that. The *chicas* are part of that scene, they go with the cars. You got the car, you get the *chica*; if you don't have the car, you gotta find some other way, see what I mean?' And he laughs, begging the obvious awkward question about gangland and drug dealing. 'Yes', he says carefully, 'there is a role for some *chucos'* (someone from El Paso) and what Alejandro calls '*Segundo Juárez* which I guess means Juárez USA, you know – overspill of what's going on over there. There's a kind of connection between Juárez and a gang this side by the name of *Barrio Aztecas.*'

'But,' Alejandro continues, 'most folks aren't involved in the other side. That's gone way heavy now. We stay this side, just *chuco* clubs, car clubs. The crazy stuff don't come over here too much, and not at all on the car scene. The car scene is family, brothers, maybe people who've been in jail, but come out again and cleaned out. We do heritage now, Chicano heritage. And I mean they're beautiful things, man, very beautiful objects and a lot of work and money to get to that condition. It's all connected in the cars, you know – brotherhood, neighbourhood, all kinds of connections.' A woman arrives and ends the conversation. 'This is my mother,' Alejandro says, introducing a cleaner for the school district, and they wander off together to admire cars and join the extended family for empanadas.

Alejandro has a point: the much-vaunted 'spillover' of violence across the Rio Grande has not occurred (yet) other than as a series of episodes. Drug traffickers and their support systems in gangland – never mind the 'legitimate' financial sector – seem reluctant, so far, to draw the authorities' attention on the border itself. Of course, there are exceptions that go beyond the daily routine of trans-border carjacking and mugging. An edition of the Juárez morning paper *El Diario*[9] in September 2009 carried a grisly picture of a pair of severed arms folded and resting on the chest of their former owner, Sergio Saucedo, aged thirty, kidnapped in the El Paso suburb of Horizon City one fine afternoon in May. Three men wearing black baseball caps and black gloves burst into his home and took him away in a maroon Ford Expedition, as recounted by his wife and a bus load of schoolchildren who bore witness to the abduction. Saucedo had convictions in the USA for money-laundering and cocaine possession with intent to distribute, and had been taken by his captors across the border to Juárez where his mutilated body was found four months later, dumped in a busy street. Soon after the kidnap, on 15 May 2009, José Daniel González Galeana was gunned down outside his hacienda-style villa in El Paso: he had been a lieutenant for the Juárez cartel, turned informant for the customs service – apparently rumbled and tracked down by his erstwhile *compadres* to become what the FBI in El Paso considers to be the highest-ranking member of a Mexican cartel to be assassinated in the US.[10] One in eight El Pasoans is employed by the military and, in August 2009, the FBI arrested an eighteen-year-old soldier based at nearby Fort Bliss for being contracted by the Juárez cartel to carry out the execution.

The fate of informants, and those in flight to the USA from direct personal threat, is among the preoccupations of a tireless man who helped organise the car club corral and works from a little office on the low-slung Yandell Drive in El Paso: Eduardo Beckett, of Mexican-Irish descent, managing attorney at the Las Americas Immigrant Advocacy law centre. Most of Beckett's clients are families facing deportation, or those with citizenship issues or the other problems of any large migrant or immigrant community – appointments with families: mum and the boys in Beckett's office, daughter staying behind in reception to take a nap. 'Most people we see here,' says Beckett, 'have spent their whole lives in the United States, commit a crime and get deported. They're not educated, and they end up taking odd jobs back in Mexico. A few get a break, others end up in whorehouses or committing another crime. Then you have the others, who have worked sometimes ten years for US government agencies in Mexico – DEA, FBI, customs, police departments – on the understanding that if they give up information, they'll get a visa in return one day. It's called an 'S-Visa', better known as 'Snitch Visa'. But in my experience, once they're found out, or after they've testified, they're just clipped off, they're garbage. The agencies I deal with won't even admit they were informants, and they're sent back to the wolves waiting for them.' These special cases that demand Beckett's energy and motivation are of people who face almost certain torture or death if they return to Mexico, having fallen foul of the narco cartels for one reason or another.

Beckett surveys the paperwork, his caseload that looks like a truckload, with the air of an exhausted gladiator. This is a man who spent his student days knocking door to door for the United Mineworkers of America in Gillette, Wyoming, where 'all these folks wondered: What's this *brown* person doing up here?' He judges that 'most of my clients are looked upon as trash by the system, and that's the starting point. With the informers, it's even worse – that they were doing it for the money, and they're snitches. They know that if they cross back over, they're going to get tortured and killed. They have nowhere else to go, they're banged away before they get to court, and they're stuck. And still the feds just say: "No, I never saw this man." We argue that they're in danger and a hell of a situation, and they just wash their hands of them or say these things can't be decided in open court because it constitutes a danger to their operations and the way they do things. They argue for internal relocation within Mexico, but there's nowhere to hide in Mexico. And if you're an honest cop, put in an impossible position and in fear of your life, they argue that if you're a cop of course the criminals will be out to get you. They say that's not persecution. We're accused of imputing some kind of politics into what the narcos are.' So the law on asylum, persecution and torture is not ready for post-political war, unable to recognise persecution unless it has a political colour. The law of the United States is not ready for, and cannot cope with, the post-political nightmare of which the narco war is herald – organised terror by branches of the state whose only political colour is white powder.[11]

Among Beckett's cases is the extraordinary story of Martín Espino Ledezma. Ledezma was a mounted police officer in Juárez but left the force due to the personal strain of his division's duty digging up the bodies of young women who had been kidnapped and murdered. He left Juárez in 1993 for his wife's native town of La Junta, to work as a singing teacher. La Junta lies at a strategic hub for the transportation of drugs into Juárez from the south and there Ledezma was approached by the leadership of the local PAN party, and asked to help in establishing order in 'a lawless town'. Then Ledezma found out, he claims in an affidavit filed in a federal asylum case in El Paso, that his sponsor in the PAN 'was a puppet for [the narcos] in La Junta'. One day, 'two individuals came to my office and said they came on behalf of Pepe Estrada [the local municipality president] to put me at his disposition, for me to work for organised crime, and for this they offered me a substantial amount of money . . . My job would consist of distracting the federal police officers at the checkpoints near La Junta. I would also have to put the officers under my authority at their disposition. When I denied this they went from being kind people as they had presented themselves at the beginning to being very overbearing and threatening.' After Ledezma refused to cooperate, 'on 3 March 2008, Mr Estrada sent some men to kill me.

This occurred that day, which was my birthday,' says Ledezma. His wife answered the door, outside which two SUVs had parked and 'at least six individuals with high-calibre weapons who had surrounded the house and pointed their guns toward it. They told her I should watch out, and wherever they found me, they would kill me, that it didn't matter where I went, that they could find me anywhere because they had connections all over Mexico.' It was later 'confirmed', claims Ledezma in the same affidavit, that Estrada was working for *La Línea*, the Juárez cartel.[12]

I wish life was still like that, my Uncle Tommy says/
But everything's gone straight to Hell since Sinatra played Juárez/
You could get a cheap divorce, get your Pontiac tuck and rolled/
You could take your dolly to the dog track in her fake chinchilla stole.

The Fiesta Club, The Chinese Palace, The Old Kentucky bar/
The matadors and baseball heroes and great big movie stars/
Those were truly golden years, my Uncle Tommy says/
Cause everything's gone straight to Hell since Sinatra played Juárez

Now Uncle Tommy Gabriel he still plays Fats Domino/
He speaks that border Spanglish well, He owns a carpet store/
He lives out on his pecan farm, 'I don't cross the bridge,' he says
Cause everything's gone straight to Hell since Sinatra played Juárez[13]

It's a song by Tom Russell, who arrived in El Paso in 1997, from Brooklyn, in a U-Haul truck. Before that, he had taught criminology in Nigeria, worked in Canadian lumber camps, took time out in Norway and elsewhere besides. But now Russell is the deep-voiced bard of the border, 'one of the people who still thinks songs should tell stories' as he says himself. And of El Paso: 'Hell, the town has been semi-dead for pretty much half a century. If you turn off towards downtown, you'll hit the central Plaza with its fountain of fibreglass sculptures of leaping alligators. Up until the 1960s, there were real gators in there, but the drunks fell in and lost their arms and legs.' Russell likes to recall Johnny Cash's song 'Mean As Hell', in which the Devil is looking for Hades on earth, and God gave him 'a plot of land near the Rio Grande which sounds like El Paso'. Notwithstanding which, Russell bought an adobe on three acres 'not to find my identity so much as to lose it', he says. Up the hillside was Cormac McCarthy, who 'lived in a rattle trap, trying to do the same thing. To be left alone to write. Unfortunately, fame and fans hunted Cormac down and chased him to Santa Fe. I'm still here.' El Paso, he says, 'is an abandoned midway of cultural impoverishment. When big corporations and big business came calling, decades ago, the city council and powers that be delivered an ultimatum, which went something like this: We'll allow you to move in here, but what are you going to do for us? Big Money squirmed with distaste and walked away.' As a result, Russell adds, 'the city fathers left in charge bought up water rights by paying off the city council and turned El Paso into one big freeway, the agricultural land both east and west chewed up to build strip mall sprawl and substandard housing'. For all that, however, 'El Paso is my own Patagonia. Outside and over the edge. Lyrical in its essence, tragic in its fate, comic in its existence. But it's a peaceful place. You find that amusing? The war has not spilled across the Rio Bravo. Life is cheap and simple. I like the people.'

We are sitting over dinner at a restaurant squeezed between the suburb of Sunland Park, just over the New Mexico state line, and the border, the other side of which is Anapra, the poorest *colonia* in Juárez. Another train rumbles by, the railway line backlit by the glow of the city Russell sings about in another song called 'The Hills Of Old Juárez' – a smuggling ballad. It is the city his fictional 'Uncle Tommy' loved until everything went 'straight to hell', and which Russell used to love to visit for bullfights and the Kentucky Club, the city where Steve McQueen died. But Russell, like Uncle Tommy, thinks twice about crossing the bridge since everything went to hell; moreover, he says: 'I wouldn't sing some of those songs now, like "The Hills Of Old Juárez"; any idea that drug smuggling was in some way dare-devil or romantic – bandits under the mesquite trees – just ain't admissible any more. But that ain't to say I don't miss Old Juárez, and the way it was.' Russell has a new song now, about drugs coming north, guns going south, and the ghost of Benito Juárez watching on, and shedding a tear.

Like Tom Russell's, my memories of Juárez are of a city that explodes at night. On a Saturday, the *Esfinge* – Sphynx – disco, shaped like an Egyptian pyramid behind what was the Holiday Inn, was pullulating with a multitude of drinkers and dancers, mostly girls spending their *maquiladora* wages like there was no tomorrow. For this is a strange economy: wages are pitiful by US standards, but not by those of the Mexican interior and if you want to go out dancing with your friends on a weekend, there might be the change with which to do so. Life on the border is all about inspection: you are forever clocking in and clocking out at the *maquila*, your productivity is overseen, your lunch break and even your toilet break are monitored, papers are scrutinised by the police, the army and at US border checkpoints if you are able to cross the bridge. You even get checked by the doorman and security guards here. But once inside, *Esfinge* is a different kind of inspection: that of a factory girl's body by every male in this ruffian ballroom tripping the light fantastic. But not all the men in their spiffed-up shirts and tight slacks will be content to admire from a distance, nor will their attentions be necessarily amorous. The horror of extreme violence against women came to curse (but also to define) this city, and predict the present way of violence in narco warfare.

In here, though, aphrodysia and the music were all that mattered. Like the concupiscence of Nero's Rome, that of Ciudad Juárez was connected in some perverse way to the impending collapse out there: the superabundance, the flowing drinks and a toss of the hair were a devil-may-care defiance of death in the streets and of hard factory grind. Kisses blown and conjoined, acceptance and rejection; tease and tussle; the chessboard diplomacy of the dance floor as it is anywhere else in the world, only in Ciudad Juárez it was lascivious like nowhere else – both in spite of what was happening outside and because of it. Those who preferred to economise or could not afford the $8 entry fee could go instead to a less lavish bawdyhouse like *El Patio* and listen to a band singing *narcocorridos* rather than the thumping techno at *Esfinge*. But *El Patio* was voluptuous enough, the debauchees in skin-tight jeans and boots of blue, red and green crocodile clinging onto the girls' fingertips as they spun them round with elastic arms but a firm grip, watching the skirts flying and breathing smoke rings in the thick, damp air. On the border, by the way, a *corrido* (masculine) becomes a *corrida* (feminine) when it is being danced to.[14] In *El Patio*, a visiting foreigner was a space alien, unworthy even of a threat – in fact, so absurd that the *bravos* would buy me a drink – just one. At *Esfinge*, though, an outsider who is not American got drawn in. It was all 'welcome to Juárez!' and clinking glasses of *'Paloma'*, which normally means a dove, but in this dive is tequila and grapefruit in a place where no one really belongs, apart from those counting the laundered money.

Back in Juárez seven years later, in 2008, the *Esfinge* was subdued. Amexica's great city of the night was ill at ease after sundown. Back again in 2009, the *Esfinge* has shut. The nine-storey hotel into which I check is empty apart from a boxing team from Chihuahua City on its way to fight in Finland. In 2008, Cardona and I went for a beer at another dive, Bar Amsterdam. There, one of the barmaids wearing the uniform red micro-dress, Giselle by name, had joined us for a drink. She told the quintessential Amexican life story about making it across the border when she was fourteen, getting as far as Denver and a decent job, only to be stopped ten years later because of a faulty rear light on her car, caught without papers, and deported. Back home, Giselle took the job in Amsterdam where she could be leered at for a living. She seethed with palpable frustration at it all. She wished the men who came to do whatever they thought they were doing here to cream their jeans would please just play Creedence Clearwater Revival on the juke box instead of that endless fucking *norteño*. Some time afterwards, in July 2009, Cardona sent a story from *El Diario* which read: 'Five men were assassinated in a spray of gunfire last night, while meeting in a bar called "Amsterdam". First reports said that two of the victims were beside the bar, and three were in the toilets . . . Word reached the first agents on the crime scene that one of the victims had been terminated with a so-called *Tiro de Gracia*.'[15] Giselle, according to the *susurro*, had apparently found herself a narco she liked and gone to work in another place, Dallas, which had been closed after its owner was kidnapped and shot dead. Cardona and I return to Amsterdam in October 2009, after the killing. We are the only customers there. We drink a quick beer and leave through the dark, deserted and menacing streets. 'The narcos,' says Cardona, 'decided to take over the night life, and in doing so, they killed it.'

Even in changed Juárez, there are still attempts at public life. In the parking lot of the *Plaza Renacimiento* there's an impromptu night rally of customised cars – not vintage classics like El Paso's, but roaring, grinding, screeching Toyota Camrys and Volkswagen Golfs, genetically modified with overdeveloped hubcaps and souped-up engines, and low-slung to make sparks against the tarmac. The young drivers race a little, but mainly just take turns to wheel around the lot making as much noise, smoke and smell of burning rubber as possible, for the benefit of onlookers. It's edgily hysterical, certainly, but 'the best fun in Juárez', says Antonio González González, proud owner of a white Ford Focus with what look like wings over the rear wheels, and a chassis millimetres from the road. 'During the day, in the maquila, it feels like everyone is driving the machines apart from me, but when I'm in my car, I'm driving,' he says. At the other end of the spectrum, 2 October 2009 was a big night when − as if Juárez hadn't suffered enough − Sarah Brightman came to sing, and close the fifth Chihuahua international festival of culture. There she was, onstage in the Benito Juárez stadium in the most dangerous city in the world, wearing a dress that seemed to come from the costume-drama wardrobe, flanked by crooning tenors and a bevy of dapper musicians. La Brightman's saccharine voice wafted across the air, heavy with sulphur fumes from the chemical works and this evening's news of seven more murders. The lyrics were inescapably bizarre in such a place: 'And I think to myself / What a wonderful world'. The finale, 'Deliver Me', rose to a crescendo of fake, packaged hope for Juárez, making way for the second elaborate and extended fireworks display in a fortnight (the *Grito* of independence was just two weeks beforehand). 'Deliver me, loving and caring / Deliver me, giving and sharing / Deliver me, the cross that I'm bearing,' she sang sweetly, into the murderous night.

And credit to Ms Brightman; many, influenced by the headlines, would have shied away from the appearance; she was right to keep it. For Juárez surprises those who come here on business or to take a peep. Journalists who arrive expecting to find a besieged Sarajevo or Grozny are disappointed (or relieved); BBC news presenters talking to cameras in bulletproof vests look downright silly. By day, not much has visibly changed in the little streets behind the cathedral and the plenteous Cerrajeros marketplace, especially on Saturday, when the shroud of work is lifted and Juárez's face is hearty and san-guine. This landscape of flotsam and jetsam for sale could only exist in a border town, and only on a border with America. Everything that is not quite *à la mode* north of the frontier lines the streets in overload quantities: sixties' furniture, soda fountains, hair curlers, Kelvinator fridges and Osterizer blenders, as though the sets of hundreds of post-war movies had been ransacked and put up for sale along Mexican sidewalks. There's a *Venta de Boilers Eléctricos y de Gas Termostatos*, a block of sixties' sofas and armchairs, another block of sixties' cookers and another lined with pre-digital electronics: reel-to-reel tape recorders and mono record players, even some early stereo. What a bloated modern city nowadays calls 'retro', Ciudad Juárez calls the Saturday market. The centrepiece, though – the masterpiece – is the car mart.

Here is Amexican border economics at its most eccentrically creative, supplying Mexico with refurbished, formerly discarded or crashed (and written-off) American cars between twenty and five years old. While the periphery of Juárez is an infinity of *yonke* auto-repair yards, the arteries running from the marketplace are lined with miles and miles of refurbished models. The man selling one stretch of them, Enrique, explains the system: 'We go all together in the back of a van, to the auctions, all over the US, then drive or tow back the cars that have been discarded. Some have been in car crashes and we rescue them from wrecking yards because we know we can do things with them the Americans won't. Others are just old, or damaged in some way, and the *gringos* offer such low prices that it's worth our while fitting them up. Sometimes, they're in a really bad state, and we need to do some work on the other side – in our relatives' workshops. That's why we usually go to the sales in North Carolina, Texas or Chicago.' One by one, the cars are fixed up to the point of being able to get them back, via a bribe to Mexican customs. In Juárez, they are made roadworthy again, driven back to the US, re-licensed, returned to Mexico and either registered with a Mexican plate or driven as a coveted American car. The export 'duty' paid to Mexican customs for this second, more delicate, crossing is usually an informal settlement with a specific officer or shift, explains Enrique. The system works: People come from all over Mexico to buy these cars.

This matey discourse carefully skirts any connection between this trade and that in drugs. As everyone knows, part of the *yonkes'* work is to fit up the ingeniously secret compartments within a private vehicle for hiding drug shipments across the border. Fitting out the cars is an expert business, with container spaces hidden in batteries, tyres, door panels and elsewhere, often treated with mustard, engine grease, hot chilli pepper or perfume in order to foil the dogs. But even without the more lucrative kitting up of vehicles for smuggling, the economy of the resale market is all the more baffling when we learn how cheap these cars retail for. I asked Enrique's understudy Emilio how much a beautifully done-up Chevrolet Impala costs. 'About a kilo,' he says, by way of a telling Freudian slip, with a completely straight face, meaning a thousand dollars. Most of this business is probably semi-legal, with customs officers working out private import duties, says Emilio, and creates badly needed jobs in a city busy training mechanics. But, given Emilio's ambiguous word for a grand, the term the Mexicans use for a car loaded with drugs for smuggling is a *clavo*, literally, a nail. And there is a bar just up the road – the local, indeed, to which the mechanics and salesmen retire for a beer and snack – with a great nail rising from its roof, called, of course, *El Clavo*.

To say that little has changed in the marketplace is not strictly true. There are army Humvee jeeps patrolling the crowds and fridges, soldiers in pale desert camouflage, weapons at the ready, safety catches off. And similar trucks driven by the federal police, in dark blue ninja uniforms, eyes peering from behind their ski masks. And nobody is quite sure what exactly the Mexican army – an enigmatic but highly potent power throughout the country's history – is up to.

One of the striking things about the spiralling violence in Juárez is that it escalated dramatically during 2009 despite wave upon wave of military reinforcements. The Mexican government's insistence that an increased military presence is the only way to confront the drug violence makes Juárez the litmus-test city of its policy. It is a test spectacularly failed. In January 2009, there were some 5,000 soldiers in Ciudad Juárez. On the first day of March, an additional 3,200 troops were deployed in the city with a massive show of force alongside 700 federal police officers, all under the banner of what the military now called Joint Operation Chihuahua. The new troops had new uniforms which could not be duplicated, said the operation's spokesman, Enrique Torres, after accusing narco death squads of dressing up as soldiers to carry out their executions.[16] There was a brief respite in the slaughter, but only a brief one, and as soon as 26 April, Mexico City sent 5,000 more soldiers to Ciudad Juárez, bringing the total to over 13,000. His efforts at police reform in ruins, Mayor Reyes Ferriz announced that the military would take over police functions and other arms of civilian authority, would man checkpoints, conduct house searches, challenge extortion rackets and guard crime scenes.[17] By 21 April, a former air force lieutenant, Jorge Alberto Berecochea, who had taken over the 6th police district, took journalists from the *Washington Post* on a tour of the Casas Grandes *colonia*, to demonstrate what the paper reported to be the 'sudden, surprising calm' in Juárez.[18] 'The cartels are basically wiped out here now,' Berecochea said, making a point barbed with half-truth. 'They're not operating, at least not in Juárez.' He explained the 'cockroach effect' the army had, scattering drug traffickers, and proclaimed: 'Ciudad Juárez: right now I'd say it's the safest city in Mexico.'[19]

It was an extraordinary claim. Two months later, the plot thickened: the army said it had captured twenty-five cartel gunmen who went about their murderous business dressed as soldiers. They were never named, and if they were ever charged, the case disappeared like almost all the others. By early June, the escalation and pattern of killing continued – often targeting teenagers. Three adolescents were among five people executed on 13 June, according to the magazine *Proceso*. Three more the following day, next day, another five.[20] By midsummer, Howard Campbell, an expert and author on the Juárez drug war at El Paso University, estimated that 90 per cent of those killed were street-level drug dealers, not smugglers of drugs into the United States.[21] And so it continued through 2009, by the end of which 2,657 deaths had been recorded in Ciudad Juárez alone.[22] From these statistics, and the nature of the executions, a second heresy arises among the attempts to explain the inexplicable in Juárez: that the violence has intensified not despite the army's increased presence, but because of it.

One especially savage massacre was meted out in August 2008, off the Avenida de los Aztecas, at a drug rehabilitation centre called CIAD No. 8. A car pulled up on the dirt track, the *sicarios* alighting and shooting to death nine recovering addicts while they were at prayer. The executions lasted fifteen minutes, and accounts from eyewitnesses reported in the local press suggested that military jeeps had blocked off any impediment to the executioners' progress, guarding their way, while others said the killers were dressed in military uniforms (something, claims the army, that cartel killers do). Certainly, the rehabilitation centre is only a few blocks from the impressive Campo Militar 5-C, on the main road. Gangland graffiti painted on the stricken building and in the alleyways give some clue as to why, perhaps, the authorities had a stake in this carnage: '*Locos 23. El Signo*', and '*Signo* RIP' read the paint-sprayed tributes. *El Signo* was a member of a street gang, apparently now penitent or at least 'clean', whom rivals wanted rubbed out, possibly with army approval. Or maybe the army wanted him and his fellow patients killed – no one knows, for the systematic massacre of the city's most wretched outcasts is Juárez's cruellest mystery. 'The army,' says Ignacio Alvarado, one of the original heretics in the Juárez media, with Cardona, 'is like Spiderman. It has a double. There is the real Spiderman, and there is his dark *doppelgänger*.' No emergency services arrived to help the wounded from the rehabilitation centre massacre – they were taken to hospital by trucks driven by staff and neighbours. Hours passed before the police arrived. No one has been arrested. It was after this attack that the Red Cross in Juárez said it would stop treating gunshot wounds in rehab centres and would not respond to emergency calls after 10 p.m. after death threats made over their internal radio network.[23]

There are three interpretations of the why, who and wherefore of mass killing in rehab centres. One is that of Pastor José Antonio Galván, who runs a rehab clinic and asylum on the outskirts of town called *Visión En Acción*: that the cartels – Guzmán's Sinaloa and the *Línea* heirs to the Juárez cartel – are picking out former *sicarios* and other operatives who once worked for their rivals. A twist to this is added by a former patient and now an assistant at another rehab clinic who wishes to remain anonymous: that the cartels have an interest in eliminating their own: the logic being that if former cartel foot soldiers are trying to clean out, rehabilitate and fix themselves a new life, they would become dangerous – no longer bounded to the organisation and knowing too much. And there is a third possibility, the heresy, advanced by Cardona and Alvarado: that the Mexican army is using the crisis to either facilitate, by default, or even engage in a campaign of what they call '*limpia social*', literally 'social cleansing' of society's unwanted outcasts, the undesirables, drug addicts, street urchins and petty or more-than-petty criminals. The army hardly dispelled this notion when the general in charge of the 11th military district of which Juárez forms part described each death on his watch as that of *'un delinquente menos'* – one criminal less. The occasion was a press conference on 1 April 2008, at the State Palace in Chihuahua City, when General Jorge Juárez Loera told the assembled journalists and cameras: 'The media are very important to us. Tell the truth, say what you have to say, but say it with courage. And I know that the media are sometimes afraid of us, but they should not be afraid. I hope they will trust us, and I would like to see the reporters change their articles and where they say "one more murdered person", instead say, "one less criminal".'[24] Sandra Rodríguez of *El Diario* was herself subject to a terrifying slander by the army in 2008, after she began investigating human rights abuses by the military in Ciudad Juárez. When she raised a question about the violations at a press conference, a Mexican army general singled her out and said: 'You look suspicious to me'. 'They were suggesting that I work for a criminal group', says Rodríguez. 'They had even been talking about it with the delegate of the federal prosecution service in Juárez, suggesting that I was compromised.' Such an affiliation – an outrageous allegation in the instance of Ms Rodríguez, of all people – is a death sentence in the Mexican media – a number of journalists have been killed not because they were crusaders for truth but because they were placements by one cartel or another, taken out by a rival. Requests were made for access to the army for this book, to ride with its patrols, discuss general strategy as well as these allegations in Juárez – including a request at the highest level with President Calderón's adviser, Ms Sota, in Mexico City – but were not granted.

One of the most compelling public figures to emerge from Juárez's war believes that all the above explanations of the killing in rehab clinics and of the poorest on the streets can be concurrently true, including the heresy of *limpia social* by the army. Gustavo de la Rosa Hickerson is a fascinating man. Born to a middle-class family in rural Chihuahua, he came to Ciudad Juárez as a boy to do two things: live rough and train as a lawyer. De la Rosa explains all this over an Italian dinner after his second day in exile in the USA – in flight from death threats by the Mexican army. During the 1990s, he was appointed governor of Juárez jail, a formidable task and dangerous position for anyone. He brokered a truce between street gangs that confronted each other within the prison walls, and so presided over a period of peace, shattered only after he left, when, in March 2009, a riot between gangs caused twenty-one deaths.[25]

In April 2008, de la Rosa was appointed legal director of the Chihuahua branch of the National Human Rights Commission, a rare institution of self-policing by the Mexican government. Established in 1989 by the Interior Ministry, the commission has independent judicial power and can refer instances of human rights abuse to the appropriate prosecuting authority, and this was de la Rosa's role in Chihuahua – in theory. Soon after the arrival of the military in Ciudad Juárez, during early 2008, de la Rosa began to open files on what he believed to be abuses by the military. From January of that year, he collected 154 complaints against the army, including 'allegations of house searches without warrants, arbitrary detentions, torture, abuse and even killings during the detention of victims'.

De la Rosa was on his way home from work on 4 September 2009, he says, when he stopped at a traffic light. A driver pulled up alongside him, rolled down his window, and imitated a pistol with his hand – 'like this', says de la Rosa, and he makes as though to fire through a barrel made of two outstretched fingers, with recoil. The motorist said: 'Quieten down, or we'll kill you.' When de la Rosa asked his own commission for physical protection, he was refused; indeed, his superiors in the state human rights commission headquarters at Chihuahua City ordered him to stop taking statements from alleged victims of army abuse. Soon afterwards, one of de la Rosa's bodyguards was shot dead. On 22 September 2009, de la Rosa walked across the bridge into El Paso, and exile. He stayed with his brother, resident in the US, and on Thursday 24, had lunch with his son and daughter in the restaurant of the century-old *Camino Real* hotel, downtown. After eating, he kissed his children and bid them goodbye that they may cross the bridge into Juárez and return home before dark. Then he sat down to talk.

He has an imposing stature, a wild mop of white hair and white beard – everyone, including him, says he looks like Father Christmas. But there is severity too, and in this circumstance even a certain vulnerability. De la Rosa talks about the notion of *limpia social* – social cleansing – going back a long way in Juárez, to the 1950s when, he said, undesirables and criminals 'would be taken up in aircraft, and simply thrown out into the desert'. De la Rosa does not believe that *limpia social* can account for all or even most of the deaths in Ciudad Juárez's war. But, he says, 'I believe the police know who the expert executioners are, who the people are fighting the cartel war at street level. I believe they know who is in the Azteca gangs, and who is in their assassination squads. When I was at the jail, the adminstration, CERESO, had a map in the office showing which *colonia* gangs affiliate to which cartel, and quite a lot on specific individuals, which means that when they affiliate to a cartel, they know exactly who the rivals are. The information that we have is that when the killings involve known members of the Aztecas, they are carried out by Guzmán's people, and vice versa. And as we know, elements of the police will themselves be at the disposal of one or the other.'

But, de la Rosa continues, ordering a fourth coffee, 'another group of killings, about four to five hundred this year, are of *malandros* – common delinquents, junkies, nothings – such as those in the rehabilitation centres, crack dens and abandoned houses, taking drugs. They are always people expelled from society: low-lifes, addicts, dressed shabbily, often homeless. They play no part in this war, beyond the fact that they are drug addicts, they have no affiliations and their deaths have no logical explanation. And they are killed in a different way to the drug dealers or informers. They are not ritually murdered or mutilated, and I don't think these killings are the work of *sicarios* for the simple reasons that I don't think anyone would want to pay the money the cartel *sicarios* charge in order to kill *malandros*, and the style of killing is entirely different. You would not need a *sicario* affiliated with Guzmán or *La Línea* to kill *malandros* who had gathered to try to clean out in a rehabilitation centre. Cartel *sicarios* either use a few bullets or fire sixty bullets accurately through a small area, like a car window. The *malandros* are also killed by experts in killing – but differently, in ways characteristic of soldiers or the police, in a hail of bullets, sprayed all over the place, mechanically but without regard to the amount of ammunition spent, as is characteristic of military commandos or death squads. The victims are nothing, but their murders are systematic and cruel. I don't have any hard evidence of this beyond ten homicides and fourteen disappearances, but they are all humble people, poor people, not narco traffickers, and I observe that this kind of mechanical killing of the *malandros* suggests training in the army or federal police. They're always after poor people in the poor *colonias*, breaking down doors, taking the young men away and if there's no young man, they take the father, and hardly ever a drug dealer or serious criminal – always *malandros*, low-life.

'I would say,' he observes, less forensically, 'that the army has come to defend the politicians, not the people. I said publicly that a culture of delinquency is growing in the army. My mistake, or my offence, was that I got involved in military matters. Let me say, though, I don't think the soldiers are necessarily directly responsible for many of the killings, but I am convinced that the assassination units are operating with their knowledge, or trained by them, and often you can see the killers working on one side of an army checkpoint, then on another. I notice this when killers go into the rehabilitation centres on some occasions, and more often into houses to kill maybe four or five people, day after day: they often do this within three hundred metres of an army checkpoint.'

De la Rosa asks where I am staying. The *La Quinta* on Geronimo Avenue, as always, I reply, nowhere fancy, but it's good and clean, with a fantastic view of Juárez. 'I'll come there too,' says de la Rosa, without so much as a toothbrush. 'The family and I will only get in each other's way; I need to be alone to think.' He checks in, half-recognised by the girl on night duty who comes from Ciudad Juárez, goes to his room on an upper floor and makes a phone call sitting on the bed. The news is not encouraging: an intermediary through whom de la Rosa communicates with General Loera urges him to stay away from the city. 'I must try and get hold of the general, then my wife, in that order, so I know what to say to her,' he says, shifting from the bed to the desk. This tower of a man seems suddenly vulnerable; these are clearly private calls, so the best thing to do seems to be to get him a beer from the fridge in that room of mine, number 262 on the other side of the motel. '*Negra Modelo* or Bud light?' I ask. 'Bud light', he answers quickly, 'with lime.' De la Rosa's room faces out directly onto Interstate 10, cutting virtually across the open doorway, trucks roaring by a short distance from where his head will be, with luck, sleeping. Mine, as always, is at the back, tranquil, over-looking the border and a panorama of Juárez by night, twinkling lights and belching smoke beneath my favourite balcony in America. I offer to get de la Rosa's room changed to the rear, in the interests of slumber and the view. 'No, it's fine.' He smiles as another truck grinds by his doorway. 'I prefer to look at El Paso.'

CHAPTER FIVE

The Human Junkyard

The procession of the possessed sets out soon after the quickening of the eastern sky, while the sun is still low, and meanders its way along the littered bank of dying grass beside Highway 45, as the road departs the raggedy outskirts of Ciudad Juárez heading towards Nuevo Casas Grandes. There are 113 of them: walking like marionettes, some mumbling to themselves, some shrieking out loud, others laughing awkwardly or else silently lost in fretted, crazy thought. They are patients of *Visión En Acción*, a rehabilitation centre and mental asylum on the chewed-up edges of the city, for people enduring the hallucinogenic horror of withdrawal from crack cocaine, crystal meth, heroin, methamphetamine, 'blue water' glue – and the rest. Some are just schizophrenics to whom no other place would open a door, who have found themselves in the company of the recovering addicts. And they all love this walk, three times a week for exercise. And no wonder: the patients spend most of the rest of their lives within the concrete walls and behind the iron doors of the rehab compound where the desert strewn with old tyres and garbage meets the gangrened urban outskirts, just past an army checkpoint and one last Oxxo convenience store before the open road. Some of them even live behind bars – in cages, padlocked, for the safety of others and themselves. Some are former killers, some are former nurses, some are former drug traffickers, some are former strippers – but almost all were drug addicts, now 'clean', but journeying through an inner landscape of nightmare and cold turkey. Indeed, it has been quite a night, punctuated by cries, screeching and laments piercing the still of the desert, and the rattling of metal bars against the chains and locks that bind them.

But night has passed now, its phantoms dispelled with the dew on the creosote bushes and discarded tyres. And as the caravan of the mad makes its way along the roadside, the walkers gesticulate wildly at passing cars, at each other, at thin air or whatever monstrosity or delight they see in their mind's wayward eye. Some motorists look aghast at this surreal parade, and swerve away from it, across the carriageway, lest something untoward happen at close range through the car window. Others, though, are regulars along the route and are acquainted with the procession and even some of the individuals. The driver of a white tanker carrying drinking water hoots and waves, and those walkers who notice the greeting wave back, and call out strange acknowledgements in return. Alejandro, wearing leather headgear and goggles for vintage automobile driving, bursts into a jog in pursuit of the truck, then stops suddenly, distracted by something in the distance that has caught his eye, or at least his imagination. He used to deal drugs, he says, 'all over the world – in China, Japan, and of course France'. There is Manuel, striding along – scary Manuel, who keeps trying to kill his mother, on advice from a rapper called Mr Bone, who visits his visions escorted by 'four little witches'. And there is Becky, 'Crazy Baby' as she calls herself, one of the team leaders and in high spirits this morning, singing '*Escucha la canción de la alegría*!' – listen to the song of happiness. A man called Antonio needs to wear a diaper, only it has come loose and flaps around his thighs as he walks, bare-legged, in a motion of semicircles in alternate directions, leaving a trail rather like that of a snake but occasionally barking like a dog. A twenty-one-year-old called Olivia arrived only this morning, and now tries to make what she can of her new circumstances, clutching at a doll. Crazy Baby Becky takes it upon herself to keep the newcomer company and make sure she feels welcome. Up on the road itself, at the edge of the tarmac, is Josué Rosales, the man who keeps *Visión En Acción* ticking over, day to day – a former heroin dealer and street gang fighter in Los Angeles, he now sees to the running of the refuge, and this morning must act as sheepdog, to ensure no one wanders onto Route 45 and under a truck. Like the one carrying groceries, a big one, which now passes by with a hooting salute to the parade that sounds like a great mechanical fart, and the more cognisant walkers call back, knowing this driver well: 'Señor Oxxo! Hola, Oxxo!' – the name of the store chain emblazoned on the vehicle's side. But Marisela, once a topless dancer, prostitute and crack addict, lags behind in silence; she has had a hard time so far today, troubled by *'muchas memorias'* and had been tearfully worried that the pastor who runs this remarkable institution might be late, and the walk not happen.

But she worried needlessly, for there he is, up front, leading the way, José Antonio Galván, who established and directs *Visión En Acción*. He has a full head of silver hair which he wears 1950s style; he has his trousers tucked into his boots and carries a long wooden staff to steady his long stride, adding a biblical feel to this exodus to nowhere in particular along the road, 3 kilometres and back again. He, too, from time to time, breaks into a jog, then walks to talk awhile. 'This is the human junkyard,' says the pastor, with a sweep of the arm towards his flock. He was one of them once, a street-wise kid from Juárez who lived illegally in Los Angeles and El Paso, got deported, became a drug addict on the streets back home and 'hit rock bottom, man, the very bottom before I was saved by the Lord.

'We are the people no one wanted,' he says with a kind of pride, 'cast out. This is where they send the trash that no one else wants. I run a recycling centre for human trash. I take the scrap people off the street, and treat them like human beings. When they come to us, they're not junkies or working women any more, they're not orphans, they're as much God's children as anyone. So just you think about this, brother: back there in the city, the *sicarios* are killing children, people are kidnapping and raping and killing young girls, and people are torturing other people to death, and people are cutting each other's heads off. In here, we're not doing any of that; here we are still alive, helping each other, not killing each other. Here, you can shout out loud, walk around naked with your diaper falling off, and no one will judge you or bother you. In fact, we'll hug you. We're crazy here, but we have love, and we have been saved.' All things being relative, the pastor has a point: in the human junkyard of Ciudad Juárez, the procession of the possessed is, in its peculiar way, a procession of the saved.

To drive south-west out of Juárez towards *Visión En Acción* is to journey through contaminated desert dust along boulevards of shopping malls, nightclubs and rooms-by-the-hour with names like 'San Judas

Quick Motel', past more compounds of prefabs built to house labour fodder for the *maquiladoras*, sprawling *colonias* built from scrap and wastelands controlled by gangs. In the dust of early morning, the Boulevard Oscar Flores passes the so-called 'green spaces' that a civic forum of more enlightened business people called Plan Juárez wants to 'reclaim', on which football is sometimes played, but which are more often becoming *dompes* for trash. *'Di No A Las Drogas'* reads a large hoarding – say no to drugs. Another displays an emergency number, o66, which few citizens care to call, because the people manning the hotline are universally believed to be working for the cartels or the security personnel under their control. People joke that calling o66 is the best way to talk to the kidnappers in the event of the abduction of a relative. The road skirts a hillside into which a giant white horse is carved in imitation of that in Wiltshire. It was done by order of Amado Carrillo Fuentes, the Lord of the Skies. Through the outlying military checkpoint, one arrives at a half-built breeze-block structure in the middle of nothing and nowhere declaring itself in careful paintwork to be an *'Albergue Para Discapacitados Mentales'*, a shelter for the mentally disabled – invariably for those fallen prey to drugs. On the wall beside the iron doorway are painted the logo of *Visión En Acción*, a sword breaking and a passage from St Paul's Epistle to the Ephesians, Chapter 6, Verses 11 to 17, which begins: 'Put on the whole armour of the God, that ye may be able to stand against the wiles of the Devil / Because we wrestle not against the flesh and blood, but against principalities, against powers, against the rulers of darkness of this world, against spiritual wickedness in high places.'

As the rust-coloured iron door is pulled aside by those who welcome us, it reveals what seems at first to be a courtyard of narco bedlam. People in various states of derangement and decay either cower and jabber to themselves, dancing around like puppets on strings, or rooted to the ground, just stare incredulously at the very air in front of them. Some come forward, as though propelled by electric shocks, to greet us. First is toothless Rebecca, in a red beret. *'Yo soy* Becky! Crazy Baby!' Then comes another man, diaper flying about his exposed not-so-private parts, with skin pitted by warts and scars. Then another, in a dirty track-suit top and shorts starts to talk, but whatever his story, which he tells in fits and starts, my Spanish is nowhere near understanding a word of it. But neither is anyone else's for whom Spanish is a native tongue. All around is the stench of tribulation, excretia, sweat, grime and a sense of miracle against all odds.

Pastor Galván, who founded *Visión en Acción*, has yet to arrive at this point. But the keeper of the lodge, Josué Rosales, starts to explain how these people came here. He has an inexplicable inner calm behind the intensity with which he speaks, in faultless American English, punctuated by Crazy Baby's contributions. 'Most of them have been addicted to drugs for years,' he says, 'crack cocaine, crystal meth, heroin; and some take stuff that can blow your fuse with just one hit. All of it made here in Mexico, intended for the US, but it only gets as far as the streets of Juárez. See that woman sitting over there, with white hair? She don't say much. She was a strip dancer in a club, got raped, got into crack, went to jail – but she's getting along better now.' Sometimes these people just roll up at the gates, some voice inside telling them they're desperately in need of help, 'which is why I live here', says Josué, 'to welcome them, 'cause they could come any time. Sometimes we find them on the street, talk 'em through it, and bring 'em in, to get 'em off whatever they're on, get 'em some food, attention, and get 'em off drugs. The hospitals, they don't want to know, and someone has to. I ain't got no medical training, but I need to know what to do with 'em, what kind of medicine to give 'em, how to book 'em in and calm them down if they're freaking out or having bad visions, before the doctor and psychiatrist come to check 'em out. Recently, we've had the Mexican consulate bring 'em in after they get deported, the police too – just bring 'em here, like junk, er . . . well, garbage, I guess I should say' – and Josué allows himself a smile – ' 'cause I'm a recovered heroin addict myself!'

So first comes Josué's own story, which he takes time out to tell, first on a rickety bench outside his little breeze-block and sleeping quarters 'office' on the outside of the heavy iron gates – a story he tells during four visits made over a year. The pastor keeps a video of Josué arriving at the home on a stretcher, unable to move, heavily bearded and skeletal, his skin like dry parchment folded over his bones. 'Sometimes,' Josué begins, 'you can be on both sides. You can think you're fine, and go back over to the other side. You flip, or take drugs just once, and you're back in the dark. Me, I'm fine now. I think. I do my best. I do my very, very best, and I'm still here, on this side of them gates.' He gestures towards the door through which he arrived as a patient some three years ago; his veins swimming with heroin and flesh punctured by needles, his bones broken after a car crash. He was in death's waiting room. 'When Josué came,' Pastor Galván would recall later, 'he couldn't walk – he could barely move. I had to amputate his finger myself. I kept it for a while, to show him, but eventually threw it away.' 'I arrived on St Valentine's day, I later learned,' says Josué. 'February fourteen, three years ago next year [2010]. I've seen the video; I was dying. I was in a coma. I was one of *them*.' And he gestures across the yard, as afternoon deepens, and a woman who has just eaten asks where the line for food is. 'I'd had a car accident and I couldn't walk, couldn't move. I lay here for a year on a mattress in a corner with the door open, watching all these crazy people jumping around the patio, just like I'd been jumping around downtown. And a voice said to me, "Kill this person inside you who is destroying you." And the Lord told me not to go back to being one of them again. All I wanted to do was walk, and get my life back.'

Born in Ciudad Juárez, Josué went to the San Gabriel Valley in California, to live and work. 'But I grew up with heroin,' he says. 'Heroin is always the same thing, wherever you take it – Juárez, LA, it's always heroin. I used to do heroin in California, and deal it too. I did cocaine, angel dust and all the other stuff, too, but got stuck with heroin. And when you get stuck with heroin, you're hanging out with heavy fellas. Some of them junkies have big houses and nice cars, but some again they sleep in the trash and empty houses. For a while, I had a job in an auto body shop, and I used to lift weights. I had a '62 convertible and a 1946 customised truck. In 1982, I got first place in a low-rider show. But I was doing heroin, I got busted, I went to jail, and that's where I blew my mind. I remember thinking, I'm too young for this – 'cause jail is all about gangs. I was given a knife, and I was fighting. Jail is where I went crazy. When I came out, I knew every gang in east LA and the San Gabriel Valley, and after a while out, I knew every barrio. Serious shit, shit, shit.' And Josué lifts his shirt and sleeves to show the scars from bullet wounds. 'That one happened in San Dimas, there was a battle in the middle of the night. A gang from La Susa shooting at us, but I got to take off, running right up the side of the highway, like that' – and he shoots a flat hand through the air, cutting.

Josué's recollection of his past keeps getting interrupted by reminders of his illness: patients. 'There are a lot of feelings in this place for me. I'm only the person I am now because I've been there and I know their feelings.' The narrative continues: 'I had to come back from LA because my mother was sick, but I kept taking the drugs – man. I was part looking after my mother, and part not looking after myself. By the time I got hit by the car, I was spending 250 pesos a day on heroin, that's almost a gram a day, five or six shots. I was in that scene; some of them got AIDS. Some got gangrene, like me. There's always heroin around for fifty or sixty pesos a shot, and you got people needing a fix, seeing other people carrying a load of money around and they're thinking, Hey, what's going on here? Hey, hey, hey – I can have some of that money if I shoot what I need and sell on the rest. That's what happens when you're totally hooked, totally fucked up. If you found some work and got fifty dollars, you'd spend it all on getting a fix. It was just: I've got to get fifty dollars so I can get fixed up.'

Even though this conversation happens in stages, months apart, Josué's narrative is punctuated by feral sounds from within the yard and dormitories looking onto it, sounds from some zone between a scream of pain and a peal of laughter. He continues: 'When a car hit my back three years ago next February, something else hit me too. I told myself that if I hadn't been using drugs, that car would never have hit me. I realised there was no one to blame, no one said "hey, try this", no one pushed me. I'd done this all to myself. They brought me here and I just wanted to go to sleep for ever. But I didn't sleep for months, I just watched and listened to the people who were like I'd been, for days, nights, weeks and months – feeling the pain, and watching. Then really I woke up, something exploded, *gracias* to the Lord. I'm fifty years old now, and I feel better than I've ever felt. When I go downtown, I always see four or five of 'em. People I used to shoot up with. And they call me *Güero* – blondie – just 'cause I lived in the US. Then someone'll say, "You looking good, man! Wish I could look like you. Wish I could stop taking all these cocktails, shooting all this junk." That's when my life gets weird, man, very weird. So I get glad I went through that pain, so I can help the others.'

From Josué now comes the street-level explanation of what is happening in Juárez. 'The market now for drugs in Juárez — it's very tough competition 'cause the drugs are getting so much stronger — and you go round the houses: "Hey, mine's better!" they say, "mine's stronger", and people have so many options. And especially in Juárez. If you're somewhere else, you'll come all the way to Juárez to get the good stuff. That's what a lot of these people were doing. Most of these people were addicts, selling drugs to feed their own habit. But they never see the big fellas. They buy it off people one step up the line, and here, you don't need to sell pure like the stuff that crosses the border. They buy it cut with rat poison, fertiliser or whatever; take some then cut the rest again to sell on. Cut it ten times, you get ten times the money; sell it in the wrong place, you get shot. The big guys are nothing to do with this level, I know that. They don't even know what Juárez looks like. They just make the $250,000 a day, the next guy down $10,000 a day, and so on, down to ten dollars a day. You know who you buy from, and who you deal to, but you never know beyond that, or who is moving all that coke or meth into the USA. Only other folks know that, way above the street.

'Do you want to see where I lived on the floor for a year?' Josué asks. And we walk through the iron gates again, into the world that was his, and from which he is now separated by the thin veils of his conversion, his responsibilities and a wall. To say that the stench is unbearable is no insult, it is just to admit that there is nothing like the suffocating stink of misery. A man speaks, Manuel — a former but now part-time crack and heroin addict on a high wire between saving himself and the abyss. When he hears the voice of a rapper called Mr Bone, he explains, coherently, 'Mr Bone tells me to kill my mother. "Kill Your Mother!" he says. "Kill Your Mother!" He comes into my room, and tears fall from my eyes. And when I get with my friends and we smoke some, the four little witches arrive, and Mr Bone too, and they order me to fight with guns.' For four years, Manuel has been here to try to exorcise Mr Bone and the little witches, and exchange the drugs for religion, or at least survival. 'He's getting there,' says Josué, 'but he ain't there just yet.'

A man wearing a football shirt joins us, Luis Noreto. 'He was a problem for a while,' says Josué, 'tried to kill someone three or four times, and tried to kill his mother.' (It seems to be a rite of narco-passage, this matricide.) 'Yes,' recalls Luis, 'I hit some bad luck. My mother was praying for me with a candle, but I thought it was a sword, so I tried to kill her, and she brought me here.' Luis was on crystal meth, 'rock' (crack) and sniffing paint-thinner. 'But now,' he says, 'I listen to Josué and have found Jesus Christ, and when my mother comes to visit me, I see my mother. I want to stay here forever, and help people like I was, to be like Josué.'

So just as Josué modelled himself on the pastor, so Luis models himself on Josué. And now, the pastor himself arrives. There is a term in African-American preaching: the 'charismatic' style, and the pastor is its Hispanic mutation. Galván has little (earthly) backing for what he is doing here, hardly any money, but 'with love in our hearts, smiles and hugs, and holding them close to our chest, we do what we do in here', he says, by way of introducing himself. The patients call out: *"¡Papi!"* – Daddy – with excitement, run to him, and he clasps them to his breast, kissing them, heedless of their weeping sores, stroking their matted hair. He looks a bit like a movie star acting the role of a former street-wise kid from the barrios. Which is exactly what Galván is – the former barrio kid. He has a tattoo of an Indian squaw on one arm. 'I was born in Ciudad Juárez, it's my city and I love it. But I was fourteen years over there, from 1972. I was an illegal in Los Angeles and El Paso. Yeah, the wild years! Man, I was making money, operating a crane, hanging out whatever; there were drugs and babes to spend it on and that's what I spent it on.' He was jailed for a period – he implies it was for drugs – and deported. 'And after I got deported and I was back home in Juárez,' he says, echoing Josué and gesturing towards his patients. 'I was one of *them*, completely lost.'

Galván's conversion happened on the streets upon which he was dying, found by street missionaries just as he now finds others for *Visión En Acción*. ' "The Lord Wants You," they told me. "Wants *me*?" I figured. *"Wants* me?" I used to tell those Bible people to get the hell away from me. "Get the fuck off my back!", I'd cuss 'em – but they treated me in a different way to how I'd ever been treated, so I started treating myself differently. Found a whole lot of needs I didn't have before.' There were several spiritual and physical adventures, culminating in an experience that led to the founding of *Visión En Acción*, an echo of the Good Samaritan: 'I was driving through the cold one night, and saw people sleeping by the wayside wrapped in blankets of snow. That was when the Lord gave me this mission.' The shivering roadside outcasts were Pastor Galván's calling to establish *Visión En Acción*, which he believes to be his destiny. 'The task,' says Galván, 'is to dignify the lives of these people, and to return those lives to them. Sixty per cent of them have completely lost their identity. They don't know their own name, age, who they are, where they came from or why they're here. They don't know what they were doing before they came here, but many get very aggressive when they arrive. That guy there, the big guy, he was brought by eight cops, handcuffed by the hands and feet — he'd tried to kill a guy in the USA. That one there had a problem with heroin, his arms were all pitted with holes and all them holes infected. And when we go inside their heads, we find that no one ever loved them or hugged them, their mothers didn't care and their stepfathers hated them, they never went to school — they sold Chiclets and newspapers on street corners or worked in clubs if they were girls. They started out on glue and paint-thinner, then different drugs, more expensive and dangerous drugs, then they're hooked.

'But we show 'em the path, the way out, because we've been there too, we know where they are, and how to find the path. I was there; I was living on the streets, trying to work out where the next hit was coming from, and the next meal, looking for food in trash cans. Josué, too — the director of the hospital brought him saying: "I'm giving you this man to die." No, I thought, he's already dead but we can bring him back to life. Now he's my right arm here, and my greatest fear is he'll slide back and start taking drugs again. He says he won't, he won't even use tranquillisers, but we're all on the edge here.'

The pastor finds it 'weird that there are also people here who know me from my old life', he says with a strange expression of disdain, whether for them or himself. 'They've seen me on the street and lying in a bed, and some of them try to take advantage of me; at first I had trouble with a couple of guys and a woman — I could see into their thinking: We used to change this guy's diapers and spoon feed him and now he's a boss? But mostly now they see me as a boss – they have to learn that's what I am. There's a hierarchy here, there has to be for it to function.'

There is a man called Alejandro Valencia García with electric-blue eyes who washes all the cars parked outside the centre, obsessively – wiping them down, polishing them; the visiting relatives' cars, our car and especially the pastor's. He's the man wearing vintage driver's headgear, a leather cap with earflaps, and tells the pastor: 'You fool everybody.' 'Why?' retorts the Pastor. 'Because I'm the only one who knows that you're even crazier than the rest of us,' Alejandro replies, and walks away laughing. 'He was a big drug dealer,' says Pastor Galván. So it was true, what Alejandro had said, out along the highway, though maybe not about China, Japan and France.

One Sunday, they await the pastor again. The iron gate is open, it being the Sabbath, and the patients mill around in the shade of trees they have planted, surrounded by benches made of rocks they have set and painted white. And when the pastor's car pulls up in the driveway, they surround it, clapping. Others stream through the doorway from the courtyard calling: '¡Papí! ¡Papí!' Others again, on the edges of the throng, wander and wonder, staring with a flicker of recognition, whispering confidences for themselves alone to hear. Because it is Sunday, the pastor is wearing a Zoot-style blazer in a paisley design, and black suede shoes. He looks as though he is about to sing 'Rock Around The Clock', but instead – once the multitude is settled – he gets out his acoustic guitar, sits down on the painted concrete bench in the shade of a mesquite tree and begins to sing. 'Who is your friend when you need Him?. . .' A woman sits at his feet, unties his shoelaces and ties them up again – a deranged but poignant echo of Mary Magdalene at the feet of Christ. '*Cristo Sí, Cristo Sí, Cristo Sí, Sí, Sí. . .*' The singalong is extraordinary – uplifting and disturbing. Some sing beautifully, and in tune; others wail like coyotes in a fit of lunar-induced ecstasy. 'Crazy Baby' Becky bashes a tambourine hopelessly out of time but with feeling, singing louder than anyone else, while a lady with a black shawl and cropped hair and a smock stares into mid-distance, smiles, drops the smile and weeps. Becky puts down the tambourine, takes her head and lays it in her lap.

Pastor Galván sits down to talk about things that have happened in the eight months since my last visit. 'The big thing now,' he says, surveying the bedlam around him, slightly stilled by Sunday hymns, 'is synthetic labs, synthetic drugs: we're seeing people's brains getting fried by crystal meth and ice; it's easy to transport, easy to hide, but it's causing a lot of dead people, lots of orphans and widows, and a lot more people like you see here. There's been an invasion of addiction in the city – they're everywhere, like human cockroaches crawling around looking for synthetic drugs. Juárez – it's sinking under a flood tide, a tsunami of addicts, all crazy. They've been given video games if they're lucky, so they know how to kill virtually, and when they're out of their heads and need another hit, they'll take the money to go out and kill for real jus' like they learned in the games.'

I ask about Manuel, Mr Bone and his little witches. 'He suddenly recovers his mind, and suddenly loses it,' replies the pastor. 'When he's doing well, he knows who he is. Then he hears the voices, telling him to go and kill his mother, and starts masturbating all the time, in front of people. He's been doing it since he was seventeen years old and started on crack, and now he's twenty-five.' One time, says Pastor Galván, 'I took him to the store to get cigarettes, and on the way back we stopped at the checkpoint and as we descended he was at the soldiers trying to get their weapons so he could kill the people in his head, and when I told them I was a pastor, they said, "What are you doing with this guy, motherfucker?" They never want to see me with him at the checkpoint again. Yeah, a lot of problems, Manuel.'

Manuel is a heavy-set man who sometimes contorts his face as he speaks, and at other times smiles as though concealing a secret. It has been some ten months since he explained about Mr Bone and the four little witches, and now he talks quite lucidly, though the content follows his own logic. 'I don't have so many problems now, but I do want to go back and party and I still have a big problem with my mother about witchcraft. She also says I beat her, which I do; I like to beat her. My brother was attacking me with witchcraft, but I don't have the papers to escape to the US. My wife is in Texas, living with my sister.' ('Rubbish,' says the pastor.) Mr Bone, says Manuel, continues to 'use spells and magic against me. And he's very tall, as tall as I am. My new mission is Thai boxing.' Manuel veers into a new theme. Can you box against Mr Bone? 'Hmm. If I recognised him and he made me angry, I could fight him. I'm dangerous when I'm angry.' And Manuel stops screwing up his face, and smiles that secretive smile. 'They gave me the weapons to do it, but I never intended to spray people with bullets.' We have to let that go. Manuel presses his nose against his face, squashing it, then pulls and stretches it – kneading it between his fingers as he talks. 'And then come the four little witches again, telling me I should go home, to have money and women.' Would he ever try to fight the four little witches? 'I want to fuck the four little witches,' replies Manuel. 'They look so sexy, they're *gringa* witches, blonde ones, Americans.'

We walk back, with the pastor, into the yard, the human junk-yard, the concrete quadrangle where the mad and the scared people roam. In a room off to the right, a man rattles the bars of his pad-locked cage, growling in short bursts, then suddenly conversing in a winning way, feigning lucidity, asking for help to be let out to return home to his family. 'Don't get involved,' counsels the pastor, 'he knows how to manipulate, even though his brain's gone. He tried to stab someone, so we call him '*Cholo*', the gangbanger. He can get very violent,' the pastor continues relaxedly, a matter of inches away from the cage. 'And Josué's problem is that he's not that strong yet, and if he tried to intervene between *Cholo* or Manuel and one of the other patients, he could get killed. When *Cholo*'s in a crisis, it's ugly, hard to stop him, so we keep him locked up.'

Bounding across the yard comes Rebecca, Crazy Baby, who, says the pastor, is usually 'more than half in command of herself', and is thus a supervisor of the thirty-six women patients. You can see her taking to her role – that girl crying during the singing this morning, whom Becky rested upon her lap. 'Ah yes, Lety,' says the pastor. 'Lety and Elia – they're sisters. They were found chained up in an aban-doned house. They'd been chained up all their lives, like dogs, ever since they were babies. Their parents were addicts and finally left them, abandoned.' We pass the line for food served by big Oscar, now a prefect for the men's wards, and we enter one of those for the women. The rows of mattresses and bodies stink noticeably less than the men's quarters, but the insects are just as populous and, as with the men, there is little distinction between being clothed and unclothed, although Becky's regime tries to keep things decent. On one mattress, Lety and Elia cling to one another. Both have shaven heads and wear long frocks. They speak – or rather, make squeaking noises – in fits and starts, staring hard and quizzically. They are like two little children, although they are in their early thirties. 'They're afraid of everyone,' says Pastor Galván. Apart from, it seems, Becky, who approaches them, and strokes their cropped hair. 'I take care of them,' says Becky, who is about the same age as they are, 'they are my little babies.' In this world, it matters not where affection comes from, only that it exists at all.

Becky has a deputy in her task as prefect: Marisol, who wears a woolly hat despite the September heat, and closes her eyelids when spoken to with a shy, childlike sweetness – and sadness. 'She was a waitress at a strip joint,' the pastor informs, 'a dancer, doing cocaine and smoking crack, and prostitution to feed the habit.' Now she sweeps the yard and cleans surfaces with a dirty rag, in silence. Marisol seems to know where and who she is, but keeps it all to herself. 'I'm jealous of Marisol,' says Becky. Oh yes? 'Yes I am, because she has a little baby, who they bring to visit her. I fell in love with him when he was three years old.' (Marisol's child is a girl.) Marisol also plays an important role here, adds Pastor Galván, organising the women's wards, their food, dressing and washing. 'But she's schizophrenic; terrible depressions, fits, loses herself completely. She had to be locked up for a year, she was so violent.' It seems unbelievable – this placid, timid, apparently crushed but gentle soul, but there is no such thing as a surprise in this place – only the threat of the worst surprise of all.

'Now we're in the firing-line,' says the pastor. 'Yes, us – mental hospitals, rehab centres. You had ten killed at the *Anexo* the day after the *Grito*; and seventeen were lined up and shot in August at the *Aliviane* – just little addicts, like we have. They're going round the rehab centres taking out people who had any business with the other cartels, and anyone else they take with 'em.' There have already been some 'funny phone calls', says the pastor, on another occasion – at dinner in El Paso, where he lives for safety. 'They called up and said they were the police – but that can mean anything in Juárez. Now we're in danger, we who run help for the addicts and crazy people, we're on the front line, just by being here and doing what we're doing. They could come for us any night now.'

Night falls over *Visión En Acción*, and the pastor has left. Josué – delegating some tasks to Oscar, Becky and Marisol – administers medication and shuts things down before retiring to his quarters. The darkness that falls is a deep one, out of which the pastor's fears of what has happened to so many other rehab centres loom larger than they do in daylight. The room, or rather the little cubicle of breeze-blocks, in which I am graciously hosted to sleep is, as Cardona points out as he leaves, 'right next to the entrance; the first they'd get to if they come tonight'. But the iron bed is already made up, and there's nothing for it but to settle in with Josué and chat away the evening by torchlight. We talk about Led Zeppelin and The Who. 'Man, they come from England? I never knew that. I used to love that stuff, but we don't get it in here.' He talks about his family, while we eat cold burritos, and about his cousin's husband, a US marine, who had 'fought in Afghanistan and against that other guy, Saddam Hussein – he kicked his ass too'. Josué makes as though to fire a machine gun: 'I heard from him all about those countries, it sounds like fun.' But Josué had recently attended his cousin's funeral: he died not in warfare, but 'in Pinkie's bar, having fun, you know [Josué shakes his hips, as though to jive], and in they came, looking for someone. Sprayed the place with bullets.' And Josué talks about his work and some of the people in his care. 'Look, what I do here is part of my testimony. A lot of people come through here, and we stare at each other in the eyes, and we can see the drugs; we know, yes we know we've been there. In that stare, I say it with my eyes that I've been even worse'n you are now. I say to 'em – staring hard with my eyes, 'cause they wouldn't understand if I spoke it – I say: "You've come through fire and water and so have I, so I know what you are doing here." And even though they're crazy, and can't hear a word, I think they kinda understand.' He lets on that the benign ones are not always what they seem. 'Becky can be real dangerous. Usually she's fine, but when she flips, she flips real bad, she's a violent one. When she gets angry with me she's threatening to kill me and all sorts. Oscar, he's desperate to make it. He really wants to succeed. But man, when he explodes, he explodes. He needs putting down real hard, real difficult to deal with.'

Josué wants to watch a home-view movie. He goes to his cubicle, next to mine, rummages around for his DVD player and sifts through the black wallet containing his collection. 'I got some titty ones, but, hey, how about this? It's about the crucifixion of Jesus, man, this one's gonna blow your mind; I saw it but not really properly.' It is Mel Gibson's *Passion of The Christ*, and into the player it goes. The bloodier the sufferings of Our Saviour get, the more Josué's devotion deepens. The flagellation is an especially savage and prolonged episode, Jesus lacerated to the bone. Josué is transfixed. A pitiless depiction of Calvary makes Josué sweat with empathetic rage, so that by the time of Jesus' convulsions of pain on Golgotha, Josué's eyes are popping out of his head. Only with the storm clouds, and winds that rent the temple shroud apart, does Josué relax again, and prepare for bed. There is one last tour of the courtyard, under the stars. However haunted their slumber may be, those tortured in the mind rather than by nails to the hands and feet are mostly asleep. The occasional groan of anguish drifts from the dormitories, on the desert breeze, sometimes ascending into a whine. Josué shines his flashlight through the bars of *Cholo*'s cage – he is motionless, under a heap of blankets. All told, it feels as though some untamed animal is at rest, its afflictions abated a moment, by the quiescence of unconsciousness. There is quiet, but the smell still lingers, though even that is tempered by the chill hanging from the desert night. Josué makes his way back through the kitchens to our adjacent sleeping quarters, and we exchange good wishes for the night, so dark in these windowless quarters, with nothing but desert out there, that even with eyes-wide-open one is blind as a mole.

The occasional truck rumbles by towards Nuevo Casas Grandes or back into Juárez, but otherwise there is silence. Josué has been both disturbed and excited by the sufferings of his Saviour, and the dark feels darker just for the fact of being on the edges of the murder capital of the world with 113 recovering maniacs for company, and only Josué and a wall between us. But it is not the maniacs that constitute the unquiet in the night, what with the events at *Anexo* and *Aliviane* a few days beforehand, and the trick is not to think too hard about those bloody bootprints all over the courtyard back there, the sticky crimson pools in the infirmary or the pastor's fears about this place. So long as the door remains shut, one will survive the night. Sleep comes (with a little chemical assistance), but for the laments that pierce the black from within the dormitories – the wailing, yowling, winnowing sounds of visions disturbing the sleep of the mad.

Josué's shuffling heralds the day. Through a crack in the door, now ajar as he begins his duties, a first hint of silver-blue across the eastern horizon makes its entry into my cubicle. The hills to the west, into which the Lord of the Skies' white horse is etched, respond with a pink hue, and dawn arrives. And into the morning, as the sun rises, they emerge into the courtyard to begin another day; mumbling, grunting or singing but mostly silent as they depart the land of sleep. The first task is to deal with the excretia that night has generated, the stench of which is best removed before it is intensified by sunrise. This involves teams organised by Josué, big Oscar and others, swilling buckets of water across the dormitories and floors. Part of the same operation is to change the diapers of those who use them, mostly men. The afflicted are lined up in a row outside their sleeping places while those with an awareness of where to direct the body's rejected matter wipe them down and apply new nappies. Then, with the sun bolder, come the showers. There are two of them, attached to the courtyard walls, and all 113 people line up to wash, men under one waterfall, women under the other — the line therefore twice as long on the male side. They leave their clothes in a pile on the concrete slabs, stand under the cold water, and may or may not be scrubbed down by the team of prefects, Oscar and his male assistants for the men, Becky and Marisol for the women. Some, of course, have to be unlocked from their cages for washing down, and this is supervised by Josué himself, working in overdrive. Some of them rattle the bars and scream to be let out; others, like *Cholo*, just wait in sullen silence to be called and temporarily released for cleansing. When the bathers are finished, they clutch their own shrivelled, crinkly bodies against the cold, dry dawn with their clothes or a towel if they can get one, go back round to their underwear and pile of rags and put them back on. It all works estimably well and smoothly, there is order in the mayhem. All the while, the patients acclimatise themselves to morning, test their walk, stop, reflect, walk a little more, stop again, look around them and work it out, whatever it is. They may smile or they may cry at the conclusion they draw. A man called Julio has been completely blinded by the cocktails of drugs he has taken, and complains of cold and the noise the others are making. Josué, working like there'll be no tomorrow, now appears with a collection of brooms, which he distributes. Becky commandeers one and sweeps every corner of the courtyard she can reach. Others follow her, some just stand there, holding their brooms. Alejandro, the former drug dealer, has already donned his open-top driving headgear and started cleaning cars again — the only one parked here and others abandoned in the desert. 'See that radio over there?' He points to a car stereo lying in the dirt. 'I got that from the truck with a broken window. I'll tell you something,' and Alejandro draws near, his breath heavy with something smelly, 'it's not a car, it's a plane. It flies.'

The sun is risen, it is time for the walk along the highway, and the pastor is late. They gather outside the gates, sit under the trees and wait. *¡El Pasco! ¡El Pasco!* they shout excitedly. Marisol stands alone, clutching a broom and weeping. 'If *Papí* doesn't come, we can't walk,' she sobs. Then she crawls back into her cave of silence. What's troubling you? 'Many things.' Memories? 'Many memories.' Bad ones? 'Very bad.' But the pastor will be here soon, and we can all walk! 'I just want to walk. It's so beautiful, the walk. My baby came to see me. But she's gone now. All I want is to have a nice walk, but *Papí* is gone too.' She cries again. 'It happens suddenly,' says Josué, 'you don't know what or why, just hurtin' inside.' But not for long, for a maroon car pulls into the driveway and here he is, pulling his staff off the back seat and off we go.

'We need money,' Pastor Galván cuts to the quick. 'People like you come and say they care, but we need money.' We stride out to the highway, and Alejandro stays behind to wash the pastor's car. 'Let's go all the way to Argentina!' Josué shouts from the roadside as the procession of the possessed winds its way to nowhere in particular, Pastor Galván to the fore, trousers tucked into his boots and pounding his staff into the ground. Out on the road, they talk, even Lety, who amazes: 'When we were chained in the house, we were like birds in a cage. When we walk we are alive,' she warbles.

And by the time we return, 3 kilometres down the road and 3 back to the centre, big Oscar has supervised the creation of a plentiful breakfast. There are vegetables, fruits, beans and rice. There is water and there is singing, led mainly by Becky who has not stopped her '*Canción de la Alegría*', song of happiness, since halfway down the road. The sun is high, the air is warm at last, and another day of heterotopia in the human junkyard begins.

We agree that whatever one believes or does not believe, the bedrock of Christianity is a progression from Crucifixion, via Descent into Hell, to Resurrection – essentially: Good Friday, Easter Saturday and Easter Sunday. And that whatever is happening here is hopefully some stage between Saturday and Sunday morning. But by the time we get to this conversation though, impending night covers the land, the gloaming begins to fall, the witching time arrives, darkness is visible to the east. We say our farewells, and make to go, until the next time. 'You call this a mental institution, but when you get back to the city, you're in the real madhouse,' says the pastor, 'back in the real human junkyard.' But he is interrupted by a figure who has clambered out of the yard and is now lurking on the roof, leaning over the eaves and silhouetted against the deep golden flare of last light on the desert horizon. '*Yo soy* Rebecca!' comes a voice between a croak and laughter. 'Crazy Baby!'

CHAPTER SIX

The Wind of Knives

In Aztec lore, life was a brief passage through a world of pain and malice, prelude to reunion with the ancestors after death. Beyond the boundaries of the world was a universe made from death, whence the winds blew from the four directions. Death had three realms: The House of the Sun, in the sky; a paradise on earth called Tlalocan, and Hell, named Michtlan. Most people − apart from those killed in battle or women at childbirth; those struck by lightning or lepers − began their journey in death through the underworld, in and out of Michtlan. The journey of the dead out of hell was a long and arduous one, across rivers and mountains, encountering devils demanding tribute. But it began with a voyage along a road guarded by a green lizard called Xochitonal, Sign of the Flower, and proceeded across eight icy deserts, through a wind so cold that the deceased needed to burn all his or her possessions − weapons, gifts of passage and the remains and clothing of any captives they had captured in war. The name of the wind was Izchecaya, the Wind of Knives.[1]

When the authorities finally gave Paula Flores back the medallion of the Virgin of Guadalupe which her daughter María Sagrario had worn around her neck, it was terrible proof of that from which Paula had been hiding some five weeks, refusing to believe that María Sagrario was dead. Paula held the medallion in her hands and implored the Madonna: 'Where were *you* when they did that to my little girl?'

Paula and her husband, Jesús, had last seen their seventeen-year-old daughter when she rose for work shortly before 4 a.m. on 16 April 1998, at their gimcrack home in Lomas de Poleo, a shanty of dwellings sprawled across high desert. Sagrario worked, like hundreds of thousands of other local girls, at one of the new factories, the American-owned *maquiladoras*. Normally, María Sagrario González Flores would leave for the afternoon shift with her father and elder sister Guillermina, but the CapCom company had changed her routine. Instead, Sagrario now took the lonely mile-long walk down unlit dirt tracks to the main route through another shanty, Anapra, where she would wait for the company-chartered bus to take her and her fellow factory girls to work. After Sagrario failed to return that afternoon, Paula went to the police. 'Did she like to stay out late?' they asked. 'Did she wear miniskirts and go dancing?' Paula, disgusted, made 2,000 flysheets: 'Missing Teenager. Please Help.' Eventually, she learned not from the authorities but a newspaper article that Sagrario's corpse had been dumped near her *maquila* on the other side of town.

There is a new word in the Spanish language as spoken in Juárez: *femicidio* – femicide – the systematic mass slaughter of women. There is no other word to describe the iniquity of a singular and savage phenomenon which appeared at first unique to this city at the heart of Amexica – mystifying and vile: some 340 young women found murdered between 1992 and 2001, when I first went to report on these events. Killed in different circumstances and varying degrees of sadistic savagery, with a further 180 or so missing. 'They have been dumped in public places, not even like animals; more like trash,' says Marisela Ortíz, from one of the groups campaigning to bring the killers to justice. The victims, she says, fit a pattern: 'they are poor, young, working class'. And when they are found, she says, some 'have been tortured, mutilated, bruised, fractured or strangled and violated'. 'The killers,' adds Marisela's colleague Rosario Acosta, 'take no trouble to cover up evidence. With these, the evidence is brazen, right there, every time. Whoever is doing this knows they are immune from the law.' 'When our search teams fail to find a body, one will appear next day,' says Marisela Ortíz. 'There's some code or language: "Just letting you know we are here." ' One body discovered in 2002, that of Erica Pérez, was found with her purse strings tied around her neck and underwear around her knees. The authorities say she died 'of an overdose', but would not confirm the results of toxicology analysis. Another, unidentified, girl was found wearing clothes belonging to a different teenager whose body was found along with seven others in 2001. Another, Esmeralda Juárez Alarcón, shut down the little market stall at which she worked in January 2003 in order to catch her computer class. It was dusk; plenty of people to intervene, police officers to be seen around, including a special downtown patrol. But Esmeralda vanished. Gabriel Alonzo, her boyfriend, still works at the stall opposite hers: 'I watched her as she left that day to walk to the school.'

And that same month in 2003, I stumbled into further horror, and a more sinister implication of apparent official complicity: yet more bodies found, and either outright denials or silence from the authorities over their existence – as if there were something to hide; something worse than ineptitude. On a visit to Lomas de Poleo, only to say goodbyes and pay respects to Paula Flores and present flowers before leaving Juárez one time, there is news. It comes from E.P. (whose name must be protected), one of the vigilantes patrolling the area in the absence of any police interest. E.P. had found three more bodies in the hinterland behind the town a few days ago. Strange, because the official number of bodies recovered for that month, January 2003, was zero. E.P. puts on a cap reading *Jesús Cristo Te Ama* – Jesus Loves You – and heads out to show us the location of his latest, grievous find. We set out, accompanied by María Sagrario González's remarkable sister, Guillermina, who has returned from work and is seeing to her mother, but for whom E.P.'s narrative is a recurrent nightmare and was once her work too. In rage and grief at her sister's murder, Guillermina had, she explained, established an organisation called *Voces sin Echo* – Voices Without Echo – to mobilise search parties in the deserts above Lomas de Poleo, and pressurise the authorities. But, explained Guillermina as we left the shacks behind and drove up into the desert, 'we disbanded it as a formal group. We were being used by the media, by the NGOs [non-governmental organisations]; people were profiting from us, pretending to help, raising money which never arrived.'

We pass through a gate marked in Spanish 'Private Property', and out onto land known to have connections with the Juárez cartel and to contain an airstrip, says Guillermina, for light planes carrying cocaine heading north, as well as roads used by no one except the *traficantes*. In this desert expanse, *Voces sin Echo* would comb the land day in day out, and E.P.'s tireless group still keeps watch for circling buzzards above a possible cadaver. He guides us to a bush to which plastic police ribbon has been attached, and demonstrates how he works, and worked last week, he says, pawing the fine sand: 'Suddenly there was a hand, then a severed arm.' The bodies were arrayed on their backs in a row, each in the shape of a cross, naked and recently killed, with two *maquiladora* uniforms strewn nearby. 'Their arms were chopped and stomachs ripped out,' E.P. says. 'You get used to finding them,' he adds. 'I've done this so many times.' E.P. radioed the police and fellow vigilantes, with some thirteen witnesses to his call, and the authorities duly arrived to take the bodies into official custody. 'When they came,' says E.P., 'they told us: "That's your work done. You guys can go now." If we hadn't found them,' he insists, 'nothing would have been done.' As we leave the accursed terrain, a motorcycle rider who has left a plume of sand as he headed to cross our path, waits at the gate to ensure our departure. He wears a balaclava mask, says nothing – and nor do we. Just get out.

Marisela Ortíz, who founded the campaigning group *Nuestras Hijas Regreso a Casa* – may our Daughters Return Home – had asked the authorities about rumours of bodies found that January. 'They denied it, outright,' she reports. Marisela Ortega, a journalist from the paper *El Norte De Monterrey*, was told the same, also Diana Washington Valdez from the *El Paso Times*, across the US border. 'We will provide any pertinent information to the public . . . except for whatever is considered confidential,' Valdez was told. To me, despite instant cooperation from the prosecutor's office on other questions, and offers to respond any time, not a word – until later, when E.P.'s terrible find was admitted to – on this latest discovery. Only one thing emerged as certain from this rueful development: the authorities of Ciudad Juárez were, for whatever reason, covering up the discovery of bodies of murdered women. And so another word in the Spanish tongue came to be oft spoken in Ciudad Juárez during these days: '*el encubrimiento*' – the cover-up.

The *femicidio* became a badge of Juárez: doctoral theses were published across university departments in the United States; films were made, including Bordertown starring Jennifer Lopez; many books were written, and the cause of the women and bereaved mothers in Juárez, trying to seek the truth against a wall of official resistance and suffering continual menace, became a rallying cause for the women's movement in America and worldwide. In the recent explosion of violence in the city – and implosion of the city – the *femicidio* continues still; unfortunately, it never went away. Only now it is everywhere across Mexico, directed against all ages of women, subsumed into the hurricane of violence and yet a distinct strand within it. An investigation by *Proceso* magazine in December 2009 showed that as narco-related violence spirals, so too does the intensity and cruelty in the killing of women.[2] They are related: deeply and terrifyingly so, argues one of the leading Mexican-Americans currently writing on these matters, Cecilia Ballí. 'The murders of the women in Juárez revealed a certain *style of killing*,' she says. 'The fact that many of the killings were sexualised in some ways related to the broader wave of violence we're seeing now against both men and women. It has to do with an expression of power, and a particular form of masculine power.' Ms Ballí is descended from one of the formerly great ranching families of the Rio Grande Valley (as will feature in Chapter Nine). She has garnered recognition for her brand of narrative journalism and teaches in the anthropology department of the University of Texas at Austin. 'Some of the media coverage of the women's killings made me cringe,' she argues. 'It perpetuated this idea of Mexico as an exotically violent place; the idea that only Mexican men are capable of these terrible things. The truth is that people in Mexico are struggling as much as anyone to understand this chilling type of violence. I'm trying as an anthropologist to understand what is happening, what it means, where it's coming from. Not that violence always means something, but specific types of violence exerted on the body can serve as a form of communication. I think the message has more to do with the killers than with the victims, which is why I think the *femicidios* ultimately signal a crisis of masculinity in Juárez, not a crisis with women.

'For me,' she continues, 'the killing of the women in Juárez is about power more than it is about sexual pleasure. The style of the violence demonstrates a specific kind of male performance and a complete domination of the other person.' 'Style' is not a word Ballí deploys lightly, and she will use it later to define the 'social performance' of the new generation of narco bosses and footsoldiers. 'Before, the violence in Juárez was merely functional, but now it's also meant to publicly display a specific kind of masculinity, and to reassert that male power at a time when the traditional forms of masculinity along the border are under threat. You see a similar thing happening between men; the way men are tortured by the military and police and by people in the drug world is often highly sexualised. So I personally see a relationship there between the two. Of course, since men and women's bodies and social status is different, the violence takes different forms and is experienced differently. But all of it is focused on violating the body and on displaying this kind of masculinity that is not simply what we usually think of as "machismo".'

As we have seen, it was the legitimate global economy that wrought fundamental change in Juárez, and provided raw material for the *femicidio*: the arrival of the *maquiladoras* factories brought to town a workforce that was at the outset almost 80 per cent female. According to an undeclared stereotype, women's hands are more dextrous, and women can be paid less than men and be more easily exploited. *Maquiladora* work is relentless, concentrated and hard on the eye: tiny adjustments to microchip boards, under a searing artificial light. 'We cannot really talk because then you would slip behind,' says Cinthia Rodríguez, who works at the same *maquila* as María Sagrario González. Two visits to the bathroom a day, no independent unions and production lines demanding punishing quotas which are then slowed down when inspectors visit from US parent companies. 'But it's good work,' Cinthia concludes. The arrival of so many young women workers plays hard with the *machista* foundations of Mexican society. For within the enslavement of the *maquilas* was a liberation of sorts. Esther Chávez Cano (who passed away in December 2009) established *Casa Amiga*, the city's first and only centre dealing with sexual and domestic abuse. She explained: 'Men found themselves no longer the breadwinner. Women exchanged subordination at home for subordination to the factory boss, but this offered a certain independence; they could buy clothes, leave their abusive boyfriends, wear mini skirts, go out alone. And, with middle-aged men unemployable in Juárez, this created frustration, a backlash against women exhibiting independence for the first time. Being financially independent and wearing a mini skirt, however, is not an invitation to one's death.'

'The *maquilas* provided meat for the killers,' says Dr Arminé Arjona, trying to gather evidence of the slaying. 'They bring girls from all over, and they're easy to get hold of, for whatever purpose.' 'From the *maquilas*,' says Marisela Ortíz, 'comes the culture of dispensability that underwrites the murders. The *maquilas* see women who work much as they see our city, as something expendable. So what if a woman is murdered? Ten, or a hundred? There are always plenty more.' 'If you want to beat, rape or kill a woman, there is no better place than Juárez,' Esther Chávez told me. 'There are thousands to choose from, plenty of opportunities and, thirdly, you can get away with it. The lives of women, especially poor women, have no value. They are faceless.'

The wind, cold as a wind of knives, whips up sand on the main road through the desperately poor *colonia* of Anapra, which lies beneath Lomas de Poleo, and to the edge of which the dirt road leading to the city arrives. When daylight comes, this road will be heaving with buses and trucks, kicking up the dust; but in the hours before dawn, the shadowy, huddled figures of young women emerge from makeshift homes, moving through the side streets and down to await the special buses which transport them en masse to work. It was down such a road that María Sagrario González walked after saying her last goodnight to her family. Along these dark pathways, many a young woman has disappeared, to be found, weeks later, violated and lifeless, in the scrub beneath the mountain, now a hulk against coming sunrise. At first light, three women from Veracruz explain that they are not even going to work; rather, they get up every morning and go to the *maquilas* in the hope of doing so, having been laid off by a company that went to China, where labour is even cheaper and more compliant. Another, Rosa López Contreras balks when approached by two males, then explains how she never waits for the bus alone now, preferring to stick with friends or else her dog, trained to raise the alarm. These women have forgotten the names of most of their murdered workmates, but María Sagrario González rings a bell. 'I remember her,' says Rosa, 'everybody knows her mother.'

Paula Flores has a singular, disarming way of talking about her daughter's murder; she moves her eyes across mid-distance and a strange, distant smile crosses her face when reaching the most heartsick passages of her narrative. The González Flores family arrived from Durango in 1995. Jesús had worked in a sawmill, but 'we wanted to come to Juárez to make our lives', says Paula, 'although of course the reality is different. After all, the boss of a *maquila* is like a government official; not a normal human being because he has everything he needs. All he cares about is that you arrive on time and work. That's all.

'This area is famous,' proclaims Paula. 'People say, "Oh, that's where all the murdered girls come from!"' It is a place of hutches on borrowed land; there are spirited little *abarrotes* – basic stores – here and there; Paula has managed to open one of her own. After her daughter was killed, she retreated even from the neighbourhood she had made home: 'My first reaction was to close off completely, thinking only about Sagrario. Her father was in a terrible state; awful physical problems. But then some mothers from the neighbourhood asked me to be their representative, and to act. And I did.'

From somewhere, somewhere remarkable, Paula drew insistent strength. The resultant 'Committee of Neighbours' meets every Sunday. Rather than dwell on the murders, it seeks to find 'ways to protect the living'. It has forced the authorities to install a few electrical lines, some water pumps, and even a kindergarten school. Not that the authorities had much to do with the latter, exactly: merely to give Paula a registration licence number. She found a teacher, and men of the neighbourhood built the little hut to which children are brought at 9 a.m.

'When I deal with the police about my daughter,' says Paula, 'I never know whether I am dealing with a criminal or a cop – probably both. But I feel they have the obligation to tell me what is going on. It's hard to go there every day and see how bored and hostile they are. We don't expect help from the authorities any more. All we can do is awaken the citizenry.' Along the main *Ruta Anapra* are painted black crosses on a pink background – 'Less to commemorate the dead,' says Paula, 'than to warn young women that they are in danger. I do everything for Sagrario,' she reflects. 'Sagrario was in the chorus at church and taught catechism class. She gave the children sweets, therefore so do I. From Sagrario. . .' And Sagrario is staring out from the photograph overhead, with serious, dark eyes. Paula wrings her hands. There is little point in asking for the big things, so we fight for the normal things in life.

'Only one thing,' laments Paula: 'I would love to have taken Sagrario back to Durango so she could have seen her roots. It is so beautiful there, and she was only fifteen when she left. But now it is impossible even for me to go alone.' Why? 'Because of Sagrario I cannot go. We're a tight family, and they always insisted that if I went back to Durango, I would take Sagrario with me. So that if I returned alone, she would have left them.'

'Everything still astonishes me,' said Esther Chávez at the domestic abuse crisis centre. 'Even though I have been fighting this for ten years.' Chávez had returned from Mexico City to her native Juárez to look after her sick mother, intending to leave again. But her mother lived until the age of 102; Chávez established herself, in Juárez, worked as an accountant, wrote a column in the *Diario* newspaper and opened a dress shop. As she heard about the lives of women in the city, she set up *Casa Amiga*. When the *femicidio* began, she tried to push the authorities for answers. The official response was to advise women not to dress provocatively, avoid walking the streets and: 'if you are sexually attacked, pretend to vomit. That will be repulsive to the attacker, and he will probably flee'. The unofficial answers came in a more distinctive tone. For a girl to go out alone is 'like a little treat', said former prosecutor Arturo González Rascón. 'Like putting a candy at the entrance to a school.' The former deputy state attorney general, Jorge López, remarked: 'When a young woman goes missing, more often than not, the parents will tell you that she was practically a saint! But then we start making enquiries and find out that she was out dancing every night.' The mother of one girl murdered last year was appalled to find her daughter's clothes tossed, some mornings later, over the fence of the back yard. When a police officer came to collect them, he remarked: '*La chava andaba de cabrona*' – roughly: that slut was asking for it. 'You must remember,' Chávez had counselled in 2002, 'that this is a state in which wife-beating was not a criminal offence until a year ago. Not unless the wounds were "visible for longer than fifteen days". And even since then, we have failed to get one conviction, because the cases are always said to be too "complicated".'

The tragic farce of the authorities' professed attempts to find the killers began in October 1995. Abdel Latif Sharif, an Egyptian former *maquila* engineer, was arrested and accused of seven murders. Despite a record of sexual violence, he pleaded innocent. The case hit problems: one of the women he was accused of murdering, Elizabeth Ontiveros, turned up alive. The police forensic expert on the case, Irma Rodríguez, said that the bite marks on his alleged victims did not match Sharif's teeth. Police then arrested a group of nightclub workers belonging to a gang, *Los Rebeldes* – the rebels – charging that Sharif paid them to kill seventeen women while jailed. They were accused of seven murders, including that of María Sagrario González, while Sharif's conviction for a single murder was overturned in 2000. The case against the rebels also collapsed, but the authorities claimed another break in February 1999, when a peasant opened his door one night to the sight of a fourteen-year-old called Nancy González, blood streaming from a wound above her eye. A bus driver had violated her, tried to strangle her and left her for dead. The abuser, Jesús Manuel Guardado, a.k.a. 'The Toltec' and other members of his gang, 'Los Ruteros' (The Trackers), were arrested and accused of fifteen murders, to which they admitted but later withdrew their confessions – extracted, they said, under duress and torture. Subsequently, the bus driver Guardado was convicted and jailed in January 2005 for his part in the murder of 113 women in Ciudad Juárez, along with nine other members of the Toltec gang, two others were also bus drivers.

Events then twisted along a strange course. On 13 May 1999, Sharif's lawyer, Irene Blanco, received a strange telephone call saying there had been a shoot-out between narco gangs and a victim, Eduardo 'Blancas' (an error in the name). She went to the hospital to find her son, severely wounded from three gunshot wounds. He had been driving when the would-be assassins opened fire. Injured, he stepped on the gas, making it to the emergency ward. While he was being operated on, agents from the state police arrived to ask the doctors whether he was dead or alive. A month after the attempted murder, a newspaper in Mexico City, *Reforma*, published the account of a whistleblower from the Juárez police, Víctor Valenzuela.

Valenzuela had gone to his superiors saying that he knew who was behind the murder of scores of women in the most horrific and sadistic circumstances: people close to and members of the Juárez cartel. The group was, moreover, protected by the police and government officials, including two police officers on the Sharif case.

They stand silent and spectral in the light of dusk: a rose-coloured hue in the sky reflecting the colour with which eight upright crosses are painted. They were placed in what was once a cotton field, now a dumping ground for old tyres, chemical drums, and stinking flotsam and jetsam. On the crosses – by contrast – sweet, fresh flowers are attached. Names are painted in careful script: Claudia Yvette, Brenda, Bárbara, *Desconocida* (unidentified), Laura Bernice, Lupita, Esmeralda, Verónica. They are the names of eight women whose mutilated bodies were found here on 21 November 2001. The land is exposed, at a busy road junction; rows of windows on the upper storeys of houses in a walled community overlook the site. No one wanted to see, or tell about, whoever left these cadavers.

Yellow police tape is still strung out along the ditch behind the crosses and there's another cadaver, that of a dog. The stench of rotting rubbish fills the air, along with the evensong of birds and hum of traffic. But whatever message those who dumped the bodies wanted to deliver, there is one from those who erected these crosses: they do not only mark and mourn, they stare, hush as death itself, in accusation, straight across the scrappy land to the cylindrical offices of the *Asociación de Maquiladoras* – the bonded factories' employers' federation. In the evening, the pink paint becomes luminous, reflecting the light of the building, and that of the twilight sky. During another dusk, on Mexico's Day of the Dead in November 2002, women from the movement for justice gathered here in tribute 'not just to the eight, but to all the dead women', as Marisela Ortíz said. Two torches were lit and planted in the ground. A cross made in stones was carved into the dirt and surrounded by candles. Flowers were strewn and the Requiem Mass said by two priests: 'Lamb of God who takest away the sins of the world, grant us thy peace . . .' 'It is,' says Marisela, 'a funeral rite, a dignified burial for all of them.'

After years of little headway, prosecutor Arturo González held a sudden press conference, declaring that he had cracked the case.

Within five days of the 'cotton-field' discovery, two bus drivers were arrested: Víctor Javier García Uribe and Gustavo González Meza, and charged with all eight murders. Confessions to rape, killing and dumping the bodies were quickly secured, videotaped and shown to the press, with a suspense movie-style soundtrack. The drivers said they had been tortured, the authorities retorted that the wounds were 'self-inflicted'. The drivers retained counsel, Sergio Dante Almaraz and Mario Escobedo, ready to prove the procurement of invalid confessions under duress. On the night of 5 February 2002, Escobedo found his car being tailed by the police. He was on the cell phone to his father as the shooting started; the old man heard his son being murdered by a burst of automatic fire. The police insisted that Escobedo was mistaken for a dangerous fugitive and had shot first at their officers' car. There were bullet holes in the police car to prove it. Co-counsel Dante Almarez says he was advised, meanwhile: 'If you do not drop the case, we'll kill you the same way we did Escobedo.'

'It was an execution,' says the man at the heart of the case, Óscar Máynez Grijalva, former forensic chief for the Chihuahua state assistant attorney general, who handled the case of the two drivers. Máynez, having resigned in disgust at the end of January 2002, holds one of the few keys to this serpentine story. He is a young, curiously puckish man who, for all his passionate involvement, talks with the professional's air of detachment when we meet in the lobby of what was then the Holiday Inn. As tutor of police cadets and later chief forensic scientist, Máynez was the first to alert his own masters about the likelihood of a powerful consortium of killers behind the slaughter: he connected fifty-six murders between 1993 and 1999.

Máynez says the supposedly self-inflicted cigarette burns to the bus drivers' bodies and genitals were twin-pointed injuries made by two-pronged electrodes used by the police. As regards the Escobedo shooting, Máynez noted that bullet holes in the door of the police car allegedly fired by Escobedo were on the *other side* (the driver's side) to that which was supposedly attacked, and on the other side from the wreckage of the lawyer's car — making it a defiance of physics for Escobedo to have made them. And anyway, adds Máynez, 'whoever shot those holes in the police car, they were not there immediately after the incident. Pictures, even those in the paper, clearly show no holes'.

Máynez points to no specific culprit, but he is lucid on that about which he is certain, even as far back as 2002. One: that 'the authorities and business interests in Juárez have been thoroughly "narcoticised". Big drug cartels are a force you need to deal with if you go into government. You can't fight that, and – more important – you are able to make a lot of money out of that.' Second: 'I think behind many of the murders lies an organised group with resources. There are big, powerful forces behind this. The only certain thing is that fact, and that they will continue killing.'

The eight bodies in the 'cotton field' were a last straw for Máynez, even before the torture of the bus drivers. When he checked their DNA, in only one case did forensic evidence give a positive identification (the others either misidentified or the samples contaminated). Five of the bodies, moreover, were covered in 'big pieces of concrete rubble. I thought inevitably possible connections to the construction industry, heavily "narcoticised", with concrete easily traced. But those leads were never followed up. After two days, "case closed".'

With Óscar Máynez gone, the forensic burden fell upon Irma Rodríguez Galarza, who examined body after body, and even spent time roaming the streets under cover. But on 25 July 2001 – two years after she had forensically discarded the case against Sharif – Dr Rodríguez was preparing a lecture in Mexico City when someone asked her if she had seen the news: 'They shot up the family of some forensic scientist in Juárez.' Irma's daughter, Paloma Villa Rodríguez, and her husband, Sotero Alejandro Ledesma, had been gunned down on the porch of the family home in a brazen execution by men firing AK-47 rifles from two vehicles. The authorities expressed regret that the pair were caught in the crossfire of a drug-related shoot-out. No suspects were identified or interviewed.

There is one case that particularly disturbed Óscar Máynez, as it did his opposite numbers at the FBI in El Paso: the killing of seventeen-year-old Lilia Alejandra García Andrade, abducted on St Valentine's Day 2000 outside a television shop, her body found a week later. The murder, says Máynez, bears the same signatures as those of the women in the 'cotton field'. An FBI report on Andrade's killing was leaked to Mexico City's *Reforma* newspaper based on the testimony of three witnesses who, failing to gain a satisfactory audience in

Juárez, crossed the river. Lilia was abducted by hit men working for the Juárez cartel, said the report. The television store was known to be used as a conduit for cocaine dealing and among the attackers was a certain 'Raul', known to the authorities. After the girl was bundled into a white Thunderbird car, sounds of a struggle were heard, and a lookout disappeared into the shop. Taxi drivers parked on the other side of the street looked on, said the witnesses, doing nothing. 'Someone must have seen something,' says Norma Andrade, Lilia's mother, 'and the only people who could possibly get away with this is someone who had some connection to the police.' The FBI document was dismissed by Juárez authorities as 'erroneous'. But across the river, the *El Paso Times* newspaper reported that people in Juárez, falsely claiming to be FBI agents, were knocking on doors in search of the witnesses.[3] Lilia's body was dumped 300 yards from a *maquila* factory owned by the ProMex company. She had been held alive for an estimated five days, raped, tortured and strangled. Forensic reports suggested she had been bound by police handcuffs.

Norma Andrade is a wounded but formidable woman, in stature, gesture and courage. 'What kills me,' she says, 'is that the people who did this are out there somewhere, maybe doing it again to some other girl. But I am sticking with my determination that whoever did this be punished. I am fighting impunity, that the authorities are allowing this to happen.' Over the years there have been endless suspicions as to who is behind the malefaction of Ciudad Juárez. There are theories about narco-cartel 'Juniors', male heirs to big landowning and *maquila* management families, about police cadres, common domestic violence, snuff videos and occult connections. 'Only one thing is certain,' presumes Norma Andrade, 'that whoever is killing is killing for pleasure.'

A primary school teacher, Norma lives on the southern edges of Juárez in a house so nearly joyful, filled with the sounds of playing children; children of neighbours, nieces, nephews, and Lilia's own two children, Jade, now three, and Kaleb, aged two. They call their grandmother 'Mamá', while their real mother's portrait sits on a shelf, inquisitive, gentle, bespectacled. 'The authorities never bothered to call,' recalls Norma of the day they found her daughter's corpse. 'I heard from someone out of the blue, and went down to the morgue. Even now, they never call me. I feel they have lied to me about my daughter's case. They said she had been tied with shoe-laces, but I believe it was police handcuffs. They said there were no marks of strangulation but I know there were. It's up to me to go down there and pester them. If I didn't, I'd never hear from them again.' Lilia's murder has been categorised as a 'crime of passion'. Her (separated) husband was accordingly interviewed and struck off any suspect list – but the crime not re-categorised. 'He wouldn't have the trousers to do it anyway,' sneers Norma, allowing herself a hol-low laugh. 'It's hard to think too much about it.' She exhales a deep breath. 'The facts speak for themselves. She had been dead thirty hours when they found her, but had been missing a week. My life has totally changed,' she reflects. 'You know, I was so happy; I enjoyed everything. But I saw the world through rose-tinted spectacles. Now, I trust no one. I could count them on one hand. Only two, actually, Martha Cabrera at the school where I teach, and Marisela Ortíz.'

After Lilia was murdered, Norma went to her daughter's former high school teacher, Marisela Ortíz, to urge her to become involved. An elegant woman who hides rage beneath a bushel of civility, Marisela founded *Nuestras Hijas* in the belief that 'it's time to chal-lenge the entire order here, and meanwhile try to take care of the mothers; and the children who are orphaned. Many of those are now growing up to be drug addicts, or gang members.' Marisela has her-self become the target of harassment. One night recently, she was driving home, trailed by an SUV. It followed her bumper-to-bumper, until she gave it the slip. 'I was terrified,' she says. 'I . . . well, it was a clear signal.' But it is not threats, says Marisela, that deter her. Nor even the response of the authorities, whom Marisela believes to be complicit anyway. Rather, it is the response of the *maquiladoras* that 'takes away our hope'.

Three thirty in the afternoon: shift change at the *maquilas*. The buses line up outside each factory, waiting to take their load downtown or back up to the *colonias*. The girls emerge from the fluorescent-lit world within. Some stay to chatter, one young woman simply boards the bus, sits down, rests her head against the pane of the bus window, closes her long eyelashes and sinks into sleep. Half an hour later, up the *Ruta Anapra*, the buses grind in convoy, kicking up great clouds of dust, old American schoolbuses, marked *'trans-porte de personal'* and household names: Philips, TDK, Delphi, Lear.

Occasionally, they pull over, fart a puff of exhaust and drop off workers who then weave their onerous way home between the shacks climbing the hillside.

The silence of the *maquila* companies over the slaughter of their employees was perhaps loudest in the case of seventeen-year-old Claudia Ivette González, one of the eight found in the cotton field. She had worked for Lear, but was sent away one morning for being three minutes late, having missed the works bus. That was the day Claudia, turned away alone, disappeared. The company's official response to her subsequent death was that 'González's murder did not happen on Lear property'. In response to the attempted murder of the fourteen-year-old bus rape survivor Nancy Illaba González, her employer said only: 'It is not our policy to hire anyone under sixteen.' The company even filed legal papers against the family for helping Nancy to forge false identification.

Outside the Juárez offices of the Chihuahua state authorities, a forest of little crosses was planted in a scrap of lawn, no longer there. Each cross, beginning in 1993, bore a name, starting with 'Ivonne Estrada Salas'; one for each recovered corpse, and towards 2003, they bunched for lack of space. Many were unidentified because, explained Rosario Acosta of *Nuestras Hijas*, 'so many girls came alone from the south, and have no one here that knows them'. Inside, there are frosty handshakes with the head of the special office for sexual homicides, young Ángela Talavera, in a smart skirt suit. She is happy, she says, to answer questions. 'Many were seduced by men who . . . took advantage of the situation. Most were seduced, but others taken by force. There is no fixed pattern.' Ms Talavera gets little opportunity to speak, as most questions are answered in perfect American English by a bullish, discomforting man, former head of the unit, now an aide in charge of 'liaison'. The aide details the categories of sexual homicide, and statistics involved. There have been 229 during the period under discussion, of which, he insists, 163 have been solved, leaving 66 ongoing investigations. Of these 229, 70 were sexual homicides, of which 24 have been solved, with 46 pending. The other categories include 'argument related', 'accidental death' and the largest, 'crimes of passion'.

I ask about the case of Lilia Andrade, categorised as a 'crime of passion'. When we talk about this particular subject, he says only, with contempt, 'her mother always misinterprets what we are saying'. On the recent 'overdose' case of the girl with panties pulled down and handbag strings round her neck, Ms Talavera pitches in: 'It is true her pants were slightly above the knee, and her handbag on her arm close to the neck. The medical examiner did the autopsy on the body. She did not have any type of sexual assault on her.' Óscar Máynez finds the argument laughable: 'I have seen no end of overdoses; they do not have panties halfway down their legs and purse strings around their necks.' The question of possible connections to weighty families or to the authorities is quickly dismissed. 'When I was in charge of this unit,' the aide butts in again, 'we did have information about a spe-cific powerful person. It didn't lead anywhere. It was one of these powerful people, but that didn't stop us then, and it wouldn't stop us now.' And the murdered lawyer, Escobedo? 'He wasn't the attorney,' snaps the aide. 'The attorney was his father. I don't know how it tran-spired, but unfortunately the younger lawyer was killed. However, it had nothing to do with the bus drivers.' 'Mario Escobedo *junior*,' affirms Óscar Máynez, 'was the registered attorney for one of the bus drivers. That is in the records.' The meeting concludes with an assur-ance from the aide that only three of all the bodies recovered between 1993 and 2003 were mutilated. The FBI, he says, is welcome in Juárez, 'for training' – but not to help with investigations. Meanwhile, the movement outside is preparing to act above the heads of the prosecu-tion team.

A year later, Rosario Acosta came to Washington DC for the first hearing at the headquarters of the Organisation of American states, as *Nuestras Hijas* endeavoured to consider legal action through the OAS Inter-American Court of Human Rights, sitting in Costa Rica and established by a Holocaust survivor, the formidable Thomas Buergenthal, now the presiding judge representing the United States at the International Court of Justice in The Hague. Rosario's journey turned out to be a first step down a long road, but when we met for lunch in Starbucks amongst the glass and steel of Washington, the pellucid light in Rosario's eyes was already fading. 'It is a desolate landscape now,' she says. 'There's no one to turn to in Mexico any more. While this game goes on, more women die. No, that road has ended now. We need to play a bigger game, or nothing. This can only be solved if we challenge the mechanism whereby the law is enforced. What drives me,' she says, 'is not "activism" any more, it is rage and sorrow. Sometimes I feel the organisation is full of women working together, sometimes that we are just a few, and sometimes that I am totally alone.' Rosario talks not only about the crimes, but their impact after ten years on Ciudad Juárez – and this in 2003, four years before the outbreak of the present narco war: 'This is a decomposing society. We are witnessing its destruction – women in pain who cannot turn to society, suffering cancer through stress, children to take care of, and domestic violence against women rampant.' The battering of women in Juárez is through the roof, she says: even those rare instances reported to the police increased by 300 per cent during the month after the eight bodies in the cotton field. 'It's logical,' says Rosario, 'if they can kill women and get away with it, then why shouldn't they beat them close to death? It's common now for men to taunt their wives: "If you tell on me, I'll dump you in the Lote Bravo" ' – referring to a canal where a number of bodies were found.'

'This message of complete impunity is having terrible effects in all directions,' said Esther Chávez at the crisis centre around the same time. 'It is now so bad that women come to me who cannot do anything about being beaten because their husbands threaten to kill them. What can I say if a woman says, "I can't come again, because he says he'll dump my body in the cotton field?" If the police would only intervene in these cases, we might start to break that cycle of impunity.'

Back again at Norma Andrade's lovely but poignant home. As Shakespeare would say, she 'bears it out even to the edge of doom'. 'I'm proceeding with my own investigation,' she insists with four-square resolve, 'looking into that *narco* television shop.' Down at the police station, 'their attitude gets worse and worse, but I won't let this go, whatever that means for me'. She slams the palms of her hands onto her knees, and turns her attention to Lilia's children, sticking pieces of yellow paper onto a stencil drawing. 'My husband doesn't like what I am doing. "Think of the children," he says. But that's the whole point. I do it for the children. So long as they look at me and call me *Mamá*, I have Lilia with me, and a reason to get up each day and fight on.'

In December 2009, The Inter-American Court of Human Rights ruled against the Mexican government in three test cases involving murders of young women in Ciudad Juárez. The court found that Mexican authorities failed adequately to investigate the murders of Claudia Ivette González, seventeen, Esmeralda Herrera Monreal, fifteen, and Laura Berenice Ramos, twenty – all killed in the 'cotton field'. The report, running to 167 pages, also said Mexico failed to protect the victims, and that the government must publicly acknowledge its responsibility, publish the sentence in official government records and build a monument in memory of the victims. Authorities must also investigate the murders and bring those responsible for the slayings to justice. The case was without precedent, the first time the court has ruled against Mexico on a human-rights complaint, and the first ruling to recognise murder according to gender – whereby women are killed only because they are women.[4] Benita Monárrez, the mother of Laura Berenice, had petitioned the United States for asylum such were the threats from police officers and government officials menacing her to drop her case. The ruling came just as mothers of some of the victims and their supporters set out on a march from Ciudad Juárez all the way to Mexico City. Two months previously, however, in mid September, President Calderón had undertaken a cabinet reshuffle, and appointed Arturo Chávez as attorney general of the Republic to replace the outgoing Eduardo Medina Mora. Chávez was formerly the lead prosecutor of Chihuahua state, a post he held during the 1990s, when investigations into the murders of young women went nowhere. 'It is like sending a wolf to protect the lambs,' said an opposition parliamentarian. In testimony before a Senate committe, Chávez had acknowledged failings by his former agency, but said he did his utmost as state prosecutor to investigate and prosecute the slayings.[5]

'This year, however,' Marisela Ortíz reflects, two weeks before the ruling in Costa Rica, 'the number of murders of women is higher than in the previous year, and that was an increase on 2007. We have had more than two hundred this year now; the violations and killings are of a different kind, many kinds – in the home, on the street, on the way back from work, and some directly connected to narco trafficking. But one thing is consistent: there is always a reason for not investigating. The police will always find a reason to wash their hands of the crime.' We meet in Sanborns, as we almost always did over nine years — only this branch is in an outlying shopping mall, not downtown, because it is evening. 'I can't get safely to the one we went to before,' she explains. 'I had to move out here, because of all the threats.' Marisela is dressed elegantly and exudes resolve and charm, but she looks exhausted. 'The state has found a way to be a little less offensive about the killing,' she continues, 'there are not the same insults about the girls inviting the kidnaps and tortures with their dress.' But 'we are still having to investigate all the cases ourselves, and they're different from before, more varied. Some are university students taken off the street, some are even of school age. Most are taken when they go downtown looking for work, especially since the recession, because that's where all the buses go, and they have to change buses after dark. They're not always raped, sometimes killed in the style of Mafia executions. But to be honest, it's not important to me how a woman is killed; what is important is WHY: and the fact is that these men kill women because they are women, and because they can.' And she echoes Cecilia Ballí's point: 'The killing of the women here was an indication of how things would go. That men would think this was a way to exert their power, to overwhelm women and other people with such violence, until such point as that kind of violence spreads like cancer and becomes a part of the culture. So you end up with this madhouse: there was an execution across the street from where I teach in September, and the *sicario* came to pick up his child so it could watch the execution.'

Marisela's own life continues to be threatened. 'My car was shot at twice, from a black vehicle with tinted windows, but I wasn't hurt,' she says, switching from coffee to a modest liqueur. 'I had to move house, and live apart from my daughters to keep them safe. And I have a couple of escorts, but they work indirectly to Arturo Chávez, so that since he was ratified as attorney general, my enemy is protecting me! Maybe that should make me doubly afraid. But I can't stop. The day I stop means that I have accepted that this is the right way.'

On 16 December 2010, Marisela Escobedo Cortíz, a mother who had struggled for two years to bring her daughter's killer to justice, was shot to death by masked men pulling up in a car in front of the governor's office in the state capital of Chihuahua, where she was staging a vigil. The murder took place while security guards at the portal to the governor's headquarters looked on. Ms Escobedo's daughter, Rubi Frayre Escobedo, had disappeared in Ciudad Juárez in 2008, only for her remains to appear a year later – burned and dismembered.

Ms Escobedo Ortíz was mounting a protest commemoration for her daughter outside the office when she was attacked; she tried to flee by running across the street, but the gunmen chased her down and shot her in the head. The principal suspect, Sergio Barraza, was the man Ms Escobedo believed had killed her daughter, but been released – to Ms Escobedo's horror – by the authorities she was picketing.

I revisit Paula Flores near Christmas, and she has a model nativity scene laid out on the floor. A centre for children in Anapra, which was merely a gleam in her eye and a piece of cleared desert scrubland in 2002, has been completed, thanks to private donations, and named after Sagrario. A sign of restored faith? 'Maybe,' replies Paula pensively. 'At the beginning, I prayed a lot, and I still do. Not in church, but here at home, to the Virgin of Guadalupe. I have always been a very religious woman, and believed in the resurrection and miracle of Guadalupe. But I never really recovered my faith after that moment, when Sagrario's Virgin came back to me, the one she wore around her neck. Maybe with time, I will get it back.' Her deep, comfortless eyes move across the photographs of her dead daughter, and back to mid-distance. 'Because justice is what I crave. Justice against her killer, and against all of the killers. There is no justice in Juárez, so I have given up on that. I have my work to do here, meanwhile, and wait for the justice of God.'

The Road It Gives and the Road It Takes Away

'What do the coyotes mean when they yodel at the moon?'
Edward Abbey, Desert Solitaire

I had always wondered about those people who sit next to motel pools that are only a couple of hundred yards from an interstate. But I did just that, after a long stay in Juárez, for a whole four hours, applying factor 15 and listening to the clamour of trucks thundering down Interstate 10 at very close range. The more exhausting Juárez gets, the more wonderful it is to sit by the *La Quinta* pool inhaling aromatherapeutic emissions from the chemical smokestack just over the border, embarrassed by hard-working cleaners, and soaking up ultraviolet, it feels like near wild heaven. This was the last day in El Paso for a while, and that before an evening with the singer Tom Russell, whose music I played after towelling down, on my way to Cowtown Boots and the Luccese factory outlet – and continued to play during the next several thousand miles, in various loop-de-loops across the Texas borderland on one side, Chihuahua, Coahuila and Tamaulipas on the other. One song made me especially sad and another made me especially happy. The first went:

> Then he finally got married and he had two little girls /
> But he didn't see 'em much cause he had to see the world /
> And the lie that he told 'em is I'm like most men /
> It's always down the road that the dream begins /
> And the girls grew up to be pretty and wise /
> They said 'you could've seen the dream by looking in our eyes'[1]

And the second:

But we'll sing 'Hallelujah!' — we'll sing it in the morning /
And thank the Lord for giving one more day /
For ones who passed on through, we'll sing this one for you /
For the road it gives, and the road it takes away[2]

Next morning after dinner with Russell and his wife, Nadine, I left El
Paso an hour before sunrise, right in my face along Interstate 10, heading into the eternity of Texas, which accounts for the entire eastern
half of the United States side of the border, the Rio Grande's left bank,
all the way to the sea. From El Paso to the mouth of the river and the
border's end is 645 miles as the crow flies, but as the Rio Grande flows
it is 1,254 miles, and eight times that by automobile, if one is zigzagging to and from the hinterland on either side. Driving alone in
America, the car radio is one's companion, channels changing of their
own accord as one proceeds from one signal range to another. So that
without touching the dial, one is serially accompanied by classic rock,
apocalyptic fundamentalist Christian soothsaying, country music,
pulsating *Norteño* and windbag talk radio. Every now and then there's
a public broadcasting station, discussing health care or playing Sibelius (why it's always Sibelius, I don't know). Channel-surfing is achieved
not by flicking the dial but by one of the main themes on any journey
through Amexica: boundless distance. The kind of distances film
directors can only measure with receding telegraph poles by day; the
kind of distances to which private cars surrender after dark, their drivers tucked up in motels, so that one shares the night highway almost
exclusively with trucks and the coloured lights with which each teamster makes his sixteen-wheeled monster distinctive. Distances across
which the endlessly long, thrilling freight trains rattle and surge so
that sometimes in the desert night, I would pull over just to wonder at
their thunderous passing — an excitement that never wears off — 'Nine
hundred thousand tons of steel' — as the Grateful Dead song goes — of
which an iron horse of the Santa Fe, Kansas City Southern or Union
Pacific is made, virile, all-conquering, ploughing and hooting through
the desert night.

For the Aztecs, Tezcatlipoca was the supreme God of the sky. He
was a 'Smoking Mirror', and no wonder, for the Aztecs made their
mirrors of gossamer-thin obsidian, and obsidian is black. It is at night,

heralded by the sumptuous colours of sundown and twilight, that the sky comes alive above the desert. In the skies over Amexica, one can attempt to learn the ancient Native American art of stargazing. I remember seeing Indians sitting alone in South Dakota, staring skywards for hours – and envying them. So I bought myself a metal chair from Walgreens for eleven dollars to try it myself. I parked, walked, and kept walking – although no landmark butte or rock seemed to get any closer, such is desert distance – until the dark blue band that is the earth's shadow opposite sunset rises and fades into the mauve light above it, which is that of the sun illuminating the atmosphere. After dark, there are three fundamental rules: 1, Wait at least fifteen minutes until you really start looking into the depth of the constellations of so many stars like God is throwing sugar at you from the deep; 2, Never forget that it is all moving (or rather, as Galileo realised and for which he was excommunicated, you are moving) and that you can watch this happen by keeping your eye on the horizon; 3, Always take your empty beer bottles with you back to the car. There is nothing more depressing than finally finding what one thinks is a spot of mystical isolation, only to discover that frat-brats and *cholos* have already turned the place into a venue for Miller Lite drinking contests and/or a landfill for the disposal of condoms and Burger King packaging.

Somewhere near Coyanosa, Texas, I recalled my father telling me as a child that many of these stars were extinguished millions of years ago, yet the light they emit continues to reach us, and there are only 350 million years before we in the Milky Way collide with our next-door-neighbour Andromeda. It all seems to make sense in the desert, as though the universe was almost as big as Texas itself. The endlessness of Texas: where there is nothing like the feeling that one is entirely alone – until suddenly, behind the constellations, fulminate the sounds of the creations of man: the roar of fighter planes and sometimes even a sonic boom. Or, after hours of nothing but signs by the roadside warning, with a gratifying existentialist twist, that 'Dust Storms May Exist', frantic lights flash ahead, where the border patrol has pulled someone over and has him pinned, spread-eagled at gunpoint, against his vehicle. Above all, after nightfall, there are the coyotes, the prairie wolf whose name derives from the Náhuatl word *coyotlinaut* – an Aztec deity whose followers wear the animal's fur – and is the jester and

'God's dog' of a thousand Native American stories. The trickster whose resilience has defied all erosion by modern man of its habits and habitats, by outwitting him at every turn. The jackal of America which unleashes its flesh-creeping range of haunting sounds across the desert night: howling, yipping, yapping – sometimes almost laughing. Their chorus, whether it is sung for territory or for fun – no one knows – seems to bring the night to a standstill, unless there are domestic dogs around, which can be sure to go into a frenzy, knowing something deep down about these wild cousins with whom they have so much – though so little – in common. But keep going, until daybreak – for the loneliness can be sublime when a lilac light of dawn fades the constellations in the vast sky, by way of fanfare for the golden desert sunrise, like firelight across the land.

Turning off I-10 at Van Horn, via the truckers' travel centre, the railroad and Highway 90 run hand-in-hand back towards the border through scrub and grassland. An incongruous roadside shrine at the entrance to a ranch containing and advertising for Prada shoes gives some idea of the upcoming arty settlement of Marfa, south of which the landscape changes dramatically. Suddenly it is huge and isolating again, with horizon after horizon, layer upon layer, of mountain ridges ahead, turning green to blue to grey into the distance, as the frontier comes back into view. After miles of savannah and scrub, the first ocotillo since Arizona appear again, and buttes rise against the skyline.

If only TV teenaged soaps hadn't kidnapped the word 'awesome' – for that is what these mountains are, such is the dread, southwards along Highway 67. Only the awe emanates not just from nature; it has also to do with the arrival at dusk in the most remote of the twin towns along the border, clinging together and surrounded by an expanse of mountainous wilderness and what feels like infinite nothing: Presidio on the Texas side and Ojinaga over the river. Although they live as one, clinging together in the emptiness, Presidio's clocks are an hour ahead of Ojinaga's, which often leads to confusion. Here, the Rio Grande ceases to be the trickle that divides El Paso from Juárez, its waters back there plundered by the farmers of New Mexico, for it is now joined by the Conchos river and a lusty current. In fact, what is from now on called the Rio Grande or Rio Bravo is almost all water from the Conchos. Presidio by night is a place of mobile trailer homes to which cling canisters of butane gas, a place lit by isolated fluorescent lights against the glow from over the river of the larger Mexican town, behind which rises a steep, impassable escarpment.

It was that mountain slope on which the joint US and Mexican operation against drug baron Pablo Acosta was banking, for it gave him no way out. What the SWAT teams on the American side did not know was that the operation over the river was in part arranged and paid for by Acosta's trusty lieutenant, 'Lord of the Skies' Carrillo Fuentes, who needed to be rid of his mentor in order to reform the Juárez cartel under his authority. The history hangs heavy in the deep valley, into which a mist rises from the river after the sunrise.

Perhaps surprisingly, behind the corrugated iron Subway sandwich store in Presidio is a small villa with a diplomatic plaque above the portico and cloister within, up the walls of which bright flowers climb, with a fountain in the middle of it. This is the Mexican consulate, where Héctor Acosta Flores presides, supported by his tireless aide, Elsa Villa, who busies herself with 'a massive workload, mostly protection of Mexican nationals, their documentation, what they need to present themselves to the US authorities, birth certificates, ID, labour rights, family rights – the everyday machinery of Mexican life on the border'. The office handles 300 cases a day and covers eighteen prisons, to which it organises visits for the Mexican families of inmates. 'We had to get involved in riots recently,' says Acosta, 'in Pecos jail – most of those involved were Mexican. The rise in numbers detained for deportation, or with cases pending, adds to convicted criminals – it's a lot of work. But we did manage to have nine independence *Grito* ceremonies in nine jails this year – that was quite something!' In Presidio and Ojinaga, it is Health Awareness Week, which Acosta is helping to organise on both sides of the river. Today's business opens with a seminar in Ojinaga on health and migration, for which we, of course, arrive an hour early because of the time difference we both forgot, allowing for a breakfast of sickly sweet cakes. There follows an interesting and edgy exchange in which the director of the Ojinaga hospital (also called Acosta) and some of his paramedics quiz a man from Mexican customs called Porfidio about delays in getting the migrants home once they have been deported, leaving them stranded in Ojinaga. 'If they don't have any money, how are they going to get home?' asks the director. Apparently there is a plan afoot to help, but 'I know of no such plan', grunts the customs man. 'How many millions of dollars do these people send back to Mexico?' protests a paramedic called Clara, lambasting the 'functionaries', while Consul Acosta looks a little shamefaced, adding: 'I am arguing that the government do all it can to help.' There's a Woody Guthrie song called 'Deportee' about the nameless people made to 'ride the big airplane', but the truth is that they don't get their names back when they reach the borderland of their own country either.

Apart from the migrants who roam the streets looking to earn a fare home, Ojinaga is one of those places that looks entirely normal, and probably is 'unless you're here on bad business', says a man called Raul in Kick Ass Pizza. The bar and pizzeria – one of many here, pizza clearly a favourite in the middle of nowhere – is quiet and friendly, with curiosity getting the better of suspicion. Raul is keen to talk about melons and onions, for which the surrounding area is famous, and about the annual onion festival held in town, rather than any illegal form of commerce. A random compliment along the lines that because of Pablo Acosta, famous Ojinaga is where it all started is greeted by silence, a swift change of subject to The Beatles and, oddly, a peal of laughter from a man at a table in the corner by the pretty lace curtains who then buys me a shot of tequila, insisting to the barman that it be a good one, and leaves.

As we had returned over the bridge to Presidio earlier, Mr Acosta the consul explains that his is an 'itinerant consulate', meaning that its constituency includes two towns away from the border, but very much part of Amexica: Midland and Odessa – the names rang a bell after covering the Bush administration for several years, for these towns were the New England dynasty's western colony, cradle for its recent money and the place where two of its most recent political sons, Jeb and George W. were raised. Odessa and Midland require a detour north, through a landscape of desert mountains that cast a blue shadow over the heat, then becomes a barren scrub across which dust devils fly and trains rumble like iron snakes. I took a walk towards a railroad line, just to watch them forge a way through the now crepuscular light, their own lights visible and the sound of their hooting audible at least ten minutes before reaching a deafening crescendo as they thunder by. I stayed until way past dark, then on into the country of apparently humble origins in which the Bush dynasty entwined with the energy barons of Texas. America likes to think of the Bush era as distant past already, whether with regret or relief, but until recently, a member of the Bush family had for half a century occupied the White House, a Senate seat or governor's mansion and the family continues to fascinate here around its fortress in this corner of the Lone Star state's wild west, nowadays very much part of 'Amexica'. It was here that a young pilot back from the Second World War called George Herbert Walker Bush was sent by his father, Senator Prescott Bush, to a trainee job with the International Derrick and Equipment Company. Derrick was a subsidiary of Dresser Industries, controlled by the Bush family and selling more oilrigs than anyone in the world, later absorbed by Halliburton, of which future Vice President Dick Cheney became chairman, keeping things in the family, so to speak. The Bush family settled in Midland, although the workshop of the area was scrappy Odessa, where the White working class live on one side of the tracks, Blacks and Hispanics on the other.

The world did not hear much about Odessa until one fateful day in December 1998 when George W. Bush was governor of Texas and the sky turned black after an 'upset' at the Huntsman chemical plant which was literally on the wrong side of the railroad tracks it shares with poor housing, where the Mexicans live. (An 'upset' is an unplanned accident releasing pollution, not part of the plant's normal running procedure, and which does not count in its regulatory tally.) Lucia Llánez, whose family came from Tabasco and thereafter the border, lives in this tightly knit community of bungalows squeezed between the chemical plant and the railroad. She will never forget that day: 'It was dark all over; cars on the Interstate slowing down and putting their lights on because they couldn't see, though it was day. There was a rumbling like trains that rattled the windows, and people were going to hospital for watering eyes, allergies and problems breathing. The cloud stayed two weeks.' In Odessa, where Mexico came to live on the Bushes' doorstep, I ate one of the best fajitas I had eaten along the entire road, found a motel with a room looking straight across the parking lot at a railroad line and — by now a hopelessly addicted trainspotter — sat propped against the wall drinking beers and watching them crash by, dividing Mexican Odessa from white Odessa, until turning in and allowing the rattle and hum of Union Pacific to hammer me to sleep.

Next day, I hear the story of how Huntsman goes back to the days of George Herbert Bush's arrival, when Odessa was a town of what retired fireman Don Dangerfield calls 'wildcatters'. In the forties, the US Air Force bombed deep holes in the giant Permian oil basin in a search for oil, which then attracted a stampede of speculators who would, recalls Dangerfield, 'spend the nights in a hotel, the End of the Golden West, and gamble their lots in rooms so thick with cigar smoke you could hardly see'. Among them was a man he remembers well: John Ben Shepperd, a former attorney general of Texas and member of the White Citizens Council come to seek his fortune out west by setting up the El Paso Products company, later Huntsman.

George Herbert Bush landed in this mayhem but quickly decamped 20 miles north to Midland, where new millionaires like him established a country club, a Harvard and a Yale club, met at the Petroleum Club and played golf on irrigated lawns. Midland was, at the time, one of only two towns in America (the other was Los Angeles) with its own Rolls-Royce dealership and more millionaires per capita than any other town, out here in the dusty desert. This was where Bush Senior built his oil fortune, launched a political career on its shoulders and raised his sons Jeb and George W. in the art and language of power, which the latter feigned to speak from the White House over two terms. These were decades during which the Mexicans arrived to work the chemical pipelines in Odessa and water the lawns and golf courses of Midland, so that now more people speak Spanish in Odessa and Midland than English.

Driving back to Presidio and the border, I parked up at that same spot from which I had walked to watch trains roll through the twilight two nights before, only to find that I was walking against the tracks of my own still perfectly indented footprints, coming at me in the opposite direction, as though walking backwards against time. It was the strangest feeling out there in forever, Texas, and not out of place, for in this desert, time and space curve into their own endlessness.

Southbound from Presidio, Highway 170 leads to one of the most famous and famously spectacular natural monuments in America, Big Bend National Park, but there are lovelier and less crowded wonders to behold on the way, past Redford in the less celebrated Big Bend State Park, and a stretch of border at once baffling and gratifying. Past Palo Amarillo Ranch, the winding road, deep in a valley, runs right alongside the bubbling brook that the Rio Grande has become. Here, you could play a game of catch between the United States and Mexico, and no one would see or interrupt you. There is no fence, no border patrol, no sign of any sensors, but that could be a trick. If a child kicked a ball across, you could kick it back, or you could bring as much cocaine or as many Salvadoreans as you wanted. Of course, the roads north are no breeze, but you would be inside the United States. At the Coronado River Access Point, the Rio Grande flows by like a pleasant pastoral stream in which you could wash your face (try doing that in El Paso). The only fence is a wooden one put up by the state parks service, and the only signpost is that instructing: 'Do Not Block The Boat Ramp. Pets Prohibited. By Order.' On the far bank, 20 feet away, rocks rise to a small hill, and that is Mexico. The road passes red-headed buttes at the foot of which red-headed vultures pick at the carcass of a desert fox by the road. It climbs, and overlooks the great ravine that is Madre Canyon, where a picnic area looks across the running water at Mexico on the other bank, with toy teepees instead of parasols for shade and tables set for a riverside snack. Then, to stay on course (for this is no tourist trail to the Big Bend), my route swings north towards Alpine, Texas, and into a moonscape, a flat horizon punched by Kokernot Mesa and the 5,000-foot peak of Hen Eggs Mountain. Along these liberating stretches of road, not only is there no phone signal, but the digital 'radioset' channel-surfing function just whizzes through the numbers which it thinks locate a radio station, finding nothing. Heading east between Marathon and Sanderson, even the railway track is like an oxbow lake left behind by a river: cut off, going nowhere, home to an abandoned, idle row of freight boxcars painted with graffiti in the rust.

The destination is not a butte or a mountain, it is one of the very few people to whom one can talk and who can say they met Pablo Acosta and the Lord of the Skies himself, Amado Carrillo Fuentes. Don Henry Ford farms a ranch at Belmont, near the agricultural centre of Seguin, Texas, once the high, arid plains have become grassland through which runs the Guadalupe River. Ford was a dope smuggler from near Fort Stockton, a way north from Hen Eggs Mountain. It was a trade he chose, for which he was jailed, escaped and was jailed again, and about which he wrote a book called *Contrabando*. His meetings with the drug lords over the river were both remarkable. The first with Carrillo Fuentes, during his years of apprenticeship to Pablo Acosta in Ojinaga, was part of an attempt by Ford's smuggling partner Oscar to get into the big time. They meet in a motel room for negotiations over mountains of cocaine, during which Ford has the temerity to say he prefers not to get into any business that involves killing people. He and another smuggler are left, but then returned for, taken out into a parking lot stark naked, interrogated and then into another room where Oscar is in the process of being beaten senseless by Carrillo Fuentes's men. 'I had no idea then how powerful Carrillo would become,' says Ford. The meeting with Acosta comes later, while Ford is on the run from prison and guarding a stash of marijuana, is spotted and taken by Acosta's men, then recognises the man himself. 'Don't look into my face,' snaps the drug lord. Ford is interrogated, held, and in an extraordinary exchange asked by Acosta whether (and why not) he had never killed a man. The dialogue is knife-edge tense, Ford pleading only for his life – which he is granted, Acosta also insisting that he take his load of marijuana 'as a gift from me', even though Ford has said he would rather leave without it. 'Yes, sir,' agrees Ford, when Acosta presses the offer.[3]

The gateway to Ford's ranch is open, flanked by the Lone Star flag of Texas. The access road winds through the green, deepened by a day of steady rain, past a lake, to the house Ford and his wife have only recently completed. There is no one there at first, just a noisy greeting by a pack of dogs and countless cats and kittens. Eventually, Ford arrives, in his old pickup, the gentleman cowboy farmer, with a difference. Quite a few differences, actually. It is afternoon, and a grey one, and there is a quick glance around the immediate vicinity, with a full tour of the property promised for tomorrow. Ford also breeds, and loves, racehorses at a stable near Seguin, from which a horse he feeds in a field here has retired. 'He can't race any more, this old sack of shit,' says Ford. 'But he's a good man, gentle soul, so the kids love to ride him.'

If there is one thing Ford does not want to talk about over the three days and two nights he graciously hosts me at his ranch, it is his book and his life as a narco trafficker. But we have barely finished our first cup of tea at the table in his great kitchen before he begins to talk about the CIA, cocaine and Iran-Contra, and about his own second work, *Ruminations From the Garden*. He writes: 'I have had a hard time convincing people that I dislike revisiting my past. I did write a book about it, I'm not looking for pity. I chose my path then and now.' In conversation, Ford does, however, reflect on the old trade, as darkness falls and we eat spicy stuffed jalapeño peppers to die for. Leah Ford and I drink beer, Don is teetotal, and prefers tea. 'The area I was living in, that was south-east of Ojinaga, you kill someone, and that makes you Somebody. But the thing was, I never ran cocaine. I refused to run cocaine. It's a fucker, and I wouldn't do it. I put that in my deposition, my plea, but they edited it out of the tape. The cops were trying to turn me into this coke dealer, and I said no, I'm against hard drugs. But they didn't want the judge to see that. No mitigation . . . Yeah,' Ford reflects, without much relish or even interest, 'I still meet some of those people. I met someone recently and I said: "Who do you work for?" and he said: "I don't work for no one." He was just like the Mexicans you meet in my yard. He said he'd love to go back, but couldn't take the risk, back into the middle of it all now. They can kill you just because you were once a name they knew.

'Look,' says Ford, leaning across his kitchen table, 'I know the business I was involved in. You hear about all these people backpacking across country with the dope, but that's all shit. That stuff is going right through customs, I know it is. Taxi drivers going back and forth, the same cars getting waved through every day by people on the US side who know. And as for the trucks – Jeezus Christ! All you have to do is get paid to do what you'd do anyway, wave ten per cent of the trucks right on through. I've heard that if you have the money and you know the Zetas, you can get anything you want into the United States – you can get it waved through, and they might even ship it on up for you in a nice fucking border patrol vehicle.' Ford remembers: 'In my day, a place like Ciudad Acuña was run by *Chapo* Guzmán, but now it's all Zetas. And it's not just drug dealing. You got taxis sit there all day, and have to show one hundred per cent occupancy even though they haven't taken a single fare. The taxi firm works for the Zetas, the Zetas launder their money, and the driver registers busy all day without driving anywhere.'

This being a dairy ranch, Leah churns butter in a big porcelain jar as we talk. It is turning slowly, and Ford takes the bowl, and talks about the cash paid for all these drugs crossing back into Mexico. An investigation by the Associated Press in December 2009 found that only a fraction of the river of cash flowing through the border was being intercepted.[4] During 2008, the customs and border patrol in El Paso alone confiscated $2.8 million in cash, but most of it was in a single, massive $1.9 million load heading to Ciudad Juárez from Kansas City, Missouri.

'I read that two hundred million dollars is crossing the bridges,' says Ford. 'That's two hundred kilos of cash if it's in hundreds, 'cause a bill weighs a gram. If it's in twenties, that's a thousand kilos. How are you gonna spend that in Mexico? You can't get rid of that kind of money! They say there's five hundred billion dollars a year in this business. Dammit, there's only eight hundred billion dollars of currency circulating in cash at any time, so am I gonna believe that five-eighths of that is drug money? Of course not. So how does all that money get back into circulation? It does through legal funds, don't it? How else? Or am I just dumb? But, you can't bank all that cash. You can't roll into a bank and say, "I gotta deposit a truckload of dollars, quick". You got to find someone who's gonna launder that money and take a cut, you got to find someone who's going to re-introduce it into legal channels. If you've got a semi-articulated truck full of cash, you go to Mexico City and you find the representative of a big-assed American bank to do you a favour for a big-assed cut. And the money's gonna go via that representative to some even bigger smart-ass on fucking Wall Street. How else is it gonna work? You gonna find guys driving round Mexico spending cash out of a semi truck? I don't think so. It's Bob Dylan, ain't it: "Steal a little and they put you in jail / Steal a load and they make you a king".'

But what compels Ford now, and the real subject of his book, is self-sufficiency. Like many Americans electing to live and farm in reclusion, in enviable quarantine, from the hullabaloo. 'When I came out of prison, after five years surrounded by the constant noise, stress and confusion of a federal joint, I found the idea of living alone in a forest kind of appealing,' Ford says. But he is watching hard; watching the oil run out, what he believes to be the guzzling of a finite resource by the planet generally, even by his own peers 'turning too much diesel into too much of the wrong kinda food, with bigger and bigger machines. Well, if all this breaks down, I'm gonna be prepared. I'm gonna be able to feed myself, my family, my children and even a few of my favourite people. We receive an inheritance, and, God willing, we get to leave a legacy.'

Morning starts especially early for Ford as a farmer, and he begins the day with darkness outside and a scour of his overnight email before we go out through the misty chill smelling of moist, fresh earth, Jack Frost underfoot, and milk the cows, which Ford does by hand, into a bucket, squelching. After breakfast – a warming bowl of rice, egg and the freshest, creamiest milk I've ever tasted – we prepare to go to Gonzales, the nearest town.

There is word again of Texan secession from the union, as is the formerly confederate Lone Star state's constitutional right. It never happens, but is much discussed in these parts, on a cyclical pattern depending on who is in the White House and especially since the election of Barack Obama. Before that, the secessionists had quietened, not least because one of the guiding characteristics of the Bush presidency was the fact that George W. 's team was led by his father's Texan men of steel, Karl Rove and Dick Cheney, the heavy hand of Texan big oil, and many who had served Bush's governorship – the idea being that if Texas has to be part of the union, then one might as well forge the union into being Texas. But it's not like that anymore – Obama is not only black and Democrat, he's a Yankee. And so the language and threat of secession now re-enters Republican politics, and the battle for the party's nomination in gubernatorial elections. And as the lexicon of secession that accompanied the Clinton years resurfaces, Ford's neighbourhood becomes the secessionist heartland. This is logical: Gonzales is where in 1835, the first battle of the Texan revolution against Mexico was fought. The Mexican army asked for a cannon it had loaned the Texans to fight off Apache raids be returned, to which the Texans retorted what became a legendary taunt: 'Come and Take It.' When the Mexicans tried to do just that, in Ford's words, 'they got the shit shot out of them'. So as Ford and I drive to Gonzales to pick up cattle feed and deal with the bank, we pass a flag flying from a ranch gate with a Lone Star, a cannon and the slogan written on it: 'Come and Take It'. 'The government can say whatever it fucking wants,' spits Ford. 'We're all disaffected, we're too far from Washington DC, we feel left out of the equation and over-taxed by too much federal government.' Only Ford is wary of the 'redneck secessionists'. 'I sure ain't one of them,' he says. 'I don't go to things like the secessionist Tea Parties they have – they got over five thousand people to that.' In American political parlance, to be left wing tends to entail a sympathy for federal government, while right entails libertarianism. Ford, though, produces an ingenious four-way 'political compass' quiz whereby one answers questions about various issues and is then placed on a grid between left and right on a vertical scale, and 'authoritarian' and 'libertarian' on a horizontal one. He comes out in the bottom left-hand corner, a left-wing libertarian, and while that stakes out a vertical difference between him and his anti-government neighbours, it binds him to them on the horizontal scale. Ford's other distinction is his fluent Spanish, and deep love for Mexico; Ford is a horseman and man of the borderland, he is not unlike the principal characters in Cormac McCarthy's epic and remarkable 'Border Trilogy' – John Grady and Billy Parham. 'Over on the other side, you got people who are as far away from Mexico City as we are from Washington, and that man is our neighbour. What I see is that we end up with a bunch of counter-cultural rebels on both sides of the border with more in common with each other than we have with the capital cities.' Ford wants to hear some of that counter-cultural rebel stuff, so we head off to see a young singer-songwriter whom Ford has taken under his wing somewhat, scheduled to play a gig in New Braunfels, over the other side of Seguin, Ryan Bingham. Bingham's songs have become the soundtrack to the whole stay, two discs Ford and Leah play over and over again. 'Found him on the circuit here, playing to just a bunch of people, and wrote him up in a cowboy music magazine I contribute to. He's the real thing. Parents ran a roadhouse in South-East New Mexico. He grew up sleeping in the same beds where prostitutes worked. His uncle was a rodeo rider and he was riding competitive rodeo in Mexico by the age of five, but got thrown by a horse, messed his hands up. Now Ryan writes songs, sounds a bit like Dylan and making a name for himself.'

It's a drive, the night is cold, the support acts endless, the crowd small when the boy comes on, in a Dylan 'rolling thunder' white hat, a Dylan voice and Dylan looks. The songs, sung in a small yard under an avenue of pecan trees, are poignant, deep-felt and of the frontier ground they come from: 'Tell my mother I miss her so', sings Bingham; Ford leans over and whispers: 'His mother died just recently.' Bingham swigs from a can of Shiner beer, fairy-lights wink from the branches of the pecan trees, the frat-brat audience is barely listening, but he sings on: ''Cause hard times they come and they go / Most of the time they're in the middle of your road'.[5]

One can feel Ford's tough love for this boy; immersed, it appears, not only in the young singer's music, life and words, but also his own youth, after a fashion – there is more than a faint echo of the dope-smuggling cowboy in this son-of-a-roadhouse on stage, assailing his acoustic guitar and straining his larynx, even for these jocks with their beers and bimbo blonde girlfriends. These jugheads should get work as speed bumps lying in the road: they have no idea what they are listening to, giving an authentic cowboy rocker like Bingham the pronged-horn metal rock salute with one hand and raised Bud can with the other as he sings a heartbroken but gritty song called *For What It's Worth*. And as we leave, which has to be early if the cows are going to get milked in the morning, the young man begins to sing 'The Times They Are A-Changing', written by his muse in 1962 when his father was probably younger than Ryan is now. 'I can't say I don't worry about Ryan,' muses Ford. 'There's a side of him that stays detached, then there's a side of him that's like Jim Morrison, auto-destruct. Be interesting to see how he handles success. Funny thing, capitalism: takes a protest song by a poor boy and turns it into big business. Bit like the Church, I guess, taking something as revolutionary as Christianity and turning it into a religion.' And he thinks back instinctively to his own past. 'Drugs are a symptom, not a cause. Ask the addicts, they'll tell you. What the hell happened, and why? What's the root cause of that stuff I was smuggling?' He leaves his question hanging from the night as we drive through the gates of the ranch.

The sun beats down, next afternoon, through bigger, older pecan trees than those around Ryan Bingham's stage, with older, venerable trunks. There's been a bumpy ride around the now luminous meadows and woodland, refreshed by rain. Now the sun is out and down by the lazy-rolling Guadalupe River, Ford's foreman on the ranch, Manuel García Guajito, and his assistant Abraham are cutting dead branches. They take a break as Ford applies the brakes and alights to chat. For some reason the conversation turns from wood clearance to the Zetas, about whom Manuel has things to say. 'I don't think the Zetas are bad people,' he asserts. Why? 'Well, they're not. They're good. My brother was driving a bus in Tamaulipas once, which broke down. And the Zetas helped him, they got help, and helped him fix the bus.' After this eccentric account of Zetas as an emergency roadside service, there's also unusual word from the underworld of migration, a steady current through these parts as reliable as that of the Guadalupe River. 'In the old days', says Manuel, 'when the *coyotes* brought people over, there was always trouble. They got robbed by the *polleros*, the women were violated, everything was trouble. Now, the Zetas have taken over, and it's all under control. Everyone coming through says the same. They take more money, *claro*' – certainly, of course – 'but it's much safer. You keep your things, and the women keep their honour.' But the surface of things is of little interest to Manuel García, who has worked with Ford many years and whom Ford respects greatly, 'good a land manager as you'll ever find'. What interests Manuel are the happenings and phenomena in the extraordinary world he inhabits while he runs this ranch, seeing not the beauty of the pasture and wildwood, the shafts of sunlight that shine through and illuminate the leaves of oak and pecan trees, nor hearing the mellifluous singing of birds. For Manuel has his visions.

'I saw gold and silver mosquitoes,' he relates, 'and others of fluorescent colours, biting people and taking out their DNA. Taking our DNA elsewhere, bit like Noah's Ark. But there was no ark, they were taking each of us, and every animal, to another time, or another place.' Some might nod politely and leave Manuel to his chopping, but on a long afternoon, Ford and I stay rooted to the spot and wait for more. Ford is a man with a short bullshit endurance fuse, and he not only wants to talk more to his foreman, but says this: 'He said he'd seen a tornado of eagles, going round and round, upwards. And the funny thing was that two years later, there was one. Most far-out Godamn thing I ever saw: like a cyclone of eagles, swirling in a circle towards the sky, just like Manuel said.' Now Manuel continues: 'I've seen a lot of people walking down the highway there. Their clothes are all torn, and they're hungry, and we offered them some food, but they didn't know what to do with it. They were walking like zombies, right along the road.' And he sweeps his arm towards Highway 80 and the distant border. 'Thing is, I'm not afraid of dying, what I'm afraid of is being alive and not being able to help these people out on that road.'

CHAPTER SEVEN

Eat off the Floor

In May 2000, shareholders of the giant Alcoa aluminium company assembled in Pittsburgh, Pennsylvania, to hear their chief executive, Paul O'Neill, for the last time. O'Neill had served the company well and those who had invested would be sad to see him go. On the other hand, there was a great honour awaiting him: President George W. Bush would soon announce O'Neill's appointment for the post of Treasury Secretary in what the business community regarded as a powerhouse administration, at the commanding apex of his economic and financial agenda. Alcoa and its subsidiaries had plants all over the world, including a number of *maquiladoras*, mostly automotive assembly plants and joint ventures just inside Mexico. One of those was in the city of Ciudad Acuña, opposite Del Rio, Texas, which made electrical distribution systems for light and heavy vehicles – 'electrical octopuses', as the workers call them.

The twin cities of Ciudad Acuña and Del Rio are the first in what now becomes the eastern third of the borderland, after the deserts and mountains descend in altitude towards rolling Texas ranch land and the vast Mexican state of Coahuila. The land becomes greener, semi-tropical and on the US side more densely scattered with towns and industrial settlements from now on, to the sea. On the Mexican side, the cities of Acuña and, a little further downriver, Piedras Negras have been transformed by the arrival of *maquiladoras*, an industrial revolution in what was horse and cattle hacienda country, now assembling the contents of America's supermarket shelves and auto-dealerships. Ciudad Acuña was, until the recession of 2009, the fastest-growing city in the country.

Reports of protest against poor conditions and wages had emanated from Alcoa's plant in Acuña since two chemical exposures in 1994, one of which had caused a three-day shutdown with 179 workers sent to hospital for evaluation. Despite a reputation for concern with workers' safety, O'Neill had reportedly brushed these whispers aside at another shareholders meeting in 1996, saying that conditions at Alcoa's plants were so good the workers could 'eat off the floor'.[1] But at that meeting in 1996, also in Pittsburgh, a shareholder rose to speak. He was no ordinary shareholder: his name was Juan Tovar Santos and he was himself a worker for Alcoa in Ciudad Acuña. Tovar Santos addressed the assembly with a bulletin from the shop floor of the *maquiladora*. He spoke about intoxication of the air by materials used in the factory. He spoke of relentless working hours and pittance pay. He described punishing production quotas and the iron regulation of breaks – to rest the eyes and fingers, to eat, even to use the lavatory. He spoke about discrimination against pregnant women, and workers having to leave after industrial injuries without compensation. Matters had become so bad, said Tovar, that riot police had had to be called in to quell a demonstration in the factory yard with tear gas.

The intervention had been carefully and long planned. The clutch of shares enabling Tovar Santos to speak had been bought by a support network for workers in the *maquilas* led by the Quaker American Friends Service Committee, and a group of Benedictine nuns in San Antonio led by one extraordinary Sister Susan Mika. Both teams worked in concert with one of the most impressive and cogent organisations along the border, the only one of its kind, the *Comité Fronterizo de Obreras*, Frontier Committee of Women Workers or CFO, based downriver from Acuña at Piedras Negras. The committee had come to represent men, too, and Tovar had been one of the driving forces behind it. The CFO is not a union but a pressure group and cadre of people working in, or sacked from, the *maquilas*, and devoted to harassing, educating, agitating, inciting, motivating, fomenting, prompting and blandishing. In Mexico, trade unions are traditionally affiliated to the central *Confederación de Trabajadores de México*, the confederation of labour or CTM, a vast bureaucracy. The CTM-affiliated unions are known by democratic currents and militants as *charros*, for which there is sadly no translation other than the literal 'horseman' – 'union hacks,' perhaps, or even 'scabs'.

Such institutionalised organisation of labour is a legacy of the seven decades of power invested in the PRI, which proclaimed a veneer of sympathy with organised labour, not unlike that of the Peronist system in Argentina, with unions ceding a measure of control to the corporatist state. The PRI President Salinas de Gortari talked about 'the indestructible historic pact between the Revolutionary government and the working class', sealing it with the union leader Fidel Velásquez in 1988.[2] When the *maquilas* were brought to Mexico by the PRI, there was little changing the notion that a union is not there to rock the boat. Quite the reverse, it was from now on there to keep the PRI's industrial peace, even with the new wave of investors from north of the border. In Ciudad Acuña, however, even this is luxury: the city boasts itself to potential investors in North America as being the only one along the border in which the *maquilas* are entirely 'union free', which is music to the ears of boardrooms across the USA but is a red rag to the bull of the CFO. In the postmodern, globalised marketplace, just as in the post-modern drug war, there is little place for the old lexicon. In the world of globalised production, the idea of structures to negotiate pay and conditions sits uneasily within a doctrine of profit free from restraint which carries a big stick whereby if the Mexicans get too difficult, an employer can simply move to China, or some other place where the wages are even lower and the workers docile. Only it takes longer, and costs more, to cross the Yangtzee into Texas than it does the Rio Grande, and for this reason, *maquilas* are spreading south within Mexico, into the interior, where the decrease in wages payable on terrain of abject poverty more than offsets increased costs of transport. In his excellent book on *maquilas*, Alejandro Lugar found that 'the life of working-class people at the US–Mexico border is so fragmented, and yet so systematically inspected, that a culture of rebellion, or of class mobilisation, was not found . . . The ruthless working conditions, the cutthroat competitive performances among workers, and the struggle over decadent tools of production often led to the unmaking of class.' His conclusion, based on years of work on and in the factories, no doubt describes the landscape accurately and in justified despair.[3] Strangely, though, the arrival of a new workforce on the border worked in two directions. On the one hand, the generally rural agricultural population that came north to work in the factories had no experience of unions or organised labour when they confronted their new transnational employers. On the other hand, the new workforce 'undermined old spaces of union control, while opening up a space for non-PRI militant unionism', wrote Altha Cravey in a study of *maquila* labour.[4] Into that space, the CFO emerged to try to ensure the basics of decency and fairness at work; that the endangered species enshrined in its slogan, 'Dignity, Justice, Solidarity', were not banished entirely, as the employers avowed, from the globalised industrial landscape in borderland Mexico.

Juan Tovar Santos has now left the border and settled in Torreón, at the southern tip of Coahuila, of which Acuña is the far north. But I caught up with him two years after a second visit to Pittsburgh in 2000, tending to the engine of a car propped up on blocks of wood and concrete outside his home in the *Colonia 28 Junio* on the edge of Ciudad Acuña. 'I'm a mechanic now, and have been since they sacked me,' he said, with both wariness and a hint of humour. 'I was never an activist before, I just came here from Zacatecas to work in the *maquila* eleven years ago, and was hired the following day — the wages were one hundred and fifty pesos a week in 1991, about fifteen dollars; they were seven hundred when I left, about fifty dollars, but worth much less in the shops.

'We'd all come from the same farms in the south of the state, we knew each other and had had enough shit from landowners during the privatisation. There were nine of us in a local factory committee, and we started trying to get direct meetings with the managers.' The things he remembered best about the Alcoa plant were the poisonings and untreated industrial injuries, the sacking of workers after being injured, the lowest wages in Ciudad Acuña and 'having to apply for toilet paper, being allowed one piece per go, only being allowed to go to the toilet twice a day and not being allowed to spend more than a minute about one's business in there. It was particularly hard on the women'. There was only one thirty-minute break for lunch and two five-minute breaks in the nine-hour working day. Tovar and his committee 'tried to talk to managers in the factory, but no one wanted to listen. Then we had an idea that we would try and get the board itself, in the United States, to listen. The CFO got involved; they said that if we wanted that, they could make it happen, with their contacts.' The CFO, he says, had been contacting workers inside the plant since 1994: the shares were duly bought by the AFSC and San Antonio nuns and the plan laid to attend Mr O'Neill's shareholders meeting in 1996. 'A number of people were invited to go to Pittsburgh,' says Tovar, 'but they were too afraid to do it, so I said okay, I'll tell the boss what's wrong in this company. So with Sister Mika and the Quakers we wrote down a list of complaints, they brought translators and off we went, to an old hotel downtown, I don't remember its name. We went to the new company headquarters and had a great time – our problems were back here, not there. Only when I stood to speak, there was an argument between O'Neill and the chairman of the meeting, and the chairman said the people should hear what the workers have to say.'

Once Tovar Santos had spoken, Alcoa's response was immediate. The following week, O'Neill fired the chief executive of his Acuña plant for failing to inform headquarters about the intoxications in 1994, and made sure that toilet paper and soap were available across all eleven of his Mexican borderland factories. 'The week after we got back,' says Tovar, 'the Alcoa human resources people showed up. They offered us a choice to work in all different places, any shift we wanted. They asked how much we wanted just to leave all this alone. I said that didn't interest me. A man called José Juan Ortíz offered me 100,000 pesos just to quit, and I said no.' O'Neill was eventually replaced by a tough new CEO, Alain Belda, but negotiations through the religious shareholders continued. Alcoa promised, says Tovar, that 'nothing would happen to those of us who had campaigned for better conditions'. However, he says, 'those conversations occurred just a few weeks before the attacks on 11 September, so that no one was really looking when the company turned against us. I was accused of sabotage,' Tovar says. 'Almost immediately afterwards they sacked the ringleaders involved. The plant was locked down tight so that the CFO could hardly get a foot inside.' Tovar has a brother in Dallas – 'and I'd like to go across. I tried to get a visa but there's not much chance of that now! My brother says to try and cross as a wetback and I'm thinking about it, but there's an issue with my mother and father. So I earn my living this way now, fixing cars. I'm quite good at it, actually; I don't have anyone to boss me around like in the *maquila*; if I work hard I can operate my own bonus scheme, if I fix up a car for myself I have a travel subsidy, the days off are more generous and I can wipe my ass as often as I want.'

On New Year's Day 1994, the same day as the Zapatista revolt at the other end of Mexico, the North American Free Trade Agreement came into effect, evaporating duty barriers and tarriffs between Canada, the United States and Mexico. As the great historian of Mexico, Enrique Krauze, writes: 'Even coming up with the idea of the North American Free Trade Agreement was a violation of the Eleventh Commandment of official Mexican mythology: Thou Shalt Not Trust Americans.'[5] Barack Obama is the first president since 1994 to show any sign of wanting to 'upgrade' NAFTA, in other words tighten the flow in favour of some protectionist measures aimed at protecting American jobs and manufacturing. His mention of the possibility proved to be a sticking point during a meeting the week before Obama's inauguration with President Calderón.[6] NAFTA was a boon to business and free trade, a blow to jobs in America and transformed the economies of Mexico and the border. For the narco cartels, NAFTA was a gift: the perfect cover for their traffic, which multiplied overnight while the bureaucracy required to ship it diminished. But it had all started with the *maquiladoras*, three decades beforehand. Although they are now the emblem of the NAFTA treaty, the *maquilas*, which defined the border's new economy by bringing the millions north (and now define it in reverse, as recession and competition from Asia cause depopulation), were NAFTA's pilot scheme, and symbol of Mexico's subjugated but dependent relationship to the US economy.

In 1961, after thousands of former migrants returned across the border when the United States ended the Bracero Program, Mexican president Adolfo López Mateos drew up the PRONAF, or *Programa Nacional Fronterizo*, seeking to lure American corporations to northern Mexico. It offered loans, tax concessions and free zone status for the import of goods into the US. The United States was hardly going to spurn the occasion to enjoy bargain-basement Third World wages and industrial costs on its doorstep, and the US Border Industrial Program was duly drawn up on the American side, and put into effect in 1965. Mexican fortunes could also be made, leasing to the North Americans, and jobs created in a 'developing' country. As we saw in Juárez, the necklace of *maquilas* was accordingly built along the border, where cities burgeoned with those come to seek employment, but little or no attempt was made to create infrastructure capable of sustaining the new labour force – neither water nor roads, electricity nor adequate housing. As profits soared, the wage gap and that in family budgets between workers on either side of the border widened, thus antagonising relations across the frontier in 'Amexica'. The early *maquilas* thus became a scale model not only for NAFTA but for the global economy, staring the First World in the face across the Rio Grande. While the *maquilas* paid wages close to slave labour by US standards, people in the impoverished villages of the south and interior – Oaxaca, Zacatecas, Chiapas or Durango – viewed them as money indeed. Whole communities in the Mexican interior were left as ghost towns as their populations headed north, not to try to cross the border, but to work on the Mexican side, creating not only an explosion of trade, but also the busiest border on earth and work that is both comparable to factory labour around the world but also unique in its way. The collective edifice of the *maquilas* is calculatedly impregnable. The factories are architecturally ugly and soulless, homogenous and monolithic, reflecting the toil undertaken within them and the human condition required to perform it. They are invariably surrounded by fencing, barbed wire and security lodges or gates manned by guards, not so much to protect as to control. They are collated into 'parks', the ambience of which could not contrast more strikingly with the cluttered streets from which most workers commute: sterile, colourless, angular and clean. The 'parks' throttle the towns to which they have moved, built around their edges in locations that bring fabulous wealth to those who own the land, and strangulation to everyone else.

The only spoke in this wheel of production – wheel of life, indeed, as envisaged by the transformation of the borderland by the *maquiladoras* – is that the human race, and especially the Mexicans among it, has not quite yet been reduced to the automaton this cybernated model demands. Even in the *maquiladoras* of Amexica, these servo-system feeder plants of globalisation, little irritants are at work, such as unofficial lotteries, under-the-counter cosmetics sales, jokes about line managers or flirtation during stolen breaks. Dangerous in different ways to the new corporate uniformity is the questioning of this bludgeoned order by the CFO, and the indefatigability of a woman called Julia Quiñónez.

Of all the big cities on the Mexican side of the border, Piedras Negras, 60 kilometres downriver from Ciudad Acuña, is to date the easiest to be in and the safest. One can stay at the *Autel Río* with families in transit and walk out at night to eat or relax in bars where staff are fully clothed. Tourist shops are open, and a few Americans still browse the bric-a-brac. The name of the city means 'Black Rocks', but, says Julia Quiñónez, who runs the CFO from its office some twenty benign blocks from Bridge No. 1 over the Río Grande, 'though we are Piedras Negras, we are also called the *Frontera Blanca* – the white frontier. For some reason, touch wood, the narco war has not greatly affected us. No doubt they are here, but not in our everyday lives.'

Julia Quiñónez is on one hand effervescent, with her ready laugh, boundless energy and mischievous fun-poking, but also resilient and indurate when dealing with her subject matter – abuse of the rights of labour and human beings – and pretty tough, too, when dealing with her own people. After nearly a decade of visiting Piedras Negras, it is always wonderful to find her again, not a volt of her energy gone, nor a jalapeño sting from her severity – though she has developed a sparkly smile that was missing from the earlier days of struggle. From its humble office, and with its stretched resources, the CFO has had an influence against all odds and entirely against the zeitgeist. For instance, says Quiñónez, at one point in 2004 during the dialogue with Alcoa, the company said it needed to make cuts to wages and extend working hours by trimming benefits. Such measures, it claimed, were necessary to avoid a decision to move the plant to Honduras. The CFO organised a ballot, asking workers which they preferred between two options: to accept the changed conditions or to refuse them and challenge the company to leave. 'We called their bluff,' says Quiñónez. 'Of those that voted, eighty-nine per cent told them to go to Honduras. Part of the company did go to Honduras, but it came back again.'

In Mexico, 'it had always been the men that worked', says Quiñónez, yet from the outset 'the *maquilas* employed mostly women. The idea was that women were more careful, with smaller delicate hands. Of course it was also thought, but not said, they were easier to manipulate in the workplace. This caused social disruption and resentments — men unused to looking after kids were staying at home cooking while their wives were out at work — often harassed at work by male supervisors.' The proportion of female workers was at its highest during the 1970s, she says, when the first generation of *maquilas* were built as assembly plants. A next generation would produce more complex products, such as electronics and electrical auto-parts, and a third, latest round would involve 'new technologies and computer chips'. The CFO, she explains, was originally formed in 1979, in the state of Tamaulipas, backed by supporters in Edinburg, Texas, knocking door to door in the sprawling new *colonias*, collecting information and offering advice on conditions, hours, pay and domestic disruption. Although CFO was not a union as such, union branches affiliated to the CTM found themselves unable to accept wage cuts and quota increases because of pressure by the CFO.

In 1980, aged fifteen, Quiñónez took her first job in the Piedras Negras *maquila* operated by Johnson & Johnson, sewing hems for medical fabrics and bandages. 'We had a union,' she recalls, 'affiliated to the PRI and functioning in the interests of the company.' She was paid by productivity, and after five years 'I was exhausted, and fed up with always having my finger punctured by the needle on the machine and pulling it back so the needle tore even more'. Julia was seventeen when the CFO organised its first assembly workers in her plant, suggesting that they vote on whether to accept a wage cut. 'I thought: Why don't we always do this?' In 1986, Quiñónez joined the new CFO regional committee covering the states of Tamaulipas and Coahuila, and the following year established a local CFO organisation for the two cities of Piedras Negras and Ciudad Acuña — made up 'mostly of women', she says. 'Our first aim was to give the workers a voice of their own, not through a union which was beholden. Our second aim was to make workers aware of the law and their rights and the third was to work in the *colonias* to support people, and stop their lives being like a parade of ants to and from work. The *maquila* depends on us being machines and the CFO was formed here to tell the workers they were human beings, and the first thing that makes you a human being is knowing what your rights are. At first, there was no hope, complete apathy. But we started by talking about sexual harassment by the managers, and taking up cases. Then we took the logic of that into the *colonia*: if it's not okay for the supervisor to yell at you and abuse you, it's not okay for your husband to do that either. So we became a force in the *colonias*, and the more that happened, the more we became a force in the *maquilas*, talking about wages, health and safety, pregnancy and conditions.'

With time, the CFO moved its headquarters to Piedras Negras, and Quiñónez became its primary, later full-time, mover and shaker. Guided by the CFO, an unprecedented series of thirty face-to-face dialogues began between employee representatives and Alcoa, after Tovar Santos' intervention. They were deftly handled by the man who had always led the initiative for the Quaker American Friends Service Committee, Ricardo Hernández, and more enlightened managers at Alcoa proved willing to venture to the Mexican side of the border for seventeen meetings – seven in Acuña and ten in Piedras Negras – for discussion about hours and conditions, on which some important agreements were reached over renewal of protective clothing, sexual harassment, holidays and injury benefits. 'The workers were speaking directly to the company,' says Hernández, 'prompted by the CFO, though the CFO organisers weren't allowed themselves to come to the meetings. The workers were there, I was there, Sister Mika was there, but the CFO did all the work.'

The Colonia Luis Donaldo Colosio in Piedras Negras is a shanty town made up of one long street, a continuous strip of wooden shacks built with planks and tarpaulin roofs tumbling into one another and sharing each other's back yards. The *colonia* is sandwiched between the Airport Industrial Park and the main railway line, along which freight trains roll through from Mexico City and Monterrey so that, Julia Quiñónez says, 'children quite often get run over and killed'. The estate has been so well located that it suffers from regular flooding whenever there is heavy rain to turn the dirt that makes up the street and most people's flooring into mud. In addition to houses tucked behind the slat-wood fence that runs parallel to the railway line, there are corrugated-iron *bodegas* selling household basics.

A roll-call of the industrial park and its neighbour, the *Parque Industrial Piedras Negras*, reveals a backyard production line making the icons that adorn the temple of America. The Mex-Star factory

makes wrapping for straws in McDonald's. Another factory, South-
west Manufacturing de Mexico, makes wiring for Harley Davidson
motorcycles. Dimmit Industries, which closed in 2001, made jeans
for Levi's. And there's a factory called FAMX, formerly the Fujikura
half of Alcoa's interest, which makes the electrical circuits that keep
America switching on the ignition.

Three thirty in the afternoon: and it's shift change again, in
another town. Rows of school buses past their sell-by date north of
the border line up outside each factory, waiting to take their load
downtown or back up to the *colonias*. The workers emerge from their
windowless, fluorescent-lit world within, down a flight of steps and
into the forecourt, blinking into the sunlight. There is a crush waiting to get through the chicane of an exit, everyone dressed in either
a blue or a green tunic, patient, but anxious to get past the security
fence that is supposedly to keep people out – but that's unconvincing –
and the guards. Some girls pick out a waiting face, and blow a kiss at
a boyfriend through the chainlink before taking a walk, arm-in-
arm. Others chatter amongst themselves as they board the buses;
others again stare, hypnotised with fatigue.

It is here in Colonia Colosio between the factory and the railway
that Leticia Ramírez lives, and here that Leticia works. She takes
some finding – four visits before she is finally home. She works so hard:
all the overtime she can get, and her house is a four-generational
revolving door of two visiting sisters, their children, Leticia's daughter and her children, other relatives come to visit, and her mother
from Zacatecas trying to have a holiday with the brood – plus the
dogs chilling out in the dirt. She has a striking appearance: flame-
red hair, a skin condition which has affected her face, the figure of a
sixteen-year-old even though she is forty and a grandmother, a lambent smile and vice-grip handshake. Leticia has the aura of Semtex
or some compressed plastic explosive. She was with Alcoa for eight
years until 2003, and now works at the Elektrokontak factory from
which she has just returned, the rear wall of which is visible from the
yard where her teenaged nephews are sitting around barefoot, countless girls tend countless babies, and old Mum takes in the evening sun
in a rickety chair wanting dinner, so we cannot be too long and we're
lucky to have caught Lety at all. 'I was involved in the CFO right
from the start,' she affirms. 'I was like Julia – asking questions,

challenging them: "Why should you take away a day's wages if I'm five minutes late?" "How can you reduce my bonus just for talking?" I was always asking the CFO for advice, and soon people were coming up to me for tips on how to get round this problem or that. What we did was to know our rights and educate the others, house-to-house in the *colonias* mostly. There was knowledge to learn from books, and there was the question of confidence at work. The managers have these two big problems: they think they're smart and they've convinced themselves you can't resist their masculine charms. Both are nonsense, so if you have your wits about you, you can run rings around them, or at least put up a fight, even if they win in the end. They started talking to us, granting better benefits, but I was blacklisted, and left. And things started to slip back after we, the CFO crowd, had left the factory. We need to be on the inside and the outside. Right now, we're campaigning on Mex-Star over there.' And she waves at another stark wall enclosing another factory within view. 'The McDonald's straw place – it's dangerous,' she claims, 'something they use in a glue to make the plastic that wraps the straws.'

Now, says Leticia, finally in work again after five years on the blacklist, 'I get better pay, but only because I work longer hours.' Her ten-hour shift is 7 a.m. to 5 p.m., which brings home 600 pesos, about $50, for a five-day week. 'I work as late as they will let me every evening [as we know, she is never home when we call] and at weekends if possible. I have to, to feed everyone. I'm a mother, a grandmother and a daughter – families to feed here, parents to feed in Zacatecas.' The *colonia*, she says, 'is quite a place to live. We're all on top of each other, as you can see, and there's not much sleep with the trains two metres away – they're on their way from Mexico City to Kansas, and even Canada.' Two little boys idle on the rail tracks, torturing a frog. 'You!' shouts Lety. 'Get off the line! Idiots, they're always getting killed.'

There was one creepy *maquiladora*, says Julia Quiñónez, 'which gave me the spooks when I visited it. They made body bags for the American military. The ones they use to bring the dead soldiers back from Iraq and Afghanistan. There was a problem, they closed it. It was the strictest of all: no chewing gum, no music. No wonder: the boss was an evangelical Christian.'

* * *

By 2008 and 2009, the *maquiladora* landscape has changed in Piedras
Negras since my early visits here nearly a decade previously. Although
gains had been made at Alcoa, the company responding to the CFO's
initiatives, a new arrival in Piedras Negras, the Lear Corporation, has
brought with it new problems, says Quiñónez: 'paying wages under a
new "flexible architecture" management model, of $46 for a fify-hour
week. Among the lowest of all,' says Julia, 'in terrible conditions. We
are having to work with victims of serious industrial accidents and
injuries with no recourse to compensation.'

And there is further turbulence for those employed, or formerly
employed, by Alcoa in both Acuña and Piedras Negras. Alcoa's interests had been in part a joint venture with the Japanese Fujikura
company. But in 2009 Alcoa, wanting to divest and focus on aluminium production, sold its share of operations in Ciudad Acuña, Piedras
Negras and other borderland cities to a California-based company
called Platinum Equity. One immediate problem on the ground in
Piedras Negras and Acuña is that the AFSC and Benedictine nuns
in San Antonio were, as Hernández says, 'owners of stock in Alcoa,
using those shares to speak to the company and bring the workers to
the table. Now, there's a whole new board of directors, of an equity
company without stakeholders, so we no longer have a formal platform for discussion.'

Piedras Negras' appealing architecture after crossing from Eagle
Pass dissipates as one progresses into the miles of drably uniform
INFONAVIT housing, built and mortgaged by the government to
maquila workers, designed either deliberately or by happenstance to
be without character. In one such forlorn terrace of cuboid habita-
tions, Dora Luz Córdoba lives in a relative's house, rain lashing the
leaking roof. She has a pink streak in her hair. It's a gesture of defiance, in its way, and she needs to be defiant, unable to work after
suffering an industrial injury at the new Lear factory, and laid off
without compensation, she claims. 'I only got to work there two years,'
she complains, though it wasn't much fun. Her job was to operate a
machine punching nails into a metal plate, only one day last year the
nail punched into her hand. You only get gloves, she says, 'so as not to
contaminate the circuits', and she didn't qualify for a pair. 'I suppose
I have myself to blame, but I'm angry that no one trained us, just put
us in front of that machine; it was never explained how to use it. And

I'm angry that they didn't give me any protection for my hands, especially after a man near me lost his finger.' The accident happened at 2 a.m., and Dora was bundled off to an emergency doctor chosen by her employer, though she was made liable for the taxi fare. She claims she was told she was fine and could carry on working, though she had lost the use of a thumb, and laboured on with one hand. It was her personal doctor who insisted on an appointment with social security, but Lear declined to accept that Dora's injury was an industrial accident, as she claimed, and no benefit was forthcoming. 'So now I do what I can. I clean, mostly, people's houses, front yards, or I mind kids, anything.' Quite often while doing the rounds in Piedras Negras, one will come across Dora, in one neighbourhood or other – sweeping, scrubbing, wiping, polishing or dusting like an outdoor scullery maid with a shock of pink hair in a town where everyone works for someone else.

Dora is from Monclova in the south of Coahuila. She came here to work in the *maquilas*; she is only in her early thirties, but looks wearier. She recalls the main meal breaks, described in most *maquiladora* contracts as something to be 'enjoyed' – *disfrutar*, it says in the workplace rulebook – as especially stressful. 'If the workers exceed the thirty-minute limit, they will receive disciplinary action,' reads the rulebook.[7] 'It's supposed to be half an hour,' says Dora, 'but okay: you have to line up to clock your card out, then you line up to use the bathroom if you want to wash your hands before eating, then you line up for the food and then line up to clock back in again. That leaves about five minutes to bolt your food. Everything has to be done to the second, even your meal break. If you're late back from lunch three times at Lear, you lose a day's wages. The managers are always on your back, inspecting you, checking you, throwing their weight around and, of course, trying to make a pass. All we could do to get rid of the stress was dance. Every Friday. I'd go out with the special people I bonded with at work, the ones I had friendships with, jokes and sometimes romance. And I used to lose myself in the music and a drink, and in a dance club you could take it out on the ones who were sneaks, sucking up to the bosses. I'd work all evening, come off a shift at 2 a.m., dance all night, and sleep all next day. It was heaven.'

If there's one thing worse than Dora's *maquila* working life, it is being thrown out of it. For how different is the life of young Sara González Noriega, in a similarly tiny but well-kept house on *Calle Mar Muerto*, Dead Sea Street, making racks that enable car seats to recline. The shift, from 5 p.m. to 2 a.m., pays her 700 pesos (about $55) a week, plus the $6 bonus she keeps to spend strictly on herself, for treats or outings with friends. 'I don't like the job, but I like going to work,' says Sara, 'because I get bored at home now that my son is in school, and I like the jokes we make about the bosses, the *jefes de línea*. They're mostly vulgar, but not always. There's one who really fancies himself, always flirting and bossing us around, but he's so short and we call him *Dobico*, after a dwarf on TV. We do it every time he passes, and collapse laughing.' The managers are mad, she says, 'really insane: they have to regiment everything, enforce a strict dress code – no bracelets or anything. They might let us chew gum, but if they make us stop, we squash it into the machines! If you miss a single day, they dock twenty dollars' pay, nearly half the week. I have to start at five but there can be problems leaving my son, only if I am five minutes late, they dock a whole day's wages. You have to sign this form accepting whatever discipline they give you.'

'Article 107 of the Labour Law,' interjects Carmen Luria Vidal, a CFO organiser who accompanies us, 'prohibits arbitrary fines for workers, whatever the reason – did you know that?' 'I do now,' replies Sara, flashing a smile. 'Only sometimes people are scared to talk about things like that, in case they get sacked. When they find out that a worker is studying their rights, they ask: "How do you know? Where did you learn that?"'

Men were at first a minority of 25 per cent of the *maquila* workforce along the border, which is now about evenly balanced. Reynaldo Bueno Sifuentes is part of that equation, after thirteen years with Alcoa and now at AEES, the acronym name of the factory owned by Platinum Equity, with his baseball cap on backwards, buzz cut and red T-shirt, and piles of breeze-blocks propping up a car on which he is working in the front yard. He earns 'the same pay as when I started', about 940 pesos ($80) a week including overtime if there is any, and is happy to be driving a forklift truck stacking crates rather than on the production line. But even that is insufficient for a young family – who soon join us, his wife and two children – and so Reynaldo joins the procession over the bridge each weekend to Eagle

Pass to sell plasma and raise extra cash. 'I go twice, for sixty dollars,' says Reynaldo, 'two-thirds of what I earn all week at Alcoa. It pays for small things and extras, details, fixing up the bathroom and car, toys for the kids. But you have to be careful selling plasma. I've seen people who don't eat right or sell too much, and they're dizzy all the way home. I've seen them falling over on the bridge coming back.' Reynaldo's dream, he says, 'is to be a mechanic. In the *maquila*, though it's much more dangerous than driving, and eventually for myself, just fixing up cars back there.' I think of Juan Tovar Santos, the original troublemaker, fixing cars and wiping his ass whenever he wants. Reynaldo was part of the CFO dialogues with Alcoa executives, and one of the plant delegates nominated by the *charro* union leaders. As such, he was supposed to attend what Ricardo Hernández calls the parallel 'pantomime negotiations' supposedly to prepare the workers' positions and brief the union leaders who would themselves negotiate. In reality, these meetings were held so that workers could be briefed on what the leadership had decided, and says Reynaldo, 'when the time came for the contract negotiations at the Alcoa plant in Piedras Negras, which is unionised, no one would tell me when the negotiations were happening, because I'm with the CFO and I know the book of labour law. So how was I supposed to brief my shift if I can't go to the negotiations? So I'm walking a high wire now – there are threats, but only verbal ones so far. The snitches'll say: "Let's kick this guy in", right in front of the manager, to please him. So we'll see, but I ain't backing down.'

Behind Julia Quiñónez's offices, there is a *maquiladora* run by the CFO with a modest workforce of eight. With a difference, as one might expect: the *Maquiladora Dignidad y Justicia* – of dignity and justice – employs women sacked or retired from the jungle *maquilas* out there, working to timetables that fit their lives, making goods for sale on the Internet, made of organic, 'fair-trade' materials. 'Once,' says Julia, 'we got an offer to make holsters for guns, from a company called Maverick Arms. We turned it down because it was part of the arms industry. Shame, we'd have made them much better holsters.'

Two ladies have come to work at the CFO's *maquila* this morning: Sonia, who made Levi's for eleven years at the Dimmit factory, and Herlinda, who worked as a seamstress for Barry Industries in Ciudad Acuña, making slippers for America's favourite family mall megastores. Where will America be without them? Who knows, but both ladies have meanwhile been retrained by a third woman, Ofelia, suggested by Julia Quiñónez. Sonia and Herlinda remember the days of the twelve-hour *maquiladora* shift that has now been reduced to nine by most employers. Twelve hours from 6 a.m. to 6 p.m., that is, punctuated by a ten-minute break at 9 a.m., thirty minutes at midday and another ten at 3 p.m. Sonia was eventually promoted to quality control, 'inspecting miles and miles of fabric, having made it myself for many years. They got more and more strict "do it quicker, do it quicker" – so there's a chain of pressure, which I had to pass on. There was one we called Jalapeño, because he was always stinging us. The twelve hours got you five hundred pesos [$42] a week; you had to work weekends to get the extra two hundred. Eventually, I had to leave because I lost my eyesight from concentrating all day – before, I could see like an eagle, now I'm blind as a bat – and because the bones in my ankle got all messed up from standing for eleven years. I'm not a small lady,' she laughs, 'and I started having trouble walking.'

Herlinda spent twenty-two years making slippers, seven days a week. 'Sometimes we had to increase production because there was an emergency, like when the buyer first started ordering them by the thousands, and if we didn't complete the order in time, the buyer might go somewhere else.' Interestingly, to wrap a straw for McDonald's is a much slower process than stitching a slipper. Herlinda would sew a base figure of eighty-four slippers a minute. In a day of 720 minutes minus 50 minutes for breaks, that is 56,280 slippers per day and 393,960 slippers in a seven-day week. This level of productivity paid a basic wage of 600 pesos a week – 0.0015 pesos (0.00011 cents) per slipper. 'But we could earn an extra three hundred pesos a week if we increased our productivity by an extra thirty slippers a minute, which I learned to do,' says Herlinda – 114 slippers per minute, totalling 76,380 slippers a day, or 534,660 in a seven-day week. Herlinda almost certainly didn't do this, but if she had worked at the higher rate for all her twenty-two years, and not accounting for any days off she must have taken, she'd have amassed what in baseball would be called a career total of 613,331,400 – well over half a billion – slippers, over a career average of 27,878,700 (nearly twenty-eight million) slippers a year. But that was not enough, not fast enough, not cheap enough. Suddenly, says Herlinda, 'the factory closed. It went to China, and after twenty-two years I lost my job. But everyone kept talking about this Julia, who had helped the workers and was retraining specialists who had lost their jobs, so here I am.' And she beams through her spectacles, a woman now in her forties, with the fingers of an eighty-year-old, but nimble as a child's as she serves herself from the aluminium trays containing a hearty lunch of fajitas that Julia has brought from a *taquería* round the corner.

Of course, this workshop could not begin to try to compete in the service of America's appetite for slippers. But it is a going concern, it has its catalogue and its business: T-shirts, tote bags, handbags, sweaters, blouses and shirts. 'My dream is to grow this workshop into an export business,' says Ofelia, who was herself a seamstress but self-employed in her house, 'because I had six sons', making school uniforms and habits for monks and priests and once, even, the bishop's robe. The CFO *maquila* has carved itself important partners like the Minnesota-based 'North Country Fair Trade', and a high point came when the Mexican fashion designer Juan Pablo López asked the women in Piedras Negras to realise his designs for various haute couture shows in Paris. The ladies take an intake of proud breath at the very thought. 'We made a summer and winter collection,' purrs Ofelia, 'all fair-trade materials, all organic: blouses and dresses for the women, and some shirts for the men. And there they were on the DVD, on a catwalk in Paris, paraded by models!' López's design drawings are on the wall, garments named after and reflecting the planets and their qualities. 'Earth is men's stuff, as you can see,' enthuses Ofelia; 'Mercury is a lovely blouse and Mars this sexy mini-dress. Jupiter's very pretty, a blouse with big baggy sleeves, but look at Pluto, a frock with a high waist, hem above the knee and designs from Chiapas.'

A hard few days in Piedras Negras end with a get-together in a dimly lit room at the back of a house in another shanty town, Colonia 28 Junio where Juan Tovar Santos lived, of buildings made of wood and this one, belonging to the Ozilla family, of concrete. The walls of the room are covered by the Virgin of Guadalupe, Club América and children's drawings, and it is hard to tell which of the people dangling their legs from both storeys of bunk-beds and sitting across the floor are Ozillas and which are family, friends or workmates. This is a social occasion, not another collective gripe, though the two tend to overlap. Arturo and Luis, two of the old guard, sing the praises of lotteries that operate in most *maquilas*. Arturo says that tickets for the official state-run lottery sell for less in the *maquilas* than they do on the street, but with the same prize money, because the salesman's commission is lower. To be caught selling tickets, though, 'gets at least a four-day suspension, and usually the sack'. Marginally less risky are the sweepstakes held, and odds offered, on horseracing and football. 'I won fifty pesos on a nag running in Torreón last year,' says a man called Adrian, 'for a stake of only five, though I've probably spent another hundred since.' Gabriela and the girls are dependent on thriving cosmetics markets that operate unofficially in the *maquilas*. 'The older ladies who can cross to Eagle Pass buy them in bulk and bring them back to sell in the toilets. The only snag is going into the bathroom two at a time to check out what they've got without being seen. Usually, the sales and raffles are on pay day, but it's getting easier now to pick up your winnings or perfume after work.' 'Better to go to Eagle Pass to buy cosmetics,' says Julia Quiñónez drily, 'than to sell your blood.'

The old baseball stadium in Ciudad Acuña is a rickety but precious one; the kind of ground that would melt the heart of an ageing American aficionado of the game who feels out of step with electronic scoreboards and a thumping disco beat through the seventh-inning stretch. The Acuña stadium didn't make it into Ken Burns's series on the history of baseball, but it reminds one that this is still a pastoral game, though invented in the city: there are little windows in the brickwork through which to buy tickets, scuffed concrete steps into the stands off which the paintwork has been worn by decades of boot heels. The crowd is arraigned on wooden bench seats without numbers; *Krakejak* is on sale from an ad-hoc stall for ten cents and Tecate with lime and salt in a can for thirty-five cents instead of the seven dollars that Americans pay for Bud Lite in plastic cups. This afternoon's game is a Coahuila state cup knockout fixture between Acuña's Atléticos and Saltillo, and the crowd is full of piss and vinegar with Acuña winning 8–1, sitting pretty with bases loaded at the bottom of the eighth. A third strike collapses the chance to go 12–1, but the standard is high, the signalling and second-guessing sophisticated and at the close range afforded by this stadium, you get to savour those moments of sudden acceleration and deceleration, after the tension of carefully calculated nothing. Across the scrap of land outside, a market is in full swing, selling *ropa usada* – literally 'used clothes': second-hand clothes brought from Del Rio across the border – knock-off CDs and very unofficial soccer kit: those in Acuña who are not fans of baseball tend to be devoted to the *Santos de Torreón* soccer team. Boys accordingly play football in the dust wearing either local green or Club América yellow, and a crowd of tambourine-bashing evangelicals sing on a corner, *'los aleluyas'*, as they are jokingly called. Jehovah's Witnesses – *Los Testigos de Jehovah* – are more commonly known as *Los Testículos de Jehovah* (which shouldn't need translating), jokes Oscar Gonzáles, our companion.

In June 2009, after the sale by Alcoa to Platinum Equity, the workers in Ciudad Acuña supported by the CFO, uncertain about the future of their forum for dialogue with company executives, made a decision: they would seek recognition to a trade union – that of Mexico's coal miners – a fly in the ointment of the city's selling point north of the border. This is not a shift away from the CFO, which is not a union and cannot legally organise a workplace. Quite the reverse, the CFO is as usual part of the plan. The CFO's office in Ciudad Acuña is located at the end of a dusty stretch of road along which a *pulga* (literally: flea) market sprawls, blaring music by our *narcocorrido* friends Los Tigres del Norte (Julia Quiñónez is a big fan). And inside the CFO office, on two consecutive September afternoons in 2009, groups of mischief-makers meet to discuss the progress of the idea to organise the first union in the city's *maquilas*, before moving on to work their shifts. These were all members of the dialogue forum, the legacy and tribe of Juan Tovar Santos and his day out in Pittsburgh. A man called Juan Carlos Palomino remembers the riot back in 1999 in the parking lot: 'they came in with guns, attacked us by force'; he feels his blood rush even now. 'People were fainting from the tear gas, women too, they didn't give a damn about the women.' And 'after they sacked 240 people, they thought the problem had gone away – ha ha! All they'd done was steel our nerve and spread 240 people to fight in other *maquilas*!'

The group on the second afternoon included Sergio from Veracruz who works in plant 2 of AEES, with a red T-shirt and ruddy face, and Javier from Tabasco with a pony tail pulling back the hair from his handsome face and a baseball cap on back to front, leaning forward, elbows on knees throughout the discussion. 'There were numerous advances as a result of our meetings with the executives,' says Sergio, citing a few: deals over pregnant women and protective shoes, time out for medical emergencies and recognition of grades and differentials. 'But there's been a change since the company was sold by Alcoa, noticeably by supervisors and managers, going back to the old ways.' The men use the term *prepotencia* – bullying, throwing their weight around. 'We're worried about the recession, but especially the way they respond. Laying people off, increasing the quotas, constantly repeating the threats to leave for Honduras or Asia, whether that comes from the top or not.' The uncertainty takes a social toll on Acuña as it did on Riveras del Bravo in Juárez, Javier talking about 'people returning to Veracruz or the south of Coahuila, nine out of ten of the empty homes left being invaded by gangs and addicts. It all helps organised crime sink roots into the *colonias*. Kids don't go to school, and things disintegrate socially. It's not Ciudad Juárez, but we're on the road to Ciudad Juárez.' The fact that things are quieter here, and the CFO's minds are on other things, does not mean the Zetas are any less active. Joe Morales, a former security coordinator for US and transnational companies investing in *maquilas* across Piedras Negras and Ciudad Acuña, said that the narco traffickers were 'in complete control of the streets and get very little resistance from those they extort. It's every citizen for himself if they are confronted by the drug lords. If the drug dealers need to kill someone, they take them outside Acuña so they don't attract attention of the Mexican federal officers or the military.'[8] In 2007, the Zetas organised a street party for children's day, with food, cakes and drinks. A banner was posted: 'Happy Day to All, from Osiel Cárdenas.'

'Because of who we are,' says Javier, 'we think the solution to all the problems has to start where the problem starts: in the workplace. We need to improve the quality of life, and that starts at work. It all begins with that.' Hence the aim to create a union branch, but why the miners' union? 'Because it's a strong union,' says a man called Nicolás Rojas Romero. 'It's less *charro* than the others, doesn't kiss the boss's ass and has a history in Coahuila – the coal mines in the south of the state were always well organised.' Ciudad Acuña's promise north of the border was that such a thing would never be tolerated. But contact has already been made with the miners' union in Mexico City, which is now ready to recognise a local branch of the union across the AEES plants belonging to Platinum Equity, in union-free Ciudad Acuña. How Platinum Equity will react is anybody's guess. 'It feels like back to Pittsburgh!' laughs Juan Carlos Palomino, like an old trooper called back to the front after too long in the rear echelon.

Once past the usual ring of Pemex stations and Oxxo convenience stores that flank any Mexican border town, and the Colonia 28 Junio where Juan Tovar Santos lived, the road out of Acuña and back to Piedras Negras crosses flat land reaching towards the border, through groves of mesquite trees and nopal cacti, wholesome and delicious with beans, and the pretty little town of La Purísima – the most pure. But before reaching the most pure, there is a sudden jolt. A white-painted chapel stands on the south side of the road, alone. Julia Quiñónez presumes it to be just another Virgin of Guadalupe and pays it no heed, puzzled at my demands we pull over.

The skeleton within is shrouded in a cloak of colours, the spectrum of the rainbow. In one bony hand, her right, she holds a globe – the earth, the whole world, the sphere of continuum and eternity. In the other, the left, a bunch of white flowers someone has placed there, roses and lilies, the flower of purity presented by the archangel Gabriel to the mother of Christ. At her feet, candles burn in glass holders bearing her image, only in the pictures, the cloak is hooded and black and she carries a scythe. Also on the ground, in homage, offerings of oranges, Tecate beer, ashtrays full of cigarette ends and scratch cards. An iron grille across the face of the chapel is locked. To partake in this homage, in this petition for protection and blessing, one needs access to a key, one must be initiated. On the side of the chapel is painted an oration which reads: You who await the exact moment/ To extend your hands to me/ To enter the time ordained/ Protect me from evil and all memory.

The skull of *Santísima Muerte* – most holy death – is unadorned. This is rare. She is usually crowned, at least with flowers, if not a mitre. She stares north, with her hollow eyes. And the black light of her gaze stares through those eye sockets of bone towards the river, the Río Bravo, Rio Grande – call it what you may, under this gaze it matters not a fig. The river: the flowing border, its waters now moving towards a new chapter in this war, a new terrain – that controlled by the Gulf cartel and Los Zetas, where all the rules change, the landscape changes, and the air itself is heavy with the cartel's power, deadly and, until very recently, intact. The skeleton's eyes stare towards the river as it winds now towards a bridge called the Gateway to the Americas, where the war began.

CHAPTER EIGHT

Gateway to the Americas / *Pax Mafiosa*

The headlights aimed along Highway 85 coming in from Monterrey throw bedazzling beams through the dust kicked up around truck stop *Veintiséis* – Twenty-six – so that the encampment of drivers, roadside cafés and police officers at their checkpoint is coated in a thick, illuminated mist of powdery, pulverised dirt. Although the trucks are parked up like a military column, many of their drivers have kept the engines loading so the granulated dust is also heavy with noise and fumes, chugging Volvo and belched Pemex diesel. There is no daytime or night in the truckers' world, only daylight and darkness; there is no clock apart from that which measures pick-up and delivery times, delays. North of the border, the commandment is set in stone and monitored by tachometer, an accord between the Teamsters and haulage companies: after ten hours' driving, you rest ten hours. But this side, in Mexico, things are more flexible. Or maybe not so flexible, there's just a different kind of rule: you drive all the hours God gives, pep yourself up with chemical cocktails to do so and make as much money – that is, drive as many kilometres – as you are physically capable of, Devil take the consequences. But even a Mexican trucker must eat, sleep a little and do other things while off the road.

Veintiséis is the name given to the truckers' republic that has sprung up around the customs post and police checkpoint 26 kilometres south of Nuevo Laredo, the city that, with its twin on the US side, Laredo, makes up the gateway to the last, industrial, leg of the border journey. The bridge between the two downtown areas of each city is called the 'Gateway to the Americas', because this is the border's commercial fulcrum, at which you arrive either by freeway up from Monterrey in the south or down Interstate 13 from Dallas to the north. Or, of course, as I did: along the flat border road from Eagle Pass, Texas. The railway bridge and three other road bridges between these cities form the umbilical cord of trade connecting Mexican and Latin American freight, and Chinese exports, with North America. Forty per cent of all trade between the US and Mexico – totalling $367.4 billion – crosses the Rio Grande here every day, loaded onto thousands of rail cars and 8,000 trucks crossing daily in both directions, converging from all over the US and Mexico to transfer their payloads to shuttle-trucks at vast freight-forwarding yards on either side of the border. More than a million barrels of crude oil a day cross the line here, along with 432 tonnes of jalapeño peppers, 11,000 ATM cash machines, 16,000 television sets – all this and more through a town that on the Mexican side didn't light the streets until recently and on the US side was a sleepy cowboy town famous for the song, 'The Streets of Laredo'. Now, neither side can mix concrete fast enough. *Los Dos Laredos*, as the twin cities are called, form a commercial DMZ full of freight containers as far as the eye can see. There is charisma and excitement in the whole thing – trucking – in both these twin cities.

Laredo, Texas, is the fourth biggest port – and the biggest land-locked port – in the USA, after New York, Los Angeles and Detroit. Some 5,000 trucks a day cross north, and 5,000 south, over the busiest bridges in the world. But here's the rub: although 97 per cent of the goods transported is legal, an estimated 3 per cent is contraband – invariably drugs northbound, guns and cash southbound – making this the principal crossing point for narco-cartel exports. And these drivers are their witting or unwitting transporters. The cartels' war – which began here in earnest in 2005 – was for the prize corridor, the most important Plaza of all. The authorities' war is against a simple logic: the more trade that comes through *Veintiséis* and across the border, the more drugs come with it.

Behind the rays of the headlamps at *Veintiséis* are other lights, the pale yellow or bright fluorescent lanterns of the *comedores*, places to eat, each marked with a hand-crafted sign. Approaching night, the place is all bustle and hustle. Exhausts farting, brakes screeching, reverse gears grinding and the drivers checking out the deals in the *comedores*. In the middle of this arcade is a little chapel, lit from within by flickering flames of candles burning on its floor and in alcoves in the side walls. On the back wall are painted the images of the Virgin of Guadalupe and San Judas Tadeo, beneath whom is written an oration: *Pros mi por San Judas Tadeo / Dame la mano firme y migrada vigilante / Para que llegue a mi destino / Sin accidentarme ni dañar a los demás / Líbrame de los conductores bandidos y agresores.* Grant me a firm, vigilant hand to lead me to my destination, without hurt to myself or the others — and deliver me from bandit and aggressive drivers — for thine is the eternal ribbon of asphalt, for ever and ever, Amen.

In the *Comedor Johanna*, two drivers sit on red plastic chairs at a red plastic table eating fajitas. They are Juan Gabriel Morales from Tabasco, driving a load from the Pacific port of Lázaro Cárdenas, and Alfredo Cornelio from the gulf port of Veracruz, hauling a container from a depot outside Mexico City. Juan Gabriel has two front teeth missing from the upper tier, a chest thick with hair and a ring with a crown of thorns on it. Alfredo wears a Chivas T-shirt and shorts despite the damp drizzle. Neither is told what their load is nowadays, they complain. Both men are exhausted and glad to have made it. 'The road gets harder,' says Juan Gabriel, the older man, 'more checkpoints, more delays, more *mordida* [bribes to pay along the way.] 'It's crazy,' says Alfredo, 'there's more work than ever, but more hassle on the route — because of the problems.' Their friend Jorge emerges from the gloom of the desert and backyard behind *Comedor Topo Chico* next door, zips up his flies and re-clasps his belt buckle with a hand of four Aces on it. It's too late to eat, he says; he'll have breakfast in the morning and a beer for now. Jorge looks the part: black pony tail, Durango boots with a harness and buckle, tight jeans.

Beyond the banter, no driver wants to get into an involved discussion about anything until morning, that is to say in five hours' time, at 5 a.m., same place. There are things to talk about, says Juan Gabriel, the older man, with glasses, but for now we'll just exchange team news between Chivas and Napoli, and talk about Barcelona. Barca's following in Mexico and among Mexican Americans is ubiquitously passionate, not least because the Mexican national captain, Rafa Márquez, played at left back for the Catalans. But the issue now is to find somewhere to sleep, not having available the cabin of a truck personalised with religious articles and pictures of women wearing only cowboy hats and boots. The first hotel on the north-bound carriageway was the *Campo Real*, but the din and squealing from the adjacent Bar Jaguar, from which one presumably adjourns in company to bed, made us U-turn back to the 8km line and the Motel California, with courtyard walls painted ochre yellow with a touch of pastel green to give the chipped cement that south-west adobe feel. The man at reception gives us the keys to rooms 05 and 07 in exchange for 200 pesos each and asks, how long we want them for. 'For the night,' I reply and his reaction says it all: part shrug, part compliment at the prowess entailed by a rental longer than an hour.

By 5 a.m., *Comedor Johanna* is in full swing as ebullient *Veintiséis* gears up for another day of NAFTA. Of last night's company, only Jorge from Puebla, looking chipper in a clean Wrangler shirt with embroidered horseshoes, has kept the 5 a.m. rendezvous. 'So you stayed at the Motel Californicada!' he growls with laughter, raising a thick eyebrow as though to ask: And how was she? Jorge calls hook-ers not the usual *putas* but *arañas*, which means spiders, and reports that the ones at *Veintiséis* are particularly *garrapatas*, literally ticks, meaning pushy. 'Not my type,' I offer, trying to sound more macho than prudish. 'You should've stayed in my truck and put me in the motel,' retorts Jorge, who says he's fed up with the food at *Johanna's* so we take a stroll across the pitted roadside tarmac through a battleship-grey dawn to the first eatery inside the line drawn across the highway by police inspection booths.

Jorge started driving after losing his job as a mechanic in Cór-doba, in the state of Veracruz. 'The Mexican driver,' says Jorge, 'is the best in the world because he has to be. It's not like the USA — there's no job protection, no guaranteed rest, no limit on the time you can drive. The company will never pay for a second driver, so it's all down to you. The pressure comes from both the company, and the other drivers. The crazier they are, the crazier I have to be. We set our own pace, always driving further to make more money, always stretching it, pushing it.' Jorge has been driving trucks the length of Mexico for eleven years: 'I know every metre between here and Monterrey, Monterrey and Mexico City, and down from my town to Guatemala. I know every trick — ha, and I know every *cachimba*.' That's a new one. It means literally fireplace or hearth, but Jorge means the kind of roadhouse where you can get fed, drunk and laid – and score drugs – all in one. 'In Zacatecas and the south, you get everything money can buy whenever you want,' assures Jorge. One hardly needs to ask how Jorge and his comrades perform these miracles of itinerant sleeplessness over weeks, months, years, for they are not miracles. 'How much do you get paid for this?' I ask. Jorge looks around him, checks that the cook is stirring eggs, and pulls out a plastic bag full of pills and little packets of silver foil. 'This much.' He smiles with a grimace.

At that moment, Juan Gabriel comes in and orders coffee. Juan Gabriel being a family man, Jorge explains that we're just talking about driving, a lot of driving. And Juan Gabriel has seen the highways change, he says, especially of late, since the drug war began, in 2005, here in Nuevo Laredo. 'The timing is stressful. You have your load, your deadline and delivery date. If you fuck it up, you don't get paid. After five years, I think I know every trick, and suddenly: new checkpoints, new hassle. And it gets scary,' though Juan Gabriel seems ashamed to admit it, for Mexican truckers are supposed to be unacquainted with fear. 'You're coming out of San Luis Potosí towards Saltillo and there's a checkpoint that wasn't there before. You've no idea who it is. If it's the army, you can usually talk your way out of it, even if you have to pay. But what if it's the police? Or the police working for the bad guys from here who are big in that area?' (No one utters the word 'Zetas', we shall see why.) 'You just have to get the papers out and give them what they want – you can try, but the company won't pay it back.'

What both Juan Gabriel and Jorge want to talk about more than anything is the moment that, as it happens, first brought me to Laredo in 2001. In a narrow window of time between his election and the attacks of 11 September that year, George W. Bush, as former governor of Texas and devotee of free trade, had made the first overtures of his presidency to Mexico. Vicente Fox was the first foreign head of state with whom he met and President Bush proposed the unthinkable: he wanted to admit Mexican trucks into and throughout the United States. Instead of a drayage system of forwarding yards and shuttling loads across the border, the long-haul trucks containing goods from the south and from China via Lázaro Cárdenas would simply line up for inspection and roll over the bridges. The proposal drew flurries of reaction from all sides and in all directions. US haulage firms accelerated their already substantial financial stakes in transporters based in Mexico. The Teamsters union was outraged: jobs regulated by years of negotiation were threatened by drivers working to timetables that were recklessly non-existent. Ironically, the left and right swapped sides: the former isolationist and the latter wanting to tear down the border while environmental groups joined the fray with dire warnings about Mexicans, the trucks they drove and the way they drove them. In the event, the proposal was scotched by 9/11, but it had begged all kinds of questions about not only NAFTA and the vagaries of free trade but about the border itself. It sent particles of interest flying about like those in a nuclear reactor, smashing into one another from all directions.

At every truck stop in Mexico, the passing moment fuelled a conversation that will never end. 'Let me drive to Chicago!' enthuses Jorge, eating breakfast like a bear. 'We could beat those *gringo* truckers' asses off their cabin seats!' Juan Gabriel says, with more deduction: 'If they let us cross the border, that would change everything. We'd make more money than the *gringos* even though their wages are higher, just because we'd drive so hard. We'd drive them out of a job with equal competition. That's why it'll never happen. But I respect them. They're doing what we would do – I wish we had the Teamsters instead of a *charro* union. They're drivers, we're drivers, we're the same people. If I was a Teamster, I wouldn't want crazy Mexicans driving everywhere, popping pills.'

We walk back to the parking area, past the police checkpoint, behind a very different eating joint which amalgamates Church's Chicken, Subway and Daily Roast. Along the way, an entire village has been built up around the *Veintiséis*, with houses where *comedor* owners, cooks, dishwashers, waiters and waitresses, used-clothing dealers, prostitutes, engine repair mechanics and their children live, and yards where rangy dogs, cats, cows, goats, pigs and rats cohabit with them. The *Comedor La Güera* – the blonde – also operates a full service market for detergents, shaving gear, batteries, penknives and knock-off audio and video entertainment, while the *Restaurante Jaliciencse* is attached to a *Yonke La Maroma*, fixing up cars and exhausted engines. And all along the way, the ground is littered with discarded little aluminium packages that once contained pills, the overnight dosage of downers to sleep and amphetamines to get you going again. There are hundreds of them strewn across the dust, but they are only the slightest micro-shaving off the great block of narcotics pulling up at *Veintiséis* and moving on through. The drugs are aboard the trucks, in bulk, heading straight into the United States of America. There is no reason why, if 40 per cent of cross-border trade moves through here, 40 per cent of the drugs shouldn't either, if not more. That is why the drug war began in Nuevo Laredo, and that is why the Gulf cartel and Zetas made sure to win it.

The battle for Nuevo Laredo was the beginning of the current phase of Mexico's agony. It announced a new level and a new kind of violence: some 2,000 were killed in 2005 across the country. The Sinaloa cartel sent a lieutenant called Edgar Valdez Villarreal, aka *La Barbie*, to lead its siege of the Laredo trade route, who used the Internet to show videos of four Gulf cartel killers being beaten, and ending with one being shot in the head. Valdez had been raised in Laredo, Texas, and been given his nickname – because of his pale complexion and blue eyes – at High School, where he was a cheerleaders' favourite and football star. *El Barbie* was the only American citizen to reach these heights of a Mexican cartel, until he was captured in Mexico City in August 2010. After one firefight late in 2006, the dead in Nuevo Laredo 'lay in pools of blood flowing into the Rio Grande', after which men with assault rifles 'picked up the bodies of the victims, threw them in the back of pickup trucks and headed out of downtown.'[2] In June 2005, President Vicente Fox sent in a token military force, but as a commander of the police department, Enrique Sánchez, said when asked by journalists where the soldiers were during the fighting: 'That's a good question. Where are they?' It was a barbed remark, with Mexican federal officials at the time briefing that the Nuevo Laredo's police department was at the disposal of the jailed Osiel Cárdenas, leader of the Gulf cartel and creator of the Zetas. At the same time, Alejandro Domínguez Coello, a former federal law-enforcement official and president of the chamber of commerce, became chief of police in Nuevo Laredo. He was honest, unaffiliated to the cartel – and assassinated seven hours after taking office.[3] Within days of the police chief's murder, the US government closed its consulate, comparing Nuevo Laredo to Baghdad, a city of 'bazookas, grenades and machine guns', said a businessman after watching a twenty-minute battle.[4] Throughout, the cartel hung their *narcomensajes*, one of which promised that the Zetas served 'Better Food Than Noodle Soup', the standard fare consumed by serving soldiers.[5]

But the war has, in 2009, abated. Nuevo Laredo is calm, or has the appearance of calm that could blow at any moment. When the human rights campaigner Raymundo Ramos Vásquez shows off a narco villa in the exclusive Madero neighbourhood whose owner switched loyalty to the Sinaloa cartel five years ago – attacked with bazookas, incinerated and still empty – he does so as though it were both a cautionary tale and a tourist attraction. But Nuevo Laredo lives the peace of the tomb, or what in Italy would be called *Pax Mafiosa*. 'There has been a truce,' says Ramos. 'I don't know the details, and I don't want to know, but the Gulf cartel has won, the Sinaloa cartel has lost, and they have reached an accord. I can only guess that Guzmán pays some kind of tax to use the corridor, if he uses it at all. The Gulf cartel controls the corridor again, and the federal army patrols every block of the city, twenty-four hours a day, 365 days a year. During 2010, the *Pax Mafiosa* ruptured as fighting broke out between the Gulf cartel old guard and elements loyal to Los Zetas, who eventually took the town.

But this nevertheless remains a monolithic society in which no one dares speak the word *Zeta*. In every town under their control, the Zetas have another name in everyday parlance, a codeword used as a vain insurance policy by the few who dare speak of this subject; here it seems to be *La Pirámide*, or just the generic 'bad guys', as everywhere else. It is an absurd charade – anyone who talks about the Zetas is at risk whatever they call them – but the shying away from the word is fundamentally important. It shows that the faux-mystique of the Zetas works and intimidates; that their name has become an evil talisman, and to avoid uttering it is a primal act of superstition. To speak it, on the other hand, feels like self-condemnation. Ramos talks about the Gulf cartel, but never uses the 'Z' word. There are, though, exceptions of insane courage.

Driving back with Raymundo Ramos into town one day, there was an extraordinary coincidence, speaking of brave people. I asked after a mutual friend of ours, Elisabeth, and Raymundo said he hadn't seen her for nearly a year, since the three of us were last together, in fact. At that very moment, in a little street behind the Church of the Holy Infant downtown, there she was. Elisabeth was once a leading attorney in town, fighting domestic violence, as a public defender for five years and four years in jails on cases of wrongful conviction. She was the first woman from Nuevo Laredo ever to volunteer for national military service. But in this city, her curriculum vitae makes Elisabeth unemployable, a transgressor of the values that sustain this society (which she is). No *curia*, tribunal or court will touch her, though she still carries her résumé round every forum in town.

In her hurt and rage, Elisabeth is another rare soul who testifies to what is happening, but unlike Raymundo she does so with a Devil-may-care fury heedless of consequence. After the joy at the serendipity of the meeting, we adjourn to a friend's house in an alleyway behind the church for coffee and incautiousness. 'I watch them control everything, different people but always the same interests. First the police, then the Zetas — let's call them by their name [she is the only person who does] — beating the city into silence. They control everything in this town, everything that moves, every particle of our lives.' Shouldn't you be careful, saying all this, Elisabeth? 'It's driven me mad being careful. If I am so dangerous, let them kill me. If they do, at least I'll die with a clean conscience.' People know Elisabeth, as we walk around and towards the church. They greet her from underneath the parasols that shade their taco stands, but make sure not to tarry too long talking, lest someone see or hear.

On the back of a truck, there is a sticker of *Santa Muerte*, and the words: *'Dios mé guía, Ella me proteje'* — God guides me, she protects me. 'Just look,' spits Elisabeth, 'there's a cult of death across this town. It is sick, dying from within.' We enter the church and breathe the musky air with relief. Elisabeth caresses the feet of the saints with fervent exhalations. 'Here, I am safe,' she says beneath the figure of the *Virgen del Carmen*, and the words: *'En la vida protejo / En la muerte ayudo / Y después de la muerte salvo'* — in life I protect, in death I help, and after death, I save.

Nuevo Laredo's peace is a hideous, precarious but browbeaten calm, yet it serves as a model which the Mexican government, or any future Mexican government, keeps on as an option, especially if the

PRI were to return to power by beating President Felipe's Calderón's PAN party out of popular exhaustion with his war. Put starkly, and in the extreme: Mexico's choice may one day be between the implosion in Juárez, where the war grinds on, or the *Pax Mafiosa* of Nuevo Laredo. The only problem is that a national *Pax Mafiosa* would be entrusted to Guzmán for safe keeping, so what deal to cut with the Gulf cartel, and/or Zetas? (These latter two were synonymous — until 2010, when an as yet unresolved internecine power struggle exploded further downriver and at the time of writing was about to arrive in Nuevo Laredo.)

When I return to see Raymundo Ramos a year later, in 2009, the 'peace' is one year older, the town almost buzzing, such is the façade of the *Pax Mafiosa* and the determination of these people to live as best they can. Raymundo and I convene in the front room of the house of a friend of his. He is an intriguing man — secretive about his life, but boldly forthright in his utterances and analysis. He runs the beleaguered Nuevo Laredo Committee for Human Rights, working as a *rapporteur* to the United Nations human rights commission, but his casework mainly involves complaints against the army — he stays well clear of problems caused by the Zetas. 'The difference between here and Juárez,' he begins, 'is that there, the Plaza is still contested — a battle between gangs, cartels and the army. Here, we don't have that problem. The Plaza is tranquil, it's peaceful now compared to three years ago. Here, there's one cartel and the army. But the volume of traffic going through Nuevo Laredo doesn't change. All it means is that the accord between narcos at the highest level must be holding, between the Gulf cartel, Guzmán and the *Familia*.' But, he warns: 'Laredo is the main crossing point for trafficking throughout all the USA, we're right in the middle of the distribution network here, and no one wants to give it up entirely. The Gulf cartel and Zetas hold the terrain, and anyone else must pay a tax. The army is here, but that doesn't affect the traffic either: you notice that President Calderón is fighting a war against the narco traffickers, but not the narco traffic!' And he echoes Ignacio Alvarado in Juárez: 'It's a strategy to control the traffic, not to eradicate it. Calderón's war is a political flag, a battle against the impunity of the narco traffickers. He's lowered their status in society, but it has done nothing to interfere with the economy the narco generates, the transportation and delivery networks that come through here – a structure that remains intact – and the infrastructure that has been established to launder money. All that is untouched. So the drugs cross over, and then what? The supply chain is in Mexico, and the distribution and demand chain is in the US, where the infrastructures are also intact. The US wants to try and stop the drugs coming over, but like Calderón, they don't go after the money or the infrastructure. Laredo – San Antonio – Houston: it's a seamless supply chain, and a seamless financial system.' And here in *Los Dos Laredos*, the essential link in the equally seamless transportation chain, 'the smuggling is closely tied to NAFTA. We supply the US with goods, and we supply the US with drugs, through the same corridor, aboard the same trucks.' The more goods, the more drugs, the percentage is consistent. 'The US has friends, and it has interests,' says Raymundo. 'In the cases of both goods and drugs, Mexico is not a friend, we are an interest. Depending on who you are in the USA, Mexico produces the goods and delivers the drugs.

'But things have changed,' he goes on. 'Before the war, and during the PRI time, the narco was granted impunity, so he thought he was the boss, but actually the politicians and the police were the bosses of the narco. Now, after the war and with PAN, the cartel in Tamaulipas has become a parallel structure; they are not subject to the political parties, they are a parallel government. Before, the policeman and politician were the bosses of the narco. Now, the narco is the boss of the policeman and politician, and does what he wants.'

The sudden rupture of the *Pax Mafiosa* and fighting between the Gulf cartel and Zetas from February 2010 came as a surprise in the apparent vice grip of the apparent alliance between the two over Nuevo Laredo. Although the worst violence was further downriver, opposite deep south Texas, Nuevo Laredo felt the tremors of the rift, for which one possible explanation, advanced by US and Mexican intelligence, is that the Zetas had become almost victims of their own success – too ambitious and greedy for the other cartels to tolerate further. Incuding that which they were supposed to serve as an enforcement wing. Indeed, the *Pax Mafiosa* had been so complete, there was little active enforcement to do, so that the Zetas became a cartel in their own right. Elements within the Gulf cartel's old guard, cut out of the loop, were even seduced into joining their old enemies from Sinaloa in a front against the Zetas. It even had a name: 'Carteles Unidos'.

Ramos was once a journalist for the local paper with a reputation for fearless reporting on the narcos, *El Mañana*. But, he says, 'I just couldn't carry on. It became too dangerous to be a reporter here. What would be the point risking it? The papers can't publish the news – it's too dangerous for them to do so.' In imploding Juárez, people banded around the words '*Línea*' and 'Guzmán' with relative ease in public, for all the raging violence. Here, barely anyone speaks and in the local press, nothing.

As any visiting reporter trying to cover Nuevo Laredo – and all Zeta or Gulf cartel territory – knows, this terrain is harder and more frightening than Juárez. Juárez has a functioning, albeit assaulted, mass media; a visiting journalist has reason to be there. In Juárez, there are press conferences, interviews and articles about the violence. The tabloid arm of the *Diario* newspaper, PM, makes a point of getting to the latest atrocity first, for a gory front-page photo. In Nuevo Laredo, the opposite prevails – the press has been bludgeoned into silence by the Zetas.

Nuevo Laredo is one of those towns in which the local paper is a local institution, as is the family which owns it: one of the most prominent and respected in the state, along the border indeed: the Cantú family, the head of which is Heriberto Ramón Cantú, with his wife Ninfa Deánder as its matriarch. The executive editor of the paper, and others the family owns, is their son Ramón Cantú, an impressive man, something of a good-living rake, charming, clever, forceful and unreliable in his appointments. But the doors of his newspaper are protected by a bullet-proof, bomb-proof screen, atop which is an understated memorial plaque commemorating an attack on the paper by the Zetas with grenades and guns in February 2006, targeting and injuring a veteran journalist investigating narco smuggling and conditions in the *maquiladoras*, Jaime Oscar Tey. Two years previously, in March 2004, the editor, Roberto Javier Mora García, was stabbed to death in his SUV, outside his apartment. The case developed a gruesome momentum of its own, after the arrest of a homosexual couple living in the apartment above Mora's, one of them a US citizen, Mario Medina. Both were convicted for the murder, and Medina himself stabbed to death in a hallway in Nuevo

Laredo's state prison. He had accused the Tamaulipas police of torturing him, and gave an interview the day before his death to *El
Mañana*, saying he was confident of being proved innocent.[6] And it
was not only in Nuevo Laredo that journalists were being attacked
and killed. In January 2010, Mexico's National Human Rights Commission published a tally of fifty-six reporters killed over the previous
nine years, with eight missing and seven newspaper offices attacked.[7]
In most cases, the assailants were narco-trafficking cartels hitting
reporters investigating drug traffic, corruption or crime, said the
report. But the *susurro* in Mexican journalistic circles is that in a few
cases, reporters put themselves at the disposition of one cartel, or had
been threatened into doing so, and were thereby targeted by another.
The Committee to Protect Journalists has assiduously traced the
attacks, and in its report for 2008 came up with a lower casualty figure, and damning indictment of the Mexican authorities: 'Powerful
drug cartels and escalating violence made journalists in Mexico more
vulnerable to attack than ever before,' read the report. 'Most crimes
against the press remained unsolved as Mexican law-enforcement
agencies, awash in corruption, did not aggressively investigate
attacks. With no guarantee of safety, reporters increasingly turned to
self-censorship to protect themselves.'[8]

Ramón Cantú defends his ground with estimable tenacity, though
takes care to do so on the US side of the border, on the public occasion of a 'War-on-Drugs' conference in El Paso. In private, he
confides, 'I'm sick of the whole thing. I want to talk about something
else, about the future of this place, trucks and trade.' But on the conference podium he bites the bullet: it was made clear, he says, 'that
we should not use the word "Zetas". And I took the view that the
lives of our staff are more important. This war is not going to be won
by a newspaper or magazine. We have to be aware of our safety as
well as benefit the community. We spend a lot of time looking out for
our own safety so as to avoid more complicated situations ... We're
censoring the newspaper, because we have to get our children to
school. If we get some anonymous tip or call, we have to decide what's
correct and what's incorrect. These people' – he reminds his audience in case it urges him to brandish the sword of truth at all costs,
as many do – 'they just kill you. They don't make up a slander that
you're having an affair, or taking money from the Mafia. If they

don't like you, they kill you. We have to be very calm. Yes, I've received complaints: "Why don't you publish this or that?" And I try to explain that I feel bad that we're not doing our job, and then: a lady calls, and we must report something. Next day, THEY call and tell me that two of my reporters have been kidnapped, and advise me to keep silent. I'd like to say I had a bit of courage, but these are innocent reporters covering social affairs – what am I going to do?'

Other journalists in Nuevo Laredo do speak what they cannot write – off the record. One editor says of the crossings into the United States: 'The Mexican government can put all the money it wants into the customs and inspections posts, it's all useless. A customs officer is as afraid of organised crime as anyone else. What are they to do when a convoy of fifteen Suburban SUVs pulls up at the forwarding yard or even at the bridge? And men get out wearing paramilitary uniform and ski masks, carrying AK-47s. If it's a forwarding yard, they're told to open the truck. If it's on the bridge, they're told just to let a truck through across the river. They're not asked, they're told. What do they do? They move to one side. They open the door. They let the truck cross, they don't ask or say anything. They just look the other way. Who wouldn't? This is a military unit; they wear hand grenades in their vests. They don't need to ask people to cooperate. This is what happens here, this is how it's done.' He hypothesises: 'How can you deal with a military formation? You can militarise customs instead of having civilian law enforcement, and have regular shoot-outs on the border bridge, but I can't see that – you'd be having battles all day. You can check every truck, but what happens to NAFTA if you check four thousand trucks a day? The line would go all the way to Chiapas!' We are talking late. There's an edition due. None of this can be broadcast locally. 'When the truck reaches the US side,' he continues, an impeccable source, 'they have their corrupt officers among the honest ones. They are approached, offered money and threatened. You play and get paid or you refuse to play and pay with your life; they're bought the old-fashioned way.'

At the end of a street running through the Colonia Victoria and down to the reeds along the riverbank and the border is a migrant shelter called the House of Nazareth, run along similar lines to the CCAMYN in Altar, catering mostly to desperate Central Americans waiting to cross, or else deported back. Over the road is a blue wall tagged with graffiti, not of gang names but those who have died. '*El Veracruz* RIP' – the implication being that this was a migrant from the state or city of that name who perished in the desert. Wrong.

A posse of lads is shallying around the wall, apparently nonchalant but watching over the stretch of land between the end of the street and the border. Presuming them to be something to do with the migrant shelter, and the priest in charge not available, I saunter over for a chat. 'No,' says a rapscallion youth in a grey zip hoodie and jeans. 'They died here in accidents, in this *colonia*.' 'That's my brother,' says another, in perfect English, pointing at a name on the wall. So you're not migrants, then? 'No, we're from here.' These boys need to be spoken to, but carefully. 'Antonio' lived in Houston awhile. 'Came back after a few years – got deported.' So these people were killed? 'Yeah.' So the Victoria *colonia* was bad during the war. And when I ask where's a place to eat, Antonio talks about a restaurant called the *Esquina*, now a shell, which 'closed during the killing and never re-opened because the owner was shot'. A slim boy is standing on the corner wearing nothing but a pair of dirty shorts, a red baseball cap on backwards and expensive new sneakers. He has said nothing so far, but suddenly a walkie-talkie in the pocket of his shorts crackles to life. He takes it out and walks away round the corner to talk. There's a feeling that I'm not supposed to be here while this communication takes place, so we shake hands and I leave, saying I'll come back to see the padre.

I return a week later, to find Antonio speaking to a friend at the Fox motorcycle service station near the memorial wall, to which we walk back together, talking about Houston and his deportation, past houses made out of wooden slats. I am alone – probably not a good idea, but being a clueless *gringo* can be a form of protection, as is the proximity of the House of Nazareth, where I feign an appointment for which I have been stood up again. I am therefore obliged to wait around. I thought it might help to be European, which apparently makes me a *gabacho* rather than a *gringo*, and wear a Barcelona shirt with 'Márquez' and a number 4 on the back, the Mexican captain's shirt. The fact that it is official merchandise is worth twenty minutes of valuable conversation, which rolls along sufficiently as to have me slouch up to the *Abarrotes El Brego* for some beer. We pour down a couple of cold ones as the sunlight sweetens and deepens, and

I take a risk. I ask the boy wearing the hoodie if they might be able to sell me something '*de la buena*', some '*trueno verde*', green thunder. There's a frisson. Antonio looks at the boy with the walkie-talkie. My move: It's your work, no? Silence. 'Maybe, yeah,' says Antonio, 'but we don't do weed.' *Coca*? '*Chiva*', heroin, he replies immediately in Spanish, 'but not us, other people. We watch.' And in English again: 'For export only.' And he laughs. The boys address each other as '*carnal*', a form of 'bro', but apparently thicker since it implies common blood. If these are not smugglers, they are *halcones* – falcons, lookouts. Well, I say, respects and God bless your brothers, and cross myself looking over at the names on the wall. 'It was heavy,' says Antonio. 2005? 'Yeah.' Guzmán's people? Silence.

Next day, the shelter is shut so I tell the boys I have to wait. They don't believe me, nor do they want to talk about Barcelona. Okay, I ask, but getting nervous: tell me just one thing and I'll go. Do you work for yourselves, or are you part of the pyramid? Antonio screws up his face as though he has just eaten a jalapeño too far. Then he stares back. 'Kind of connected,' he says in English, 'everyone is.' The walkie-talkie crackles in the young boy's pocket again, and I leave for the last time.

On the outskirts of another town, he balances his weight in the shade of a walnut tree, through which dappled sunshine falls. 'Oliver' is a big man, with a belly and a second one beneath it. He moves slowly, and wears a yellow T-shirt and grey track-suit trousers. One would like to be able to say that he had the keen, darting eyes of an executioner, but he hasn't. Like him, they are slow but not languid, they are considered. They do, however, have a certain extinguishment in them. He was, so his employer had said, a member of a gang affiliated to the Gulf cartel, and a *sicario* – an executioner – though Oliver doesn't like the word. He prefers *asesino*.

For all its importance and size, Nuevo Laredo lies in a far northwest corner of the state of Tamaulipas, the Zetas' home territory, but it is not their bastion – that lies further downriver. And it was in Nuevo Laredo that the war showed how little sense of brotherhood there really is within the cartels, happy to kill out of factional greed within the same organisation. Guzmán's attack on Nuevo Laredo in 2005 was an opportunist push several years after the arrest and extradition of Osiel Cárdenas, but the arrest led also to an internal struggle within the Gulf cartel, as the seizure of a *capo* often does. Cárdenas's power base was Matamoros and his soldiers were the Zetas he founded, with Nuevo Laredo far away and run by an old guard in the Gulf cartel, some of them loyal to Chava Gómez, whom Cárdenas killed to assume supremacy. They had their own deals with the local police and, crucially, with the haulage industry, and needed subjugation by the Zetas from down the valley. Oliver's gang served a network which the Zetas from Matamoros needed to bring to heel, but his faction fought its ground. The fault line across which Oliver was fighting was more or less that which broke open again in spring 2010, his Gulf cartel faction being that which appears to have been seduced by former rivals among the old Sinaloa foe to pitch once again against 'the people from Matamoros' – the Zetas.

Oliver won't say for whom he worked, only that he was one of *Los Texas*, which he sometimes calls *Texanos* – Texas and Texans. It was, he says, 'a gang' ('*pandilla*', he calls it), 'on Calle Leona and Calle Vicario in the Victoria *colonia*. We carried out tasks for the organisations in this area of Tamaulipas, in Nuevo Laredo; it also has connections over the river.' Oliver had been a truck driver in the United States, and a drug addict – he is now a born-again Christian. 'I looked up the *Texas* guys there in San Antonio while I was trucking over there,' he says. 'I was taking some heavy stuff, and suffered mental problems. I got deported.' Back in his home town of Nuevo Laredo, in need of work, Oliver hooked up with the gang again, by now formally affiliated to the Gulf cartel. The 'truck driving', it seems, had involved distribution of drugs. 'We were in the *colonia*; we were safe in the *colonia*, but only in the *colonia*. Outside of that, you don't know who you're dealing with. You don't know who's armed and who isn't. So you work for the organisation and they work for you. First, they get you dealing. Then they get you dealing a little more. But if you're good, the real money is in killing.' How much? Silence. Oliver stares back, waiting for another question. He could just get up and go, but he doesn't, he just sits and waits. There are other people around; his boss isn't far away. It's not easy to talk – Oliver is on probation for promotion at work – back to a post he held, but lost. He wants it back a lot more than he wants to talk to me.

How did it start? 'It started with fights against the gangs from other *colonias*. They were creating problems. We got told they were shaving the product, or going over to the guys from Matamoros who were coming in [the Zetas]. I killed one guy in a parking lot, between Victoria and the *Puente* 2. I shot him.' And? (There's no point in asking those daft 'how did it feel?' questions, Oliver would probably knock my head off with a flick of his finger.) 'And he died.'

Until 1994, says Oliver, 'the organisation was straightforward. I wasn't involved in smuggling. Most of the drugs were going through the POEs, and they were taking care of that, but some of the gang would organise for distribution with people we knew on the other side in San Antonio. What they needed to make things run smooth was enforcement.' What's enforcement? 'Enforcement is getting problems off the cartel's back.' There's another silence, which Oliver finally fills of his own accord, heaving his huge frame from one side to the other and rolling his eyes. 'I killed a guy on orders – he was *drogado*.' Here the slang kicks in: in border street talk, *drogado* can mean 'in debt' as well as 'drugged'. 'He hadn't paid, he was moving stuff and he wouldn't pay back what he'd sold. He died.' Where? 'In his house.' Why? 'For the money he owed the cartel.' That is all.

The reason I am at this place, a medical institution, is not to talk to Oliver but to his employer and manager about the wonderful work he does with drug addicts – of which Oliver was one. Oliver was doing well, and about to become one of the manager's top assistants, but rescinded back to his friends in the gang, and to drugs again. Then he returned, like the prodigal son, desperate to get back to where he was, said the employer, 'But it had to be on my terms: "I'll take you back," I told him, "but you'll have to start at the beginning."' 'It's hard,' Oliver says softening, almost confiding, 'always that temptation.'

After 2003 and Osiel Cárdenas's arrest, 'there was more to do,' says Oliver, 'just more to do. Now I know it was because the people from Matamoros didn't like my people, and my people didn't want the people from Matamoros moving in. I never tortured anyone. I beat the shit out of people. But I never tortured anyone, like they do now.'

Oliver speaks in short phrases; his breaths do not accord with the beginning or the end of a sentence. As he speaks, he rolls his heavy head back, and adjusts himself and his weight on the metal seat around the tree-trunk. 'I ran a guy down with my truck,' he says, 'I made a big mess.' There is no point fishing for details. 'This'll only stop when people stop taking drugs,' says Oliver. The body language is a strange mixture of sloth and strength, like a drowsy animal that can become dangerous in the blink of an eye. 'I was never part of the people who were cartel and police,' he goes on, at last exhibiting some pride in himself. 'We were on the street, in the *colonia*. The cops didn't trust us. I was in it for the *territorialidad* [defence of the turf]. That's why we were trying to stop the guys from Matamoros. I'd seen my friends die, I was doing it for the *Calle Leona* and for my brothers [*carnales*] in the gang, and because it paid.'

Oliver says he played no part in the war between the Zetas and Guzmán between 2005 and 2007; he had begun his road to recovery from drugs and endeavoured to live his new life by then. But memories are long and the danger remains, says his employer. 'He's a threat to us all. He was a *sicario*, he was one of the gang affiliated to the Nuevo Laredo Gulf cartel faction, and the Zetas could come for him any time. Which is very dangerous for all of us.' 'I was not a *sicario*,' insists Oliver, 'I was an *asesino*. I didn't kill enough for a *sicario*, and I didn't get the money a *sicario* gets. I did other things. I was an *asesino*' – an assassin, but not an executioner.

One of the things the editors and reporters on *El Mañana* are eager to talk about is the 97 per cent of merchandise crossing the river that is legal. Not just because it changes the subject, but also because 'trade is the only viable solution to the problems', says Ramón Cantú, 'good jobs and a strong economy for the city'.

The four road bridges that make this the Gateway to the Americas are: the Colombia Bridge to the east over the Nuevo Leon state line; the World Trade Bridge towards Laredo, which carries the bulk of traffic; the Gateway to the Americas itself (also known as Bridge 1), which connects the two main streets downtown and has a pedestrian pathway, and Bridge 2, a short way east. A fifth is planned. The railway bridge or *Puente Negro* runs between the Gateway and World Trade bridges, owned by Union Pacific, which charges the other principal user, Kansas City Southern, for its use. But with Kansas emerging as the new rail hub of the United States, the muscular KCS line, which had bought into Mexico's network during privatisation, is masterminding plans for a second rail bridge, its own, connecting Lázaro Cárdenas to Laredo.

'It's been a flag of this paper as the voice of the city: Get the New Rail Bridge,' says *El Mañana*'s editorial director, Antonio Martínez Santoyo. 'It will complete the infrastructure we need to cope with future traffic. It's now more than just trade between Mexico and the US, it's China, too – some of the goods not even destined for the United States: a route has expanded over the past five years bringing goods from China, through Lázaro Cárdenas, up through Laredo and out through Galveston or New Orleans to Europe, by sea and train. It's quicker than coming through the Middle East, and the new 'Post-Panamax' generation of ships are too big to get through the Panama Canal and sail the Atlantic. So it all has to dock in Mexico and proceed by rail. For now, trucking is the bedrock of this town, and Laredo over the river. Every one of those truckers and workers in the yards has a relative who works in freight over the other side. However, there'll come a time when the fuel situation will change, making sea and rail the future, and we can be part of that. The whole thing is a lesson of history. For centuries, Valparaiso in Chile was the stepping-stone between Asia and Europe, then the Panama Canal, and now it can be *Los Dos Laredos*.' It can. But for the problem: Nuevo Laredo is a place in which almost every business is shaken down by extortion rackets run not by the local *cholos*, as in Juárez, but by the Zetas or the Gulf cartel. Bigger business needs protection by a bigger stick, but the Zetas's attention to detail is thorough.

In the maze of alleyways behind the border parking lot downtown, a group of ladies engage busily in one of the most established businesses throughout the borderland, *ropa usada*, used clothes. They are called *chiveras*, and they work in every city on the Mexican side, going over to the US to pick up second-hand clothes to bring back for sale – which is, unbelievably, against a Mexican law forbidding the import of used clothes for retail.[9] Nevertheless, in every Mexican border town, garden fences and roadside railings are lined with jeans, shirts, blouses, baby wear, skirts and frocks for sale.

In Laredo, on the US side, in a low grey building with a brick-red sloping roof, a team of women and girls overseen by an Anglo manager sort mountains of *ropa usada*. The warehouse is one of many along Santa Isabel Avenue beside the Union Pacific railway sidings and inspection yards. It is hot, hard work, which the women undertake with genially high spirits: piles and piles of clothing, tied together in bundles, are sorted according to type, thrown into canvas containers marked with labels like *'Mujeres* Leisure', 'Western' or 'Teen'. There is even an Amexican word for this process, a verb: *'clasear'*.[10] The ladies are helped out by their daughters after school's out. Rick, the supervisor, is wary of any conversation that gets too detailed, but the money is fair, and the labour done with gusto. Then the problems begin.

Over the bridge in Nuevo Laredo, a woman cooks chicken and corn for her daughter and friends in a little house near the bridge car park. All these ladies know and visit the warehouses and sorting depots along Santa Isabel Avenue from which they collect *ropa usada*, and bring it over the Gateway to the Americas bridge, in big zip-top bags. Some of the women then sell their loads to people who retail it from their fences to boost the punishing family budget. Others sell directly themselves, but none escape the tap on the shoulder. Unbelievably, the Zetas and Gulf cartel − an international criminal syndicate dealing drugs into the USA and to Europe worth billions of dollars − has the *ropa usada* ladies firmly in its sights. Of the women in the whitewashed room, none pays less than one peso in ten as a tariff on the sale value of what she brings across the bridge from Laredo, most pay two pesos and one pays three, probably because she sells direct. This is not a street-corner crew of teenaged thugs, this is *La Pirámide*, the Zetas, though of course not even the boldest-speaking of these women, wearing her headscarf would consider using the word. 'The customs is right there in the parking lot,' she says with a dry laugh. 'And if they're not on duty, they come to the place where we distribute. That's how it is. What's the point of arguing? I need the work to get the money that's left to eat and send my daughter to school.'

But this is just the small fry. Raymundo Ramos and I are driving through the horizons of forwarding yards and containers, when the strangest thing happens: a sudden storm of little moths fill the air as far as the eye can see flying into the windscreen like hailstones. They almost eclipse the pale, hazy sun, and make the panorama of haulage and rungs of yellow cabins behind the chicken wire, dust and dirt even more surreal. Still, we keep passing the yards, at a slower pace: ALA, Carga Consolidada, Trasportes Mineros de Coahuila, Fletes México, FEMA, Aeromexpres. Ramos chooses his words carefully, alternating on and off the record with meticulous attention to what he is saying. We have been talking about 'the cartel' levying *cuotas* or *mordidas* (bribes) from local businesses. Do these freight companies pay the *cuota* – extortion money – as well? 'Everyone,' replies Raymundo. To who, the police or the cartel? 'The cartel.' Is that on or off the record? 'On the record.' Are you sure? 'Yes.' Is that normal? 'It's totally normal. It's the system. Those who get killed in Nuevo Laredo now,' he says, 'are not part of any turf war; they're usually businessmen who have problems with the cartel. But none of this has had any impact on the drug traffic or the *cuota* that everyone must pay.'

On another occasion, the line of shuttle trucks waiting to cross the busiest bridge in the world, *Puente Comercio Mundial*, No. 3, a couple of weeks later stretches back for miles, the truckers expecting at least a five-hour wait today and alighting for coffee and breakfast tacos at the roadside buffets. A group snacking at a little roadside stall called *Takos Kora* have just been hauling plasma TV sets and domestic white goods from Korea and China. They complain that enhanced security makes two runs a day more strenuous to complete if not impossible. They object to the amount of tracking devices and checking the shuttle companies are now obliged to carry out to make sure the load goes straight from the forwarding yards to the bridge, not via some other place where the load may be tampered with and a little extra put on board. 'If there are drugs in the container,' says a driver called Luis, 'they'll have been there all the way, and you'll know nothing.' And anyway, says another man, these new seals they put on the containers are all very well; 'but the bad guys know how to break the seal, do what they want and put everything back looking like nothing had happened'. The conversation, already a bit awkward, winds down. Then a driver wearing a brown bomber jacket and smoking silently until now says: 'Sometimes, the bad guys just come into the yard in a *troca*, and just say: "open the container." There's nothing you can do but turn away, wait, get in the cabin and drive.'

Thirteen miles north of the border, Bill Sanderson shoots a dart of spittle through his front teeth onto the tarmac and points his cowboy boots towards the entrance to the Pilot Travel Center. A Teamster of twenty-three years, Sanderson was born in southern Missouri, raised in Little Rock, Arkansas, 'but now I live in Carlisle, Pennsylvania, 'cause it's the crossroads of trucking and it makes life easier. I get to see more of my wife and kids that way, if I'm living right on the depot.' Crossroads it certainly is; Carlisle should be twinned with Laredo: I remember interviewing Jimmy Hoffa Jr. there once in a diner at 3.30 a.m., president of the International Brotherhood of Teamsters made famous by his father, who is believed to be entombed within the concrete of a bridge over the New Jersey Turnpike. 'I love it,' says Sanderson without hesitation, 'doing this job. Right amount of freedom, right amount of home. I can say I know every mile between here and Dallas, Dallas and Little Rock where my parents are, Little Rock and Nashville and Louisville, and between Louisville and Pennsylvania pretty much every inch. I know just where to stop when the hours are up and the clock's gonna catch me out. But it's always different: different weather, different time of day. And there's always an adventure, up to Montana, always some place you don't know yet.' Sanderson wears a great T-shirt: 'Born Free. Taxed to Death.'

This is Port Laredo, the truckers' lair, US equivalent of *Veintiséis*, 13 miles north of Laredo up Interstate 35, the spinal freeway that connects the freight yards with San Antonio, Houston, Dallas and all stations north. And it could not be more different. You can choose between McDonald's and Subway to eat right here, or any number of other chain favourites within a couple of miles down the 1-35 business loop. If you don't care to eat in, your meal can be ordered and your number called by loudspeaker into the forwarding yards. You can buy special phone cards called 'Truckerbucks'. You can buy a T-shirt reading: 'Christ is the ROCK ON which I stand'. A voice comes over the Tannoy: 'Shower customer number 114, your shower is ready. Please proceed to shower ten.' There are slot machines and a bewildering range of scratch cards. 'Pumpkin Spice Capuccino is Back,' says a sign, as though it ever went away. Sanderson acknowledges a man wearing a fluorescent orange jacket and combat fatigues; he is travelling with his wife and child, in defiance of the lonesome trucking stereotype, but Sanderson leaves him to his itinerant family Sunday lunch. 'There's places I'd rather be than Laredo,' says Bill, who is down collecting a mixed load for Yellow Freight. 'But it's an interesting enough town, on the edge, kind of thing, seen a few problems but that don't affect me. People is kind, that's for sure, though

I can't say I like the food. Some of the boys like it, and used to visit over in Mexico, too. But you never caught me going across there, oh no, not even when it was quiet. I'm a family man, got responsibilities; far as I'm concerned, you kiss goodbye to all your rights as a human being soon as you cross that border.'

In the old days, says a driver called Mitch from Springfield, Illinois, a taxi would take you in a group of four for $25 each, over the border to what is called the *Zona de Tolerancia* in Nuevo Laredo – 'he'd wait for everyone to finish their business and bring you back. Only twenty-five bucks, and you didn't spend much more'n two times that over there,' says Mitch. But, happily for the Mexicans, that caper has ended since war started – one of its few welcome beneficial side effects. Maybe it is coincidence, but since I was last here, a new building has risen over the road from the Pilot Travel Center: the multi-storey 'City Limits Adult XXX' complex. This is an air-conditioned hypermarket for sex aids, S&M appliances, blue DVDs, the lot – open twenty-four hours, with dark reflective glass and an ATM machine. On a sweaty Saturday afternoon it is fairly well patronised: on a Saturday night, it's teeming. 'They hang out in the motels around the Howard Johnson's down there,' Mitch had said. 'You'll see a bunch of guys parked up at the 610 truck stop on Santa Maria next to the movie theatre and that's them.'

The Dos Laredos freight system works like this: once past the *Veintiséis*, Mexican long-haul truckers take their loads towards the border and fan out along the two great *Anillos Periféricos* ring roads that circumvent the south of the city. From these yards operates the system of 'drayage' – the Mexicans have adapted the word to *'Drayaje'*. Shuttle companies – some locally and independently owned, others belonging to the big long-haulers – operate smaller, usually older, cabins to which the containers are affixed and which take the merchandise over the river, via a long wait, as becomes clear, skirting the edges of a city to which 10,000 men have come to live as shuttle truckers in the freight yards that extend the length of the Airport Boulevard, Pan American Boulevard and the giant ring roads mile after mile of stack upon stack of containers waiting to go; row after row of little cabins returned having just handed over their load north of the border or else waiting to go. And row upon row of bigger, newer cabins also parked, ready to head back through *Veintiséis* to the south or Lázaro Cárdenas, pick up another container, bring it back and do it all again. At any time, there are 30,000 containers in Nuevo Laredo awaiting transportation, and easily tampered with, loaded with freight that does not appear on the ledgers. Once through customs and on the US side, the drayage drivers take the load over the flyovers and overpasses connected to the international bridges and deposit them at any one of the miles and miles of forwarding yards on the US side, flanking Mines Road, officially known as FM1472, to the west, and Port Laredo to the east of the freeway. Even the street names on which the yards are located have ambitious names like Inter American Boulevard, Pan American Boulevard and Trade Center Boulevard. Many of these yards are US-owned with names like Swift Transportation, but an increasing number are Mexican, like *Despachos del Norte*.

Aldo Fernández has the rare distinction of being a trucker who actually lives in Laredo, among these yards where Pan American Boulevard meets Mines Road. 'Right in the middle of them,' he says. 'You'd never know there was residential housing in here.' He does so not only because he comes from Nuevo Laredo, so that this is home, but for reasons similar to Bill Sanderson's: 'If you live near the depot, you get more time at home.' Employed by Tri-National, or just 'Tri-Nat' as the drivers call it, of St Louis, Missouri, Aldo is a committed Volvo man. 'This is 2009,' he beams, 'best truck I ever drove.' His usual route is to Oklahoma City, but last night he came back from Detroit, and tomorrow, he's going to Canada, 'where they open the border at eight a.m., so you have more waiting around than here, but less paperwork. I see the whole of America, but I know how it works here.' There is 'total camaraderie between truckers', Aldo says. 'I'm Hispanic and I speak Spanish on the CB, someone else may be black, someone else may be white, but if you're a trucker, you're just a trucker. When you get into trouble, the nearest guy helps you out.' However, there is 'no camaraderie between the long-distance *gringos* and the drayage drivers who bring their loads over from Mexico. The Americans never speak to them when they switch the loads cause they're just in little four-wheelers. It's more like "hey, mother-fucker, out the way!" when they're backing up.' But they need to be careful, watch their language. 'If you come to Laredo and talk shit about Mexicans on the CB, that's not a good idea,' says Aldo. 'There was some guy a couple of years back talking all that wetback stuff and hairy Mexican women. He was doing it on the CB radio and parked up. Only his truck didn't move from the truck stop, and six days later they had a look inside and found him stabbed to death in the cabin.'

In Laredo, too, there is no avoiding frequent offers to transport smuggled drugs from cartel contacts in the forwarding yards. 'You get offered money according to how far you'd go,' says Aldo. 'So much to take a load to San Antonio, more to New York. It's a dumb game to get into – a couple of my friends are in jail for that. They get the offer, think it's easy cash, get caught.' Are the drugs loaded up in the Mexican forwarding yards, or do they come all the way? 'Usually they've come all the way,' replies Aldo, preferring to change the subject, since this is a social dinner with a friend from Nuevo Laredo over for the evening. He takes us down by the river to show us a trick the drayage drivers play. Beneath the Gateway to the Americas bridge connecting downtown Laredo with its Mexican neighbour, they have parked their cabins overnight. 'They walk back across the bridge, get drunk, sleep in Mexico and walk back across to start from this side and avoid the morning rush-hour line on the bridge.'

The Czech composer Antonín Dvořák wrote his greatest string quartet – No. 12 in F major, op. 96, 'The American' – in a little town called Spillville, Iowa. He had gone there by way of a retreat from New York, where he was not always happy, knowing that he would find there a community of fellow Czechs. It was a blissful summer in 1893: Dvořák would take a bucket of ale down to the banks of the Turkey River at five each morning and compose, so that moments in the quartet's *molto vivace* third movement replicate in music the exact notes of the birdsong to which he listened. No piece of music ever written evokes the scale and lyrical serenity of America's open spaces more than the quartet's mellifluent *lento* second movement. The arrival in Laredo of the internationally acclaimed Bellas Artes Quartet of Mexico City to perform Dvořák's masterpiece one evening in October 2009 was hailed in a series of speeches as a cultural high watermark in the city's long history. 'A wish come true,' said the host, the provost, in the hall of Texas A&M university campus. The freight business elite of the Gateway to the Americas made sure to

be there for the occasion, resplendently dressed. Many spoke Spanish, and continued to do so through the music, although the woman
next to me who asked out loud, as we approached an especially lovely
moment in the Allegro: 'Why is everyone being so QUIET?' did so
in broad Texan. Sitting in the front row was Laredo's first citizen,
who looks like an FBI agent with his quarterback frame, spivvy suit
and shaven head; probably because he was an FBI agent. Raúl Salinas' position keeps him so busy that he is obliged to look into his
computer screen and tap away throughout most of our interview, but
this is a man who can chew gum and walk at the same time, for he
makes a salient point about 'the high wire we're on, between needing to keep goods coming through, and stopping that illegal
percentage. We've had problems on the border, sure. We have crime
statistics that tag us.' When Salinas qualifies this by insisting that
'bad news sells, and that's been our problem' and that 'the drug and
violence situation has been exaggerated', he sounds like a bad salesman. But when he insists that 'I won't accept a compromise in the
fact that we and our Mexican neighbours need to support each other
as cities and keep the bridges open', then he sounds like a mayor. 'We
can't slap our neighbour then ask for his help – that's a mistake we
constantly make with Mexico. We're the number-one inland port in
America, and we don't need a damned wall between us and the
number-one inland port in Mexico.' He says that 'it's more difficult
being mayor than an FBI agent. As an agent, you investigate crimes
and send people to jail. As the mayor, you gotta run Laredo.'

In Mayor Salinas' city hall, an estimable diplomatic system operates: an office is occupied by a consul from Nuevo Laredo, a Mexican
ambassador from the twin city, Gerardo Lozano. Born in Laredo,
Texas, raised in Nuevo Laredo and educated in San Antonio, he would
appear perfect for the job. He also talks straight, less convinced about
what Mayor Salinas called the 'exaggeration' of drug trafficking.
Lozano puts it the other way round: 'Amazingly, the narco war hasn't
affected trade. More traffic is arriving in Nuevo Laredo than we have
the infrastructure to deal with, and that's our great challenge – to
build and provide it. But it hasn't affected drug smuggling either.
Let's say that only three per cent of the merchandise is illegal, that's
probably about it, despite all the technical devices. But three per cent
is three per cent of whatever's coming through. Imagine: if eight

thousand trucks a day cross the border, and three per cent of what they bring is contraband, that's a hell of a lot of contraband.' But Lozano's crusade now is to ensure for Nuevo Laredo the fourth road bridge, the implications of which are being weighed by Miguel Conchas, director of Laredo's all-important Chamber of Commerce.

Conchas keeps the figures, and they are staggering. Truck crossings: 0.6 million in 1990, 3.2 million in 2008. Rail car crossings: 90,000 in 1990, 335,000 in 2008. Percentage share of all US–Mexico Trade: in 2007, Laredo, 39.8 per cent, all other ports, 60.2 per cent. In 2008: Laredo, 40.9 per cent, all other ports, 59.1 per cent. US–Mexico total trade: Exports in 2007, $136.5 billion-worth; in 2008, $151.5 billion-worth. Imports in 2007, $210.8 billion-worth, in 2008, $215.9 billion-worth. Total trade: in 2007 $347.3 billion-worth, in 2008, $367.4 billion-worth. Conchas ponders: 'The problem is always one of logistics – how to ship it all, and to ship it fast enough. That will be Laredo's task as long as the Mexican long-haulers are prohibited from coming over. The recession has affected us slightly, but the amount of cargo will grow now that Kansas City Southern have bought the railway line from Lázaro Cárdenas to Nuevo Laredo and we're getting the new bridge; that'll mean a big increase. It's part of talk we're hearing about a super-corridor – bringing less in through the US ports like Long Beach and New Orleans, deepening the Mexican pacific ports and bringing it all straight up through here to Dallas and Chicago, cheaper and faster. We're on the brink of that.' This 'Super-corridor' is much discussed, with its potentially cataclysmic impact on the US docklands and other jobs in the support industries that support them. 'But just as all this is happening,' says Conchas, 'business is confronted by the major problem of the drug trade. Legitimate business knows that you can't always guarantee what your drivers are bringing across.'

If the Rio Grande, which unites and divides Amexica, has a living human son, his name is Keith Bowden. Bowden navigated the watery borderline by kayak, from El Paso to the sea, as war raged through Zeta country in 2005. He was trying to experience the beauty and power of the river in the wake of the loss of his young wife to slow and painful cancer. Bowden kept and published a record of his voyage, which he called *The Tecate Journals*. There is an intensity, an existential solitude, about Bowden which draws one in rather than orders one away. He is strikingly good-looking, and physically trim – a sports coach as well as a teacher of English at Laredo Community College. On the wall of his windowless office is a photograph Bowden took of a moment in the river's flow as it rounds a colossus of red rock along the Big Bend, on which one inevitably comments. He takes it down and says, 'Have it.' Although Bowden is more afraid of rapids than of Nuevo Laredo, he speaks as someone who knows the narco footsoldiers well, as a baseball coach in Ciudad Acuña and in Nuevo Laredo, where he could hardly avoid the young men's other interests and activities. 'In one year,' he remembers, 'I lost fourteen ex-students or players. Kids I'd coached or taught.'

Among the young baseball players he coached was a boy named Ricardo who 'made a swift descent into the Nuevo Laredo drug-trade underworld, and his transformation from innocent adolescent to cold-blooded killer was total'. Ricardo's uncle was a standing member of the FBI's Ten Most Wanted list, and Ricardo bragged to coach Keith Bowden one day that he used the baseball team as cover to smuggle 'a hell of a lot of loads. The last time I saw him', writes Bowden, was 'a chance encounter at the same Nuevo Laredo baseball fields where we were once team-mates – he boasted that he was killing fifteen people a month "as part of business". I assailed his barbarism as "chicken shit" and demanded he explain the logic . . . "People with babies and mothers and little sisters. That's what you do. You kill people and you brag about it. I can't accept that." Ricardo buried his head in his hands and wept like a child.' Bowden never saw Ricardo again. 'A rumour surfaced that he had been hacked into five hundred pieces.' The body of another student, Alicia, was found beneath a construction site, to which police were led by yet another boy who studied with Bowden. He likewise vanished; 'his specific instruction leading to the discovery of her corpse were the last words he ever uttered'.[11]

Between this world and his, the river, says Bowden, 'there's a kind of oblivion, even hostility, towards the natural elements. Nature's a hard sell to people on both sides of the river. By the time people are five years old, they dislike the river, distrust it, they're afraid of it – they're told it's filthy and polluted, it's something migrants cross, it's where bodies wash up . . . Only when you're out on the river for days do you get a sense of it, both as nature and as the border.' So one gets a strange view of a war from a kayak. 'When I came through here, it was during the crazy time,' he says of his river passage between *Los Dos Laredos*, 'the middle of the war, wondering whether I'd see bodies floating on the river. But what really worried me were things like currents, things I had to have a sense of and could do something about. My fear did not come from people, it tends not to when you're trying to kayak through Big Bend or facing down a charging mountain lion. The person who could do me the most damage was myself, by making one tiny mistake.'

In days not long ago when the *Houston Chronicle* was one of the great newspapers in the world, it carried weighty, definitive supplements on a burning issue of the day in western America, one of which, in October 1993, was about the Rio Grande. The supplement followed the river from its source to the sea at Brownsville: 'A Clean Start in Colorado, A Filthy Finish in the Gulf', ran the opening headline. But there was beauty and poetry too, as the Rio Grande, 'like any river, it keeps trying to shed itself of the filth dumped into it. Given enough time, enough water, enough air, any river can remedy many pollution problems'.[12] But if one talks now about a river full of metal as the Rio Grande flows into its final, tropical stretch of borderland, people will not think you are talking about pollution. A river of iron, in these parts, means something else.

CHAPTER NINE

Iron River / Tell Them Who You Are

Metalwork and metalware strewn across every table, stretching all the way to the back of the hall – weaponry of matt, gunmetal grey. The guns are expertly made, all of them – although it is much easier to feel affection and admiration for the venerable collector's items with worn wooden butts, or the latest hunter's shotguns, than it is the wholly inorganic steely weapons that only make sense in combat. Quite apart from what an AR-15 is designed to do so effectively, its steely, glaucous grey emanates a sombre foreboding all of its own. Apart from the fact that a Czech vz.58 Military Folder Polymer is said to be among the best-value variations of a Kalashnikov, its leaden slatiness commands menace in itself. Apart from the full-time rimfire boasted by the new Colt M4, its griseous coldness is itself intimidating, just to look at – even before it is picked up, sized up, deftly handled and wiped down by a hefty-framed man demonstrating his sure touch of familiarity with the heavy weapon's ways and whimsies. It is a citizen's right to bear arms in America, whether you like it or not. Matter of fact, this gun show at Pharr in October 2009 is far less brazenly militaristic than another three times the size held a few weeks back at the Pima County fairgrounds outside Tucson, Arizona. There, the Blackwater Company – some of whose guards were acquitted late in December 2009 of murder in Iraq, where they opened fire on a crowd – had a stall abundantly stocked with tactical combat gear, night-vision equipment, body armour and other stuff you need for all-out warfare rather than duck-hunting. There, it wasn't just a matter of the AR-15 semi-automatics being lined up for sale as here in Pharr. There was a banner hanging from the ceiling beckoning buyers to a wide range of the deadliest weapons available on the open market, at reduced prices.

But there are nevertheless a couple of twists to holding a gun show in Pharr during October 2009. The hall is about six miles from the Mexican border and eight miles from Reynosa, Mexico, fortress city for the Zetas and scene of ferocious fighting a few months later, in spring 2010. Back in January 2009, three off-duty police officers were enjoying a drink at the El Booty Lounge in Pharr when a man lobbed a grenade into the bar. The explosive was traced to Monterrey an hour across the border.[1] In March 2009, seven months before this gun show, the first coup in President Obama's then week-old offensive against gun-running, Project Gun-Runner, was a haul of semi-automatic barrels, firearms accessories and gunpowder crossing from Pharr into Reynosa aboard a tractor-trailer. A seller at the Pharr gun show called Billy — a courteous and friendly man with a pony tail — is extolling the virtues of the body armour he has for sale, the intensity of the fusillades it can withstand, the specific kinds and calibre of ammunition. He has an especially rare weapon on his stand: a Heckler and Koch M3 Super 90, but made under licence by Berelli in Italy. 'There's not so many of them out there,' assures Billy, 'I got it off a guy was ex-military. Just shows how badly the armed forces need these weapons — must've been Heckler and Koch were running to max capacity, so they got 'em made under licence by Berelli.' Billy talks me through the advantages: he likes this thing called an 'annular knurled ring', which would enable me to 'switch to the semi-automatic recoil system' thereby moving from a manually operated pump-action mode 'to being able to fire full-power combat loads in rapid semi-automatic mode'.

There's an 'underbarrel magazine', which can hold 'eight rounds for police or military versions. That's a rare piece' — a snip at $1,300. Another man takes me through the benefits of an AR-15: 'the ultimate urban rifle', adaptable to thirty-round Magpul magazines, as used by 'our troops in the Middle East'. A new model he has on the table has a forearm design enabling the shooter to 'fit rails at all twelve-clock positions', he says. I tell him I'm not a US citizen, so there's a problem. He gives me his card and says to call so we can 'work something out'. Just as one must not be Euro-sanctimonious about guns in Texas, one must not engage in racial profiling. But what do those Mexican lads over there with shaven heads and tattoos on their scalps want with an SHF R50 magazine-fed bolt action .50 BMG rifle with a 22-inch barrel? How many farmers and antelope hunters really need, from the same stall, an ASA M4A3 Top 16 .223 calibre carbine machine gun, a *Santa Muerte* wallet and an ammunition pouch adorned with '*Arriba Tamaulipas*' – Go Tamaulipas – a favourite Zeta slogan on YouTube?

At the back of the hall, up a small flight of steps, is a bookstall. In amongst the many catalogues and trade volumes are US army manuals on counter-insurgency warfare, with tips on bomb-making, how to blow up bridges and other useful things to know while out hunting deer. For $25, there's a *Militia Battle Manual*, with a second chapter on 'Combat Operations'. 'An ambush is an active form of a defensive position,' it counsels. There are sections on 'Bounding Overwatch', 'Immediate Assault' and 'Urban Assault': 'when entering an enemy building, always throw a fragmentation grenade first'. In the section on 'Acquisition of Military Equipment', the manual says: 'In this section we are talking about the theft of military equipment from military bases. Sounds hard? Well, it isn't.' There is, of course, a section on explosives and how to blow up buildings, and diagrams like that showing 'Electrical blasting cap attached to car battery'.[2] It is hard not to flashback a moment, to the night of 19 April 1995, the year *before* this manual was published, when I landed in Oklahoma City. The killers of 169 people, including nineteen children, in the Alfred P. Murrah federal building in Oklahoma came from this constituency of militia manual readers and they were not lone wolves, they were part of a fomenting culture – Americans killing Americans in the name of America. Now, here's a variation on that theme: Americans selling guns that arm the cartels that kill each other so as to peddle the drugs that kill Americans. The cartels' guns of choice are the AR-15 and AK-47. The automatic versions, of course, the sale of which is illegal in the United States. But what are these manuals, selling for fifteen dollars a copy, six miles from the Mexican border in Pharr, expertly written and cheap at the price? With a white cover is volume one of the *Full Auto* manual series, telling you how to 'modify' your AR-15. 'The purpose of this small book is to clarify and explain the procedure and parts needed to convert a semi-automatic AR-15 assault rifle to be a selectable, fully automatic weapon.' In figure 11, it reads, 'an auto sear is being inserted into the pocket of the lower receiver where the take-down pin engages the lug of the upper receiver. Figure 12 shows the auto sear fully installed.'[3] Also for fifteen dollars, with a blue cover, is the conversion manual for the all-time favourite *cuerno de chivo*, the AK-47. Step six is 'Reassembly' of your fully automatic Kalashnikov: 'You are now ready to check the timing of the bolt with the movement to auto sear, which should release the hammer.'[4] But there are waivers. In the AR-15 manual, the publisher affirms that he 'produces this book for informational and entertainment purposes and under no circumstances advises, encourages or approves of use of this material in any manner'. The AK-47 booklet advises that 'all conversions must be done by a licensed Class II manufacturer'. Zetas: Do Not Try This At Home.

Since the election of Barack Obama, discussion of the flow of weapons from the United States to the cartels has found a place on the US political agenda, become a recurrent theme for the Mexican government and almost de rigueur in media coverage of the border crisis. But all this is recent, part of President Obama and his Secretary of State Hillary Clinton's final acceptance of some 'co-responsibility' for that crisis – as Mrs Clinton put it on her visit to Mexico City soon after taking office in 2009. Until very recently, however, such a suggestion was almost taboo. Certainly, gun-running to Mexico and 'co-responsibility' for the drug war had played no part in Mrs Clinton's husband's agenda when he was President between 1992 and 2000. President Obama is pressing the Senate to ratify the Inter-American Arms Treaty, which was to be fair, signed by President Clinton in 1988 but stalled on Capitol Hill, and which seeks to crack down on illicit firearms with a regulation of the import and export of weaponry across the hemisphere, and to increase cooperation between law-enforcement agencies. To gun lobby hardliners, even the discussion is seen as yet another attempt at creeping gun control; while others who support the Second Amendment's guarantee of the right to bear arms nonetheless recognise that gun-running to Mexico is a separate and justified discourse. President Obama has made no effort though to reinstate the domestic ban on semi-automatic weapons imposed by Bill Clinton in 1994, but which expired in 2004, just as the war began in Nuevo Laredo. As recently as 2008, Raymundo

Ramos was a near lone voice making the point that while 5,000 truckloads a day were crossing from Nuevo Laredo to Laredo, 5,000 also came back, and that this counterflux current of goods exported from the USA into Mexico involved smuggling in the other, southerly, direction: not of drugs, but guns. The few US law-enforcement agencies taking the threat seriously call that counterflux 'the Iron River'.

'It's obvious,' Ramos said on that occasion, 'that without the drugs, there would be no war. We all know that. But without the guns, there would be nothing to fight the war with.' It is indeed obvious, but apart from the US Bureau of Alcohol, Tobacco, Firearms and Explosives (ATF) and a report by Lora Lumpe, well ahead of its time, in *Covert Action Quarterly* in 1997, few people north of the border realised it as an issue. Lumpe's work demonstrated that the Arellano Félix brothers' weapon that killed Cardinal Posadas Ocampo in Guadalajara had been smuggled from the USA.[5] Not too many in Mexico made much noise either, though the Iron River did gain some diplomatic traction after the appointment of a forthright ambassador to Washington, Arturo Sárukhan, in 2006. But Ramos was able to say as late as 2008: 'I've been campaigning for five years now for tougher action against smuggling guns. I raise the matter every time I meet with the authorities on either side of the border. The Americans don't see it as a major problem; and the Mexicans? Every time they find an arsenal, they act all surprised! For the Americans, it's a billion-dollar business, and the Mexicans do not have the political will to get serious with gun-running.'

It is of no disadvantage to the narco cartels that the four states bordering Mexico – Texas, New Mexico, Arizona and California – cherish the lore of firearms as part of their heritage and identity. It is of no disadvantage that they are among the states in which it is easiest to buy weapons. Speaking to a conference in El Paso in August 2008, Michael Sullivan, then acting director of the ATF, said the US and Mexican governments were cooperating in an effort to trace weapons seized in Mexico's narco war, finding – to no one's great surprise – that between 90 and 95 per cent of them originate in the United States – 'mostly from the four south-western states. Two-thirds of them were traced back to Texas.' That year, 90 per cent of 20,455 weapons seized by Mexican authorities for which traces were requested showed a purchase in the US, with Texas, Arizona and California accounting for most of them. The irony and tragedy was that they had also already been used. The gun smugglers were described by the prosecutor in one case involving a gun dealer in Arizona shipping hundreds of Kalashnikovs as operating 'like a parade of ants'.

Ironically, too, the ideological right which stands so firm on people − and, of course, drugs − crossing the border northwards also opposes restrictions over marketing the hardware the narcos need to shift southwards, and the frequency with which they can buy weapons. Although the Justice Department brands the narco cartels as a 'security threat' to the United States, there are more than 6,700 arms dealers within half a day's drive of the border − three dealers per mile of frontier. One of them called X-Caliber, a distance away in Phoenix, was shut down in spring 2008 for allegedly dispatching hundreds of AK-47s and other weaponry to Mexico. The dealer, George Iknadosian, won a reprieve, however, when in March 2009, a judge threw out the case against him, finding no evidence of fraud or illicit dealing, even though some of the 700 weapons he was accused of selling to smugglers were identified in a shoot-out in Sinaloa in 2007 in which eight police officers were killed. The state of Arizona was appealing the decision at the time of writing.

Known as 'Straw Buyers', agents for the narco cartels and gangs cruise gun stores and fairs to buy the weapons. Court records from innumerable trials tell the story of the iceberg of which they are but a minuscule tip: Adán Rodríguez, aged thirty-five, was struggling as a carpet-layer in Dallas when he was tapped by two men called 'Kati' and 'César' from the Gulf cartel. They came up with the idea, with $12,000 cash up front, that if he went around telling gun dealers he was a private security employee and showing them his ID, he might need the 112 assault rifles, Beretta handguns and other weaponry he managed to procure for them. All he had to do was take the hardware to a safe house in Dallas and pick up a commission of between $30 to $40 per gun, in cash, with marijuana stored between the bills. At the time of his arrest, Rodríguez's contacts were hoping to upscale their order to include hand grenades and rocket-launchers. 'The temptation got over me,' Rodríguez told the judge in Dallas who sentenced him to five years in jail in 2006. The ATF's special agent in charge in Arizona, Tom Mangan, had said candidly: 'Gun shows have become particularly troublesome. You see the Sinaloan cowboys come in, you see them with their ammunition belts, and their ammunition boots. You can see the dollies being rolled outside to their cars. Why do they need high-powered guns? Because the Mexican military is armed too, and they need to pierce that armour.'[6]

In June 2009, the US Government Accountability Office published a report that left no rational room for doubt: 'Many of the firearms fuelling Mexican drug violence originated in the United States, including a growing number of increasingly lethal weapons.' The agencies responsible for combating gun-running 'do not effectively coordinate their efforts', said the GAO, 'in part because the agencies lack clear roles and responsibilities'. Moreover, 'agencies generally have not systematically gathered, analysed and reported data that could be useful to help plan and assess results of their efforts to address arms trafficking to Mexico'. The GAO notes that for the very first time, the National Southwest Border Counternarcotics Strategy only recently includes a chapter on combating arms trafficking and that 'while US law-enforcement agencies have developed initiatives to address arms trafficking to Mexico, none have been guided by a comprehensive, governmentwide strategy'. While the violence in Mexico 'has raised concern, there has not been a coordinated US government effort to combat the illicit arms trafficking to Mexico that US and Mexican government officials agree is fuelling much of the drug-related violence'.[7]

From Laredo eastwards, deep into Zeta country, the border becomes tropical and urban, palm trees and concrete. The road on the Texas side of the river winds its way through the town of Zapata, where, appropriately, the local auto repair shop is called 'Guevara's Garage' but where many humble Mexican-American residents suddenly found themselves to be rich, after oil was found on their patches of land. The next town is Roma, where – the Vatican will be pleased to hear – the Church of the Holy Family is full to bursting on a Sunday morning, only next door there is a raid by five flashing police cars on a branch of Mr Pollo's fast-food chicken. Next comes Rio Grande City, where the popular, moustachioed Starr County sherriff, Reymundo

Guerra, was taken out of his office in handcuffs and pleaded guilty in May 2009 for using his position as a law-enforcement officer to help the Gulf cartel. Guerra was friendly with an operative for the Zetas called José Carlos Hinojosa, and took money in exchange for giving Hinojosa tips on the movements and tactics of his colleagues, information on upcoming raids on stash houses and closing a case against one of Hinojosa's associates.[8]

On the Mexican side, the same Highway 2 that left Tijuana for Tecate way back west now finds a way through tropical flatland beneath a huge sky, and a daunting town called Miguel Alemán, where every pair of eyes seems to follow a stranger. Now the borderland reaches its most easterly and most southerly terrain, the tapered southern-most tip of the United States, from which Mexico City is only 470 miles. The Rio Grande Valley on the Texas side and tropical Tamaulipas on the Mexican right bank combine to weave the border's richest historical narrative and most complex social tapestry; it is a land apart and a special place, fiercely proud of its heritage and identity astride the border, past and present.

On the Mexican side of the valley, the road heads towards two cities: Reynosa, which has become a bustling industrial centre, and Matamoros, which despite industrialisation has held true to its roots in estate ranching and commerce. The Texas side is also dominated by a pair of cities, McAllen opposite Reynosa, and, facing Matamoros, Brownsville. They could hardly be more different: both are poor, but McAllen has sprung from almost nothing in no time, a sudden player threatening to rival Laredo with a proposed second trade corridor from Reynosa into the heart of Texas, along a new Interstate 69. Brownsville, on the contrary, is seeped in epic history and for all the strip-sprawl along the highways is at heart sedate and unarguably the most charming city along the border, enchanted by laden, lush palm trees and ubiquitous ox-bow lakes known as *resacas*, left behind by the slow-winding river as it strolls and slouches its way out to sea. McAllen is new money, Brownsville is old, and each rather resents the other for it.

The observances, remembrances and rites begin early on the Day of the Dead in Reynosa, in the Church of Our Lady of Guadalupe and in the main Plaza into which its steps descend. Last night in

McAllen, Mexican-American children had celebrated Halloween like any other American children, dressed in their ghoulish best, and out for a treat at *Taco Palenque* dressed as Count Dracula, his brides and victims. The Day of the Dead in Reynosa, however, is unchanged, uncoloured by orange and black bunting, even on the border. Inside the church portal is a special exhibition of *Los más famosos Santos Incorruptos mexicanos* – the most famous incorrupt saints – but not all saints, only the Mexican ones. The stories of their lives and martyrdom are told along with the guarantee that 'Death is not an entity / It is a simple transition from the elemental life to the celestial homeland'. But in Mexico, the dead are never far from the living, especially after the night when the veil is drawn back. In Reynosa of late, the Reaper has been given a helping hand by years of violence. Today belongs, however – though the menace is never entirely dispelled – to everybody's departed ones; the sky is deep blue, the special bread of the dead is baked, and it tastes good.

Outside in the square, altars are being built and decorated, the first thing being to lay thousands of petals in patterns on the flag-stones, of flowers called Zempazáchitl ('flower of a hundred petals'), representing the rays of the sun illuminating the path to a celestial home, and *Garra de León* – lion's paw – so that the sidewalk is ablaze with white, representing the sky, golden yellow, representing the earth and resonant purple, the colour of mourning. Around the bases of the altars are abundant offerings and ritual matter: incense, sticks of cinnamon, bowls of rice and of carefully chosen minerals, semi-precious stones and common pebbles. The food is 'to nourish the soul of the dead', explains Patricia Espinoza, aged fifteen, and the water to 'quench their thirst'. The cross symbolises not the crucifixion but 'the four directions'. On the ground, salt is scattered so that the bodies of the dead will not rot, and candles arranged to light the way of their souls. Twigs and sticks are included so that the dead can bat away malicious spirits.

An especially splendid altar has been made by the Antonio Repizo high school, steps made of cardboard flanked by tables like wings decorated with skulls sculpted out of newspaper, flour and water. The steps are covered in offerings – dolls, bottles of tequila, dancing skeletons, books – and a New York Yankees shirt – atop which is a framed photograph of Guillermo López Treviño who lived from the

10 January 1907 until the 18 July 1983. 'He was my great grandfather,' says Lorenzo Martínez Rendez, aged fifteen, in broken
English, 'a cowboy, farmer and very hard worker. He is my hero, he
is always with me.' 'It's important to all of us,' says his schoolfriend,
Mario López Villarreal. 'It's a celebration of those who bore us, to
thank them and heed their advice. We've made the shrine to Lorenzo's great-grandfather, but he represents all of our ancestors, so we
feel part of a chain.' 'This is not superstition,' says their teacher, Ana
Teresa Luebbert, helping to arrange bowls of spices on the tarmac.
'The eyes of the dead are always upon us. They watch everything we
do. If the young can reach them, they will be guided – though I
sometimes wonder what the ancestors must be thinking now, with
all that's going on.'

By now, it is mid-morning, and buses out to the cemeteries on the
edge of town are filling with families, couples and ladies carrying
flowers, mementoes, picnic chairs and children's toys as offerings to
those who died in infancy. Everybody carries a bunch of little
mauve-coloured flowers special to this day, called *Jesusitas*. There is
piped music aboard the retired American school bus, not the local,
lilting *ranchero* dance music one might have hoped for, but grinding *soca* from the West Indies. 'It's specially for the *Día de los
Muertos*,' says my companion Mario Treviño, a man with many
strings to his bow, on both the city's dark and bright sides, working
for a human rights office dealing mainly with deportees, and on
cultural events in Reynosa, such as poetry readings here in Zeta
country. The bus pulls up on a stretch of land between the baseball
stadium and Reynosa's largest complex of cemeteries, on which a
multitude is assembled, a great throng in the dusty heat, making its
way to the headstones past stalls selling floral arrangements of
every kind, and *pan de muerto* to eat.

In Reynosa, like everywhere else, you live by status and wealth –
and here you are buried that way too. Our souls may arrive as equals
to be either admitted through or turned away from that last pearly
border checkpoint in the sky, but the corporeal remains are interred
according to the ducats you left behind with them. First comes the
resting place for those at the bottom of the pile – blessed are they, for
they shall be buried here in the potter's field. Around the modest
headstones of the *Panteón Sagrado Corazón*, cemetery of the sacred

heart, families hold something between a dirge, wake, party and grave-cleaning. Bands of musicians hawk their services, playing mariachi music, local *ranchero* and traditional ballads of the departed, depending on the mood. The Hernández family sits in silence and the girls cry as musicians sing '*Amor Eterno*', usually reserved for a departed mother. Another group over in the corner is whooping it up – the ladies tapping their feet to the music while sitting on deckchairs beside the graves, the men and boys standing with their beers, and every so often pouring a few drops into the earth under which Manuel Ramos López is buried, that he may whet his lifeless lips as he used to. The Morales family is serving a meal for eleven people around the memorial stone to its matriarch, Lucía, which is draped in a pair of dungarees. 'She used to sell *ropa usada*,' explains a daughter, 'so each year we bring some to put on the grave.' The girls are studying a flyer for the special *Día de los Muertos* celebration at Frida's Disco Club later on.

Those leaving behind a slightly bigger stash of mint leaves are laid to rest in God's mid-ranking acre. Here families hold picnics too: some pensive and restrained, others exuberant and vivacious. Two musicians accompany one family sitting in silence, and sing a lachrymose but soothing ballad of remembrance by a famous Argentinian singer Alberto Cortez called '*Mi Querido Viejo*', My Dearest Old One. And finally, we reach the *Panteón Español*, the Spanish cemetery, 'where the business families are buried', says Treviño. Here is respite from the clamour. Once inside the gate, one is greeted by girls emerging from a gazebo. They're dressed in smart air-hostess-like uniforms only with a higher hemline and appropriately black neckscarves, shoes and stockings of mourning, and they asked if one would like to participate in a raffle to win a voucher towards the funeral of a relative. Elegantly dressed people walk with decorum through the Jardín Juan Pablo II, wherein perfectly pruned roses climb wire latticework. The lawns of the Jardín Padre Nuestro and Jardín Navidad – Christmas garden – into which the cemetery is tastefully divided, are impeccably manicured. No one wants a raucous *ranchero* band here; instead there are silent uniformed ushers and 'sanitary officers'. At the rear are mausoleums and family vaults as would line a big Italian cemetery containing centuries of the deceased, in mock monumental classical design. But even this is not the executive class of dear departed. There is yet another cemetery, says Treviño, 'for the very rich'. It is out of town, beyond the reach of the *soca*-rocking bus. 'There, the people we don't want to meet come to mourn, and who don't want us there today. It's where the top bad guys go, and the police, to be buried and settle their accounts.' We have no car, but I express a foolish interest in going, somehow. 'If you go, you're going alone,' says Mario, suddenly firm. 'Not me. They'll spot you right away; they'll ask: "What are you doing here, *gringo*?", they'll ask.' I'll tell them I'm reporting on the Day of the Dead. 'And they'll tell you no you're not, you're DEA, and they'll find a place for you to stay in the cemetery.' Mario is a much braver man than I, and this is his town, not mine; this is also a moment to defer to local knowledge rather than to arrive at the pearly checkpoint ahead of schedule, on 1 November of all days. Instead, we eat delicious *chiles rellenos* from a stall manned by a friend of Mario's, find a bus stop, and head back to town. Mario also buys a bunch of *Jesusitas*, and on the bus back a lady explains in detail how he must put them in a vase and let them dry until 24 June next year, the day of St John the Baptist, then bury them – and they will grow again in time for next year's Day of the Dead.

In the covered market downtown, the Dark Side store stands out from the others, selling food, magazines and tourist bric-a-brac (though there are no tourists, not even today). It is a Goth shop, at first sight of the kind you would find in New York's East Village. The owner, Zombie Raul, wears long, jet-black hair, mascara and a black leather coat. His wife dresses in black lace and violet chiffon, and wears black nail varnish. Apparently even their child wears Goth baby clothes. All of which takes mettle and feistiness in a place like Reynosa. So we talk about the local Goth scene, for which *Día de los Muertos* is a keynote day in the calendar. It being Sunday, Raul's shop is the only one in his arcade that is open, lest anyone be caught short, on this important festival, of a Metallica T-shirt or a pair of fingerless gloves with luminous bones. I ask about the cultural ancestry. 'No,' he says, 'not so much Iron Maiden, more Sisters of Mercy and Beethoven.' Well, so be it, and we have a terrific time talking about how Wagner's Niebelungs hammering on their anvils really was the first great heavy-metal riff, and as for that big double-punch in 'Siegfried's Funeral March', say no more. Raul was not a music student, he had studied the visual arts, 'but when I heard that stuff, I knew it was part of what I believe in'. Which is not strictly Goth, he hastens to add, it's Dark Side. 'It's a way of life, being aware of the beauty of things, and that all things are transient and must die, so obviously we're engaged in the Day of the Dead, but in our own way.' The Dark Side people in town are, he says unsurprisingly, 'the educated people who can think for themselves. We like to think beyond this culture in Mexico, we're open to new ideas, horror movies and different kinds of music.' This is an extremely refreshing young man to meet on the Day of the Dead, but how does all that go down in Reynosa? 'It means we have to live in our own world, but that's okay — because the fact that we refuse to participate in the compartmentalisation sets us apart from all that shit.' All we need to do is exchange a glance to know what 'that shit' is. There is one point over which that shit intrudes, however: *Santa Muerte*. 'They took our iconography. The hooded skeleton, the scythe — that's ours; that was metal and Goth long before it got to be anything to do with that shit.' Mario Treviño's tour of the marketplace, arts centre and historical museum inevitably leads to some discussion of what his Goth friend Raul called 'that shit'. We adjourn for food and coffee, over which he speaks courageously while carefully looking over his shoulder, and stopping whenever anyone comes within earshot. 'What you see on the bridge is a circus,' he says. 'The soldiers standing there — it's a farce. Everyone knows the drugs go north and the guns come south across the bridge all day. People who earn hardly any money can get a hundred dollars cash for bringing a gun over for the Zetas. The region is a hub for guns all over Mexico. They're supposed to be illegal in Mexico, unlike the US, but everyone here has a gun, some people have six guns. They get them from the army, too — the soldiers are poor, and for ten thousand dollars they let the bad guys in, and they take what they want.' A man selling *Pan de Muerto* for the *Drogadictos Anónimos* counselling service on Day of the Dead, had said: 'But the army's good, we can trust them. The police, they're just the troops of the Zetas. They tell them where the soldiers are going. You see them on the corner, waiting, watching the troops go by, then radio the movements through to the Zetas, so if they ever had a chance of catching anyone, it's too late. The only way they ever get them is with an inside tip-off.'

That is what the Zetas presumed to have happened in November 2008 when federal army troops arrested one of the founding commanders of the Zetas, Jaime González Durán, aka '*El Hummer*' (as per his preferred SUV), after a fifteen-minute shoot-out in Reynosa. The paramilitary unit that took *El Hummer* also hauled 428 guns of every kind and capability (including 288 assault weapons, and automatic or semi-automatic machine guns), anti-aircraft missiles, 287 grenades and bombs, and half a million rounds of ammunition. With the betrayal said to have come from within, the Zetas went on a rampage of violence.

Within weeks, the bodies of a long-time Mexican army general and two of his associates were found executed beside a road into Cancún. General Mauro Enrique Tello was the highest-ranking military scalp to be claimed by any assassination thus far; he had been methodically tortured, driven to the jungle and shot in the head. A week previously, he had been appointed by 'Greg' Sánchez, the mayor of Cancún, a Caribbean vacation playground, to face down the penetration of the tourist economy and transport routes by the Zetas, which threatened the ability of Mexico's number-one beach destination to attract visitors.[9] The general had led the initial military crackdown in December 2006 against *La Familia*, and now Mayor Sánchez wanted him to organise a hundred-strong armed unit to confront the Zetas. Anyone who feared the worst in Cancún was on the right track: within a week of the general's murder, federal agents had arrested Cancún's chief of police, Francisco Velasco, known as 'The Viking', and six other officers, and flown them to Mexico City for interrogation about their alleged roles in the general's murder. Federal prosecutors compiling the case still pending against Velasco estimated that as many as 1,700 of his officers in Cancún's police force were working for the Zetas.[10] He was known locally for driving around in his black Nissan Armada SUV playing *narcocorridos* glorifying the Zetas; his favourites were said to be 'Z Dynasty' and 'Pact Of Honour'. Although painted with police logos, the vehicle had been reported stolen in Mexico City in 2006. A week after the murder of the general, police arrested a cell of seven Zetas from Tamaulipas who had set up stall in Cancún.[11] The Zetas accelerated their operations against the Sinaloa's cocaine routes in central and Southern Mexico, arriving suddenly and horribly in places like the small, lazy agricultural town of Ixtlahuacán del Río near Guadalajara, where five decapitated heads were found in beer coolers with messages such as 'I'm coming for you, Goyo'.[12] The Zetas' offensive had meanwhile hit neighbouring Zacatecas, with the most audacious prison break since that by *Chapo* Guzmán in 2001. A convoy of seventeen vehicles backed up by a helicopter approached Cieneguillas prison. Thirty men alighted, most of them dressed in police uniforms, marched into the jail, where they rounded up and freed some forty prisoners affiliated to the Gulf cartel.[13] The Zetas escalated their war in Central America, too, killing ten Guatemalan agents in an attempted police ambush on a Zetas drug consignment in April 2009. When the killers finally fled, they left behind a truck containing 700 lbs of white powder and – perhaps more significantly – an arsenal of eleven M-60 machine guns, a stash of claymore mines, a Chinese-made anti-tank rocket, more than 500 grenades as well as uniforms, bullet-proof vests, commando uniforms and thousands of rounds of ammunition.[14]

The Central American front is crucial to the Zetas for many reasons: it secures control of a land route for cocaine from the producing countries, it provides a strategic outlet for smuggling to Europe and Africa and it is the source of another Iron River, weaponry of a different, heavier, calibre. Although the Iron River's deepest flow is from the United States into Mexico, an investigation by the *Los Angeles Times* showed what amounted to an arms race between cartels in military-grade weapons from Central America. The attack by the Zetas on the Independence Day celebrations in Morelia used fragmentation grenades – a weapon of war. In Mexico itself, industrial explosives plants are robbed of material that can be used to make car bombs and roadside ambush devices. Grenades used in three attacks in Monterrey were linked to a single warehouse in the city, reportedly belonging to the Gulf cartel and raided in October 2008. Much of the cache seized on that occasion was made in South Korea, including fragmentation grenades.[15]

As with Raymundo Ramos upriver, it is abuse by the army and the concerns of migrants and deportees which most preoccupies the organisation for which Mario Treviño works, the *Centro de Estudios Fronterizos y Promoción de los Derechos Humanos* – centre for border studies and promotion of human rights, run by Rebeca Rodríguez. Ms Rodríguez directs her rage not at the Zetas specifically but at the circumstances that have turned the town into 'a combat zone, in which the human rights situation is critical; a war between the military and the criminals, in which the civilian population has no stake but is held to ransom. The first human right to be trampled in Reynosa is the right to feel safe when you take a bus ride, or walk the street. Look at my hands: we don't wear jewellery, we don't wear expensive clothes – if you do, you could be kidnapped. In other countries, when a crime is committed you go to the police – but we daren't do that, because we have no idea who we're talking to. In February [2009], we had a shoot-out in an elementary school, between the soldiers and organised crime, innocent children caught in the crossfire. We live in fear of organised crime, and equal fear of the military.' The battle in the Felipe Carrillo Puerto elementary school happened on 20 February after men driving an SUV opened fire on federal police attempting to stop their vehicle. Soldiers took positions on the school patio and inside its low-walled compound for a shoot-out, lasting two hours with grenades exploding in the street and teachers ordering pupils to lie on the floor while they stacked desks against the windows to trap stray bullets. 'The bad guys feel they are lords of the streets', the sixty-one-year-old principal Martha Aguirre, had said.[6] The battle was but one of many spasms of fighting between the army and Zetas. But in the spring of 2010, a new and bloody front opened up: between the Gulf cartel leadership and the Zetas, who had until now been – in theory – the cartel's enforcement arm. The internecine violence which for a moment blew open Nuevo Laredo hit Reynosa and the surrounding area much harder. During the fighting in February that year, eight reporters were kidnapped around Reynosa, of whom two vanished and one was tortured to death. From the city, Mario Treviño sent a message reading: 'Reynosa is in mourning . . . For the moment the city is a no-man's-land, the caravans of death rolling through the streets.' Armoured cars cruised around town staking out territory, respectively marked CDG for the Gulf cartel and XX for Los Zetas – fighting pitched battles against each other and the army. Later, in November 2010 after the assassination of Antonio Ezequiel Cárdenas (Osiel's bother) by the marines, the small town of Ciudad Mier nearby was subject to the first instance of wholesale 'cleansing' by the Zetas — all its civilians ordered out of their homes at gunpoint, more than 300 fleeing en masse to encamp on the border town of Ciudad Aleman opposite Roma, Texas. A few months later, Zeta units stormed into Ciudad Aleman — firing indiscriminately in an apparently recriminatory raid on the entire population for siding with the cartel leadership — and killing an unknown number of people. Across Tamaulipas, other villages and communities had been cut off by gunmen's roadblocks, their gas stations incinerated and shops closed as the scourge of 'cleansing' territory by the Zetas and Gulf cartel, each staking out its territory, became more common. Violence of this kind also spread across the Mexican interior; in February 2011, an entire village in Durango was torched.

Ms Rodríguez meanwhile echoes the arguments of Gustavo de la Rosa in Ciudad Juárez: 'The cartel is growing and expanding, and increasing its weaponry. But you can't fight crime with crime,' she says of the army's record of 'state torture and murder' in Reynosa. 'They don't protect us: they are around our houses, but they are not around the houses of the narcos. If you say that out loud, you're the fifth column — they call me the fifth column. But the worse the army, the more the criminals will organise the people against them.' There have been large demonstrations against the army here and in Matamoros, downstream, which the cartel has been suspected of organising — blockades by taxi drivers, for example, known to be under their control. In February 2009, demonstrations against the army blocked nine bridges connecting Ciudad Juárez and various towns in Tamaulipas to the United States, with federal authorities accusing the Juárez and Gulf cartels of paying the demonstrators in order to mobilise them. In the same month, anti-army demonstrations mobilised by the Zetas extended to the state capital of Nuevo León, Monterrey, blocking the centre of the richest and second biggest city in Mexico.[18] Although Monterrey is seen as too cleanly built of glass and steel, too much an embodiment of the new Mexico, too peppered with sushi restaurants, to be a proper Zeta fortress, an investigation — the only one of its kind — into the city's undergrowth by Tracy Wilkinson of the *Los Angeles Times* found the Zetas to have sunk deep roots in its poorer barrios like that of Independencia. The barrio's long history of small-time drug dealing has allowed it to be penetrated by the Gulf cartel, which paid residents to stage huge demonstrations blocking the roads.[19] The '*tapados*', as they were called, were paid small amounts of cash (about $13), or with cell phones and even school knapsacks filled with domestic supplies, to turn out against the army. Meanwhile, back in Tamaulipas, came a warning from the US and Mexican authorities: the Zetas were said to have procured forty bullet-proof vests emblazoned with the letters FBI and DEA.[20]

Monterrey, though, is the centre for what one might call the underground of artists that exists in cautious defiance of the narcos — a group of remarkable bravery and innovation. One is Francisco Benítez, who collects (or takes) photographs of the *narcomanta* banners hung in public places, also making his own, in protest or pastiche. He is fascinated by the new, perverse literacy of the *narcomantas*, of which he says: 'they are, in their own way, messages. Some of them are directed at the civic population, in order to spread fear, showing a certain bluff of power over these official authorities. It is a means of telling everyone that they own these territories, that there is nothing to do against them.' Benítez collects his photographs into a book/installation that has become almost a historic archive of the strange, vile, macabre humour, menace and obscenity of the *narcomantas*.

Except that Francisco also makes his own, by way of pastiche and comment. 'My *narcomantas* are a reflection on the situation that exists in Mexico,' he says. 'Some of them are black — black thread embroidery on black material — because they are related to the black flag of anarchy.' One of the embroidered messages reads: *Soldados de Plomo y Policías de Paja* — tin soldiers and straw cops. 'It used to be a common line on the *narcomantas* messages, a derogatory way to indicate the authorities,' says Benítez, 'and in a certain way, it happens to be true. Any kind of crime committed by the criminals goes unpunished. The authorities do nothing but co-operate with the criminals. More than a message for peace, this work is a critique of the whole situation.'

Benítez adds: 'Personally, I think the *narcomantas* reflect several social situations that have not to do just with narco cartels, but with issues of basic education, employment and social indifference,' especially among, he says, quarters of the artistic community.

Though sometimes, the real thing can blow horribly close, as happened to one of Benítez's students. 'I teach at several institutions and workshops,' says Benítez, 'and one day I took a call on my cell phone. It was one of my students asking how to spell a word correctly. I told him, and he asked me for some other word. No word in particular. So I was curious, and asked him what he was doing, and after an odd attempt to explain, he told me that someone knew he was studying art and asked him to make a *narcomanta*. For good money. The student already knew this person, and tried to avoid problems, because this was an offer he couldn't refuse. Fortunately, he heard no more from this guy.'

Benítez works alongside a friend, Tomás Hernández, who carves reliefs in wood, in a constructivist style. One especially graphic one shows two pipelines, one dripping black oil, the other red blood. 'It's hard to find artists or artwork that challenges these issues,' he says. 'Sadly, the artistic community avoids them, or the references are shy and lateral.' Not Tomás, however, who collects 'discarded pieces of wood and cardboard from squatter ghettos. My materials were part of improvised houses abandoned by their inhabitants, and by this means I try to give the materials a second chance.' Of his pipelines relief, called *Hole In The Ground*, explains Tomás: 'A machine gun cannon targets the viewer and in the background we can see stylised veins, one of them drips oil, and the other drips blood, and in the meantime, everything is consumed in flames. It is about economic interests, and neo-liberal politics combining together to perpetrate chaos everywhere.' Tomás picks up on the themes of post-industrialisation in Juárez: 'what is happening here in Mexico is post-political and post-industrial. I choose the constructivist aesthetics for my artwork so as to relate to the idea of an industrial world. Monterrey is a post-industrial city, but the common people are still attached to the values of the nineteenth century. It generates despair when people don't understand why they cannot have work as safe as their grandparents had – and in this awful war, teenagers make up the death squads, the consequence of lack of education, and social failure.' As this book got to press, Hernández reports a terrifying episode outside his parents' house: two black trucks arrive, firing machine guns, returning two hours later to dump two bodies, one of a teenager sliced in two at the waist.

Third in this trio of bold innovation in Monterrey is Jessica Salinas, whose work is starkly and shockingly terrifying. It divides into two categories: one shows portraits of beauty queens crowned, ensnared and killed by narco gangs, their posed bodies fading into decorative wallpaper, which is what they were. The others are assertively grotesque sculptures of machine guns and pistols with erect phalluses for barrels. Jessica works, she says, 'with the subject of criminality out of control, and its collateral damage from a feminine perspective – pieces intended to graphically portray the phenomenon of cartel beauty queens as trophies for the capos, until such point as women take the cartels under their own leadership, flashing firearms all the time. It is a situation I portray by relating the male anatomy to machine guns and firearms.' She certainly does, with such sculptures as *Anatomic Plates: Missile Gun and Smith and Wesson* – handle, trigger, then stretched back foreskin and all.

'So we're balancing here,' says Ms Rodríguez back in Reynosa, 'which is a difficult task.' She discusses the cartel with extreme care: 'They're doing what they are doing for the money, for the girls, the lifestyle and the power of money. But they have become a military formation, not a social formation.' The sage Treviño has been listening, and says something simple, but of importance: 'They're doing it for the money, yes, but more than that. They're doing it for kudos, to show they can wear this T-shirt by this designer worth this much money – instead of that one that the other guy is wearing. It's like stripes on a military uniform – corporal, sergeant. You walk around and everyone knows what rank you are, because your T-shirt is worth three hundred dollars, or your sneakers. They're doing it for the money, so they can show off the things the money can buy. It's a system of rank: if you have this T-shirt, you get a cute girl to show off; if you have an even more expensive T-shirt, you get an even cuter girl. But you can't be seen in the T-shirt you wore last year, which has gone out of style – that would mean you hadn't climbed the ladder. Same with the cars, gadgets and haircuts. They're disgusting people, high on amphetamines, but in Reynosa they can wear the uniform of their rank, and they're somebody.' It is a simple, but crucial and cogent analysis.

Meanwhile, 'the economy has become dependent on illegal money', asserts a lawyer working in Reynosa who prefers to remain anonymous. 'Drugs, guns and people-smuggling: it's a cycle of illegal money.' In contrast to the criminal anarchy in Juárez, 'if you work on the domestic drug market, just selling a little on the street, you pay a commission to the narcos. If you are in legal business, you pay a quota to the narcos. They control the police, so the police don't protect you, then the narco comes to you and says: "The police can't protect you, so we will." ' (Or as a businessman over the river in McAllen puts it: 'They say: "We'll protect you from us, if you pay us to do so." ') 'That way,' continues the lawyer, 'the narco is in total control of the economy. Likewise the political parties: there are elections between the PRI and the PAN, but they are no more than a matter of Calderón and the army supporting PAN, so the narcos back the PRI. You have the army on one side, the narcos and the police on the other, and the middle — the economy, education, political life — collapsing, normal communication broken down.' Although the spring of 2010 saw a sudden and ferocious internecine conflict between the old guard of the Gulf cartel and Cárdenas' military wing, the Zetas, 'our problem', says Rodríguez, 'is not like elsewhere. In most places, there is a war between different gangs.' Despite the internecine tensions, 'this has always been the territory of the Gulf cartel. Reynosa is a one-company town'.

Not only a one-company town, but now an insurgent one-company town, at all-out war with the Mexican state and only lately, with itself. If it was ever the determination of the Mexican government that the crisis should be solved by the restoration of the PRI's old narco order, under one strong cartel with tacit licence to operate from the government, such a strategy has now been overtaken by events. If, as the *susurro* has it, *Chapo* Guzmán was — or may one day be — intended to be that one licensed monopoly cartel, then the plan has failed, thrown off course by collapse in Juárez and the ferocity of the Zetas. The Zetas can be bought off — anyone can in this game — but at what price? And if the Zetas are to preserve the *Pax Mafiosa* in this territory, what price Guzmán? The mysterious treaty in Nuevo Laredo offers a tantalising but terrifying answer: an uneasy arrangement between the cartels, with the loser paying a tax to the winner, and the price of peace being the kind of public submission Ms Rodríguez and the lawyer describe, of society and the economy to the cartel.

The word 'Zetas' is conspicuously absent from this discourse in

Ms Rodríguez's office, although it has gone well beyond what most people in Reynosa dare to speak. Another human rights worker in town who cannot be named says it privately: 'We call them The Last Letter of the Alphabet; we don't call them Zetas – it's too dangerous to acknowledge their existence or use their name, which is mad, since they're so proud of who they are, and boast it around all the time themselves. It is like this: if someone crosses them, they pay the price, either in cash or with their life.'

Around the centre of Reynosa is a system of canals built partly for irrigation and partly to channel floodwater from the Rio Grande. Along the canals are banks of grasses, and over them are bridges with yellow railings. To have a city surrounded by a system of moats is warfare's most tried and tested defence – as the Zetas realise only too well. The activist speaks of displays of strength of which no word has hitherto escaped Reynosa: 'it was February thirteenth [2009] when they did it for the first time,' she says. 'They just sealed off the city centre, as a gesture of intimidation, with road blocks at the bridges. To show they can do what they want, and to show the army they can do a training excercise. They did it again on the seventeenth – this time they hijacked buses across the bridges over the canals: boarded the buses, ordered the drivers to swing them round and everyone to get off, then took the keys. Usually they do it for two or three hours at a time, but once the buses stayed there for fifteen hours, no one dared move them; the city felt in a state of siege.' Some days later, a woman dared to speak, if only briefly, about being on one of those buses: 'We jerked to a stop. There was banging on the door and four men jumped on, shouting at the driver. They wore balaclava masks, but we all knew immediately who they were. They ignored us; it happened quickly: they shouted at us to get off the bus, quietly and no one would get hurt. One lady insulted them because she was late, but nothing happened. A few stayed and watched the driver steer the bus across the road. He got down and was sent away. They just left the bus there, empty, in the rain.'

'One time it happened,' said the activist, 'a male friend of mine was getting married, and his bride couldn't get to the church! She was coming downtown when the Zetas shut the bridge, and everyone got worried, especially my friend, because his bride arrived so late for the wedding!' Over the bridge in McAllen, Texas, the narrative of the

Zetas and the bridges becomes even more serious: it is not only those into downtown Reynosa that the narco militiamen are blocking in their shows of strength; they have another audience to impress, which involves a more audacious display across other bridges: those into the United States. 'It was a bad day here, about April or May [2009]. They blocked several bridges, the international bridges into the US. It's never happened before, they just shut 'em down.'

The businessman in McAllen talks on condition of anonymity, as well he might. But his knowledge and veracity are unimpeachable, and what he knows has never been leaked. 'They called us here at the company, and they told me that whatever I got to get over, I had to get it over by 2 p.m. Just get your stuff across, they said, 'cause we ain't reopening for a while. They said it would be peaceful, they were just making a point. And boy were they. What they were really saying was: "We're running the show." These are people who roll up with rocket-propelled grenades, and can stage a four-hour shoot-out with the military. When they roll up to close a bridge, people do what they say. The only bridge they left open was the one over from Progreso, because of the tourism that still crosses there.' No word of this ominous manoeuvre was spoken by US authorities at the other side of the bridge, or the local Texan politicians or press.

McAllen is becoming a city that looks north as well as south, turning in the direction the trucks will one day be going, it hopes, past the signs posted along Highway 281 towards Houston reading 'Future Interstate 69'. Which is also the direction that the genealogy of businessman Sam Vale's family has taken: his ancestors are from Reynosa, but his office now sits atop the only tower in McAllen from which Spanish language news, football and showbiz feed into almost every household in the Rio Grande Valley. Vale is director for the region of the Mexican Telemundo televison network and also owns the ultimate piece of Amexican real estate: a border bridge – that between Camargo, Tamaulipas, and Rio Grande City, Texas, for which each crossing vehicle pays him a toll. Mr Vale, who typifies the new, muscular McAllen, tells the story with gusto: originally the bridge was co-owned with another businessman, Vale's father holding a minority 40 per cent, but through a series of clever manoeuvres, threatened law suits and hard-faced verbal duelling, each episode increasing the stake by increments, the Vales secured majority and then sole ownership. All other bridges across the Rio Grande are the property of the federal government, apart from one other, whose owner's name happens to be Sam Sparks, says Vale, 'so that to own a bridge, you gotta be Sam, Sam or Uncle Sam'.

Vale's office is decorated with artwork and antiquities from Mexico's recent and distant past: paintings, religious artefacts and carvings. 'They're the result of what I call the Mexican way of doing business,' says Vale. 'You see something you like, you name a price you know the guy can't accept, then you ask: what else you got?' The family, however, was Mexican ranching and later commercial aristocracy from another world. 'My grandmother used to send her dresses by steamship to be cleaned,' says Vale, 'in Paris.' He is a man of presence, wears a full moustache, an open shirt and gold jewellery, talks entertainingly and with ease. He is Tex-Mex, big on the Tex, is generous with his time and believes passionately in McAllen, Texas. Throughout the family's rise in the real estate business, he says, it had been surrounded by 'people who wanted South Texas to be California – but hell no, I always said, we are what we are – that was the first principle'. The second was that 'whatever we do, we do with Mexico, rather than spend billions of dollars building a damned wall, like this is Israel and Gaza'. Laredo, he says, 'always had that integrated mentality, and did well out of it'. And he looks at the sweep beneath us, out beyond the heavy oak desk in his top-storey office. 'When I was in high school, all this was fields.' It sounded lovely, compared to the vista of concrete sprawl and the strip mall next door shared by Country Omelette, Viva Life Christian Booksellers, The Armory Guns 'n' Ammo, signs on stalks advertising AutoZone and a hoarding that reads: 'Your Wife Is Hot. Tint Her Windows'. But that is not what Sam Vale means about the fields; he means the opposite: build all over them.

'McAllen lives or dies on the basis of international trade, starting with the fact that forty per cent of retail in this town is Mexicans coming over here to buy stuff.' But that is not where it ends. 'We have people sitting there working out how to make money for this city. What next? What else? This valley is churning big time,' says Vale. 'The city must be part of the action that Laredo's part of,' and establish its own inland port along its own trade corridor. 'Laredo has a system it likes, but we can make it cheaper by letting the Mexican long-haul truck come straight across to the point of delivery, cutting out the shuttle.' No drayage trucks here: this will be the boys from *Veintiséis* crossing over as far as the Pilot Travel Center – the mind boggles.

Vale has no illusion that 'all the money is lily-white, because it's not. But around here, the cartels only affect you if you're involved in some way, you owe them, or sold them computers. The people who pay the cartels on this side have a part of their business that's illicit, some extension of the system over there, where no one can function without agreement with the Zetas.' And, of course, there is the Iron River: 'The biggest industry the cartel is involved in this side of the border is the import of guns from the US. You've got a family – you get the Gulf cartel six to ten weapons at $50 per gun per week – that's good money. A lot of people, myself included, have been clamouring for the ATF to be given more resources in this region. The government talks about sending a hundred more – dammit, we need a thousand – we need people working undercover on the other side, we need men on the ground who can root out the people selling the weapons around here, and the gangs who are buying the weapons and getting them to the cartels. They're buying up parts and assembling them on the other side of the border. But all this hardware has to be stashed somewhere, it has to be taken to Mexico one gun at a time. There has to be a collection and distribution network, and it's got to be broken.'

But the Zetas' penetration of the legal economy runs deep. One astonishing story, told by an attorney in McAllen with good connections, affords a rare insight into the world of Zeta Inc. It involves them stealing condensate from oil terminals belonging to the Petróleos Mexicanos company, and exporting it to the USA. The scam was said to have been personally overseen from jail in Houston by Osiel Cárdenas himself. 'They got the contacts inside the Petróleos Mexicanos company,' says the attorney, 'and were literally siphoning off the condensate, bringing it from Monterrey to terminals in the US, with all the correct paperwork. Coming up through Pharr, up to Houston. How do we know this? Because something happened: a man called Manuel Gómez was found decapitated.' The background to the murder, says the attorney, swearing inside knowledge: 'Gómez was working with the cartel to provide transportation. He never used his own vehicles, always smaller trucking companies. He was responsible for hauling these tankers to refineries in Houston, for use in jet oil products. He even had a name in their circles: '*Manolo*'. After a while, the cartel operatives on the receiving end in Houston 'started to notice a shortage of product arriving at the refineries; a shortfall in the cartel shipment. And what did they find out back in Monterrey? That Gómez was siphoning off his own stash. They figured it out, and cut his head off.'

According to one assessment of the Zetas, in a briefing by the DEA in 2009, such is the extent of their criminal empire that only 20 per cent of the syndicate's turnover is now generated by drug trafficking. This can be seen as a terrifying corruption of the economy, but Vale insists it can be looked at another way. 'If the economy is right, they'll condemn themselves to respectability. They'll realise that the big money is mainstream. As things are, the Zetas and cartels are infiltrating the US side – they're in Houston, they're in New York City, they're all over the Indian reservations. But these gangsters are going to have children and these children are going to have to learn legal business. Of course I'm not saying we make agreements with them, but you wait for them to condemn themselves to legality, then instead of fighting about it, you find some way to settle it. At the moment, you have a battle over an illegal product, with the profits going into semi-legal business. It's painful, and we have to face that down. But it's a growing pain, they can't fight for ever. They're already buying up houses on South Padre Island like the British do in Spain, and when the war is over it'll be like the waterfront in New York – they'll start doing things in a more licit way, then go legal.'

In defining McAllen as the town figuring out how to make money, swashbuckling Sam Vale had said: 'Brownsville, by the way, doesn't think like we do, it's more old fashioned.' Such generalisations will always need to surrender to exceptions, but they are not without their grains of truth, and Vale's remark defines the curtain that divides the two cities on the Texan side of the valley, connected by the sprawling concrete overgrowth along Highway 83 or, running parallel right along the borderline: the big sky and long story of the

Old Military Highway. It is one of the great roads in America, not because of the curious border towns it passes through, or the sweeping palms and tobacco fields that line the way, not even for the fact that Mexico and the river are never more than half a mile away, and sometimes a few feet. Indeed, if there is anything that makes the highway surreal, it is the border fence, cutting like a gash across the landscape, and often across the back of people's gardens. What makes the Old Military Highway so richly agreeable to travel are the Historical Markers erected by various institutions at various stages along the way. It was an Indian trail used by Spanish explorers in the sixteenth century, initially established to connect settlements to one another; later a military road connecting the Texan and US forts at Laredo and Brownsville during the Mexican wars; then a stage-coach, mail route and inland supply line for cotton during the Civil War.

By definition, the narrative followed by an eastward journey along the Old Military Highway to Brownsville is not a chronological one. Past a glorious avenue of palm trees to the south, one arrives at the site of Toluca Ranch, founded in 1880 by Florencio Cano, on land owned by his Spanish ancestors, once covering 10,000 acres. There is high drama at the next marker, Río Rico. In 1906, says the plaque, the Rio Grande Irrigation Company dug a canal that 'altered the natural course of the Rio Grande', abandoning 419 acres to the south of the river, in Mexico. After a treaty of 1884, says the marker, the 'popular gambling community of Río Rico, which flowered in the 20s and 30s, became subject to Mexican jurisdiction'. Later, in 1970, the USA ceded the communities of Río Rico and El Horcón to Mexico, starting an eight-year legal battle that ended in the granting of US citizenship to 200 natives of Río Rico born prior to 1970. Nature's border does not always coincide with mankind's, and the river knows best.

As one nears Brownsville, the road is marked by the site of the *Rancho de Santa María*, commandeered as a military sub-post by Fort Brown, and a mile further is the site of Villa de Reynosa, built by Juan Miguel Longoria (1815–1875), who fathered seventeen children with three wives, the last of whom was Teresa Guerra, one of the great 'matriarch ranchers of Texas'. Two miles further along, two markers and a cannon stand together. One plaque marks the route taken by Spanish general Alonso de León, fighting French incursions in 1685. Another marks the spot where 'American blood was shed on American soil. April 25th 1846. Here, Captain Philip Thornton and 62 dragoons were attacked by Mexican troops.' The cannon, aimed at the border, was placed there in 1846 by Lt. Thomas Barlow Chapter, against the Mexicans. Three miles (and eighteen years) later, 'Col. John S. Ford of the Confederate Army defeated the Union forces. June 25 1864'. Now the border fence almost touches the road, passes through Garco's construction yard, then behind a car wash and auto sales outlet in La Paloma and back right up against the road, which then runs past Dark Side of the Moon Tattoo and into Brownsville.

One marker along the way had located the Battle of La Bolsa, fought in 1859, which ignited a conflict that was named after the man who fought here, Juan Cortina. The Cortina Wars witnessed the only seizure by land of US territory in the nation's history. In 1859 and early 1860, reads the plaque, a 'series of raids led by Juan N. Cortina (1824–1894) led to skirmishes with companies of Texas Rangers and US soldiers.' Here at La Bolsa, it says, 'a battle occurred between Cortina's raiders and Capt. John S. 'Rip' Ford's Texas Rangers'. Cortina, a Mexican from north of the border, led a raid on Brownsville in 1859, occupying Fort Brown with 200 men and hoisting the Mexican flag from its ramparts. He was eventually thwarted by a mobilisation of Texas Rangers.[21]

'*Diles quién eres*,' says Dr Antonio Zavaleta, special assistant to the provost at the University of Brownsville – Tell Them Who You Are. It was the title of a paper he gave to a conference on border identity, and a *dicho* he heard in childhood – as well it might be, for Dr Zavaleta's paternal great-great-grandfather was General Juan Cortina. His academic post is therefore all the more apposite because the university campus occupies the site of the old Fort Brown captured by his ancestor.

Dr Zavaleta's office is a museum to both his ancestry and his imagination. The room is a wonder: if Sam Vale had wheeled and dealt his way into a collection of artefacts, Zavaleta has accumulated a treasure trove. He works surrounded by totem poles, icons, painted panels, carvings and masks representing deities, saints, spirits, sprites and banshees – presided over, of course, by the Virgin of

Guadalupe. Here is a roomful of the syncretism – mumbo-jumbo, if you prefer – of multiple and multilayered faiths that has defined the border's history and the road, and infused the air it breathes even more than the violence. It has done so all the way from the demolished *Santa Muerte* chapels above Tijuana to this room: a council of the incorporeal at the border's far Eastern edge end. General Juan Cortina looks down with a commanding and perfectly somatic aspect from a portrait by the window – *'Diles quién eres'* indeed.

Zavaleta is captivated, personally and professionally, by what he calls 'folk Catholicism', as believed and practised by the people of Mexico and the border, rather than the kind issued in Papal bulls and edicts. Folk Catholicism retains elements of pre-Columbian faith, which have remained as part of Christian iconography and practice in Mexico, whether it please the Vatican or not. Zavaleta is an expert in a central part of this overlay of faiths: *'curanderismo'* – the work of *curanderos*, faith healers – as embodied by the *'Niño Fidencio'*, who practised in and around Espinazo, Nuevo León, during the 1920s. And when I arrive to talk, by coincidence, copies of a new book have just been delivered: a selection by Zavaleta of petitions sent by email to the *curandero* healer Alberto Salinas, an acquaintance of his, almost entirely from Mexican Americans, together with the *curandero*'s responses. They range from requests for advice on schoolwork to that on demonic possession, from injuries to a baby by a lunar eclipse to dancing with death and, inevitably, in pursuit of deliverance from the power of *Santa Muerte*. Most correspondents, one infers, are young.[22]

'I went through over seven thousand emails,' says Zavaleta, 'and noticed a subliminal pattern that had a lot to do with very traditional *curanderismo*. They had come to this through word of mouth, at home, in schools, villages or churches, and what they sought was a subtle mix of spiritual, artistic and scientific or medical treatment and advice, a holistic process. We could only choose 190 of them, but they are 190 lives, very particularly expressed in a way that was modern to the eye, but ancient.' He makes the connection by waving an arm around the room: 'All this is pervasive in our culture. It's in every being on the border. This stuff' – which seems either distant or exotic to the modern eye – 'is very real to people, every day,' says Zavaleta. 'Dancing with the devil, feeling the eyes of the dead upon you, the patron saints of your home or travelling, saints' days, magic numbers and colours, protective talismans – it cuts deep and is always close to the surface. It plays a role in your life and community. These are poor people, but throughout, there's this deep understanding, even in the world we live in, of forms of faith and belief that go way back, from which the healing and magic traditions of all religions in Mexico including Catholicism are drawn.' Zavaleta has a professorial air, for sure – but there's something more than that: this is not academe, this is a life's faith as well as a life's work, ever since, he says, 'I was raised a Catholic in Brownsville, Texas, but of Mexican ancestry, and educated by a priest from Ireland.[23]

'I know priests who admit that it's not a problem if people don't believe what they're doing, so long as they keep doing it,' says Zavaleta. 'But we're not like that – folk Catholicism is something primal that never leaves you. It doesn't leave even people who go off to become born again evangelicals. They sing in chapel, they go to Bible classes, then they come back, to their roots in the primal mystery. They'll take in the great work – food stalls in the barrio, soup kitchens, all good. But then they come home. To not wanting to disappoint their patron saint, feeling unlucky at the eye of a certain animal on you – not Bible class, but *this*!' And again, a sweep of the hand across the room, past the dancing skeletons, the plumed serpents, the bright birds – and mesmerising figure of the Virgin of Guadalupe, standing atop the new moon. 'It's like asking someone on a beautiful warm evening,' says Zavaleta, ' "what would you like to drink, a cup of coffee or a nice cold beer?" '

Zavaleta's book contains the case of a boy who feels trapped by a pledge he has made to *Santa Muerte*. He petitions the *curandero* Salinas 'as a matter of life and death', fearing that *Santa Muerte* will 'collect on a broken promise'. 'He knows there's a payback,' says Zavaleta, 'and is afraid it will be with his life. He's terrified, and reaches out for help in a desperate way, but one which understands the deep history of what he is doing.' And at last, here is the conversation I have been waiting to have since that fearsome afternoon above the dam with the F-150 truck drivers guarding the ruins of *Santa Muerte's* chapel in Tijuana. '*Santa Muerte* was resurrected in Mexico City twenty-five years ago, in the poor Tepito neighbourhood. And was adopted by the narcos – that's what everybody knows,' says Zavaleta. 'It's a huge cult now, among the young – it's become a way of identifying with power, with easily accessible evil. For the narcos, it's obviously something more sinister and dangerous, but it's them who've mutated *Santa Muerte* into this image. She's been made into a pop saint by the drug traffickers to sublimate their cult of death.

'If you go back, *Santa Muerte* was not evil. She was, strictly speaking, the representation of a folk saint to which a woman prayed to get her wayward husband back – of course she means more than that! She represents a holistic relationship between life and death, a cycle and totality. The image of the reaper is inaccurate. That's something new – if you see *Santa Muerte* as a black-hooded reaper on the back of a car, it's more likely from Tamaulipas than Mexico City. *Santa Muerte* originally wears not black but the colours of the rainbow. It's important that she represents the universality of the colours. Originally, she holds not a scythe – that's another narco creation – but the world, the globe. Her power is that she holds everything in her palm.'

The appeal of the cult to young people, says Zavaleta, 'reminds me of when, as a fifteen-year-old, I brought home a copy of Aleister Crowley's satanic bible and showed it to my mother. And I can see that sentiment everywhere now. The gold standard in folk religions is to see what's selling – it's as true now in the marketplaces as it ever was with the sale of indulgences and relics. Now, you'll find shops broken into and the only thing missing the thieves wanted to steal is a statuette of *Santa Muerte*. There's been a rash of these thefts in the valley. Here in Brownsville, you have little kids in elementary school third grade who are doing *Santa Muerte*, they wear the gold chains, they talk to the statues, and it's obvious that their fathers are drug dealers; if you talk to them, they'll tell you their fathers work for the cartel. This is serious, and dangerous, but our reaction is different to that of the mainstream Church.' How so? 'If you ask someone who practises *curanderismo*, they will distinguish between this new cult of *Santa Muerte* and her original meaning. But the Church will not – they'll give you a blank look, dismiss it all and offer you God with the right hand or the devil with the left – that's the way it is. If you ask someone who believes in *curandero* healing, they'll grapple with it, engage in cognitive discussion, go back to the original meanings of what is really happening, understand them and find a way out.'

Where does '*diles quién eres*' come from? I ask. 'My grandfather said it to me once, in Spanish. I was about twelve years old. I asked him what it meant, and he looked at me sternly: "Tell them who you are." I asked him to tell me the story, of this Juan Cortina I was descended from, and he did. I felt like a new-born child.'

Elizabeth Street in Brownsville, running a block north of, and parallel to, the border, is a destination point for shoppers from across town, of course, but also the north-east corner of Tamaulipas. Cross-border shopping is a theme that defines the frontier, and as in Calexico, as in Laredo and everywhere in between, there is this delicate balance between what is more affordable (or less unaffordable) on the US side and on the Mexican side. Quite apart from which side the bargain might hide, or the little luxury that doesn't appear on the list prepared in advance.

The Signature store is a cavernous adventure, miles of fluffy bears, zip-up bags for *ropa usada*, marker pens, Tupperware and cutlery, towels with designs of Sylvester Stallone, Marilyn Monroe or Club América to choose from, flashing antennae and model New York yellow cabs. El Toro Sports is stacked with perfumes, soccer shirts and bags with Mickey Mouse or the Dallas Cowboys' star on the back. And in this marketplace of essentials, little luxuries and junk, stands the temple, HEB. A Texan supermarket chain that strides the frontier, with consulates in every Mexican border town, HEB is an institution. The parking lot in Brownsville is a social scene at sundown, a gossip exchange, a chat-up opportunity, a place to compare phone applications and bets on horses. About half the car plates are Texan, the other half from Tamaulipas, while over in Matamoros, the percentage is about two-to-one in favour of the indigenous Mexican shoppers. Over in Matamoros, the HEB is more department store than supermarket: an array of electronic goods more expensive than in the US, sofas and armchairs at much higher prices and a spectacle of cheap chilli and jalapeños without rival. But the pièce de résistance is over in the corner, the *Pastelitos*, the bakery. Here, at apparently reasonable prices, is a fanfaronade of cakes decorated electric pink, yellow or blue. This is the cake department to end all cake departments: cakes shaped like racing cars, Spiderman and Cat woman, Mickey and Minnie Mouse, with inscriptions in sugar icing like '*Machito*', in blue, for little boys and '*Florecita*', little flower in pink for girls. A corpulent man in a chef's hat who looks quite like the pastry he is baking heaves a humungous cake over the counter covered in sugared Technicolor, received with difficulty on the other side by two girls – this is Brian César's birthday cake, personalised in turquoise icing.

At the end of the row of shops on Elizabeth Street back across the border is a Pandora's Box of a shop. Written above the door: 'AZTECA: *Yerbería*. Gifts Dolls *Regalos Muñecas. Se Leen Las Cartas*' – Herb-shop. Gifts. Mannequins. We read cards. Azteca is an omnium gatherum of spiritual, religious and magic accoutrements and a child's dream made real. Hidden among flowers or lined up on shelves are dolls of every kind. There are white plaster statuettes: of Venus, of fine ladies in ball gowns, of the three Magi, amorous cherubs and mischievous putti as well as Christ both in manger and on cross. There are shelves of remedies for every ailment of the mind, body or soul: herbs, oils and essences of cactus. Four shelves are devoted to devotional candles to every saint, angel and archangel, including *Santa Muerte* in all her incarnations. But guiding and presiding over all of this – framed, sculpted, painted onto candles, cast in silver, gold, plaster and plastic – is the figure who oversees it all, and everything along the border, standing on the moon: the Queen of Mexico and Empress of the Americas, the Virgin of Guadalupe.

The first of many prayers offered on Saturday 12 December 2009 in Brownsville was spoken through a megaphone and chilly, damp fog hanging from the dark sky – unusual for a tropical night in America's poorest neighbourhood. But the people of Cameron Park had awoken and converged nevertheless, in the parking lot behind the Church of San Felipe de Jesús on the outskirts of town to prepare for the procession of Our Lady the Virgin of Guadalupe. And they did so, they knew only too well, along with tens of millions of others across Mexico and along the borderline. As the Christian world prepared to commemorate the Nativity, Mexicans – including twenty-eight million Mexican Americans and probably the same number of Mexican citizens living legally or illegally in the US – celebrated what is for them a more spiritually cogent and enchanted day. 'In the name of the Holy Virgin Mary, Mother of God and *Nuestra Reina* [our Queen],' implored

Father Hector Cruz down the megaphone, 'and please keep to the side of the road': three years ago a drunken driver ploughed into the parade, injuring three pilgrims. Accordingly, behind a pick-up truck leading the way, they set off, just after 3 a.m., in pilgrimage to the Church of Our Lady of Guadalupe, on 12th Street downtown. We walk at a pace, for this is no stroll and there is a way to go. Pounding those three hours through the dark are mostly young people, couples in hoodies holding hands, fathers with little children, women and girls clutching bunches of roses in December (for such was one of the Virgin's miracles when she first appeared) and the striking image of the Queen of Mexico standing on a crescent moon among the rays of the sun. A young man called Luis walked − he now has to commute to work as an ironworker 'way north in Alabama and Georgia' because there were no jobs left locally, his wife four months' pregnant; he had returned specially for this pilgrimage. A young woman called Gabriela Méndez had two weeks ago been laid off by HEB; she is now wondering what next, only glad to be able to concentrate better on basket-making class. Wearing a splendid 1994 World Cup Mexico bomber jacket, Alfonso − a steward keeping the parade in line − had been on all thirteen *Guadalupana* pilgrimages from Cameron Park since their inception, but just lost his job as a chandler in the harbour at nearby Port Isabel. 'This', he insists, however, 'is the day of *esperanza* [hope] for us all, and for all Mexicans.'

Cameron Park was until recently a Mexican-American *colonia*, which simply means 'neighbourhood' but on the US side means that it was too poor to be 'incorporated' and granted services such as lighting, running water or paved roads, because it raised no tax revenue. A movement by civic groups in the 1970s, later spearheaded by the remarkable man who was until recently parish priest at San Felipe de Jesús, Michael Seifert (he has since left the priesthood), registered Cameron Park's residents as voters and won the attention of the city, county and even the state of Texas, so that the trailer homes gradually grew permanent extensions and the oil lamps became electric light.[24]

The area remains in many ways a Mexican *colonia* as we walk first along pitted byways past little *bodega* kiosks which are windows of private homes, past guard dogs barking at the pilgrims as they wander the empty streets like a spectral procession towards the city.

Then out onto the main artery into town, Rubén Torres Boulevard, past dark stillness on the *resacas* – the ox-bow lakes left by the winding Rio Grande – past deserted Wendy's and golden arches unlit, we are joined by tributaries of other pilgrims. It is strange and welcome to see this city becalmed at night: in motionless abeyance and wrapped in damp darkness, depopulated but for our muffled steps past mute buildings and dwellings. A twenty-four-hour Valero gas station is lit and open, though, selling famously good breakfast tacos, which tempt a few folks in search of nourishment and warmth to tarry behind. All along the way, the pilgrims sing; in fact, the choir on the back of the truck is not deemed good enough and as we pass Coffee Port Road, the hooded, anorak-clad choristers are ejected and stewards appeal to the now several hundred pilgrims: '*Quién canta?*' – Who can sing? – in search of substitutes. The special hymns duly continue, with greater glow: '*Y eran Méxicanos*' – 'They were Mexicans', goes the hymn – to whom the Virgin of Guadalupe appeared in 1531. Past Don Quixote Street they walk, alongside the freeway, and even that is deserted. After three cold hours, the procession enters a bath of fluorescent light, the church resplendently decorated for Mass, which begins during darkness at 6 a.m. There is a justifiable sense of authenticity among those who walked, even if the best seats have been taken by others who drove. The altar is gleaming white, the choir dressed in bright indigenous Mexican colours and the priest has the image of the Virgin embroidered on his cream-coloured robe as he reads, apocalyptically, from the Book of Revelations. Drummers wearing lambent golden Aztec costumes and dancers in head dresses of peacock feathers perform, presided over by the icon of Guadalupe.

Icon of Mexico in the deepest sense, the Virgin of Guadalupe is at once dynamic, mystical and omnipotent. She appeared to what is commonly referred to as a 'poor Indian' – a Náhuatl peasant baptised as Juan Diego – in a number of encounters in 1531, during which she tasked Juan Diego to convince a doubtful archbishop to build a sanctuary in her honour.

But the Virgin of Guadalupe is much more complicated than that. After Mass, there is a hearty breakfast of *huevos a la Mexicana* with a man who has thought, preached and spoken about the image of the Empress of the Americas and the Virgin Queen it portrays in his former parish of Cameron Park. 'Cameron Park is in, but not of, Brownsville,' he says. 'Surrounded on all sides by one of the poorest cities in Texas, Cameron Park is so poor that not even Brownsville wants to have anything to do with the place.' It is pertinent, then, that the Virgin of Guadalupe appeared to a peasant in the cotton fields. 'She is the cry of the poor and the redemption of the poor. But it is not that straightforward: the poor Indian was from a warrior caste, vanquished and converted by another warrior caste [the Spanish conquistadores] and in this, the Virgin is the child of rape, but pregnant — both queen and outcast, pregnant with the mixed-race Mexican *Mestizos* people, after what was not an immaculate conception. So the Virgin of Guadalupe is both spiritually and ethnically syncretic: a *mestizo*, icon of both pre-Columbian and Catholic spirituality, and of the indigenous and Spanish people. Indeed, in one of the great works of Mexican literature, the Náhuatl-language *Huei Thamahoicoltica*, or *Great Event*, she is defined only in terms of pre-Columbian, Mexica lore — an echo of Coatlicue, Goddess of the Aztec pantheon, who lived among the moon and stars, and gave birth to the primary god Huitzilopochtli after being impregnated by a 'brilliant hummingbird feather carried on the wind', and who, like the Virgin of Guadalupe, had her sanctuary on the mountain of Tepeyac.

'And the Virgin of Guadalupe,' says Seifert, 'is also a symbol of defiant hope in the dark days of now. She is a social lament, and helps us in our resistance. She is what stands between places like Ciudad Juárez and total despair. And unlike any other Madonna, she is standing. If you look at her left knee, she is even dancing.' It is an extraordinary proposition. Yes, says Seifert, she is 'a young woman, dressed as an Aztec Queen, we know this from the colours and the style of dress, from the sun and the moon and the stars. This cosmic princess is standing, while amongst the people of those days, royalty sat, always and especially in the presence of the lower classes. [As do portrayals of the Madonna in European art.] She is, of course, pregnant, as we can tell from the way her robe stands forth, and from the dark sash, and she has her hair down. But she is in a dance, as well, her knee lifted forward.'

Equally unexpected is Seifert's sudden about-turn: 'Then I think to myself: Is it all opium? Opium of the people, to keep them servile?'

What a thought – heresy on 12 December from a former priest – and what a terrible moment for Seifert to have to leave. His wife, a paediatrician, has arrived and they must record pictures of a newborn baby to send by internet to grandparents in Mexico, who cannot get papers to cross the border and visit. But some weeks later, Seifert sends further thoughts on the Virgin of Guadalupe. He goes back to the Náhuatl equivalent of her name, 'Coatlaxopeuh', pronounced 'quatlasupe', which he constructs as 'Mary Who Crushes the Serpent'. 'At the heart of the Spanish conquest,' concludes Seifert, 'is rape. I don't mean the figurative rape of the country and the culture, but the rape of Indian women by Spanish soldiers.' And the child of that rape, he argues, 'would be a bastard, in the harshest technical sense of the word – a child without a past, without a people, for she is not an Indian, she is Other. This child, however, would be the most lasting reminder of the first, violent encounter between Europeans and the Aztec nation. She was Mexican, and she and her brothers and sisters would become yet another nation, another great people, a new people. In the humiliation of rape, a new race was born, a *mestizo* race, the Mexican race.' *Diles quién eres*: The Virgin of Guadalupe, telling Mexico who it is.

In the sign of peace at the end of Mass after the pilgrimage from Cameron Park, there is flesh-creeping poignancy after a year of violence across and along the border. But a woman in the front row shatters any rip-tide of thorns with a cry of redemptive defiance: *'Viva La Virgen de Guadalupe!' 'Viva!'* roars the congregation, as the sky quickens outside. *'Viva San Juan Diego!' 'Viva!'* they respond, as grey dawn breaks. *'Viva Cristo Rey!'* – Christ the King – *'Viva!'* comes the reply. Sitting in a pew on the nave is the writer Cecilia Ballí, who has narrated the trials and triumphs of poverty and resilience in Cameron Park. 'You notice,' she says, 'how today, Jesus Christ comes third, after the *Virgen* and Juan Diego.'

The Rio Grande Valley was ranched and farmed by a small number of great families before the border was drawn across it: two of which were the Ballí and Hinojosa dynasties from whom Cecilia is descended – great ranchers and owners of land. In many ways, both grandiose and bitter, the history of the valley and the border is the history of the Ballí family, which once owned – but was swindled out of – Padre Island, and proved so in a lengthy court case, a judge in Brownsville ruling in favour of the extended family in 2000. Ms Ballí wrote in the magazine *Texas Monthly* that the victory 'was for all of us to relish. In a way, its story is universal. For it is a story about how some people are washed out of their own histories.' Even more important, though, was the 'deep sense of pride and rootedness that these families share'. Cecilia's father had 'died sick on a hospital bed, and other than a little bit of pride and lots of love, he couldn't leave us much. He was a cab driver with cancer. He was forty-one. But he left us a special last name, and there lay the treasure.'

Cecilia Ballí and I drive across the land her own immediate family comes from, south of the border, stretching like low polder under an expansive but leaden winter sky towards the sea. We pass a small store – 'That belongs to a relative,' she says – then a huddle of green houses where her mother was raised, and further down the ranch where her father grew up. Along a fence beside the road, a man wearing a straw cowboy hat has hung a particularly up-market selection of *ropa usada* for sale, with a fine old Wrangler shirt to buy. 'I remember your grandfather,' he says. 'I drove a tractor on his ranch; I pasteurised and sold milk.' Past a gas station and the inevitable Oxxo store on Highway 5, a road leads off to the left. At its entrance are a buvette selling beer called Minisúper Bisby and three parked buses. It is not a road down which one turns, says Cecilia – it leads to the ranch where Osiel Cárdenas was raised. The ranch along that road itself constitutes a kind of wayside 'historical marker' in the narrative of Mexico's narco-cartel culture. Ms Ballí argues that it helps explain a shift in the social composition of the region's drug cartel, which she believes perfected the style of violence now seen in all of Mexico. 'Osiel Cárdenas comes from a very poor family that lived just on the fringes of a Mexican border city, literally and metaphorically. His predecessors in the Gulf cartel tended to be businessmen and to come from the middle-class, or at least from well-connected families. Osiel didn't initially have the same kind of access to politics and politicians. His way into the business was by becoming a federal cop. He represents the poor urban underclass that the Mexican government has always neglected, whose men basically have two options to genuinely climb out of poverty: go work on the other side of the border or join the trade.'

And what happens to these poor young men coming into the business for the first time? 'They finally get to experience power, what it is to be respected, and they're not as invested in the old social networks or political debts, in the old way of doing things. They don't just co-opt, they confront. The first thing Osiel did to become the boss was kill his associate; that's a departure from the past. People talk about him being particularly violent as a person, and once his enforcers, who came to be known as the 'Zetas', formed, they began branding a new style of violence, and it's a style that other cartels in Mexico have learned to match.' 'Style' is not a word Ballí uses lightly; she develops her own point in Chapter Five about the murders of women in Juárez. 'People say this is all about money,' she notes, 'but I think it's about money and something more. It's a social performance, a show of power, a very masculine form of power. They are saying, "We are somebodies," in a country where that was not supposed to be possible for men of their class. I think in some ways, the willingness of Mexico's rich to ignore the poor is coming back to haunt them. This isn't the poor's revenge on the rich; they are simply finding their own way to wealth and to social recognition. Especially since the old avenues for becoming a man in Mexico – you got married, found a job and supported your family – are shifting. Some men are now opting to establish their manhood this way, and this is hurting everyone.'

And yet even the cartel forms part of this narrative, of heritage, place and identity, argues Ms Ballí. 'The cartel here does still have ties to the community. People here know their names, they know who they are. Maybe they grew up or went to school together, or married distant relatives. And although they've gone national and international, their leadership is still from north-eastern Mexico and they're proud of it. They celebrate its music, its language. Regional identity is extremely strong in Mexico, and these guys like to assert the fact that they're from Tamaulipas and from the border, a place the rest of Mexico has always shunned. You see this pride displayed on the Internet, in YouTube clips extolling the Gulf cartel and the Zetas, and in the way they decorate their trucks. We like to talk about 'imagined communities' in academia, and I think the Mexican cartels have done an impressive job of harnessing those regional and communal identities, so that people almost root for them the way they would root for their soccer teams. And so when we talk about their struggles to retain control of their territories, we're not just talking about drug routes; we're talking about their ability to say, "This is our place." I think this is something that distinguishes the Gulf cartel from others. Aside from *La Familia* in Michoacán, the other cartels are made up of people who have moved around various states in northern and north-western Mexico, many of them originally from Sinaloa. The guys who took over Tijuana were from Sinaloa, not from Tijuana.' *Diles quién eres*: the Zetas, too, are telling who they are.

'People here don't condone drug trafficking,' says Ms Ballí, 'but they understand where it comes from. I think we're at an interesting crossroads now, though. The community is more silenced than ever, and everyone understands that something has been lost – something pretty big has been lost. The cross-border life that was so special about this place is changing every day.'

There's a joke they tell in Matamoros: first day of term and the schoolteacher welcomes the new children, supervised by the principal. 'All children with names beginning A to M sit over here,' says the principal, and they do. 'All children with names beginning N to Y sit over there.' And they do. 'What about children with names beginning with Z?' asks the teacher. 'Oh, they can sit wherever they want,' replies the principal crossly. The alternative, more sinister ending goes: 'Children with names beginning with what?' replies the principal, terrified.

The claw marks of artillery shells that pock-marked the walls of Sarajevo or Grozny do not usually form part of the landscape of the narco war, but in Matamoros they do, at the site of a shoot-out between the Zetas and the army during autumn 2009, beside a construction site and *Tacos al Vapor* stand on Primera Street in a smarter neighbourhood of town not far from the river, nor very far from army headquarters bunkered down in a storage depot, with its heavy gate, security lodge, sentries and visible fleet of parked jeeps. According to eyewitnesses, the shooting lasted two hours after the army tried to stop a car, which then ran the soldiers' roadblock. The Zetas, apparently already in position to cover the car, reportedly took nine casualties, according to the unconfirmable *susurro*, the army admitting to none. After the incident, the Zetas are said to have sealed off the area and – giving tactical purpose to the exercises in Reynosa – boarded buses, ordered passengers off and took the keys.

I talked for a while, sitting on a wall, with a man called 'Arturo', from Monterrey, now living in Matamoros and the only person I met there prepared to discuss the Zetas. If they call them the *'Pirámide'* in Nuevo Laredo and the 'last letter of the alphabet' up the road in Reynosa, I asked him, what are they called here? 'We just say "The Letter",' said 'Arturo'. 'Half the town works for The Letter one way or another. The only way to avoid them is do things like make sure that your car insurance is in order, because some day either you're going to get hit or someone'll make sure you get hit, and there's a fifty per cent chance that the owner of the other car will be working for The Letter. You better make sure that any damage gets paid off quick, with full third-party insurance because you don't want to be owing anything to anyone in Matamoros.' By the end of 2010, during the first months of 2011 and as this edition goes to press, the internecine war between the Gulf cartel leadership and Los Zetas had torn Matamoros and the rural reaches to the south of the city apart, ravaging whole areas, with reporters simply unable to reach or chronicle the worst of the violence as it happened. But the extent of the killing, and its ferocity, could be hinted at by the emerging, awful aftermath: the gruesome discovery of mass graves containing – at the time of writing – up to 167 corpses at various locations in the San Fernando valley, south of Matamoros, not far from the location of the massacre of the 72 migrants who had refused to pay the Zetas an extra 'cuota' in October 2010. Now, in scenes reminiscent of the wake of wars in Bosnia or Central America, relatives of people who had gone missing – from all over Mexico – would assemble at the morgue in Matamoros hoping against hope that they would not find what they were looking for – but very often doing so. Mexican authorities briefed that the victims had been riding passenger buses through Tamaulipas, had been hijacked and press-ganged into service with the Zetas, and then executed for whatever reason.

The PRI mayor of Matamoros, Erick Silva Santos, graciously agrees to meet me and a colleague – Dudley Althaus of the *Houston Chronicle*, for whom this is familiar terrain – without an appointment. Mayor Silva insists: 'We are not in a war zone. This is a conflict between the government armed forces and a group of

narco traffickers,' who, he concedes, 'have very sophisticated equipment and weapons'. But, he says, 'I have nothing at all to do with
this fight. The law does not permit us in the municipal city hall to
intervene. The law does not permit me to mobilise the municipal
police to intervene in narco traffic.' How very convenient.

After this encounter with a man really grappling with the crisis,
Althaus and I adjourn for lunch at a restaurant that is a silent
Matamoros landmark. Only Althaus can remember why, from his
days as a reporter on the *Brownsville Herald* over the river. The
simmering violence in Matamoros was inevitably part of his beat,
and Althaus covered the murder of a gangster called Casimiro
Espinoza – reportedly on orders from the Godfather of the old-time
racket in town, Juan N. Guerra. 'This was nineteen eighty-four,'
remembers Althaus. 'We heard the news and came right across – it
was my first ever story in Matamoros. "*El Cacho*", they used to call
Espinoza. He was the only other serious gangster in town that was
anything like a threat to Guerra. And Guerra made sure to rub
him out. I think that was when we first heard the name of Juan
García Ábrego, who was said to be behind the killing: he was
Guerra's nephew, and ran the Gulf cartel until ninety-six, after
which Osiel took it from there. Looking back, that killing of Espinosa was when they consolidated power. Félix Gallardo was still
running the federation down in Guadalajara, but that murder was,
with hindsight, the birth of the Gulf cartel. This is when the old
man Guerra used to sit at the back of this restaurant, holding court,
and talk horse-racing.' The restaurant has thus been renamed 'Don
Juan's', and the sign represents his favourite horse, riding crop and
hat. The real hat hangs from the wall inside. We eat well, the service is polite, only the man behind the bar fixes us all the while
with dead, unshining eyes, cold as steel and ice.

Back from the sentry posts leading to Osiel Cárdenas' ranch, Cecilia
Ballí and I sit at a beach café on a windswept winter afternoon, the
sun throwing spears of light, which children call 'ladders to heaven',
onto the sea from behind battleship-grey clouds, creating ponds of
light on the ocean's indigo surface. The rain comes ashore, and clusters of Sunday trippers bring their seafood, fries and chowder
beneath the shelter that was built to be shade from sunshine – this is

Padre Island, proven by the court in Brownsville to have been the rightful property of the Ballís. 'There are special dynamics on the border that you don't find anywhere else,' Cecilia says. 'For instance, there's a different sense of time along this part of the border. These communities in the valley, especially the ones on the Mexican side of the river, date back to the eighteenth century, which in Europe may not seem old, but in the United States means a lot. We've been here almost as long as the Thirteen Colonies.

'But ever since Mexico lost this region to the United States, Mexican Americans in Texas have always been made to feel like foreigners, even though this has been their home – our home – for generations. After the border was drawn, we began to psychically experience a gradual process of separation from Mexico, though of course culturally and socially some of the ties remained. Because Mexico is right there all the time, there's always that sense of threat of the "Other", and Mexican Americans constantly have to prove that they're American enough. When I was growing up we were made to feel embarrassed that our parents didn't speak English, even though most people in Brownsville were Mexicans. That's changing now with more immigration and the rise of a public Latino identity in the United States, which allows us not to have to hide who we are. The valley itself has changed a lot; now you hear Spanish regardless of where you are. But there's still that double movement happening. There's a cultural and emotional connection with Mexico, but most people live it on this side of the border, with other Mexicans who are here. Those of us who actually cross the border back and forth are statistically a minority. So here in the valley, Mexican Americans are becoming both more Mexican and more American at the same time, if that makes sense. I always wonder: Why are people so surprised when they come to the valley and find that Mexican Americans are really patriotic? That all our kids are signing up for the army? Well, if all your life people have questioned whether you belong, you find yourself having to *prove* that you're an American.'

One of the ways for teenaged boys to prove their American-ness has been to play the all-American game better than the Anglo-Americans – high school football. The book, film and television series *Friday Night Lights* was set in Midland and Odessa back in west Texas, but nowhere is Friday-night fever for the local team fiercer than in two small, poor towns joined at the hip in the Rio Grande Valley, Elsa and Edcouch. Sam Vale had said: 'The problem with Elsa is it's too far north from the border, too far east of McAllen and too far west of Brownsville.' But he was talking about the town's battered economy, not about the Yellow Jackets football team.

Indeed, Elsa is not on the way from anywhere to anywhere in particular. Most major employers, apart from the school district, have left or gone bankrupt – but the place has a sanguine, resilient feel to it; it is gladsome and vivacious. There is no way a visitor is going to get in and out of the Valero gas station or Stripes store without an affable interrogation, and the boys at the Elsa Body Shop fixing up cars that most garages would give up for dead are happy to carry on a companionable chat about the Yellow Jackets, even when they are lying back under the vehicle, spanners in hand.

In the Gladiator's stadium at Roma, the home stand is sparsely populated, for all their cheerleaders in mini-togas and a march-past by male pupils dressed as legionnaires and centurions carrying plastic imperial *fasci* and standards. The away stand, though, is another matter: packed, the brass band giving it what for, cheerleaders waving golden pom-poms, crowds whooping and yellow-and-amber flags waving, with pictures of bees on them. Roma is a good ninety minutes' drive from Edcouch-Elsa, but it feels like half the population has made the journey, even on a Thursday evening. Among the crowd are four generations of the Montalvo Flores family, from seventy-seven-year-old great-grandma Ida to little Deena, aged six. 'I graduated from Elsa high school in nineteen fifty,' Ida rasps above the noise, 'and hardly missed a game. I watch 'em wherever they go. You got to support the kids. We're such a small town, and we may be poor, but we're rich enough to buy our season tickets.' Her eyes glint from behind her spectacles. 'I'm sorry about my ugly *gringo* name,' she offers out of the blue, though Ida had sounded just fine to me. 'My mother's best friend was the midwife and my mother promised to name her baby after her.' An additional excitement is that one of the family, Isaac Prado (it is too complicated to work out how he fits genealogically, there are twenty of them in the party) is playing his last game before graduating. 'It's hard to take,' says his father, Enrique. 'He's wanted and waited to play for years and years, and so have we all, and this is the last time.' Isaac's girlfriend is a cheerleader, now sitting with the family.

So this thing between the cheerleaders and team stars isn't just a myth from *Friday Night Lights*, I ask my host for the evening, José Saldívar, who has driven all the way and will drive all the way back. 'Oh no,' says José, 'it's almost a requirement.' He hastens to add that he married a librarian. His father, also named José, has come with us, also a fanatic, season-ticket holder since he moved to Elsa in 1988. 'I could count on one hand the games I've missed.' Mr Saldívar fixes up classic and vintage cars for a living; mounted on bricks in his front yard. 'I'm working on a 55 Chevy right now.' The Edcouch-Elsa team for which José played in the 1990s is the envy of the valley, 'even though our town is not,' he says. 'Everyone resents us and everyone wants to beat us because we have the best record.' Elsa has won six district titles and made the state play-offs sixteen times, a tally unequalled by any team in the valley and for which the Yellow Jackets became more widely known as *La Máquina Amarilla* – the yellow machine.

Elsa and Edcouch, says José, were agricultural communities dating back to the 1920s; Elsa once boasted the largest fruit-packing shed in the world. In the 1970s and 80s, however, the fruit-picking and packing, and industries related to them, went into decline. In the period since, 'unemployment has been high and opportunities are scarce – the school district is the biggest employer, and they let two hundred people go last January [2009]. We're said to have the highest teenaged pregnancy rate in Texas. There's a lot of alcoholism even amongst the kids, a lot of drug abuse – a couple of my friends are in jail for dealing.' (In 2006, a mother in Elsa was targeted and killed in front of her children. In revenge, members of her family went in pursuit of the murderers and killed them. 'Zeta business,' says José.) 'But the more this defines the town, the more passionate it has become about the football,' he says. 'The nineteen fifty-nine team had been a legend during the good times, but now it's obvious why people are so enthused – football is all there is. *Friday Night Lights* was a story that needed to be told – we here just think it was told in the wrong town!'

Tonight, *La Máquina Amarilla* prepares itself for the sack of Roma – another 100 per cent Hispanic team, but Roma has never beaten Edcouch-Elsa and although 2009 has not been a good year for the Yellow Machine, 'even on a bad season, it's a big thing to beat

Elsa'. A scrappy game fails to impress either José or his father: 'It ain't the team it used to be,' laments José. Final score: Roma 14, Edcouch-Elsa 21. On the radio driving home, Elsa's famous sports show host Hugo de la Cruz hits the airwaves, reading the scoreboard as on any show, but diverting for a build-up of fanfares and *corridos* before announcing that from Roma tonight. A lady named Helen calls in and accuses Hugo of bias in favour of a team that didn't play that well. 'We're not supposed to diss the kids,' retorts Hugo. 'Anyhow, who won?'

'It's interesting that it was American football,' José says, at the wheel, Dad in the back, as we pass through Rio Grande City on the way to the game. 'The town is poor and Mexican American, and soccer is the Mexican sport, but it never really got hold in Elsa, and in the valley only as first-generation migrants arrived. The people that were born here grew up with American football and wanted to play American football.' In the mid '80s, Hugo de la Cruz began doing commentaries of games on local radio – 'He became an institution across the valley,' says José, 'a must-hear for all football fans, but everyone knew he was Elsa through and through so he got people pissed, and the more he got people pissed, the more they wanted to hear his show – it was a bit like the team.' But beneath this burning sporting ambition cuts a rip-tide of ethnic identity. 'Our town is one hundred per cent Mexican American,' says José. 'Our team was always one hundred per cent Mexican American and one hundred per cent working class. And I can remember the coaches being pretty up front about it, when we went to play teams that were Anglo and more affluent. We wanted to beat the pants off them, being who we were and where we came from. One coach in particular used to tell us in the dressing room: "Come on, guys, do it for the *Raza*", for the race. He'd say it even if there was only a handful of white kids in the other team! And oh man, we wanted to beat them so bad; there's no doubt it made us play harder. In the 'fifties, playing football was a way to prove that you were an American, to break the segregation barrier. I've heard about Mexican Americans walking into the chemistry class and being told to 'get out to your cotton fields where you belong!' – and that's where it started, needing to prove yourself on the football field. But it carried on after desegregation. So long as you were Latinos you were made to feel foreigners in your own

country, and playing the Anglos, you were going out there to make a
point and beat their ass. It helped, to be honest, that the game is
physical – who's the toughest, who can beat up who. It was a way of
knocking someone out legally, without getting arrested.'[25]

José Saldívar now teaches at Harlingen College, at a midway
point between McAllen and Brownsville, a town very much in the
Rio Grande Valley, but at its portal. When you turn your back on
Harlingen and drive north, the palm trees thinning and eventually disappearing into the great flatlands of south-east Texas,
towards the metropolis of Houston, you leave the border behind
you, but not the borderland.

There is a perverse beauty in the landscape arraigned below the iron
bridge where Highway 255 strides the Houston Ship Channel: great
towers of light and fire as far as the eye can behold; sinewy steel pip-
ing, plumes of smoke and flame twinkling into a Texas night
wrapped by a shroud of pollution hanging from the sky. It has long
been said that, as the author Sam Quiñones puts it, 'Los Angeles is
Mexico's culture factory.'[26] And that the gangland style and 'pseudo-
romantic culture of drug trafficking' are in many ways exports from
Los Angeles to Mexico.[27] This is no doubt true. But in the new landscape, according to the new and altered maps since war broke out
first in Nuevo Laredo and then across Mexico in late 2006, the Mexican narco capital of the United States has moved to the citadel of oil:
Houston, Texas. As the Tijuana cartel collapses, and arteries of the
narco transport routes into the heart of America follow those of
trade, Houston becomes the gateway, the hub of the wheel. If LA is
the old Imperial seat of Amexica, Juárez/El Paso its fulcrum, *Los
Dos Laredos* its spinal cord, the capital metropolis of Amexica is now
Houston.

In April 2008, Special Agent Carla Mayfield of the Bureau of
Alcohol, Firearms, Tobacco and Explosives testified to a court in
Houston about an investigation into serial purchases of 328 weapons
from two branches of a gun dealer called Carter Country by a circle
of twenty-two people, notably one John Philip Hernández. Hernández was an unemployed machinist, arrested a few weeks beforehand,
with most of the rest of his ring still at large. According to Special
Agent Mayfield, twenty-eight of these firearms – purchased for a

total of $352,134.04 – had been recovered in Mexico and Guatemala. The case was only the tip of an iceberg, but one of the very few that documented and illustrated the flow of the Iron River from Houston to the Zetas – for once, named in open court. Hernández had himself used his Texas driver's licence number 15436960 to buy twenty-three firearms costing nearly $25,000. One reappeared in Puebla, 'during an incident in which a businessman was kidnapped and murdered'. Another emerged in Oaxaca, 'during an incident in which Los Zetas . . . opened fire on the Mexican army'. A weapon Hernández bought on 12 July 2006, read the court papers, 'was recovered in Acapulco, Guerro (sic) Mexico. This incident is commonly referred to as the "Acapulco police massacre", due to the fact that more than a dozen armed assailants attacked two offices of the state attorney general and executed four police officers and three secretaries.'[28] In November 2009, another case came out of the sting at Carter Country: a windscreen repairman called Christian Garza was charged in Houston – and pleaded guilty – with a role in a wider conspiracy to traffic more than 300 weapons across the border to the Zetas.[29]

In 2008 alone, 200 indictments were issued against straw buyers working for twelve arms-trafficking rings along the US border with Mexico. Border checks of southbound vehicle crossings have been stepped up by both US and Mexican customs. But there remain elements integral to US national gun law which militate against effective action. A ban on assault weapons passed by the Clinton administration in 1994 expired in 2004, with no attempt by George W. Bush to re-impose it and President Obama shying away from a confrontation with the gun lobby. There is no computerised national gun database or registry in the USA – investigations and convictions depend on a paper trail. Records of gun sales remain with dealers, so that it is up to the ATF to take the initiative if a gun is recovered at a crime scene, or the dealer if he or she suspects a buyer – indeed, the system depends on tips and audits, with most dealers happy to cooperate with the ATF.

'All our investigations show that Houston is the number-one source for firearms going from the US into Mexico, number-one source in the country,' says the man in midstream of the Iron River's flow, Dewey Webb, Special Agent in Charge of the ATF's Houston office, which covers a vast tranch of east Texas and the borderland as far as Del Rio, opposite Ciudad Acuña – in effect, the territory controlled by the Gulf cartel and Zetas. It is the largest ATF region and the easternmost on the border, neighbouring those run from Dallas, Phoenix and Los Angeles.

Webb is an interesting man, a Native American from Oklahoma City (he wears his ATF ID on a tag round his neck made of turquoise jewellery). He has devoted his life to the Bureau, having joined in the 1970s and worked all over Texas. He is a large man and chooses his words carefully but talks with estimable transparency and honesty about the scale of the problem facing him, and with that mixture of moral contempt and professional respect for his quarry that makes the difference between a good and a great cop. He turns a scheduled one-hour briefing into a three-hour conversation on a wet December afternoon in his unmarked office near Houston Intercontinental airport. In the reception area are plaques honouring the four agents the ATF lost in the siege of Waco up the road in 1993.

Webb opens, against the received wisdom, by saying that the smuggling of arms to Mexico is now more commonly achieved by buying from licensed dealers than from gun shows, and that the ports of entry used by everyone else far outstrip consignments across open land. Smuggling guns, he says, is an entirely different kind of operation to smuggling drugs, demanding different expertise, 'mainly because a gun just weighs so much, and it's so bulky', needing to be dismantled, taken through the border in parts for reassembly. When he first joined the service, Webb recalls, the drug gangs were serviced with 'occasional trafficking from the US. People would call relatives to get weapons, and there were arms going down for political unrest in Mexico.' Often, weaponry would be trafficked by boat. Recently, though, 'we've seen an upsurge in this war, fighting for territory and needing the weaponry to fight for territory, and I've seen both a surge in the volume and a change in the nature of the weaponry: we're now looking at high-calibre rifles, high-quality equipment – AR-15 rifles and a couple of dozen variations. They want the top of the line, very high-quality weapons.' Some of the guns are bought in Houston, he says, but 'a lot is carried down here to Texas from places like Chicago, Minneapolis-St Paul and Michigan – Washington State was always a hot spot. This happened after we put a lot of effort into this area after it started off in Laredo in 2005. So Houston is both source and hub city, while in the Rio Grande Valley it's a smaller fish bowl and easier to see what's going on, the flags get raised quicker.'

It is not Webb's job to comment on gun, or gun control, policy – not least because he relies in part on the cooperation of the vast majority of honest dealers and to an extent on the industry. Besides, no one knows guns better than he does. But he asserts clearly: 'So long as we in the United States make it easy for these people to buy weapons, we will be the easy touch for these criminals. Texas has 8,000 gun dealers, and in the city of Houston, there are 1,500. The pattern we're seeing is that they'll go to the shows to buy ammo and supplies, combat gear, and so on, and to the dealers to get their weapons, using straw buyers for fifty dollars per gun, on up. They come, and they just keep coming back . . . It's simple because we make it simple. There's no black market in the US, the guns are not being stolen – it's all legal: you can make fifty dollars a day going to two or three dealers. But there are still red flags: when a woman goes asking for a large rifle or if the dealer just asks the right questions.'

'Don't Lie For The Other Guy' is a campaign Webb's agency has launched as it starts to punch into the straw-buying networks like that run by Hernández, along with the National Safety Shooting Foundation. Webb needs to work with gun-owners and users, not against them. Yes, he concedes, much of the military-calibre hardware comes from Central America: 'If they need a weapon, and they can't get it in the US, they'll get it from somewhere else.' But, he insists, 'the bottom line is that the United States is the nearest, the cheapest and the easiest place to buy – for the cartels to get their weapons. But there is at last a wind of change, for the better,' says Webb. 'For one, the agencies on our side are on the same page.' Secondly, 'we're working with the Mexican authorities in a more proactive way, we got more people in Mexico, running more agents'. The vetting procedures for Mexican hires have improved, he says, gratefully. And accordingly: 'we're getting more results', and understanding the cartels better: 'They're very smooth in their operations and the way they do business. They're managed like corporations, until it gets to the violence. Sometimes they want a gun because they want a gun. We're seeing them wanting the best: Mac 10s, Mac 11s, AR-15s, 9mm pistols – they want high-quality weapons. They want better weapons than I've seen in thirty-three and a half years. But then sometimes they want a gun because they saw it on TV. Then they get kind of like a wannabe Scarface. Then there's the fact that they all have the same trend: they have to defend their territory. And for that, they are busting each other's heads, and I know for a fact that it's costing them dear.' The cartels, says Webb, 'are also looking for alternative sources of income: human trafficking, kidnapping for ransom, and I've seen the cartels involved in oil'. But in the end, it comes down to the drugs. 'If people were not buying the dope, they wouldn't have the money to buy the guns, that's the bottom line.'

So far, Webb's efforts against the smuggling from Houston itself have focused on three cells, including Hernández', and 328 traced weapons taken across the border by them alone. In January 2009, the authorities in Houston also arrested ten members of a gang called Tango Blast Houstone, indicting four more on the run, for distributing marijuana and cocaine for the Gulf cartel from Houston. The arrests highlighted the position at the centre of the wheel of Houston's gang culture and gangland in the business of the cartels, using their contacts across the state, and thence the country, to distribute drugs. The arrests followed an investigation by both Webb's agents and those of the FBI − who noticed important differences between this new gang and those to which they had become accustomed over time − markedly the old-guard Texas Syndicate, established across jails in Texas and California during the 1960s. The differences between the two gangs echo the changes between the 'classic' and the new wave narcos across the border. Behind the glass façade of its new headquarters in Houston, FBI agents involved in busting both generations of gangs talk about the varied ways in which they put themselves at the disposition of the cartels, with very different structures. The agents give their names, even present business cards, but prefer not to be named. The expert in the Texas Syndicate − we'll call him 'James' − is chisel-jawed, terrifyingly fit with a vice-grip handshake and as courteous as he is direct. The agent who masterminded the bust of Tango Blast is more quietly spoken and considered, and we'll call him 'Mark'. There is also a woman at the briefing, who studies gangland patterns, movement and psychology, by the name of 'Angela'.

The Texas Syndicate, says James, 'has a leadership structure, its members have ranks – the *Sillón* or chairman for each region, like a lieutenant, and soldiers called *carnales*. It's blood in, blood out – you kill to join, and you can never leave. You wear the tattoo and the gang is your family, even if you get old, leave jail, go into business or have a proper family. Many of them live a low profile – they'll be family men in regular houses who hold down jobs, don't draw attention to themselves – some of them are middle-aged by now. They'll hold *Juntas* – meetings and assemblies – where they hold votes or discuss disciplining members.' The Texas Syndicate, which grew in response to the power of other criminal gangs in California's jails, fits into the national network of gang affiliations and rivalries which an annual report by the Justice Department monitors in its role as distribution network for the narco cartels. James says that sometimes, 'if there is a business opportunity, you'll see the gangs put their differences aside.

'It's historical,' continues James – 'formed in California and grew in Texas, and they have been major dope traffickers over the years. Some are very big drug dealers indeed – and they are killers.' Tango Blast, however, is a bigger, wider, looser organisation. 'It's more fluid than the Texas Syndicate; a bit like Facebook,' says Mark. 'The gang changes according to what you need that day, from who, to do what. There's no blood in, blood out, no initiation rite that we know of, no set rules. One day, you need a guy who can bring in five kilos, so you deal with him, and make the contacts you need to get it where you need. Next week, you need to pick up and shift twenty kilos from someone else, and you may use different contacts. That's what makes it the biggest gang in Houston – we estimate about twenty thousand members in the city of Houston, a lot of people doing different criminal activities, that don't necessarily know each other like in a traditional gang structure. It's part of the time we're in – they're kids, they have no code, no rules.' Sometimes, says Angela, 'you'll get kids committing crimes just so they can get sent to jail to find the gang, and join. We're seeing a lot of young guys trying to join, it's the cool thing to do, the in thing to be. So in addition to the gang members, you get a lot of wannabe gang members who then become criminals, go to jail, and become gang members. There's a lot of prestige, there's the opportunity to make money, there's a intimate sense of belonging to a brotherhood – knowing that if I would kill for them, they would kill for me.'

Ironically, 'the tight structure of the Texas Syndicate makes it possible to plan strategies against them, dismantle cells by filling in the spaces', says James, while, 'the fact that Tango Blast doesn't have that kind of structure makes it harder to catch them', says Mark. 'Only the thing that makes it a little easier, is that they don't know how to hide. Not like [James] said about the Texas Syndicate keeping a low profile. When we bust these guys, they had luxury cars, Bentleys, Maseratis, diamond jewellery.' One of the men this team is most eager to find is one Raul Madrigal, who taunts them from file photographs: basking in a bubblebath, posing on a beach and even sticking up a finger – all from Mexico. Madrigal allegedly made so much money helping the Gulf cartel pump marijuana and cocaine into the US through Houston that the FBI has sequestered £18 million in assets and nine luxury cars, including a Bentley Sedan and two Maseratis, and a three-wheel motorbike with ostrich-skin seats.[30]

Dane Schiller of the *Houston Chronicle* monitors the city's underworld connections to the cartels across the border as both a job and a personal fixation. Schiller's work locates the narco hub of Amexica firmly in Houston – not just for the distribution of drugs and cash, and the procurement of guns, but for killing. Killing like that of Santiago *'Chago'* Salinas, a Gulf cartel operative shot in the head at point-blank range in 2006 at the Baymont Inn and Suites on the Gulf Freeway, three weeks after his brother-in-law was found dead, charred in a barrel of diesel near Monterrey across the border in Mexico. It had been the third attempt on Salinas' life in one year – he had been left for dead after the first, in Mexico, when a bullet intended to kill him went through his jaw. According to Schiller, the person believed responsible for that first shooting was Daniel 'Danny Boy' Zamora, who had grown up in Houston and was part of an enforcement crew for the Sinaloa cartel – himself later killed in a shoot-out in Mexico. A second attempt on Salinas' life was made in 2006 at a Mexican seafood restaurant in Houston called *Chilos* – also on the Gulf Freeway, only this time the spotters got the wrong man, killing a maintenance worker in front of his family. But the third attempt killed Salinas, as he answered the door of room 142 at the

Baymont: this time the killer was believed to be Danny Zamora's younger brother, Jaime, a former employee of the Houston Parks Department – accused of the murder and that of the innocent man in the seafood restaurant car park. Jamie Zamora has since pleaded guilty to trafficking in cocaine and awaits trial in Houston for capital murder, to which charge he pleads not guilty. In another case, a married couple were found tortured to death in their home on East-wood Drive in north-west Houston, 220 lbs of cocaine found in the attic, and the nephew of Osiel Cárdenas himself, Pedro Cárdenas, was left dead in a ditch in nearby Madden County.[31] What intrigues Schiller most, though, are two things: how the profits from all these drugs, the spoils of this war, vanish into the economy of the United States, and the figure of Osiel Cárdenas himself.

In 1999, Schiller learned, two agents from the FBI and DEA were escorting an informant around Matamoros in a jeep, and were surrounded by Zeta troops. Cárdenas appeared, and – thinking bet-ter of executing all of them – demanded that the informant be handed over. The agents argued: 'If you do that, it'll be Kiki Cama-rena and Félix Gallardo all over again. They'll fight you to the bitter end.' Osiel Cárdenas let the convoy go. At every hearing of Cárdenas' trial, which ended with his conviction in February 2010, Schiller was there and at every hearing, he was asked to leave. 'It happens every time: there I am, the only person in the public or press gallery. And every time, the marshal comes and tells me to go and wait outside. So I wait, and then it's over and time to go. It's all being done in secret again, and it's getting kind of interesting that everything is being done in secret,' says Schiller of the days before the conviction. 'That whatever plea bargains Osiel Cárdenas is being offered, he must be giving them something pretty good in return. If this man is who they say he is, and what they say he is, then he's in a position to answer quite a few questions in front of the jury box. But it never happens, and it's incredibly frustrating. This man holds the secrets of what is going on, this unlikely Al Capone, and they're making damned sure to keep them from us.' Finally, on 23 February 2010, Schiller got to write this story: 'Behind armed guards and locked doors – in a secret hearing of judicial privacy not even given to some 9/11 terrorists or east-coast Mafia dons – Osiel Cárdenas Guillén, one of the most feared drug lords in history, was sentenced to twenty-five years in prison Wednesday. In a Houston courtroom sealed to the public, he also was ordered to forfeit $50 million, a small slice of his estimated earnings.[32]

'The famed drug lord has not been seen publicly since he was ushered in shackles into a Houston courtroom in 2007 to be read his rights when he arrived in Texas,' wrote Schiller. 'Despite a protest from the *Houston Chronicle* on Wednesday that the public had a right to be present for the sentencing of one of the most hunted men in recent times – in a case that has cost American taxpayers millions – US District Judge Hilda Tagle kept the hearing closed without explanation.' Which brings Schiller to his other point. 'Where does it all go, the cash?', he asks rhetorically, over breakfast in a diner next to a Shell gas station west of downtown Houston.

'I'm no accountant,' says Dave Schillen back at the gas station. 'The fifty billion dollars' profit from dealing drugs into America. It blows my mind. Or am I crazy? What I'm thinking is: If you, the United States, are not lying to us, then where is this money? Where are these people handling the money? Who are they? I know that the guys on the ground in law enforcement in this town want to go through that door. They know this is the centre of things now, in this war, and that's where the answer lies. But that's a hell of a door to go through.'

CHAPTER TEN

Blood Money

*Of the Sin of Usury: To take usury for money lent is unjust in itself,
because this is to sell what does not exist, and this evidently leads to
inequality which is contrary to justice . . . Money, according to the Philosopher, was invented chiefly for the purpose of exchange: and
consequently the proper and principal use of money is its consumption
or alienation whereby it is sunk in exchange. Hence it is by its very
nature unlawful to take payment for the use of money lent . . . and just
as man is bound to restore ill-gotten goods, so is he bound to restore the
money which he has taken in usury.*

—St Thomas Aquinas, *Summa Theologica*

Just before sunset on 10 April 2006, a DC-9 landed in the port city of
Ciudad del Carmen, on the Gulf of Mexico. Soldiers from the Mexican army, waiting to intercept it, found 128 cases packed with 5.7
tons of cocaine, valued at $100 million.[1] But something else — far
more important and far-reaching — was discovered in the paper trail
behind the purchase of the plane by the Sinaloa narco-trafficking
cartel.

During a twenty-two-month investigation by US agents from the
Drug Enforcement Administration, the Internal Revenue Service, and
others, it emerged that the cocaine smugglers had bought the plane
with money they had laundered through one of the biggest banks in
the United States: Wachovia, now part of the giant Wells Fargo.

The authorities uncovered billions of dollars in wire transfers,
traveller's cheques and bulk cash shipments through Mexican
exchanges into Wachovia accounts. Wachovia was put under investigation for laundering the proceeds of crime. Of special significance

was that these activities began in 2004, when the firstescalation of violence along the US–Mexico border ignited the drugs war.

Criminal proceedings were accordingly brought against Wachovia, though not against any individual, but they never came to court. In March 2010, Wachovia settled the biggest case brought under the US Bank Secrecy Act, through the US District Court for the Southern District of Florida. In March 2011, when the year's 'deferred prosecution' expired, the bank was in effect in the clear.

All told, Wachovia paid US authorities $110 million in forfeiture, for monies proved to be connected to drug smuggling, and a $50 million fine for failing to monitor the former sum used to ship twenty-two tons of cocaine.

More shocking, and more important, the bank was sanctioned for failing to apply the proper and necessary anti-laundering strictures to the transfer of $378.3 billion – a sum equivalent to one-third of Mexico's gross domestic product – into dollar accounts from so-called *casas de cambio* (CDCs) in Mexico, currency exchange houses with which the bank did business.

'Wachovia's blatant disregard for our banking laws gave international cocaine cartels a virtual carte blanche to finance their operations,' said Jeffrey Sloman, the federal prosecutor who handled the case. Yet the total fine and forfeiture was only 1.3 per cent of the bank's $12.3 billion profit for 2009. On 24 March 2010, Wells Fargo stock traded at $30.86 – up 1 per cent on the week of the court settlement.

The conclusion to the case – greeted by a deafening silence across the US media apart from the estimable Bloomberg financial news service – was epic. But it was only the tip of an iceberg, demonstrating the role of the 'legal' banking sector in swilling hundreds of billions of dollars – the blood money that is a result of the murderous farrago of Mexico and other places in the world – around their global operations, now bailed out by the taxpayer.

At the height of the 2008 banking crisis, Antonio Maria Costa, then head of the United Nations Office on Drugs and Crime, based in Vienna, said he had evidence that the proceeds from drugs and crime were 'the only liquid investment capital' available to banks on the brink of collapse.

'Interbank loans were funded by money that originated from

drugs trade,' he said. There were 'signs that some banks were rescued in that way'.

Wachovia was acquired by Wells Fargo during the 2008 crash, just
as Wells Fargo became a beneficiary of $25 billion in taxpayers'
money. Wachovia's prosecutors were clear, however, that there was
no suggestion that Wells Fargo had behaved improperly; it had cooperated fully with the investigation.

Mexico is the United States' third biggest trading partner, after
Canada and China, and Wachovia was understandably interested in
such a volume of legitimate trade.

But José Luis Marmolejo, who prosecuted those running one of
the *casas de cambio* – called Puebla – at the Mexican end, said,
'Wachovia handled all the transfers. They never reported any as suspicious.' He added, 'I am sure Wachovia knew what was going on. It
went on too long and they made too much money not to have known.'

While doing research on the Wachovia Mexican case, I obtained
documents that had previously been provided to financial regulators.
It then emerged that the alarm that was ignored came from, among
other places, London, thanks to the diligence and integrity of a man
who, with this case, emerges as potentially one of the most important whistle-blowers of our time. A man who, in a series of interviews
over several weeks, adds detail to the documents, laying bare the
story of how Wachovia exposed itself to one of the world's biggest
laundering operations.

Martin Woods, from Liverpool, England, now in his mid-
forties, joined the London office of Wachovia in February 2005, as
a senior anti-money-laundering officer. He had previously served
with the Metropolitan police drug squad, where he excelled. As a
detective, he then joined the money-laundering investigation
team of the National Crime Squad – Britain's equivalent to the
FBI – where he worked on the British end of the Bank of New
York money-laundering scandal in the late 1990s. The investigation into Lucy Edwards (a former Wachovia executive) and her
husband, Peter Berlin, who were laundering millions of dollars of
Russian criminal money was mounted jointly with the FBI, after
the couple moved from Queens, New York, to London.

Woods is still a cop in the best sense: punctilious, exact, with a roguish humour and passion for the city's football team, but moral to the core. Thus he was an ideal appointment for any bank eager to operate a diligent and effective risk-management policy against the lucrative scourge of high finance: laundering, knowing or otherwise, the vast proceeds of criminality, tax evasion and dealing in arms — and drugs.

Woods had the eyes and instincts of a police officer — not those of a banker. This influenced not only his methods but also his mentality. 'Maybe it's just something that comes from having once-Catholic roots in Merseyside,' he says. 'I want to be comfortable, but I think that a lot of things matter more than money — and that marks you out in a culture that appears to prevail in many of the banks in the world.'

Woods was set apart by his modus operandi. His speciality, he explains, was his application of a 'know your client,' or KYC, policing strategy to identify dirty money. 'KYC is a fundamental approach to anti-money laundering, going after tax evasion or counterterrorist financing. Who are your clients? Is the documentation right? Good, responsible banking involves always knowing your customer.'

When Woods looked at Wachovia's operations, the first thing he noticed was a deficiency in KYC information. And among his first reports to his superiors at the bank's headquarters in Charlotte, North Carolina, were observations on a shortfall in KYC among Wachovia's operation in London, which he set about correcting. At the same time he implemented what is known as an enhanced transaction monitoring programme, gathering more information on clients whose money came through the bank's offices in the City, in sterling or euros.

By August 2006, Woods's new monitoring program had identified a number of suspicious transactions 'relating to *casas de cambio* customers located in Mexico.' Primarily, these involved deposits of traveller's cheques in euros. The cheques had sequential numbers and the deposits were larger than any innocent traveller would need, with inadequate or no KYC information on them and what seemed to a trained eye to be dubious signatures. 'It was basic work. They didn't answer the obvious questions: "Is the transaction real, or does it look synthetic?" "Does the traveller's cheque meet the protocols?" "Is it all there, and if not, why not?" '

Woods discussed the matter with Wachovia's global head of anti-money laundering for correspondent banking – a bank receives deposits and makes payments on behalf of a foreign bank – who believed the cheques could indicate tax evasion – a criminal offence in most countries. Woods undertook what banks call a 'look back' at previous transactions and submitted a series of SARs, or suspicious activity reports, to the authorities in the UK and his superiors in Charlotte, urging the blocking of named parties and large series of sequentially numbered traveller's cheques from Mexico. In 2006, Woods issued fifty SARs related to the *casas de cambio* in Mexico.

To Woods's amazement, the response from Wachovia's Miami office, the centre for Latin American business, was, at best, antagonistic. One senior US manager in Miami called the SARs 'defensive and undeserved'. The documents say that Woods 'came under pressure from the business to change to develop a better understanding of Mexico.'

'Wachovia,' says Woods, 'had totally ignored all the factors that signalled they should not have been doing this business in this way in this place. Instead of thinking, "This is how drug trafficking works," they would say, "This is how the textile business works." "This is textiles, I am in Mexico" was the message I was getting. "I know Mexico better than you." "I'm in Mexico, you're not." To which I thought, "Well, I know money laundering better than you do." My job was to use my abilities to try and spot money laundering through the bank that was employing me. That's what I was paid to do, and that's what I was doing. But that didn't matter. They were interested only in how to make more money for the bank so that they could make more for themselves. Their reaction could have been, "You are exactly the kind of person we need to work for this bank," but instead some held the view, "You'll never work for this bank again." It was reverse logic and a continued endorsement of the criminality.'

As it turned out, Woods was on the right track. Wachovia's business in Mexico was coming under closer and closer scrutiny by US law enforcement. Wachovia was served with a number of subpoenas for information on its Mexican operation. Woods has subsequently been informed that 'Wachovia had six or seven thousand subpoenas, an absurd number. So at what point does someone at the highest level not get the feeling that something is very, very wrong?'

In April and May 2007, Wachovia – as a result of increasing interest and pressure from the US attorney's office – began to end its relationship with some of the *casas de cambio*. But rather than launch an internal investigation into Woods's alerts over Mexico, Wachovia hung its own money-laundering expert out to dry. According to Woods, the records show that during 2007, 'I continued to submit more SARs related to the *casas de cambio*, and I continued to come under pressure from the bank to "develop a better understanding of Mexico." '

In July 2007, Wachovia's remaining ten Mexican *casa de cambio* clients operating through London suddenly stopped doing so. Woods did not believe this simultaneous action was coincidental; indeed, he was concerned that the abrupt cessation of business was a response to a tip-off as the feds advanced on the bank. Later in 2007, after the investigation of Wachovia was reported in the US financial media, the bank finally ended all remaining relationships with the Mexican *casa de cambio* globally.

By this time, Woods's personal situation within the bank had become untenable. While the bank acted on one level to protect itself from the federal investigation into its shortcomings, on another it focused on the man who had been among the first to spot them. Woods sought guidance from a London law firm, which, he says, 'agreed with my concerns', upon which he filed further SARs relating to the money from Mexico, requesting information from the bank that would assist him with his inquiries. 'I was given nothing,' he recalls. 'Many of my e-mail requests to senior managers went unanswered.' On June 16, Woods was told by Wachovia's global head of compliance that his latest SAR need not have been filed, that he had no legal requirement to investigate an overseas case even if the money involved was coming through London, and no right of access to Wachovia documents held overseas.

Woods's life went into free fall. He was hospitalised with a prolapsed disc and notified the office, yet he was told by the bank that he had not done so in the appropriate manner as directed by the employees handbook. He was off work for three weeks, returning in August 2007 to find a letter from the bank's compliance managing director, dated August 7, which was unrelenting in its tone and words of warning. The letter addressed itself to what the manager called 'specific examples of your failure to perform at an acceptable standard'. The 'performance failures are more than just repeated instances of your continuing performance problems but are now operating to put the business for which you are the registered Money Laundering Reporting Officer in serious potential regulatory jeopardy. You are also putting the entire London AML [anti-money-laundering] Compliance Programme at risk by your failure to perform.' The letter even predicted, in a twist of ultimate irony, the upcoming federal case against Wachovia: 'I have explained in detail,' wrote the manager, 'the potential regulatory jeopardy (large fines, regulatory sanctions, reputational damage, etc.) that can result from failures in a regulated firm's AML programme.'

The managing director added, 'Your continued failure to concentrate your work efforts on agreed upon priorities is placing the business for which you are the MLRO in an unacceptable position.' Woods was accused of 'failure to review our high risk customer population,' of all things. The letter made further — now bitterly ironic — reference to 'this serious situation in which we find ourselves' and threatened 'the formal setting of a disciplinary hearing' in which to resolve it. The date was set for August 12, but it was postponed. Woods, on the verge of a breakdown, was put on sick leave by his doctor on August 11.

In his written responses, which began on September 2, Woods set out his case and related all that had come across his desk from Mexico, only to be told that the hearing would take place on August 26, in Woods's absence if necessary. Woods applied for an extension and was granted one 'until such time as I had returned to work'. Woods was duly given psychiatric treatment, enrolled in a stress management course, and put on medication. His doctor advised him that returning to work 'would have a severe adverse impact upon my health'.

Late in 2007, Woods attended a social function at Scotland Yard, where colleagues from the United States were being entertained. There, he sought out a representative of the Drug Enforcement Administration and told him about the *casa de cambio*, the SARs and his employer's reaction. The feds and officials of the office of the comptroller of the currency in Washington, DC — the part of the Treasury Department that regulates and supervises all national banks – then 'spent a lot of time examining the SARs' that Woods had sent to Charlotte from London.

'Their liaison people in London got back in touch with me a while afterward, and we began to put the pieces of the jigsaw together. The money coming through London, in euros, was a drop in the ocean of Wachovia's business with the Mexican *casa de cambio*,' says Woods, 'but it was a small window through which the parent organisation could and should have looked at the dollar operation' – which was exactly what the U.S. authorities were now doing. What they found was, according to Antonio Maria Costa, former head of the UN Office on Drugs and Crimes, merely the tip of the iceberg of what was happening to drug money in the banking industry, but at least it was visible and it had a name: Wachovia.

Back in June 2005, the DEA, the criminal division of the Internal Revenue Service, and the US attorney's office in Miami began investigating wire transfers from Mexico to the United States. They were traced back to correspondent bank accounts held by *casa de cambio* at Wachovia. The accounts were supervised and managed by a business unit of Wachovia in the bank's offices in Miami. A CDC, explained the court documents in the case, 'is not a bank'. It is a 'licensed nonbank currency exchange business' that does not hold deposits, maintain accounts or issue lines of credit, but does allow for exchange from, in Mexico, dollars to pesos and vice versa.

'Through CDCs,' said the court document, 'persons in Mexico can use hard currency . . . and wire transfer the value of that currency to US bank accounts to purchase items in the United States or other countries.' The 'nature of the CDC business allows money launderers the opportunity to move drug dollars that are in Mexico into CDCs and ultimately into the US banking system.'

The document continues, 'On numerous occasions, monies were deposited into a CDC by a drug trafficking organization. Using false identities, the CDC then wired that money through its Wachovia correspondent bank accounts for the purchase of airplanes for drug trafficking organizations.' The court settlement of 2010 would detail that 'nearly $13 million went through correspondent bank accounts at Wachovia for the purchase of aircraft to be used in the illegal narcotics trade. From these aircraft, more than twenty thousand kilograms of cocaine were seized.'

All this occurred despite the fact that Wachovia's office was in Miami, designated by the US government as a 'high-intensity money laundering and related financial crime area' as well as a 'high-intensity drug trafficking area'. Since the drug cartel war began in 2005, Mexico had been designated a high-risk source of money-laundering activity.

In April 2006, say the court papers, FINCEN – Financial Crimes Enforcement Network, an agency of the Treasury Department responsible for fighting money laundering – 'warned the US banking and financial industry of potential misuse of correspondent banking relationships with Mexican CDCs. FinCEN specifically warned of the repatriation of bulk cash, multiple wire transfers initiated by CDCs remitting funds to jurisdictions outside of Mexico that bear no apparent business relationship with the CDC.' 'As early as 2004,' the agreed court settlement would read, 'Wachovia understood the risk that was associated with doing business with the Mexican CDCs. Wachovia was aware of the general industry warnings. As early as July 2005, Wachovia was aware that other large US banks were exiting the CDC business based on AML [anti-money-laundering] concerns.' But 'despite these warnings, Wachovia remained in business'.

Not only that, they then took over the business of another bank that was pulling out because of difficulties with dirty money. 'In September 2005, Wachovia purchased the right to solicit the international correspondent banking customers of Union Bank of California (UBOC). Wachovia knew that UBOC was exiting the CDC market due to AML problems. Wachovia hired at least one person from UBOC who had a significant role in the CDC business at UBOC. After UBOC exited the CDC business, Wachovia's business volume increased notably.'

On 16 March 2010, Douglas Edwards, senior vice president of Wachovia Bank, put his signature to page ten of a twenty-five-page settlement, in which the bank – but no individual – admitted its role as outlined by the prosecutors. On page eleven, he signed again, as senior VP of Wells Fargo. The documents show Wachovia providing three services to twenty-two CDCs in Mexico: wire transfers, a 'bulk cash service' and a 'pouch deposit service' to accept 'deposit items drawn on US banks, e.g., cheques and traveller's cheques,' as spotted by Martin Woods in London.

Between 1 May 2004, and 31 May 2007, Wachovia processed at least $373.6 billion in CDCs and $4.7 billion in bulk cash, a total of more than $378.3 billion, more than a third of the state of Florida's GDP. The damning settlement document gives a fascinating insight into how the laundering of blood money works. It details how investigators 'found readily identifiable evidence of red flags of large-scale money laundering'. There were 'structured wire transactions' in which 'it was commonplace in the CDC accounts for round-number wires to be made on the same day or in close succession, by the same wire senders, for the benefit of the same account'.

Over two days, 'ten wire transfers by four individuals . . . went though Wachovia for deposit into an aircraft broker's escrow account. All of the transfers were in round numbers. None of the individuals or [the] business that wired money had any connection to the aircraft or the entity that allegedly owned the aircraft. The investigation has further revealed that the identities of the individuals who sent the money were false and that the business was a shell entity. The plane was subsequently seized with approximately 2000 kilograms of cocaine aboard.' And there was more to come: 'On another occasion, over a seven-day period, a CDC sent more than $1.3 million in wire transfers through Wachovia for deposit into a plane broker's accounts. These were a total of fifteen wires, and they ranged in amount from $63,000 to $127,500. All of this money was intended for the purchase of an aircraft, but the money was seized by law enforcement before the deal was completed.'

According to the document, many of the sequentially numbered traveller's cheques, of the kind dealt with by Woods, contained 'unusual markings' or 'lacked any legible signature'. Meanwhile, 'Many of the CDCs that used Wachovia's bulk cash service sent significantly more cash to Wachovia than what Wachovia had expected. More specifically, many of the CDCs exceeded their monthly activity by at least 50 per cent.'

Recognizing these 'red flags', the US attorney's office in Miami, the IRS and the DEA began investigating Wachovia, later joined by FinCEN, while the office of the comptroller of the currency carried out a 'parallel investigation.' The violations they found were, says the document, 'serious and systemic and allowed certain Wachovia customers to launder millions of dollars of proceeds from the sale of illegal narcotics through Wachovia accounts over an extended time period. The investigation has identified at least $110 million in drug proceeds were funneled through the CDC accounts held at Wachovia'.

The document cited seven areas: (1) 'lack of policies, procedures, or monitoring controls governing the repatriation of nearly $14 billion of United States dollars in bulk cash for high-risk CDCs and other foreign correspondent bulk cash customers'; (2) 'failure to conduct monitoring of over $40 billion in monetary instruments flowing through international foreign correspondent accounts in the form of RDC [remote deposit capture] for a two-year period'; (3) failure to conduct adequate levels of due diligence of high-risk CDC customers'; (4) 'failure to adequately monitor . . . to fulfill suspicious activity reporting obligations'; (5) 'failure to implement monitoring controls or limits for sequentially numbered traveller's cheques'; (6) 'failure to detect and report suspicious activity in a timely manner on the $373 billion in wire transfers that were processed by Wachovia for the CDCs'; and (7) failure to implement effective anti-laundering audit coverage. The staggering $373 billion was overlooked, according to Wachovia, because its Philadelphia office, which was tasked with monitoring wire transfers, had only a month for its investigation. The anti-money-laundering unit 'could not keep up with the volume of wires. The suspicious activity went effectively unmonitored.'

With regard to bulk cash: 'Wachovia had no formal written policy or procedure for the monitoring of bulk cash to ensure that suspicious activity was reported.' Wachovia continued to accept $47 billion in 'remote deposits' such as traveller's cheques and money orders, although 'none of these instruments were subject to examination for "smurfing" [executing financial transactions in such a way that they do not leave a paper trail], structuring, or other common money-laundering techniques associated with these types of instruments.' The authorities found that 64 per cent of the cheques 'contained unusual markings' of the kind that are 'readily identifiable patterns of money laundering activity'. Wachovia 'failed to establish any internal policy or monitoring procedures to implement or enforce' its own rules on standard pouch activity.

The settlement concludes by discussing Wachovia's 'considerable cooperation and remedial actions' since the prosecution was initiated, after the bank was bought by Wells Fargo. 'In consideration of Wachovia's remedial actions,' concludes the prosecutor, 'the United States shall recommend to the Court . . . that prosecution of Wachovia on the Information filed . . . be deferred for a period of twelve months.'

While the federal prosecution proceeded, Woods had remained out in the cold. On Christmas Eve 2008, Woods's lawyers filed tribunal proceedings against Wachovia for bullying and detrimental treatment of a whistle-blower. The case was settled in May 2009, by which time Woods felt as though he was 'the most toxic person in the bank . . . no one would talk to me'. Wachovia agreed to pay an undisclosed amount, in return for which Woods left the bank and agreed not to make public the terms of the settlement.

After years of tribulation, Woods was finally formally vindicated, though not by Wachovia: a letter dated 19 March 2010 – three days after the settlement in Miami – arrived from John Dugan, then the comptroller of the currency in Washington. Dugan said he was 'writing to personally recognize and express my appreciation for the role that you played in the actions brought against Wachovia Bank for violations of the bank secrecy act . . . Not only did the information that you provided facilitate our investigation, but you demonstrated great personal courage and integrity by speaking up when you saw problems. Without the efforts of individuals like you, actions such as the one taken against Wachovia would not be possible.'

The so-called deferred prosecution detailed in the Miami document is a form of probation whereby if the bank abides by the law for a year, charges are dropped. So in March 2011 the bank was in the clear. The week that the deferred prosecution expired, a spokeswoman for Wells Fargo said the parent bank had no comment to make on the documentation pertaining to Woods's case, or his allegations. She added that there was no comment on prosecutor Sloman's remarks to the court; a provision in the settlement stipulated that Wachovia was not allowed to issue public statements that contradicted it.

But the Wachovia settlement leaves a sour taste in many mouths, in law enforcement and especially in Woods's. The deferred prosecution is part of this 'cop-out all round', he says. 'The regulatory authorities do not have to spend any more time on it, and they don't have to push it as far as a criminal trial. They just issue criminal proceedings, and settle, so it never has to go to trial. The law enforcement people do what they are supposed to do, but what's the point? All those people taking all that money from drug trafficking and murder, and no one goes to jail? You are not going to stop them that way, because there's no incentive for them to do so. And you are not making my job any easier trying to stop this from happening, nor are you making it any easier for law enforcement.'

One of the foremost figures in the training of anti-money-laundering officers is Robert Mazur, lead infiltrator for US law enforcement of the Columbian Medellín cartel during the epic prosecution and collapse of BCCI in 1991 (his story was made famous by his memoir, *The Infiltrator*). Mazur, whose firm Chase & Associates works closely with law enforcement and trains officers for bank anti-money-laundering efforts, cast a keen eye over the case against Wachovia and, in an interview, he says now that 'the only thing that will make the banks properly vigilant to what is happening is when they hear the rattle of handcuffs in the boardroom'.

With the DEA in Miami declining to return calls relating to the Wachovia case, Mazur's view is all the more compelling. 'Why did [Wachovia] think they were getting $400 billion from Mexico? Did they really think all that money was coming from family transfers?' Mazur asks, 'I know a lot of people like Martin Woods, who are very well intentioned. I know three people who worked for Wachovia and were doing the same thing as he was – former law enforcement, brave souls. But ultimately, the bank's actions are determined by the business model – how can the bank ultimately make a profit? – and that will undermine the work that people like Martin are trying to do.'

Mazur found that 'a lot of the law enforcement people were disappointed to see a settlement' between the administration and Wachovia. 'But I know that there were some external circumstances that worked to Wachovia's benefit, not least that the US banking system was on the edge of total collapse.'

What concerns Mazur is that what both law enforcement and

politicians can hope to achieve against the cartels is limited and falls short of the obvious attack the United States could make in its war on drugs: follow the money.

'We're thinking way too small,' Mazur says. 'I train law enforcement officers, thousands of them every year, and they say to me that if they tried to do half of what I did, they'd be arrested. But I tell them, "You got to think big. The headlines you will be reading in seven years' time will be the result of the work you begin now." With BCCI, we had to spend two years setting it up, two years doing undercover work, and another two years getting it to trial. If they want to do something big, like go after the money, that's how long it takes.'

But, says Mazur, 'If you look at the career ladders of law enforcement, there's no incentive to go after the big money. People move every two to three years. The DEA is focused on drug trafficking rather than money laundering. You get a quicker result that way – they want to get the traffickers and seize their assets. But this is like treating a sick plant by cutting off a few branches – it just grows new ones.

'Going after the big money is cutting down the plant – it's a harder door to knock on, it's a longer haul, and it won't get you the short-term riches.' It is the same for politicians, Mazur adds. 'Congressmen and women have to get elected every two or six years, so they're on the same short-term career ladder, needing to show short-term results.'

The office of the comptroller of the currency is still examining whether individuals at Wachovia are criminally liable. Sources at FinCEN say that, as directed by the settlement and agreed to by Wachovia, a look back is in process into the $378.3 billion that was not directly associated with the aircraft purchases and cocaine hauls, but neither subject to the proper anti-laundering checks. A FinCEN source says that $20 billion already examined appears to have 'suspicious origins'. But this is just the beginning.

Antonio Maria Costa, executive director of the UN's Office on Drugs and Crime from May 2002 to August 2010, charts the history of the contamination of the global banking industry by drug and criminal money since his first initiatives to try to curb it while at the European Commission during the 1990s. 'The connection between organized crime and financial institutions started in the late 1970s, early 1980s,' he says, 'when the mafia became globalized, with the economy.'

Until then, criminal money had circulated largely in cash, with the authorities making the occasional spectacular "sting" or haul. During Costa's time as director for economics and finance at the EC in Brussels, from 1987, inroads were made against penetration of banks by criminal laundering, and criminal money started moving back to cash, out of the financial institutions and banks. Then two things happened: the financial crisis in Russia, after the emergence of the Russian mafia, and the crises of 2003 and 2007–08.

'With these crises,' says Costa, 'the banking sector was short of liquidity, so the banks exposed themselves to the criminal syndicates, who had cash in hand. It was pure quid pro quo: banks needed cash, and criminal syndicates needed somewhere to put their cash. And we are talking about huge amounts of money.' Criminal syndicates, he says, 'will penetrate where there is least resistance, where the banks' need is greatest. So it was Western Europe in 2003 and the USA and UK in 2007–08. It's not suddenly one moment, one place; they get in progressively and they get in deep, buying up shares, buying up major assets.'

Costa questions the readiness of governments and their bank regulatory structures to challenge this large-scale corruption of the global economy: 'I wonder to what extent government regulators accepted – for want of a better term – this situation and were aware of what was going on. If money was coming into the banking sector, they seem to have adopted a policy of 'Don't ask, don't tell'. They knew that once the money is in the system, it is in the system – and you do not have the right to ask questions. Governments,' he adds, with a perceptive sting, 'certainly showed what they were capable of when the issue suddenly changed to laundering money for terrorism. Suddenly they became serious and changed their attitude.'

It's hardly surprising, then, that with regard to Mexico, Wachovia does not appear to be the end of the line. In August 2010, it emerged in quarterly disclosures by the giant bank HSBC that the US Justice Department was seeking to fine HSBC for anti-money-laundering compliance problems reported to include dealings with Mexico. On 7 October 2010, Reuters put out the following report:

The Federal Reserve issued an order on Thursday against HSBC North American Holdings Inc, requiring the bank to improve its practices to prevent customers from laundering money . . . through its accounts. The US Office of the Comptroller of the Currency issued a related order against the US subsidiary of HSBC, for violating a law governing how the company reports and assesses suspicious activity around its accounts, including international wire transfers and large cash withdrawals. HSBC is Europe's largest bank.

The regulators have not fined HSBC for the violations, but they could in the future. The OCC said its order 'does not preclude' it from assessing a civil money penalty against the bank. The regulators' orders come amid heightened US government attention to how major banks monitor and report suspicious activity, including signs of money laundering, from their accounts . . .

The OCC said in its complaint that HSBC Bank USA's 'compliance program and its implementation are ineffective, and accompanied by aggravating factors, such as highly suspicious activity creating a significant potential for unreported money laundering or terrorist financing'.

The regulator cited inadequate staffing, incomplete reviews and reporting of suspected suspicious activity from HSBC accounts, and insufficient monitoring of funds transfers and the financial activities of the bank's 'high-risk' customers. HSBC said in a statement it was cooperating fully with its regulators and it was 'committed to prompt resolution'.* Mazur, for his part, says, 'My information is that this investigation will go much deeper than the Wachovia case.'

'Wachovia had my résumé, they knew who I was,' says Martin Woods. 'But they did not want to know. Their attitude was, "Why are you doing this?" They should have been on my side, because they were compliance people, not commercial people. But they weren't, really; they were commercial people all along.'

'We're talking about hundreds of millions of dollars,' Woods continues, his police officer's mind-set affording him a moment of rage. 'This is the biggest money-laundering scandal of our time. In a

---

* Maria Aspan and Glenn Somerville, 'Fed Orders HSBC to Improve Anti-Fraud Controls,' Reuters news wire, 7 October 2010.

global context, there has never been anything like this. And we need to ask some fundamental questions: where does the money come from and what is the message if no one goes to jail? Responsibility for the failures is admitted, but no one is held accountable? Isn't that how the global crisis happened? Because no one at the banks was held accountable?

'These are the proceeds of murder and misery in Mexico, and of drugs sold around the world,' he goes on. 'All the law enforcement people wanted to see this come to trial. But no one goes to jail. What does the settlement do to fight the cartels? Nothing – it doesn't make the job of law enforcement easier and it encourages the cartels and anyone who wants to make money by laundering their blood dollars. Where's the risk? There is none – there is only an upside.

'Is it in the interest of the American people to encourage both the drug cartels and the banks in this way? Is it in the interest of the Mexican people? It's simple: if you don't see the correlation between the money laundering by banks and the thirty thousand people killed in Mexico, you're missing the point.'

Woods feels unable to rest on his laurels. He tours the world for a consultancy he now runs, Hermes Forensic Solutions, counselling and speaking to banks on the dangers of laundering criminal money and how to spot and stop it.

'New York and London,' says Woods, 'have become the world's two biggest laundries of criminal and drug money, and offshore tax havens. Not the Cayman Islands, not the British Virgin Islands, not the Isle of Man or Jersey. The big laundering is right through the City of London and Wall Street.

'After the Wachovia case, no one in the regulatory community sat down with me and asked, "What happened?" or "What can we do to avoid this happening to other banks?"

'In fact, on the face of it they are not interested. They are the same people who attack the whistle-blowers, and this is a position the FSA at least has adopted on legal advice: it has been advised that the privacy and confidentiality of banking and bankers take primacy over the Public Information Disclosure Act. That is how the priorities work: secrecy first, the public interest second.

'Meanwhile, the drug industry has two products: money and suffering. On the one hand, you have massive profits and enrichment.

On the other, you have massive suffering, misery and death. You cannot separate one from the other. When I saw what I saw, I wasn't caught between a rock and a hard place; I was in a difficult place, and I only had one honourable option: to speak up.

'What happened at Wachovia was symptomatic of the failure of the entire regulatory system to apply the kind of proper governance and adequate risk management that would have prevented not just the laundering of blood money but also the global crisis.'

EPILOGUE

El Sol Negro – The Black Sun

In ancient Mexican lore, there lies behind the sun that shines, a Black Sun which leaves this world to shed light upon another, beneath. The Mexica believed the Black Sun was carried by the god of the underworld, and was the maleficent herald of death, though not death as finality. The Mexica lived in a condition of expectation of calamity and catastrophe, yet their preoccupation with death was a blend of fear and devotion to the moment of reunion with their ancestors, in the land upon which the Black Sun shines. And behind the sunlight of the deserts of Amexica – which turns to fire during eventide – there is some maculate, black light that gives nothing back; un-shining behind the eternities of space and sky, or the bustle and music in all those labyrinthine streets lined with hot peppers and freshly gathered pistachios tumbling from every open storefront.

And one feels the rays of that dichotomous black sunshine especially after talking to Dr Antonio Irán Muñoz, of the forensic autopsy team back in Tijuana, where all this began. This is a man who sees the world very clearly, from the slabs on which the saprophytic corpses are laid for inspection. Dr Muñoz defines his work as: 'spending my life trying to scientifically interrogate people who cannot talk,' he says, 'who have suffered terrible pain, but now feel nothing. They can only communicate silently through the terrible things that have been done to them. I have to look for a cause, not a result. I have to rewind the movie, work out what was done, and why.' Why did he choose this job? 'Because I love medicine, and I love the law. And because I lost my father when I was eight years old, and in his last words, he told the doctors: "Whatever you do, do it freely, but with exactitude." '

Muñoz is a man of courtesy and exceptionally good humour. After discussing the various mutilations and their significance, he says that 'the principal message is to the other cartels. They want respect, they want to say "this is what we do", and sometimes they say it in written messages, too, perhaps a joke, like the emergency number to call. There's also a message to their own people, of course: "Toe the line, or we will do this to you. The more brutally we get you to do things, the more brutally they could happen to you." '

But there are gradations within these barbarities, and this is what fascinates Dr Muñoz. 'Sometimes they are done by a medical student, sometimes just by a butcher. It is the medical students who have something to say. They are the ones trying to speak to us. I look at a cut-off toe. How was it done? Was it done well? Was it done from the left or the right? If it was done well, exactly between the bones, the person is more dangerous. If the finger was wrapped up tight before it was cut, we know we are dealing with the medical student, employed by the cartel hierarchy. If it's just hacked off, we're dealing with a *mana*, a street thug. You need to cut it properly if you are going to send it to the victim's family, or the police.'

'That Alejandra girl,' he says, 'the model and cheerleader, I really don't think that was the work of someone working for *El Teo*, as we're told. There was nothing one could do with fingers broken that crudely. When we see women and children mutilated, that is very serious – it's probably not a direct target; they're doing it to show someone else they know how to do it, and to drive them mad.' Decapitation, 'as I told you last time you were here, that is another matter. Again, it is significant how well it was done. If it is done badly, it shows nothing more than savagery. But if it is done well, it's a primal message: "Not only are we going to kill you, we're going to cut you in pieces." It's a message to all of the kind from which the victim came.

'The difference is this: in what I would call normal times, I kill you and make you disappear. Now, they are shouting it, turning it into a kind of grotesque carousel around their territory. In normal conditions, the torture and killing is private, now it is a public execution using extreme violence, and this is significant, I think. We need to say one thing first, however: these people are drama queens. They think what they do makes them powerful, masters of the universe. But they're not. Ultimately, what they do is pathetic. We have to remember that. They keep saying they're poor people – well, they're poor in culture, that's what they are. They have no culture. The narcos in the old days had been to school. They knew that to be kingpins, they had to provide light, hospitals and schools. That way, they could keep a low profile, win respect, and protect themselves. Félix Gallardo was a businessman, using the same commercial acumen as Carlos Slim, the mobile phone man. If you play by the rules, I leave you alone. If you cross the line, I destroy you. These new people just want luxury, power and more power until they get arrested or killed. That is why they are doomed, and that is why they say so much about our society. They reflect a society without values. I don't even think they are against our society, I think they're products of it. People without culture or values in a society without culture or values. A society that has gone from Frank Sinatra to that Fifty Cent man I see on television. They're both associated with criminals, almost everyone is if they really want to make it – but look at the difference between them! Fifty Cent is the new role model for the narco, Sinatra is old school – I know which I'd rather have. The new narcos are like Fifty Cent – he says it all, product of a society that's lost its way. Money and power are what counts.' Muñoz sees this point as reason to let out a raucous laugh. He is a big man, demonstrative. Can one be nostalgic for the golden age of corruption, I ask? There had been so much misplaced nostalgia for what Julián Cardona called the 'classical' era of narco cartels. Dr Muñoz retorts with another question: 'Do you prefer it like it is now?'

Dr Muñoz considers what this war means in historical terms I had not expected this conversation to comprise. Or maybe I had, when we met briefly and made sure to talk properly, later. 'Consider how all the great civilisations fall, the marks of their last days.' He cites ancient Rome, and 'the terrible nature of public execution in its final phase'. Torture and violent public execution had also marked, he says, 'the end of the Middle Ages and the Spanish Inquisition, as they gave way to Renaissance and science. There are these great moments of civilisation, of science, but they try to be bigger and better than they are, and when they fall, they resort to grotesque public execution. And I think we are now in a moment of crisis, in the culture of global business.'

Muñoz refers back to what he calls 'times of normality', when 'the *narcotraficante* saw himself as a kind of bandit, but also a gentleman, a *patrón*. He would distribute generously, even if it was from prison, make sure the village had electric light, gifts for Mother's Day, presents for children. But this was no different from the manager of the *maquiladora* who allowed his workers a cigarette break or free coffee machine. It meant nothing sincere, it just kept everyone making the product.' Then he reaches for what I have been calling the postmodern or late capitalist, value-free and globalised phrase of both society and the narco war: 'But what happens when this system reaches state of crisis?' asks Dr Muñoz. 'Look around you: recession, crisis, factories closing. The narco is in the same position as everyone else, and everyone else is in the same position as the narco. You must keep supremacy, you must keep control. The *narcotraficante* is the most global of all global businessmen, and now he must make you loyal or afraid. And he must do these public executions involving mutilation as a demonstration of power, as all these cultures do, in their final phases.'

I suggest that despite the heinous work he does, Dr Muñoz strikes one as a swarthy man who appreciates the sight of a pretty girl, a good wine, a good meal. 'I spend all day with the dead,' he replies, 'so I have a duty to love life, and live it to the full. When I am with my colleagues, we are always joking about death, and joking *with* death. I live like a man who sits eating a delicious taco on the street there, aware that every moment could be his last. One bullet, and he is dead.'

AFTERWORDS
AMEXICA + 10

Tijuana Revisited

On a pluvial morning at an army base in Tijuana during October 2019, an ostentatious but imposing ceremony is staged: an *'Incineración de Droga'* by combined law enforcement agencies, setting fire to 26,000 kilos of heroin, cocaine, methamphetamine and other drugs. A trumpeter blasts a salute into the morning mist, and a military band plays the national anthem. VIPs assemble beneath a canvas canopy, and a video is played, on a screen for all to see, of the seizures – piles of narcotics laid out on tables, surrounded by armed officers. Victorino Porcayo of the Federal Police calls this morning a 'historic moment', though the governor-elect of Baja California, Jaime Bonilla, prefers the more cautious 'symbolic event'. A torch is applied, flame spreads across the hillock of drugs, and black smoke billows skywards. There is no marked odour, and huddled reporters crack the inevitable joke that this pyre is not what we are told, the officers having already apportioned the proceeds of the real thing. Nonetheless, a platoon of agents from the Agencia de Investigación Criminal lines up, with K9 tracker dogs at heel, for a team photo against the backdrop of the inferno; to be fair, they look deservedly content with a tough job well done. It's been a while since this was done publicly in Tijuana, or anywhere else – but everyone knows this was a familiar scene years ago. That – gallant though the choreography is – this pyre is but straw in a haystack, a grain among millions more kilos of the same drugs, on the move, out there, around town and across the border, now as before, and forever.

The journeys of ten years ago began and ended here at the border's western edge. Víctor Clark Alfaro, from *Amexica*'s opening chapter, is a trans-border 'Amexican' citizen who is from and lives in Tijuana, but teaches classes at San Diego State University which he brings back across for 'field trips'. Clark Alfaro was an essential guide to the narco war then, and to key players involved. Now, there's a shock: 'There's no question that the big cartels are consolidated in Tijuana, but whereas ten years ago we knew their names, their heirs are now invisible. They are business people you'd meet at the country club. But for the first time in three decades, I cannot name their leaders' This is in part because the new style of narco lord is less likely to show off their prowess and wealth, and partly because, as I wrote on those opening pages, that where the river flows through people will drink: Mexico's domestic drug market – so-called *narcomenudeo* – has increased further since, and is now believed to account for more violence than competition for 'export' plazas. The killers and their victims operate at street level, while the commanders remain out of sight, if not out of mind.

'There are now 200,000 drug addicts in this city,' says Clark Alfaro, 'one in nine of the population, and that's a vast business. But these barrio dealers are not freelance. The drugs they sell are colour-coded, according to the cartel bringing them in. You see someone selling the wrong colour for that territory, you kill them.' It is 'common for the police to visit the *tiendas* and take a percentage', says Clark Alfaro, and the authorities, he adds, 'may well know who's running them. But they are not mentioning any names publicly – perhaps as a way of protecting them.'

This was not always the case. When I interviewed him in 2008, Lt. Col. Julián Leyzaola Pérez strutted with a military gait. As he should have, as a former lieutenant colonel in the Mexican army, summoned to take over the police force and then public security in Tijuana – we met on his first day in the job. Leyzaola – one of the most intriguing and controversial figures to emerge from Mexico's carnage – wielded office with famous (some say infamous) ruthlessness and efficacy, driving down murder rates in Tijuana, then Ciudad Juárez. But in 2015 came the payback: while with his wife and son in Juárez, Leyzaola was ambushed by a hit squad, and has since been paralysed from the waist down. Now, he arrives in a wheelchair to talk, at a favourite restaurant of his beside the Pacific shore, for juice, coffee and *pan dulce*, on a windswept day, the ocean beyond the window under a leaden sky. Col. Leyzaola, brought in by a man with the spine of a soldier, is palpably furious at his immobility.

Back in 2008, Leyzaola was everywhere to be seen on the streets of Tijuana. Whenever there was a shootout or bodies dumped – and there were plenty – there he would be, surveying the crime scene, consulting his officers and addressing the press, prowling the beat. 'What I can do,' he said back then, 'is increase a police profile to avert the social psychosis the narcos want to generate.'

From a military family in Méxicali, Leyzaola grew up in Culiacán, fortress of the Sinaloa cartel. 'We lived near the Red Cross clinic, with ambulances forever bringing the latest victims of the violence,' he recalls. 'I grew up with the impact of narco culture, and realised there was no middle ground – that these cartels have to be destroyed.' When he took over public security in Tijuana, Leyzaola says, 'I studied the criminal groups, their own rules, language, even religion – their cult of excessive violence, how they penetrate society. And I devised a strategy with the then mayor to neutralise them, and recover the city.' At first, this meant coordinating wings of law enforcement at odds with one another.

With the Arellano Felix Organisation in decline, 'my real war was against the Sinaloa cartel', he recalls now. 'They offered me money' – reportedly $80,000 a week – 'as they had done to my predecessors, but I refused, for which they tried to kill me five times.' After the third attempt on his life, Leyzaola moved his family across the border to San Diego, and took up residence in a military base.

By 2011, homicides in Tijuana had halved. There are two explanations: one, that the Sinaloa cartel won the war and established a *Pax Mafiosa* in town. The other, that Leyzaola applied a *mano férrea* – iron hand – with such force that it worked. An exhaustive report by a trans-border team of academics working under the umbrella 'Justice in Mexico' allows for both.[1]

Leyzaola brought in military officers with limited police experience to lock down zones in the city, barrio by barrio, arresting and jailing drug dealers and smugglers. But he waged another war: against many of his own corrupt officers. He purged some six hundred officers and departmental personnel – nearly a third of the force. 'I adopted a policy of zero tolerance in applying the law,' says Leyzaola, 'against no matter who, whether they wore uniform or not.

By the end, it was harder for police officers to serve the cartel, and harder for the cartel to move around safe houses in this city.' But Leyzaola's purges provoked allegations of human rights abuses and even of his own presence during the torture of police officers believed to be on the cartel pay roll. Challenged about these allegations that he abused human rights of suspect officers, Leyzaola retorts: 'The only way to fight crime is to apply the law. It was these people who violated human rights — why defend them, and not the law?'

By 2011, Ciudad Juárez was the murder capital of the world. Leyzaola was duly transferred there after the departure of the army from the city's streets, and sought to repeat his Tijuana performance. Leyzaola's welcome was a mixed one: within forty-eight hours of his arrival, a mangled corpse was dumped in the city centre with the message 'Leyzaola, Welcome to Juárez'. He took a call from José Antonio Acosta, a former senior police officer working for the Sinaloa cartel, saying: 'I am at your service.' Four months later, Acosta was arrested along with a number of his collaborators, among them police officers. Leyzaola told the *New York Times*: 'You can't apply a strategy from a desk. You have to apply it on the street.' His officers mounted, he says now, 'intense harassment patrols', as in Tijuana, 'block by block, *colonia* by *colonia*. To take back the city zone by zone.'

But that was not all. Leyzaola speaks like no one of his ilk about corrupt Mexican law enforcement operating as a crime syndicate. 'When I arrived, I set myself against two cartels,' he recalls, 'the Juárez and Sinaloa cartels. Then I realised there was a third cartel: the Federal Police cartel. Yes, the Federal Police had a force of five thousand officers, moving drugs, running extortion rackets. Like the other two cartels, they occupied territory by violence and fear. I confronted all three, head-on.' And it worked, albeit drawing the same allegations of abuse as Tijuana. During Leyzaola's three years in office, murders in Juárez plunged from 1,926 to 514. The city took a deep breath of hope, thinking (wrongly) that the worst was over.

On 8 May 2015, two years after leaving his post, Leyzaola was shot for his endeavours. Having opened a private security company in Juárez, he was arriving at a money exchange office with his wife and son when two gunmen opened fire. Diving to protect the child, Leyzaola took two bullets. The men were arrested, and jailed after the briefest of trials; they said they had been paid for the hit, but claimed they did not know by whom. Leyzaola, wincing at the memory, insists that the attempted execution was 'by the authorities in Juárez, on orders of the Chihuahua state government, because of its connections to organised crime'.

Leyzaola returned to Tijuana in 2017, aiming not at the apex of law enforcement, but political authority, to become Tijuana's mayor. He narrowly lost, twice, as he sees it, 'to the political machine'. Mexico's current murder capital is also one of the country's fastest-growing conurbations, integral to the vibrant cross-border economic area known as 'CaliBaja'; the second-largest city on the Americas' Pacific coast, after Los Angeles, where 40 per cent of all audiovisual goods in North America are manufactured. Nearly 200,000 people a day cross this border into San Diego and back, legally.[2]

Leyzaola regards the surge in violence as a mark of the latest encroachment into Tijuana by the Cartel Jalisco Nueva Generación, 'filling a vacuum' left by the fragmentation of the Sinaloa cartel after the trial and jailing of Joaquín 'El Chapo' Guzmán in the United States. 'At the moment, the Jalisco cartel wants to dominate Tijuana, and that's the biggest problem. But they are franchises, like McDonald's – everyone is replaceable. Same scenario when Chapo's people arrived in my day – ad infinitum.'

Unlike most of his peers who think it harder to confront disparate, street-level groups than organised criminal pyramids, Leyzaola thinks it 'more difficult to fight a big organisation. Small groups can be taken down on my territorial model; but the great problem in Mexico is the power of the big cartels and their corruption of the institutions of state.'

His next step, personally? 'To try again to get elected. Surrender is not in my vocabulary.'

But narco traffic and homicide have been overwhelmed in the news, as have resources in Tijuana itself, by the surge in numbers of migrants arriving in the city, with intent to cross into the United States, either by claiming political asylum, or illegally. The faces and points of departure have changed, as will unfold during these latest excursions along the border.

By far the most impactful migration, in terms of numbers and the visceral pain of their stories, is that of the arrivals from Central

America, in flight from the ravages of drug-gang warfare among rival cartels in El Salvador, Honduras and Guatemala: the Mara Salvatrucha, or MS-13, and Barrio 18. They began coming en masse during 2018, in caravans organised for safety in numbers.

In January 2019, the landscape of political asylum along the border was transformed by a stroke of policy from the Trump administration. The Montevideo Treaty of 1939 on political asylum had been signed – and ratified by the United States – after shiploads of Jews were turned back by the USA to perish in Europe. Under the treaty, an asylum seeker has the right to a 'credible fear' interview, after which they can wait in the country of application for a court hearing and decision on their case. But in 2019, Trump began to enforce the so-called Migrant Protection Protocols, MPP, which required Spanish-speaking, non-Mexican applicants to 'remain in Mexico' – a term the system came to be known by – after entering the system, while they await their court hearing, often months away. The plan was rolled out between Tijuana and San Diego in January 2019, thereafter in Ciudad Juárez and El Paso, then along the Rio Grande Valley in July. The new left-wing Mexican government of Andres Manuel López Obrador cooperated enthusiastically with the policy, and was subsequently congratulated by the Department of Homeland Security for its 'spectacular results'. By the end of 2019, some 59,000 asylum applicants under MPP were stranded on the Mexican side of the border, clutching their 'Notice to Appear' documents. Access to asylum was further restricted by a system called 'metering', which limited the numbers that could apply for asylum on a given day. This led to the drawing up of waiting lists – official, semi-official and unofficial – on the Mexican side.

Chapter Two of *Amexica* ended with a three-year-old girl called América being deported alone back to Nogales, Sonora, from Arizona. Since then, jails along the US side of the border and shelters across northern Mexico have contained thousands of children, some separated from their parents, others travelling alone, or waiting to be 'processed'. The enforced the separation of children from their parents at the border, incarcerating them thousands of miles apart, is one of the darkest moments in US immigration policy within living memory. The policy provoked outcry, was ruled illegal by US federal courts and abandoned, though hundreds of children remain separated after their parents were deported to Central America without them. Internal documentation leaked from inside US Customs and Border Protection shows that the government was well aware of the traumatic effects this deterrent policy had on children, early on during its implementation.[3]

Minors cannot be returned under MPP and have instead been kept in custody in the USA to await their hearings. There is evidence of them being held in appalling conditions. Late in 2019, the news organisation Pro Publica published shocking leaked CCTV footage of the death of a teenager, Carlos Hernández Vásquez, left to die in his cell while the Border Patrol apparently falsified records of 'Welfare Checks' or conducted them but did not notice the boy was lifeless. Others on the Mexican side wait for whatever the borderland may bring. For the young, in particular, the streets of Tijuana are every bit as perilous as those they came from.

On a Saturday afternoon in December 2018, three Honduran boys walked out through the gates of the blue stucco 'Casa YMCA' shelter for unaccompanied child and teenaged migrants, in which they were staying, and turned into Cuauhtémoc Boulevard for a walk. Their destination was the camp at a sports centre, to visit people they'd met on a caravan from Central America. Two of them never returned: the deaths of Jasson Ricardo Acuña Polanco and Jorge Alexander Ruiz Duban, aged sixteen and seventeen, were reported two days later, as was the subsequent arrest of three people for their murder. Hitherto publicly unknown, however, until Jorge Fregoso (from Chapter One) and I visited the shelter, was the return here of the third boy who, though his throat bore wounds from attempted strangulation, had survived. Also overlooked, therefore, was how the two had died: one garrotted by wire, the other by having a stick driven repeatedly into his mouth – by people who had ensnared, abducted and tortured them.

I traced the cruel narrative of these murders on the basis of the account from the surviving child – we'll call him Lázaro – as told to management and staff at the shelter and the *suprocurador*, district attorney, for Tijuana, José Alberto Álvarez Mendoza. 'They had been with us two or three weeks,' says Uriel González, who runs a group of four shelters for unaccompanied child migrants operated by the YMCA along the borderline. 'It was a time when our capacity for fourteen or so kids was stretched to accommodate fifty. They left the *casa* by themselves, and two women started talking to them, commenting on their physical appearance – one had electric blue-green eyes.' 'They approached the boys to hook them,' informs Prosecutor Álvarez, 'saying: "Have you seen a little puppy?" ' As told to González: 'One offered them sex; they said no, then she said that rich ladies pay well to be with boys like you.' Eventually, 'she took them to a house and when they became frightened they were not allowed to leave, and realised they'd been kidnapped'.

'It appears the motive was to steal whatever money they might have, and possibly for the men to rape them,' says Álvarez. 'They were asked for money,' says González, 'and said they had none. "We can get money from your relatives in the USA," said their captors – then they started to torture them.' 'The assailants were all intoxicated, high on drugs,' says Álvarez. The Hondurans were tied to chairs and undressed; the lead woman in the entrapment took scissors to the throat of one of them; another suffered blade wounds to the back. 'They put a stick into the mouth of one of them wrapped in a sock, and hammered it in,' says González. 'The other was strangled by wire, turned by a stick,' affirms Prosecutor Álvarez. 'Lázaro' found his way back to the shelter, says González, 'traumatised, in a terrible condition, and on Monday went to the child protection services. That same day, I received a call they had found the bodies. The families were contacted – I had to tell them what had happened and refer them to the Honduran consulate in Saltillo [in Coahuila, Mexico].'

The police then 'arrived at our Casa YMCA', says González, 'and when Lázaro had completed his declaration, they took him to where they had been held'. 'We asked him to follow the route he took, and find the place,' says Álvarez. 'And, unbelievably, there was the same woman, walking the same street, doing the same thing – two days later. She told us where the house was, and there we found one man who took us to the other guy. We arrested all three, now detained and charged with abduction and murder.'

They were: Esmeralda García, known as 'La Keily' as in Kylie Minogue; Francisco Zavala, known as 'El Zanahorio', the carrot; and Carlos Martínez 'El Morral', the backpack. Their features are blacked out in detention photographs, but not those Prosecutor Álvarez shows on his phone; one of the men has dead, red eyes, jaw dropped, an expression both blank and brutal.

Prosecutor Álvarez confirms: 'These were small-time drug dealers working the street, themselves intoxicated. What they did – and these terrible murders – illustrate the social decomposition we see in Tijuana; the kind of killing typical of those which occur more in this city, sadly, than anywhere else in Mexico.'

Both men arrested had records of drug dealing, and had previously admitted to lowly connections with cartels. 'Usually, no one ever speaks; families will not come forward,' says Álvarez. 'The irony is that we are only able to prosecute this case because there was a survivor to take us to the scene; we have a witness. It has attracted attention because the victims were Hondurans. If they had not been, no one would know about this – they would probably be just two more murder victims in Tijuana.'

Casa YMCA is a poignant place, in shock despite the spirits of the boys and girls seated for lunch at a long table, grinning at cartoons on television. The meal cleared, volunteer Guadalupe Sepulveda supervises washing-up; girls repair to their dormitory and braid one another's hair; boys to theirs, where most, including one wearing a red cap – call him José – remember the victims well. 'They were the same as us, who came here hungry and thirsty with God's help,' he says. 'We came for lack of work and because gangs back there threaten you with a knife to your neck, even if it's for fifty quetzales.'

With González off supervising his other charges, Casa YMCA is left under the authority of its permanent manager, Maynor Contreras Estrada. 'There's no limit to the depravity these children flee in Central America,' he says, citing the case of a fourteen-year-old girl here who was gang-raped, told to sell drugs and deliver the profits. 'If she didn't, they'd take her younger sister. The two of them fled, without consulting their parents, and joined the caravan.'

There is a cruel twist to the tragedy. On Monday 17 December 2018, two Californian Congress members, Nanette Barragán and Jimmy Gómez, came to the border crossing at Otay Mesa, Tijuana, to join a protest against US authorities' refusal to allow asylum seekers to stake their claim, as was still then their right. After waiting all night at the crossing, they finally accompanied twenty migrants through, including eight minors. There were supposed to have been nine – also on the list was 'Lázaro'.

'He should be in the United States now,' says Uriel González, 'processing his asylum claim, as was his plan. Instead he is here, traumatised, living this nightmare.' And Prosecutor Álvarez has more: 'I'm afraid that one of the deceased was dressed in women's clothes,' he says. Álvarez shows a lifeless body, bloodied and horribly strangled, wearing a bra and red skirt. 'Not only that, but when the survivor took us to the house, one of the killers was still wearing the clothes and shoes of the deceased. Two days later. That's the kind of people we're dealing with.'

The most cogent allure of this land is the good people. I have reflected often since *Amexica* – during dark days in Britain and Europe – on how the United States does, unlike us, have a real opposition; it is not necessarily an ideological one, but moral, often faith-based, sometimes judicial. It tends to group by identity rather than in political structures; it is outraged, and sometimes effective.

Daybreak at the El Chaparral crossing from Tijuana into the USA has become a crossroads of the world. Sisters from El Salvador attend to one another's appearance; men from Cameroon await numbers to be called for an asylum hearing on the far side. Iranians play dice; a father from Venezuela buys his child a taco from a street stand with carefully counted coins. First sun and chill wind cut across the plaza, and groups of young Americans also converge, carrying armfuls of papers. They are an unsung story in the narrative of migration towards America; coming from all over the USA, encamped in Tijuana to volunteer for an organisation called Al Otro Lado, To the Other Side.

One of the women propelling Al Otro Lado arrives to greet her troops. Border Rights Project Director Nicole Ramos, from New Jersey, is here – via six years as a federal public defender in Alabama – 'to do work that never ends'. The principle of that work becomes, she says, 'to get the courts and federal law enforcement to follow federal law. To stop the people whose role is to uphold the law from routinely breaking it.'

Ramos exudes tireless purpose. She wears a ring made of bullet casing and obsidian. 'I came here to apply what I knew about the broken system,' she says. She teamed up with two immigration attorneys working in southern California: Nora Phillips and Erika Pinheiro, who founded Al Otro Lado in 2011. 'We've counselled over two thousand migrants. This is the new normal. People are going to keep coming, and so many people are hurting so bad.'

Al Otro Lado 'works as much on the US side as we do in Mexico', Ramos explains, and south of the border 'it's a question not of representation, but of ensuring people know their rights under US law, giving them a clear picture of what to expect and what not to expect on the other side'. There's no attempt to feed dreams or delusions that may have got migrants thus far. 'We'd be violating our own ethos if we didn't warn people and explain the grim realities of detention.'

Al Otro Lado's Tijuana premises occupy three storeys of Enclave Caracol, a food co-op and free vegan café, bike workshop and music venue. Now the food offered here to people in need goes to migrants and deportees who arrive 'for advice and things nothing to do with law', says Ramos, 'like a warm welcome, a big smile, a place to rest among friends — to get practical advice and medical needs'. The latter tended to in a clinic by Rosanne Hebert, a nurse from Vermont, practising, she says, 'down and dirty nursing, thinking outside the box'.

'A day here is like a week anywhere else,' says Millicent Hoffman, a legal observer for the National Lawyers Guild. 'We're drinking from a firehose, working with a system that's either broken or deliberately dysfunctional. It's nothing new, but the Trump administration is ramping it up, breaking all the norms.'

Litigation director Erika Pinheiro is the daughter of Portuguese immigrants to the US, a long-time specialist in child and immigrant detention in Los Angeles. Pinheiro speaks with apprehensive sagacity in her Tijuana office. 'I've worked many years in detention facilities in the US,' she says, 'immigrant detention for adults and kids, county jails in LA, and it's been very hard. But what we had until now was the US government following the law, more or less. People were in danger, but there were rules. Now it's very different: we have another level of desperation among those applying, and we just don't know what the rules are. We keep following the law and statutes, but the government is not following the law. I've been practising law a good while, and I've never seen it so routinely broken by those who make it.'

We talk, inevitably, about the abomination of child and family separation. This has always been the case — the difference now is that the government is separating families deliberately to 'deter asylum seekers'. Much of Pinheiro's work has been with deported parents of children who remain, often in custody, in the US. 'We now know that thousands of children have been separated from their parents at the border in the past year, some before and after "zero tolerance".' The timing of this work in Pinheiro's home life has been visceral. 'While on these cases, I was in the late stages of pregnancy, and gave birth to a son. There I was, becoming a mother, receiving daily texts from Central America, from mothers and fathers who had been torn away from their children. To be honest, there were moments where it became unbearable.' Ramos sees me out into the Tijuana night; I ask: Does it all get too much? 'When I think of what the asylum-seeker migrants have been through, nothing is too much.'

On a Friday night, the cavernous Zacazonapan bar in the down-at-heel red-light district is thick with marijuana smoke, and packed as always with Tijuaneros plus gringos in town for cheap drink and whatever – but the band up tonight is different from usual.

Five-piece Resistencia Migrante was formed in the Espacio Migrante shelter nearby. Oscar plays keyboards with a voltage he communicates less through the amplifier than by drawing on two years of travelling from El Salvador and seven months in Tijuana. He has given up trying to cross the border; Oscar's flight from threats by the MS-13 gang back home was insufficient to impress the US court system; he then tried to cross illegally but was apprehended and deported. 'We've abandoned the American dream as a nightmare,' he says, 'and it's okay here.' The set done, Oscar and I share a cab through early hours, dropping him off at his lodgings in an outer *barrio* to which Victor Clark Alfaro said he only goes with a police escort. 'I manage here *mas o menos*' – kind of, says Oscar, alighting, 'we are survivors.'

The epilogue to *Amexica* comprised that interview in Tijuana with Antonio Irán Muñoz, whose macabre expertise at the prosecutor's office was to analyse mutilations of cartel victims to decode messages they might contain. I always meant to see him again – forensic expert, but also droll philosopher. We meet now at the Ateneo de Ciencias Universitarias y Artes – a college since founded by Muñoz 'to train young people to blend "criminalistic" – what is found at a crime scene, scientifically – and "criminological", which is psychological, why the criminal did what he did', he says. 'Ten years ago, we talked about terrible things happening in this city. But I was failing to change things at the prosecutor's office, so decided to create my own university and impart what I knew to the next generation.'

Muñoz was 'decoding mutilations', he says, 'because they were a controlled way of communicating messages. This still happens in southern Mexico, but no longer here. In Tijuana now, they just shoot each other on street corners like dogs; now you find bodies – usually killed in one place, and dumped in another.' Before, he posits, 'the narco only killed who he needed to kill. Now, anyone can be a narco, so they kill anyone. The drugs don't just fly to the north, they also stay here, so that now there's a war for the streets – and this contributes to the general collapse. There is no message to send; I just erase you from the point of sale, and it works. Kill one, and I have four more waiting to replace you.' But, I suggest, the export market is unaffected. Who controls that business now? 'We don't know,' replies Muñoz, echoing Clark Alfaro. 'The government says it doesn't know, but I think they know, and do nothing about it. I'd prefer it if they did, because if they don't, we are lost.'

Muñoz notes the arrival of fentanyl on the domestic and export markets. 'It's cheap to make and easy to smuggle. I also come across it in my forensic investigations – more deaths from fentanyl, often mixed with cocaine, without the addict knowing. Dealers cut other drugs with fentanyl to make them even more addictive.' But this creates a problem with the business model, doesn't it? I interject. Fentanyl is too strong, and there's no point in a dead customer. 'Human beings are addicts,' he replies, 'to pleasure and power – coffee, alcohol, sex, extreme sports – and drugs are the most addictive of all. The stronger the drug, the more the addiction, the more people will crave it. One addict dies, another comes along. It's never going to go away, and what makes this war pure stupidity is that we are never going to win it unless we see the addict as a sick person, not a criminal.'

Devil's Highway Revisited

Mike Flores, of the Tohono O'odham — 'Desert People' — Nation in Arizona, cut off from his own people in Sonora, Mexico, spoke ten years ago of despondence among his Native American people in the borderlands. But Flores's resilient rage, and view of a contemporary First Nation identity, albeit rooted in ancestral wisdom, was prescient. The past five years have seen a remarkable resurgence of consciousness and activism among young Native Americans, resonant of Flores's days in the AIM and the generation to which he belongs, yet of now. The protest camp in 2016 at Standing Rock — against the Dakota Access Pipeline, which cut through ancient Lakota tribal land and crucial water supply — won a temporary victory under the Obama administration, but endured defeat under Trump. Yet it helped detonate a movement across tribal identities, and conjoined a flourishing of innovative Native activism, thinking and literature.

The renaissance in Native pride is palpable around and across Tohono O'odham territory, ten years on. The walls of the copper-mining town, Ajo, where Flores had worked, are decorated with striking, generally Native and specifically O'odham murals, showing their 'Man in the Maze' logo, wolves and Native chiefs — declaiming slogans and citing poems against borders and frontiers. One depicts, beautifully, a seamless map of the USA and Mexico, with agave, ocotillo and saguaro in flower, butterflies and bats, and the words: 'I am safe in my adobe house with its rainbow congregation of chuckling quails, pyrrhuloxia, choirs of mockingbirds, skitterish purple finches, coyotes, javelinas, rattlers, scorpions and leopard lizards, and the not so silent majority of English sparrows, who accommodate too easily to walls — there is not one passport among them.' Another mural shows a woman with hair made of desert plants and blooms, while yet another depicts a leaping mountain lion of the kind whose migration the border fence hampers, proclaiming: 'Revitalize Not Militarize. Tohono O'odham Jewed' – Tohono O'odham Earth (or Land) – from the slogan: 'Sic Has Elid g Jewed' – Respect the Land.

But this revival of consciousness among the O'odham is double-edged, for though an invocation of pride, it is also in reaction to a heinous, callous and violent intrusion. The renaissance is in resistance to echoes of that 'genocide' in our time, as America's present continues to decimate its indigenous past, as at Standing Rock, and demonstrate contempt for its Native people and First Nations. Sells is no longer that sleepy, desolate town of 2010; it has been fired into action against President Trump's proposals for a barrier that will not only cut a gash across their ancestral land, but destroy ancient burial grounds and natural habitat. In early 2020, O'odham citizens were preparing to combat a grievous violation at Monument Hill, in the Organ Pipe National Monument, where the vast silence is shattered by blasting with dynamite, the chug of bulldozers, the clatter of construction, drainage of water from a rare desert oasis and the felling of venerable cacti. The still darkness of deep, desert night is now blinded by floodlights. The cause: replacement of mesh fencing along the white man's borderline through the O'odham 'Jewed', with steel bollards and the same new, towering thirty-foot reinforced barrier as blights elsewhere along much of the frontier.

The Organ Pipe Monument was designated a UNESCO International Biosphere Reserve in 1976. Even more importantly, this is land wherein the O'odham of old buried their own dead and scattered the bones of raiding Apache they had ensnared. But the cemeteries of Native People in 'Amexica' are of no more value than water supplies on the Great Plains. The Trump administration resurrected 'national emergency' legislation passed in the wake of the attacks of 11 September 2001, the so-called REAL ID Act of 2005 and 'mega-waiver' legislation in 2008, which allow the government to waive any law in a wall's way. The legislation overrides laws protecting public lands, sacred sites, endangered wildlife and more. Here, in addition to the disturbance of ancient burial grounds, several rare desert species will have their migration patterns disrupted or even terminated.

The construction threatens Quitobaquito Springs, the only natur-
ally occurring source of fresh water in the area, an oasis inhabited
for innumerable centuries by the Hia C-ed O'odham – the Sand
People – many of whom still live in the area. They are a distinct
branch of the tribe, from whom the spring is an important spiritual
site. The chairman of the Tohono O'odham Nation, Ned Norris Jr.,
told a congressional subcommittee in February 2020: 'How would
you feel if someone brought a bulldozer to your family graveyard
and started uprooting the graves there? That is the relationship, the
significance.' With chilling understatement, Norris added that the
works had already 'resulted in the inadvertent discovery of human
remains near Quitobaquito Springs'. Democrat representative Raul
Grijalva – who chairs the House Committee on Natural Resources
on Capitol Hill – in a statement a month earlier, said: 'There has
been no consultation with the Nation. This administration is basically trampling on the tribe's history – and, to put it poignantly, its
ancestry.'

In November 2019 – on the thirtieth anniversary of the fall of the
Berlin Wall, by ironic design – there was a demonstration at the site,
at which a Hia C-ed O'odham lawyer and activist of the new gener-
ation, Nellie Jo David, addressed the crowd. 'This wall is illegal.
This wall is a desecration of spiritual and religious land. There is no
O'odham word for "wall". There is no O'odham word for "militarisa-
tion".' She led the crowd in a chant of 'Tear down the wall' and
'Water not walls'.

Among the solidarity groups that have brought political susten-
ance and environmental clout to the O'odham's campaign is the
Center for Biological Diversity, based in Tucson. The centre combines
philosophical understanding of the relationship and interdependency
between humankind and nature, not unlike a version of indigenous
wisdom, with keen local activism, knowledge of the terrain, both scientific and historical, and a record of robust legal action to protect it.
From the centre, the compelling figure of Laiken Jordahl has been to
the fore in seeking to protect O'odham land generally, and the Organ
Pipe site specifically, against this latest outrage.

Jordahl's story demonstrates not only that of the assault on this land
since *Amexica* was published, but that on the entire National Park
Service, one of America's great achievements since its foundation in

1916, under the Trump regime. Jordahl joined the service 'excited at the thought of working with the government to protect the borderlands'. He was already working at Organ Pipe when Trump was inaugurated, promising his wall, 'after which everything turned upside down'. As a scientist and technical writer with the park's wilderness stewardship plan, 'I realised that the single greatest threat to this land was border militarisation and the prospect of wall construction. I knew that if the wall was to be built, my days with the service were numbered.' Since construction started last summer 'it's been this all-consuming passion, to try and get people to understand what is being destroyed. It's not the job I signed up for, but as long as the bulldozers roll, I'll be there to document the damage and share this heartbreak with the world.'

Jordahl's voice quivers as he describes what's at stake at Organ Pipe. 'It's the heart of the Sonoran Desert, where many species reach their northernmost end. As the wall is built, these species will be trapped and isolated from the rest of their range, they'll have nowhere else to go.' Quitobaquito Springs, a rare desert oasis that has sustained 16,000 years of human history, he reminds, 'is a miraculous oasis in the hottest desert in America, home to two unique endangered species: the Quitobaquito pupfish and Sonoyta mud turtle. Under the Bush administration, the government carried out an environmental assessment affirming they didn't want to harm these unique species. Now, as wall construction tears through these lands and millions of gallons of groundwater are pumped to mix concrete, there has been no study of the impact on water levels, or of the permanent damage that will be done. The Trump administration knows perfectly well that their actions could destroy this place forever, but they just don't care.'

As with the land, the people. 'Organ Pipe holds immense cultural significance to the O'odham. Their ancestors are buried there. The lands are used for plant gathering, for ceremony, for ritual. To stop the migration of modern indigenous people fleeing conflicts our own government helped create, the Trump administration is erasing the history of the O'odham.'

Jordahl proceeds to his devastating conclusion: 'To Border Patrol and to the Trump administration, sacred sites and endangered species are viewed not as wonders worth protecting, but as obstructions to surveillance. I know how they see this landscape. For them, each saguaro cactus or mesquite stand is something that blocks their line of sight, a place a fleeing migrant can find shade and cover. For them, life is a "threat" to "security". It serves their interests to have a landscape bereft of history, bereft of life. It's this mentality that allows them to inflict so much damage without a thought to what they're destroying.'

Magnificent Los Tigres del Norte, the *narcocorrido* group which had played that concert up the road from Ajo in Tucson, has navigated an extraordinary trajectory. They've become the biggest band North America has never heard of. Their songs blare from every radio station and in every café across the hemisphere – still that spirited, surging and infectious two-step or waltz *norteño* and *ranchero* style with roots in oom-pah accordion music played by German brewers in Mexico during the nineteenth century. Here, there and *todos partes* – everywhere. When I was being driven for eight hours through mud and deepest jungle in Colombia by Marxist guerrillas from the FARC in 2016, the music on the sound system was Los Tigres. When billiard players start potting balls and downing beers from daybreak onwards in Villa San Salvador on the outskirts of Lima, Peru – on the jukebox: Los Tigres.

But dashing, swashbuckling Jorge Hernández, his two brothers and cousin have changed their cause and image: no longer narrators of narco frolicks, but *la voz del pueblo* – voice of the people. Troubadours for the poor and downtrodden, champions of refugees from Central America and southern or interior Mexico, the border-crossers, toilers in America's fields, cleaners of America's toilets, inmates of America's jails. In 2018, on the fiftieth anniversary of the famous Johnny Cash concert in Folsom Prison, Los Tigres did the same thing, producing an explosive album and film for Netflix. The demographics of the jail reflect the changes since Cash's concert of 1968: Los Tigres play to a largely Hispanic home crowd, which whoops and cheers to a song about a Salvadorean migrant, entitled 'Tres Veces Mojado' – the last lines of which are dedicated to those who have been just that: three times wet . . . swimming the Rio Grande.

3

Ciudad Juárez Revisited

Juárez: fulcrum of the borderland, whence the Rio Grande takes a south-easterly turn, and defines the border as far as the Gulf Coast. First stirrings precede first light, beyond the city's frayed edges at the desert rehabilitation centre or 'rescue asylum' Visión En Acción: mumbling, moaning, crashing of pans heating coffee and the odd scream. Things change, but remain the same. As the sun's fiery rays break over the scrub, residents appear from their sleeping quarters around the courtyard, as ten years ago, deranged but dutifully carrying soiled blankets out into the dirt, pungent, to be bleached in the heat.

The place has been run for twenty-four years now by Pastor José Antonio Galván, who joked a decade ago that the city out there was actually a 'human junkyard', while this was 'a haven of peace'. Which it still is, in a way: the addicts, penitent cartel sicarios and their odalisques, psychos, street dealers and those discarded by the city's assembly plant economy – are here refitted for life, like the cars in all those yonke auto-repair yards along the route. Last time I was here, I spent a few nights sharing quarters with Josué Rosales, who told me he had been 'dead when I got here'. Now, Josué has qualified as a nurse, and all that remains of him here is his degree certificate, framed on the pastor's wall.

Pastor Galván still looks like the Teddy boy he was – purple paisley jacket that seems out of place here, yet not – and greets me with poised fists of the boxer he also was. 'The Lord is on my side,' he says, punching air, 'you see the Devil coming, you gotta beat him up!' I say I feel ten years older, yet he seems younger. He laughs. 'Have passion, have faith, have life. These are my people, under my wing.

I feel more part of this desert now, like a lizard — you've got to look carefully, know what you're doing and move fast.' Threats from cartels and gangs seeking out patients to enact vengeance have eased, he reports, but 'they never go away'. More than 67,000 people have disappeared since 2006 in Mexico — one of the most outrageous aspects of this war — and some are found by Peludo, the asylum's pet dog. 'He keeps finding legs, then a head, different bodies in different places, of people who've been kidnapped and disappeared in the desert,' says Galván. 'Sometimes when it rains, bodies surface, and come floating.' There's been impressive building work since a decade ago; what were timeworn breeze blocks are now whitewashed walls; there's air conditioning, even a TV area for telenovelas and baseball. In the yard, 'his people' greet Galván, now as they did then, hugging his waist while he pats their matted hair, strokes their boils and scars. 'Crazy Baby' Becky is dead now, as is big Oscar, former *sicario* for the Barrio Azteca gang, street affiliate of the old Juárez cartel. But a man called Yogi is still here from before, shaven-headed ten years ago, now sporting a jester's hat — a long-termer with Down's syndrome and schizophrenia. He embraces me with a child's smile, but 'a few years ago, killed someone with a single punch', says the pastor.

The drugs are different now, says Galván — 'less crack, more cristal — meth — and synthetics', but their destruction is the same. It takes, explains the shelter's qualified nurse Imelda Castro, 'a balance between miracles and medication'. People who arrived here as patients staff the place and Pastor Galván wants to tell the story of his last decade here through their example; they are disarmingly open about where they've come from.

Vera is now the accountant at Visión En Acción, having arrived here 'completely wild', says Pastor Galván, four years ago. Born to a middle-class family in Guanajuato, 'I entered a life of prostitution and pole-dancing,' she says, 'pregnant at fifteen. I attracted bad people: narcos, *sicarios*, *jefes*.' Before long, she was one of them, selling and moving drugs, and courtesan to the bosses; 'I was VIP only,' she insists with pride and shame, at her availability to the leadership of the Knights Templar cartel. 'I saw everything: murders, kidnappings. So much violence, so many drugs, so much sex, you don't see it for what it is. I admired the power of these people, and the respect they commanded.' But such proximity was dangerous, as the Knights were overrun by the Jalisco Nueva Generación. 'They kill women because they have so much information; the favoured women know everything.'

Vera attempted suicide, but was rescued by her parents and placed in a psychiatric hospital. There, however, she learned that 'the Jalisco cartel wanted me, not to kill but hire me, because I knew the market in Guanajuato'. Her parents sold their house to pay for treatment at a shelter for women, and finally Vera arrived at Visión En Acción. She began, as most do, in *el ocho* – the eight – a row of cages, throwing her bucket of urine and excrement against the bars, but then began to trade kisses through those bars with Benito, who has worked nineteen years at the shelter, and who gave her chocolate '*y mucho mas!*' Two years ago, they were married – Vera on horseback, Benito in traditional dress – 'one of the great days of our lives here', says Galván. Helping in the office, 'Vera has a keen sense for things,' he continues, 'and she spotted something wrong with the cheques. She suspected a man called Beto, who was my right-hand man. She was right – Beto was stealing from us, he quit and I gave Vera the job. You see, my job is to find the treasure in people they don't even know is there themselves.'

That must have been hard in the case of Neor, who now runs the overnight operation, host for my nocturnal stay. He had a 'bad life' in Guanajuato, with his father 'taking drugs, whipping us all – no money, no food'. Neor started on *cristal*, crack and solvents at the age of twelve, then started 'robbing and killing for money', and inevitably did so for Jalisco Nueva Generación. 'I was a *sicario*,' he says. 'Once you've killed the first time, it gets easy – I was taking so much *cristal*, I could handle it.' Neor shows me a terrifying collection of pictures of himself on his phone, posing with heavy weaponry, sometimes two machine guns at a time, with a death-dealing squint so different from his pensive eyes now. It is unsettling to think this is the same person. 'I usually carried a 380 Kalashnikov. I killed snitches, people who'd been kidnapped, anybody the cartel told me to kill. Always with a gun – I never tortured anyone to death, though I saw them do it. I was paid well – the bigger your weapon, the better the job, the higher the tariff.' Time came for Neor to kill a man who had been tasked to sell 50,000 doses of meth, but kept and spent the money. 'It was a big hit – for some reason I didn't want to do it, but they said if I didn't, they'd kill me. I knocked at the door, the man pleaded, but I shot him in the back three times, to save my own life. I went back next day, and the police were around the body. Something happened in my head; I started having nightmares. I dreamed a bull was dripping blood over the dead man.' Three days later, there was a shootout from Neor's house, 'I took a bullet in the leg –' he shows the scar – 'and I just – I ran away.' Neor had heard about a former drug dealer called Hector, working at Visión En Acción, who arranged to bring him here through a network of contacts. How long ago? Neor beams. 'Four months.' It seems barely possible.

One recent morning, though, Neor found himself out on the highway, planning to return to Guanajuato. 'I started shaking,' he says, 'and a voice in me said: "Don't. Go back to work." ' I just hope Neor doesn't have another flashback during the night, as we turn in. 'There's a devil waiting to lure them back any time,' says Pastor Galván next morning, 'and I gotta beat that devil up.' 'I learned that,' he says, 'when I was living among the trash cans myself – when I was one of them.'

Ten years ago, Sandra Rodríguez Nieto was mourning the execution of Armando Rodríguez, no relation, a colleague on the crime beat of Juárez's daily newspaper, *El Diario*. Sandra took the same reckless risks to write the kind of stories for which her friend died, preoccupied with what she called 'the culture of impunity in this city, from its very design, to the way the economy works; from the street to the top'.

Sandra returned to *El Diario*, from Mexico City, twice, on both occasions just as the city's murder rate was climbing; once just before *Amexica*, and again before this revisitation. 'I just prefer it here,' she says. Sandra finished and published that book about *impunidad*, impunity, only that was not in the end its title; she chose *La Fabrica del Crimen* – Crime Factory – translated into English as *The Story of Vicente, Who Killed His Mother, His Father and His Sister*, which he did.[1] Rather than write about *capos* and *sicarios*, Rodríguez's subject is the pervasive brutalisation of Mexican society, with indemnity; it is the book Émile Zola would have written about Juárez, inasmuch as it addresses not the wider landscape of violence, but murder and horror with macabre intimacy, tightly focused into the frame of one family, and the commission of matricide, patricide and sororicide by a young man who said he did what he did '*porque puedo*', because I can. 'The story of Mexico is exactly as Vicente predicted,' she reflects. 'You can do whatever you want, with impunity. You can kill who you want, kill in broad daylight, kill a journalist, disappear forty-three students – and get away with it. Vicente has become a metaphor for the whole country.'

Sandra was news editor for a while, in 2018–19, and faced a dilemma during that time. 'We had a picture,' she says now, 'of two people walking past a corpse, and they don't even glance at it – this is Juárez after ten years. I wanted it on the front page, but we didn't have a story to go with it. Or we have a sixteen-year-old killed, without a birth certificate or school record. Again, this should be front-page news. But it's not. In Juárez, people being killed is no longer news, or the rest of Mexico – killing has become normal and crime has become a habit.' The reason, says Rodríguez: 'a breakdown of the rule of law. No prosecution, no intelligence – just a fight, between the state and whatever else. If the authorities want a crime solved, it's often done in moments; but there's no enforcement of law by which to measure what is going on, and no measurement of impunity. So much we just do not know.' *El Diario* reported one incident on the edge of Juárez in 2018: a family of four had been murdered, but neighbours were only alerted to the killing days later, by stray dogs preying on the cadavers.

Since Armando Rodríguez's death, Sandra has lost another colleague, Miroslava Breach, a reporter from her own home town of Chihuahua, murdered in 2017 when leaving home, like Armando. In 2019, Mexico overtook Syria as the most dangerous country in the world to be a journalist.[2] 'It's outrageous,' she says. 'It comes from the same disease, impunity. They kill journalists because they know they can, to try and silence the press.'

The culture of impunity has roots, says Sandra, 'in the nineties, with the killing of three hundred women in this city, when we realised nothing would happen to the killers'. The *femicidio* brought Juárez to the attention of the world. The misogynist 'style' of killing – the word 'style' used 'not lightly' by anthropologist Cecilia Ballí – seemed to take the ways of violence to another level, prescient of the wider carnage that followed. In a subsequent, seminal, thesis,

Ballí explored this 'sexual murder' in the light of a 'hypermasculin-ity in U.S.–Mexico border zones, informed by the history, style and logics of militarization and organized crime'.[3]

Among the mothers who suffered unfathomable grief at the abduction, violation and murder of a daughter was Paula Flores. In April 1998 the body of seventeen-year-old María Sagrario González was found dumped in the desert. My chapter on the *femicidio* opened with Paula imploring the image of the Virgin of Guadalupe which María Sagrario wore around her neck: 'Where were *you* when they did that to my little girl?' I've forwarded her question to priests and theologians since, and never found an answer.

Paula's face has changed remarkably little since I last saw her ten years ago, or indeed since I first interviewed her in 1999. It carries that same wounded but indomitable fortitude; she lives in the same well-kept house, attached to the family's grocery store atop the Anapra barrio, right against the border. 'Time passes slowly. It's been twenty-one years now,' she says, 'and everything is the same – nothing has happened. We are marked for life, and will remain so while there is no reckoning with what happened. There can be no recovery. And it continues: women keep disappearing, keep being murdered.' On the other hand, 'I have my store, and family. At week-ends we are all together, all from Durango, though my grandchildren were born here. Eleven of them now, some of the age María Sagrario was, and that can be traumatic.' Also: 'Claudia, my sixth daughter, teaches at a kindergarten school named after María Sagrario. People tell me she lives on, in the spirit of the school, in the children and the learning given to them.'

In 2005, a man called José Luis Hernández was jailed for the murder of María Sagrario – sentenced to twenty-eight years, 'but I fear he will be out much sooner', says Paula. And he is not the end of the story. 'He said he was paid $800 to be part of this. But by who? Who else was involved, and why? We have always said that everything rests with the authorities, that the authorities were complicit in the murder of women in Juárez.' The cover-ups and lies detailed in *Amexica* and by Cecilia Ballí have never been accounted for, although the apparently calculated ineptitude of the authorities in dealing with the evidence and bodies of the mur-dered women was unveiled in forensic anthropological work by experts from Argentina, to be discussed later. Paula's eldest daughter is here with us. Guillermina formed the group Voces Sin Eco – Voices Without Echo – to unite mothers of other murdered women against those cover-ups, and designed its now iconic symbol: a black cross on a pink background, painted throughout the city. A large wooden pink cross was erected beside the Santa Fe Bridge, covered in black nails, as was another, on the highway from Mexico City at the southern entrance to town. But 'it was stolen', says Guillermina. 'They say it was to sell the iron, but I think the authorities were involved.' She's less active now – 'I have a seven-year-old, and that's my life.' Not her mother: 'Every year, on the anniversary – 16 April – we get together and repaint the crosses,' she says. In 2012, the mayor of Juárez, Hector Murgía, announced he would ban this practice and 'apply the law' on defacement of public space. 'He threatened us, but we did the painting,' says Paula. Yet: 'this year only four of us turned up'.

The mothers of six murdered women from that time, including Paula, filed suit – Elena Rivera et al. v. Mexico – through the Inter-American Commission on Human Rights, over the authorities' abrogation of responsibility. A hearing was held in Washington DC on 29 September 2019, just before I revisited Paula González. It recalled that trip to Washington by other mothers when I was reporting their story back in 2002 – with some bitterness; the actions have got nowhere. 'Though my daughter's case is from twenty-one years ago,' Paula told the commission, 'I still feel the same pain of my daughter not being here. She deserves justice.' 'Yes,' Paula says now in her kitchen, 'with the other mothers, we're still pushing this. The president of the court offered his sympathies. But they've had this case since 2007, and it's a verdict we need, not sympathy. I don't think they have any idea of the emotional toll, the pain involved in all this.'

Paula seems rightly exhausted with trying to find words for the unspeakable. Two of her other daughters arrive, and there's a delicious lunch of spicy beans, cheese and tortillas, all the while a portrait of María Sagrario staring down from the back wall. There's discussion of music, grandchildren, climate crisis and life around the barrio. We're done for today with what Edgar Allan Poe called 'the hideousness of mysteries which will not suffer themselves to be revealed'. But there's one final question: where was the Virgin of Guadalupe when they did that? 'I've asked that every day since, and hear no answer,' Paula responds. 'I still believe. But how can it be? María Sagrario was not against God; she was a believer, she sang in church, and helped at Sunday school. It was Lent, and I prayed for the protection of my daughters. Three days later, María Sagrario disappeared. I try to ask myself not so much "Why did she die?" but "For what?" Maybe for the school. Maybe so that with the help of the other mothers, I can raise awareness about what is happening here. So the world would take notice – maybe.'

The *femicidio* never went away. But of late, there has been a terrifying qualitative twist to the *femicidio* in Juárez. It is as though a new generation of women is being differently targeted, not just for being what they are – women – but also for what they do, in defiance of misogynist, *machista* culture and violence. And differently murdered – not so much 'sexual murder' as investigated by Ballí, but assassinated, mafia-style, by outright execution.

They gather in the chill of a high desert night, around a bakery on a street corner in Juárez, to blend homage with mourning, love with sorrow. Opposite them: a mural of painted eyes, and the words: '*Te Observan*' – They're Watching You. And a self-portrait by the artist, Isabel Cabanillas de la Torre, shedding a tear. It is a prescient and poignant detail: at the foot of the painting is a floral tribute to Isabel, shot in the head on 18 January 2020 while cycling home. These are the twenty-five-year-old's friends, colleagues, activist sisters and fellow artists, gathered for a 'print-in' of artwork in Isabel's honour and memory. There had been days of rage: marches downtown, to that huge black cross on a pink background commemorating victims of the original *femicidio*, and blocking the trans-border Santa Fe bridge beyond it. A heart-wrenching public statement by Lydia Graco, one of the collective to which Isabel belonged, had said: 'Isa, we're sorry we couldn't stop your femicide. Forgive us, Isa, please. We owe you, comrade, we owe you.'

But now for music, conversation and celebration of Isabel's métier: art, for sale tonight at voluntary prices towards a fund for her now motherless four-year-old son. 'We're doing what she would have wanted us to do,' says Aarón Venegas, pushing a roller of ink across a lino-cut of a bicycle with a pot of flowers on the carrier. The image of the bicycle – in the organic way whereby political symbols evolve – now joins the black-pink crosses painted across Juárez as icon of resistance against the *femicidio*. Isabel's copper-coloured bike is hoisted atop the door of the bakery. 'It signifies life,' says Aarón, 'while the cross symbolises sacrifice and death.' The event is convened by the street-art group with which Cabanillas worked, 'Pure Borde' – Pure Border. 'In a city hollowed out by narco war,' says Aarón, the group's founder, 'we try to take back the streets with art, colours and visual ideas.' The event was 'already scheduled before Isabel was killed', he adds. 'It's unbearably tragic she's not here.'

Cabanillas was 'widely known' and 'much-loved' across the city, as every burrito vendor and tender of the artier bars in central Juárez will affirm. Much of her artwork decorates the concrete banks of the river border which divides Juárez from El Paso, Texas, the ever-harsher frontier against which these people and their murdered friend protest. 'She was often with us down on the border, painting images of protest,' says Aarón. Hers was a softer statement than some: visible from the bridge, beside a striking image of a soldier is another of a little boy and girl playing – the latter is by Isabel Cabanillas de la Torre. Alfredo Carrillo, at the 'print-in', had begun making a film about Pure Borde and its artists, 'not a group of people with sprays', he says, 'more a movement'. Among the interviewees recorded was Isabel, 'so I have a personal connection here, and the privilege of working with one of our most precious soldiers. It'll be so hard to edit this; I was with her a few weeks ago, crossing the same road in which she was murdered.'

The last thing Isabel Cabanillas did was enjoy a drink with friends at Eugenio's bar in central Juárez – a genial, mostly young bohemian joint. A week after the murder, it is full as usual, with chatter and banter – *charladuría* – about Isabel and not. Behind the bar, a poster shows her face, and the slogan: '*Ni como vestía*' – Nor how I was dressed – from an anti-rape chant originating in Chile. 'We can't quite believe it,' says the barman, 'that she'll never return.' 'I remember her well,' says an elderly regular, Carlos, sipping a Dos Equis. 'Charming girl, usually with her group, but sometimes chatting with we older folks. Always "*hola!*" and a smile. If the Devil had told me someone would pull a trigger against her, I'd have called him a liar.'

Isabel bade her friends goodnight and mounted her bicycle, riding two blocks northwards along Calle Ramon Corona, and turning right into Calle Ochoa, beside the office of a pensioners' association and along the — ironically — pink walls of its courtyard. Either she was followed, or someone had been positioned to ambush her; two shots from a high-calibre revolver were fired into her chest and head — a cold-blooded, targeted execution. Video cameras appear to give a view of the street, but police have not confirmed the existence of footage, or a motive for the slaying. Now, in the parched light of afternoon, a pink bicycle is attached to a lamp post on that spot in Calle Ochoa, with daffodils in its basket, for the springtime of Isabel's life, cut down. The painted slogans speak for themselves: *'Isabel vive'* — Isabel lives. *'Ni una más'* — Not one more. *'Justicia'* — Justice — but there lies faint hope. When Isabel's' friends are asked whether they expect any serious attempt at apprehension and trial of the real murderer, all reply: 'not a chance', 'unthinkable, in this city'. 'In all the decades of *femicidio*, impunity has been the rule,' says one, Arena, a school-teacher, echoing Paula Flores and Sandra Rodríguez.

Throughout the days following the 'print-in', these friends and members of the feminist collective to which Isabel belonged gather to talk by the bakery. The place itself, Rezizte, is an institution, run by Jorge and Paty — who remembers 'Isabel always here, for coffee or a pastry, and conversation. We opened four months ago and she was one of our first and favourite friends.' The feminist collective is called Hijas de su Maquila Madre — roughly: Daughters of the Factory Mothers — significant in itself, since many of the victims of the original *femicidio* in Juárez were girls working in the *maquiladoras*. While the protests and campaigns for justice then were led mainly by mothers of the victims, most members of the Hijas collective are daughters of those workers. All their mothers came to Juárez to work, and many of them in the *maquilas*. 'We are the first generation born in Juárez,' says Marte, a poet. 'Isabel too. And many of us are the first generation in our families to go to university.'

'We are the daughters of *femicidio* in the nineties and 2000s,' says Sirena, a sociologist. 'We were little then, and the young women murdered in those days would now be the age of our mothers.' 'We are the children of that generation,' says Arena, 'and with Isabel's death, it comes closer to our circles.' 'There is a difference,' observes

'Procupia' (his nom de mural), a male colleague and fellow street artist. 'This new generation is a new kind of target. Unlike the former victims, these women are organised, hold meetings, targeted not just because they are women, but for their activism.'

For all their impressive individuality, as a group these women combine deep strength with vulnerability; cautious fear fortified by life force and humbling courage. Most live together in an *ocupa* – a squat – 'working out whether our security is best served by being open, rather than hiding', says one. 'We are so precarious,' says Arena, 'we have nothing but our art and our selves.' 'Isabel came to us,' she continues; 'she felt a reason to fight in the way we do.' 'Our work with Isabel was about expressing what is happening, and why,' says Areka, describing herself simply as 'a worker'. 'So that we have a say in our story as women in this city,' adds Marte. In a video, Cabanillas herself explained further: 'One of the reasons why I paint – apart from the fact that it has helped me overcome a lot of hard times – is that one night, I woke up, and I started thinking that I needed to do something for myself and for my child. In fact, this is for him.' 'She was funny,' says Marte. 'She had what I'd call a white humour, rather than black. A pure humour, simple and sensitive. She laughed, and made other people laugh.'

'We want it understood that what Isabel was doing was *rebeldía* – rebellion – in Juárez,' emphasises Arena. 'In a *machista* city, she was occupying the streets with art, she was riding her bicycle home alone at night, she was subversive of patriarchal culture. She trespassed across the borders imposed on women in the city of *femicidio*, and challenged the reasons for the *femicidio*. She joined us to fight patriarchal violence, in her own way.' Cabanillas was active over the borderland crises around her, markedly that of migration. 'Isabel worried so much about the migrants,' says Marte. 'She had her own initiatives, collecting and delivering blankets, food and clothes to the shelters – we all supported them, but the collections were her idea.' She was also 'busy against the extraction industries in Chihuahua', says Sirena. 'When she was killed, she was preparing protest art at Salamayuca, south of here, against a Canadian company opening a copper mine.' Cabanillas designed clothes, and worked with random text on fabrics during her last weeks. Areka recounts: 'She gave me a T-shirt with three words on it – I told her then I'd never wash it, and I certainly won't now.' Areka shows a picture of Isabel model-ling a marvellous jacket she made, emblazoned with criss-crossing words in varied typefaces.

Eyes are the constant theme and trope in Cabanillas's art. 'She said eyes are two-way: our own eyes with which we observe, and the eyes that survey us,' says Areka. 'It's like: we are watching you watch-ing us.' We talk about the eyes on the mural opposite, and the self-portrait – with its prophetic tear. 'She told us she had a feeling that she herself was being watched, specifically, not long before she was killed,' says Procupia. 'But last time I saw her, Isa was full of ideas. She wanted to find new spaces for her work, and to make new connections. She had plans to go to Mexico City, and visit Berlin in April, to see the street-art scene there . . .' 'All we can do is carry on what she did,' says Sirena. 'That is what she would have wanted, and that's what her mother wants. She has the little boy now, she joined our protests, and we are in touch with her. She agrees with what we are doing: asking who killed Isabel, and why?'

'Of course, it's not just Isabel,' says Arena. 'There are so many invisible, unreported murders of women in this city. Very many women are abducted, disappear and are never seen again – often due to trafficking. The *femicidio* in Juárez never stopped. There's been a war against women on the streets of this city since the 1990s.' Sirena adds: 'This is not the same as the original *femicidio*, but I'd say the danger was now exponentially even greater.'

Weeks after I met these brave people at Rezizte, there was yet another, similar, execution in Juárez: Teresa Arcely Alcocer, thirty-seven, a well-known local radio broadcaster, was ambushed and shot dead by a group of gunmen waiting outside her house on 15 February 2020. She was known on her programme *La Poderosa* – The Powerful One – as Bárbara Greco, a card and palm reader, but often focused on violence against women generally, denounced the execution of Caba-nillas, and, just before her own murder, the atrocious abduction and murder of seven-year-old Fátima Aldrighett in Mexico City. Not long before, also in Mexico City, 25-year-old Ingrid Escamilla was stabbed, flayed and disembowelled. President López Obrador drew the ire of the women's and feminist movements with his belittling of – and manifest inability to grasp – the significance of the murders, saying: 'I don't want the topic to be only femicide, this issue has been manipulated a lot in the media.'[4] On the same day as Teresa Arcely's execution, another woman was killed in Juárez by two shots to the head, in front of her father.

The 'style' of killing in the original *femicidio* was unspeakable violation, torture, bodies dumped in the desert. But though that 'style' has expanded to include outright execution, now, as before, the question screams for an answer: who does this, and why? 'We are in no doubt that Isabel's death was a political, misogynist execution,' says Sirena. 'But the *sicarios* do not act alone, the mafia does not kill in a vacuum. They get their orders. Even if the authorities catch the killer, they will not catch the intellectual author of the crime. Who is that? There have been so many murders downtown, men and women. Who is ordering them?'

No one knows, and the authorities hardly ever arrest, let alone convict; people can only surmise. A professor, T.M., at the Autonomous University of Ciudad Juárez, notes the existence in the city of an overtly misogynist organisation called 'Imperio Alpha' – Alpha Empire – which disseminates pornography and insults women on the Internet. 'Their leader, Jesús Manuel Z.N., is in jail here awaiting trial for extortion, and there was an article in the paper about him, a video he made, the day before Isabel's murder – who knows?' The video is menacing and revolting, and begs the question: how was it dispatched from custody? 'All we know,' says Arena, 'is that Imperio Alpha is extensive in Juárez, misogynist and aggressive.'

Back at the 'print-in', delicious pastries are served, and coffee brewed against the chill of night. An emcee takes to his deck and spins a few records, to ease the solemnity, lighten the leaden reason for the gathering, bring back some of Isabel's smile. A few dance tracks, ripples of laughter and tapping feet among those assembled, then 'Paloma Negra' – Black Dove – a Tomás Méndez song famously covered by Lila Downs. 'Ah!' I exclaim. 'I love this song, but . . . ?' 'It's not Lila Downs,' says one of the young women, 'it's Isabel, recorded doing karaoke.' There's a shiver on the wind, but not from cold. 'She was just, well – lovely,' says Arena. 'That's it, really. Lovely. She should be here with us, and we just cannot understand why she had to die like that.'

The theme of migration which came to dominate the narrative of Tijuana does so in Juárez too. Tens of thousands of people from all over the world converge on the city, hoping to make a crossing into the USA that hardly any succeed in doing. The chapel at the Methodist Buen Pastor – Good Shepherd – migrant shelter has become a dormitory for women – mostly young mothers with children – among them Marisela del Carmen Espinosa, who lays her seven-year-old son Diego on a blanket; the child is visibly sick, running a fever. Marisela fled her native El Salvador when the MS-13 gang demanded she join them, the problem being that Diego's father was among those doing so.

Marisela is careful to brush her hair and apply make-up before being interviewed; she has the flare of a survivor in her eyes. 'They came to my house, armed, saying they needed me to do "tasks" for them, and if I didn't they'd kill me and take the boy,' she says. Marisela left, and has spent the past year on 'trucks and railway cars, crossing Mexico', paying $8,000 to coyotes and smugglers. To her horror, Diego's father has traced her to Juárez, 'and I am scared when I go out for food, because he said his contacts here would take our son and kill me'.

The shelter is run by Reverend Juan Fiero García. 'More people than ever are on the move from generalised violence,' he says, 'from all over the world, seeking safe places for themselves and their children. And if anyone thinks this is going to stop, think again – this is just the beginning.'

In the men's dorm, a converted storeroom, Evian Mvouba from the Democratic Republic of Congo prepares to cross and make his asylum claim. Mvouba stands a chance of speedier processing than his Central American companions at the shelter because MPP does not apply to Africans. But he does fall under the parallel US system of so-called 'metering', which limits the number of people per day who can cross to apply for asylum. It is a system which generates a waiting list of some kind at every border-crossing town; that in Juárez counted 5,500 in December 2019, and there were more than two thousand people ahead of Mvouba. He was a schoolteacher back home, until his village was attacked by government forces in summer 2018, since which he has journeyed through Angola, Brazil, Colombia and Central America – with no word of much of his family as it scattered. 'It is limbo,' he says, 'not knowing where I live, and whether they are alive.' Mvouba says that every morning, just before he wakes, 'I think for a moment that I am still there, and must get ready for work, and the children.'

A 'Little Havana' has emerged in Juárez, of those either waiting to cross, or refused asylum and returned to live. Ariel Busquet, from the eastern outskirts of Havana, kneads burritos in the Llenadora café. He was number 3,527 on the 'metered' waiting list, and on hearing from a friend who returned after three months' incarceration on the other side, elected to remain in Juárez, in a house he shares with five other Cubans. 'We Cubans left our country to work for a wage – something we cannot do there,' he says, 'but that's what I'm doing here in Juárez!' Not everyone has given up, though, nor is everyone prepared to wait.

At the age of fourteen, Jonathan Levit was given an order by the infamously brutal MS-13 gang in his native Tegucigalpa, capital of Honduras: to kill a friend he had known throughout childhood, 'like a brother, all my life'. Jonathan had, like almost every child in the city's Tela Atlantida barrio of Colonia 15, grown up in the gang's shadow; there was no avoiding it, especially if you were partial to a smoke, as he was. And now the time had come for him to execute 'a mission' for the MS-13 gang which, Jonathan says, 'doesn't just run Colonia 15, they almost run Honduras'. But, he continues, 'I'd rather have a friend than a peso in my pocket, and I refused. Whatever the price, that's something I wouldn't do.' The MS-13 death sentence was accordingly switched: Jonathan would die instead. But he lived to tell his story in the courtyard of the Casa del Migrante, operated by the Catholic diocese, having fled Honduras, determined to escape to the United States.

Jonathan wears an orange jacket and has a shock of black hair; his eyes are quick with mischief and wit. He remembers his life back home without sentiment – 'I started smoking marijuana when I was eight – I can't tell you I'm proud of my life, or that it was a good place to be, even before the death sentence. But even if I wanted to go back, I can't – ever – they'd kill me in a heartbeat.' Asked how many young people are in similarly fearful situations, Jonathan throws back his head with a hollow laugh. 'Almost everyone.' With us round a concrete table are two lads from Guatemala City with whom Jonathan has teamed up, Osman and Rodrigo, themselves in flight from 'poverty and violence' back home. By contrast, this place, though sad, is clean and organised; mothers and children sit beside a statue of the Virgin of Guadalupe; boys play football – but it's no more than a way station. All three at our table want to work in construction in the US, but while the Guatemalans left home recently, Jonathan is now nineteen, he's become an artful dodger and survivor of the road, trying to cross *la frontera* into America. 'I've been in Mexico five years now, working, saving, hiding – planning the moment. The Mexicans ordered me deported twice, but I slipped the net. The trains through this country' – he calls them, collectively, *'la bestia'*, the beast – 'have been my home. They're more dangerous for women than me; getting raped, kidnapped and killed. But now my time has come to cross.'

Jonathan has not applied for asylum or joined the 'metering' line. 'They've made it too difficult,' he says, 'and it takes too long. I'll go alone, my own way.' Osman and Rodrigo are going illegally too. 'Trump has made asylum impossible,' says Osman, in English. 'I miss it back there; my mother calls me every fucking day – it's torture – but too dangerous to stay and there's no future in Guatemala – I have to risk it.' Rodrigo, quieter, is more nervous. 'I've a wife and son back home, that's who I'm doing this for – but what if I get caught?'

Police patrol the fence around the compound, ostensibly to protect the migrants from the prying traffickers who gather there. But there's a twist: 'The police are part of the system. We all know that,' says Jonathan. He laughs and makes to slice his index finger in half. 'Fifty-fifty, that's how it works. We watch the *polleros* watching us, and the police allow the *polleros* to work on their *plaza* – turf – for a fifty-fifty cut on the money paid. If you don't believe that, you're an idiot. That's why I stay away from the smugglers and police – to be apart from that shit.'

More people arrive at the heavy gates of Casa del Migrante: families from Guatemala, including Eder Ramírez and his daughter, Leti, aged eight; and two women travelling from Panajachel, with two children each, 'running from the gangs'. Had they heard about two other children from their own country who died in US custody just across the river, over Christmas? No. A guard explains the rules: 'You must surrender your phone at reception and collect it when you leave. No weapons or drugs; no Viagra, only one smoking area.' Then they register, grateful for the wide smile on the face of a volunteer.

Leti wants a soda from the vending machine, but there's no cash; they look in a store cupboard for donated used clothes – *'ropa usada'* – that might fit. Leti chooses a pink Looney Tunes hoodie.

I say I hope Jonathan Levit's childhood friend is grateful for what he did – or didn't do. 'He is,' replies Jonathan. 'He vanished from the Mara's sight, and is still alive.' How long can you stay here at Casa del Migrante? 'Three days.' How long have you been here? 'Three days. I cross tomorrow night.'

Across that border is where these people want to be, through El Paso, Juárez's twin lung. In August 2019, President Trump's forebodings of how El Paso, one of the safest of cities its size in America, was menaced by migrants from across the border were rendered ironically outrageous, by the arrival of a white supremacist from Dallas who killed twenty-two Hispanics at a Walmart store. Weeks later, the scene of the crime is heart-stopping: flowers laid, tributes written, offerings made, of teddy bears, pens, key rings. *'El Paso Fuerte'* – El Paso Strong – read the signs, and it is.

Here in El Paso, Ruben García has seen each wave of migration arrive and try to move on since, in 1978, he first opened the doors of what is now a network of shelters for migrants, Annunciation House, across El Paso. In the current calamity, it has been further to the forefront than any other institution of its kind along the border in seeking to abate the suffering.

Without radical Catholicism, the 'liberation theology' that inspires García, far less would happen on the migrants' behalf. *Amexica* discussed the idea that a 'post-political, materialist war meets resistance from the pre-political clergy and church groups more than any other constituency of society'; Pastor Galván here in Juárez, Father Murrieta in Sonora and Father Ramos in Riberas del Bravo were central to the narrative. Yet our secular media are squeamish about religion; rather like the Victorians and sex, they pretend it isn't there, that these people are political activists. Ruben García's reflections defy that discomfort. 'Forty years ago, a group of us started this work,' he says, 'thinking to ourselves: "We are not the people with whom the God of Scripture identifies; with whom would He identify in El Paso in the 1970s? It would be the least among us, the unwanted, wanderer and outcast." And we talked to people who had crossed, but been refused by migrant shelters – "because we don't have papers".

So there was our work. We made a decision to offer hospitality to undocumented migrants.

'And forty years later, we have Mr Trump as president and below him very capable officials whose sole task is to make life unbearable for refugees. There've been days when we've received hundreds of people – that keeps me pretty full, and it makes me think of Lazarus, restored to life by Jesus, who turned to the community and said: "Unbind him." In this situation, it is the refugees who unbind us, sharing their stories, their struggles. On one day, immigration released eight hundred to a thousand people and we had to find the volunteers, the wherewithal to shelter them; we get in touch with every parish, and say: "Work for the refugees, receive them – it will help them, and in this dark time, they will unbind you." ' On a night in 2018 when those eight hundred migrants were released onto the streets around El Paso bus station, TV coverage showed García, arms wide, saying to a group: *'Bienvenidos!'* – and this welcome seemed the first kind gesture they had encountered in months. A tough-looking youth was filmed on the phone to his mother, in tears of relief.

García exudes both inner calm and burning passion, having seen generations of migrants 'flee death squads in Central America during the 1980s, when war was war and you knew who the sides were, to this new kind of undeclared war, where no one knows the rules, and you live in a state of permanent insecurity. Plus drought, and crop failure – further causes for people to flee where they live. It's hard for us to understand that one word: *"basta"* – I can't take this any more, I'm leaving. You either give up your children to those realities back there, or you pay the coyote, subjecting yourself to debt bondage and whatever risk, and leave.' So the causes of flight change, and faces with them. 'But in one sense, nothing changes,' says García, 'a person in flight is a person in flight.'

For all the arrival of the Central Americans, about half those awaiting along the border for asylum hearings in the USA are still Mexicans, not theoretically covered by MPP. Having accounted for most migrants ten years ago, the proportion of Mexicans dropped as arrivals converged from all over the world, but rose again towards the end of 2019 as narco-related, political and other violence spread across the centre and south of the country. And many of those – in three waves from Guerrero, Zacatecas and Michoacán – came to Ciudad Juárez.

Throughout the summer and autumn of 2019, a sizeable tent city of some hundred people sprang up right by the Santa Fe downtown bridge between Juárez and El Paso, entirely comprised of Mexicans. Sitting with her two children on their sleeping bag, pitched on a kerb by the bridge, Juanita C. from Michoacán waits, watching her co-citizens with US citizenship or 'Sentri' pass on their way to shop, visit relatives or study on the other side, and return that evening. Juanita decided to leave their small town (she preferred not to say which) when enforcers from Cartel Jalisco Nueva Generación left a series of severed heads in plastic bags on the streets, to warn the local gang, La Maña, of its intention to secure a trafficking route through the area. One was placed close to Juanita's home, and she feared this might signify targeting by the incomers, for whatever reason, if only that her uncle had recently 'been forced to pay a *cuota*' on his business. Reluctantly, the family bade goodbye to the small auto-repair shop, and headed for Juárez. When they crossed to claim asylum, however, they were turned back by US authorities, along with those from Central and South America, in spite of being exempt from MPP. Accordingly, there being no official waiting list as there is for applicants under MPP, Mexican migrants by the bridge began their own handwritten 'metering' list, attached to a clipboard with a red heart drawn on it.

A routine established itself by the bridge: local boarding houses allowed mothers to wash their children; roughly half the men found jobs, while other men tried to ensure a supply of food, though local women's and church groups provided hearty burritos, gratis. 'This is a community,' said one of the ad hoc leadership of the camp, a joiner and carpenter from Guerrero who had fled after gun battles raged around his barrio in the town of Tepochica during October 2019. 'Like any community, it needs organisation.'

Morale was strangely high while warmer weather lasted, but with autumn it began to be tested. From mid-December, US officials on the bridge blocked all campers from applying for asylum, and by the first week in January, some who remained had taken up a government offer to join the MPP 'Remain in Mexico' waiting list, even though they were exempt from its provision. Then, on 7

January, what felt like a squadron of officials flanked by armed soldiers, local authority vehicles, decommissioned school buses and garbage disposal trucks burst into the morning routine. The migrants were given two hours to leave, and their camp was swept away and vanished into a system of shelters. The clear-out occurred just before the arrival in town of left-wing president Andres Manuel López Obrador – to protect children against the cold of winter they said, an outburst of compassion as timely as it was unconvincing.

It was more than just the tent community that was scattered – also its school, and one of its most beloved figures, the Reverend Cristina Rathbone. A half-English half-Cuban Episcopalian priest from Boston, Reverend Rathbone, arrived in August 2019 and operated – in the broadest sense – a chaplaincy to the camp, which, organically, led to her arranging to school its children. She had for ten years operated a 'street church' for homeless people in Boston, and 'felt that I needed to be on the migrant trail in Mexico. I did not expect to be on the border.' She paid a visit to two remarkable people (whom I've had the pleasure to know), Father Peter in his nineties and Sister Betty in her eighties, who had worked in El Salvador during the civil war and known Archbishop Oscar Romero, assassinated at the altar rail in 1980 and beatified in 2018, before moving to Juárez, where Father Peter celebrated binational Mass to a congregation astride the fence. Living proof of the dictum about drinking the water of Juárez, Reverend Rathbone says: 'There was clearly just so much to do here. I had not intended to be here, but I stayed. Two weeks later the Mexicans arrived, and established their camp at the bridge.'

What, then, is 'ministry' in such a place, in need of lawyers, doctors and practical provision? 'One person's need may be to get medicine for a sick child, so you get the medicine. But another person's need may be something else, and among the most important needs for someone who has lost everything, including their home and identity, is the need to be treated as a human being. I worked with wonderful people who were doing the material things, and I did a bit of all of them, but as a priest. If you have time, the depth of those relationships evolves, and something happens. With many of the men working, my days were spent mostly with the mothers and

children, and the need for the children to do something, and for a
school, became clear.'

In the first instance, what 'happened' was Reverend Rathbone
leading 'a platoon of kids with rubber gloves and brushes cleaning
the streets around the camp, a troupe of street cleaners. They loved
it, and so did I – "When are we going to clean the streets?" they'd ask
every morning.' Then: 'I realised I had to start classes. I'm not a
teacher, but I found someone who was, a retired elementary school
teacher who was wonderful. And so it started: every afternoon for an
hour, from two to three, for four months. We began outside, then
went into a building when the weather got cold. It was known as the
"*clase de inglés*" – English class – because that is something I know.
We did "Simon Says" and "Heads and Shoulders, Knees and Toes".
But it became much more. I'm not an orderly person, but the class
became a place of order in the uncertainty, of desks, of relative nor-
malcy. A place without photographs being taken, which was a bane
of life on the street. Children felt able to talk about their emotions:
why I'm happy, why I'm sad, or happy and sad at the same time.
Then it would be time for drawing. And they all drew houses – the
houses they'd left – and next to the house would be a person, the
cousin they'd left. At the end, we'd have what was for me the high
point of the class: I'd go round and just tell them how beautiful their
drawings were, make them feel admired and proud, and I'd see their
faces, pleased with what they had done – in fact it was the high point
of the whole day.'

Unlike a journalist, says Reverend Rathbone, 'I didn't have an
ulterior motive, though I was a journalist – I do have this need to tell
their stories.' I posit that a priest does actually have an ulterior
motive, that of faith. Reverend Rathbone cuts to the quick: 'The bottom line is that the word became flesh. To a priest, each person is
potentially an expression and container of actual God. And *in extremis*, people are able to demonstrate, share and make manifest that
truth far more than when they are just trundling along.'

She cites an example. 'There was a woman who had fled her husband, a policeman and very violent. He'd tracked her down, and she
was terrified. She was far down the list, number 47, with only one
family every ten days going across. The organisers of the camp
called a meeting, for her to plead her case. And the people voted

unanimously to put her top of the list, next to cross. I asked a woman who had waited and waited her own turn for three months: Why? "Because we have to maintain our humanity," she replied.' These are the people President Trump calls 'rapists and criminals'. 'You can call them what you like,' says Reverend Rathbone, 'there's enough God in that single action to last me a year and a half.'

4

La Plaza Revisited

What a moment: after decades of building the world's largest and most powerful narco-trafficking corporation, of arrest, escape, arrest again and escape again, and the biggest manhunt in recent history, there he was. In a courtroom on the eighth floor of the East New York District Federal Court at Cadman Plaza, Brooklyn, on Tuesday 13 November 2018: Joaquín 'El Chapo' Guzmán. Looking rather dapper, it must be said, in a dark blue suit and tie, more puckish than he had been during pre-trial hearings. He tried to approach his wife, Emma Coronel, but was dissuaded by court marshals. Outside, the rain fell, and people lined the entire block from long before the grey November dawn in hope of a glimpse.

This is not the place to recount the trial of El Chapo Guzmán, about which millions of words have been written, and interesting books will yet appear. The trial was a necessary spectacle, and no wonder Eric Newman, showrunner for Netflix's *Narcos Mexico* series, was in court on occasions; how he must have wished he'd known some of this before. Such as Guzmán spying on his girlfriends with the latest encrypted tracking equipment, and leaping naked from bed, mistress in tow, down a tunnel beneath his bathtub as marines and agents from the DEA battered the door down.

The proceedings told us everything, yet nothing. For those covering the trial without much experience of the Sinaloa cartel, the revelations were of its sway over the commanding heights of power in Mexico, bribing even presidents (though Enrique Peño Nieto, named by witness and former Colombian narco Alex Cifuentes Villa, denied the testimony). When the 'drug czar' atop Mexico's anti-cartel offensive, General Genaro García Luna, was himself named by witness Jesús Zambada García as being Guzmán's closest ally in government, reporters, aghast, checked the spelling and dashed to file. We old-timers, however, mouthed to one another the word 'An-a-bel' – referring to a book Mexican journalist and author Anabel Hernández had written back in 2010, naming García Luna. While North American newspapers trumpeted the news, veteran David Books led off his report in Mexico City's *La Jornada* next morning, by saying: '*no dije nada de nuevo*' – he didn't say anything new.

Jesús Zambada was the witness that long-in-the-tooth narco watchers appreciated most. He had been the Sinaloa cartel's most senior accountant for more than fifteen years – brother of its co-founder Ismael Zambada García, aka El Mayo – and had been arrested in 2008 on drug-trafficking charges, extradited and pleaded guilty. Appositely, he testified with the cool aplomb of an astute businessman, because that's what he is, on the particulars of his delivery overheads and profit margin targets.

Zambada ran the cartel's 'Plaza' in Mexico City, with responsibility for three warehouses, including one at the airport, close to the president's hangar. He described details of how cartel leaders would combine their separate fortunes to invest in shipments of cocaine to the USA, typically of 15,000 and 30,000 kilos each. Zambada explained to the court that five cartel leaders and sub-leaders, including his brother and Guzmán, would each invest in order 'to strengthen the cartel' with a bigger shipment, but also because if the load failed to reach its destination, 'they lost some capital, but not very much'.

Different destinations in the USA demanded the calculation of varying overheads and yielded incremental levels of profit – all in cash. A shipment to Los Angeles, for instance, would sell at a street value of $20,000 per kilo, with costs of $7,000 per kilo, so that a single load of 15,000 kilos would reap a profit of $13,000 per kilo – a total of $195m to the cartel, or $39m to each of its investors. For Chicago, the overheads per kilo rose to $9,000, but the street price was higher – $25,000 – so that profits from that same 15,000 kilo shipment would be $16,000 per kilo – a net profit of $48m for each of the five investors. New York was the prize market, with costs still at $9,000 per kilo but a street price of $35,000. 'That would produce a profit of $26,000 per kilo,' explained Zambada punctiliously, 'which would produce, for 15,000 kilos, a profit per investor of $78m each' – ergo, $390m to the cartel in net profit, from a single shipment. Asked how many shipments of this kind he would arrange in a year, Zambada replied: 'Hundreds.' And the value of shipments he oversaw during an average year? Even Zambada's astute mental ledger seemed to fail him. 'Billions,' he said.

As Zambada continued, ice-cool, Guzmán fidgeted, but at one point burst out laughing. As he left court for an afternoon break, Zambada walked right past Guzmán, giving him a nod. El Chapo raised his eyebrows, and rolled his eyes towards the courtroom ceiling.

One of the stranger moments came when El Mayo Zambada's son, Vicente Zambada Niebla – 'El Vicentillo' – took the stand. Guzmán had nurtured the boy like one of his own, and here he was, turncoat state's witness, greeting the defendant with a courteous half-smile. El Vicentillo oversaw importations of cocaine, he said, from Colombia into Mexico and onward to Los Angeles and Chicago, which he made centre of operations. But Zambada Jr. was a controversial witness, to a degree that defence lawyers, oddly, failed to seize upon. His story tells us much not just about how the cartel cohabited with government, but how US law enforcement cohabits with the cartels. El Vicentillo was arrested in Mexico City in March 2009. The court did not hear that according to a US indictment unsealed in 2013, he had moved more than $1 billion's worth of drugs into the United States and operated a vast distribution and money-laundering network centred on the Sinaloa's fortress city of Chicago. Prosecutors in north Illinois say Vicentillo 'inundated Chicago with heroin and cocaine'. In April 2014, the DEA unsealed Vicentillo's guilty plea, adding that Zambada Niebla was now 'cooperating with the United States'. During the first week of the Guzmán trial, Vicentillo entered a further guilty plea for related offences, and another agreement to cooperate 'on any matter'.

Omitted from El Vicentillo's testimony was that when he was arrested, he claimed he was given immunity to provide the DEA with information about narco traffic – ergo, that he was on the America's books long before his arrest, able to continue his murderous operations with full knowledge of US authorities. A year-long investigation by *El Universal* of Mexico City traced the details of Vicentillo's dealings with the DEA, providing information in exchange for a free hand to operate. The DEA has admitted contact with Vicentillo but denies a deal allowing him to continue trafficking.[1] A book by the Mexican journalist José Reveles quotes Guzmán's then lawyer, Humberto Loya Castro, 'ventilating the fact that Vicentillo had been arrested a few hours after one of the meetings he held with DEA agents at the Sheraton Hotel in Mexico City on 18 March 2009'.[2] Reporter J. Jésus Esquivel, covering the trial for *Proceso* magazine, had quoted a US source in an issue of 27 February 2014, before any deal was announced, saying: 'Vicentillo will not be condemned.'[3] As if there had been any doubt, Anabel Hernández published a book in 2019, *El Traidor, The Traitor,* based in part on El Vicentillo's diaries, to which she had gained access, detailing in his own words a revealing – and shocking – level of collaboration with US authorities, and leniency on their part to allow their 'asset' to continue killing and drug dealing, so long as he was theirs.[4] The paradigm could mean that, once Zambada Jr. was arrested and extradited, his dealings with the DEA and pleas of cooperation were – and now are – all part of El Mayo's taking Guzmán down, and securing reduced sentences for his son and brother. Ergo: a deeper and total betrayal of Guzmán, with US cooperation, by his own people.

Behind the oft-repeated adventure of Guzmán's rise, recounted at his trial, is the less well-known story of his demise since 2010 – the how, why and wherefore of his taking. It is a tale of betrayal and treason within the cartel and the shifting demands of power on high, north and south of the border. As Javier Valdez wrote: *'La mafia no perdona'* – the mafia does not forgive. Guzmán never forgave his enemies, but nor did they forgive him. There were so many people who, even if they were not traitors to Guzmán in the first instance, proved willing to become so, trading plea bargains and sentence reductions in return for testimony to the US authorities – spine of the prosecution case in New York. It is said that upon inheriting Felix Gallardo's Guadalajara cartel during the 1990s, Guzmán's first action was to exterminate Gallardo's legal team and close entourage, a manoeuvre worthy of Greek drama that anticipated his own demise – live by intrigue, die by intrigue.

As he built the Sinaloa cartel into an organisation which controlled just not most of the US frontier but trafficking networks worldwide, Guzmán's corporate strategy faced a dilemma: his cartel needed pyramidal control, but also to operate as a federation to achieve its reach. The structure and story of the Sinaloa cartel since 2010 has been one whereby strengths became weaknesses, in a federation wide enough to become the behemoth it was, but wherein no one really knew whom they could trust.

Guzmán relied more and more on lieutenants, who in turn became crucial to his downfall. It must wound Mexican pride that so many narcos turn against their erstwhile comrades and bosses when, by contrast, in Sicily, Judges Giovanni Falcone and Paolo Borsellino inflicted serious damage to the Mafia having only managed to secure the cooperation of one major '*pentito*', Tommaso Buscetta, for which both judges were murdered. In New York, then District Attorney Rudy Giuliani did the same to Cosa Nostra's American arm on the basis of a single snitch, Sammy 'The Bull' Gravano, to bring down the organisation of its boss, John Gotti. For his trial, Guzmán hired the lawyer who at one point secured a partial acquittal of Gotti, Jeffrey Lichtman, hoping to repeat the achievement. But so many lined up from inside the Sinaloa cartel to squeal against El Chapo, in return for commuted sentences and favourable treatment, this was never going to happen. Lichtman assailed the prosecution's 'snitch' witnesses: they 'lie, steal, cheat, deal drugs, and kill people', he said. Prosecutor Amanda Liskamm said in rebuttal that 'the defence is pointing fingers everywhere', she said, 'except where the evidence points'. But these apparently contesting accounts can *both* be true. Justice may be drama, but that doesn't work in reverse; Guzmán was convicted on the facts, and those facts were overwhelmingly based not on intelligence, but on the word of what the Mafia calls 'rats'. He was convicted by several years of painstaking work behind the scenes, by Justice Department prosecutors cutting deals and exchanging information for liberty in the form of commuted sentences with some of the nastiest people in the business. Snitches are recyclable: Guzmán's lead prosecutor Andrea Goldbarg had put Colombian Jorge Cifuentes Villa behind bars, but now resurrected him as a witness – he can be used again, as can they all, even Guzmán too, in time, against whoever comes next.

Along with Guzmán, another figure towers over all this: the man who, after fifty years at the apex of the cartel, has never spent a single hour in jail, Ismael Zambada García – El Mayo – the man many believe delivered Guzmán, or at least betrayed him into a corner. El Mayo, also a protégé of Gallardo, served from the early eighties in all the offshoots of the old Guadalajara syndicate in Juárez and Tijuana. He was considered by Javier Valdez to be the cartel's business strategist, more cautious than El Chapo.

Two differences estranged Zambada from the nominal chief. First, while El Mayo remained in the shadows (apart from one interview with the publisher of *Proceso* magazine), Guzmán criss-crossed Mexico making daring appearances that became folklore. Then, famously, El Chapo went a step too far: actress Kate del Castillo caught Guzmán's eye, reciprocated in her way and became involved in discussions about a biopic that led to a meeting between El Chapo and the actor Sean Penn, and an article in *Rolling Stone.* These occurrences infuriated El Mayo. For Zambada, narco traffic was business, not show business. Second, El Mayo is said to have urged Guzmán that plans needed to be laid to hand over cartel control to capable lieutenants from the next generation, as the founding fathers aged and reeled from arrests and extraditions. Zambada had – and has – his own state and military contacts, which, like Guzmán's, not only made it possible for the Sinaloa cartel to spread, but enabled El Mayo to remove Guzmán's official protection in some quarters. Zambada is said to have been with Guzmán when El Chapo was arrested for the last time in 2016 in Los Mochis, a coastal town deep within territory controlled by El Mayo. Guzmán initially escaped the raid, disappearing into a sewer, reportedly with Zambada. And when they surfaced to hijack a red Ford Focus from a woman and her child, covered in grime, Zambada not only ensured the lady kept her purse but somehow slipped the net. El Chapo was captured, El Mayo not, fuelling rumours of a betrayal.

Sinaloa remains a formidable multinational syndicate, and mustered sufficient firepower in Culiacán to force a unit of the Mexican army to release El Chapo's son Ovidio after a raid in November 2019 – a humiliating surrender on the government's part. During spring 2018, I was working in the Colombian Pacific port of Tumaco, through which a third of all Colombian cocaine passes, and where local priests, activists, government and military sources all concur that the waterfront remains firmly under Sinaloa control. Before the trial, Alejandro Hope of *El Universal* had made the logical point that 'no one really controls the Sinaloa cartel, not even Chapo Guzmán, it now seems. If he did, it would have collapsed, and it hasn't.' But the cartel is wounded, its hegemony lost, to cede initiative to others.

The 'Plaza' chapter in this book needs no rewriting, but could be doubled in length here were I to recount in detail Mexico's *narcología* since. On the slipstream of La Familia: the Milenio cartel, the Knights Templar, Guerreros Unidos, even 'Los Viagras' – and against them a mobilisation of self-defence militias, often accused of using the cartels' methods against them, and eventually going into the business themselves. On the border, the Zetas completed their violent separation from the Gulf cartel which had spawned them – just beginning when *Amexica* was published. The Zetas squabbled between themselves after the killing of brutal Heriberto Lazcano – El Lazca, or Z3 – in a shootout with the navy at Progreso, Coahuila, in 2012; his body was snatched by gunmen from the funeral home where it awaited burial. One Zeta spin-off formed the Cartel Noreste – North-East – which inherited control of the commercial hub of Nuevo Laredo, to which the old Gulf cartel, still centred in and around its fortress city of Matamoros, lays siege, in cahoots with by the far the most significant new player since *Amexica*: Nemesio Oseguera Cervantes – El Mencho – and his killing machine, the Cartel Jalisco Nueva Generación. To update on the decade past is to report on what happened to El Chapo, but in another ten years' time, we'll be doing the same with regard to El Mencho.

I noted in 2010 the increasing share of methamphetamine in the narco market, and this has continued exponentially, pioneered by the Jalisco cartel for whom it is a prime product, rather than cocaine: cheaper to produce, with higher profit margins. The CJNG is based in the state which boasts as its slogan *'Jalisco es México'* – land of agave plantations, tequila and mariachi music. Its capital is Mexico's second city, Guadalajara, home of Mexico's book fair, of the Chivas football club – which enlists only Mexican citizens to play – birthplace of the first modern cartel, centre not only of finance (thereby money laundering) but also the pharmaceutical industry, with an ample supply of chemists and others who know how to manufacture synthetic narcotics.

Unable at first to secure a 'plaza' on the border, Oseguera duly focused on latitudinal smuggling: westward, between Mexico and Asia and Australia (where cocaine retails at three-to-four times the US street price), and to the east, Europe, across the Gulf and Atlantic. The CJNG had initially cast itself as 'Los Mata Zetas', the Zeta killers, out-shocking even the most brutal cartel of all. The CJNG's coming-out party on the Gulf coast – and announcement of presence deep into Zeta territory – was the deposit of thirty-five bound and tortured bodies during rush hour in the port of Veracruz, as El Mencho punched a hole in Zeta control of the port, access to which he needed for business in Europe. Control of the Pacific coast, necessary for shipping to and from to Asia, entailed turf wars across the seaboard states of the cartel's native Jalisco, Colima, Michoacán and Guerrero. Acapulco, a prime tourist destination, became one of the most dangerous cities in the world. Seven months after El Chapo's arrest in January 2016, his sons, Iván and Jesús Alfredo, were kidnapped by gunmen while dining with friends at an upscale restaurant in the tourist haven of Puerto Vallarta, Jalisco – CJNG home turf. Their release was negotiated by El Mayo. El Mencho was still in theory part-affiliated to the Sinaloa cartel. US and Mexican intelligence believed the kidnapping to be a sign of El Mencho's ambitions against the fragmenting cartel, a warning that it not trespass into Jalisco, and that even Guzmán's own terrain was henceforth insecure.

'Mencho' can be a familiarisation of 'Nemesio', though in parts of South America it can also describe someone of bad taste – a possible self-deprecation consistent with Oseguera's wry sense of dark humour. Recent intelligence profiles of Oseguera describe him as self-disciplined, teetotal and more economical with women than the likes of Guzmán. His ruthlessness is renowned: torturing and killing anyone he might suspect, on the slightest rumour, of being an informant. The CJNG is harder to infiltrate than less cohesive cartels, and El Mencho himself makes no public appearances – 'He's like a ghost,' says one DEA source.

Oseguera was born to an avocado-growing family in Michoacán (a business to which he has, with his cartel, returned – buying up plantations and extorting growers has become CJNG business). He left for California as a teenager, where his brother and sister's husband worked in methamphetamine 'super-labs' across the central lowland valley. Oseguera was arrested in San Francisco 1989 for selling drugs, was deported, but returned and was caught again in San Francisco, selling heroin with his brother. He pleaded guilty in order to protect other members of his family, spent five years in a US jail, then returned to Mexico. He briefly joined a small-town police force, then the Guadalajara-based Milenio cartel, a Sinaloa subsidiary controlled by Ignacio Coronel, uncle to El Chapo's wife, Emma. Oseguera climbed a brutal way through the Milenio's ranks to its apex, ready to take over the franchise when Coronel was killed during a shootout in 2010. But El Mencho was passed over and, insulted, formed his own spin-off. Thus were born both the CJNG and Oseguera's insatiable cause of vendetta. His takeover of Guadalajara was absolute, and a bloodbath.

In 2015, the CJNG went to war not only against the Zetas and Guzmán but the state, with a series of attacks more reminiscent of Pablo Escobar in Colombia than El Chapo. It posted a video on YouTube showing a veritable army, and a warning from El Mencho: 'I am coming.' Five federal police officers were killed in an ambush at Ocotlán, Jalisco, and the state's head of public security, Alejandro Solorio, narrowly escaped assassination. Shortly after Easter 2016, a convoy of police special forces was ambushed and fifteen officers killed. When the army responded with 'Operation Jalisco', eight soldiers and one police officer were killed during a single battle on May Day that year, and a military helicopter shot down.

It was only a matter of time before the CJNG lay claim to the border. Having amassed a fortune and terrorised central Mexico, El Mencho had accumulated a price of $10m on his head in the USA, and become Mexico's most wanted man, along with the patriarch of the old Guadalajara cartel, Rafael Caro Quintero, jailed for the torture and murder of DEA agent Enrique Camarena, whom a judge inexplicably released on a technicality in 2013, after twenty-eight years in jail. (The USA was outraged at this baffling act of clemency, suspected of being a trade-off for Guzmán's capture with Caro Quintero's friend, El Mayo.) As I'd heard the length of the border, from Col. Leyzoala and Dr Muñoz in Tijuana, from Pastor Galván and the addicts in Juárez: the drugs have changed. And just as El Mencho had asserted himself as principal of laboratory production of meth, the whimsy of demand in the United States then delivered into his lap another business boom: fentanyl. At first, Oseguera's organisation was insufficiently potent to challenge Guzmán's hold on major distribution routes between and from Los Angeles, Chicago and New York, so the CJNG focused its meth business around smaller networks across Tennessee, West Virginia, Oklahoma, the Carolinas and Deep South. These turned out to be exactly the places where the claw-back on prescriptions to abate the proliferation of opiate painkillers – and addiction to them – was most intense. The only problem with fentanyl's business model is that the drug is so strong, but as Dr Muñoz says, America provides a plentiful supply of addicts to replace those who die. In pursuit of them, and now also the bigger markets, Oseguera aims to do to the borderland something not dissimilar to the siege of the plazas laid by Guzmán ten years ago.

Like Guzmán, Oseguera began with Tijuana, by 2010 under Sinaloa control. According to the local Zeta magazine, CJNG used its initial attacks on the city around 2015 to forge a working alliance with Guzmán's franchise there. But after El Chapo's final arrest in 2016, CJNG abandoned the détente, aiming for control of smuggling routes. Now, analyses by the private intelligence agency Stratfor and the DEA – as well as voices on the ground – confer on a push by CJNG into Chihuahua, and its prize corridor, Ciudad Juárez, where turf wars between gangs affiliated to cartels rage, as they did ten years ago. In August 2019, and again in December, battles raged in Nuevo Laredo, with officers and cartel gunmen killed. This is El Mencho knocking at the Gateway to the Americas.

In a significant echo of the arrests of Guzmán's family and associates in the US, and of others extradited to the US, February 2020 saw the extradition of El Mencho's son, Ruben Oseguera, to the United States, then the arrest of his daughter, Jessica Johanna Oseguera, when she arrived in Washington DC for her brother's arraignment. The court papers accuse Jessica Oseguera of laundering cartel profits into a vast web of businesses, including a notable brand of tequila – Onze. Significantly, the indictment for both was drawn up in Chicago, formerly a fortress city for the Sinaloa cartel, suggesting that El Mencho has broken out from his rural distribution networks, moving in on the big-city markets, as Sinaloa influence wanes. One thing – and not much more – is certain: El Chapo Guzmán is not 'the last narco' (as the title of an estimable book of 2010 by Malcolm Beith had hoped). But what next? Today, as ten years ago, violence flares when the plaza is unquiet, when the sands shift. Jeremy Slack, at the University of Texas El Paso, puts it well in a new book about narco traffic and migration: 'La Familia Michoacana is fighting the Zetas who are fighting the Gulf Cartel, who are fighting *La Línea*, who are fighting Sinaloa, who are fighting Tijuana, Los Rojos, the Cartel Jalisco Nueva Generación and the Beltran Leyva for good measure.'[5] Phew.

The week after Guzmán's extradition in February 2017 saw a surge in violence across Culiacán especially – twenty were killed over that weekend. The year 2017 then became the deadliest on record in Mexico's narco nightmare, and 2018 began more brutally than ever in Ciudad Juárez, where I spent New Year's Eve – twenty-seven murdered within the first three days of January – and Tijuana – with ninety killed in the first three weeks of the year – both after periods of relative calm in those cities.

So not only did the mass murder and disappearances intensify after Chapo's arrest but – crucially – there has been no interruption in the flow of cocaine, methamphetamine, fentanyl and heroin into the United States and Europe – in fact, the supply is greater than ever. No commodities in the world trade at such steady, reliable prices, despite flooding the market, as do illicit drugs. Saviano was right about Copernicus: narcotics are recession-proof; they defy the laws of supply and demand, able to meet both, ad infinitum. Cocaine is always in demand and adaptable in its quality control: good stuff for the rich, crack in the ghetto. The opioid crisis can only further increase demand for heroin derivatives.

The legacy of Guzmán's conviction can be measured against a less trumpeted moment in the narco narrative since *Amexica*: the appeal by then Colombian president Juan Manual Santos to the Organization of American States, at its summit in Cartageña in 2010, to tear up the War on Drugs battle plan, and start again on the basis of 'co-responsibility' between 'producing' nations, torn apart by violence over narco traffic, and what President Santos called 'consuming' countries, where the noses, veins and pill-wrappers are, and where the money gets 'cleaned'. An exhaustive report on the micro- and macro-economies of cocaine was published in 2012 by two academics at the Universidad de los Andes in Bogotá, Daniel Mejia and

Alejandro Gaviria. They concluded that 2.6 per cent of the street value of cocaine from Colombia stays there, while 96.4 per cent swills through distribution networks and banks in 'consuming' countries. 'Colombian society,' said Gaviria in an interview, 'has suffered to almost no economic advantage from the drugs trade, while huge profits are made by distribution networks in consuming countries, and recycled by banks which operate with nothing like the restrictions that Colombia's own banking system is subject to.' None of this featured at Guzmán's trial, nor did anyone try to introduce it. Guzmán is in jail, but where is his money? Where are the Zetas' billions? Where are El Mencho's? According to the banks caught out thus far, they are under your nose, if not up it.

Among the many things Guzmán shares with El Mayo Zambada is that each granted only one interview. Zambada told Julio Scherer, publisher of *Proceso*, that he had a lifelong fear of incarceration, but pondered: 'One day I may decide to turn myself in, so they can shoot me, and there'll be general euphoria. But we all know that at the end of the day, if they catch me or kill me, nothing will have changed.'[6] Talking to Sean Penn, Guzmán said: 'this will never end' – and as so often, he was right.[7]

Blood Money Revisited

An irony hung over the trial of El Chapo Guzmán. For across the East River from Cadman Plaza – on Manhattan island, of which nearby Brooklyn Bridge affords a spectacular view – lie the US headquarters of the giant HSBC bank. HSBC is one of the most enduring commercial institutions from, and symbols of, British Empire, established in 1865 as the Hong Kong Savings Bank of China during the conclusion of, appositely, the Second Opium War, fought over British demands to open China to its merchant companies, including legalisation of the opium trade.

A century and a half later, HSBC was the bank which, alongside and even after Wachovia, embraced billions of unmonitored dollars in cash from Mexico, of which hundreds of millions were proven to be proceeds of El Chapo's cartel, for laundering and circulation across the 'legal' economy. According to the Senate report, vast sums banked by HSBC from individuals with connections to al-Qaeda, terrorism and sanctions-busting in the Middle East, without sufficient monitoring – $200 trillion in all were moved without proper controls. The first stirrings of that scandal were just breaking on the Reuters wire in time to warrant an early mention in Amexica, where I was also able, thanks to a series of interviews with whistleblower Martin Woods, to recount HSBC's predecessor, the movement of blood money by Wachovia.

To recap, for the numbers are staggering: the court settlement between Wachovia and the US government, through the District Court of Southern Florida in March 2010, found that: 'For the time period of May 1, 2004 through May 31, 2007, Wachovia processed at least $373,630,892,102 [$373.63 billion approx.] in wire activity through

CDC [*casas de cambio*, or exchange houses]. During that same time period, Wachovia processed at least \$4,728,626,300 [\$4.728 billion approx.] in bulk cash for the CDCs. For the same time period, Wachovia processed approximately \$47,000,000,000 [\$47 billion] in RDC deposits for all of its correspondent banking customers, which included the Mexican CDCs.'¹ 'RDC' stands for remote deposit capture, 'a delivery method for international check deposits' which involved scanning cheques electronically, explains the settlement. This was done, the bank admitted, without due process or checking. One of those CDCs was Casa de Cambio Puebla, with branches across Mexico, through which the Sinaloa cartel bought the cocaine-laden planes. Yet no one from the bank was prosecuted, let alone sent to jail. The same good fortune was enjoyed by HSBC. As with Wachovia, HSBC's punishments were an admonition and fine payable with its small change. No one was prosecuted or tried, let alone jailed.

HSBC's shocking (or maybe not-so-shocking) accommodation of the Sinaloa cartel is narrated in detail by three privileged documents. First came a report by the Senate Subcommittee on Investigations, answerable to the Committee on Homeland Security and Governmental Affairs, published on 17 July 2012 and chaired by Democrat Senator Carl Levin, with Republican Tom Coburn as non-dissenting Ranking Minority Member. Its title was self-explanatory: 'US Vulnerabilities to Money Laundering, Drugs, and Terrorist Financing: HSBC Case History'. Second came an agreed 'Statement of Facts', dated 11 December 2012, by way of appendix to a legal settlement between the US Government and HSBC. Then another congressional report was published in July 2016, seeking to address the US government's refusal to prosecute HSBC, compiled by the minority Republican Staff of the Committee on Financial Services in the House of Representatives. It was chaired by Jeb Hensarling and was entitled: 'Too Big to Jail: Inside the Obama Justice Department's Decision Not to Hold Wall Street Accountable'.

What HSBC did is best described by the officials themselves. Announcing his report, Senator Levin condemned HSBC as a bank wherein the culture was 'pervasively contaminated'. Presenting the criminal investigation and settlement months later, Assistant Attorney General Lanny Breuer said: 'HSBC is being held accountable for stunning failures of oversight — and worse — that led the bank to permit narcotics traffickers and others to launder hundreds of millions of dollars through HSBC subsidiaries, and to facilitate hundreds of millions more in transactions with sanctioned countries. The record of dysfunction that prevailed at HSBC for many years was astonishing.' He continued: 'HSBC's blatant failure to implement proper anti-money laundering controls facilitated the laundering of at least $881 million in drug proceeds through the US financial system.'[2]

The House minority report of 2016 would later summarise: 'Despite evidence of serious money laundering risks associated with doing business in Mexico, from at least 2006 to 2009, HSBC Bank USA rated Mexico as "standard" risk, its lowest AML risk category. As a result, HSBC Bank USA failed to monitor over $670 billion in wire transfers and over $9.4 billion in purchases of physical US dollars from HSBC Mexico during this period, when HSBC Mexico's own lax AML controls caused it to be the preferred financial institution for drug cartels and money launderers.'[3]

A press release by the Treasury considered that: 'The bank's breakdowns in anti-money laundering (AML) compliance were particularly egregious because these failures allowed hundreds of millions of dollars from Mexican drug trafficking organizations to flow through accounts in the United States. Despite HSBC's extensive global operations and the substantial resources it had available to manage transnational risk, it failed to help secure the United States financial borders and left dangerous gaps that international drug dealers and other criminals readily abused.'[4]

To put it bluntly: HSBC, as well as Wachovia, was banker to the narco-trafficking industry. The criminal investigation following on from the Senate report found HSBC to have breached three laws: the Bank Secrecy Act, the International Emergency Economic Powers Act, and the Trading with the Enemy Act. The Department of Justice established its 'Statement of Facts' on the basis of the Senate report, cited later. Paragraphs 9 and 10 of that statement, on HSBC's breaches of the Banking Secrecy Act are worth quoting.

9. From 2006 to 2010, HSBC Bank USA violated the BSA and its implementing regulations. Specifically, HSBC Bank USA ignored the money laundering risks associated with doing business with certain

Mexican customers and failed to implement a BSA/AML program that was adequate to monitor suspicious transactions from Mexico . . . As a result of these concurrent AML failures, at least $881 million in drug trafficking proceeds, including proceeds of drug trafficking by the Sinaloa Cartel in Mexico and the Norte del Valle Cartel in Colombia, were laundered through HSBC Bank USA without being detected. HSBC Group was aware of the significant AML compliance problems at HSBC Mexico, yet did not inform HSBC Bank USA of these problems and their potential impact on HSBC Bank USA's AML program.

10. There were . . . significant failures in HSBC Bank USA's AML program that allowed the laundering of drug trafficking proceeds through HSBC Bank USA, including: 'failure to adequately monitor over $200 trillion in wire transfers between 2006 and 2009 from customers located in countries that HSBC Bank USA classified as "standard" or "medium" risk, including over $670 billion in wire transfers from HSBC Mexico'. And: 'Failure to adequately monitor billions of dollars in purchases of physical US dollars ("banknotes") between July 2006 and July 2009 from HSBC Group Affiliates, including over $9.4 billion from HSBC Mexico . . .'[5]

HSBC Mexico − which is only supposed to enrol accounts in MX pesos − operated a 'branch' in the Cayman Islands, a British tax haven, which handled 50,000 client dollar accounts worth $2.1 billion by 2008. It had no staff, or offices − this was a virtual bank nominally located in Cayman, operated by HSBC Mexico for Mexican clients. However, $7 billion in cash dollars was shipped from that Cayman 'branch' − in reality from Mexico − to the United States in only two years, 2007 and 2008, despite serial warnings that they were the proceeds of drug dealing. This in addition to the $9.4 billion from Mexico proper − $16.4 billion total. This was not cyber-money, it was hard cash. In 2013, I asked a very senior Mexican official involved in the investigation into Casa de Cambio Puebla since the outset how that cash was moved. He replied, on condition of anonymity, that it was transferred as the 'proceeds of foreign exchange', in armoured vehicles over the bridge from Ciudad Juárez to El Paso, deposited, and the value wired on to New York.

Paragraph 33 of the Statement of Facts, discussing the Cayman Islands operation, connects HSBC directly with the cocaine aircraft. 'One HSBC Mexico compliance officer noted the massive misuse of [the HSBC Mexico Cayman Islands US dollar accounts] by organized crime.' One example, identified by HSBC Group's Head of Compliance in July 2008, involved 'significant USD [US dollar] remittances being made by a number of [HSBC Mexico's Cayman Islands US dollar] customers to a US company alleged to be involved in the supply of aircraft to the drug cartels'.[6]

Paragraph 35 concerns HSBC's reluctance to close suspicious accounts.

When suspicious activity was identified, HSBC Mexico repeatedly failed to take action to close the accounts. Senior business executives at HSBC Mexico repeatedly overruled recommendations from its own AML committee to close accounts with documented suspicious activity ... Even when HSBC Mexico determined a relationship should be terminated, it often took years for the account to actually be closed. In December 2008, there were approximately 675 accounts pending closure based on suspicions of money laundering activity. Closure had been approved for 16 of those accounts in 2005, 130 in 2006, 172 in 2007, and 309 in 2008. All 675 of these accounts remained open into at least 2009, with transactions being actively conducted through them despite facing pending closure based on suspicion of money laundering activity.

Then the settlement addresses the river of cash.

In November 2007, Banco de Mexico, the central bank of Mexico, expressed concerns about the volume of US dollars exported by HSBC Mexico back to the United States. Specifically, Banco de Mexico wanted an explanation as to why HSBC Mexico's US dollar exports were significantly larger than its market share would suggest.

37. In February 2008 ... HSBC Mexico's CEO [Paul Thurston] was told that law enforcement in Mexico and the United States were seriously concerned that the US dollars being deposited at HSBC Mexico might represent drug trafficking proceeds.

And Paragraph 39 goes on to say:

> Moreover, a significant amount of the physical US dollar exports
> came from Culiacan, in the Mexican state of Sinaloa. Culiacan is
> home to the Sinaloa drug cartel. HSBC Group and HSBC Mexico
> were both aware of the money laundering risks in doing US dollar
> business in Sinaloa state. In 2007, HSBC Group learned of what
> was referred to in its employees' emails as a 'massive money-
> laundering scheme' executed by HSBC Mexico employees and
> managers at multiple branches in Sinaloa state. HSBC Mexico
> closed all of the accounts involved in this scheme and terminated
> employees. However, HSBC Mexico branches continued to accept
> US dollar deposits in Sinaloa state. From 2006 to 2008, HSBC Mex-
> ico exported over $1.1 billion in physical US dollars from Sinaloa
> state to HSBC Bank USA.[7]

Then comes a damning detail. Using circuitous routes like exchange
houses and accounts in the Cayman Islands is one thing. But Paragraph 50 describes how narcos would brazenly arrive at branches of
HSBC with boxes full of cash. It deals with findings by the Homeland
Security Investigations (HSI) which 'revealed that drug traffickers
were depositing hundreds of thousands of dollars in bulk US currency
each day into HSBC Mexico accounts. In order to efficiently move this
volume of cash through the teller windows at HSBC Mexico branches,
drug traffickers designed specially shaped boxes that fit the precise
dimensions of the teller windows. The drug traffickers would send
numerous boxes filled with cash through the teller windows for
deposit into HSBC Mexico accounts. After the cash was deposited in
the accounts, peso brokers then wire transferred the US dollars to
various exporters located in New York City and other locations
throughout the United States.'[8]

The Statement of Facts had been preceded five months earlier by
the Senate report, which detailed, over 336 pages, just how HSBC
caused – or failed to prevent – this river of drug money. HSBC
Mexico, says the report, was 'the single largest exporter of US dollars to HBUS, transferring over $3 billion in 2007 and $4 billion in
2008, amounts that far outstripped larger Mexican banks and
other HSBC affiliates. Mexican and US law enforcement and

regulatory authorities expressed concern that HBMX's bulk cash shipments could reach that volume only if they included illegal drug proceeds that had been brought back to Mexico from the United States.'[9]

And the committee details HSBC's awareness of risks at the Casa de Cambio Puebla. There was apparently heated internal debate over whether the account should be closed or retained. 'In early July 2007,' reads the report, 'HBMX Compliance head, Ramon Garcia, disclosed in an internal weekly report that went to HSBC Group Compliance that the HBMX CCC [Compliance Committee] had considered closing the Puebla account, but decided instead to retain the client'. In response, 'John Root, a senior HSBC Group Compliance officer, sent him a blistering email criticizing the CCC Committee for "rubber-stamping unacceptable risks".' In the end, the matter was referred by Root to the CEO of HSBC Mexico, Paul Thurston, who did eventually close the account, although, said the report: 'Despite Mr. Thurston's July 2007 decision to close the Puebla account, HBMX did not actually close or freeze its Puebla account for another four months, allowing Puebla continued use of HBMX's correspondent account at HBUS.' HBMX only 'finally closed the account in November 2007, after receiving a seizure warrant from the Mexican attorney general seeking all funds in accounts opened in the name of Puebla or related parties'. In other words, the bank, having dithered for months, was eventually forced – rather than elected – to shed the Sinaloa Cartel's dollar pipeline.[10]

The buck does not stop with HSBC Mexico's CEO Paul Thurston, though he was the senior executive the bank paraded before Senator Levin's committee. Both the Senate report and the legal statement of facts apportion blame – and assign knowledge of what is happening – right to the top: to CEO and later chairman Stephen Green (from 2010, Lord Green) in London. The statement of facts affirms that senior executives, including Green, were 'all aware' of irregularities in dollar accounts, while page 67 of the Senate report specifies that: 'Internal HBMX and HSBC Group documents indicate that senior management immediately began to investigate the allegations. HSBC Group CEO Michael Geoghegan spoke to HSBC Group Chairman Stephen Green.' Footnotes and appendices to this and the 2016 report refer continually to emails from Geoghegan and HSBC US head of compliance David Bagley in New York to Green at London headquarters.

At least one HSBC officer tried to sound the alarm on inadequate monitoring, not only in vain – she was sacked for doing so. Her name was Carolyn Wind, HBUS chief compliance officer from 2000 to 2008. The Senate report recounts how: 'Ms. Wind was dismissed by HBUS after raising the issue of inadequate AML resources with the audit committee of the board of directors of the bank's holding company.' The report cites Wind as saying: 'I was told on November 30, 2007 that I was being terminated effective 2/28/08, due to the fact that the Board had lost confidence in me . . . If the Board has lost confidence in me based on my comments at the October, 2007 Audit Committee, why have I been allowed to continue to run this critical department without additional supervision or any direct follow-up from Group Compliance?'[11] Wind, who moved to the US arm of Bank of Scotland, did not reply to a request for interview about HSBC for this book.

HSBC responded to the Senate report with those bland, off-the-peg statements invariably served up whenever a corporation gets caught. A statement said: 'We have learned a great deal working with the subcommittee on this case history and also working with US regulatory authorities, and recognize that our controls could and should have been stronger . . . We believe this case history will provide important lessons for the whole industry.' Green's replacement as CEO, Stuart Gulliver, insisted that HSBC had become 'a fundamentally different organization' by 2012. But in 2015, he was apologising again, for 'unacceptable practices' at HSBC's private bank in Switzerland that helped clients evade tax, the discovery of which had caused, he said, 'damage to trust and confidence' in HSBC.[12]

Small-fry sacrificial lambs like Bagley were obliged to resign. The bank 'agreed to partially defer bonus compensation for its most senior officials during the five-year period of the deferred prosecution agreement'.

In the land that imprisons more people per capita than any in the Western world, hundreds of thousands of them for minor drug offences, no one from HSBC was arrested, tried or jailed. The bank was fined $1.9 billion, less than five weeks income for HSBC's

American subsidiary. There would be a five-year 'deferred prosecution', like Wachovia's yellow card, times five. Speaking at a press conference, Attorney General Loretta Lynch and Lanny Breuer insisted that the punishment met the crime. Yet Breuer was clear about why HSBC should be spared prosecution. 'Had the US authorities decided to press criminal charges,' he said, 'HSBC would almost certainly have lost its banking license in the US, the future of the institution would have been under threat and the entire banking system would have been destabilized.' Ergo: for causing the financial crash of 2008, the banks were too big to fail and needed bailing out with trillions of taxpayer dollars and pounds sterling. Four years later, they get caught and admit laundering drug and terrorist money, and are 'too big to jail'.

This was the title of the minority report of the House of Representatives Financial Services Committee in 2016, which deepened the plot, and the shame. The findings show the US government overruling its own officials' urgings to prosecute HSBC. It finds Attorney General Lynch's successor, Eric Holder, and senior officials at the Treasury Department admitting that purely financial considerations overrode a legal will to prosecute. And the minority report demonstrated an apparently successful intervention in the HSBC drug money-laundering case by UK Chancellor George Osborne. The report recounts how, before a crucial inter-agency conference call, 'George Osborne, Chancellor of the Exchequer, the UK's chief financial minister, intervened in the HSBC matter by sending a letter to Federal Reserve Chairman Ben Bernanke . . . on September 10, 2012, to express the UK's concerns regarding US enforcement actions against British banks'.[3] Osborne got his way; as Lanny Breuer had said: 'Our goal here is not to destroy a major financial institution,' rather than to prosecute El Chapo Guzmán's bank.

In 2016, a number of families of US citizens murdered in Mexico's drug wars brought a civil suit against HSBC, under an amendment in the 1996 Anti-Terrorism Act after the attacks of 11 September 2001, allowing victims to seek compensation from organisations that provide material support to groups that commit terrorist acts. The suit was filed through the Southern Texas Federal District Court in Brownsville, with a St Louis law firm, Elias Gutzler Spicer, acting for the plaintiffs. They included: the family of Lesley Redelfs, shot with her husband Arthur, when leaving a children's party at the US consulate in Ciudad Juárez in 2011; the family of Rafael Morales Jr., his brother and uncle, abducted by the Sinaloa cartel, and asphyxiated by having duct tape wrapped around their heads also in 2011; Victor Avila, former special agent for Immigration and Customs Enforcement, who survived an ambush when driving to Mexico City through San Luís Potosí with a colleague, Jaime Zapata, who was killed, again in 2011. In court papers, the complaint made the point articulately:

> As a proximate result of HSBC's material support to the Mexican drug cartels, numerous lives, including those of the plaintiffs, have been destroyed . . . Without the ability to place, layer and integrate their illicit proceeds into the global financial markets, the cartel's ability to corrupt law enforcement officials, and acquire personnel, weapons and ammunition, vehicles, planes, communication devices, raw materials for drug production and all other instrumentalities essential to their operations would be substantially impeded. Thus, by facilitating the laundering of billions of dollars of drug cartel proceeds through its banks, HSBC materially supported the terrorist acts of cartels.[14]

The case, the first of its kind relating to drug-traffickers and their proceeds, is pending after HSBC filed to have it moved from Brownsville to New York. HSBC told the *Financial Times* it intended to contest the case, and a spokesman told Bloomberg News: 'We are committed to combating financial crime, and have taken strict steps to keep bad actors out of the financial system.'[15]

At Guzmán's trial, we heard a great deal about cocaine shipments from Colombia via Mexico to the USA, but the money always goes 'back to Mexico'. One witness, Juan Carlos Ramírez Abadia, aka La Chupeta, Lollipop, of the Colombian North Valley cartel – who cut an especially bizarre figure, his face disfigured, lizard-like, by plastic surgery – said he flew planes loaded with between $8 million and $10 million in cash from Tijuana to Mexico City three times a month. Cash deposits were hidden beneath beds and even underwater. Ramírez testified that he hauled a Samsonite case filled with $10 million in cash to 'a Mexico City bank' monthly – but was never asked which bank, not by the prosecution, defence or bench. Prosecutors put Guzmán's forfeiture bill at $14 billion, a figure dwarfed by the value, over decades, of the profit on consignments described by Jesús Zambada, and the figures admitted to by Wachovia and HSBC. The US government has been looking for that money since the trial, but has yet – at the time of writing – to retrieve a single dollar. There is no search for Guzmán's billions as moved by Wachovia and HSBC. There's been no apparent attempt in the forfeiture to prise open the Pandora's boxes of the other twelve *casas de cambio* through which his cartel channelled profits as well as Puebla. There's been no reference to another indictment in southern Florida filed in 2014, *after* the Wachovia settlement there listing ninety-two wire transfers conducted by associates of Guzmán between 2003 and 2007. That was El Chapo's money; but what about the other cartels? Even if Wachovia and HSBC banks did comply with their deferment agreements, what about El Mencho's billions? Or the Zetas' fortune? Through which major banks are they being 'cleaned'?

As he handed over his file to prosecutors, Senator Levin said: 'As long as the bank just sees it is going to be dealt with kid gloves, I think we're going to continue to see these shortfalls that have been endemic.' How right he was. At big banks, the naval tradition whereby the buck stops at the top, with a ship's captain, is reversed. The big cheeses do not only avoid sanction, they get promoted. Fate as well as justice was kinder to those named in the settlement and congressional reports on HSBC than either was to the bank's client, now jailed Guzmán. Paul Thurston, head of HSBC Mexico, under whose nose the laundering took place, had been elevated in 2008 to Head of Global Retail and Wealth Management for the bank. When he retired at the end of 2012, Stuart Gulliver thanked him for having 'developed and rolled out consistent business models across multiple markets'.[16] Lord Stephen Green is shown by the Senate report to have been copied in several emails seeking to raise the alarm over what the bank was doing with regard to drug profits and is named in the Statement of Facts. He initially responded with outraged umbrage, calling the Senate report 'a singular and wholly irresponsible attack on the bank's international compliance procedures'.[17] But he nuanced his reaction a day later, once the report's details became known, telling Sky News that he had 'no case to answer' over the blood money scandal, but had the temerity to add:

'I think we must acknowledge there were some failures of implementation. HSBC has expressed its regret for that. I share that regret.'[18] But none of this had affected his nomination back in September 2010 to the British government Cabinet, alongside Chancellor Osborne, as Minister for Trade and Investment, a position he kept until December 2013.

6

Shooting the Messenger

Promotion of *Amexica* in its Spanish translation led to some interesting places, few more than Xalapa, capital of Veracruz state, where the Hay Festival held a literary fair in October 2012. Veracruz is *infamously* penetrated by Los Zetas, and was then the state in which more journalists had been murdered than any other, markedly the correspondent there for *Proceso* magazine, Regina Martínez, found beaten and strangled to death at home in April of the festival year; five other reporters were then killed in the following month.

Accordingly, while there, my colleagues Jon Lee Anderson of the *New Yorker*, the writer Peter Godwin (then chair of PEN USA) and I drew audiences which used the occasions to exhibit posters reading 'No *Más Periodistas Asesinados*' – No More Assassinated Journalists. We duly acknowledged the protesters by reciting lists of names of our colleagues murdered in the state, and dedicating the events to them. Rather than relax into 'downtime' at Xalapa, I researched the life and death of Víctor Manuel Báez, the state's crime editor for the national newspaper *Milenio*, whose mutilated body had been found in June 2012. One of Báez's close colleagues shakes as he speaks to me at a café in the centre of Xalapa, and at moments his eyes fill as he recalls: 'It's certain that the people who killed Victor were criminals. The killing had the modus operandi of organised crime.' Then that haunted, haunting question that invariably arises: 'But who sent them and why? That's the question, that's the smokescreen.'

Apart from the barbarism of his killing, Báez's death bore another hallmark of apparent narco execution: a note pinned to his torso, this one reading: 'Here's what happens to traitors and people who act clever. Sincerely, Los Zetas.' But Báez's colleague says he learned from the marines 'that the note was not there when the body was discovered by a neighbour who found Víctor's door open — it was put there later, by someone, for some reason'. All of which compounds the cruel strangeness of Báez's death, the explanation for which anguished and terrified his colleague — the possibility of official complicity. Among those also brutally killed in Veracruz was Miguel Ángel López Velasco, columnist for the daily *Notiver*, murdered along with his wife and son the same month as Báez. And Yolanda Ordaz de la Cruz, whose decapitated, tortured body was found a month later in July, dumped near the offices of her newspaper, *Imagen*, two days after she was seized by armed men as she left home. State prosecutor Reynaldo Escobar Pérez insisted the killings were not linked to the journalists' work, and state governor Javier Duarte de Ochea assured that authorities were pursuing 'multiple lines of investigation'.

Things became weird at the Hay Festival. Godwin appealed to Duarte to act over the mass murder of reporters in his fiefdom; Anderson and I declined to meet him. Then, *Proceso* magazine posted on its website a detailed account of a supposed meeting in the Crowne Plaza hotel in Xalapa, at which Duarte supposedly 'exploded' with recrimination at Godwin, Anderson and myself for bringing the name of Veracruz into disrepute. The story was a complete fabrication, and a close friend of mine, Mike O'Connor — representative in Mexico for the Committee to Protect Journalists — used his contacts to have it taken down. 'The weirder it is, the scarier it can be,' said Mike.

But there was a coda to the episode, and to the reporters' worst fears for their colleagues: Governor Duarte was in October 2016 obliged to resign over numerous allegations of corruption, affiliations to Los Zetas and threats to journalists. He was federally indicted for criminal association with the cartel and embezzlement of state funds to buy artefacts and properties, but vanished, and an aide convicted for assisting the governor's escape. Duarte was eventually arrested in Guatemala and jailed in 2017 for nine years. Yet the war against the press continues in Veracruz. On 30 March 2020, journalist María Elena Ferral of *El Diario de Xalapa* was gunned down and killed, after pleading — in vain — that her official bodyguard, who had been removed by the authorities, be reinstated.

* * *

Staying, as I did when in Mexico City, with Mike and his wife, Tracy Wilkinson of the *Los Angeles Times*, was as enlightening as it was entertaining and a privilege. But Mike would sometimes pause our intense or hilarious conversations, saying firmly, 'I have someone coming. We need to be undisturbed in my office,' and a journalist, usually from the Mexican provinces, would arrive looking like a terrified rabbit in headlights, grateful and eager for Mike's counsel. Mike summarised government officials as usually insisting that murdered Mexican journalists were corrupt or in the service of cartels – 'as if they could possibly know'. Working on the ground, he said, 'I do know that at some times and in some places, a reporter might get approached by someone with a pistol, and told to write this but not that, and there may be some money in it. And if you don't do as we say, we know where you and your family live, we know where your kids go to school. Is that working for the cartel? Well, yes and no – it's staying alive and keeping your family alive. But so far as a rival gang is concerned, you *are* working for the cartel, and federal officials use that context to make out that the dead are corrupt.'

Mike put the killing of journalists into stark strategy from the cartels' and authorities' point of view. 'The government and authorities are ceding territory to the cartels and, for the cartels to take territory, three things have to happen. First, the cartel needs to control the institutions with guns – basically, the police. Second, control political power. And, for the first two to be effective, you have to control the press. So often, then, it's the authorities who are the corrupt ones. I know reporters who get asked by the police chief, "Why are you so curious?" That's a clear threat. Every journalist I've spoken to says that the corruption of forces is such that the cartels control the politicians. I'm not quite sure what the word is to describe the relationship, but ultimately the Capo is in charge.' However: 'When I say to a roomful of journalists, "Ask the question, *Quien manda aquí?* (Who's in charge?)," they take a virtual step backwards, wide-eyed. That's the question you only ask yourself at night when you're drunk and your wife is asleep and you hope no one hears you.'[1]

Mexico has now become the most dangerous place in the world to work as a reporter. According to the CPJ, at least fifty-two have now been killed since 1992, the vast majority of those since 2004, and fourteen are missing; other organisations register much higher counts. Most of the journalists with whom Mike worked did their reporting at town, city or state level, on local papers. But some journalists attacked are national figures.

The writing of *Amexica* led me to the honour of personal acquaintance and professional collegiality with — among many others — Mexico's two most esteemed dissident journalists and authors, who have between them laid bare the range of official complicity with organised crime. Their work is differently targeted and nuanced. Lydia Cacho, Mexico's foremost and loudest advocate for women's and children's rights, investigated and revealed the role of high officials of state in sex slavery, trafficking in children and child pornography. Anabel Hernández, whose father was abducted and murdered in 2000, wrote a book in 2010 — *Los Señores del Narco*, translated as *Narcoland* — which traced and named the connections between El Chapo Guzmán's Sinaloa cartel and the upper reaches of Mexican government and state. Now, her recent *El Traidor* has, at the time of writing, topped Mexico's best-seller charts for weeks. What the two women have in common is that their work has led both to be driven into exile after threats to their lives.

Cacho's revelations appeared in several books, markedly *Los demonios del Edén* — *The Demons of Eden* (2006) and *Esclavas del poder* (2010), translated as *Slavery Inc.* in 2012. The former, especially, exposed a terrifying circuit of child exploitation and sadistic pornography among senior political and business figures, all named, centred on the state and city of Puebla.

I first met Lydia in 2014, at the book fair organised annually by the Italian magazine *Internazionale* in Ferrara. I knew her work well, and was gratefully amazed that she knew mine. She proceeded to Rome, to promote an Italian translation of *Los demonios del Edén*, and it was my honour to show her round a city in which I had once lived. *Los demonios del Edén* had cost Cacho dear. One of the businessmen named in the volume, José Kamel Nacif, sued Cacho for libel — Cacho fought the case and won, cleared of defamation.

But then, in December 2005, Cacho was approached by several police officers near her office in Quintana Roo. They bundled her into a van and drove her twenty hours to the city of Puebla, where she was illegally detained and subjected to physical and psychological torture: sexual threats and abuse. A gun was pushed into her mouth, and she was told how easy it would be for her to 'just disappear completely'. 'I kept thinking one minute I was going to die,' Cacho recalls, 'then that I would survive.'

When Cacho arrived from the police station at Puebla jail, a female guard told her she would be raped inside. But a network of friends, contacts and activists swung into action and she was bailed. Tapes later surfaced that demonstrated the arrest to have been orchestrated by the governor of Puebla, Mario Marín Torres, who was at the time linked to obscure business transactions with other politicians and members of the highest courts in Mexico. All had something in common: they attended child sexual exploitation parties in Cancún organised by another businessman named in the book, Jean Saccar Kuri. Saccar Kuri was sentenced in 2011 to 112 years in jail for paedophilia, child pornography and human trafficking; he had enslaved more than two hundred children for abuse, some as young as three years old.

In counterpoint to this trauma, Cacho was showered with honours, including the Chevalier de la Legion d'Honneur in France. In 2009, the Inter-American Commission on Human Rights granted Cacho the right to claim precautionary protective measures, and asked the Mexican government to take action to protect her as a result of continued harassment and monitoring. But in July 2012, Cacho received a call on her satellite radio from a man who told her she was a 'fucking bitch' who had 'ignored warnings', threatening to 'send you home in pieces'. Cacho reflects now: 'The way they interfered with my radio, it had to be someone who had the power and the means to do that, hack into it. Immediately I called some security experts, and told them what had happened. They said to get out of the house straight away. I called my lawyers, who urged me to run for my life, so I did. I just took my passport and a bag and got out of there, taking the first flight available. I couldn't even say goodbye to my family because my phone was hacked.'

Cacho commuted between Spain and New York, visiting London and Italy. 'I think it's absurd,' she told me then, in 2015, 'that I'm telling the truth, and though I don't scare easily, I have to flee my country.' She was offered political asylum in a number of countries, 'but I don't want to take it. It'd mean I couldn't return because I've been defeated by the narco state. I built a home, I love Mexican people, I like the music, I like to dance and drink tequila. Everything is there – my home, my dogs, my studio where I paint and write. And in Mexico, journalists are so badly needed. They want to erase journalism in Mexico. After all these years, every time my mobile phone rings and I see the name of a colleague I fear the worst: someone's been assassinated, kidnapped or disappeared. Journalism is essential in a country that lives in a silenced war, a masked war.'

Cacho returned to Mexico in 2014, and on 31 July 2018, the United Nations Human Rights Council ruled that the Mexican state was responsible for the violation of Cacho's human rights, the torture to which she was subjected and failure of due diligence in its investigations into the violence against her. Subsequent to the verdict, arrest warrants were issued on 11 April 2019 for three of the principal players in *Los demonios del Edén*: former governor Marín; the businessman who had sued her, Nacif (whose denim company makes jeans for Calvin Klein and Tommy Hilfiger, among others); and former undersecretary of Public Security of Puebla, Hugo Adolfo Karam Beltrán. They were accused as intellectual authors of Cacho's abduction and torture. The response to both the UN and the indictments was swift, and terrifying.

On 21 July 2019, a week after Interpol announced an international warrant for these men, Lydia Cacho returned home. She had written and spoken often about its balm, her dogs and chickens, and fortitude gained from the peace and heave of the turquoise sea. But that night, she found a different, terrifying scene. Cacho's paradise had been ransacked. Much of her reporting equipment, including a laptop, audio recorder, three cameras, memory cards and ten hard drives had been taken or destroyed. Most painfully, two of her dogs had been killed, slowly, by poison; a third survived.

The attack came at a time of baffling mixed signals from the Mexican government. In January 2019, it proffered an apology for what Olga Sánchez Cordero, head of the Government Secretariat for newly installed President López Obrador, conceded as 'arbitrary detention to which she was submitted by various authorities of the Mexican State, derived from the accusation of the crimes of defamation and *calumnia*, by the authorities. For the use of torture as an instrument of state revenge, intimidation and punishment that she was victim of carried out by various agents.' Cacho accepted the apology but demanded that the government similarly fulfil its obligations to all other victims, 'absolutely everyone, to whom I represent today and to whom I will continue to give voice'. But then, on the very weekend Cacho returned home to find it ransacked, the same López Obrador government, aware that she was due to do so, withdrew official protection on her home, and bodyguards.

All this, yet again, under the supposedly reformist presidency of López Obrador. 'Time is running out,' said Mike O'Connor's replacement at the CPJ, Jan-Albert Hootsen, 'for the government of President López Obrador, to provide the country's journalists with a comprehensive plan to protect them and combat impunity in crimes against the press.' Cacho posted a defiant video message on Twitter. 'I won't stop. We have to move from indignation to action. All the culprits must be detained, not only those who attacked me, but also those responsible for violence against the boys, girls and women that I have been exposing, and who are currently hiding from the law . . . Here *Nadie Se Rinde*' – no one surrenders.'

And yet, when I next contacted Lydia, to talk about the murder of Isabel Cabanillas, she had bad news: she had felt obliged to leave Mexico again.

'I have been forced seven times to leave my country to avoid being murdered as have many of my colleagues and friends,' Lydia reflects, caught by the Covid-19 lockdown while staying with friends near Los Angeles, where she is recording a series of podcasts on the history of *femicidio* in Mexico. 'I'm certain of one thing at least: no matter where I am I will not be silenced. Women have been silenced for centuries, and once we have a voice, we shall not stop proclaiming the facts and root causes of violence against women and children.' Lydia is haunted by the murder of her dogs, Ulma and Luna. Of the survivor, a stray she had taken in, she says, 'I guess Petra and I are alike. Two street rebels who will decide when death arrives to claim us, not without a fight for those we love.'

I met Anabel Hernández in 2013 when asked to moderate an event at which she was appearing, organised by the Frontline Club in London. It was my first outing in several months, after an accident had broken off more than two inches of both fibula and tibia. Anabel was in a different kind of pain, which she wore better than I did, generated by fear and rage.

Her father, Emiliano Hernández, was an engineer, 'always fighting against corruption, impunity and injustice', she recalls. 'He wasn't a journalist, or an activist. He was just an honest citizen from a very poor town, who denounced what he thought was wrong.' After making a modest amount of money, he had 'returned to his home town and fought for the basic things, for those around him: water, electricity and the rights of the people. And I grew up watching him do that. I told him: "I watched you fight against bad things, and for justice, and I want to do it my way." But he didn't understand. He wouldn't even pay for me to go to college – my mother did that.' Decades later, in December 2000, after Anabel had started work at *El Universal*, her mother called to say that her father had not returned home the night before. 'Everyone was searching, the hospitals, houses of his friends. And then they found his car. In it was one of his shoes, and there was blood on the trunk. Days passed before they found him, dumped on a highway. The police said they would only investigate if we paid them, which my mother refused to do. His killers are still free. Before this happened, he had told me he was, after all, proud of my choice, to be a journalist, and that is why I do what I do.'

Two years before she arrived for the Frontline event in 2013, Anabel's extended family held a party at a favourite café in Mexico City. The gathering was to celebrate the birthday of her niece. As one who rarely allows herself time off, Anabel was especially happy because 'the entire family was there. There are so many of us that it's extremely difficult to get everybody together in one place. It hardly ever happens.' But she had to leave early, as so often, 'to finish an article', and it was after she left that gunmen burst in. 'Pointing rifles at my family, walking round the room – and taking wallets from people. But this was no robbery; no one tried to use any of the credit cards – it was pure intimidation, aimed at my family, and at me.' It was more than a year before the authorities began to look for the assailants, and during that time the threats had continued: one afternoon in June 2013, Hernández opened her front door to find decapitated animals on the doorstep. Hernández's offence was to have written a book about Mexico's bloodletting of a different kind. What made *Los Señores del Narco* special was its relentless narrative linking the Sinaloa cartel to the apex of Mexican power. It was a book, to use one of Hernández's best words, about the 'mafiocracy' – the mafia state rather than the mafia. Her further sin against the establishment and cartels was that the book became a best-seller, with more than 100,000 copies sold in Mexico. Such wildfire interest delivers a clear message, she said. 'So many Mexicans do not believe the official version of this war. They do not believe the government are good guys, fighting the cartels. They know the government is lying, they don't carry their heads in the clouds.' On the other hand: 'Mexico is exhausted. People will pay anything to live in peace. But this is the strategy of government: sponsorship of the Sinaloa cartel, which makes the so-called "War on Drugs" one big lie.'

Only a few weeks after the Frontline event, on the night of 21 December 2013, came another, more terrifying, attack. Eleven armed men 'dressed in civilian clothes but organised like a military squadron, violently burst into my home', she said. Hernández was elsewhere when this happened, but learned later how the gunmen had 'identified themselves to my neighbours as Zetas, but then said they were federal police. They forced people at gunpoint to say which apartment was mine. While they took down the metal door of my garage and entered my home, they sealed off the street for half an hour, communicating by radio. All they took was the hard drive on which my CCTV was stored. And all this while I was being guarded by the Interior Ministry's civil protection mechanism.'

For Hernández, after the murder of her father and other threats to herself, this was a 'last straw'. She accepted a fellowship on the Investigative Journalism Program with the University of California, Berkeley, but returned to Mexico to unpeel the scandal of the disappearance of forty-three students at the Ayotzinapa teacher-training college, at Iguala in Guerrero state in 2014. Hernández told an audience in Cambridge: 'People might think that journalists like me are exaggerating, that corruption makes some people more rich and nothing worse than that. This story is about how corruption can kill. How corruption can disappear and torture people. How it can hurt a country like Mexico. So I had to do this. I saw the pictures, and heard explanations coming from the government I just did not believe.' *A Massacre in Mexico* proved, on the basis of exhaustive research, official complicity in the disappearances of the students, and appalling torture of innocent civilians in order to obtain 'confessions' to support the government's untruthful versions of events. Like Cacho, Hernández was also named a Chevalier de la Legion d'Honneur by the French government in 2017. 'A journalist who has to walk with bodyguards is an embarrassment for any nation,' she says. 'I constantly fear for my health and the health of my family, but the fear only drives me.' And yet, again like Cacho, Hernández lives as an exile from her country, in Italy. From there, she recalls how at Berkeley, 'I could think of little else but those mothers and fathers, looking for their sons, who have been taken, abducted. Vanished, suddenly disappeared – how could they bear that, without an explanation?'

7

The Unquiet Dead

One of the grievous outrages of Mexico's war inadequately treated in the original *Amexica* is that of disappearance and the disappeared. In January 2020, figures released by the Mexican government's under-secretary for human rights and a newly created National Search Committee counted an appalling 61,637 persons missing since the drug war began in December 2006. The unspeakable curse of disappearance, and the haunted, purgatorial existence to which it condemns family and relatives who remain, deprived, brings into the language of the borderline a word as spine-chilling and searing as *femicidio*. It was first used in mass public discourse in Chile and Argentina during the 1970s and 80s: *los desaparecidos* - and *las desaparecidas* - the disappeared. I had listened, learned and written much in Bosnia about the existential and emotional void wherein the families of missing personas are left unknowing, searching for a sign of either life or death, without a grave at which to grieve, tortured by hope that their loved one might somehow and sometime reappear. Time to hear that voice from Mexico.

Leticia 'Lety' Hidalgo Rea kneads the fingers on one hand through those of the other when she speaks, as though preparing corn mash between them; her gaze is fixed, and appears to focus inward as well as towards whatever distraction is in front of her. Like Paula Flores in Juárez, she exudes fortitude and defiance, but wears her wound. Our conversations span the ocean: at her home in her middle-class quarter on the north-eastern outskirts of Monterrey; a meeting of the group she help found, FUNDENL (United Forces for Our Disappeared in Nuevo León); then when a speaking tour brought her to University College, London.

Leticia was a schoolteacher in a neighbourhood called San Nicolás. She lived close to her work, with her two sons, Roy, eighteen, and his younger brother Ricardo, sixteen, at the time. Roy was a student of foreign languages in the faculty of Philosophy and Arts at the Autonomous University of Nuevo León. 'He was studious, he spoke good English, was used to living at home, perhaps a bit overprotected,' remembers Leticia. 'Different from Rici, who was more adventurous on the street.' It was a quiet life – that is, until the night of 11 January 2011 when sudden kicking and banging on the front door of their family home in the early hours were so loud, the boys 'thought they might be gunshots'. A group of ten to a dozen men wearing balaclavas and dressed in the uniforms of the Escobedo Municipal Police then burst in, and began ransacking the house. 'I thought it was just a robbery, or that they may have come to collect a *cuota*. But no, this was more than that. They beat and threatened the boys, forced them to lie on the floor, then grabbed Ricardo, and as they did so, demanded to know which was the elder. Roy raised his hand: "It's me," he said. So they grabbed him instead, hauled him out of the door, put him in one of their trucks and disappeared.' That was the last Lety saw of her son. 'When we recovered our senses, it was just Ricardo and me in the house.'

And so began Lety's entirely changed life, twisted and transformed in moments. Next day, at 4 p.m., the telephone rang. A man calling himself Alejandro demanded 100,000 pesos ransom money, and titles to two vehicles loaned by Lety's father. Leticia assembled the money, and was told to bring it and one of the two vehicles to a school bus parked outside a church, San Benito, in the Los Angeles sector, where 'they'd free Roy within two hours'. Lety did as she was asked, handed over the money and deeds to a man who appeared out of the night, but then waited past two hours, then past dawn, for nothing to happen. After that, 'All I could do was search, in order to stay breathing, and so I did.' She repeatedly called 'Alejandro's' number, and early one morning he answered. He said he would call back when ownership of the vehicles had been arranged – he never did, but another voice called from another number some days later to say that Roy would be returned, 'in pieces'. 'I started to feel everything implode. All I could do from that moment on was devote every hour to the search.'

Over the weeks and months that followed, Leticia reported the facts to the state attorney general's office, the anti-kidnapping agency, the human rights commission, the organised crime office and the search prosecutor's office. She went to the Telmex phone company, where she paid employees to help her find names associated with the numbers she had. Finally, one of them answered, 'and a voice in a room of people asked "Which of you is Roy?" Then my son came on the line. "Mama, it's me." I couldn't believe it was him, and asked the date his brother was born, to check. When he replied, I burst into tears. He told me he missed me, I replied that I loved him, and said I would make sure to see him again — then they took the phone and all I could hear was men shouting and laughing. I was dizzy, I had heard Roy's voice, but he was nowhere.'

Stung, Lety continued her search. Officers at the military barracks advised her to use a GPS system operated by Nextel, which located the addresses where a phone had been used. The army, it transpired, had carried out an operation to rescue kidnapped people in one of those areas, north of Monterrey, but Roy was not among them. Federal prosecuting authorities allowed Leticia to circulate Roy's picture among the released hostages, 'but none recognised him'. Ominously, two witnesses in the case testified that the Zetas and police forces were collaborating in a series of abductions 'to get forced recruits for the cartel'. A year after Roy's abduction, the first of a number of police officers from San Nicolás was arrested and accused of kidnapping teenagers for the Zetas. Fernando Castañeda of the municipal force confessed that he was among the cops tasked to abduct youths for a local Zeta leader known as 'El Sureño', the Southerner, who was himself later arrested. Lety asked his interrogators for information on Roy — there was none.

'We were so near, yet so far,' says Lety. 'The bad boys even met with us.' With other women from her organisation, Lety arranged for an encounter with representatives of the cartel, who admitted that kidnapping for prostitution and forced labour was part of its modus operandi. 'The army recovered one of my vehicles in an operation against the narcos,' she says, 'and keys to the other were found in a car also full of guns and ammunition.' The authorities lost interest in Lety's search, but in January 2018, she turned to the United Nations Commission on Human Rights, registered the case, and transferred it to the Mexican government. All, so far, to no avail. The crime remains 'unsolved' and Roy's whereabouts unknown. The Spanish writer Lolita Bosch has published a book about the case, not because it is 'special' but because it speaks for others, 'which is what I want to do, represent all the others', says Leticia. And because the book brings Roy to life – it talks about his favourite music groups, and love of the Tigres soccer team, whose yellow shirt he wore. Bosch uses the term *'brutal dolor'* to describe those with a loved one forcibly vanished into the ether – the brutal pain. 'I'll find Roy, even if it costs me my own life,' Leticia pledges. 'This cause is all I have. How to describe this way to live, for years now? Roy is absent, yet with me all the time. If I hear a door open, I think it must be him. I cannot admit that he is dead – I know I'd get a message from the other side if he was, a voice would come into my prayers and tell me. And until that happens, I'll keep searching. Who am I after Roy? Everything has changed. Worse than all that, though, I've imagined *his* pain, thousands of times. Sometimes I think it's egotistical of me to insist that he is alive, because if he is, it will be in such inhuman conditions. For that reason, I think it may be selfish of me to affirm that he lives.'

It is hard to erect a marker to the disappeared. But a poignant coordination takes place among the mothers and families: a series of embroidered handkerchiefs bearing their names. The project generates both public monument, when the handkerchiefs are exhibited – often hung from lines in public spaces or galleries – and testimony. By the summer of 2016, nearly three thousand had been sewn, and the project continues, now thanks to three separate but coordinated groups: Fuentes Rojas in Mexico City, Bordando Por La Paz Puebla in that city, and FUNDENL in Monterrey. That to Roy Rivera reads: 'Student at the Faculty of Philosophy, UANL. Son of my heart.' In 2015, the city of Monterrey did cede to FUNDENL the naming of a space as 'Plaza de los Desaparecidos', a block north from the state government palace. The square consists of steps towards a pool of water, from which a sail-shaped glass column rises, bearing the names of mostly young people who have disappeared from the city since 2006. At night, it is especially moving, elegantly lit, the water rippling like whispers from the void. On the sloping concrete walls around the square, there are painted portraits of some, and a mural of burning candles. On 11 January

2017, the sixth anniversary of Roy's abduction, Leticia Hidalgo stood in the Plaza de los Desaparecidos, by real candlelight, wearing a white T-shirt depicting her son's face, flanked by others holding photographs of their lost loved ones, mostly sons, and spoke to an assembled crowd. 'These have been six years of struggle and search,' she said. 'We, the families of the disappeared, will fight for our lost and loved ones, for their dignity and ours.' She read a list of demands: that the authorities step up their investigations into disappearances, and cease covering up for organised crime. That there be transparency with regard to 'all available information' on 50,000 fragments of recovered human remains. 'We who have searched for six years have met and worked with the Mothers of the Disappeared in Argentina, who have been looking for forty years . . .' Her voice, strong for some eight minutes, began to crack, but she continued: 'We who live on will pursue justice . . .'

Leticia's reference to Argentina was apposite. The search for the missing in Mexico — and around the world — has invoked one of the most impressive movements of our time: an entwinement of the methods, arts and sciences of forensic anthropology and genetic matching with other disciplines, which tries to find the deceased missing, identify them, and return their remains to the living. To close, where and when it can be done, that searing wound of uncertainty, make the unknown known, even when worst fears are confirmed.

It matters not just what is done, but *how* — with regard to both the information and the human beings it affects. A radical multidisciplinary weave of expertise and method, that has revised the story of the borderland and Mexico, has origins in the search for those forcibly disappeared during the military dictatorship in Argentina between 1976 and 1983. The Equipo Argentino de Antropología Forense — Argentine Forensic Anthropology Team, EAAF — was formed in 1984, initially to investigate cases among the 8,960 or more people disappeared by the Junta. Applying techniques established by the American forensic anthropologist Clyde Snow, the group transformed this field of work, connecting scientific efficacy and collaboration with the relatives of victims, to become leaders in the field, now in demand worldwide, including Mexico.

EAAF was forged more by commitment than experience in the wake of the hurricane of violence unleashed by the Argentinian military regime: thousands were 'disappeared' after round-ups by the feared and fearsome *'grupos de tareas'* – task forces. Those contesting the regime and those with nothing to do with the opposition were alike 'disappeared', tortured, killed and their bodies concealed, in morgues, in graves marked N.N. – no name – or else thrown from helicopters into the Atlantic, or incinerated in crematoria and open pits, or hidden in clandestine mass graves, military bases and police precincts. In April 1977, a demonstration outside the presidential palace began the movement that inspired Leticia Hidalgo and others: the Madres de la Plaza de Mayo, the Mothers of the Disappeared, and later also the Grandmothers of the Disappeared.

Clyde Snow – who had played a part in the identification of Dr Josef Mengele, the 'Angel of Death' in Auschwitz – was called to Argentina in June 1984, after the military had fallen and given way to the elected government of Raúl Alfonsín. As though by fate, a team of seven students of anthropology, archaeology and medicine drew together around Snow. 'Not one of the team had forensic training, in those earlier years, except Clyde, obviously,' says one of them, Mimi Doretti, who would proceed to work with such effect in Mexico. Snow nurtured this small collection of dedicated young people into learning fast, not in seminar rooms but digging with trowels, cleaning with toothbrushes, carefully filing and analysing what they found and matching those discoveries to desperate families of the *desaparecidos*. It was an organic concurrence of anthropology, archaeology, genetics, forensic pathology and humanitarian activism for a reason: the right of those left by the missing to know where they are, what happened to them, and to claim back their remains. The seven students soon realised that, as a book about their early work by Christopher Joyce and Eric Stover puts it: 'digging had been the easy part', to which was attached responsibility to human sensibilities.[1] At Mar del Plata Cemetery in the western suburbs of Buenos Aires, the team searched for the remains of a man called Nestor Fonseca. There, a lady came to observe the exhumation; Doretti put down her trowel and walked over to her – it was Fonseca's widow. She took Doretti's hand and whispered: 'Thank you . . . What you are doing is wonderful.'[2] Doretti would hear that again many times, in Mexico.

So the method was established: work on the remains, work with the families. Exhuming under judicial order, EAAF uncovered all twenty-five skeletons from the so-called 'Fátima massacre' of 20 August 1976. The enterprise expanded to include one of the most infamous burial grounds of all, Sector 134 at the Avellaneda Cemetery, 'a virtual city of the dead', write Joyce and Stover, where the team had to suspend digging for a short while after death threats were telephoned to the cemetery office.

In an academic paper of 2014, the group explained its approach, starting with essential 'Preliminary Information', ergo: 'the reconstruction of the event under investigation, for methodological planning, and to determine the possibilities to accomplish the main forensic goals; among these, the identification of victims is of utmost importance'.[3]

Those three decades since Argentina, EAAF has impacted the narrative in Mexico, after doing so in fifty other countries that have suffered mass disappearance, including Chile, Guatemala and Bosnia.

The Mexican work began in Ciudad Juárez, where EAAF was engaged with a view to forensic assistance on investigations into the *femicidio* by the non-governmental Mexican Commission for the Defence and Promotion of Human Rights, but under an agreement with the state attorney general's office in Chihuahua. Two experts duly arrived in Juárez: Sofia Egaña and Doretti, who in Argentina had become unofficially assigned to EAAF's most delicate human task, described by Joyce and Stover as that 'of interviewing the relatives of suspected *desaparecidos* to track down medical records and personal histories that could help in identifying skeletons'. Doretti was also, they write, the one who usually performed that walk on shards: 'informing families that a set of bones belonged to their lost relative, most often a son or daughter'.[4]

Doretti speaks with calm but firm authority; like Lydia Cacho, an infectious entwinement of resolve with *joie de vivre*, severe endeavour with effervescence. In Juárez, EAAF did what no one else had done: talked to everyone and looked for, and at, everything. 'The technical part is not new,' explains Doretti. 'But it was new to use anthropology and archaeology in forensic investigations. And it was very new to use physical evidence in human rights investigations.

It was also new to work in this multidisciplinary way, having the families at the centre of the work.

'To start with, in human rights cases,' she says, 'there are always documents. That's where you begin; if it had been the Third Reich, you'd need to look at the train timetables. It's what we always do, in every case – we always found valuable information in the documentation.' Then, crucially, there's the element that EAAF brought to both method and cause: the families of the disappeared. However: 'forensic science was cautious of our approach', she continues. 'There was this idea that involving the families would somehow contaminate the work, turn us into social workers, jeopardise our "objectivity". But that is absolutely not the case.' Not only is participation by the families a matter of principle, but 'when you work in situations when the state is the perpetrator, or the state has failed, you need to be in contact with the families. For the most part, the families have an enormous amount of information. It helps us in how we do our work'.

EAAF established that from early 1993 to 2004, between 400 and 500 young women had been killed in Juárez and Chihuahua City.

Working with an organisation called Justicia para Nuestras Hijas – Justice for our Daughters – Doretti conducted hundreds of exchanges with those left bereft or bereaved by a disappeared loved one, to establish narratives around women's disappearances, in order to connect them to the remains under examination. The interviews were, says the report, 'to gather pre-mortem (physical data of the victim when she was alive), and information on the circumstances surrounding her disappearance and/or death' – something none of the mothers or activists report the authorities as having done thoroughly. Official files 'contained this information', says Doretti, 'but it was extremely basic'. The team also reported on what its necessary understatement refers to as 'peri-mortem trauma (trauma occurring around the moment of death) and cause of death from each case to Mexican officials and families'.

'A lot of what we did in Juárez,' says Doretti, 'was basic work that had just not been done, from lack of training to tampering with evidence. That's how we found the wrong IDs. Or the authorities might have matched one set of remains against one family and said "okay, negative", whereas what you have to do is match all relevant people against *all* the bodies, if you are going to make these identifications. What we said was: let's test all these families against all the remains.'

This scrupulous work proved what reporters could not, and what the families and activists in the 'Wind of Knives' chapter had long suspected: cover-up, and official malpractice. The discovery was a liberation and vindication – however raw – for the grieving mothers and families. The team's assessment 'confirmed grave methodological and diagnostic irregularities in all phases of the forensic work on the unidentified remains' they had exhumed, 'including recovery and analysis, and technical and/or credibility problems with the results of the genetic analyses'.

Moreover, said EAAF's first report of 2007: 'Access to full files was in many cases resisted by officials in Ciudad Juárez, even though it was part of the . . . contract.'[5] The search for bodies was itself contorted by official irregularities. Originally, reported EAAF, 'the Medical-Legal Institute [in Ciudad Juárez] had sent unidentified female remains to municipal cemeteries to be buried in mass graves. Initially, the official information given to EAAF regarding this practice indicated that it had ended in 1997. However, an extensive review of morgue and cemetery records led the team to conclude that the practice continued to take place until at least 2005.'[6] It required a deposition to the state attorney general to ascertain the existence of 'more female remains . . . at the former facility of the Medical Examiner's office in Ciudad Juárez'. Yet further remains were found at the medical school of the Autonomous University. Other remains or body parts taken from crime scenes had been lost while under custody.

By 2007, after analysis of fifty-five remains at a state-of-the-art laboratory in Virginia operated by the Bode Technology Group, twenty-four women and girls were positively identified – in lay language, returned to kith and kin – a rate of more than 40 per cent.[7] In a second report of 2011, EAAF said it had recovered remains of eighty-three women, and identified thirty-three. Doretti explained: 'Unfortunately, the remaining 50 female remains had not matched genetically or anthropologically with any of the 42 families that remained unanswered.'[8] So EAAF had brought closure – insofar as it can be brought – to thirty-three families. But also, two wider truths were now established, crucial in the long term: grotesque official malpractice, a sense of the scale of *femicidio* in Juárez. In a chilling conclusion to its earlier report of 2007, EAAF noted: 'One of the most challenging aspects of the investigation is that there are more remains than reported victims' – suggesting that many disappearances have not even been officially registered. As Mexico's *femicidio* bequeaths and mutates into an appalling new phase, this will be as true now as it was then, and as it is across the country.

But the calamity and cruelty of disappearance run the length of the border. Tamaulipas state assumes first place in a ghoulish table, with 10,633 disappearances registered to the end of 2019. Most are migrants, but the figure also includes victims of cartel assaults on entire communities, and – many insist – abuses by the military and marines.

Following the San Fernando massacre of seventy-two migrants in 2010, descriptions by an Ecuadorean survivor of the brutality metered out to its victims defied the darkest imagination. The following year, in April 2011, another – worse – carnage took place, of 193 people at and around La Joya ranch in the same municipality. It is presumed that the plan was to extort the migrants, or perhaps to press-gang the men, but there is no explanation of why they were summarily executed. The remains were scattered across forty-seven clandestine mass graves. In May 2012, there was a third major massacre, when forty-nine people were horribly murdered in the municipality of Cadereyta, Nuevo León, close to the highway connecting the state with Tamaulipas.

EAAF arrived into this nightmare, at first to support the consolidation of a forensic information data bank, a joint governmental and non-governmental mechanism which sought to cross information between migrants reported missing, and remains of migrants who had died during their journeys and were recorded as anonymous by forensic services and municipal cemeteries in both the USA and Mexico. By 2011, 162 migrants' remains had been identified, and returned to their families, mostly in Central America.[9]

Now, EAAF took over analysis of the remains from the three massacres: the seventy-two bodies from San Fernando, 193 from La Joya, and forty-nine from Cadereyta – 314 in all. The organisation took charge of the scientific work, backed up by the range and depth of data and information gleaned from the migrant project, having already reached out, to civil society groups in Mexico, families and social organisations across El Salvador, Guatemala and Honduras. By 2020, they had matched eighty-four of the dead from the massacres with their families, again mostly in Central America. A remarkable achievement, and yet, says Mimi Doretti: 'Most of those IDs could have been done years ago, had the work been done, had the connections been made. Most of the information was already there in the files. In some cases, people had been identified but the families had not been contacted. There's just no follow-up. We're not geniuses, and this is not nuclear physics! We're just looking at every document, looking for the families. In most cases, the families were glad to talk to us, and we learn from what they are saying.'

The approach to the disappeared was changing, towards EAAF's multidisciplinary way of thinking. A paper on the Tamaulipas projects published by the International Committee of the Red Cross noted: 'Among the many interesting aspects of the process, particularly notable is the reversal of roles: when interviews must be conducted, DNA samples collected or an identification notified, it is no longer the responsibility of the families to travel to Mexico; rather, the responsibility is on the institutional actors and the EAAF to travel to the country of origin of the migrant.'[10] The system was likewise eased with regard to the return of remains, said the ICRC paper: 'At EAAF's bidding, Mexican authorities took responsibility for such measures as issuing documents and humanitarian visas, covering expenses, to facilitate the presence of relatives of missing migrants in Mexico.' It even noted that 'consular and diplomatic channels have been alerted and are adapting their traditional operation system to favor this process'.[11]

Yet in Tamaulipas, says Doretti: 'The more we examine the information, the more we see.' Though EAAF only has direct responsibility for bodies from those three massacres, 'there've been many similar episodes. You have entire busloads of people disappeared, and they are not the remains we have. We just don't know what the extent of disappearance is.'

The rapport between the EAAF's search for the disappeared and the authorities in Mexico was, in 2014, about to be challenged in extremis. The story of the mass kidnapping of forty-three student teachers from the Rural Normal School teacher-training college in

Ayotzinapa, abducted by the police in September that year, is infamous. It was one of the most brazen known acts of enforced disappearance in recent history, and its telling is beyond the remit of this book. What concerns us here is that with the eyes of the world upon it, the government of President Enrique Peño Nieto scrambled for a version of things. Attorney General Jesús Murilla Karam announced that the authorities had secured confessions from leaders of the Guerreros Unidos narco-trafficking clan, with regard to the 'murder of a large number of people in the vicinity of Cocula'.[12] Cocula was the site of a garbage dump some fourteen miles from Iguala where, said Murilla Karam – according to the confessions his department had secured – the students had been burned, some of them alive. Later, it was announced that members of the Mexican marines had found bone fragments compatible with the students' remains in the San Juan river into which the 'confessed murderers' had dumped them. Murilla Karam affirmed this account as 'historic truth'. But it wasn't, it was an outright lie.

Urged in large part by international outcry and enraged demonstrations, some of the most qualified experts in a range of forensic disciplines descended upon Murilla Karam's account. A team – the Interdisciplinary Group of Independent Experts, or GIEI – from the Inter-American Commission on Human Rights concluded in two reports of September 2015 and April 2016 that this official version of events was 'scientifically impossible'.

EAAF had in 2014 convened not only its own multidisciplinary experts, but assembled one of the most wide-ranging teams of its kind ever: authorities on anthropology, archaeology, anatomy, genetics, pyrotechnics, botany, ballistics, entomology, odontology and criminology, plus analysts of video, photography and satellite imagery. They came from Argentina, Mexico, the United States, Canada, Uruguay and Colombia, to pore over the garbage dump for more than a year. Part of EAAF's work also involved commissioning a remarkable digital 'cartographic platform' devised by the innovative Forensic Architecture agency at Goldsmiths College at London University. This enabled users and investigators to navigate and follow the interconnections between some five thousand events – shootings, radio communications, vehicle movements – and hundreds of actors belonging to the different organisations – state and student – concerned. Collusion and coordination between various organisms of state and organised crime in the disappearances of the students are manifest.

On 9 February 2016, the EAAF gave a press conference at which its coordinators, led by Mimi Doretti, said that confessions by detained alleged gang leaders, testimony of police officers and other witness statements to the attorney general's office did not coincide with the scientific evidence it had amassed and analysed, and that it was 'impossible' for the forty-three students to have been incinerated at the Cocula dump.

On 20 April, dispelling the confusion and blowing away the smokescreen the government appeared now to be drawing, EAAF elected to publish its full report.

The document is a mighty, at times complex, tome of 351 pages, driving towards conclusions that seem to hammer a final nail into some last coffin in the funeral march of Mexican official credibility. First, the report establishes that there had been 'numerous fires' at the dump, during the ten years that rubbish had been deposited there. Human teeth and bones were indeed found there, comingled, and with a 'level of thermal alteration' that were 'significantly varied', implying 'multiple fire events and incinerations, and/or alteration or manipulation of those remains within the site'. The previous fires raised the possibility among activists and reporters that the site had been used to dispose of bodies in the past, by narcos and/or the authorities, and that is perhaps why the official version of events invoked it.

EAAF found nineteen human remains, including teeth and bone fragments attached to a prosthetic denture, which could be immediately discounted as not that of an Ayotzinapa student, since none had a false tooth. Ammunition and spent bullet casings were found at the dump, but ballistics analysis found none of them to be compatible with weapons the supposed 'killers' – according to the government's own 'confessions' – said they had used. The PGR had said it had found forty-one shell casings that were consistent with the confessions, on a day – conveniently – when the EAAF team was away from the site. The team had previously searched the very same location at which the authorities claimed to have found the ordnance, between two boulders, and found nothing there. Botanists attached to the team examined vegetation around the alleged incineration of the students, to find that no plants were in a condition compatible with a fire there in late September 2014.

In September 2019, the office of Alejandro Gerz Manero, new attorney general in the López Obrador government, announced that there would be a fresh investigation into the disappearance of the forty-three, 'almost from scratch'.

EAAF has made its mark on Mexico through its method and ethos. 'We listen to people,' says Mimi Doretti. 'We have to listen to the families, for their sake and for the sake of our work. You see very different reactions among the families as they prepare for the worst thing that can happen in their lives. Some people say they'd rather be in limbo than know, because knowing means their missing family member is dead. If a family doesn't want us to work with them, we won't. But most people do need to know. For most families I've met doing this, it is: "I cannot live with this. I would rather know; it's going to break my life, but I cannot live with the uncertainty." We listen to these people and work with them; I think that has become our mark. Yes, you want to find the disappeared; yes, you want justice. Yes, you want the system to work better. But above all, it is about them. In the end, the families of the disappeared are the people who matter.'

Meanwhile, along the border, citizens and especially migrants continue to vanish – every day.

8

Gateway to the Americas Revisited

A score or so of migrants crouch in the dark corridor of a safe house most have called home for a month now. Today, their turn has come – on the road again, not towards or across the US border they came here to traverse, but back deeper into Mexico whence they came, to save their skins. Men and boys focus their road-worn faces nervously on the journeys behind and before them; weary mothers tend to children who draw, distracted but fidgety, in colouring books. Outside, a minivan pulls up, driven by Baptist Pastor Lorenzo Ortíz, full of supplies – corn flakes, soap, Pampers – to be unloaded and replaced with its human charge, taking the migrants to relative safety, away from ubiquitous kidnap, extortion and violation by the mafia.

This is Nuevo Laredo, Gateway to the Americas, the busiest commercial border crossing in the world. The door of the safe house opens and blinding sunlight beckons those awaiting, as does Pastor Ortíz, who arrives across the border from Laredo, Texas, each morning to take a vanload of these people, sometimes twice a day, to the larger cities of Monterrey and Saltillo. Also here to help oversee the transfer is another pastor, local to Nuevo Laredo, Diego Robles, from the First Baptist Church in the city centre. 'If they walk to the corner of the block,' he says, 'they're likely to be kidnapped.'

The safe house – its gate kept closed with padlock and chain – is crammed with some 180 people, mostly indoors, some in a backyard enclosed by breeze blocks. Their stories are at once singularly terrifying, yet consistent. Moy Eduardo left his home in El Salvador when henchmen from the MS-13 gang took his brother – whose body was later found – after they failed to pay sufficient extortion money. He arrived at Nuevo Laredo bus station, only to be forced into a car and taken to the outhouse of a farm some distance from town. There, he was pistol-whipped, his phone taken and a cousin in Atlanta contacted and asked for $8,000 ransom. 'When he asked for time, they shouted obscenities,' says Moy Eduardo. 'They said if I didn't pay, they'd hand me over to "other people in our organisation".' Four days later, his desperate relative wired the money, and Moy Eduardo was released. He told US authorities his story when applying for asylum, 'but they didn't believe me, took my fingerprint and sent me back'. Moy Eduardo has a court date several months hence, 'and I cannot stay here – they said if they saw me again, they'd kill me'.

Yaqueline and her daughter Lisbeth had been given a code by their 'coyote' traffickers en route through Mexico after fleeing gang violence in San Pedro Sula, Honduras. They were told that if approached in Nuevo Laredo, the word '*rana*' – frog – would ensure safe passage. But when three thugs halted them outside the government migrant registration offices, Yaqueline was told the word signified 'property' of the enemy; mother and child were accordingly bundled into an SUV. Relatives north of the border were again contacted. After five days, they were still unable to find the ransom money, and Yaqueline and Lisbeth were released to find their own way to Pastor Robles's church. Asked if she had been maltreated, Yaqueline lowers her eyes, gestures towards the child, and crosses herself. Again: 'The officers on the other side said: "How do we know you're not inventing this?" The Maras were bad in Honduras, but it feels even more dangerous here.' While the Zetas and their off-shoot, the Cartel Noreste, control migrant movement within the city, the Gulf or Jalisco cartels often bring the migrants to it. 'It's the ones who've been brought here by a rival cartel they're after most,' says Pastor Ortíz, 'they have to pay twice.'

In August 2019, criminals approached Aarón Méndez, a Seventh-Day Adventist managing a shelter called Casa Amar in Nuevo Laredo, demanding he hand over Cubans in his care, whose relatives in the USA might, they thought, pay higher ransoms for their release than Central Americans. He refused, vanished and has not been seen since, joining the 62,000 disappeared in Mexico's war, with Tamaulipas accounting for more than any other state. When I went to visit Casa Amar, in search of whoever had elected to replace

Méndez, a man called Alejandro Rodríguez, in charge of the property, told me the shelter had 'closed for refurbishment'.

Three reports were published within a few days of one another in early 2020: one, by Médecins Sans Frontières, found 80 per cent of migrants waiting in Nuevo Laredo under Migrant Protection Protocols to have been abducted by the mafia, and 45 per cent to have suffered violence or violation.[1] Another, by Human Rights First, documented 816 cases of rape, torture and assault of migrants in the city[2] and a further report from Human Rights Watch documented Salvadoreans abused and killed after being sent back to Mexico under MPP.[3] Although Tijuana and Ciudad Juárez are statistically more dangerous, they are also big enough to get lost in. Nuevo Laredo is a city of palpably sharp eyes; a stranger in town for whatever reason can feel them the moment you cross the bridge. *Halcones* – cartel scouts – make no effort to conceal their presence, staking out new arrivals and migrant safe houses from the street corners, at the bus station, at the government registration centre for 'metering'. And pursuing migrants across town if they dare move around.

The cooperation of Mexico's left-wing government with Donald Trump's MPP is more brazen in Nuevo Laredo than anywhere. In contrast to the pastors' vehicles helping migrants wait in relative safety, government-chartered buses depart daily from Nuevo Laredo's state migration centres to take migrants – free – back to Tapachuca on the Guatemalan border, and out of Mexico. Even one of those was hijacked in autumn 2019, surrounded by gunmen aboard pickup trucks, and migrants taken.

The Mexican National Guard – a showpiece of López Obrador's security policy – is deployed in Nuevo Laredo, but, says Raymundo Ramos, 'they are like butterfly-hunters' during mass migrations across these lowlands. 'They may snatch one or two abductors, but all the others fly away.' 'The authorities make no attempt to intervene in the abduction and extortion,' says Pastor Ortíz. 'The mafia is right there in the open, and there's nothing done to stop them. It's total impunity for the cartels.' At local and national level, governments play down the abduction emergency. The chief investigator for the Office of Disappeared Persons in Nuevo Laredo, Edwin Aceves, said he had received 'no reports of kidnapping and extortion of migrants. These are just rumours.' According to US National Public

Radio, acting commissioner for US Customs and Border Protection Mark Morgan told a round table of reporters in 2019 he was unaware of reports of kidnapping, while Mexican foreign minister Marcelo Ebrard has said kidnaps were 'not a massive number'; his department had information on twenty cases nationally.

But here at the safe house, the minivan is ready to take people to relative safety then back again to cross the border when their 'Notice to Appear' date arrives. The group shuffles out of the front door onto the sidewalk and scrambles aboard. Lisbeth, wheeling her little pink bag, throws Pastor Ortíz a glare. Pastor Robles says a prayer for the road – and off they go, in the opposite direction to that of their plans, but away from the mafia's jaws.

I had returned to Laredo late off a Greyhound bus. I checked in to the comfortable Hotel Posada, on the banks of the Rio Grande, ready to proceed over the bridge next morning, only to find – right beneath my window – not just the view of the river and bridge into Mexico, but an uncomfortable sight that was not there ten years ago: a brightly lit complex under canvas. This is what the US government calls a 'soft-sided facility' wherein migrants think they will get to have their say, convinced that they will at last tell their stories; be heard by and admitted to the USA. In reality, the 'tent court' hearings, as they are more generally known, are by video link, often perfunctory, to a judge usually sitting in – in the case of this one at Laredo – San Antonio, 150 miles away.

Those summoned to the tent court begin gathering on the Mexican side of the bridge before 4 a.m. A group from Cuba and Venezuela assembles first, then two families from El Salvador, manifestly nervous – they ask the Mexican border official who escorts them to the halfway point to take a photo on their phone. There are sixty-seven on the docket to appear at the tent court this morning, but by 7 a.m., only twenty-nine are shuffled through into the canvas corridor, to plead their case, and await judgement on a screen; the rest are presumed to have given up – returned home, decided to stay in Mexico – or disappeared. Reporters are not admitted into the Laredo tent court. 'We are fleeing a regime that imprisons us,' says Yordani from Havana, escorting his wife and son, aged fourteen, 'but if we are sent back there, the danger is greater than anything in Cuba.' A woman from Honduras with two children, who refused to give her

name, said she feared what lay behind them 'there' more than anything she had fled back home. By 'there', these people mean not the
places they left, but Nuevo Laredo.

Once his colleague Pastor Ortíz is on the road, Pastor Robles talks
in his parish office, beside the Primera Baptist church, established
in 1888. About the faith that propels his work, despite Aarón Méndez's abduction a few blocks away. 'We are a church of service, not of
domination,' he says, invoking *El Cristo Biblico*, the Christ of Scripture, who 'calls upon us to serve the weak, and here they are among
us. All we can do is create a space for them, as safe as we can make
it.' The whole enterprise – shelter, provision of food and logistics – 'is
done by volunteers, from our and other churches. Some people in
this city want to kidnap and kill migrants, but others want to help
them. We do it for God, and seek nothing in return.' 'Each one has
their different story,' adds Pastor Robles's wife, Serena, 'but there
are common themes. So many of the women are violated. They've
been beaten, mistreated, while the mafia waits for the relatives to
pay the ransom money. We've had girls as young as eight years old
who've been raped.'

'It's a very clear danger,' says Pastor Robles. 'The authorities do
nothing for their security. There's no exact figure for the disappeared
migrants from here, but very many have simply vanished. Trafficking and kidnapping migrants has become big business, 'a way for the
drug cartels to diversify. It is worse in Tamaulipas than other border
states, and worse in Nuevo Laredo than anywhere else in Tamaulipas. There's no formula to the abductions and disappearances, some
they take, others not. But it is far too dangerous for migrants to be on
the street, and for that reason, we are an open door to them.' The
danger is not only to the migrants. 'We take calls threatening us,
and they have carried on since Aarón Méndez disappeared. They
know who we are and what we are doing, they keep a list of places
where the migrants are. Our answer is always John, chapter ten,
verse ten: "The thief cometh not, but for to steal, and to kill, and to
destroy: I am come that they might have life, and that they might
have it more abundantly." '

Pastor Ortíz is of like mettle, a stonemason who came from Mexico to northern Texas aged sixteen – 'My dad brought me across as an
illegal,' he says over coffee back home in Laredo, the morning after

his latest run to Monterrey, to be repeated today, as every day. Ortíz found work as a labourer in Houston – 'I know how to stucco, stone, brick and block' – then arrived in Laredo in 1992, and 'found the church whose mission was to serve outside its parish'. He was ordained, and has devoted himself full-time to migrant work for three years. Ortíz shows me around his home and its outbuildings, which were converted – until MPP – into dormitories and showers for up to two hundred migrants waiting on the US side, right here – men's quarters, and those for women and children. MPP, which began between Tijuana and San Diego in January 2019, was rolled out to Ciudad Juárez/El Paso, then '*los dos Laredos*' in July. 'Before they got sent back to Mexico, we'd get cars to drive 'em up to New York, Chicago or wherever for their court dates,' says the pastor, showing pictures of those days, the now empty yard full of people from the planet over. 'If we knew what they'd been through,' he says, 'we'd understand this society a whole lot better.'

Since the introduction of MPP, says Pastor Ortíz, 'everything has changed, including our ministry. The problem now is they have to wait on the Mexican side, exposed to the mafia.' The cartels are 'not interested in the Africans, they know they have no money, and are less likely to have relatives in the US. The most vulnerable are those who are waiting for their court dates, under MPP. All these people who don't really know what they are doing, don't really know where to go; someone trying to cross for the first time, who won't call the police, or file a report. Who will just pay to get out of there.' Often, there's work with migrants who have had their papers taken. 'I had a lady, taken by the Zetas, and she lost her immigration permit. No one will take her without the papers, so I tried to sort that for her.'

Every day, Pastor Ortíz goes to monitor the migrant office downtown. 'They can't walk a block from there without being taken – the cartel has people right there.' Pastor Ortíz knows the mafia scouts, and they know him; he negotiates all this face-to-face with the cartel and its killers. 'I talk to the cartel. They say: "Hey, aren't you the guy who drives them around?" I know the tricks and the traps. I'm walking like a lamb among the wolves. So far, they don't seem to want to eat me up. But maybe the day'll come when they do.'

9

Iron River Revisited

Ten years ago, 'Iron River' referred to the flow of guns across it, north to south, as it still might, for that has not abated. But it could now also describe the enduring steel fortifications that continued to be built west to east under President Obama, and their massive, ponderable extensions dictated by President Trump. Whatever the outcome of Trump's threatened 'big, beautiful wall', at the time of writing new, high, reinforced steel walls were built in 2018 and 2019 between Laredo and Nuevo Laredo, between Roma and Ciudad Alemán, between McAllen and Reynosa, and between Brownsville and Matamoros, with more on the way. Aggressively robust, copper-coloured iron dug deep into the soil, towering above meadow and riverbank, churning the valley floor, confusing animals and birds, dividing people: this is Donald Trump's chainmail entrenchment. Even in the quietest places along the lovely Rio Grande Valley citizens await its coming, for it is upon them.

Diana Uribe points to the door of a stolid stone outhouse beside the old Spanish fort at San Ygnacio, Texas, built in 1830. 'My great-great-great-great-great-grandfather and his bride lived there,' she says. In those days, Mexico was trying to stop US immigration here into 'Los Tejas' – as Texas was then called – to no avail. A slope leads from the street down to the slow-rolling Rio Grande, across which you could throw a baseball into the foliage and palms of Tamaulipas. It's a lazy day in San Ygnacio, population 700: grackles swooping and sun beating down on the empty plaza where Marlon Brando once filmed a scene for *Viva Zapata*; little else. But through here, President Donald Trump orders, a new border wall must cut.

Diana – now sixty-three, a retired teacher – grew up in this village, as did her forebears, watching names change and borders drawn: her ancestors were first granted land in New Spain under royal charter from Madrid, then it was Mexico, then the Texas Republic, then the USA after 1848. She wears a red sweater and prominent crucifix. 'This place isn't as sleepy as it looks,' she says. 'It's on a direct smugglers highway, if you know the land.' Yet even so: 'I don't feel unsafe here. The last thing smugglers want is to draw attention to themselves on the border. Do we want security? Yes. Do we want or need a wall? No.' But even that is not the point. Diana tells me that the man who built this fort, Don Jesús Treviño had three daughters, one of whom married Blás María Uribe, from the town of Guerrero across the river. 'And I am being told I have to be cut off from my family and people on the other side of a frontier drawn since they arrived,' says Diana. 'We used to go to Mexico all the time, for weddings, dances,' she says, 'and clubbing in Nuevo Laredo, though my parents didn't know that bit. The wall cuts across all those generations and traditions. Also through the realities of border economics, the complete interdependency of twin communities all along the Rio Grande.' The wall would, she says, 'close off opportunities to the future of the children I've taught, and that's just crazy. It's always been no man's land here – too far for the Mexicans to control, and Washington didn't want to know.' Communities along this stretch of river are tired of being pawns in distant games: residents of this county seat, Zapata, and Guerrero over the border were in 1953 forcibly moved entirely to accommodate flooding for a reservoir under the Falcon Dam project.

The fort itself had been entered on America's National Register of Historic Buildings in 1973, but was still a ruin when, five years later, the artist Michael Tracy moved to San Ygnacio and, incrementally, bought it and undertook its restoration. Influenced by long excursions to Mexico and India, Tracy's latest work – some of it displayed in the rooms of his maze-like home a block away – reflects a troubled present. A five-panelled frieze entitled *For Mexico* is a turbulent vortex of acrylic, dedicated to journalists murdered in Mexico for their work.

Sitting in his untroubled cactus and agave garden, Tracy insists that the president's wall is 'meaningless. Yes, there's always the possibility here that someone could come to your door at four in the morning and demand all you have. But will Trump's wall stop them? Of course not – it's a distraction.' But not all in San Ygnacio share these views, least of all one of Tracy's main patrons from Los Corralitos ranch across the highway, Lannie Mecom.

A fountain at the heart of Houston's museum district bears the Mecom family name, of one of Texas's oil dynasties. Lannie's grandfather Harvey bought this ranch in 1913 just after the Mexican Revolution and her brother owned the New Orleans Saints American football club. Now Lannie, an energetic seventy-five-year-old, stands on the riverbank, after a morning loading longhorn cattle for sale at market. 'That's Mexico,' she points, two hundred yards away. 'I'm happy to donate this land to the government to build a wall,' she pledges. 'It's gotten worse and worse over there – we had the Zetas camp right there over the river, and there was something going on – something mighty scary.' Lannie too owns land on which a historic fort is built, 'and it was built for a good reason', she half jokes, 'to keep trouble out!' Her ranching neighbour, Joe Braman, joins us – he also works as a K9 unit police officer in Victoria County to the north. 'We need a solid wall bad, and I'd give my land for it right now,' he says. 'There's so many people coming through here – I've caught 284 while training police dogs in the last few months. Other day, I took my lunch break and when I came back there were thirteen sets of sign along the *sendero*.'

We settle back at Los Corralitos ranch – complete with airstrip and plans for a tourist game-hunting reserve – to sit below a score or more of deer-head trophies. But also Mexican fabrics and colours; Lannie Mecom's view is not a parrot echo of the president's, or Braman's, but more nuanced. 'We need to give security to illegal Mexicans who are here already – they've been here twenty years, they're good workers; they're our neighbours, and poor. There's a lot of good people getting hurt; my family never asked people coming to work here for papers, and I never will. We need to help them get their papers, pay taxes and contribute to our economy. Yep, help us make money – but also build that wall.' Down by the river, a *vaquero* buying Lannie's longhorns, Lalo González – riding with skill in his cowboy hat – ain't so sure. 'I watch who comes and goes,' he says. 'The bad guys'll get through whatever you build; it's the honest people that'll get stopped.'

Like other citizens of San Ygnacio, Diana Uribe wonders where the wall would be built. 'There's just no physical space for that kind of construction here, we're so close to the river. The only way they could do it would be to build the wall on the far side of the main highway. That way, we'd end up in Mexico!'

Further downriver, at Madero just south of McAllen, Rey Anzaldua walks the path, through a pluvial afternoon towards the little church where he has worshipped 'since I was five years old': the lovely chapel of La Lomita, built in 1865 on a Spanish land grant of 1767. It is a jewel: candle smoke and the musky scent of whitewashed stone wrapping the Virgin of Guadalupe icon and offerings of flowers and corn. Rey's family has been here since the 1750s: signs off the freeway a few miles north indicate an exit for the 'Anzaldua Int'l Bridge' to Mexico. 'The Anzaldua extended family had three Spanish land grants between 16,000 and 18,000 acres along the Rio Grande river,' says Rey, 'and the bridge between. We don't have much of that now.'

But Rey and his family still own land along the river border here, and nearby. That's the problem. Hard to imagine, but the levee running beside La Lomita chapel, which has been battered by hurricanes and floods, is designated to be the course of a new border wall – cutting the chapel off from its congregation. This wall was planned before President Trump's national emergency in pursuit of an even bigger one – designated by George W. Bush's Secure Fence Act of 2006 that President Obama continued to enforce. Father Roy Snipes, known locally as the 'cowboy priest' for his Stetson headgear, leads prayers for his chapel to be spared. 'It would still be a sacred place,' he has said, 'but it would be a sacred place that was desecrated.'

It would also run right through land owned by Rey's cousin Fred, cutting him off from chapel and river, ten years after another stretch of wall dissected and isolated Rey's fields a mile east. Rey has served his time and country as a special agent for US Customs – stopping contraband north- and southbound – and wears his Vietnam Veteran's cap and jacket. 'I saw it all as a customs agent,' he says. 'Working both sides of the border. Cocaine and you-name-it coming north, guns and money going south. One haul heading to Mexico was 60,000 rounds of ammunition.' So his view is that of a professional, not just a landowner. 'You got to ask yourself: why are all the drugs and illegal immigrants coming through? Why, because of the demand for illegal drugs and illegal labour, not much different from Al Capone and prohibition. Do I, as a retired customs agent, think a wall will stop that? Oh, come on.'

Among the things that mark this fiercely proud border country in the deep Rio Grande Valley is the preponderance of privately owned land along the route of proposed walls, rather than public land more easily sequestered. And many of those landowners refuse to comply, like the Anzaldua–Cavazos cousins. Fred Cavazos is unable to join us at the chapel and down on his riverfront land today; he moves thanks to a wheelchair and the mud is deep. So we convene at his home half a mile away, over maps and plans sent there by the government. Fred runs his finger along red lines that mark the wall's trajectory. 'This is where it'll go, along the levee by the chapel, taking out a couple of houses, some of the RV park – but there's a lot of businesses on the other side, including mine. What happens to them?'

'It started with letters from the government, last September,' says Fred, in early 2019. The map arrived with the first, from the Department of Homeland Security demanding 'Right-of-Entry for Survey and Site Assessment'. Three more letters followed, each one ending with a line for signature of acquiescence by the landowner. On Fred Cavazos's letters, they remain blank. 'Our strategy is silence,' he says. 'I will not agree to this.' The serial challenges by the Anzaldua and Cavazos families to walls already built or due to be built present a model for the kind of private litigation by landowners – in addition to that by sixteen states and environmental groups – President Trump would face, at the time of writing, to get his wall.

Now Fred faces loss of access to his livelihood: he has divided seventy acres of his land on the riverfront into fifty-foot-wide lots onto which thirty tenants – mostly local – have built decks and huts, for fishing and gathering, eating and camping. Among his tenants are Father Snipes and the parish of La Lomita, which leases land with several buildings for visiting seminarians in retreat. 'The tenants pay each year,' says Fred, 'and I use the rent for taxes and bills. Now I worry I won't get that money.' Fred has cattle too, which traverse the wall's proposed path, 'and we won't know where to put that cattle now'. At some points along stretches of wall that have cut across private property, gates are installed, with pin-code locks. 'But even if we're lucky enough to get a gate, who gets the code? Do all my tenants get the code? Do the bad guys make sure to get the code?'

'People far away, want the wall,' says Rey, 'but hardly anyone down here. There's less illegals than there used to be, though we do get a car chase now and then – and there's no crisis on the border. When Donald Trump came here' – two weeks before our conversation – 'all he talked to was a few people who want the wall and law enforcement. He didn't speak to a single landowner; they just don't understand our ties to the land, on both sides of the border. There's a village called Cavazos over on the other side – that's family.' 'Most of the Mexicans come across to work,' says Fred, 'in hospitality and agriculture, like they did since I was born and Grandma used to bake 'em cakes and feed rice and cheese when they came to work the ranch – cotton, watermelon and cabbage in them days.' But, he adds: 'Whatever we do, they'll win; they'll build their wall anyway.'

A definitive report on the politics and legacy of border walls and fencing was commissioned in 2018 by the American Civil Liberties Union from Stephanie Herweck and Scott Nicol, who teach at colleges in McAllen.[1] 'As we see from Fred's and Rey's cases,' says Nicol in conversation, 'sacrosanct property rights in America are inviolable, until they get in the way.' Nicol and Herweck, through exhaustive Freedom of Information applications, demonstrate 'reservations by some Border Patrol sector commanders uneasy about the levee walls. Customs and Border Protection has said themselves that a wall doesn't do the job of preventing illegal crossing.' The report follows the effects and efficacy of walls and fences built thus far, and of that REAL ID Act of 2005, which ravaged O'odham land further up the line. 'This'll be a serious catastrophe in an area renowned for its natural life,' says Nicol. 'We have framed the argument in terms of income and hotels, and so on – but must also ask: do people want to live in a world like that?' He adds: 'Communities are built on rivers – they have been for all time, here and everywhere else. But if Trump gets the wall he wants, we'll be completely cut off from the river, after centuries. The only view we'll have of it will be from the bridges to Mexico. The Rio Grande Valley will be that no longer.'

* * *

And so the road bends, along stretches of new fence, to the border's and river's end, where the twin towns of Brownsville and Matamoros face one another. A decade ago, Michael Seifert had recently left the priesthood at his parish of San Felipe de Jesús in Cameron Park, Brownsville, fallen in love with a paediatrician and married her. But he had continued to work for the community in a post-pastoral role. Seifert remains 'plugged in to Cameron Park, all the better to keep people connected', but has adapted his work to the migration crisis, for the American Civil Liberties Union, ACLU, with an 'integrated advocacy' team guiding migrants as they cross from Matamoros into Brownsville, and writing regular Internet reports entitled 'Alongside a Border'. 'These migrants came here,' he says, 'because they wanted to be safe. Yet over in Matamoros, they are prey to deadly criminals, and here they are met with a system carefully designed to fail. They can have no idea of the evil genius of our immigration and asylum apparatus, satanic in its cleverness in keeping them out, and in danger.'

Immigration courts on the US side are poignant, perfunctory and dysfunctional. Having been forbidden to enter the tent court at Nuevo Laredo, I did visit the detention centre at Port Isabel, near Brownsville: rows of sometimes shackled, confused, weary people hustled through production-line 'justice', with, in some cases, no more exchange with the bench than a nod to indicate understanding of their 'rights', before deportation. 'Oh, and another thing has happened in ten years,' says Seifert. 'A spaceport built in Brownsville, for private launches into orbit. Yes, a thing called SpaceX has disrupted an entire neighbourhood to take rich people to Mars from here one day, while we cannot accept desperate migrants from a few yards across the river.'

On the Mexican side, in Matamoros, a makeshift tent city has been established of some thousand people clinging to the Gateway Bridge like barnacles, encamped for safety in numbers, for fear of the mafia. A tent city where, says a man called Milson from Honduras, 'time passes very, very slowly'. Most are from Central America, clutching their crumpled 'Notice to Appear', given to them before they were sent back under MPP.

A higher proportion of migrants are returned to Matamoros than anywhere else on the border, for all the dangers. Seifert had put me in touch with an opposite number on the Matamoros side, the kind of person these situations throw up, hurricane heroines and heroes of the hour. Glady Cañas Aguilar is one such figure. Two young men approach, asking what I want; I'm looking for Glady Cañas, I say. They have pockmarked skin, dead eyes and 'Santa Muerte' tattoos, unlike the migrants, whom they say they've come to *'apoyar'* – support. But they don't know Glady, and clearly haven't come to *'apoyar'* anyone: these are obviously *halcones* – falcons, or scouts – from syndicates of which those encamped live in dread.

Glady comes to the 'office' in a row of shops near the bridge wearing a red T-shirt with *'Associación Para Ayudarles a Triunfar'* on the back – 'Help Them Triumph'. A crowd awaits her; everyone wants a moment with Glady. Some 80 per cent, she says, come from Honduras, fleeing gang violence – also El Salvador, Guatemala, Cuba, and some from Africa. 'People often stay four months,' crossing in groups of fifteen according to the 'metering' system. 'We have more than 250 tents and we cope – just about – but they've been here too long and it's all too much – chickenpox, hepatitis, tuberculosis, and waiting, waiting . . . Here, they're safe, but out in the town, absolutely not.' Glady blames a *'falta de amor'* – lack of love – 'in the world'.

And she must run: a group of Tzotzil Maya Indians has arrived from the Mexican town of San Juan Chumula, evicted by fighting between rival political militias; she takes control of the chaotic scene, distribution of sanitary kit and clothes.

Waiting in the office are Teresa and her son Samir, who left San Pedro Sula, Honduras, when a faction of the Barrio 18 gang declared it was time for Samir, eleven, to join them. 'If he didn't, they'd kill the whole family,' says Teresa. Has that happened to others? 'All the time – I've seen it.' It's been a journey. 'We've paid the coyotes, been abused and I've been afraid for my boy. We don't leave the camp. Three people went to meet a bus last week, at the station, and never came back' But there's no question of trying to swim the narrow river. 'Legal or nothing. We have faith in God, and I know the Americans will believe us.' I bite my lip and change the subject: Samir says he likes *'reggaeton evangelístico'* and I confess I don't know many of his favourite songs.

Milson sits with his daughter Loany on the reedy riverbank, across from which – a short distance, but a world away – is Texas.

They are tempted to wash, for lack of fresh water, with others among the same eddies and whirlpools that drowned Oscar Alberto Martínez and his two-year-old daughter Valeria in June 2019, their bodies washed up on the US side, and photographed in an image that shocked many, but caused others to entrench their support for President Trump's policies.

Milson and Loany come from Tegucigalpa. This is Milson's third attempt to cross, and we joke about that Tigres del Norte song, '*Tres Veces Mojado*'. 'That's me!' exclaims Milson. He made it to San Antonio in 2014, but was deported. Before his second attempt, he was kidnapped by the Zetas and held in the desert for eight days – he is coy about how he was released, suggesting payment by a cousin in St Louis. 'They told me that if I ever came back to the border, they'd kill me.' He crossed, was again deported, and returned to Honduras – for good, he thought. 'But then the M-13 informed me: "We're having your daughter." Loany is fourteen, and I said: come on, my love, we're leaving.' Father and daughter were separated for a week on the US side. 'They kept us in the heat by day, and as cold as the air conditioning would go by night,' says Loany, 'with filthy blankets and toilets. When we asked them to turn the cold air off, they refused.' The worry now is for Loany's brother, left at home with his mother, immobile with cerebral palsy; Milson produces documentation, to show the Americans: 'Javixson Rodríguez. *Descapacidado*' – disabled.

A disturbing narrative abounds across the camp: children – who as minors cannot be sent back under MPP – leaving their parents, with or without their knowledge, to cross alone, unsure if they will ever make it or see them again. Milson is clear: 'I know some of the parents whose children have left and gone. They're devastated, whether they knew or not. I'd never let Loany go without me – that's why we are here, so she can be safe with me. It has to be legal, and together or not at all.' Loany concurs: 'I'm staying with my papa' – as if she would say otherwise.

Over three days in the migrant camp, the conviviality of these people in conditions of extreme hardship is remarkable; there is almost no strife between them, their tents huddled and washing hung out to dry. They exchange news, views, baby care and food when there is any. Each morning, they line up for breakfast, in orderly respect of priority for women and children, served from a local *taquería* and organised by a solidarity group called Team Brownsville from across the river, founded by Michael Benavides, a former explosives disposal soldier in Iraq and Mormon missionary. 'People disappear. It's so scary,' he warns. 'You'll agree to meet someone next day, come back, ask around, and no one knows where they are. They cannot do everything to defend against the mafia, but they look after each other. Watch them,' he says, as volunteers hand out plates of beans and rice, 'not a push or shove.'

Benavides has the names of two teenagers who died in US government custody over Christmas 2018–19, tattooed above his heart; he was inspired by a group of women called Angry Tears, mobilised in response to child separation. 'Kids in cages, taken from their parents by the US government – are you kidding? That did it for me.' Team Brownsville started out cooking food in a tiny kitchen a block from the border on the US side and bringing it across, then expanded – raising money and buying tents, driven by a belief, explains Benavides, 'that this is what America should be. My grandparents came from Mexico, and raised me to think of America as a country of compassion and open arms to those in need. Whatever Donald Trump thinks, this is my idea of patriotism.' The operation now feeds more than six hundred people, for some $380 a day at breakfast and $500 for dinner. 'We just need to keep raising the funds to keep it going,' he says.

Those from the Sanctuary Movement of the 1980s to these people now – people like Nicole Ramos and Erin Pinheira, like Ruben García, Reverend Rathbone, Pastors Robles and Ortíz, Michael Seifert, Glady Cañas and many, many others – form part of the little told story of that other, compassionate, America, as quintessential to the narrative of migration to the border as are the migrants themselves, and the brutality they face.

Lining up for breakfast are pregnant Jocelyne Flores and her four-year-old daughter Imena, sent back under MPP, although Jocelyne was due to give birth at any moment. She left San Salvador after Imena's father – who beat her regularly – threatened to kill them both when he learned of the pregnancy. It is explained to her that domestic violence, after a recent ruling, is no longer grounds for asylum. But Jocelyne is confident that they'll make an exception. Glady

Cañas takes the mother-to-be under her wing and makes an arrangement with the local hospital (and a few days later sends a picture, of little Carlos).

Glady must run the list of those waiting to cross under the 'metering' policy. '*La lista, la lista*! How I *hate* it,' she says, sitting on a flight of steps, calling out names of those due to cross at 4 a.m. A tropical storm breaks over the camp, drenching it in driving rain. Puddles deepen at the entry to each tent, flip-flops left outside. A few children run and splash, but most head for what shelter they have. Night falls, and a group of people – including Milson and Loany – sits among the puddles, as torrential water lashes the concrete, softly singing a *paseo* covered by a group from Monterrey called Tropa Vallenata.

Los caminos de la vida / No son como yo pensaba
Como los imaginaba / No son como yo creía
Los caminos de la vida / Son muy difícil de andarlos
Difícil de caminarlos / Yo no encuentro la salida[2]

The roads of the life / They're not as I thought
Not as I imagined them / Not as I believed
The roads of the life / They're hard to go down
It's hard to walk them / I can't find the way through

Bibliography and References

Mexico, general

There exists, inevitably, a feast of good books on Mexico. The best overall history, by far, in Spanish and English, is an essential read, for the 'visitor' and specialist, written in the style of a great novel: Enrique Krauze, *Mexico: A Biography of Power*, Harper, New York, 2007. Krauze is the country's most astute commentator, and has also written wisely on politics and morality in Mexico, in: *Contra La Intolerancia*, Opúsculos, El Colegio Nacional, Mexico City, 2017; and *Tarea Política*, Tusquets, Mexico City, 2000.

A good collection of papers is assembled in William Beezley and Michael C. Meyer, eds, *The Oxford History of Mexico*, OUP, New York, 2000. And for a general read and a gratifying meditation, although overtaken by events: Alan Riding, *Distant Neighbours: A Portrait of the Mexicans*, Vintage, New York, 1989.

An excellent collection of essays on the current crisis, by Mexico's most compelling journalists, is gathered in English translation in Lydia Cacho, González Rodríguez, Anabel Hernández, Diego Osorno, Ruiz Parra, Marcela Turati, Juan Villoro, *The Sorrows of Mexico*, MacLehose, London, 2016.

Lydia Cacho is the foremost reporter working on contemporary Mexico, and her books are essential reading: *Los demonios del Edén: El poder que protege y la pornografía infantil*, Debolsillo, Mexico City, 2006; *Esclavas del poder*, Debolsillo, Mexico City, 2010, translated by Elizabeth Boburg as *Slavery Inc., The Untold Story of International Sex Trafficking*, Portobello, London, 2012; *Memoria de una infamia*, Debosillo, Mexico City, 2014, translated by Cecilia Ross as *Infamy: How One Woman Brought International Sex Trafficking to Justice*, Soft Skull Press, Berkeley, 2017.

Likewise a requirement, as per the text, the work of Anabel Hernández, on the Ayotzinapa students and (below, in the narco-traffic section) on the

Sinaloa cartel: *La Verdadera Noche de Iguala*, Grijalbo/Penguin Random House, México City, 2016, translated by John Washington as *A Massacre in Mexico: The True Story Behind the Missing Forty-Three Students*, Verso, London, 2018.

For readers wanting a diary from another time, there's Sybille Bedford's charming *A Visit to Don Otavio: A Mexican Odyssey*, Collins, London, 1960. And, more recently, Tony Cohan, *Mexican Days: Journeys to the Heart of Mexico*, Bantam, London, 2006.

Few countries are as seeped in their folkloric and mystical traditions as Mexico, and on the deeper history of Mexico, no book on the lore of the ancient nation compares with J. M. G. Le Clézio, *The Mexican Dream: Or, The Interrupted Thought of Amerindian Civilizations*, translation by Teresa Lavender Fagan, University of Chicago Press, 1993. On the Aztecs specifically, about whom so much has been written, I recommend, in the first instance, G. C. Vaillant, *Aztecs of Mexico: Origin, Rise and Fall of the Aztec Nation*, Doubleday, London, 1944. There is copious further literature, markedly: T. T. Waterman, *Bandelier's Contribution to the Study of Ancient Mexican Organization*, University of California Press, Berkeley (facsimile of original, 1917); and Karl Taube, *Aztec and Maya Myths*, British Museum, London, 1993. And for a visual feast: Eduardo Matos Moctezuma, *Los Aztecas*, National Council for the Arts, Mexico City, 2000. Much of the scholarship depends on Spanish narratives; but just of late, a refreshing and remarkable new study emerges, drawn entirely from indigenous sources: Camilla Townsend, *Fifth Sun: A New History of the Aztecs*, Oxford University Press, 2020.

And, of course, there are the original commentaries, by those of conscience who accompanied the conquests, translated from the Spanish of the day: Bernardino de Sahagún, *Historia General de las Cosas de Nueva España*, translated by Fanny Bandelier as *A History of Ancient Mexico*, Fisk University Press, Nashville, 1932; and Bernal Díaz, *The Conquest of New Spain*, translation by John Cohen, Penguin, New York, 1963. There's some especially enlightening commentary in Emiliano Riuz Parra, *Ovejas Negras: Rebeldes de la Iglesia Mexicana del Siglo XXI*, Oceano, Mexico City, 2012.

For wider reading to connect Mexico with the rest of Latin America, two books stand out: the classic, Eduardo Galeano, *Open Veins of Latin America: Five Centuries of the Pillage of a Continent*, translation by Cedric Belfrage, Monthly Review Press, New York, 1973; and Alma Guillermoprieto, *The Heart That Bleeds: Latin America Now*, Vintage, New York, 1995.

The Mexican Revolution remains a hinge in the country's history, along with conquest and independence, on which a good account exists in Frank McLynn, *Villa and Zapata: A Biography of the Mexican Revolution*, Pimlico, London, 2001. On the outrageous, irresistible story of *narcocorridos* there's Elijah Wald, *Narcocorrido*, Harper, New York, 2001. Finally, two books among many on the mystery of Mexico's most enduring symbol, and folklore: D. A. Brading, *Mexican Phoenix: Our Lady of Guadalupe – Image and Tradition Across Five Centuries*, CUP, New York, 2001; and Antonio Zavaleta and Alberto Salinas, *Curandero Conversations*, AuthorHouse, Bloomington, IN, 2009.

The border

There is an impressive, now growing, body of literature on the border, inevitably expanded by the mass-market interest in narco wars and the current migration crisis. Starting with the so-called Indian wars, and essential background: Brian DeLay, *War of a Thousand Deserts*, Yale University Press, New Haven, 2008; and Pekka Hämäläinen, *The Comanche Empire*, Yale University Press, Newhaven, 2008.

On the revival of Hispanic identity and culture in the United States, an important recent book, Ed Morales, *Latinx: The New Force in American Politics and Culture*, Verso, London, 2019, builds on the wisdom in: Ed Ludwig and James Santibañez, eds, *The Chicanos: Mexican American Voices*, Penguin, London, 1971; and Manuel G. Gonzáles, *Mexicanos*, Indiana University Press, Bloomington, 1999. A sumptuous collection of mural art is displayed in: Erin Curtis, Jessica Hough, Guisela Latorre, eds, *Murales Rebeldes! LA Chicana/Chicano Murals Under Siege*, Angel City Press, Los Angeles, 2017. A brace of books by the expert border reporter Alfredo Corchado explore Mexican-American identity with poetic personal reflection: *Midnight in Mexico: A Reporter's Journey through a Country's Descent into Darkness*, Penguin Press, New York, 2013; and *Homelands: Four Friends, Two Countries, and the Fate of the Great Mexican-American Migration*, Bloomsbury, New York, 2018. Above all, there is the essential classic on Latinx border identity: Gloria Anzaldúa, *Borderlands/La Frontera: The New Mestiza*, Aunt Lute Books, San Francisco, 1987.

There are interesting collections of essays on border identity: Oscar J. Martínez, ed., *US–Mexican Borderlands: Historical and Contemporary Perspectives*, Scholarly Resources, Wilmington, DE, 1996; Jane Juffer, ed., *The Last Frontier: The Contemporary Configuration of the US–Mexican*

Border, Duke University Press, Durham, NC, 2006; and Martha Oemhke Loustaunau and Mary Sánchez-Bane, eds, *Life, Death and In-Between on the US–Mexico Border*, Bergin and Harvey, Westport, 1999. Also, there's especially rich anecdotal detail in Luis Humberto Crosthwaite, John William Byrd and Bobby Byrd, eds, *Puro Border*, Cinco Puntos Press, El Paso, 2003.

The late Charles Bowden was a doyen of contemporary 'border writing', with regard to narco traffic, economic ravages and landscape. He was one of the earliest writers in the current wave of environmental awareness, and, actually, I admire Bowden's work on landscape, and human damage to it, most of all. These are his 'non-narco' titles on the borderland: *Killing the Hidden Waters*, University of Texas Press, Austin, 1977; *Blue Desert*, University of Arizona Press, Tucson, 1986; *Mezcal*, University of Arizona Press, Tucson, 1988; *Desierto*, W. W. Norton, New York, 1993; *Blood Orchid: An Unnatural History of America*, Random House, New York, 1995; *Red Line*, W. W. Norton, New York, 1989; and, best of all: *Some of the Dead are Still Breathing*, Houghton Mifflin Harcourt, Boston, 2007. Further material is collected in *The Charles Bowden Reader*, Erin Almeranti and Mary Martha Miles, eds, University of Texas Press, Austin, 2010.

And there is this partnership between text and photography in Charles Bowden and Julián Cardona, *Exodus*, University of Texas Press, Austin, 2010. Julián Cardona published a personal memory of Juárez's demolished red-light district: *Stardust: Memories of the Calle Mariscal*, Ruben Center for the Visual Arts, El Paso, 2017.

Keith Bowden (no relation), *The Tecate Journals: Seventy Days on the Rio Grande*, Mountaineers Books, Seattle, 2007, is a poetic journey, along the river, through the war – it is one of my own favourite books on the territory.

Among the first books on the current border crisis are: Ted Conover, *Coyotes*, Vintage, New York, 1987; Leon C. Metz, *Border: The US–Mexico Line*, Mangan Books, El Paso, 1989; Luis Alberto Urrea: *Across the Wire: Life and Hard Times on the Mexican Border*, Anchor Books, New York, 1993; and *The Devil's Highway: A True Story*, Back Bay Books, New York, 2004. Also: Claire F. Fox, *The Fence and the River: Culture and Politics at the US–Mexico Border*, University of Minnesota Press, Indianapolis, 1999; Miriam Davidson, *Lives on the Line*, University of Arizona Press, Tucson, 2000; and Ken Ellingwood, *Hard Line: Life and Death on the US–Mexico Border*, Vintage, New York, 2004. For more daring travelogue, there's Richard Grant, *Bandit Roads: Into the Lawless Heart of Mexico*, Abacus, London, 2008.

Two books from the same author, on Central American migrants and where they came from, are among the best in the entire border library: Oscar Martínez, *The Beast: Riding the Rails and Dodging Narcos on the Migrant Trail*, Verso, London, 2014; and *A History of Violence: Living and Dying in Central America*, Verso, London and New York, 2016. On migrants and migration: Justin Akers Jacón and Mike Davis, *No One Is Illegal*, Haymarket Books, Chicago, 2006. On those trying to stop the migrants: William Langewiesche, *Cutting For Sign*, Vintage, New York, 2009; Robert Lee Maril, *Patrolling Chaos*, Texas Tech University Press, Lubbock, 2004; Dale Squint, *My Border Patrol Diary*, AuthorHouse, Bloomington, IN, 2007; and Tim Gaynor, *Midnight on the Line*, St. Martin's Press, New York, 2009. Above all, as per the text, Lee Morgan, *The Reaper's Line*, Rio Nuevo Press, Tucson, 2005.

The best of the newer studies since *Amexica* was published tend to focus on the increase in migration as a driving theme along the border, notably Jeremy Slack, *Deported to Death: How Drug Violence is Changing Migration on the US–Mexican Border*, University of California Press, Oakland, 2019. While President Trump reinforces the border, an interesting study puts the vanity of this enterprise in the context of economic and cultural forces to the contrary: Andrew Selee, *Vanishing Frontiers: The Forces Driving Mexico and the United States Together*, Public Affairs, New York, 2018. And a useful collection of essays on migration is gathered in Xóchitl Bada and Shannon Gleeson, eds, *Accountability Across Borders: Migrant Rights in North America*, University of Texas Press, Austin, 2019. Among those slices of life that weld together, rather than drive apart, sister-cities astride the border are emergency services – ambulances, paramedics, firefighters – operating across it, as described in an excellent book, of particular relevance in hindsight, after Covid-19: Ieva Jusionyte, *Threshold: Emergency Responders on the US–Mexico Border*, University of California Press, Oakland, 2018. And there is an especially moving, confessional memoir of a former Border Patrol agent: Francisco Cantú, *The Line Becomes a River: Dispatches from the Border*, Riverhead, New York, 2018.

The best book by far on contemporary Ciudad Juárez is: Sandra Rodríguez Nieto, *La Fabrica del Crimen*, Temas de Hoy, México City, 2012, translated by Daniela Maria Ugaz and John Washington as *The Story of Vicente Who Murdered His Mother, His Father, and His Sister*, Verso, London, 2017. There is also the pioneering book curated by Charles Bowden, *Juárez: The Laboratory of Our Future*, Aperture, New York, 1998. And, with marvellous line drawings, Charles Bowden and Alice Leora Briggs, *Dreamland: A Way Out of Juárez*, University of Texas Press, Austin, 2011.

On the economy of the city, there's Eduardo Alarcón Cantú, *Estructura Urbana en Ciudades Fronterizas*, Colegio de la Frontera del Norte, Tijuana, 2000. There's also a poetic view of Juárez in a collection of essays by Judith Torrea, *Juárez En La Sombra: Cronicas de una ciudad que resiste a morir*, Aguliar, Madrid, 2011.

A rigorous analysis of the deep Rio Grande Valley comes with Milo Kearney and Anthony Kopp, *Boom or Bust: The Historical Cycles of Brownsville and Matamoros*, Eakin Press, Austin, 1991. On the Nuevo Laredo–Laredo border: Dan Robinson, *Nuevo Laredo: A Prelude to War*, Shotmakers, Fort Lee, 2009; and the more whimsical Tony Raunch, *Laredo Stories*, Eraserhead, Portland, 2008.

Two useful official US government publications are: 'Hearing Before the Committee on Foreign Relations, US Senate, US–Mexican Border Violence, March 30, 2009', US Government Printing Office, Washington DC, 2009; and 'Hearing Before the Subcommittee on Highways and Transit, US/Mexican Trucking: Safety And the Cross-Border Demonstration Project, March 13, 2007', US Government Printing Office, Washington DC, 2007.

Drug wars

On the cartels, their leaders and the 'War on Drugs', there is copious material, and discernment is needed. The classic two books remain as relevant as ever: Gary Webb, *Dark Alliance*, Seven Stories Press, New York, 1998; and Elaine Shannon, *Desperados*, Viking, New York, 1988. Another earlier book, still of value, is Michael Levine, *The Big White Lie*, Thunder's Mouth Press, New York, 1993. Among the close encounters with early narco barons is Terrence E. Popper, *Drug Lord: The Life and Death of Mexican Kingpin*, 3rd edn, Cinco Puntos Press, EL Paso, 2010.

The definitive account of the Sinaloa cartel's entwinement with power in Mexico: Anabel Hernández, *Los Señores del Narco*, Grijalbo/Penguin Random House, Mexico City, 2010, translated by Iain Bruce as *Narcoland: The Mexican Drug Lords and Their Godfathers*, Verso, London, 2013. And from the same author, deep inside the cartel: *El Traidor: El Diario Segreto del Hijo del Mayo*, Grijalbo/Penguin Random House, Mexico City, 2020.

Unsurprisingly, there is plenty on 'El Chapo' Guzmán, with more to come, no doubt. Best are: José Reveles, *El Chapo: Entrega y Traición*,

Debolsillo, Mexico City, 2014; and Rafael Rodríguez Castañeda, *El Chapo: El Señor del Gran Poder*, Proceso, Mexico City, 2012. There's also: Malcolm Beith, *The Last Narco: Hunting El Chapo, The World's Most Wanted Drug Lord*, Penguin, New York, 2010; and Andrés López López, *Joaquín El Chapo Guzmán: El Varón de la Droga*, Penguin Random House, Miami, 2015.

For El Chapo addicts, there's an audacious book whose authors claim virtually sole credit for Guzmán's capture! Andrew Hogan and Douglas Century, *Hunting El Chapo: Taking Down the World's Most Wanted Drug Lord*, HarperCollins, New York, 2018. Never mind *Desperate Housewives*, there's also a (very readable) thriller from the wives of Guzmán's operatives in Chicago: Mia and Olivia Flores, *Cartel Wives: A True Story of Deadly Decisions, Steadfast Love and Bringing Down El Chapo*, Grand Central, New York, 2017.

Two good histories of the Sinaloa and Zeta cartels come from the same author, Diego Enrique Osorno: *El Cartel de Sinaloa: Una Historia del Uso Politico del Narco*, Grijalbo/Penguin Random House, Mexico City, 2009; and *La Guerra de Los Zetas: Viaje por la Frontera del la Necropolitica*, Grijalbo/Penguin Random House, Mexico City, 2012. Also on the Zetas: Ricardo Ravelo, *Crónicas de Sangre: Cinco Historias de Los Zetas*, Random House/Mondadori, Mexico City, 2007; Jorge Fernández Menéndez and Victor Ronquillo, *De Las Maras a Los Zetas*, Grijalbo/Penguin Random House, Mexico City, 2007. And another, on the Zetas as commercial enterprise: Guadalupe Cabrera-Correra, *Los Zetas Inc., Criminals Corporations, Energy and Civil War in Mexico*, University of Texas Press, Austin, 2017. One of the best books to come out of the whole war, though, is this reporting on the Zetas' investment and intervention in horse racing: Melissa del Bosque, *Blood Lines: The True Story of a Drug Cartel, the FBI, and the Battle for a Horse Racing Dynasty*, HarperCollins, New York, 2017.

A useful guide to border wars comes from Howard Campbell, *Drug War Zone*, University of Texas Press, Austin, 2009. And from the same university, UTEP, Tony Payan, *The Three US–Mexico Border Wars*, Praeger, Westport, 2006.

A marvellous read from one of the only people to have met two drug lords and survived to tell the tale: Don Henry Ford, *Contrabando*, Cinco Puntos Press, El Paso, 2005.

Javier Valdez Cárdenas paid with his life to write these wonderful books: *The Taken: True Stories of the Sinaloa Drug War*, translation by Everard Meade, University of Oklahoma Press, 2017; *Periodismo Escrito*

Con Sangre, Aguilar, Madrid; *Narco Periodismo: La prensa en el medio del crimen y la denuncia*, Aguilar, Mexico City, 2016; *Malyerba: La Vida Bajo el Narco*, Jus, Mexico City, 2016. There is also the estimable Emiliano Riuz Parra, *Los Hijos de la Ira: Las victimas de la alternancia mexicana*, Oceana, Mexico City, 2016.

Proceso reporter J. Jesús Esquivel here describes the 'normal' citizens in the USA who deliver the drugs: *Los Narcos Gringos: Una Radiografia Inédita del Trafico de Drogas en Estados Unidos*, Grijalbo/Penguin Random House, Mexico City, 2016.

Charles Bowden's books on the borderlands are listed above. Here are his important contributions on drug violence: *Down by the River: Drugs, Money, Murder and Family*, Simon & Schuster, New York, 2002; *Murder City: Ciudad Juárez and the Global Economy's New Killing Fields*, Nation Books, New York, 2010; Bowden and Molly Molloy, *Sicario*, Bold Type Books, New York, 2011.

Also two views from a DEA agent, Michael S. Vigi: *Metal Coffins: The Blood Alliance Cartel*, Ishmael Tree, New York, 2016; and *Deal*, I-Universe, Bloomington, IN, 2014. And there's a more academically rigorous analysis in Carmen Boullosa and Mike Wallace, *A Narco History: How the United States and Mexico Jointly Created the 'Mexican Drug War'*, OR Books, New York, 2015. In Colombia, meanwhile, a biography of the man who tried – laudably but in vain – to rewrite the war on drugs: María Jimena Duzán, *Santos: Paradojas de la Paz y del Poder*, Debate/Penguin Random House, Bogotá, 2018.

Femicidio, maquiladoras and the disappeared

The appalling themes of *femicidio* in Ciudad Juárez and beyond, and of disappearance, have been written up, but not of late. The place to start is Diana Washington Valdez, *The Killing Fields*, Peace at the Border Press, Los Angeles, 2006. Also: Alicia Gaspar de Alba, *Desert Blood: The Juárez Murders*, Arte Público Press, Houston, 2005; Stella Pope Duarte, *If I Die in Juárez*, University of Arizona Press, Tucson, 2008; Julia Estela Monarrez Fragoso, *Trama de una injusticia. Feminicidio sexual sistematico en Ciudad Juárez*, Miguel Angel Porrua, Madrid, 2009; Marcos Rampal and Jean-Christophe Fernandez, *La ciudad de las muertas: La tragedia de Ciudad Juárez*, Debate, Bogotá, 2008. There's also a film, starring Jennifer López, directed by Gregory Nava, *Bordertown* (DVD), Möbius Entertainment, El Norte Productions, Mosaic Media, Berlin, 2007.

On the *maquiladoras*, and the brutal culture of their operation – suddenly so relevant again after they were ordered to stay in production during coronavirus – there is: Alejandro Lugo, *Fragmented Lives, Assembled Parts*, University of Texas Press, Austin, 2006; also Altha Cravey, *Women and Work in Mexico's Maquiladoras*, Rowman & Littlefield, Lanham, MD, 1998; and Clara Jusidman, ed., *La Realidad Social de Ciudad Juárez*, Universidad Autónoma de Ciudad Juárez, 2008.

On disappearance: Lolita Bosch, *Roy Desparecido*, Ediciones B, Mexico City, 2015, tells the story of Roy Rivera; and there's the marvellous book on Clyde Snow, the formation of the EAAF and the revolution in how the missing dead are sought, identified and returned to the living: Christopher Joyce and Eric Stover, *Witnesses from the Grave: The Science of Identifying Human Remains*, Little Brown, New York, 1991. For academic rigour on the same subject: Bradley J. Adams and John E. Byrd, eds, *Comingled Human Remains: Methods in Recovery, Analysis and Identification*, Academic Press/Elsevier, Oxford/San Diego, 2014.

And the disappearances in Argentina: Jill Hedges, *Argentina: A Modern History*, I.B. Tauris, London and New York, 2015; James P. Brennan, *Argentina's Missing Bones: Revisiting the History of the Dirty War*, University of California Press, Oakland, 2018.

Native Nations

There is some lovely writing on the Tohono O'odham Nation: Winston P. Erikson, *Sharing the Desert: The Tohono O'odham in History*, University of Arizona Press, Tucson, 1994; Frank Russell, *The Pima Indians*, Nabu Press, Tucson, 1979; Gary Paul Nabhan, *The Desert Smells Like Rain: A Naturalist in O'odham Country*, University of Arizona Press, Tucson, 1982; Ruth M. Underhill, *The Papago (Tohono O'odham) and Pima Indians of Arizona*, Filter Press, Palmer Lake, 2000, originally published as *The Papago Indians of Arizona and Their Relatives, The Pima*, US Bureau of Indian Affairs, Washington DC, 1941; Anne Moore Shaw: *Pima Indian Legends*, University of Arizona Press, Tucson, 1968; and *A Pima Past*, University of Arizona Press, Tucson, 1974.

More widely, and of the utmost importance, there has been a recent flurry of wonderful indigenous writing that redefines the role of First Nations in American history, bringing them into a contemporary setting and urban present, and a narrative of agency, rather than victimhood: Tommy Orange, *There There*, Vintage, New York, 2018, which follows a group attending a powwow in Berkeley; Nick Estes, *Our History is the Future*, Verso, New York, 2019, which draws lessons from the Standing Rock pipeline protest camp; Mark Dowie, *The Haida Gwaii Lesson*, Inkshares, San Francisco, 2018, which charts the successful strategy of a First Nation in British Columbia; and the most important among these: David Treuer, *The Heartbeat of Wounded Knee*, Riverhead Books, New York, 2019, which challenges genocidal policies against Native people – but also any notion that they succeeded.

Blood money

To my amazement, there is no book on the details of the Wachovia and HSBC drug-money laundering scandals. But the outrage of money laundering, and its place in the overall narrative of banking and the financial crash of 2008, is relevant, of course, and written about in a selection of books. The best by far, specifically on narco traffic as corporate enterprise, is Roberto Saviano, *ZeroZeroZero*, translated by Virginia Jewiss, Penguin Random House, New York, 2015. Another excellent account of narco traffic and capitalism comes in Dawn Paley, *Drug War Capitalism*, AKA Press, Oakland, CA, 2014. There is also the thrilling story of infiltrating the Medellín cartel of Pablo Escobar, and its bank, BCCI: Robert Mazur, *The Infiltrator: My Secret Life Inside the Dirty Banks Behind Pablo Escobar's Medellín Cartel*, Little Brown, New York, 2009. And among the others: Tom Wainwright, *Narconomics: How to Run a Drug Cartel*, Ebury, London, 2016; Jesse Eisinger, *The Chickenshit Club: Why the Justice Department Fails to Prosecute Executives*, Simon & Schuster, New York, 2017; Oliver Bullough, *Moneyland: Why Thieves & Crooks Now Rule the World & How to Take it Back*, Profile Books, London, 2018; Matt Taibi, *Griftopia: The Story of Bankers, Politicians and the Most Audacious Power Grab in American History*, Spiegel and Grau, New York, 2010; Tom Feiling, *The Candy Machine: How Cocaine Took Over the World*, Penguin, London, 2009; Ken Rijock, *The Laundry Man*, Penguin, London, 2012; Marc Roche, *La Banque*, Albin Michel, Paris, 2010; Sergio Ferragut, *A Silent Nightmare: The Bottom Line and the Challenge of Illicit Drugs*, Lulu, Washington DC, 2007; Peter Lilley, *Dirty Dealing: The Untold Truth About Global Money Laundering, International Crime and Terrorism*, Kogan Page, London and Philadelphia, 2000; Susan Grossey, *Anti-Money Laundering: What You Need to Know*, Susan Grossey Books, London, 2015.

Academic papers

Academic research for a smaller readership has made a significant contribution to our understanding of the borderland, narco wars and migration. There is a wealth of material, from which I would recommend, and am grateful for, the following: Anna Marta Marini, 'The materiality of the wall(s): counter-space appropriation in El Paso's South side', presented at 'Exploring the Transnational Neighbourhood: Integration, Community, and Co-Habitation' conference, Humanities Institute, University College Dublin, 25–26 September 2019; Alison Elizabeth Lee, 'US–Mexico Border Militarization and Violence: Dispossession of Undocumented Laboring Classes from Puebla, Mexico', *Migraciones Internacionales*, Vol. 9, No. 4, July–December 2018; Jennifer G. Correa, 'Unheard Voices at the Texas–Mexico Wall: Fragmentation, Citizenship, and Opposition in a War on Terror', dissertation presented to the Faculty of the Graduate School at the University of Missouri-Columbia, July 2011; Raquel Rubio-Goldsmith, M. Melissa McCormick, Daniel Martinez, Inez Magdalena Duarte, 'The "Funnel Effect" & Recovered Bodies of Unauthorized Migrants Processed by the Pima County Office of the Medical Examiner, 1990–2005', Binational Migration Institute, report submitted to the Pima County Board of Supervisors, 2006; Josiah Heyman, 'The Border Network for Human Rights: From Community Organizing to Public Policy Action', *City & Society*, Vol. 26, Issue 1, pp. 73–95, 2014; Robin C. Reineke, 'Naming the Dead: Identification and Ambiguity Along the US–Mexico Border', dissertation submitted to the Faculty of the School of Anthropology, University of Arizona, 2016; Małgorzata Poks, 'Home on the border in Ana Castillo's *The Guardians:* The Colonial Matrix of Power, Epistemic Disobedience and Decolonial Love', *Revista de Estudios Norteamericanos* 21 (2017), Seville, pp. 119–43; Josiah McC. Heyman, 'Constructing a Virtual Wall: Race and Citizenship in U.S.–Mexico Border Policing', *Journal of the Southwest* 50, 3 (Autumn 2008) pp. 305–34; Guillermina Gina Núñez and Josiah McC. Heyman, 'Entrapment Processes and Immigrant Communities in a time of Heightened Border Vigilance', *Human Organization*, Vol. 66, No. 4, 2007; Abby C. Wheatley & Ruth Gomberg-Muñoz, 'Keep moving: collective agency along the migrant trail', *Citizenship Studies*, Vol. 20, 2016.

Notes

Author's Note

1. Security Ministry figures cited by Anthony Esposito, 'Murders in Mexico hit record as Lopez Obrador seeks justice system reform', Reuters, 21 January 2020. • **2.** Survey by the Citizens' Council for Public Security and Criminal Justice cited by Kate Linthicum: 'Five of the six most violent cities in the world are in Mexico, report says', *Los Angeles Times*, 14 March 2019. • **3.** Edith Lederer, 'Crime Rates Plummet Around the World as the Coronavirus Keeps People Inside', *Time*, 11 April 2020. • **4.** Roberto Saviano, 'Why the Mafia is Taking Care of Everyone's Business', *Observer*, 26 April 2020. • **5.** Oscar López, Christine Murray, 'Murders of Women Rise in Mexico Amid Fears of Lockdown Violence', Reuters, 27 April 2020. • **6.** Kate Linthicum, Wendy Fry, Gabriela Minjares, 'U.S. factories in Mexico are still open. As the coronavirus spreads, workers are dying', *Los Angeles Times*, 18 April 2020. • **7.** Roberto Saviano, *ZeroZeroZero*', paperback edn, foreword by Ed Vulliamy, Penguin Random House, New York, 2016, p. xiii. • **8.** United States of America v. Wachovia Bank, N.A., Case 1:10-cr-20165-JAL Document 13, entered on FLSD Docket 03/17/2010, case no. 10-21065-CR-Lenard, Exhibit A: Factual Statement, p. 5, paragraph 22.

Prologue: Amexica

1. Molly Molloy, New Mexico State University, Las Cruces. 'Fronterizo List' bulletin, 31 December 2009. The only reliable count of the dead is that assiduously compiled for Molloy's invaluable 'Fronterizo List'. Molloy's collection of documents is the definitive historical record of the carnage in Juárez. • **2.** Annual Report, Chamber of Commerce of Laredo, Texas, 2009 • **3.** A good guide to border Spanglish can be found in *Cabo Bob's Mexican Slang*, published on slang101.com. • **4.** Tomás Ybarra-Frausto: 'Rasquachismo', published in *Puro Border*, Luis Humberto Crosthwaite, John William Byrd and Bobby Byrd, eds., Cinco Puntos Press, El Paso, 2003, p. 191. • **5.** Gloria Anzaldua, *Borderlands – La Frontera*, 1987, third edition, Aunt Lute Books, San Francisco, 2007, p. 25. • **6.** As narrated throughout the English translation of Bernardino de Sahagún, *Historia General de las Cosas de Nueva Espana*, aka *A History of Ancient Mexico*, trans. Fanny R. Bandelier, Fisk University Press, Nashville, 1932. • **7.** Eduardo Matos Moctezuma, *Los Aztecas*, Consejo Nacional para la Cultura y Las Artes, Mexico City/Jaca, Milan, 1989, pp. 31–51. • **8.** Interview with Dr Miguel Olmos Aguilera. See his *'Imaginando Fronteras: Representación y Ficción en la Frontera del Norte'*, paper presented at *'La Frontera: Una Nueva concepción Cultural'*, conference Universidad Piloto de Colombia, 2004. • **9.** Alejandro Lugo, *Fragmented Lives, Assembled Parts*, University of Texas Press, Austin, 2008, pp. 20–24. • **10.** The best history of the frontier itself is Leon C. Metz, *Border: The US-Mexico Line*, TCU Press, Fort Worth/ Mangan Books, El Paso, 1989, p. 31. • **11.** Ted Conover, *Coyotes*, Vintage, New York, 1987, p. xviii. • **12.** Conversation with Roberto Saviano, Rome, 2008. • **13.** Daniel Borunda, 'El Pasoans Stay Uneasy as Slayings Continue', *El Paso Times*, 17 August 2008. • **14.** Chris Kraul, 'Captain Nemo is Grounded', *Los Angeles Times*, 14 December 2008. • **15.** Laurence Iliff, 'Mexico Drug Cartels' Banners Escalate Attacks Against President Calderón's Government', *Dallas Morning News*, 13 December 2008. • **16.** Diana Washington Valdez, 'Firearms in Mexico Have Ties to El Paso', *El Paso Times*, 13 December 2008. • **17.** 'Gunmen Kill Family of Mexican Drug Hero', CBS News/Associated Press, 23 December 2008. • **18.** 'TV Station Targeted in Attack', *Los Angeles Times* wire, 7 January 2009. • **19.** CNN/ World Co., 4 February 2009. • **20.** Dan Glaister, 'US Surge Plan to Contain Mexico Drug Violence', *Guardian*, 10 January 2009. • **21.** Molloy, 'Fronterizo List,' 5 December 2009. • **22.** Stewart Powell et al., 'Mexico to Begin Receiving Drug-fighting Aid', *Houston Chronicle*, 4 December 2009. • **23.** Dudley Althaus, 'Zetas Terrorizing Border Outposts', *Houston Chronicle*, 14 December 2009. • **24.** 'Police Arrest Man Linked to Slayings of 2000', *El Paso Times*, 11 December 2009. • **25.** Committee to Protect Journalists, Press Release, 2 November 2009. • **26.** Mark Stephenson, Associated Press bulletin, 18 December 2009. • **27.** Tracy Wilkinson, 'Mexican Drug Raid Hero's Family

Slaughtered', *Los Angeles Times*, 23 December 2009. • **28**. Associated Press, 8 January 2010 • **29**. Molloy, 'Fronterizo List'. • **30**. Associated Press, 31 December 2009.

1 La Plaza

1. Various articles by Alfredo Corchado in the *Dallas Morning News*, especially 30 May 2008, and Elaine Shannon, *Desperados*, Viking, New York, 1988, pp. 31–42. • **2**. Dudley Althaus, 'Cartels Have Mexican Citizens Trembling', *Houston Chronicle*, 19 July 2008. • **3**. For a full account of the American secret services' role in cocaine dealing and the contras, see Gary Webb, *Dark Alliance*, Seven Stories Press, New York, 1998; Shannon, *Desperados*; and Michael Levine, *The Big White Lie*, Thunder's Mouth Press, New York, 1993. • **4**. Don Winslow, *The Power of the Dog*, Arrow, New York, 2005, p. 103. • **5**. See Terrence Poppa, *Drug Lord*, Demand Publications, Seattle, 1990, pp. 135–238. • **6**. Statement by Anthony Placido, assistant administrator for intelligence, US Drug Enforcement Administration, before the US Senate Judiciary Committee on Crime and Drugs, 17 March 2009. • **7**. Tony Payan: 'The Drug War and the Border,' in *The Last Frontier; South Atlantic Quarterly*, Jane Juffer, ed. Fall 2006. Duke University Press, 2006, pp. 864–865. • **8**. *Proceso*, no headline – part of summary of killings, 25 February 2009; and *Los Angeles Times*, wire service, 26 February 2009. • **9**. Tracy Wilkinson, 'Women Play Bigger Role in Mexico's Drug War', *Los Angeles Times*, 10 November 2009. • **10**. Marcela Turati, 'Chapos Contra Zetas', *Proceso*, 30 June 2009, and various articles by Alfredo Corchado, *Dallas Morning News*, during 2008. • **11**. Jorge Chabat, op-ed, *El Universal*, op-ed leader article, 20 December 2009. • **12**. Ken Ellingwood, 'Drug Cartel Boss Arturo Beltrán Leyva And The Luxurious RIPs of Mexico's Narcos', *Los Angeles Times*, 21 December 2009. • **13**. Tracy Wilkinson, 'Mexican Family Slaughtered As Drug Lords Take Revenge', *Los Angeles Times*, 23 December 2009. • **14**. See full account in Poppa, op. cit., 1990. • **15**. For a full account of Carrillo Fuentes's takeover and running of the Juárez cartel, see Charles Bowden, *Down by the River*, Simon and Schuster, New York, 2002. • **16**. Tracy Wilkinson, 'El Chapo' Has Left the Building', *Los Angeles Times*, 3 December 2008. • **17**. *Los Angeles Times* wire, 18 June 2009. • **18**. *Corriere della Sera*, Milan, 2 October 2008. • **19**. Quoted on Fox News/Associated Press, 3 April 2009. •

20. Julia Preston and Samuel Dillon, *Opening Mexico*, Farrar, Straus and Giroux, New York, p. 500. • **21.** Ibid. • **22.** Dane Schiller, 'DEA Bribes Taint Late Mexican Drug Czar', *Houston Chronicle*, 13 May 2009. • **23.** Speaking on MSNBC Television, 9 April 2009. • **24.** Quoted in Leslie Berenstein and Sandra Dibble, 'Border Bloodshed Likely to Worsen', *San Diego Union-Tribune*, 5 October 2008. • **25.** Ken Ellingwood, 'US Shares Blame for Mexico Drug Violence', *Los Angeles Times*, 18 March 2009.

2 Aquí Empieza la Patria – Here Begins the Homeland

1. Pablo Vila: *'Identificaciones de Región, Etnia y Nación en la Frontera entre México-EU'*, Universidad Autónoma de Ciudad Juárez, 2004, p.47. • **2.** See Luis Alberto Urrea, *Across the Wire*, Anchor, 1993. • **3.** For a full account of the 'Institute Set' and AFO drug smugglers, see Anne-Marie O'Connor: 'Seduction of a Generation', *Los Angeles Times Magazine*, 28 July 2002. • **4.** For a full account of Alfredo Hodoyán's abduction, and of what the US Embassy in Mexico City did and did not know about it, see Julia Preston and Craig Pyes, 'Witness to Evil', *New York Times*, 18 August 1997. • **5.** Redaccion, *El Universal*, 25 January 2009; Marc Lacey, 'Mexican Man Admits Using Acid on Bodies', *New York Times*, 26 January 2009. • **6.** Rafael Morales Magaña, *'Edecán Era Informante'*, *El Mexicano*, 13 August 2009. • **7.** Dudley Althaus, 'With Mexico's Violence, Nothing is Sacred', *Houston Chronicle*, 2 July 2009. • **8.** See Tim Gaynor, *Midnight on the Line*, Thomas Dunne Books/St Martin's Press, New York, 2009, 'Where Midnight Meets The Road', pp. 77–100. • **9.** See Alfonso Cortez Lara, Megan K. Donovan and Scott Whiteford, 'The All-American Canal Lining Dispute: An American Resolution over Mexican Groundwater Rights', *Frontera Norte* journal, Vol 21, num 41, Enero-Junio, 2009.

3 El Camino del Diablo – The Devil's Highway

1. Ruth M. Underhill et al, *Rainhouse and Ocean: Speeches for the Papago Year*, University of Arizona Press, Tucson, 1997, pp. 89–115. • **2.** Pinau Merlin, *Desert Holes*, Arizona-Sonora Desert Museum Press, Tucson, 1999, pp. 51–53. • **3.** Stephen Trimble, *The People*, School of American Research Press, Santa Fe, 1993, p. 131. • **4.** Luis Alberto Urrea, *The Devil's Highway*,

Little Brown, New York, 2004, p.85. • **5**. Richard Felger and Bill Broyles, eds., *Dry Borders*, University of Utah Press, Salt Lake City 2007, p. xiii. • **6**. For full accounts of the Wellton disaster, see Ken Ellingwood, *Hard Line*, Vintage, New York, 2004, and Urrea, op.cit. • **7**. See Metz, *The Border*, op.cit. pp. 385–395. • **8**. Quoted in Urrea, op.cit., p. 12. • **9**. Josh Meyer, 'Sinaloa Cartel May Resort To Deadly Force In US', *Los Angeles Times*, 6 May 2009. • **10**. Interviewed in Salt Lake City, November 2009 – real name withheld. • **11**. Joel Millman, 'Immigrants Become Hostages as Gangs Prey on Mexicans', *Wall Street Journal*, 10 June 2009. • **12**. Ibid. • **13**. For a history of Pitiquito and its mission and church, see Claudio Murrieta, 'Las Paredes Hablan,' Pitiquito, 2004. • **14**. *Periódico Expreso* (Hermosillo), by La Redacción, 30 October 2009; and Tracy Wilkinson, 'Mexican Farm-Workers Activist and 14 Others Slain', *Los Angeles Times*, 1 November 2009. • **15**. Winston P. Erickson, *Sharing the Desert: The Tohono O'odham in History*, University of Arizona Press, 1994, p. 25. • **16**. ibid, pp. 69–70. • **17**. Underhill et al, op. cit., pp 17–37. • **18**. Ralph Vartabedian, 'US Soldiers, Law Officers Snared in Border Drug Sting', *Los Angeles Times*, 13 May 2005. Also Brenda Norrell, 'US Soldiers Ran Border Cocaine Operation', *Censored News* 23 July 2007, and 'Army Soldiers Sentenced In Drug Sting', *Arizona Daiy Star* • **19**. Carol Ann Alaimo, 'FBI: Military Recruiters Ran Cocaine', *Arizona Daily Star*, 17 December 2006 and Narcosphere.com, 'FBI: Recruiters Caught in Drug Probe' www.unsolvedmysteries.com/usm469076.html?t=conspiracy. • **20**. For a history of the *narcocorrido* genre and Los Tigres' career, see Elijah Wald, *Narcocorrido*, Harper Collins, New York, 2001. • **21**. Randal Archibold, 'Mexican Cartel Violence Spills Over, Alarming US', *New York Times*, 22 March 2009. • **22**. Interviewed by Martin Hodgson, 'Death in the Midday Sun', *Observer*, London, 19 September 2009. • **23**. Tracy Wilkinson, 'Song Banned, Band Pulls Out', *Los Angeles Times*, 29 October 2009. • **24**. Dudley Althaus, 'Singer Shot to Death After Surgery In Matamoros', *Houston Chronicle*, 4 December 2007.

Intermission: The Business End of a .12-Gauge – Barrett and Morgan's War

1. Lee Morgan II, *The Reaper's Line*, Rio Nuevo, Tucson, 2006. • **2**. Interview with former agent Jaime González, Austin, 2009. • **3**. Quoted in

Sebastian Rotella in 'Mexican American former Anti-Drug Chief's Reputation On Trial', *Los Angeles Times*, 22 November 2009. • 4. Stan Tekiela, *Mammals of Arizona*, Adventure Publications, Cambridge, Minnesota, 2008. • 5. Associated Press, 18 September 2009.

4 Urban Frankenstein

1. Quoted in Steve Fainaru and William Booth, 'An Army Takeover Quells Violence in Mexico', *Washington Post*, 21 April 2009. • 2. Associated Press, 24 February 2009. No byline. • 3. CCPSSJ report, quoted in *El Diario de Juárez*, 11 January 2010. • 4. For an excellent discussion of the city's origins and name, see Lugo, *Fragmented Lives, Assembled Parts*, University of Texas Press, Austin, 2008. • 5. Quoted in Metz, *Border*, TCU Press, Ft. Worth/Mangan Books, El Paso, 1989, pp. 168–69. The book also contains a detailed account of the development of the twin cities of Juárez and El Paso. • 6. Charles Bowden, *Murder City: Ciudad Juárez and the Global Economy's New Killing Fields*, Nation Books, New York, 2010. • 7. Redacción, *El Diario de Juárez*, 14 November 2008. • 8. See various entries by Bill Conroy on narcosphere.com. Search 'Ramírez' or click on Conroy byline. • 9. Redacción, *El Diario de Juárez*, 11 January 2009. • 10. Alicia Caldwell, Associated Press, 9 September 2009. • 11. United States Court of Appeals for the Eighth Circuit, No. 06–1569, 12 January 2007. *See also* Guillermo Eduardo Ramírez-Peyro, Petitioner, v. Alberto Gonzales, Attorney General of the United States of America • 12. A brief in support of asylum application in the matter of Espi. no Ledezma, Martín. Case no 0 74–816–432 (El Paso, 6 July 2009) • 13. Tom Russell: 'Since Sinatra Played Juárez,' from the album *Borderland*, Frontera Music/Hightone Records, Oakland, 2001. • 14. Alejandro Lugo, *Fragmented Lives*, p. 119. • 15. *El Diario de Juárez*, 17 July 2009. • 16. For a full account of troops dressing up as criminals and vice versa, see Ignacio Alvarado Álvarez '*Desapariciones y Masacres*', *El Universal*, 8 April 2008. • 17. Ken Ellingwood, *Los Angeles Times*, 27 February 2009. • 18. Fainaru and Booth, 21 April 2009, op. cit. • 19. Ibid. • 20. *Proceso*, no byline, 15 June 2009. • 21. Ramón Bracamontes, 'Mexican Cartel Battle Shifts', *El Paso Times*, 23 June 2009; see also Howard Campbell, *Drug War Zone*, University of Texas Press, Austin, 2009, especially chapter on 'Selling Drugs in downtown Juárez', pp. 96–107. • 22. Molly Molloy, New Mexico State University, Las Cruces. 'Fronterizo

List' bulletin, 31 December 2009. • **23**. Redacción, *El Diario de Juárez*, 9–11 February 2009; and Associated Press, 11 February 2009. • **24**. Alejandro Salmón and Orlanda Chávez, *Ejecutados son un delincuente menos"*, *El Diario de Juárez*, 4 April 2008 • **25**. Jo Tuckman, 'At Least 20 Dead in Mexican Prison Riot', *Guardian*, London, 5 March 2009.

6 *The Wind of Knives*

1. As narrated in the English translation of Bernardino de Sahagún, *Historia General de las Cosas de la Nueva Espana*, aka *A History of Ancient Mexico*, Fisk University Press, Nashville, 1932. Also J.M.G. Le Clezio: *The Mexican Dream*, trans. Fagan, University of Chicago Press 1993, chapter two, pp. 41–93. • **2**. *Proceso*, various articles in special edition, 9 December 2009. • **3**. The articles were part of a series over many years by Diana Washington Valdez, narrated in the book *The Killing Fields: Harvest of Women*, Peace at the Border Productions, Burbank, 2006. • **4**. Ken Ellingwood, 'Court Cites Rights Failure by Mexico In Juárez Killings', *Los Angeles Times*, 12 December 2009. • **5**. Ibid.

Intermission: The Road It Gives and the Road It Takes Away

1. Tom Russell: 'Where The Dream Begins', from the album *Borderland*, Frontera Music/Hightone Records, Oakland, 2001. • **2**. Tom Russell: 'The Road It Gives And The Road It Takes Away', from *Borderland*, ibid. • **3**. Don Henry Ford, *Contrabando*, Cinco Puntos Press, El Paso 2005. • **4**. Alicia Caldwell, Associated Press, various reports during 2009. • **5**. Ryan Bingham: 'Hard Times,' from the album *Mescalito*, UMG music, Nashville, 2007.

7 *Eat off the Floor*

1. *San Antonio Standard*, 10 March 1996. • **2**. See Enrique Krauze, *Mexico: Biography of Power*, trans. Hank Heifetz, Harper Collins, New York, 1997. Especially the chapter on Miguel Alemán, pp. 526–600. • **3**. Alejandro Lugar, *Assembled Parts, Fragmented Lives*, University of Texas Press, Austin 2008, pp. 148–52. • **4**. Altha J. Cravey, *Women and Work in Mexico's*

Maquiladoras, Rowman and Littlefield, Lanham, MD, 1998, p. 49. • 5. Krauze, op. cit. pp. 697–8. • 6. Todd Gillman, 'Obama Talks of "Upgrade" to NAFTA With Mexico's Calderón', *Dallas Morning News*, 13 January 2009. • 7. *Reglamento Interior del Trabajo*, Article 13, 1980. • 8. Quoted by Diana Washington Valdez, *El Paso Times*, 2 February 2009.

8 *Gateway to the Americas/Pax Mafiosa*

1. Ginger Thompson, 'Rival Drug Gangs Turn the Streets of Nuevo Laredo Into a War Zone' *New York Times*, 4 December 2005. • 2. Sara A. Carter, 'Here, We are Prisoners', *San Bernardino Sun*, 28 December 2006. • 3. Ricardo Ravelo 'Los Zetas: Ejército de Osiel', *Proceso*, 15 September 2005, and Dudley Althaus and James Pinkerton, 'Violence in Nuevo Laredo', *Houston Chronicle*, 7 August 2005. • 4. Susana Hayward, 'Drug War Rages in Border Town', *Miami Herald*, 31 July 2005. • 5. Ricardo Ravelo, Los Zetas, op. cit., and Manuel Roig-Franzia, *Washington Post*, 7 May 2008. • 6. *Frontera NorteSur,* website, 15 May 2004. • 7. Alicia Caldwell, Associated Press, 28 January 2010. • 8. Committee to Protect Journalists, Mexico Annual Country Report for 2008. • 9. See Cecilia Ballí, *'Ropa Usada'* in *Puro Border,* Crosthwaite, Byrd and Byrd, eds. Cinco Puntos Press, El Paso, 2003, pp. 183–190. • 10. Ibid, p. 187. • 11. Keith Bowden, *The Tecate Journals*, The Mountaineer's Books, Seattle, 2007. See chapter 'Symbols of Power', pp. 219 ff. • 12. Dudley Althaus and James Pinkerton, 'River to Ruin: Descent of the Rio Grande,' *Houston Chronicle* special supplement, 17 October 1993.

9 *Iron River / Tell Them Who You Are*

1. Tracy Wilkinson, 'Mexico Drug Gangs Turn Weapons on Army', *Los Angeles Times*, 15 March 2009. • 2. Thomas Koch, *The Militia Battle Manual*, Desert Publications, El Dorado, Arizona, 1996. • 3. *Full Auto*, Volume One. 'AR-15 Modification Manual', Desert Publications, 1981. • 4. *Select Fire AK-47 Gigil and Vamlet Conversion Manual.* Desert Publications, 1994. • 5. Lora Lumpe: 'The US Arms Both Sides in Mexico's Drug War,' *Covert Action Quarterly,* No. 61. Summer 1997. • 6. Richard Serrano, 'Guns From US Equip Drug Cartels', *Los Angeles Times*, 10 August 2008. • 7. United States Government Accountability Office, 'Firearms Tracking: US Efforts

to Combat Arms Trafficking to Mexico Face Planning and Coordination Challenges,' Report no. GAO-09-709, June 2009. • **8**. FBI press release, 2 May 2009. • **9**. Tracy Wilkinson, 'Ex-General, 2 Others Found Shot To Death Near Cancún', *Los Angeles Times*, 4 February 2009. • **10**. Dudley Althaus, 'Cancún's Top Cop Is Grilled In Retired General's Killing', *Houston Chronicle*, 13 February 2009. • **11**. Ken Ellingwood, 'Killings Uncover Seamier Side of Cancún', *Los Angeles Times*, 2 March 2009. • **12**. Dudley Althaus, 'Beheadings Shake Mexico Town', *Houston Chronicle*, 15 March 2009. • **13**. Tracy Wilkinson, 'Mexico Sees Inside Job in Prison Break', *Los Angeles Times*, 18 May 2009. • **14**. Ken Ellingwood, 'Drug Violence Spilling Into Guatamela', *Los Angeles Times*, 7 June 2009. • **15**. Tracy Wilkinson, 'Mexican Cartel Weapons from Central America', *Los Angeles Times*, 15 March 2009. • **16**. Dudley Althaus, 'Gunfight Near Mexican School Leaves Pupils Traumatized', *Houston Chronicle*, 21 February 2009. • **17**. Lynn Brezosky and Dudley Althaus, 'Blood Flows in Streets of Reynosa', *Houston Chronicle*, 19 February 2009. • **18**. Marc Lacey, 'Drug Tie Seen to Protests in Mexico', *New York Times*, 18 February 2009. • **19**. Tracy Wilkinson, 'Mexican Cartels Buying Public Support', *Los Angeles Times*, 13 March 2009. • **20**. Dane Schiller, *Houston Chronicle*, 1 April 2009. • **21**. Milo Kearney and Anthony Knopp, *Boom and Bust: The Historical Cycles of Matamoros and Brownsville*, Eakin Press, Austin, 1991, pp. 106–130. • **22**. Antonia Zavaleta and Alberto Salinas, *Curandero Conversations*, University of Texas at Brownsville/Authorhouse, Bloomington, 2009. • **23**. For a discussion of the competing influences of Mexican and Irish Catholicism in the United States, see Manuel Gonzáles, *Mexicanos: A History of Mexicans in the United States*, Indiana University Press, 1999, p. 241. • **24**. See Katherine Boo, 'Letter From South Texas', *New Yorker*, 29 March 2004. • **25**. For an analysis of high school football and Latino identity on the Rio Grande Valley, see Joel Huerta, 'Red, Brown, and Blue: A History and Cultural Poetics of High School Football in Mexican America,' Ph.D. dissertation, University of Texas at Austin, 2005. • **26**. For an analysis of Los Angeles as style capital for Mexican narcos, see Sam Quinones, *True Tales from the Other Mexico*, University of New Mexico Press, Albuquerque 2001. • **27**. Tim Rutten in the *Los Angeles Times*, 28 February 2009, discusses Quinones' theory. • **28**. US District Court/ Southern Texas, *USA v Hernández*, case H-08-317M, filed 24 April 2008. • **29**. Dane Schiller, 'Windshield Repair Man Admits Gun-Smuggling', *Houston Chronicle*, 21 November 2009. • **30**. Dane Schiller, 'Suspected Drug Boss "taunting" Feds', *Houston*

Chronicle, 12 July 2009. • **31**. Dane Schiller, 'Mexican Cartels Infiltrate Houston', *Houston Chronicle*, 17 October 2009. • **32**. Dane Schiller and Jacquee Petchel, 'Drug Cartel Chief Sentenced in Secrecy', *Houston Chronicle*, 24 February 2010.

10 Blood Money

1. Michael Smith, 'Banks Financing Mexico Gangs Admitted in Wells Fargo Deal,' Bloomberg news wire, 29 June 2010.

Amexica+10

1 Tijuana Revisited

1. Jaime Aredondo Sánchez, Zulia Orozco, Octavio Rodríguez and David Shirk, 'The Resurgence of Violent Crime in Tijuana', Justice in Mexico Policy Briefing, February 2018. • **2**. CaliBaja Region Initiative, Center for US–Mexican Studies, 'Jobs Without Borders: Employment, Industry Concentrations, and Comparative Advantage in the CaliBaja Region', conference minutes, Colegio de la Fontera Norte San Diego-Tijuana, 2014. • **3**. Susan Ferris, 'The Trump administration knew migrant children would suffer from family separations. The government ramped up the practice anyway', *Texas Tribune*, 16 December 2019.

3 Cuidad Juárez Revisited

1. Sandra Rodríguez Nieto, *Fabrica del Crimen*, Temas de Hoy, Mexico City, 2012, translated as *The Story of Vicente, Who Murdered His Mother, His Father, and His Sister*, Verso, London, 2017. • **2**. Carrie Kahn, 'Mexico Surpasses Syria as the Most Dangerous Country for Journalists', National Public Radio, 10 September 2019. • **3**. Cecilia Ballí, 'Murdered Women on the Border: Gender, Territory and Power in Ciudad Juárez', PhD thesis, Rice University, Texas, 2009. • **4**. Kirk Semple and Paulina Villegas, 'The Grisly Deaths of a Woman and a Girl Shock Mexico and Test Its President', *New York Times*, 19 February 2020.

4 *La Plaza Revisited*

1. 'Le Guerra Segreta de la DEA', *El Universal*, 27 October 2017. • 2. José Reveles, *El Chapo: Entrega y Tración*, Debolsillo, Mexico City, 2014. • 4. Anabel Hernández, *El Traidor: El Diario Segreto del Hijo del Mayo*, Grijalbo/Penguin Random House, Mexico City, 2019. • 5. Jeremy Slack, *Deported to Death: How Drug Violence is Changing Migration on the US–Mexico Border*, University of California Press, 2019. • 6. Julio Scherer, 'Si me atrapan o me matan, nada cambia', *Proceso*, 3 April 2010. • 7. Sean Penn: 'El Chapo Speaks: A Secret Visit with the Most Wanted Man in the World', *Rolling Stone*, 10 January 2016.

5 *Blood Money Revisited*

1. United States of America v. Wachovia Bank, N.A., Case 1:10-cr-20165-JAL Document 13, entered on FLSD Docket 03/17/2010, Case no. 10-21065-CR-Lenard. Exhibit A: Factual Statement, p. 5, paragraph 22. • 2. Assistant Attorney General Lanny Breuer, quoted in United States Department of Justice, Press Release 11 December 2012, '**HSBC** Holdings Plc. and **HSBC** Bank **USA** N.A. Admit to Anti-Money Laundering and Sanctions Violations, Forfeit $1.256 Billion in Deferred Prosecution Agreement'. • 3. House of Representatives, 'Too Big to Jail: Inside the Obama Justice Department's Decision Not to Hold Wall Street Accountable', Report prepared by the Republican Staff of the Committee on Financial Services, US House of Representatives, Hon. Jeb Hensarling, Chairman, 114th Congress, Second Session, 11 July 2016. • 4. Department of the Treasury, Press Release, 'Treasury Department Reaches Landmark Settlement with HSBC', 11 December 2012. • 5. United States of America v. HSBC, Case 1:12-cr-00763-ILG, Document 3-3, Filed 12/11/12, Appendix A, Statement of Facts (paragraphs as specified in text). • 6. Ibid. • 7. Ibid. • 8. Ibid. • 9. United States Senate Permanent Subcommittee on Investigations, Committee on Homeland Security and Governmental Affairs, 'US Vulnerabilities to Money Laundering, Drugs, and Terrorist Financing: HSBC Case History', Majority and Minority Staff Report, Carl Levin, Chairman; Tom Coburn, Ranking Minority Member, released in conjunction with the Permanent Subcommittee on Investigations hearing, 17 July 2012, pp. 33–5. • 10. Ibid., p. 83. • 11. Ibid., p. 21. • 12. 'HSBC boss apologises for "unacceptable" practices', BBC

Business News, 25 February 2015. • **13.** House of Representatives, 'Too Big to Jail: Inside the Obama Justice Department's Decision Not to Hold Wall Street Accountable', op. cit. p. 14, and Appendix 4, p. 42. • **14.** Mary M. Zapata et. al v. HSBC Holdings, Case 1:16-cv-00030 Document 1 Filed in TXSD (Texas Southern District, Brownsville) on 02/09/16. • **15.** Greg Farrell, 'HSBC Sued Over Drug Cartel Murders Laundering Probe', Bloomberg News, 9 February 2016. • **16.** Sarah Miloudi, 'HSBC Wealth Chief Thurston to Retire', Citywire, 3 December 2012. • **17.** Ned Simmons and Mehdi Hasan, 'Stephen Green, Ex-HSBC Boss Now Trade Minister, Has "Questions to Answer" Over Money Laundering Claims, Huffington Post, 18 July 2012. See also: Ben Laurance and Aimee Donellan, 'The Two Faces of HSBC', *Sunday Times*, 15 February 2015. • **18.** Rosa Prince, 'Lord Green: I regret HSBC money laundering failures', *Daily Telegraph*, 24 July 2012.

6 Shooting the Messenger

1. Mike O'Connor died on the penultimate day of the year 2013. I lost a friend and the funniest person I had ever met. Also, he and Tracy had accumulated an assemblage of animals from war zones, at their home in Mexico City: a cat from Bosnia called Buha, the word for a flea in that language, 'because she was more a bundle of fleas than a kitten when we found her', another stray called Habibi from Gaza, and a little dog called Busby, whom Tracy noticed running around over time, abandoned, at Mexico City airport. When Mike died I was laid out horizontal for twenty-three hours a day, dosed up on morphine but still unable to move without extreme pain. Mike had sent me a number of supportive emails, the first of which read: 'Sorry to hear about all this, Ed. Most importantly, do you have the company of a cat?'

7 The Unquiet Dead

1. Christopher Joyce and Eric Stover, *Witnesses from the Grave: The Science of Identifying Human Remains*, Little Brown, New York, 1991, p. 237. • **2.** Ibid., p. 296. • **3.** Mercedes Salado Puerto, Sofia Egaña, Mercedes Doretti and Carlos María Vullo, 'A Multidisciplinary Approach to Comingled Remains Analysis: Anthropology, Genetics, and Background Information', in *Comingled Human Remains: Methods in Recovery, Analysis, and Identification*, Bradley J. Adams and John E. Byrd, eds, Academic Press/Elsevier, Oxford and San Diego, 2014. • 4. Joyce and Stover, op. cit. p. 283. • 5. EAAF Annual Report for 2007, Mexico, p. 3. • 6. Ibid., pp. 3–4. • 7. Ibid., p. 6. • 8. Sofia Egaña and Mercedes Doretti, EAAF Concluding Report on Ciudad Juárez, 2011. • 9. Ana Lorena Delgadillo, Alma García, Rodolfo Córdova Alcaraz, 'Rebuilding Justice We Can All Trust: The Plight of Migrants', in *Accountability Across Borders: Migrant Rights in North America*, Xóchitl Bada and Shannon Gleeson, eds, University of Texas Press, Austin, 2019. • 10. Gabriella Citroni, 'The first attempts in Mexico and Central America to address the phenomenon of missing and disappeared migrants', *International Review of the Red Cross*, 2017, pp. 735–57. • 11. Ibid. • 12. Anabel Hernández, *A Massacre in Mexico: The True Story Behind the Missing 43 Students*, Verso, London and New York, 2018, p. 205.

8 Gateway to the Americas Revisited

1. Médecins Sans Frontières, 'The Devastating Toll of "Remain in Mexico" Asylum Policy One Year Later', Paris, 29 January 2020. • 2. Human Rights First, 'Deported to Danger', Los Angeles, 29 January 2020. • 3. Human Rights Watch, 'US: Deported Salvadoreans Abused, Killed', New York, 5 February 2020.

9 Iron River Revisited

1. Stephanie Herweck and Scott Nicol, 'Death, Damage and Failure: Past, Present and Future Impact of Walls on the US–Mexico Border', American Civil Liberties Union, New York, 2019. • 2. Lyrics trad arr. Omar Geles, from the album *Tropa Vallenata: '20 Reales Superéxitos'*, D Disa Latin Music, S. de R.L. de CV. Reproduced by kind permission of EDIMUSA / Big House Publishing.

Index